1984
SEASON

THE COMPLETE HANDBOOK OF BASEBALL

1984
SEASON

THE COMPLETE HANDBOOK OF BASEBALL

EDITED BY ZANDER HOLLANDER

A SIGNET BOOK
NEW AMERICAN LIBRARY

ACKNOWLEDGMENTS

It is the Year of the Mouse—to the Chinese—but Yankee fans view 1984 as the Year of the Yogi. There could be a connection if Yogi Berra plays mouse to George Steinbrenner's bear. That is one of the many uncertainties that lend intrigue to a new season that offers a rainy-day option for the fan—Robert Redford playing baseball in the movie, *The Natural*.

For helping achieve this 14th edition of the handbook, we thank contributing editor Howard Blatt and Frank Kelly, Nick Peters, Tracy Ringolsby, Pete Alfano, Joe Gergen, Phil Jackman, Phil Pepe, Joe Castellano, Rick Wolff, Robert Redford and David Horowitz of Tri-Star Pictures, Lee Stowbridge, Mike Ruberg, Red Foley, Dot Gordineer, Beri Greenwald, Phyllis Hollander, Peter Hollander, Richard Rossiter, Pete Sansone, Steve Wisniewski, Seymour Siwoff, Bob Rosen, Bob Wirz, Chuck Adams, Rick Cerrone, Bob Fishel, Phyllis Merhige, Blake Cullen, Katy Feeney, the publicity directors of the 26 major-league teams, and the staff at Westchester Book Composition.

Zander Hollander

PHOTO CREDITS: Cover—Tri-Star Pictures (Jurgen Vollmer); back cover—Richard Pilling. Inside photos—George Gojkovich, Nancy Hogue, Steven Jenner, Richard Pilling, the Joe Castellano Collection, Tri-Star Pictures, Jon Simon, UPI, and the various club photographers, including Dennis Burke. The photos of Robert Redford on pages 7, 11 and 12 were taken by Jon Simon.

SIGNET, SIGNET CLASSICS, MENTOR, PLUME, MERIDIAN AND NAL BOOKS
are published by New American Library, 1633 Broadway
New York, New York 10019

First Printing, March 1984

1 2 3 4 5 6 7 8 9

PRINTED IN THE UNITED STATES OF AMERICA

CONTENTS

Editor's Note: The material herein includes trades and rosters up to final printing deadline.

Playing Ball With Robert Redford In "The Natural"

By JOE CASTELLANO with RICK WOLFF

Joe Castellano, a Brooklyn native who works for the U.S. Customs Service in New York's World Trade Center, had two dreams when he was growing up.

Joe wanted desperately to play in the big leagues some day, like so many Brooklyn-bred ballplayers had done before him. And Joe wanted to be a movie star, like the many other Brooklynites who had found stardom on the silver screen.

To those ends, up until last July, Castellano was the top relief pitcher and a reserve infielder for the New Rochelle (N.Y.) Robins, a semipro club, and had appeared in some local community theater productions.

Now in his late 20s, Joe realized he was still a long, long way from either the big leagues or Hollywood.

But when he heard from a friend last summer about the casting call for The Natural, *starring Robert Redford, Joe jumped into his Robins' uniform and headed uptown for the audition. Out of some 1,400 hopeful ballplayer/actors, Castellano was selected to play the role of Allie Stubbs, the second baseman in the movie, a Tri-Star production to be released this spring.*

By the end of shooting, Joe had seen both his childhood dreams come true: he had played second base for the New York Knights of the National League in a hot pennant race, and, at the same time, he had found himself in the movies, surrounded by—and rubbing pine tar with—several well-known stars including Robert Redford himself. The following is Joe's account of his experiences in The Natural.

First, let me say that Robert Redford knows how to play baseball.

I don't mean that he just has a passing fancy for the game or

Robert Redford looks for a signal from the dugout.

that he picked up a bat and surprised everyone by knowing which end of it to swing.

I mean the guy knows how to play the game. Knows how to throw. How to hit. How to field. How to look, talk, and—let's face it—act like a ballplayer.

But I guess I should start at the beginning. Well, a friend of mine had read in *Backstage* last summer that they were conducting a casting call for ballplayer/actors. Immediately intrigued, I showed up at Fordham's Frisch Field one Saturday with all the other hopefuls.

But it was more of a baseball tryout than an audition. We were hit grounders, did a little batting and ran the bases. Most of the

---

Rick Wolff, senior editor at the Alexander Hamilton Institute, wrote What's a Nice Harvard Boy Like You Doing in the Bushes?

A winning pair: Joe Castellano and teammate Redford.

actors were told "Thanks, but no thanks" and were dismissed. The few lucky ones, including myself, were asked to come back the following Saturday, this time to Columbia's Baker Field.

Again, more baseball drills, more hitting, more fielding. Still more of a tryout than an audition—I mean, nobody asked us to recite any lines or sing or anything like that.

We were told we'd be notified if they could use us, and I remember how thrilled I was when I found out I had been selected. I quickly got permission to take a leave from my Customs job and boarded a plane with my wife, Terri, for Buffalo—and my movie debut.

It always seems that whenever Hollywood attempts to put together a baseball movie, the actors unintentionally reveal on screen that they don't know the difference between a double and a double play.

Heck, I remember reading that, when they produced *The Pride of the Yankees*, the filmmakers had to bring in special advisors to show Gary Cooper how to swing a bat or throw a ball. They even had to resort to reverse film editing, because Cooper, who played Lou Gehrig, never really mastered the art of swinging a bat left-handed.

That was hardly the case with the filming of *The Natural*, which is based on Bernard Malamud's best-selling novel. Redford plays Roy Hobbs, a 35-year-old rookie slugger who finally makes it to the majors and immediately thrusts the New York Knights into the thick of the National League pennant chase of 1939.

If there's one thing that I've been totally impressed with during the production of the film, it has been the careful attention given to details.

I remember when I first met Barry Levinson, the director (who also directed *Diner*), he commented that he'd "never seen a baseball movie that had really authentic baseball scenes." Because of that concern for realism, Levinson, along with the producer Mark Johnson, went to great lengths to ensure the film's believability.

For example, since the movie takes place in the late '30s, it was essential that the ballpark reflect that era. Buffalo's ageless War Memorial Stadium was selected for that purpose.

And, of course, all the ballplayer/cast members were quickly given 1930s haircuts, along with baggy, pinstriped baseball uniforms with KNIGHTS across the chest, heavy woolen stirrup socks with hardly any stirrup, and small, fingers-only, no-web gloves.

In addition, we had to dip chaws of tobacco out of old-style tobacco bags (Beechnut, of course), smoke hand-rolled cigarettes ("Spuds"), rub Wildroot Cream Oil into our hair in the clubhouse scenes and shag flies in front of outfield billboards that displayed the products of those times. Even the baseballs we used had distinctive red-and-black stitches, which I learned were the kind they used in those days, as contrasted with the all-red stitching used today.

Naturally, whenever we raced off the field after a half-inning was complete, we left our gloves right on the field—just as ballplayers did in that era.

Redford's ability on the ballfield won't disappoint any moviegoers who are baseball fans. Redford's a lefty—both batting and throwing. And even though he's 46 years old (which, admittedly, would have made him an elder statesman of the "Wheeze Kids"), his innate athletic instincts make him, well, a natural for the movie (no pun intended).

Redford has a good, short stroke at bat, and he throws with the fluid motion of a ballplayer. It was obvious to all that he was no stranger to a ballfield.

In fact, when I first found out that I was going to be in the film, I did some research about Redford. I found out that he had been quite an athlete in his high school days in the Los Angeles area where he grew up. Apparently, he was a pretty decent first baseman and quarterback, and used to follow his favorite big leaguers in *The Sporting News*.

Redford even went to the University of Colorado with the intention of playing college baseball before his acting aspirations shortstopped his ballplaying.

In the movie, you'll see Redford, not his stand-in, doing most of his own swatting from the plate. Roy Hobbs, the character Redford plays, is a home-run hitter and even though Redford showed he was more of a line-drive hitter when he took batting practice every day, he was still able to jack a few out of the park—while the cameras were rolling. It's 310 feet down the right-field line in War Memorial—not a bad shot.

I was also impressed with Redford's physical conditioning. Whether he was fielding, hitting, or running the bases, he never asked for time, for a breather, or for any other kind of pampering that might befit such a star. Of course, he's in great shape—not a drop of fat on his body—and even though his face is beginning to show the lines of his age, he doesn't wear glasses, either when hitting or fielding.

Still, they did cast a stand-in for Redford, because there are some scenes in which Roy Hobbs has to bang into an outfield wall or break up a double play at second. But most of the action Redford handled himself. And did it pretty well, too.

In fact, if anything, it was usually the "real" ballplayers who kept lousing up some of the scenes. In keeping with their attention to detail, Levinson and Johnson had cast ballplayers who had some acting ability. The director and producer wanted authentic baseball scenes with real ground balls being hit and fielded by real infielders, real line drives being hit off real hanging curves.

To accomplish this, former big leaguers such as outfielder Joe Charboneau (AL Rookie of the Year with the Indians in 1980) and third baseman Phil Mankowski (four years as a Tiger and eight games as a Met) were cast as members of Redford's Knights.

There's one scene which spoofs the mild-mannered Mankowski. According to the script, he's supposed to be playing third in the middle of an inning when he spots a good-looking gal up in the stands. Unfortunately for Phil, while he's standing there and ogling her, he gets hit with a ball in his groin.

Phil reassured the director that he knew how to "act" the part, and that he really didn't need any "authentic action" to motivate him to appear pained. We all got a good laugh.

However authentic I may have been as a ballplayer, I was still

Redford used to look it up in The Sporting News.

Redford stroked a few out of Buffalo's War Memorial Stadium.

a rookie as an actor, and like any other rookie on a movie set, I was fascinated by what these stars are like, up close and in person. In addition to Redford, who was on the set just about every day, there were Robert Duvall, who plays Max Mercy, the conspiring, snoopy sportswriter; Kim Basinger (*Never Say Never Again*), the sexy star who plays Memo Paris, Hobbs' heart-throb; Wilford Brimley (*Absence of Malice*), who plays Pop, the manager of the Knights, and Glenn Close (*The Big Chill*), who plays Iris, the woman whom Hobbs finally falls for.

That's a pretty good lineup for any movie, and I was sorely tempted to rush up to the stars and ask for autographs myself.

We started filming last Aug. 1 and went at it, day after day (sometimes nights) for up to 12 hours a session. I was lucky because my role as Allie Stubbs, although a minor one, involved me in many of the baseball scenes. So I was usually around the set. Since we didn't finish until mid-October, I had a rare opportunity to observe the stars up close and see them in a more realistic light.

Redford, for instance, treated everybody in such a polite and courteous fashion that you couldn't help but like him. He never played the role of the "big star"; in fact, if anything, he would poke good-natured fun at himself or his baseball ability.

I recall one scene we were filming in which Redford had to field a ball in the outfield. But just as he was ready to catch the ball, it fell out of his glove and an unexpected error resulted. Caught offguard by this turn of events, Redford simply laughed and said, "Well, that's the real story of my baseball career!"

Redford was constantly being mobbed by curious fans who wanted to get a glimpse of him "in person." Even when they filled the War Memorial stands with "extras," Redford was constantly under the microscope. And talk about star magnetism—he was cheered spontaneously, just for throwing a ball, or swinging a bat, or even walking out on the field.

Still, there were times, especially late in September, when we filmed at night under the lights from 5 P.M. to 5 A.M., that Redford was actually greeted with some jeers and catcalls from some of the cold and hungry fans. Again, Redford, always the consummate professional, never lost his cool.

I was impressed with the other stars as well. One night I came across Glenn Close and my wife sitting in the dugout exchanging recipes for homemade bread. And by the way, every so often, whenever there was a lull on the set, Glenn would grab a bat and glove herself and head out onto the field.

Believe me when I say that she is one of the finest female ballplayers I've ever seen. She's a good looker, too.

Joe Charboneau, 1980 AL Rookie of the Year, found a role in the New York Knights' starting lineup.

Of course, I kept a close eye on Joe Charboneau, whose off-the-field antics at Cleveland had drawn national attention. In one of the later scenes, fireworks are shot off to help celebrate a home run hit by one of the Knights, and Joe and I along with some teammates gather around home plate to welcome him. Unfortunately, in one of the takes, some of the fireworks fell to the ground before being entirely burned out, and some of the falling debris actually singed Joe's hair.

He started jumping around, afraid that his scalp was on fire, but when he realized that no serious damage had been done, he muttered to me, "Geez, if they wanted me to shorten my hair, I would have gladly gone to a barber."

One day, we were standing around the batting cage and some of us mentioned to Redford that Roy Hobbs' magic bat—Wonderboy—was only a 32-incher and probably too small for a true home-run hitter. Redford listened attentively, was most appreciative and switched to a 34 right away. It added some distance to his pokes, too.

By the time the filming came to an end, the leaves were already turning color and a cold northern breeze was beginning to whip off the shores of Lake Erie. It was time to head back to Brooklyn, wondering whether I'd be staying in my secure job at the Customs Department or grabbing my sunglasses and suntan lotion and heading off to fame and fortune in Hollywood.

Oh well, only time will tell. But after three months of being involved in the making of *The Natural*, one thing remains clear in my mind—anytime Robert Redford gets the urge to throw the ol' horsehide around again, I hope he gives me a call.

Between takes, the southpaw warms up.

Kittle & Strawberry: Home Run Kings Of the '80s

By PETER ALFANO

There hadn't been this much excitement in the Mets' clubhouse in nearly 10 years. It still was four hours before game time, but the reporters already had arrived and were now chatting among themselves like expectant fathers in the waiting room of a maternity ward. The photographers were here, too, nudging one another for some information. "Which one is he?" they wanted to know. "Where is the kid's locker?"

Some of the players seemed amused by all the fuss. Rusty Staub, however, muttered an obscenity and wondered aloud about whether the phenom that everyone had come to see would be suffocated by all the attention. Twenty years ago, when he was only 19 years old and a phenom himself, Staub played his first game for the Houston Colt 45s, as the Astros were known then. He remembered the expectations people had for him; he knew how intimidating it could be for a young man making his first appearance in the major leagues.

But now, it appeared as if Staub were worrying needlessly. The phenom was taking everything in stride. Darryl Strawberry, the young man with the home-run swing and storybook hero's name, walked quietly through the clubhouse, getting a feel for his new surroundings. He smiled politely and said "hello" to the strangers who greeted him. In an hour, Strawberry would be formally introduced to the New York media in a special press conference to be held behind home plate.

As a podium was being erected and microphones put in place, Strawberry bounded up the dugout steps dressed in his uniform and a windbreaker. He was tall and lean, but the scouts said he

---

Peter Alfano hits his home runs as a sports feature writer for The New York Times.

Most Valuable Rookies: Darryl Strawberry and Ron Kittle.

also was deceptively strong. He took long, loping strides out to right field, where he jogged on the warning track. He was alone with his thoughts in an area of Shea Stadium he is expected to call home for the next 10-to-15 years.

Darryl Strawberry was a sophomore at Los Angeles' Crenshaw High School in 1978, the year that Ron Kittle's baseball career apparently ended.

Kittle was a product of William Wirt High in Gary, Ind., where he had also been an all-state basketball player. He was signed by the Dodgers as a free agent in 1977 and soon faded from attention playing in one of the richest farm systems in baseball.

He batted .229, with seven homers and 24 RBI in 56 games in his first season, playing for Clinton, Iowa, (Midwest League) and Lethbridge, Alberta (Pioneer). He was big (6-4, 200) and strong and looked a little bit like Clark Kent when he wore his glasses, but he struck out too much and his fielding was suspect. Even worse, he suffered from a chronic pinched nerve in his neck.

During the offseason it was discovered that the pinched nerve was caused by two crushed vertebrae in Kittle's back. He underwent delicate spinal fusion surgery and the doctors told him it would be three years before he could play again. Kittle, however, would not wait that long. He began the 1978 season with Clinton and was released after 13 games. At a time when Strawberry was enjoying his summer vacation, Kittle was playing semipro baseball in hometown Gary. He earned a living working in the steel mills of that industrial city.

But Kittle loved baseball too much to give up. His back continued to heal and he became the scourge of the semipro leagues. "Over fifty percent of the balls I hit were out of the yard," he said proudly. And people noticed. A friend of White Sox scout Billy Pierce suggested that he take a look at this young slugger. Pierce did and he recommended that the White Sox give Kittle a tryout. In the fall of 1978, Kittle signed a contract to play in the White Sox farm system.

Torn tendons in a thumb hampered Ron in 1979, when he played for Knoxville, Tenn. (Southern) and Appleton, Wisc. (Midwest). He averaged .267 in 85 games, with a total of eight home runs and 38 RBI. But he started to blossom in 1980, with Appleton and Glens Falls, N.Y. (Eastern), hitting .314, with 16 homers and 65 RBI.

It was at Glens Falls the following season that he excited the White Sox organization when he batted .324, had 40 homers and 102 RBI, and was voted the league's Most Valuable Player. Moved up to Triple-A in 1982 with Edmonton, Alberta (Pacific Coast League), Kittle walloped 50 homers and drove in 144. But some of the skeptics said that the Edmonton ballpark was conducive to hitting home runs. "If it was so easy," he retorted with understandable annoyance, "how come no one else did it?"

Entering the 1983 season, the White Sox believed so much in Kittle's potential that they didn't try to re-sign outfielder Steve Kemp, who eventually signed with the Yankees. And the decision proved to be a wise one. Early in the season, when the team struggled and it was rumored that Tony LaRussa would be fired as manager, only Kittle helped keep the White Sox from collapsing altogether. He carried the hitting attack while Greg Luzinski and Carlton Fisk slumped. Thus the White Sox never fell far behind in the divisional race.

"A lot of hitters have physical ability," said Charley Lau, who was the team's hitting instructor. "But Ron's got something else. He's got that inner confidence. If he strikes out four times, he doesn't go into a shell. He goes up the fifth time knowing he's going to do something special."

Home-run hitters have to feel that way. With one swing, they can change the course of a game. With one swing, they can erase the memory of a strikeout and become the hero of the day. "I always followed home-run hitters," Kittle said. "That's what peo-

ROOKIES AT THE BAT

Here is how these illustrious home-run hitters, past and present, stacked up in their first full seasons as regulars.

Contemporaries

Player	Year	Games	BA	HR	RBI
Darryl Strawberry	1983	122	.257	26	74
Ron Kittle	1983	145	.254	35	100
Mike Schmidt	1973	132	.196	18	52
Reggie Jackson	1968	154	.250	29	74
Johnny Bench	1968	154	.275	15	82
Dale Murphy	1978	151	.226	23	79
Andre Dawson	1977	139	.282	19	65
Jim Rice	1975	144	.309	22	102
Eddie Murray	1977	160	.283	27	88
Dave Winfield	1974	145	.265	20	75
Dave Kingman	1972	135	.225	29	83
Greg Luzinski	1972	150	.281	18	68

Old-Timers

Player	Year	Games	BA	HR	RBI
Frank Robinson	1956	152	.290	38	83
Mickey Mantle	1951	96	.267	13	65
Willie Mays	1951	121	.274	20	68
Hank Aaron	1954	122	.280	13	69
Ted Williams	1939	149	.327	31	145
Joe DiMaggio	1936	138	.323	29	125
Willie Stargell	1963	108	.243	11	47
Eddie Mathews	1952	145	.242	25	58

ple come out to see. When I was in Little League, I was the same size as the other kids, but I always had the biggest bat, because I wanted to hit the ball out."

They may have taken different roads to the major leagues, but Strawberry and Kittle arrived during the same season. And each, in his own distinct style, made a big impression. They were the outstanding rookies in their respective leagues last year and are expected to continue to develop into superstars this year. Strawberry and Kittle could very well become the home-run kings of the '80s.

Kittle, of course, made the biggest splash playing for the White Sox, winners of the American League West title. It was the White Sox' first championship of any kind since they won the pennant in 1959. In a city starved for a winning team, the Sox became overnight heroes. Comiskey Park, which once threatened to become an abandoned building on Chicago's seamy South Side, was filled as it had never been before as more than two million fans came to watch the team play.

And from the moment that he won the starting job in left field during spring training, Kittle became a crowd favorite. As a youngster growing up in Gary, which is located near Chicago, he had rooted for Ernie Banks, Billy Williams and Ron Santo, three sluggers who played for the crosstown Cubs. Some day, Kittle had hoped, he would be the one hitting those home runs over the ivy-covered walls in Wrigley Field. Instead, he would hit those towering home runs into the left-field seats in Comiskey Park—and sometimes completely out of that park.

Kittle batted .254 last season, with 35 home runs and 100 runs batted in. And if some observers were surprised by the output, Kittle was not. He is a light-hearted young man with a confidence that some people call arrogance. But Kittle says that he's always believed strongly in his own ability, even when it looked as if he would never play baseball again.

While Kittle came up on the local and had to endure several detours on the way to the bigs, the 6-6, 190-pound Strawberry took the express, making only a few whistle stops.

As a high-school star in California, he displayed the many talents that gave him a "can't-miss" tag. His long strides gobbled up the ground and made him faster than he looked. His left arm was strong and accurate and not too many base-runners challenged it. When the Mets made him the first overall selection in the 1980 amateur draft, he immediately was touted as the finest hitting prospect they had ever had in the organization.

The Mets, remember, were always rich in pitching. Tom Seaver, Nolan Ryan, Jerry Koosman, Tug McGraw and Jon Matlack were some of the strong arms who came up through the farm stystem. When the Mets had an opportunity to draft Reggie Jackson in 1967, they passed up the opportunity to select a catcher whom they thought would eventually handle those young pitchers. But an injury cut short Steve Chilcott's career.

The Mets were not about to overlook a hitter like Strawberry, though. There were some who thought he could step into a major-league lineup without playing in the minors. Strawberry tried to be patient. But even when he got off to a slow start in his first full minor-league season in 1981 (.255, 13 homers, 78 RBI with

Kittle was third in the league with 35 home runs.

Strawberry hit 26 homers in 122 games.

Lynchburg, Va., in the Carolina League), Strawberry maintained that he thought he was ready to play in the majors. When the Mets acquired Ellis Valentine from Montreal to play right field that year, Strawberry voiced his objection.

Soon, Valentine realized that he was only keeping right field warm until Strawberry arrived. In New York, the media was comparing the youngster to Willie Mays even though most of the reporters had never seen Strawberry play.

The reports from the minors, however, were becoming more encouraging. Playing for Jackson, Miss., in the Double-A Texas League in 1982, Strawberry was named the Most Valuable Player after leading the league in home runs (34) and slugging percentage (.604), tying for second in stolen bases (45) and finishing third in RBI (97). He batted .283.

He was the most impressive player in the Mets' camp during spring training last year. But management was in a quandary. GM Frank Cashen didn't want to rush Strawberry. He wanted him to play a full season for Tidewater, Va., in the Triple-A International League.

George Bamberger, who was the Mets' manager at the start of last season, thought that Strawberry was ready to help the team immediately. Cashen won, however, and Strawberry accepted his demotion gracefully.

"My mother always told me, 'Don't let things get you down. Be the person that you are. Don't let troubles, or a little success, change your life,'" he said.

"So even when the Mets drafted me, I didn't let it change my life. I didn't want people to look at me as being a fresh person because the New York Mets had drafted me first. I want to be recognized as a person. A kind-hearted person."

The Mets were having a typically poor start when Cashen finally agreed with Bamberger that it was time to bring Strawberry to New York. On May 4, he arrived, carrying one suitcase and the hopes of the organization. It was too much pressure even for a level-headed rookie to bear. As Kittle was tearing up the American League and earning votes for the All-Star team, Strawberry's batting average was lower than his weight. For the first time in his career, he was faced with adversity on the playing field.

"It was tough for him," Rusty Staub said. "They didn't allow him to come up under the guidelines that he was a rookie making the team. He was supposed to be the salvation.

"I don't think he expected the big leagues to be that tough," Staub added. "He was striking out a lot. He was put under tremendous pressure. It just took him seven or eight weeks to iron it out."

For most of that time, Strawberry suffered in silence. He continued to be polite and available to the reporters but often he looked depressed and confused. How could the game he loved so much become such a chore?

"He wasn't worried," said his mother, Ruby Strawberry. "But he had to sort it out in his mind. We sat down and he said, 'Mom, you can't know how many things go on in my head.' But he didn't complain. It takes a lot to upset him."

Her son had spent too many days during his childhood playing baseball to remain discouraged for long. Instead, Strawberry looked for advice. Jim Frey, now the Cubs' manager, was the Mets' batting instructor last season. He and Strawberry spent hours together during those troubled times, trying to correct the flaws. Strawberry has long arms and a natural arc to his swing. It will make him an authentic home-run hitter, but it also means he will strike out a great deal. Like Kittle, he had to learn to forget about the strikeouts.

"Mostly, Darryl and I would sit and talk," Frey said. "It began in Montreal in June, when he was hitting .167. He was confused about why he wasn't getting any hits. I told him he wasn't working hard enough. The next day, he came to me and said, 'I thought about it all night. Let's work.'"

Slowly, Strawberry began to emerge from the prolonged slump. In one game he had three hits and all were bloops, but they counted anyway. For the most part, however, he would get one hit a game, but it would be an important one. He had power to all fields and he showed an ability to hit with men in scoring position. He began to catch up to the statistics being posted by such other promising rookies as the Dodgers' Greg Brock and the Reds' Gary Redus.

"I had to learn that it wasn't going to be easy," Strawberry said. "I'm still learning the fundamentals of baseball."

By the end of the season, however, those comparisons to Mays and other former greats were seen in a new light. Strawberry finished with a .257 average. In just 122 games, he hit 26 home runs and drove in 74. "He went through a long transition," Tom Seaver said. "He's learning what it takes, intellectually, to make it. He's learning that you can't have a good rookie season and settle for it, that you have to do it over and over again."

Kittle and Strawberry seem capable of repeating their success over and over again. Kittle said he was not pleased with his batting average and would like to raise it. "People still haven't seen the real Ron Kittle," he said.

He already is so popular that he cannot fulfill all the requests the White Sox get for public appearances. He has his own radio show, "Kittle's Corner." Those are some of the rewards that come to a home-run hitter, even one who struck out 150 times. "People don't come to the park to see singles," he said.

"You hear people say that he can be pitched to," LaRussa said. "In one form or another, theoretically, there are ways of pitching everyone. But it's a game of mistakes and Kittle does some awesome things with mistakes."

Among his contemporaries, perhaps only Fred Lynn and Jim Rice had better rookie seasons—1975 with the Red Sox. Lynn hit .331, drove in 105 runs and had 21 homers. Rice batted .309, with 102 RBI and 22 homers. Mike Schmidt of the Philadelphia Phillies batted just .196 as a rookie in 1973 and hit only 18 home runs. Dale Murphy of the Atlanta Braves batted .226 in 1978 and hit 23 home runs. Eddie Murray of the Baltimore Orioles, one of the most consistent players of his generation, batted .283 as a rookie in 1977. He hit 27 home runs and drove in 88 runs.

Both Kittle's and Strawberry's statistics compare favorably to their peer group's. Strawberry's big swing may hold down his average and contribute to his strikeouts (he struck out 128 times), but his speed will enable him to beat out some infield grounders and stretch doubles into triples. By the end of the season, many teams no longer challenged him and were pitching around him, taking their chances with George Foster and Keith Hernandez instead. "He's going to be great for a long time," Jim Frey said.

And success did not change Strawberry's perspective. "For a while I thought I would have one of my worst seasons," he said. "The pitchers are so smart. They have a lot of tricks. You've got to mature fast here or you're lost."

Kittle paid his dues in the minor leagues and took the majors by storm. Strawberry was a child protege who stumbled during his first couple of months in the big time. The two players may become the most feared sluggers in their respective leagues. Kittle is just 26 years old and Strawberry is only 21. And both have the drive to improve.

"Fifteen years," Strawberry said, "Then I'll feel I've made it."

Computer in the Dugout

By JOE GERGEN

Davey Johnson came to play—with his computer.

It was earlier in the 1990 season, at a special ceremony held in conjunction with the annual Hall of Fame inductions in Cooperstown, N.Y., that "The Book" was burned. This was no easy feat in itself because there never was a book as such. Mostly, it consisted of oral history, baseball precepts passed down from one generation of managers to the next.

Although no one ever had packaged these teachings between covers, baseball men had treated "The Book" with the reverence fundamentalist Christians accorded the Bible and Moslems saved for the Koran. Its authorship was a matter of speculation which ranged from a Union soldier under Abner Doubleday's command at Fort Sumter to Connie Mack's haberdasher to Charles O. Finley's mule. As with every other form of organized religion, it survived heretics, managers who would scandalize the community by intentionally putting the winning run on base or bringing in a right-handed reliever to pitch to a left-handed batter.

"The Book" was considered the moral approach to the conduct of the sport, a walk down the old straight-and-narrow. Its alleged truths were based on percentages, or what people perceived to be the percentages, because there were no statistical records to support them at the time. The man who preferred to rely on his intuition, his hunches, had better have been very secure and/or independently wealthy before defying all that was good and holy in "The Book."

Exactly when "The Book" fell out of favor is difficult to determine. But the erosion seemed to start in the early 1980s, when baseball first began to pay heed to the computer. By 1990, of course, every team in the major leagues was functioning with a highly-advanced system at the manager's fingertips and more than one organization was flirting with the idea of dismissing the manager entirely in favor of an electronic memory bank. The Yankees, it was said, were awaiting only a prototype which could kick dirt and throw punches before firing Billy Martin for a fifth time.

Clearly, the new era required a show of symbolism. It was Peter O'Malley, the second-generation owner of the Los Angeles Dodgers and the trusted counsel of commissioner James Watt, who suggested the burning. For the occasion, the people at the National Baseball Library, which was being replaced by the National Baseball Control Center, were asked to assemble a collection of the most arcane volumes in their collection and place them on the patio inside a huge plywood mock-up of a book. There, the newest Hall of Famer, Pete Rose, who earned everlasting fame

---

Sports columnist Joe Gergen's printouts appear regularly in Newsday.

by computing his career batting average while running to first base, struck the first match and thousands of spectators sang "Auld Lang Syne."

But if that represented the end of an era, it was the World Series three months later which really opened eyes to the brave new world of baseball. This was the first fully-automated Fall Classic, where everything from the number of warm-up tosses to the length of a lead off first base was spelled out on special video screens in the opposing dugouts. Good, old country hardball had embraced software.

The series was a particularly meaningful one, because it incorporated two geographical rivalries. Not only were the Oakland A's and the San Francisco Giants meeting for the first time in the postseason, but American and Japanese computer systems were going disk to disk in front of a huge television audience on the planet and select international crews in the six space laboratories shot into orbit in the previous 12 months. Although the teams were separated only by a bay and a bridge, it was labeled the first Galactic Series. And, said California governor Steve Garvey before throwing out the first ball, let the silicon chips fall where they may.

Game One marked the initial Series game played without the presence of umpires. In their places were strands of tiny photographic cells which could record the location of a pitch or catch a baserunning play from several angles. The evidence would be evaluated by the new Arbiter II system installed in each major-league park and a decision rendered instantaneously. The players called the computer Big Brother. Denizens of the press box, inspired by an old line of Grantland Rice, dubbed the new wunderkind The One Great Scorer.

Since there was no home-plate umpire, the managers didn't bother to leave their dugout to present lineup cards. They merely punched the information into the computer terminal arrayed in front of their desks and it appeared on the huge DiamondVision scoreboard. Of all the ballparks in the big leagues, Candlestick Park had the worst record of computer failures, because of the extreme cold at night. For this reason, a special glass enclosure had been built around the managers' consoles.

In the first tentative years of computer baseball, managements had been reluctant to turn the teams over to computer specialists. Invariably, the front offices would hire a recycled baseball man from the old school to manage and assign him a computer coach who could present him with a detailed analysis of the situation and a list of options in order of preference at the snap of a finger. Slowly but inevitably, managerial responsibilities were seized by the computer coaches, who made all the important decisions except where to spit the tobacco juice.

There were only a few of the old-timers left in the game by 1990. Martin still was hanging on, but his days appeared numbered after he purchased a large bloc of stock in a new company called Dictator Computers. The company founders had completed preliminary plans for systems "which take matters into their own hands." The new products, according to the company's public relations consultants, would make the logical choice and issue orders without prompting. The units also were being built with arms and hands to "admonish those who disagreed with technological policy."

Another of the survivors was Davey Johnson, who came to his position with the Mets in the Orwellian year of 1984 prepared for the future. He had a degree in mathematics from Trinity University in Texas and a fondness for computers. While still a player for the Baltimore Orioles, in fact, Johnson borrowed time on the system of the National Brewing Company, which owned the Orioles, to demonstrate that he should be batting second instead of sixth, which was the opinion of manager Earl Weaver.

"I put all the printouts on Earl's desk and I left a note saying, 'You might want to take a look at these figures.' In two seconds, they were in the garbage can."

Ironically, Weaver had been one of the forerunners of the computer revolution. He had kept an index-card file on every player on his team and what each did against all the pitchers in the league. By this laborious method, he started what seemed to be the best possible lineup every day. What those cards did not take into account, however, was the nature of the hits. Bloops counted as much as line drives.

Johnson wanted to improve on the concept, to figure in more probabilities. So, while managing the Mets' top farm club in 1983, a time when innovative major-league teams such as the A's and Chicago White Sox were learning to adapt a computer to baseball use, Johnson was doing his own programming in the Tidewater area of Virginia.

And the following season, Johnson became the first true push-button manager in the big leagues. He not only knew how to read a printout for the answers it supplied, he also knew what questions to ask. Unfortunately, the Mets didn't look much better on paper than they did on the field.

Still, Johnson was notable in that he did not need a computer coach when the game opened up two years later. Other managers scouted talent in the instructional leagues after the season. Johnson went back to school and became proficient at operating larger systems that befuddled amateurs. The excitable Tommy Lasorda finally was released by the Los Angeles Dodgers for repeatedly kicking a brand new unit which gave a two-letter answer to a question about the identity of the Big Dodger in the Sky. The answer? Me.

By 1988, virtually all the franchises had turned to specialists in their fields. Managing computers became of greater significance than managing people. What made the 1990 Series the source of such fascination is that it matched two of the great minds in baseball.

Bill James, the noted author of the annual *Baseball Abstract* and one of the first men in the country to analyze the sport through computers, was finishing his third full season as manager of the A's. This was fully in keeping with the progressive attitude of club president Roy Eisenhardt, the former law professor at Berkeley who had pioneered the use of a computer with the franchise in 1981. Originally, it had been used to feed interesting statistics to the A's broadcasters and later, when Steve Boros replaced Martin in the dugout, for managerial use.

In James, who had built a cult following with the yearly analyses he dispatched from his home in Lawrence, Kan., Eisenhardt had the perfect man for the job in baseball's most efficient organization. The A's, after third-place and second-place finishes in James' first two seasons, swept to a division title and the American League pennant almost without opposition. "We dazzled them with our data," joked Dwayne Murphy, the only player remaining from the Martin ("No machine's going to tell me what to do") era.

The Giants received most of the media attention before the start of the Series because they had rallied from a dreadful start after the surprise selection of Bobby Fischer as manager on July 30. He was hired after he had walked out on the Tampa Bay Twins when Calvin Griffith billed him for excessive computer time. In his first baseball season, the former chess champion had the Twins challenging the A's for the lead when Griffith decided the cost of competing was too high.

After years as a recluse, Fischer had been drawn to baseball by the mathematical progression of the game. Even in his position, he remained something of a loner, barely nodding to his players, shunning postgame interviews and—unlike the bearded James, who delighted in wearing a uniform—he dressed in the mode of old Connie Mack, with a three-piece suit, celluloid collar and a straw boater.

But no one doubted his capacity to run a baseball team in the computer age. The Giants had finished 45–12 under Fischer to

Tommy Lasorda's epitaph: Fired for kicking the computer.

overtake the Dodgers on the final day of the season. They had, in fact, beaten the Dodgers, 5–4, in the ninth inning of the deciding game on a three-run homer by Joe Morgan. The 47-year-old Morgan had not had a single at bat since Fischer took over the club. "I was saving him for just such an opportunity," Fischer said in a rare postgame meeting with the media. He had agreed to speak, in fact, only because his players had threatened to give his computer console a champagne bath if he didn't come out of his office, where he was said to eat, sleep and replay each game 10 times through the night.

The Series rocked back and forth between the teams, whose rosters in the age of two-platoon, situation-substitution baseball had been raised to 40. The National League had long given up the fight against designated hitters. Now, there was nothing but DHs in the lineup. That, combined with the extra pitchers in the bullpen and the occasional system crash, had raised the average

Bobby Fischer left chess with Bob Hope to become manager.

length of a game to four hours and one minute. More than ever, baseball had become the national pastime.

Still, there was growing excitement as the Giants and A's split the first six games with no team able to win two in succession. Game Seven, postponed by two days of power outages at Candlestick, finally got underway on the night of Oct. 20. "It looks like this Series," said broadcaster Joe Garagiola, "is going down to the last printout."

And so it did. The A's, manipulated brilliantly by James, carried a 6–5 lead into the last of the ninth. But Oakland had expended most of its pitching staff in the effort and now, with two out and the bases loaded, Fischer had Morgan to bat against a relatively inexperienced right-handed pitcher. Or so the crowd presumed.

But there was an inexplicable delay in the Giants' dugout. Morgan could be seen gesturing at the tall, skinny man in the boater and, finally, he had to be restrained by teammates when he picked up a bat and took a violent swing at Fischer's Chessmaster 500 console. Instead of Morgan, it was Rabbit Armstrong who walked to the batter's box. Armstrong was a weak-hitting shortstop who rarely got to bat in a game. He also was a right-handed hitter.

Armstrong had to wait approximately 15 minutes to fulfill his destiny. That's how long it took to clear the field of debris, consisting mostly of batteries from the portable computers on which people had been following the clash of minds. And when it was over, after Armstrong had struck out looking on three pitches, a special police detail had to be assigned to Fischer for 24 hours.

It was only several months after the game that Fischer, reached at a monastery in the Andes, explained what had happened. He had known in his heart, the manager said, that Morgan was the right man. But after feeding all the information to the dependable computer, the machine had spit out Armstrong's name. Again and again, no matter how Fischer had challenged it. "It had never been wrong before," Fischer said. "And I've never been able to beat it at chess."

Two weeks after that story appeared, the truth was unearthed. As part of a nationwide crackdown on computer thieves, the FBI broke into a grammar school in Palo Alto and arrested three second-graders. After 24 hours of questioning, they confessed.

It seems that they had grown tired of maneuvering millions of dollars from one account to another in the Bank of America and no longer were amused by breaking into the computers of the Strategic Early Warning System. So, after sneaking back into school late one evening and turning on the computer, they had come upon the baseball game. The two boys didn't know much about it, but the girl happened to be a Giants' fan. She had decided to add a few glowing statistics to the player named Armstrong, who was the first man on the team alphabetically. "We didn't mean any harm," she said. "Honest."

And so was decided the memorable season of 1990, the year baseball pulled a Rabbit out of a computer or, as one newspaper headlined the caper, Bugged Bunny.

The Remarkable Ripken

By PHIL JACKMAN

It seemed only fitting that when the Phillies' Garry Maddox hit the soft liner that ended the 1983 World Series and crowned the Baltimore Orioles, the final out should end up in the glove of Cal Ripken Jr.

After all, when Cal was playing Little League ball in North Carolina, didn't his team win the state championship?

And when he was in high school, didn't he pitch Aberdeen (Md.) to a state title by fanning 17 batters in a game?

And when he was playing Double-A ball, didn't he lead the Charlotte Orioles to the Southern League crown?

And when he reached the majors, didn't he make history by following up his AL Rookie-of-the-Year performance of 1982 with an AL MVP-winning season?

The championship season—significant as it was—meant one more accomplishment to be taken in stride by the 23-year-old shortstop.

In his fashion, Cal listens to the praise and speculation about his future and all but stifles a yawn when he explains he doesn't see himself as a finished product yet. "I've got a long way to go," he assures.

There is no false modesty in Ripken. Just a calm, almost laid-back belief in the physical and mental prowess which he possesses and the faith that he can surmount any obstacle posed by the game.

Pressure? Mention the word to him and he simply chuckles. "I always had the big build-up and hype," he says, "and I've never let it bother me."

As a high school star, Cal made the headlines more than his dad Cal Sr. ever did as a minor leaguer or, since 1977, as the third-base coach of the Orioles. Young Cal pitched and played

---

Phil Jackman has followed the Ripkens and the other Orioles from his perch as a sports columnist on the Baltimore Evening Sun.

Cal Ripken: Rookie of the Year and MVP back-to-back.

shortstop at Aberdeen, where in his senior year he posted a 7-2 record and hit .492. (He also starred in soccer.)

"I was in baseball from the day he was born," his dad says, "and I've never seen anybody enjoy the game as he does. He used to sit in the stands as a kid following our games. Around the house we were always knocking over lamps, because he was practicing with a whiffle ball."

"I never wanted to be anything else but a big leaguer," says Cal Jr. "Dad couldn't have stopped me. Not that he tried. But neither did he push me. It was all my idea."

The Orioles picked Cal in the amateur draft in June 1978 and inevitably there were comments about nepotism. "I didn't even know the ballclub was drafting him," Cal Sr. notes. "We were playing in Anaheim at the time and, on a call home, my wife [Vi] mentioned it almost in passing."

Naturally, young Cal had always followed the Orioles. "I couldn't see how anybody could possibly like any other team," he says. "I pictured myself in an Oriole uniform some day. Another team? Deep down I knew it had to be the Orioles."

He wasn't an instant success in his first professional summer—playing for Bluefield, W. Va., in the Appalachian League (D). After a slow start he ended up hitting .264. But in 1979 he batted .303 for Miami (A) and joined Charlotte, N.C. (AA) late in the season. His Miami performance brought his selection to the all-Class-A All-Star team. With Charlotte the next season, he hit .276, had 25 homers and was the Southern League's All-Star third baseman. Upped to Triple-A in 1981 with Rochester, N.Y., in the International League, Cal became Rookie of the Year (.288, 23 homers, 75 RBI) and was all-league third baseman. He missed the last three weeks of the season for good reason—the Orioles called him up to the big leagues.

Along the way, from Little League through high school to the minors—Cal Sr. didn't get to see his son play that much. "Hell, I was always working," he says. "When I began coaching with the Orioles, I could pick up a couple of innings of a high-school game, but then I'd have to head for the park."

Dad claims he didn't have that much influence on Cal's rise to the bigs. But "JR," the nickname his Oriole teammates gave him, says, "I'm reaping the benefits of dad's experience. He's always left a lot up to me and the coaches and managers I've played for. He'll tell me when he thinks I haven't handled a situation well. He'll say, 'That doesn't look good,' and I don't question it because almost everything he's ever told me was right on the money."

Ever since Cal Sr. moved into managing and coaching more than 20 years ago when a shoulder injury cut short his playing career, he has had a credo. "As long as I'm in this game," he says, "I'll continue to try to put 40-year-old heads on 20-year-old bodies."

JR says he's heard the line maybe a million times since he was a kid, but he admits it took a while to sink in. "We'd be sitting watching the World Series or some other big game and I'd be wondering what was going on in the mind of Pete Rose, Reggie Jackson or Steve Garvey in pressure situations," he recalls.

"All dad would say is 'It's the same as a regular-season game. The game doesn't change.' I couldn't understand what he was trying to say back then. Now I know."

When he was younger and impressionable, folks took a look at Cal's size—6-4 and over 200 pounds—and figured he was a home-run hitter. "I wasn't, but I tried to be, just to please people," he says.

"Actually, what I try to do is hit doubles, hit the ball hard and sometimes it goes out. I almost never try to hit a homer and, when I do, I usually pop up or ground out."

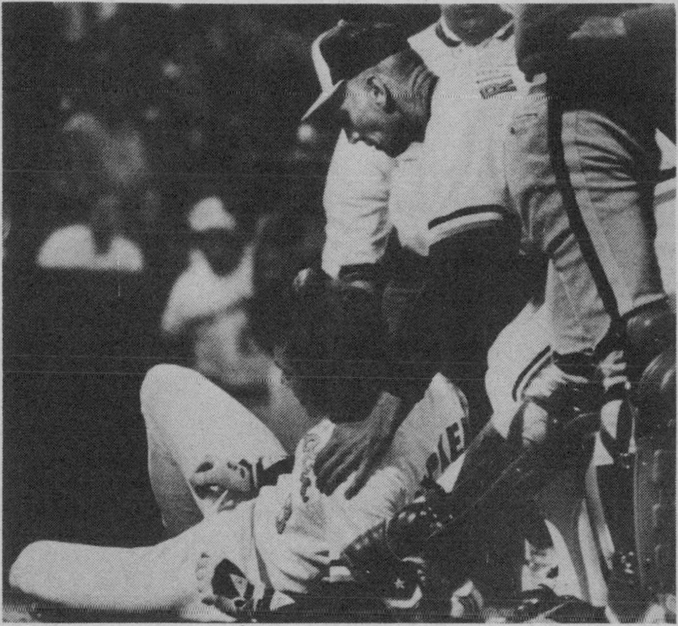

Cal Sr. rushed to his son's side after the beaning in 1982.

In his first at-bat in 1982, his rookie season, Cal rocketed a two-run homer over the left-field fence and Cal Sr., coaching at third, was the first to congratulate him.

"Had two other hits that day, too," Cal quips. "Then had four more the rest of the month. I was just over .100, so I guess I was 7-for-68."

Worse, he got his head in front of a fastball one day and, though he came out fine physically, there was the usual concern about how he would react to the next high-and-inside pitch.

He quickly dispelled all doubts. And suddenly the batting slump was over.

"Instead of bothering me," Cal reasons, "the beaning was probably a blessing in disguise. I was playing badly until I got hit. I had something to prove. I came back more determined. And good things started to happen."

He had begun 1982 as a third baseman, having replaced the traded Doug DeCinces, but was moved to shortstop in early summer. He wound up with a .264 average, 28 homers, 93 RBI and the Rookie-of-the-Year award. He played in all but two games.

Young Cal was the starting shortstop in 1983 All-Star Game.

There was the exciting prospect of a father managing a son in the big leagues in 1983—in Baltimore! Cal Sr. was among those mentioned as a possible successor to Earl Weaver. But the fantasy—imagine dad fining a son—never became a reality. Joe Altobelli got the job and Cal Sr. remained at his third-base coaching berth, a perfect spot to welcome JR as he rounded the base en route to 27 home runs.

JR hit .318, drove in 102 runs and played in every inning of every game. And he was the starting shortstop—ahead of Milwaukee's Robin Yount—for the American League in the All-Star Game.

He never dreamed he would be this successful this soon, however. "I figured myself for .280, .290, that kind of a hitter," he says, "but .318 with 211 hits, that seemed out of the realm of possibility."

Cal, an extremely disciplined and intelligent hitter with power, patience and quick wrists, benefitted greatly from batting in front of Eddie Murray. Clearly, the combination paid off.

Cal's World Series' bat (.167) was notable by its absence, but teammate Eddie Murray came through when it mattered. The two enjoy good-natured bantering. "Eddie and I don't actually have a competitive thing going—although we both want to do our best naturally—but we are big on negative statistics," reveals Cal. "For instance, strikeouts. Any time either one of us strikes out three times in a game, he has to carry this red plastic bat around. It gets embarrassing."

The post-championship winter is always a busy time. But even with all the activity of the baseball dinner season, the Orioles' full slate of basketball games and other local commitments, Ripken leads a quiet, almost reclusive life away from the ballpark, much as he does in season.

His townhouse at the very end of a development in an off-the-beaten-path section of Baltimore County suggests that this isn't the digs of a swinging bachelor bent on burning the candle at both ends.

The only trips he had planned, apart from banquet appearances, were a short vacation and a visit to Florida to check the progress of younger brother Billy, 17, an Oriole farmhand taking part in the Instructional League.

In the past, probably due to the O's low-key way of getting things accomplished on the baseball field, Ripken didn't have too much trouble blending in with his surroundings. That has changed dramatically. "I'm starting to get recognized, which is nice, but with it comes responsibility," he said.

"I used go out and get milk and eggs or something, and leave the house in a warm-up suit and an old wrinkled shirt. People come up to me now and say hello and suddenly it dawns on me what I'm wearing, and I begin to feel self-conscious."

It wasn't too long ago when Cal was painting the inside of his house and he came up about a gallon short in the paint department. He hustled to the nearby hardware store to rectify the situation and ended up giving out autographs to a line of fans.

"It was crazy," he recalls, "me in my oldest clothes, moth-eaten sneakers, paint all over me and speckled in my hair, trying to act dignified. But I still say the attention is great."

And the money isn't bad, either. He was paid the minimum of $33,500 for his rookie season, but last year he was up to $200,000. With two years in the big leagues, he qualifies for arbitration, so the O's were going to have to dig deep into the vault this time around.

Cal's goal is "to play 20 years, like Rose and Yastrzemski, and be remembered like they will be. Meanwhile, I'm going to enjoy it."

Where Have You Gone, Jim Bouton?

By PHIL PEPE

". . . you spend a good piece of your life gripping a baseball and in the end it turns out that it was the other way around all the while."—Jim Bouton in Ball Four

As a Yankee rookie in 1962.

As president of Big League Cards in 1983.

The book seems so tame now, so mild, so inconsequential, but at the time it was published, in 1970, it kicked up a fuss, all right. It was controversial, it was sardonic, it was irreverent; it desecrated the great American game; it was unpatriotic, blasphemous and scandalous; its author was a traitor, a Judas, a Benedict Arnold, a deviant.

It would have been just fine if the book had lived out its normal life, then slipped into oblivion on its own. It didn't. *Ball Four* sold almost 300,000 in hard cover, three million in paperback. It was a smash best-seller, "an American classic," as the publisher humbly dubbed it. What's worse, people refused to let it die, the very people who wished it would go away. They were the ones who breathed new life into it—baseball commissioner Bowie Kuhn, who called the author in on his elegant, plush carpet; players

---

As reporter and columnist for the N.Y. World Telegram and Sun *and the* N.Y. Daily News, *Phil Pepe has followed the bouncing ball with Jim Bouton from his first days as a Yankee.*

mentioned in the book, who beat their chests in outrage and climbed aboard soap boxes to decry the audacity of the author who dared tarnish the image of the game's most beloved heroes; the baseball establishment, which descended its wrath on the author and blackballed him.

All of this only stimulated sales, brought the book to the attention of greater numbers of readers, widened the distribution of the very book these people wanted to quash and amplified the stories they wanted hushed.

If *Ball Four* was controversial, sardonic and irreverent, it was only because its author, James Alan Bouton, was controversial, sardonic and irreverent. He was also creative, inventive, witty, intrepid, anti-establishment and iconoclastic, a combination that, when presented in one package to the single-minded, narrow-thinking rank and file that make up the rosters of major-league baseball teams, immediately got him branded as a "kook" and a "flake."

I first met Jim Bouton in the spring of his rookie season in the major leagues, with the Yankees in 1962. To my knowledge, I wrote the first full-length article that ever appeared about him in a New York newspaper, the *World Telegram & Sun*. I found him refreshing, youthfully vibrant, articulate, outgoing, brash, witty, ambitious and cooperative, all characteristics that made him a marked man with his peers.

To his teammates, Jim was "different," although it is necessary to explain their definition of the word. Different meant he read books instead of *The Sporting News*, he went to concerts instead of movies, he drank imported wine instead of beer, he preferred French restaurants to McDonald's; different meant he chose the company of sportswriters, because they were his intellectual equal, over the company of his teammates, who were not; different meant he talked openly and willingly with the press after a tough defeat rather than retreating to the sanctuary of the trainer's room, which was off-limits to the press; different meant when the Yankees were preparing to elect a new player representative, he had the nerve to openly campaign for the job, with a platform and all, because he cared deeply about players' rights and he had ideas he wanted to implement. Naturally, he was defeated.

You see, playing major-league baseball was a pleasant interlude in the life of Jim Bouton, hardly the be-all and end-all of his existence. It was a fantasy for him, the fulfillment of a dream he had never even dared dream. It was not something he had hoped for or had planned on, not something he ever had believed was remotely possible. Considering all that, it was impossible for him to take it, or himself, seriously, which is not to suggest that he

During CBS stint, Jim Bouton was visited by Tom Seaver.

gave less than his all on the playing field. He was, in every sense of the word, a competitor. Bulldog Bouton.

Time has mellowed Jim Bouton somewhat. At 44, he is still brash, witty, articulate, ambitious, inventive, irreverent, sardonic and iconoclastic. But no longer does he cling to the fantasy of a baseball comeback by playing in a semipro league on New Jersey sandlots ("I haven't done that in four or five years," he says, adding that the extent of his athletics these days is "playing touch football on Sundays and an occasional game of tennis"); no longer does he maintain a once-fervent interest in baseball ("I see maybe four or five games a year, at most, and I'm never invited to official baseball functions"); no longer does he think of himself as a jock. Jim Bouton's fantasies these days are in the business world. He is the president of something called "Big League Cards," and he did not even have to campaign for the title. He simply formed the company and gave himself the title of president.

I caught up with Jim Bouton late one night last fall, at the end of another hectic business day. We met at his newly-opened office, on the third floor of a brick building in Teaneck, N.J. Wearing a dark business suit and tie and sitting behind his desk, he could not have appeared farther removed from a baseball diamond and Yankee pinstripes. He hardly even thinks about his playing days any more.

"Those days are over," he says. "That's a different part of my life. When I call on clients now, they don't even know I once pitched. A few weeks ago, a man recognized me and told his small son that I was a Yankee pitcher and the kid said, ''Is that Ron Guidry?' "

His Yankee days are remote now, but he is fortunate that he never suffered the withdrawal pains that trouble most big-league ballplayers after their playing days have ended.

"That's because I never even dreamed of making the major leagues," he says. "When I made it, it wasn't a dream, it was a miracle. In high school, I barely made the team. I was a skinny kid with pimples and glasses and they used to call me 'Warm-up Bouton' because all I did was warm up, I never pitched. In college, I studied art. I was going to be an artist."

The major-league career he never planned encompassed 10 seasons, including a short and aborted comeback with the Atlanta Braves at age 39 in 1978, eight years after he had "retired." There were some good years—21 victories for the Yankees in 1963 and 18 in 1964, plus two more in the World Series—but mostly mediocre ones, and a career record of 62-63.

Because he was intelligent enough to recognize that there is life after baseball, Bouton planned early for the future. While he was still a player, he formed a company, with relatives and friends as investors, that bought and sold real estate in New Jersey.

The creative juices were always flowing freely through Bouton's body and *Ball Four* was published in 1970, not coincidentally his final year in the big leagues until his comeback. The book was, in effect, his "farewell to baseball," but while *Ball Four* closed a lot of doors for Jim Bouton, it opened certain others.

He ventured into the world of broadcast journalism as a sports reporter for the New York affiliates of ABC and then CBS. And he dabbled—lecturing at college campuses and at business seminars; writing a syndicated, weekly sports column that appeared in as many as 30 newspapers; trying his hand at politics as an elected delegate to the 1972 Democratic Convention in Miami and serving as vice chairman of the New Jersey delegation; appearing in a movie, "The Long Goodbye," starring Elliot Gould, and playing the role of a playboy killer; writing a television situation comedy treatment of *Ball Four* and playing the lead in the show that was canceled by the CBS network after only five weeks.

Like baseball, these were all mere interludes in the life of Jim Bouton, who continued to search for the one career that would satisfy him creatively and financially.

He gave up the sports column, Bouton says, "because there was no money in it. Plumbers make more than sportswriters."

If money was so important, why did he give up sportscasting, which has been known to reward some people with salaries of

Bouton won two games against St. Louis in 1964 World Series.

$1 million a year?

"I did TV for six years, then I found I had nothing else to say," he explains. "I was a good sportscaster in New York, but my message was that sports was over-inflated. One of my ideas about sports is that it's something you play yourself, not just watch others do on television. So I did stories about girls' basketball teams and old men lifting weights in their basement. This is the kind of thing that would never go over on the network, which is where the big money is. I might have been able to make that big money if I wanted to conform to their way of doing things."

Again, the iconoclast, the idealist, the rebel.

"I'm not knocking people like Marv Albert and Howard Cosell, because I respect what they do and they are good at what they do," Bouton says. "But Marv Albert and Howard Cosell get paid by the hour, by what they are able to produce. As soon as they stop producing, they stop getting paid. I wanted to create something that has a life of its own, something that would live beyond me. It's fun to create. It's a tremendous challenge. It's harder to do than to make the major leagues."

All of which is a roundabout way of bringing us to Jim Bouton's current project, "Big League Cards," which, of course, is an outgrowth of "Big League Chew."

"Big League Chew" was conceived in the bullpen of the Portland Mavericks, an appropriate nickname for Bouton. In his comeback attempt, Bouton had perfected a knuckleball and had taken it to the Mavericks, that rarest of professional baseball teams in these times—a minor-league independent.

"Some of the guys were sitting out there in the bullpen and chewing tobacco and getting sick on it," Bouton recalls. "I asked them why they chewed if it makes them sick."

"Because," one guy said, "it's good for my image."

"Later I was talking with one of my teammates, Rob Nelson, and I mentioned that we should come up with something that looked like chewing tobacco, felt like chewing tobacco, but tasted good; something that kids all the way down to Little League could chew to enhance their image."

The result was "Big League Chew," shredded bubble gum in a roll-up pouch that can be stored in the back pocket of a uniform, just like the big leaguers do. It was a smash, and, in its fourth year, is still a successful product, doing $15 million in sales a year.

The success of "Big League Chew" led, quite naturally, to the next step, "Big League Cards."

"I remembered the feeling kids got when they chewed 'Big League Chew,'" Bouton said. "I started to wonder how I could let everybody get that feeling, and that's when it came to me. Personalized baseball cards."

He took his idea to a printer and was told it couldn't be done on the small scale he required.

"It was impossible I was told," says Bouton. "Too expensive. It couldn't be done. That's when I knew I was on to something."

Don't challenge Jim Bouton. Bulldog Bouton. Now "Big League Cards" lives, not only in the fertile mind of its creator, but in the third floor of a brick building at 121 Cedar Lane, Teaneck, N.J.

His clients are business executives, skaters, high-school athletes, waitresses, marathon runners, babies, authors, grandmothers, housewives. They send in a photo for the front of the card and anything they want to say about themselves for the back.

"What these cards do is give anyone who has them a sense of importance, the feeling that they are in the major leagues," Bouton says. "It puts them on a par with Reggie Jackson. What these cards say are events in an individual's life that he feels are significant and worth documenting. It's a useful item because by handing you a card, I can tell you anything I want to tell you about myself. In five seconds, you have my phone number, my credits, my address, my interests and my picture. They can be used as business cards, as trophies, as invitations, as greeting cards, as birth announcements."

It would seem Jim Bouton has another winner in a series of winners. Don't get the idea, however, that he will retire undefeated. Jim Bouton has had his share of failures—an idea for a spoof of Rubik's Cube called "Rodney's Cube," that turned only in three planes and was named after, and endorsed by, Rodney Dangerfield; a computerized statistical computation of baseball statistics printed on a cardboard slide rule called "The Baseball Brain" that helps fans predict trends and probable results when certain hitters face certain pitchers; and the cancellation of his TV series.

About "Rodney's Cube," Bouton says, "How was I to know that it would come out just when the Rubik's Cube fad was fading?"

About "The Baseball Brain," he still insists it is a good idea whose time has not yet come. "I haven't given up on it," he says. "I just put it on the back burner for now."

As for the TV series, "It was a failure in the sense that it didn't become a hit show," he says. "But I don't consider that a failure because we got on the air and not many shows get that far. A network gets something like 2,000 ideas a year. Of those, about 30 become pilots and of those 30, four shows get on the air. Ours was one of the four."

Bouton insists that he is not haunted by fear of failure, not reluctant to take a chance. On the contrary.

"I recognize how important failure is," he says. "It's an important part of success because you can't know success unless you have known failure."

As for future successes and failures, Jim Bouton is not talking. Another book?

"I don't have one planned," he says, "but I never had *Ball Four* planned. Right now, I'm so heavily involved with 'Big League Cards' that I can't think about future projects. I can't even tell you what I want to be doing ten years from now. But I have a lot of ideas that I'd like to try."

And don't dare tell him any, or all, of them cannot be done. That will only pique his interest, present a greater challenge for Bulldog Bouton.

INSIDE THE AMERICAN LEAGUE

By TRACY RINGOLSBY
Kansas City Star

	West	East
PREDICTED ORDER OF FINISH	Chicago White Sox	Baltimore Orioles
	Oakland A's	Toronto Blue Jays
	Kansas City Royals	Milwaukee Brewers
	California Angels	Detroit Tigers
	Texas Rangers	New York Yankees
	Minnesota Twins	Cleveland Indians
	Seattle Mariners	Boston Red Sox

Playoff winner: Chicago

	WEST DIVISION	Owner		Morning Line Manager
1	**WHITE SOX** Best of weak field	E. Einhorn/J. Reinsdorf Navy, white & scarlet	1983 W 99 L 63	3-2 Tony LaRussa
2	**A's** Trying to regain old form	Roy Eisenhardt Forest green, gold & white	1983 W 74 L 88	5-1 Steve Boros
3	**ROYALS** Fading fast	Ewing Kauffman Royal blue & white	1983 W 79 L 83	8-1 Dick Howser
4	**ANGELS** Better in stud	Gene Autry Red, white & navy	1983 W 70 L 92	10-1 John McNamara
5	**RANGERS** No staying power	Eddie Chiles Red, white & blue	1983 W 77 L 85	30-1 Doug Rader
6	**TWINS** Not ready to move up	Calvin Griffith Scarlet, white & blue	1983 W 70 L 92	75-1 Billy Gardner
7	**MARINERS** A swayback's sadness	George Argyros Blue, gold & white	1983 W 60 L 102	150-1 Del Crandall

WHITE SOX are no powerhouse, but look like Man o' War against these nags. **A's** trying hard to provide competition. **ROYALS** just seeking to maintain respect after year of disillusionment. **ANGELS'** age becomes bigger problem every year. **RANGERS** can't stand the heat of midsummer to stay in race. **TWINS** are in constant player turnover, never get to know the course. **MARINERS** can't get out of starting gate.

Winning Ugly Stakes

84th Running. American League Race. Distance: 162 games plus playoff. Payoff (based on '83): $44,000 per losing player, World Series, up to $65,000 per winning player, World Series. A field of 14 entered in two divisions.

Track Record: 111 wins—Cleveland, 1954

EAST DIVISION

	Team	Owner		Morning Line Manager
1	**ORIOLES** Black & orange Knows the track well	Edward Bennett Williams	1983 W 98 L 64	**3-2** Joe Altobelli
2	**BLUE JAYS** Blue & white Ready to make a move	R. Howard Webster	1983 W 89 L 73	**5-2** Bobby Cox
3	**BREWERS** Blue, gold & white Change in saddle a boost	Bud Selig	1983 W 87 L 75	**3-1** Rene Lachemann
4	**TIGERS** Navy, orange & white Needs stretch drive	John Fetzer	1983 W 92 L 70	**7-2** Sparky Anderson
5	**YANKEES** Navy blue pinstripes No magic with Yogi	George Steinbrenner	1983 W 91 L 71	**4-1** Yogi Berra
6	**INDIANS** Red, white & blue Not even early foot	Pat O'Neill	1983 W 70 L 92	**90-1** Pat Corrales
7	**RED SOX** Red, white & blue Seen better days	Mrs. Jean Yawkey	1983 W 78 L 84	**100-1** Ralph Houk

Amounts to five-horse race. **ORIOLES** show it down the stretch. **BLUE JAYS** move up strong along the rail. **BREWERS** always pose threat, but won't make winner's circle. **TIGERS** need hot flashes to surprise. **YANKEES** remain own worst enemy. **INDIANS** appear out of the running. **RED SOX** fade fast.

BALTIMORE ORIOLES

TEAM DIRECTORY: Chairman of the Board: Edward Bennett Williams; Exec. VP-GM: Hank Peters; VP: Jack Dunn III; VP: Joseph P. Hamper, Jr.; Dir. Pub. Rel.: Bob Brown; Trav. Sec.: Philip Itzoe; Mgr.: Joe Altobelli. Home: Memorial Stadium (53,208). Field distances: 309, l.f. line; 385, l.c.; 405, c.f.; 385, r.c.; 309, r.f. line. Spring training: Miami, Fla.

SCOUTING REPORT

HITTING: Eddie Murray and Cal Ripken Jr. alone would give the Orioles a potent attack. Murray hit .306 with 33 homers and 111 RBI last season, typical numbers for him. Ripken (.318, 27 homers, 102 RBI) performed a worthy encore to his 1982 Rookie-of-the-Year exploits, becoming the 1983 AL MVP by leading the league with 121 runs scored, 211 hits, 47 doubles and 76 extra-base hits.

But the Orioles have more weapons than just those two. They do not create fear with their speed on the basepaths (61 stolen bases), but they don't have to be sneaky. They simply pound their opponents into submission (AL-leading 168 home runs.)

They use the platoon system to the hilt, splitting time at all three outfield spots and now at third base, following the winter acquisition of Wayne Gross from Oakland. Nothing typifies the Orioles' success better than the production they get out of their left-field platoon. Last season, John Lowenstein and Gary Roenicke combined for 34 homers and 124 RBI at that position. Designated hitter Ken Singleton, idle in last year's World Series, will get his swings again this season.

PITCHING: The T-shirt reads "31 says work fast, throw strikes, change speeds. Hold 'em close." Ray Miller, pitching coach, is No. 31 and the motto is a way of life for the Oriole pitching staff. In compiling the second-lowest team ERA (3.63) in the AL, the Orioles issued the fewest walks (2.8 per nine innings).

A solid rotation became even more solid when last season's injuries to Mike Flanagan (12-4) and Jim Palmer (5-4) gave Mike Boddicker a chance to pitch in the big leagues. Boddicker (16-8, 2.77 ERA) won Rookie-of-the-Year honors.

The big development, however, has been the work of the bullpen tandem of Tippy Martinez and Sammy Stewart. Martinez, who has saved 37 games during the last two years, has become the premier left-handed reliever in the big leagues. Stewart re-

Emerging Mike Boddicker won 16, plus two in postseason.

directed his life shortly after the All-Star break and it worked wonders (7-1, 2.39 ERA after July 20).

FIELDING: They may not look pretty doing it, but the Orioles seem to get the job done. They play sound, fundamental baseball. The outfield is as solid as any club's, even if the arms of the six platooning semi-regulars aren't the strongest. Center fielder John Shelby (.981) covers plenty of territory.

Ripken has gotten better every day he has played shortstop and second baseman Rich Dauer is solid. Back-to-back Gold Gloves have finally given Murray (.993) his due as a first baseman. Third baseman Gross isn't smooth, but at least the Orioles can replace him in late innings with converted shortstop Todd Cruz, who has the strongest arm of any AL infielder. And don't forget sharp catcher Rick Dempsey, who has thrown out 42.9 percent of potential base-stealers since he joined Baltimore.

OUTLOOK: Earl Weaver left the Orioles with a solid system and Joe Altobelli managed last year's team to the seventh divisional title in club history and brought home the Birds' first world championship since 1970.

Now that the Orioles shored up their most obvious weak spot by adding Gross, don't bet against the Baltimore formula—a deep pitching staff, flawless fundamentals and three-run homers—producing a title-winning encore.

BALTIMORE ORIOLES 1984 ROSTER

MANAGER Joe Altobelli
Coaches—Elrod Hendricks, Ray Miller, Cal Ripken Sr., Ralph Rowe, Jimmy Williams

PITCHERS

No.	Name	1983 Club	W-L	IP	SO	ERA	B-T	Ht.	Wt.	Born
52	Boddicker, Mike	Rochester	3-1	24	18	1.90	R-R	5-11	172	8/23/57 Cedar Rapids, IA
		Baltimore	16-8	179	120	2.77				
59	Brown, Mark	Rochester	6-1	53	44	3.54	B-R	6-2	190	7/13/59 Bellows Falls, VT
34	Davis, Storm	Baltimore	13-7	200	125	3.59	R-R	6-4	207	12/26/61 Dallas, TX
41	Dixon, Ken	Charlotte	8-7	130	73	3.95	B-R	5-11	166	10/17/60 Monroe, VA
		Rochester	3-6	64	34	4.48				
46	Flanagan, Mike	Baltimore	12-4	125	50	3.30	L-L	6-0	195	12/16/51 Manchester, NH
—	Gonzalez, Julian	Charlotte	10-6	106	105	3.32	L-L	5-11	205	5/13/60 Tampa, FL
		Rochester	5-3	67	61	4.43				
30	Martinez, Dennis	Baltimore	7-16	153	71	5.53	R-R	6-1	185	5/14/55 Nicaragua
23	Martinez, Tippy	Baltimore	9-3	103	81	1.35	L-L	5-10	175	5/31/50 La Junta, CO
16	McGregor, Scott	Baltimore	18-7	260	86	3.18	B-L	6-1	190	1/18/54 Inglewood, CA
21	Morogiello, Dan	Rochester	1-1	33	16	5.73	L-L	6-1	200	3/26/55 Brooklyn, NY
		Baltimore,	0-11	38	15	2.39				
22	Palmer, Jim	Baltimore	5-4	77	34	4.23	R-R	6-3	194	10/15/45 New York, NY
36	Ramirez, Allen	Rochester	4-5	90	78	3.80	R-R	5-10	190	5/1/57 Victoria, TX
		Baltimore	4-4	57	20	3.47				
53	Stewart, Sammy	Baltimore	9-4	144	95	3.62	R-R	6-3	208	10/28/54 Asheville, NC
32	Swaggerty, Bill	Rochester	9-6	118	25	4.64	R-R	6-2	186	12/5/56 Sanford, FL
		Baltimore	1-1	22	7	2.91				
51	Welchel, Don	Baltimore	4-12	111	61	4.64	R-R	6-4	205	2/3/57 Atlanta, GA

CATCHERS

No.	Name	1983 Club	H	HR	RBI	Pct.	B-T	Ht.	Wt.	Born
24	Dempsey, Rick	Baltimore	80	4	32	.231	R-R	6-0	184	9/13/49 Fayetteville, TN
17	Nolan, Joe	Baltimore	51	5	24	.277	L-R	6-0	190	5/21/51 St. Louis, MO
56	Pardo, Al	Rochester	56	1	31	.255	B-R	6-2	187	9/8/62 Spain
		Charlotte	44	4	19	.312				
64	Stefero, John	Baltimore	5	0	4	.455	L-R	5-8	185	9/22/59 Sumpter, SC
		Rochester	19	2	5	.196				

INFIELDERS

No.	Name	1983 Club	H	HR	RBI	Pct.	B-T	Ht.	Wt.	Born
2	Bonner, Bob	Rochester	44	1	15	.222	R-R	6-0	185	8/12/56 Uvalde, TX
		Baltimore	0	0	0	.000				
10	Cruz, Todd	Sea.-Balt.	87	10	48	.199	R-R	6-0	175	11/23/55 Highland Park, MI
25	Dauer, Rich	Baltimore	108	5	41	.235	R-R	6-0	180	7/27/52 San Bernardino, CA
—	Gross, Wayne	Oakland	79	12	44	.233	L-R	6-2	205	1/14/52 Riverside, CA
11	Gulliver, Glenn	Rochester	127	11	63	.309	L-R	5-11	175	10/15/54 Detroit, MI
		Baltimore	10	0	2	.213				
3	Hernandez, Leo	Baltimore	50	6	26	.246	R-R	5-11	170	11/6/59 Venezuela
		Rochester	69	8	25	.343				
65	Jones, Ricky	Rochester	78	7	38	.230	R-R	6-3	186	6/4/59 Tupelo, MS
33	Murray, Eddie	Baltimore	178	33	111	.306	B-R	6-2	200	2/24/56 Los Angeles, CA
8	Ripken, Cal Jr.	Baltimore	211	27	102	.318	R-R	6-4	200	8/24/60 Havre de Grace, MD
—	Rodriguez, Victor	Charlotte	170	14	77	.298	R-R	5-11	173	7/14/61 New York, NY
12	Sakata, Lenn	Baltimore	34	3	12	.254	R-R	5-9	160	6/8/53 Honolulu, HI

OUTFIELDERS

No.	Name	1983 Club	H	HR	RBI	Pct.	B-T	Ht.	Wt.	Born
27	Ayala, Benny	Baltimore	23	4	13	.221	R-R	6-1	195	2/7/51 Puerto Rico
1	Bumbry, Al	Baltimore	104	3	31	.275	L-R	5-8	175	4/21/47 Fredericksburg, VA
28	Dwyer, Jim	Baltimore	56	8	38	.286	L-L	5-10	175	1/3/50 Evergreen Park, IL
15	*Ford, Dan	Baltimore	114	9	55	.280	R-R	6-1	185	5/19/52 Los Angeles, CA
39	Landrum, Tito	St. Louis	1	0	0	.200	R-R	5-11	175	10/25/54 Joplin, MO
		Louisville	126	18	77	.292				
		Baltimore	13	1	4	.317				
38	Lowenstein, John	Baltimore	87	15	60	.280	L-R	6-1	180	1/27/47 Wolf Point, MT
35	Roenicke, Gary	Baltimore	84	19	64	.260	R-R	6-3	200	12/5/54 Covina, CA
—	Sheets, Larry	Charlotte	145	25	87	.288	L-R	6-3	217	12/6/59 Staunton, VA
		Rochester	2	0	2	.154				
37	Shelby, John	Baltimore	84	5	27	.258	B-R	6-1	175	2/23/58 Lexington, KY
29	Singleton, Ken	Baltimore	140	18	84	.276	B-R	6-4	212	6/10/47 New York, NY
43	Young, Mike	Rochester	106	14	66	.284	B-R	6-2	195	3/20/60 Oakland, CA
		Baltimore	6	0	2	.167				

*Free agent unsigned at press time

ORIOLE PROFILES

CAL RIPKEN JR. 23 6-4 200 Bats R Throws R

Was silenced in World Series, going 3-for-18, but made plenty of noise in second major-league season . . . Led AL in at-bats, runs scored, hits, doubles and extra-base hits (76) . . . Set Oriole records for hits and doubles and compiled third-highest batting average in club history . . . Has played every inning of every game since July 3, 1982 move to shortstop . . . Consecutive-game streak of 253 actually dates back to May 29, when he was still third baseman . . . Didn't appear tired late last season . . . Hit .394, with 10 homers, 30 RBI and 42 runs scored in final 43 games of regular season . . . Reached base safely via hit or walk in 143 games . . . Selected AL Rookie of the Year in 1982 and AL MVP in 1983 . . . Born Aug. 24, 1960, in Havre de Grace, Md. . . . Father Cal Sr. is Oriole third-base coach and brother Bill is infielder in Oriole system.

Year	Club	Pos.	G	AB	R	H	2B	3B	HR	RBI	SB	Avg.
1981	Baltimore.	SS-3B	23	39	1	5	0	0	0	0	0	.128
1982	Baltimore.	3B-SS	160	598	90	158	32	5	28	93	3	.264
1983	Baltimore.	SS	162	663	121	211	47	2	27	102	0	.318
	Totals		345	1300	212	374	79	7	55	195	3	.288

EDDIE MURRAY 28 6-2 200 Bats S Throws R

Shed World Series ghosts in big way . . . Went 0-for-21 in final five games of 1979 Series vs. Pittsburgh and 2-for-16 in first four games of 1983 Series, but had two homers and single in guiding Orioles to championship-clinching victory in Game 5 against Philadelphia . . . Also had three-run home run that ignited Orioles in 11-1 rout of Chicago in Game 3 of Championship Series . . . Finished second in AL in runs scored, fourth in home runs and fifth in RBI . . . Has averaged 28 homers, 99 RBI in seven years with Baltimore . . . Turns it on during September and October, sporting career mark of .335, with 49 homers and 178 RBI in 208 games . . . Went career-high 31 games without hitting homer before connecting May 27 off Kansas City's Larry Gura and beginning binge of four homers in five games . . . First baseman shares Oriole career grand-slam record with Boog Powell with seven . . . AL Rookie of the Year in 1977 . . . Born Feb. 24,

1956, in Los Angeles . . . Brother Rich played in San Francisco and Cleveland systems.

Year	Club	Pos.	G	AB	R	H	2B	3B	HR	RBI	SB	Avg.
1977	Baltimore	OF-1B	160	611	81	173	29	2	27	88	0	.283
1978	Baltimore	1B-3B	161	610	85	174	32	3	27	95	6	.285
1979	Baltimore	1B	159	606	90	179	30	2	25	99	10	.295
1980	Baltimore	1B	158	621	100	186	36	2	32	116	7	.300
1981	Baltimore	1B	99	378	57	111	21	2	22	78	2	.294
1982	Baltimore	1B	151	550	87	174	30	1	32	110	7	.316
1983	Baltimore	1B	156	582	115	178	30	3	33	111	5	.306
	Totals		1044	3958	615	1175	208	15	198	697	37	.297

MIKE BODDICKER 26 5-11 172 Bats R Throws R

Capped brilliant rookie season by pitching five-hit shutout during 4-0 victory over Chicago in Game 2 of AL Championship Series . . . Then pitched three-hitter against Philadelphia, giving up only an unearned run during 4-1 triumph in Game 2 of World Series . . . Injuries to pitching staff prompted his recall from minors in May . . . Went on to lead AL rookie pitchers in wins and become first rookie to be sole AL leader in shutouts (five), since Horace Lisenbee did it for 1927 Washington Senators . . . Finished second in AL in ERA . . . Finished with 12-4 record, 2.23 ERA in 17 starts prior to postseason play . . . Was 11-3 with 2.09 ERA at Memorial Stadium . . . Finished second in International League with 2.18 ERA for Rochester (AAA) in 1980 . . . Born Aug. 23, 1957, in Cedar Rapids, Iowa . . . Spends winters working in grain elevator in Norway, Iowa.

Year	Club	G	IP	W	L	Pct.	SO	BB	H	ERA
1980	Baltimore	1	7	0	1	.000	4	5	6	6.43
1981	Baltimore	2	6	0	0	.000	2	2	6	4.50
1982	Baltimore	7	26	1	0	1.000	20	12	25	3.51
1983	Baltimore	27	179	16	8	.667	120	52	141	2.77
	Totals	37	218	17	9	.654	146	71	178	3.01

TIPPY MARTINEZ 33 5-10 175 Bats L Throws L

Earned two saves in three World Series appearances . . . Also pitched six shutout innings in playoffs, earning pennant-clinching win against Chicago with four-inning stint in 3-0, 10-inning victory in Game 4 . . . Missed three weeks after All-Star Game because of appendectomy . . . Still set career high in wins and amassed his second-most appearances in a season . . . Established career highs in innings pitched and strikeouts, too . . . Came back from surgery to go 4-0, with 11 saves and 1.46 ERA in 31 appearances during second half . . . Pitched in seven straight games in September, including both games of two doubleheaders . . . Picked off three Toronto runners off first base during 10th inning of Aug. 24 game . . . Before that, he hadn't picked off a runner since Aug. 23, 1980 . . . Born May 31, 1950, in La Junta, Colo. . . . Originally signed by Yankees after he attended Colorado State . . . Acquired along with Scott McGregor and Rick Dempsey in nine-player, June 1976 deal the Yankees certainly regret . . . Real name is Felix Anthony Martinez.

Year	Club	G	IP	W	L	Pct.	SO	BB	H	ERA
1974	New York (AL)	10	13	0	0	.000	10	9	14	4.15
1975	New York (AL)	23	37	1	2	.333	20	32	27	2.68
1976	N.Y.-Balt (AL)	39	70	5	1	.833	45	42	50	2.31
1977	Baltimore	41	50	5	1	.833	29	27	47	2.70
1978	Baltimore	42	69	3	3	.500	57	40	77	4.83
1979	Baltimore	39	78	10	3	.769	61	31	59	2.88
1980	Baltimore	53	81	4	4	.500	68	34	69	3.00
1981	Baltimore	37	59	3	3	.500	50	32	48	2.90
1982	Baltimore	76	95	8	8	.500	78	37	81	3.41
1983	Baltimore	65	103	9	3	.750	81	37	76	2.35
	Totals	424	655	48	28	.632	499	321	548	3.04

MIKE FLANAGAN 32 6-0 195 — Bats L Throws L

Won first six decisions in 1983 before being sidelined for three months with stretched ligaments in his left knee, suffered while trying to field a grounder . . . Best start by Oriole pitcher since Dave McNally won club-record 15 in a row to open 1969 and the only time in Flanagan's eight-year, major-league career he won more than one in a row to start a season . . . After going 1-3 following return, he won five straight from Aug. 28 to Sept. 17 . . . Had made 157 consecutive starts before suffering torn muscle in left forearm in August 1981 . . . Won AL Cy Young Award in 1979, when he led majors with 23 wins . . . Born Dec. 16, 1951, in Manchester, N.H. . . . Wife Kathy gave birth to first test-tube baby born in United States by normal delivery, July 9, 1982.

Year	Club	G	IP	W	L	Pct.	SO	BB	H	ERA
1975	Baltimore	2	10	0	1	.000	7	6	9	2.70
1976	Baltimore	20	85	3	5	.375	56	33	83	4.13
1977	Baltimore	36	235	15	10	.600	149	70	235	3.64
1978	Baltimore	40	281	19	15	.559	167	87	271	4.04
1979	Baltimore	39	266	23	9	.781	190	70	245	3.08
1980	Baltimore	37	251	16	13	.552	128	71	278	4.12
1981	Baltimore	20	116	9	6	.600	72	37	108	4.19
1982	Baltimore	36	236	15	11	.577	103	76	233	3.97
1983	Baltimore	20	125	12	4	.750	50	31	135	3.30
	Totals	250	1605	112	74	.602	922	481	1597	3.77

SCOTT McGREGOR 30 6-1 190 Bats S Throws L

After losing openers of Championship Series and World Series by identical 2-1 scores, he came back to clinch world championship with 5-0, five-hitter against Philadelphia in Game 5 . . . Also had departed Game 7 of 1979 World Series after seven innings, trailing, 2-1 . . . Compiled lowest ERA of career during regular season and fifth-best mark in AL . . . In 20-start span from late May through early September, he was 13-2 with 2.20 ERA, pitching nine complete games and going 10 innings in another without getting a decision . . . Has best winning percentage in majors over the last five years (.672) . . . Born Jan. 18, 1954, in Inglewood, Cal. . . . Was MVP of El Segundo High School team that also featured George Brett, now of Kansas City . . . Originally signed by Yankees and was part of 1976 blockbuster deal.

Year	Club	G	IP	W	L	Pct.	SO	BB	H	ERA
1976	Baltimore	3	15	0	1	.000	6	5	17	3.60
1977	Baltimore	29	114	3	5	.375	55	30	119	4.42
1978	Baltimore	35	233	15	13	.536	94	47	217	3.32
1979	Baltimore	27	175	13	6	.684	81	23	165	3.34
1980	Baltimore	36	252	20	8	.714	119	58	254	3.32
1981	Baltimore	24	160	13	5	.722	82	40	167	3.26
1982	Baltimore	37	226	14	12	.538	84	52	238	4.61
1983	Baltimore	36	260	18	7	.720	86	45	271	3.18
	Totals	227	1435	96	57	.627	607	300	1448	3.59

RICK DEMPSEY 34 6-0 184 Bats R Throws R

Forget about weak-bat rap . . . Won World Series MVP honors by setting five-game record with five extra-base hits (four doubles and one home run) . . . Also threw out Phils' Joe Morgan on two-of-three theft attempts . . . Holds Oriole record for catchers, playing 861 games . . . Led AL catchers in fielding percentage for second time in three years . . . Threw out 30-of-83 runners attempting to steal, giving him total of 249-for-582 since joining Orioles . . . Stole his first base since 1980, in April against Chicago . . . Broke jaw of pitcher who was upset when interim manager Dempsey pulled him from a game in Puerto Rican Winter League . . . Born Sept. 13, 1949, in Fayetteville, Tenn. . . . Brother Pat spent six years in Oakland organization before playing for Baltimore farm teams in 1983 . . . Has performed hilarious pantomime routines during rain delays that have been big crowd-pleasers.

Year	Club	Pos.	G	AB	R	H	2B	3B	HR	RBI	SB	Avg.
1969	Minnesota	C	5	6	1	3	1	0	0	0	0	.500
1970	Minnesota	C	5	7	1	0	0	0	0	0	0	.000
1971	Minnesota	C	6	13	2	4	1	0	0	0	0	.308
1972	Minnesota	C	25	40	0	8	1	0	0	0	0	.200
1973	New York (AL)	C	6	11	0	2	0	0	0	0	0	.182
1974	New York (AL)	C-OF	43	109	12	26	3	0	2	12	1	.239
1975	New York (AL)	C-OF-3B	71	145	18	38	8	0	1	11	0	.262
1976	N.Y.-Balt. (AL)	C-OF	80	216	12	42	2	0	0	12	1	.194
1977	Baltimore........	C	91	270	27	61	7	4	3	34	2	.226
1978	Baltimore........	C	136	441	41	114	25	0	6	32	7	.259
1979	Baltimore........	C	124	368	48	88	23	0	6	41	0	.239
1980	Baltimore........	C-OF-1B	119	362	51	95	26	3	9	40	3	.262
1981	Baltimore........	C	92	251	24	54	10	1	6	15	0	.215
1982	Baltimore........	C	125	344	35	88	15	1	5	36	0	.256
1983	Baltimore........	C	128	347	33	80	16	2	4	32	1	.231
	Totals..........		1056	2930	305	703	138	11	42	265	15	.240

JOHN LOWENSTEIN 37 6-1 180 Bats L Throws R

Homered in fourth inning of Game 3 of World Series to start Orioles on their way to 4-1 comeback triumph . . . Teamed with Gary Roenicke to form left-field platoon that gave Orioles a potent attack . . . They combined for .291 average, 35 homers, 130 RBI as two-headed left fielder . . . Has thrived in platoon set-up in Baltimore, hitting .286 since joining Orioles in 1979, after compiling .238 mark for first eight seasons in majors with Cleveland and Texas . . . Went 142 games without an error before making one May 21 . . . Played second for first time since 1975 in 10th inning of Aug. 24 win over Toronto. Roenicke played third and Lenn Sakata made his pro debut as a catcher in that inning . . . Became first player to hit pinch-hit home run in an AL Championship Series when he connected off John Montague for three-run shot in 10th inning of 6-3 victory over California in opening game of 1979 playoffs . . . Born Jan. 27, 1947, in Wolf Point, Mont.

Year	Club	Pos.	G	AB	R	H	2B	3B	HR	RBI	SB	Avg.
1970	Cleveland.....	2B-3B-OF-SS	17	43	5	11	3	1	1	6	1	.256
1971	Cleveland.....	2B-OF-SS	58	140	15	26	5	0	4	9	1	.186
1972	Cleveland.....	OF-1B	68	151	16	32	8	1	6	21	2	.212
1973	Cleveland.....	3B-2B-OF-1B	98	305	42	89	16	1	6	40	5	.292
1974	Cleveland.....	OF-3B-1B-2B	140	508	65	123	14	2	8	48	36	.242
1975	Cleveland.....	OF-3B-2B	91	265	37	64	5	1	12	33	15	.242
1976	Cleveland.....	OF-1B	93	229	33	47	8	2	2	14	11	.205
1977	Cleveland.....	OF-1B	81	149	24	36	6	1	4	12	1	.242
1978	Texas	3B-OF	77	176	28	39	8	3	5	21	16	.222
1979	Baltimore.....	OF-1B-3B	97	197	33	50	8	2	11	34	16	.254
1980	Baltimore.....	OF	104	196	38	61	8	0	4	27	7	.311
1981	Baltimore.....	OF	83	189	19	47	7	0	6	20	7	.249
1982	Baltimore.....	OF	122	322	69	103	15	2	24	66	7	.320
1983	Baltimore.....	OF	122	310	52	87	13	2	15	60	2	.281
	Totals.......		1251	3180	476	815	124	18	108	411	127	.256

KEN SINGLETON 36 6-4 212 Bats S Throws R

Since DH was not allowed in 1983 World Series, he was limited to two pinch-hitting appearances . . . Struck out once, but walked with bases loaded in Game 4 to force in tying run in Orioles' 5-4 victory . . . Has been DH almost exclusively the last two years and hasn't appeared in the outfield since Sept. 28, 1982 . . . Deterioration of muscle in right forearm limited him to .177 average, no homers and only 13 RBI from right-hand side of plate in 1982, but last year he hit .262 with five homers and 25 RBI against left-handers . . . Finished second in AL in walks for fifth time . . . Recorded 1,000th career RBI at Chicago in August . . . He and Mickey Mantle are only two switch-hitters to hit as many as 35 homers in a season . . . Born June 10, 1947, in New York City . . . Has spent recent winters working for Baltimore television station.

Year	Club	Pos.	G	AB	R	H	2B	3B	HR	RBI	SB	Avg.
1970	New York (NL)	OF	69	198	22	52	8	0	5	26	1	.263
1971	New York (NL)	OF	115	298	34	73	5	0	13	46	0	.245
1972	Montreal	OF	142	507	78	139	23	2	14	50	5	.274
1973	Montreal	OF	162	560	100	169	26	2	23	103	2	.302
1974	Montreal	OF	148	511	68	141	20	2	9	74	5	.276
1975	Baltimore.	OF	155	586	88	176	37	4	15	55	3	.300
1976	Baltimore.	OF	154	544	62	151	25	2	13	70	2	.278
1977	Baltimore.	OF	152	536	90	176	24	0	24	99	0	.328
1978	Baltimore.	OF	149	502	67	147	21	2	20	81	0	.293
1979	Baltimore.	OF	159	570	93	168	29	1	35	111	3	.295
1980	Baltimore.	OF	156	583	85	177	28	3	24	104	0	.304
1981	Baltimore.	OF	103	363	48	101	16	1	13	49	0	.278
1982	Baltimore.	OF	156	561	71	141	27	2	14	77	0	.251
1983	Baltimore.	DH	151	507	52	140	21	3	18	84	0	.276
	Totals		1971	6826	957	1951	310	24	242	1029	21	.286

SAMMY STEWART 29 6-3 208 Bats R Throws R

Excelled out of bullpen in postseason . . . Pitched four shutout innings to save victory over Chicago in Game 3 of AL playoffs . . . Pitched five shutout innings, striking out six, in three World Series appearances . . . Arrested for drunken driving July 8 and decided to enter chemical dependency program . . . Recovery coincided with turnaround on mound . . . From July 20 to end of season, he was 7-1 with 2.39 ERA . . . Set Baltimore record by pitching 140 innings in relief . . . Eight times in his career he has pitched seven or more innings in relief . . . Had lowest ERA in AL based on actual innings pitched in 1981, but lost title to Oakland's Steve McCatty in disputed decision because number of innings was rounded off ... Born Oct. 28, 1954, in Asheville, N.C.

Year	Club	G	IP	W	L	Pct.	SO	BB	H	ERA
1978	Baltimore	2	11	1	1	.500	11	3	10	3.27
1979	Baltimore	31	118	8	5	.615	71	71	96	3.51
1980	Baltimore	33	119	7	7	.500	78	60	103	3.55
1981	Baltimore	29	112	4	8	.333	57	57	89	2.33
1982	Baltimore	38	139	10	9	.526	69	62	140	4.14
1983	Baltimore	58	144	9	4	.692	95	67	138	3.62
	Totals	191	643	39	34	.534	381	220	576	3.47

TOP PROSPECTS

MIKE YOUNG 24 6-2 195 **Bats S Throws R**

Another young Oriole outfielder who can fly ... Spent month with Orioles (.167) cutting his season at Rochester (AAA) to 102 games, but he still hit .284 with 14 homers, 66 RBI and 18 stolen bases in minors ... Has to make better contact. Struck out 93 times at Rochester in 1983 after leading International League with 140 strikeouts in 1982 ... Born March 20, 1960, in Oakland ... Attended Chabot Junior College before being drafted by Orioles in January 1980.

MARK BROWN 24 6-2 190 **Bats L Throws R**

Unimpressive-looking sinker/slider pitcher who lives by Oriole motto of working fast and throwing strikes ... Was 6-1 with five saves in 19 games at Rochester (AAA), after compiling 8-2 mark with 2.08 ERA for Charlotte (AA) during 1982 ... Born July 13, 1959, in Bellows Falls, Vt. ... Sixth-round draft pick in June 1980, out of University of Massachusetts.

MANAGER JOE ALTOBELLI: Had quite an act to follow after

being named Earl Weaver's successor as manager and did quite a job ... Didn't worry about creating his own philosophy. Worked with same basic approach that Weaver used and wound up winning world championship in first year, something Weaver accomplished only once in 14½ seasons ... Was given a two-year contract ... Worked in Yankee organization from

1980-82, managing at Columbus one year and serving as Yankee third-base coach the next two . . . Managed San Francisco from 1977-79, earning NL Manager-of-the-Year honors in 1978, when Giants compiled their best record since 1971 (89-73) . . . Prior to that, he spent 14 years in Oriole organization, including 11 as a manager in their system . . . Guided Rochester to four first-place finishes in six years and was selected Minor League Manager of the Year in 1974 . . . Originally signed as a first baseman by Cleveland and played 15 years, mostly in the minors . . . Appeared in 166 major-league games with Cleveland and Minnesota . . . Born May 26, 1932, in Detroit . . . Owns 323-303 overall managerial mark in majors.

GREATEST STEALER

In recent years, the Orioles have lived by the Earl Weaver credo—you win games with strong pitching and three-run home runs. They haven't had much interest in stealing bases. But a couple of decades ago, the Orioles boasted one of the premier base-stealers in baseball history, Luis Aparicio.

Aparicio, who ranks 28th on the all-time stolen-base list with 506, led the American League in stolen bases a record nine times. Seven of those titles came when he was with the Chicago White Sox from 1956-62, but he added two more after joining the Orioles in 1963. He led Baltimore in stolen bases all five years he played for the club, including a club-record 57 in 1964, when he led the AL for the final time. And, even though he was with the Orioles only five years, Aparicio ranks third on the club's all-time list with 166, one behind Paul Blair's 13-year total.

The Orioles' all-time leader is Al Bumbry, who has stolen 243 bases in 12 years with the club. Like Aparicio, he has led the team in stolen bases five times, but with nowhere near the single-season rate Aparicio managed.

ALL-TIME ORIOLE SEASON RECORDS

BATTING: Ken Singleton, .328, 1977
HRs: Frank Robinson, 49, 1966
RBIs: Jim Gentile, 141, 1961
STEALS: Luis Aparicio, 57, 1964
WINS: Steve Stone, 25, 1980
STRIKEOUTS: Dave McNally, 202, 1968

BOSTON RED SOX

TEAM DIRECTORY: Pres.: Mrs. Jean R. Yawkey; Exec. VP-GM: Haywood Sullivan; Exec. VP-Adm.: Edward (Buddy) LeRoux; VP-Dir. Play. Dev.: Edward Kenney; Dir. Scouting: Eddie Kasko; Dir Pub. Rel.: George Sullivan; Dir. Publ.: Dick Bresciani; Trav. Sec.: Jack Rogers; Mgr.: Ralph Houk. Home: Fenway Park (33,583). Field distances: 315, l.f. line; 379, l.c.; 390, c.f.; 420, r.c. corner; 380, r.c.; 302, r.f. line. Spring training: Winter Haven, Fla.

SCOUTING REPORT

HITTING: Last season, the Red Sox had the AL's leading hitter in Wade Boggs (.361), its top two home-run hitters in Jim Rice (39) and Tony Armas (36) and its co-RBI champion in Rice (126). But they also have a lineup that is unbalanced and lacks diversification.

The outfield combo of Rice, Armas and Dwight Evans hit 97 of the club's 142 home runs. The starting infield of Dave Stapleton,

Wade Boggs was AL batting champion with .361 mark.

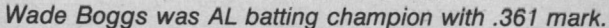

Jerry Remy, Glenn Hoffman and Boggs combined for only 19. And Boston's left-handed hitters managed only 19, 10 of which came from since-retired Carl Yastrzemski. The Red Sox hope winter addition Mike Easler, a lefty hitter who was a platoon player with Pittsburgh, can fill some of that void with his opposite-field power stroke as a designated hitter.

There's nobody to help alleviate this club's lack of speed. Not only did the Red Sox steal only 30 bases, they tied the AL record they set in 1982 by grounding into 171 double plays.

PITCHING: The Red Sox never have been a frontrunner in the arms race, but they seem to be carrying the deficiency to greater extremes these days. To get Easler, they gave up John Tudor, who has led the Boston starters in wins the last two seasons and led the staff with 240 innings last year. That leaves them with a rotation of lefties Bruce Hurst (12-12) and Bob Ojeda (12-7), and right-handers Dennis Eckersley (9-13), Dennis Boyd (4-8) and injury-riddled Mike Brown (6-6).

But that's better than the bullpen, where Bob Stanley (33 saves, 2.85 ERA) is the only reliable alternative for manager Ralph Houk. Mark Clear still strikes out plenty of batters, but he's not dependable in the clutch and nobody else has picked up the slack. Don't look for an improvement on last year's 4.34 team ERA.

DEFENSE: The imbalance of the Red Sox shows again. With Rice, Armas and Evans backed up by Reid Nichols and Rick Miller, nobody comes close to matching arms or patrolling abilities with the Red Sox outfielders.

Second baseman Remy is the only other Red Sox player who would rate as solid defensively. Hoffman was moved from third to short because he doesn't have enough punch, but now he might go back because of his lack of range. First baseman Stapleton is less impressive the more he plays and Boggs would be better at first than third. There is some hope, thanks to rookie shortstop Jackie Gutierrez. The catching will improve if Gary Allenson is given a fulltime shot.

OUTLOOK: The tradition has crumbled at Fenway. It's no big deal that the Sox haven't won a World Series lately. Heck, they haven't done that since Ted Williams was born (1918). But it is significant that, after 16 consecutive winning seasons, they fell all the way to sixth place.

With no pitching help on the farm, the loss of Tudor for a parttime player and, of course, no Yaz, things may be even bleaker in '84.

BOSTON RED SOX 1984 ROSTER

MANAGER Ralph Houk

Coaches—John Pesky, Eddie Yost, Walt Hriniak, Tommy Harper, Lee Stange

PITCHERS

No.	Name	1983 Club	W-L	IP	SO	ERA	B-T	Ht.	Wt.	Born
45	Aponte, Luis	Boston	5-4	62	32	3.63	R-R	6-0	185	7/14/54 Venezuela
42	*Bird, Doug	Boston	1-4	68	33	6.65	R-R	6-4	189	3/5/50 Corona, CA
23	Boyd, Dennis	Pawtucket	5-8	123	129	4.04	R-R	6-1	155	10/6/59 Meridian, MS
		Boston	4-8	99	43	3.28				
27	Brown, Mike	Boston	6-6	104	35	4.67	R-R	6-2	195	3/4/59 Haddon Township, NJ
38	Burtt, Dennis	Pawtucket	4-5	110	66	5.30	R-R	6-0	185	11/29/57 San Diego, CA
25	Clear, Mark	Boston	4-5	96	81	6.28	R-R	6-4	200	5/27/56 Los Angeles, CA
28	Crawford, Steve	Pawtucket	8-11	155	104	5.18	R-R	6-5	225	4/29/58 Pryor, OK
31	Denman, Brian	Pawtucket	8-11	154	76	5.02	R-R	6-4	210	2/12/56 Minneapolis, MN
43	Eckersley, Dennis	Boston	9-13	176	77	5.61	R-R	6-2	190	10/3/54 Oakland, CA
47	Hurst, Bruce	Boston	12-12	211	115	4.09	L-L	6-3	215	3/24/58 Saint George, UT
48	Johnson, John Henry	Boston	3-2	53	51	3.71	L-L	6-2	210	8/21/56 Houston, TX
—	Johnson, Mitch	Winston-Salem	15-8	214	146	3.11	R-R	6-5	210	8/2/62 Colombia, PA
49	Nipper, Al	New Britain	4-3	67	42	2.82	R-R	6-0	188	4/2/59 San Diego, CA
		Pawtucket	9-4	109	58	4.45				
		Boston	1-1	16	5	2.25				
19	Ojeda, Bob	Boston	12-7	174	94	4.04	L-L	6-1	190	12/17/57 Los Angeles, CA
44	Schoppee, Dave	Pawtucket	3-2	66	32	6.58	R-R	6-3	200	4/24/57 Bangor, MA
46	Stanley, Bob	Boston	8-10	145	65	2.85	R-R	6-4	215	11/10/54 Portland, ME
—	Woodward, Robbie	Winston-Salem	13-11	198	157	4.14	R-R	6-3	185	9/28/62 Hanover, NH

CATCHERS

No.	Name	1983 Club	H	HR	RBI	Pct.	B-T	Ht.	Wt.	Born
39	Allenson, Gary	Boston	53	3	30	.230	R-R	5-11	193	2/4/55 Culver City, CA
10	Gedman, Rich	Boston	60	2	18	.294	L-R	6-0	215	9/26/59 Worcester, MA
—	Malpeso, Dave	New Britain	111	9	72	.258	R-R	6-0	200	12/18/60 Franklin, VA
5	Newman, Jeff	Boston	25	3	7	.189	R-R	6-2	215	9/11/48 Fort Worth, TX
15	Sullivan, Marc	New Britain	63	7	43	.229	R-R	6-4	205	7/25/58 Quincy, MA
		Pawtucket	13	1	7	.186				

INFIELDERS

No.	Name	1983 Club	H	HR	RBI	Pct.	B-T	Ht.	Wt.	Born
17	Barrett, Marty	Pawtucket	41	1	18	.345	R-R	5-10	175	6/23/58 Arcadia, CA
		Boston	10	0	2	.227				
26	Boggs, Wade	Boston	210	5	74	.361	L-R	6-2	185	6/15/58 Omaha, NE
7	Bustabad, Juan	Pawtucket	46	1	24	.214	L-R	5-10	150	8/16/61 Cuba
		New Britain	57	0	19	.265				
16	Davis, Mike	Pawtucket	56	5	35	.228	R-R	6-0	170	7/18/59 Janesville, WI
41	Gutierrez, Jackie	New Britain	69	4	25	.278	R-R	5-11	175	6/27/60 Cartagena, CO
		Pawtucket	62	1	17	.266				
		Boston	3	0	0	.300				
18	Hoffman, Glenn	Boston	123	4	41	.260	R-R	6-2	190	7/7/58 Orange, CA
22	Jurak, Ed	Boston	44	0	18	.277	R-R	6-2	185	10/24/57 Los Angeles, CA
—	Lyone, Steve	New Britain	112	7	62	.246	L-R	6-3	190	6/3/60 Tacoma, WA
3	Remy, Jerry	Boston	163	0	43	.275	L-R	5-9	165	11/8/52 Fall River, MA
11	Stapleton, Dave	Boston	134	10	66	.247	R-R	6-1	170	1/16/54 Fair Hope, AL

OUTFIELDERS

No.	Name	1983 Club	H	HR	RBI	Pct.	B-T	Ht.	Wt.	Born
20	Armas, Tony	Boston	125	36	107	.218	R-R	6-1	192	7/12/53 Venezuela
50	Burgess, Gus	Pawtucket	121	8	66	.269	L-L	5-11	189	12/18/61 Boynton Beach, FL
—	Easler, Mike	Pittsburgh	117	10	54	.307	L-R	6-1	196	11/29/50 Cleveland, OH
24	Evans, Dwight	Boston	112	22	58	.238	R-R	6-3	205	11/3/51 Santa Monica, CA
12	Graham, Lee	Pawtucket	140	11	59	.276	L-L	5-10	170	9/22/59 Summerfield, FL
		Boston	0	0	1	.000				
3	Miller, Rick	Boston	75	2	21	.286	L-L	6-0	180	4/19/48 Grand Rapids, MI
51	Nichols, Reid	Boston	78	6	22	.285	R-R	5-11	172	8/5/58 Ocala, FL
14	Rice, Jim	Boston	191	39	126	.305	R-R	6-2	205	3/8/53 Anderson, SC
1	Walker, Chico	Pawtucket	119	18	56	.269	B-R	5-9	179	11/25/57 Jackson, MS

*Free agent unsigned at press time

RED SOX PROFILES

JIM RICE 31 6-2 205 **Bats R Throws R**

Led AL in home runs and total bases (344), tied for lead in RBI . . . Was second in slugging percentage (.550) and fifth in hits . . . Left fielder's production rose as he benefitted from presence of Tony Armas behind him in lineup . . . Marked first time Red Sox have had power threat to complement him since Fred Lynn left for California . . . Slowed for a month with back problems, but still managed to play 155 games . . . Has driven in major-league-leading 640 runs in the last six years . . . He and Johnny Pesky are only Red Sox to have three 200-hit seasons . . . Voted AL MVP in 1978, when he became first AL player in 37 years to amass more than 400 total bases (406) . . . Led majors in home runs, triples and total bases that year . . . Missed 1975 postseason because of broken hand . . . Born March 8, 1953, in Anderson, S.C. . . . Minor League Player of the Year and International League MVP in 1974, when he won Triple Crown for Louisville (.337, 25 homers, 93 RBI).

Year	Club	Pos.	G	AB	R	H	2B	3B	HR	RBI	SB	Avg.
1974	Boston	OF	24	67	6	18	2	1	1	13	0	.269
1975	Boston	OF	144	564	92	174	29	4	22	102	10	.309
1976	Boston	OF	153	581	75	164	25	8	25	85	8	.282
1977	Boston	OF	160	644	104	206	29	15	39	114	5	.320
1978	Boston	OF	163	677	121	213	25	15	46	139	7	.315
1979	Boston	OF	158	619	117	201	39	6	39	130	9	.325
1980	Boston	OF	124	504	81	148	22	6	24	86	8	.294
1981	Boston	OF	108	451	51	128	18	1	17	62	2	.284
1982	Boston	OF	145	573	86	177	24	5	24	97	0	.309
1983	Boston	OF	155	626	90	191	34	1	39	126	0	.305
	Totals		1334	5306	823	1620	247	62	276	954	49	.305

WADE BOGGS 25 6-2 185 **Bats L Throws R**

Has never hit under .300 in seven professional seasons . . . Led AL in hitting and on-base percentage (.444) . . . Was second in hits, second in doubles and third in walks . . . His .355 big-league career mark is fifth-highest average in history for any player after two seasons in majors . . . Led AL third basemen in runs produced and got runner home from third with less than two outs on 18-of-28 occasions . . . Hit .349 in 1982 to set an AL rookie record . . . Got chance to play regularly in rookie season when Carney Lansford was hurt and was so impressive, Red Sox decided to trade Lansford to Oakland in winter of 1982 instead of worrying about signing him after 1983 . . . Doesn't show much power now, but scouts expect it to come as he gains confidence and strength . . . Born June 15, 1958, in Omaha, Neb. . . . Creature of habit . . . Eats chicken every day of season . . . Was placekicker on high-school football team.

Year	Club	Pos.	G	AB	R	H	2B	3B	HR	RBI	SB	Avg.
1982	Boston	1B-3B-OF	104	338	51	118	14	1	5	44	1	.349
1983	Boston	3B-1B	153	582	100	210	44	7	5	74	3	.361
	Totals		257	920	151	328	58	8	10	118	4	.357

TONY ARMAS 30 6-1 192 Bats R Throws R

Target of Boston boobirds because of low average . . . May not have had enough hits to keep his average up, but the ones he did have were big ones . . . Was second in AL in home runs and seventh in RBI . . . Did tie for AL lead in one unfortunate category with teammate Jim Rice by grounding into 31 double plays . . . Like Rice, he hits the ball hard and, with batting champ Wade Boggs at top of order, he had plenty of men on base ahead of him . . . Has compiled at least 49 extra-base hits in each of the last four years . . . Right fielder for Oakland became center fielder for Boston with minimal problems . . . Combines with Rice and Dwight Evans to give Red Sox strongest arms of any outfield in majors . . . Set major-league record for right fielder with 11 putouts against Toronto in 1982 . . . Born July 12, 1953, in Anzoatequi, Venezuela . . . One of 14 children . . . Came in five-player deal that sent Carney Lansford to Oakland prior to 1983.

Year	Club	Pos.	G	AB	R	H	2B	3B	HR	RBI	SB	Avg.
1976	Pittsburgh	OF	4	6	0	2	0	0	0	1	0	.333
1977	Oakland..........	OF-SS	118	363	26	87	8	2	13	53	1	.240
1978	Oakland..........	OF	91	239	17	51	6	1	2	13	1	.213
1979	Oakland..........	OF	80	278	29	69	9	3	11	34	1	.248
1980	Oakland..........	OF	158	628	87	175	18	8	35	109	5	.279
1981	Oakland..........	OF	109	440	51	115	24	3	22	76	5	.261
1982	Oakland..........	OF	138	536	58	125	19	2	28	89	2	.233
1983	Boston	OF	145	574	77	125	23	2	36	107	0	.218
	Totals		843	3064	345	749	107	21	147	482	15	.244

DWIGHT EVANS 32 6-3 205 Bats R Throws R

Posted lowest average since his rookie season, but did manage to surpass 20 home runs for fifth time in six years . . . Missed last two months of season with torn muscle . . . Critics questioned decision to sit out final month . . . Has won six Gold Gloves in right field . . . Tied for AL home-run title and led majors in RBI in 1981 . . . Also led AL in walks (85) and total bases (215) that year, becoming fifth AL player to lead in those two categories in same season. Others were Babe Ruth, Ted Williams, Jimmie Foxx and Mickey Mantle . . . His 1977 season was cut short by knee surgery . . . Owns strongest and most accurate arm in AL . . . International League MVP with Louisville (AAA) in 1972 . . . Born Nov. 3, 1951, in Santa Monica, Cal. . . . Member of the Massachusetts Statewide Advisory Council to Office for Children.

Year	Club	Pos.	G	AB	R	H	2B	3B	HR	RBI	SB	Avg.
1972	Boston	OF	18	57	2	15	3	1	1	6	0	.263
1973	Boston	OF	119	282	46	63	13	1	10	32	5	.223
1974	Boston	OF	133	463	60	130	19	8	10	70	4	.281
1975	Boston	OF	128	412	61	113	24	6	13	56	3	.274
1976	Boston	OF	146	501	61	121	34	5	17	62	6	.242
1977	Boston	OF	73	230	39	66	9	2	14	36	4	.287
1978	Boston	OF	147	497	75	123	24	2	24	63	8	.247
1979	Boston	OF	152	489	69	134	24	1	21	58	6	.274
1980	Boston	OF	148	463	72	123	37	5	18	60	3	.266
1981	Boston	OF	108	412	84	122	19	4	22	71	3	.296
1982	Boston	OF	162	609	122	178	37	7	32	98	3	.292
1983	Boston	OF	126	470	74	112	19	4	22	58	3	.238
	Totals		1460	4885	765	1300	262	46	204	670	48	.266

MARK CLEAR 27 6-4 200 **Bats R Throws R**

Collapsed in 1983, losing confidence during a long string of bad outings . . . Held a tie or lead in only 7-of-21 opportunities . . . 60-of-65 runners attempting to steal against him have been safe during last three years . . . When he throws strikes he is tough to hit, especially for right-handed hitters, because of big wheeling motion and sharp breaking ball . . . Has 475 big-league strikeouts in 493 innings . . . Voted AL Rookie Pitcher of the Year for California in 1979 . . . Born May 27, 1956, in Los Angeles . . . Originally signed by Philadelphia in 1975, but was released after season of rookie ball . . . Signed by Angels . . . Started in first five pro seasons at A level and was about to be released when he was promoted to AA and made into a reliever in 1978 . . . Compiled 4-2 record and 13 saves in 31 games at El Paso that season . . . Made Angels' roster the next spring . . . Nephew of Angel bullpen coach Bob Clear.

Year	Club	G	IP	W	L	Pct.	SO	BB	H	ERA
1979	California	52	109	11	5	.688	98	68	87	3.63
1980	California	58	106	11	11	.500	105	65	82	3.31
1981	Boston	34	77	8	3	.727	82	51	69	4.09
1982	Boston	55	105	14	9	.609	109	61	92	3.00
1983	Boston	48	96	4	5	.444	81	68	101	6.28
	Totals	247	493	48	33	.593	475	313	431	4.02

BOB STANLEY 29 6-4 215 **Bats R Throws R**

Compiled losing record for first time since coming to majors . . . With bullpen mate Mark Clear falling apart, he had to carry full load . . . Has become a fulltime reliever, making only one start in last three years after bouncing between bullpen and rotation since joining Red Sox . . . Was strictly a starter in minors . . . Set AL record by pitching 168⅓ innings in relief in 1982 . . . Was at his best in August 1981, when he did not allow a run in 23⅓ innings . . . Has a consistent sinker that baffles hitters . . . Born Nov. 10, 1954, in Portland, Me. . . . Turned down offer from Dodgers in June 1973, then signed with Boston after Red Sox made him first-round pick in secondary phase of draft in January 1974.

Year	Club	G	IP	W	L	Pct.	SO	BB	H	ERA
1977	Boston	41	151	8	7	.533	44	43	176	3.99
1978	Boston	52	142	15	2	.882	38	34	142	2.60
1979	Boston	40	217	16	12	.571	56	44	250	3.98
1980	Boston	52	175	10	8	.556	71	52	186	3.39
1981	Boston	35	99	10	8	.556	28	38	110	3.82
1982	Boston	48	168	12	7	.632	83	50	161	3.10
1983	Boston	64	145	8	10	.444	65	38	145	2.85
	Totals	332	1097	79	54	.594	385	299	1170	3.41

DAVE STAPLETON 30 6-1 170 **Bats R Throws R**

Valuable utility man who has seen his production tail off since assuming a fulltime job at first base the last two years . . . Posted lowest professional batting average since 1977 . . . Had to have operation for removal of bone spur from back of hand . . . When he first came up, he played everywhere, seeing time at all four infield positions, in the outfield and as a designated hitter . . . Finished second in AL Rookie-of-the-Year voting in 1980 . . . Co-MVP in International League with Pawtucket (AAA) in 1979 . . . Born Jan. 16, 1954, in Fair Hope, Ala. . . . Played for former major-leaguer Eddie Stanky at South Alabama, where he lettered in football and basketball . . . Lifts front foot when hitting and reminds oldtimers of Mel Ott with his swing, but results aren't quite the same.

Year	Club	Pos.	G	AB	R	H	2B	3B	HR	RBI	SB	Avg.
1980	Boston	INF-OF	106	449	61	144	33	5	7	45	3	.321
1981	Boston	INF	93	355	45	101	17	1	10	42	0	.285
1982	Boston	INF-OF	150	538	66	142	28	1	14	65	2	.264
1983	Boston	INF-OF	151	542	54	134	31	1	10	66	1	.247
	Totals		500	1884	226	521	109	8	41	218	6	.277

DENNIS ECKERSLEY 29 6-2 190 **Bats R Throws R**

His once-promising career has fizzled . . . Has not had a complete-game victory since July 1982 . . . Has 11-18 record since July 27, 1982 . . . Finished 1979 by going 1-5 and has posted 43-48 record since then . . . Became only Red Sox pitcher to win 20 games in last six years, in 1978 . . . Did not allow an earned run in first 28⅔ major-league innings, earning AL Rookie-Pitcher-of-the-Year honors for Cleveland in 1975 . . . Pitched 1-0 no-hitter against California and Frank Tanana, May 31, 1981 . . . That feat was part of 22⅓ consecutive no-hit innnings, second-longest no-hit string in AL history to Cy Young's 25⅓ innings in 1904 . . . Also had two one-hitters in 1977, tying AL record for low-hit games in single season . . . Born Oct. 3, 1954, in Oakland . . . Came to Red Sox from Indians as key figure in six-player deal prior to 1978 season.

Year	Club	G	IP	W	L	Pct.	SO	BB	H	ERA
1975	Cleveland	34	187	13	7	.650	152	90	147	2.60
1976	Cleveland	36	199	13	12	.520	200	78	155	3.44
1977	Cleveland	33	247	14	13	.519	191	54	214	3.53
1978	Boston	35	268	20	8	.714	162	71	258	2.99
1979	Boston	33	247	17	10	.630	150	59	234	2.99
1980	Boston	30	198	12	14	.462	121	44	188	4.27
1981	Boston	23	154	9	8	.529	79	35	160	4.27
1982	Boston	33	224	13	13	.500	127	43	228	3.73
1983	Boston	28	176	9	13	.409	77	39	223	5.61
	Totals	285	1900	120	98	.550	1259	513	1807	3.64

JERRY REMY 31 5-9 165 **Bats L Throws R**

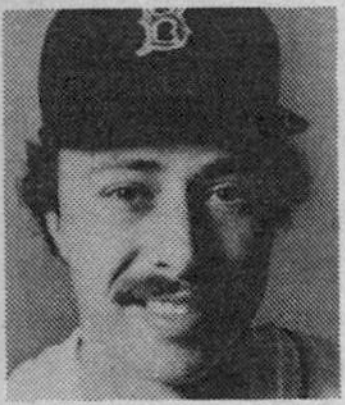

Most proficient bunter in majors . . . Had 19 bunt singles for second year in a row and has 53 bunt hits in last three years . . . Bad back forced him to miss all of 1983 spring training and early part of season . . . Didn't get average over .250 until end of July . . . Needs to walk more often to take advantage of base-running abilities . . . Averaged 35 stolen bases per year in first four major-league seasons . . . In 1979, he joined Tommy Harper as only two Red Sox players to steal 30 bases in a season since Bill Werber stole 40 in 1934 . . . Theft ability was stymied by 1979 knee injury, which required surgery in 1980. Says he's 100 percent now, but doesn't get much of a chance to run because of conservative Red Sox attack . . . Born Nov. 8, 1952, in Fall River, Mass. . . . A June 1970 draft choice of Washington Senators, but didn't sign until after the draft the following January, when he was picked by California Angels.

Year	Club	Pos.	G	AB	R	H	2B	3B	HR	RBI	SB	Avg.
1975	California	2B	147	569	82	147	17	5	1	46	34	.258
1976	California	2B	143	502	64	132	14	3	0	28	35	.263
1977	California	2B-3B	154	575	74	145	19	10	4	44	41	.252
1978	Boston	2B-SS	148	583	87	162	24	6	2	44	30	.278
1979	Boston	2B	80	306	49	91	11	2	0	29	14	.297
1980	Boston	2B-OF	63	230	24	72	7	2	0	9	14	.313
1981	Boston	2B	88	358	55	110	9	1	0	31	9	307
1982	Boston	2B	155	636	89	178	22	3	0	47	16	.280
1983	Boston	2B	146	592	73	163	16	5	0	43	11	.275
	Totals		1124	4351	597	1200	139	37	7	321	204	.276

MIKE EASLER 33 6-1 196 **Bats L Throws R**

Came to Fenway from Pittsburgh in December swap for pitcher John Tudor . . . "Hit Man" remains one of the most lethal platoon players in the majors . . . Played less last year, yet still produced eight game-winning RBI in 115 games . . . Belted two grand slams . . . A .363 June turned into his second .300-plus season in majors . . . Born Nov. 29, 1950, in Cleveland . . . Left fielder had a distinguished minor-league career, but didn't reach majors to stay until age 28 . . . Made up for lost time with Bucs, being named club's MVP with a .338 year in 1980 . . . His 10 years in minors were highlighted by winning batting titles for Tulsa (AAA) with .352 mark in 1976 and Columbus (AAA) with .330 average in 1978.

Year	Club	Pos.	G	AB	R	H	2B	3B	HR	RBI	SB	Avg.
1973	Houston	OF	6	7	1	0	0	0	0	0	0	.000
1974	Houston	PH	15	15	0	1	0	0	0	0	0	.067
1975	Houston	PH	5	5	0	0	0	0	0	0	0	.000
1976	California	DH	21	54	6	13	1	1	0	4	1	.241
1977	Pittsburgh	OF	10	18	3	8	2	0	1	5	0	.444
1979	Pittsburgh	OF	55	54	8	15	1	1	2	11	0	.278
1980	Pittsburgh	OF	132	393	66	133	27	3	21	74	5	.338
1981	Pittsburgh	OF	95	339	43	97	18	5	7	42	4	.286
1982	Pittsburgh	OF	142	475	52	131	27	2	15	58	1	.276
1983	Pittsburgh	OF	115	381	44	117	17	2	10	54	4	.307
	Totals		596	1741	223	515	93	14	56	248	15	.296

TOP PROSPECTS

DENNIS BOYD 24 6-1 155 **Bats R Throws R**

Don't let his numbers deceive you . . . Was 5-8 at Pawtucket (AAA), but 4.04 ERA was lowest on team . . . Also struck out 129 batters and walked only 41 in 123 innings . . . Was 35-7 with 3.09 ERA and 424 strikeouts in 460 innings during first three years in minors . . . Born Oct. 6, 1959, in Meridian, Miss. . . . A 16th-round draft choice in June 1980, out of Jackson State, where he played for former big-leaguer Scipio Spinks.

ROGER CLEMENS 22 6-3 210 **Bats R Throws R**
Coming in a hurry . . . First-round draft choice of Red Sox last June . . . Made strides through minors in a hurry . . . Compiled 7-2 record at Winter Haven (A) and New Britain (AA), walking only 12 and striking out 95 in 71 innings . . . Born Aug. 4, 1962, in Dayton, Ohio . . . Product of University of Texas . . . Has 90-plus-mph fastball, good slider, curve and change-up . . . Needs to improve stamina.

MANAGER RALPH HOUK: "The Major" came out of two-year retirement to become 35th manager in Red Sox history after 1980 season . . . Played 12 years of pro ball, despite missing four years for military service . . . Served in the Ranger 9th Armored Division in Europe during World War II, rising from rank of private to major, and was awarded the Silver Star, Purple Heart and Bronze Star . . . Spent parts of eight seasons in big leagues with Yankees, but played in only 91 games . . . Appeared in only one game, as a pinch-hitter, despite being on Yankee roster the entire 1954 season . . . Managed three years in minors before embarking on big-league managerial career, which has spanned 19 seasons and produced 1,533-1,455 record . . . Replaced Casey Stengel as Yankee skipper in 1961 . . . Guided Yanks to AL pennants from 1961-63 and won world championships in 1961 and 1962 . . . After stint as Yankee vice-president and general manager in 1964 and 1965, he returned to Yankee dugout in May 1966 . . . Went to Detroit for five-year term as Tiger skipper, beginning in 1974, then retired briefly . . . Born Aug. 9, 1919, in Lawrence, Kan.

GREATEST STEALER

With hitters like Ted Williams, Carl Yastrzemski and Jim Rice having made themselves at home in Fenway Park over the years, it has been hard for a Red Sox base-stealer to seize much time in the limelight. This is a team that stole only 30 bases in 1983 and has had only four individuals break the 30 level since 1914.

There was Tommy Harper, who set the club record of 54 in 1973 and also led the Red Sox in stolen bases his other two seasons in Boston. But in the long term, Boston's greatest stolen-base artist was Hall-of-Famer Harry Hooper.

He played for the Red Sox from 1909-1920 and led the team in stolen bases six times, stealing 300 during his stay in Boston. During that time, he was a member of four Red Sox pennant-winners. He finished his career with the White Sox, with whom he raised his career stolen-base total to 375 before retiring after the 1925 season.

ALL-TIME RED SOX SEASON RECORDS

BATTING: Ted Williams, .406, 1941
HRs: Jimmy Foxx, 50, 1938
RBIs: Jimmy Foxx, 175, 1938
STEALS: Tommy Harper, 54, 1973
WINS: Joe Wood, 34, 1912
STRIKEOUTS: Joe Wood, 258, 1912

CLEVELAND INDIANS

TEAM DIRECTORY: Chairman of the Board: Pat O'Neill; Pres.-Chief Exec. Officer: Gabe Paul; VP-GM: Phil Seghi; Treas.: Dudley S. Blossom; VP-Dir. Play. Dev./Scouting: Bob Quinn; Dir. Pub. Rel.: Bob DiBiasio; Trav. Sec.: Mike Seghi; Mgr.: Pat Corrales. Home: Cleveland Municipal Stadium (74,280). Field distances: 320, l.f. line; 377, l.c.; 400, c.f.; 395, r.c.; 320, r.f. line. Spring training: Tucson, Ariz.

SCOUTING REPORT

HITTING: Punch, meet Judy. The Indians epitomize offensive ineptitude. Their 86 home runs were the fewest of any team in the AL. Gorman Thomas, who didn't arrive until June 6, still tied Andre Thornton for the team lead in home runs with 17. And now Thomas is in Seattle, after his demand for a trade was granted during the winter.

The Indians can get on base (.265 team batting average and AL-high 605 walks), but they don't get very far (1,168 left on base, third-highest mark in the league). There are some decent hitters—Thornton (.281, 77 RBI), Toby Harrah (.266), Julio Franco (.273, 80 RBI), Pat Tabler (.291, 65 RBI), Mike Hargrove (.286) and Atlanta import Brett Butler (.281)—but this team has got to get some drive in the lineup.

There is hope for improvement, however, even with the loss of Thomas. Franco and Tabler will have a year of experience under their belts; Tony Bernazard, the AL's second-most productive second baseman in 1982, was obtained from Seattle for Thomas and two rookies—catcher Jerry Willard and third baseman Brook Jacoby—have shown signs in the minors.

PITCHING: The Indians went all out to sign Rick Sutcliffe (17-11) to a long-term contract—and with good reason. He has won 31 games during the last two years and this is a team that can not afford to lose a quality pitcher.

The only thing standing between the Indians and the worst ERA (4.43) in the majors last season was the Minnesota Twins, who at least had the excuse of playing half their games in the Metrodome. Again, youth offers a glimmer of sunshine. Neal Heaton (11-7) showed flashes of excitement in his rookie year and Rick Behenna, acquired from Atlanta in the Len Barker trade, is expected to provide aid in 1984.

But where the Indians need help the most is in the bullpen,

Shortstop Julio Franco drove in 80 runs.

where the never-say-die arm of Dan Spillner (2-9, 8 saves) finally went belly up in 1983. Without him at top form, the Indians are without hope.

DEFENSE: While the pitching staff fizzled in 1983, the defense wasn't as much to blame as it had been in years past. The arrival of Franco provided stability to the middle of the infield and the shortstop played a big part as the club increased its double-play total from 129 in 1982 to 170.

Franco's 28 errors ranked second among AL shortstops, but nobody's complaining. In his first year in the big leagues, he showed more consistency than anyone expected after racking up 112 miscues in his three previous years in the minors.

Whomever manager Pat Corrales picks to catch, he'll be well-armed. Willard led International League catchers in throwing out base-runners. Chris Bando caught 12-of-28 last year and Ron Hassey threw out 43 percent of potential base-stealers in the second half. The speedy Butler will cover plenty of ground in center field.

OUTLOOK: The last time Cleveland was in a pennant race, Dwight Eisenhower was in the White House, Hawaii had just become a state and the Beatles were still in Liverpool.

It's not a tendency that anyone should expect to change. But the Indians' approach to the game will. Corrales is a no-nonsense guy who makes the decisions he feels are right, without regard to the consequences. He will make this rag-tag team play hard. During one of the Indians' typical dry spells, he announced in a clubhouse meeting: "I don't want half you guys. I've talked to the front office and nobody else does, either."

CLEVELAND INDIANS 1984 ROSTER

MANAGER Pat Corrales
Coaches—Johnny Goryl, Don McMahon, Ed Napoleon, Dennis Sommers

PITCHERS

No.	Name	1983 Club	W-L	IP	SO	ERA	B-T	Ht.	Wt.	Born
51	Anderson, Bud	Charleston	1-0	20	15	3.60	R-R	6-3	210	5/27/56 Rockville Centre, NY
		Cleveland	1-6	68	32	4.08				
41	Baller, Jay	Charleston	4-12	79	62	8.81	R-R	6-6	215	10/6/60 Stayton, OR
		Buffalo	1-2	35	35	7.53				
27	Barnes, Richard	Denver	11-6	131	62	4.10	R-L	6-4	186	7/21/59 Palm Beach, FL
		Charleston	1-0	12	3	3.65				
		Cleveland	1-1	12	2	6.94				
32	Behenna, Rick	Atlanta	3-3	37	17	4.58	R-R	6-2	170	3/6/60 Miami, FL
		Richmond	6-5	95	50	4.47				
		Cleveland	0-2	26	9	4.15				
28	Blyleven, Bert	Cleveland	7-10	156	123	3.91	R-R	6-3	205	4/6/51 Holland
40	Comacho, Ernie	Vancouver	0-2	24	16	6.85	R-R	6-1	180	2/1/56 Salinas, CA
		Charleston	4-0	33	27	1.35				
		Cleveland	0-1	5	2	5.06				
64	Doyle, Rich	Buffalo	5-7	99	80	4.65	R-R	6-5	205	2/4/63 La Mirada, CA
36	*Easterly, Jamie	Mil.-Cle.	4-3	69	45	3.67	L-L	5-10	180	2/17/53 Houston, TX
13	Eichelberger, Juan	Cleveland	4-11	134	56	4.90	R-R	6-2	195	10/21/53 St. Louis, MO
58	Farr, Steve	Buffalo	13-1	112	108	1.61	R-R	5-10	198	12/12/56 La Plata, MD
44	Heaton, Neal	Cleveland	11-7	149	75	4.16	L-L	6-1	205	3/3/60 Jamaica, NY
54	Jeffcoat, Mike	Charleston	12-8	167	96	4.53	L-L	6-2	187	8/3/59 Pine Bluff, AR
		Cleveland	1-3	33	9	3.31				
65	Roman, Jose	Waterloo	6-7	126	132	2.56	R-R	6-0	175	1/23/63 Dominican Republic
50	Romero, Ramon	Buffalo	10-4	98	92	3.95	L-L	6-4	170	1/8/59 Dominican Republic
33	Smith, Roy	Charleston	6-8	155	95	5.16	R-R	6-3	200	9/6/61 Mt. Vernon, NY
38	*Sorenson, Lary	Cleveland	12-11	223	76	4.24	R-R	6-2	200	10/4/55 Detroit, MI
37	Spillner, Dan	Cleveland	2-9	92	48	5.07	R-R	6-1	190	11/27/51 Casper, WY
43	Sutcliffe, Rick	Cleveland	17-11	243	160	4.29	L-R	6-7	200	6/21/56 Independence, MO
52	Thompson, Rick	Buffalo	3-7	79	61	2.86	B-R	6-3	225	11/1/58 New York, NY

CATCHERS

No.	Name	1983 Club	H	HR	RBI	Pct.	B-T	Ht.	Wt.	Born
23	Bando, Chris	Cleveland	31	4	15	.256	B-R	6-0	195	2/4/56 Cleveland, OH
9	Hassey, Ron	Cleveland	92	6	42	.270	L-R	6-2	195	2/27/53 Tucson, AZ
53	Willard, Jerry	Charleston	119	19	77	.301	L-R	6-2	195	3/14/60 Oxnard, CA

INFIELDERS

No.	Name	1983 Club	H	HR	RBI	Pct.	B-T	Ht.	Wt.	Born
—	Bernazard, Tony	Chi. (AL)-Sea.	141	8	56	.265	B-R	5-9	160	8/24/56 Puerto Rico
22	Fischlin, Mike	Cleveland	47	2	23	.209	R-R	6-1	165	9/13/55 Sacramento, CA
14	Franco, Julio	Cleveland	153	8	80	.273	R-R	6-0	155	8/23/61 Dominican Republic
21	Hargrove, Mike	Cleveland	134	3	57	.286	L-L	6-0	195	10/26/49 Perryton, TX
11	Harrah, Toby	Cleveland	140	9	53	.266	R-R	6-0	190	10/26/48 Sissonville, WV
26	Jacoby, Brook	Richmond	154	25	100	.315	R-R	5-11	175	11/23/59 Philadelphia, PA
		Atlanta	0	0	0	.000				
55	Noboa, Junior	Waterloo	115	1	29	.256	R-R	5-10	155	11/10/64 Dom. Republic
15	Perkins, Broderick	Cleveland	50	0	24	.272	L-L	5-10	180	11/23/54 Pittsburg, CA
—	Quinones, Luis	Albany	51	6	23	.239	B-R	5-11	155	4/28/62 Puerto Rico
		Tacoma	35	2	14	.263				
		Oakland	8	0	4	.190				
29	Thornton, Andre	Cleveland	143	17	77	.281	R-R	6-2	205	8/13/49 Tuskegee, AL

OUTFIELDERS

No.	Name	1983 Club	H	HR	RBI	Pct.	B-T	Ht.	Wt.	Born
7	Bannister, Alan	Cleveland	100	5	45	.265	R-R	5-11	175	9/3/51 Montebello, CA
25	Butler, Brett	Atlanta	154	5	37	.281	L-L	5-10	160	6/15/57 Los Angeles, CA
59	Carter, Don	Memphis	128	0	30	.303	B-R	5-11	160	2/11/60 Kansas City, KS
		Buffalo	16	0	10	.267				
8	Castillo, Carmelo	Charleston	40	4	22	.270	R-R	6-1	185	6/8/58 Dominican Republic
		Cleveland	10	1	3	.278				
26	*McBride, Bake	Cleveland	67	1	18	.291	L-R	6-2	185	2/3/49 Fulton, MO
12	Rhomberg, Kevin	Charleston	158	1	60	.311	R-R	6-0	175	11/22/55 Dubuque, IA
		Cleveland	10	0	2	.476				
10	Tabler, Pat	Charleston	3	0	2	.214	R-R	6-2	195	2/2/58 Hamilton, OH
		Cleveland	125	6	65	.291				
62	Taylor, Dwight	Buffalo	136	8	38	.302	L-L	5-9	160	3/24/60 Los Angeles, CA
24	Vukovich, George	Cleveland	77	3	44	.247	L-R	6-0	198	6/24/56 Chicago, IL
61	Washington, Randy	Waterloo	120	19	89	.291	R-R	5-11	190	8/7/63 Stockton, CA

*Free agent unsigned at press time

INDIAN PROFILES

TOBY HARRAH 35 6-0 190 **Bats R Throws R**

Had played in 476 consecutive games before a pitch by Orioles' Dennis Martinez broke bone in his hand April 18, limiting him to 138 games . . . One of only four former Washington Senators who began last season as active major-leaguers (Jim Kaat, Jeff Burroughs and Aurelio Rodriguez were the others) . . . Has averaged 17 stolen bases per season in his 13 full major-league seasons . . . Was an All-Star in 1982, but was only non-pitcher who didn't see action for AL . . . Had made All-Star team three previous times, but all as shortstop . . . Moved to third base in 1977 . . . In 1982, he became first Indian to score 100 runs in a season since Dick Howser in 1963 . . . Born Oct. 26, 1948, in Sissonville, West Va. . . . Played football at Ohio Northern before signing first pro contract with Philadelphia in 1966 . . . Came to Indians from Texas for Buddy Bell after 1978 season.

Year	Club	Pos.	G	AB	R	H	2B	3B	HR	RBI	SB	Avg.
1969	Washington	SS	8	1	4	0	0	0	0	0	0	.000
1971	Washington	SS-3B	127	383	45	88	11	3	2	22	10	.230
1972	Texas	SS	116	374	47	97	14	3	1	31	16	.259
1973	Texas	3B-SS	118	461	64	120	16	1	10	50	10	.260
1974	Texas	SS-3B	161	573	79	149	23	2	21	74	15	.260
1975	Texas	SS-3B-2B	151	522	81	153	24	1	20	93	23	.293
1976	Texas	SS-3B	155	584	64	152	21	1	15	67	8	.260
1977	Texas	3B-SS	159	539	90	142	25	5	27	87	27	.263
1978	Texas	SS-3B	139	450	56	103	17	3	12	59	31	.229
1979	Cleveland	3B-SS	149	527	99	147	25	1	20	77	20	.279
1980	Cleveland	3B-SS	160	561	100	150	22	4	11	72	17	.267
1981	Cleveland	3B-SS	103	361	64	105	12	4	5	44	12	.291
1982	Cleveland	3B-2B-SS	162	602	100	183	29	4	25	78	17	.304
1983	Cleveland	3B-SS	138	526	81	140	23	1	9	53	16	.266
	Totals		1846	6464	974	1729	262	33	178	807	222	.267

JULIO FRANCO 22 5-11 155 **Bats R Throws R**

Had been hailed for several years as best prospect in minors and didn't disappoint . . . Had strong rookie season for Indians, who acquired him from Philadelphia as part of five-player package for Von Hayes prior to last season . . . Had most RBI by an Indian shortstop since Lou Boudreau's 106 in 1948 and most home runs by an Indian shortstop since Woody Held's 17 in 1963 . . . Led Indians in six offensive categories and was second on club with nine game-winning RBI . . . Only player in AL to hit at least eight homers, steal at least 30 bases and drive in at least 80 runs last season . . . Settled down defensively, too, after committing 112 errors in three previous years in minors . . . Hit .315 and averaged 11 homers, 63 RBI and 26 stolen bases during five minor-league seasons . . . Earned MVP honors in Carolina League in 1980, when he hit .321 with 99 RBI and 44 stolen bases for Peninsula (A) . . . Born Aug. 23, 1961, in San Pedro de Macoris, Dominican Republic.

Year	Club	Pos.	G	AB	R	H	2B	3B	HR	RBI	SB	Avg.
1982	Philadelphia	SS-3B	16	29	3	8	1	0	0	3	0	.276
1983	Cleveland.	SS-3B-2B	149	560	68	153	24	8	8	80	32	.273
	Totals		165	589	71	161	25	8	8	83	32	.273

MIKE HARGROVE 34 6-0 195 **Bats L Throws L**

Lack of production led to least amount of playing time since 1974 . . . Finished seventh in AL in walks and sixth in league in on-base percentage (.393) . . . Hit .324 with men in scoring position . . . First baseman has committed total of only 12 errors in last two years . . . Nicknamed "The Human Rain Delay," because of all the time he takes between pitches when he is hitting . . . Set Indian record with 111 walks in 1980 . . . Born Oct. 26, 1949, in Perryton, Tex. . . . Did not play baseball in high school, but took up sport at Northwestern Oklahoma due to father's insistence . . . Was drafted by Texas in June 1972 as the 572nd selection . . . After two years in minors, he jumped directly from Class A to majors by hitting .486 in spring training of 1974 with Texas . . . Went on to earn AL Rookie-of-the-Year honors for Rangers that season . . . Acquired by Indians from San Diego for outfielder Paul Dade in June 1979.

Year	Club	Pos.	G	AB	R	H	2B	3B	HR	RBI	SB	Avg.
1974	Texas	1B-OF	131	415	57	134	18	6	4	66	0	.323
1975	Texas	1B-OF	145	519	82	157	22	2	11	62	4	.303
1976	Texas	1B	151	541	80	155	30	1	7	58	2	.287
1977	Texas	1B	153	525	98	160	28	4	18	69	2	.305
1978	Texas	1B	146	494	63	124	24	1	7	40	2	.251
1979	San Diego	1B	52	125	15	24	5	0	0	8	0	.192
1979	Cleveland.	OF-1B	100	338	60	110	21	4	10	56	2	.325
1980	Cleveland.	1B	160	589	86	179	22	2	11	85	4	304
1981	Cleveland.	1B	94	322	43	102	21	0	2	49	5	.317
1982	Cleveland.	1B	160	591	67	160	26	1	4	65	2	.271
1983	Cleveland.	1B	134	469	57	134	21	4	3	57	0	.286
	Totals		1426	4928	708	1439	238	25	77	615	23	.292

ANDRE THORNTON 34 6-2 205 Bats R Throws R

May have been pitched around more than any other hitter in big leagues the last two seasons, drawing 31 intentional walks . . . Had career-high batting average last year . . . Led Indians with 12 game-winning RBI . . . Designated hitter began to play some first base again, spelling Mike Hargrove against certain left-handers . . . After missing all of 1980 and most of 1981 with injuries, he was voted AL Comeback Player of the Year in 1982 . . . Hit for the cycle, April 22, 1978, getting each hit off a different Boston pitcher . . . A late bloomer, he appeared in more than 100 games only once in his first seven minor-league seasons . . . Born Aug. 13, 1949, in Tuskegee, Ala. . . . President of Christian Family Outreach and member of Board of Professional Athletes Outreach . . . Obtained from Expos for pitcher Jackie Brown prior to 1976 season.

Year	Club	Pos.	G	AB	R	H	2B	3B	HR	RBI	SB	Avg.
1973	Chicago (NL)	1B	17	35	3	7	3	0	0	2	0	.200
1974	Chicago (NL)	1B-3B	107	303	41	79	16	4	10	46	2	.261
1975	Chicago (NL)	1B-3B	120	372	70	109	21	4	18	60	3	.293
1976	Chi. (NL)-Mtl.	1B-OF	96	268	28	52	11	2	11	38	4	.194
1977	Cleveland.	1B	131	433	77	114	20	5	28	70	3	.263
1978	Cleveland.	1B	145	508	97	133	22	4	33	105	4	.262
1979	Cleveland.	1B	143	515	89	120	31	1	26	93	5	.233
1980	Cleveland.					Disabled List						
1981	Cleveland.	1B	69	226	22	54	12	0	6	30	3	.239
1982	Cleveland.	1B	161	589	90	161	26	1	32	116	6	.273
1983	Cleveland.	1B	141	508	78	143	27	1	17	77	4	.281
	Totals		1130	3757	595	972	199	22	181	637	34	.259

TONY BERNAZARD 27 5-9 160 Bats S Throws R

Swapped for Indian outfielder Gorman Thomas and second baseman Jack Perconte in December . . . Acquired from the White Sox last June in exchange of second basemen . . . Had complained frequently about move and expressed dislike for Seattle . . . Did get a chance to prove he could still steal bases, despite broken ankle suffered in September 1982 . . . Had only two thefts when he came to Mariners, but stole 21 in Seattle; Julio Cruz stole only 15 for White Sox . . . Had postseason arthrogram on left shoulder . . . Was second among AL second basemen in runs produced . . . Has trouble making double-play pivot . . . Has been criticized in native Puerto Rico for not playing winter ball every year . . . Began switch-hitting while playing in Puerto Rican Winter League in 1977-78 . . . Born Aug. 24, 1956, in Caguas, Puerto Rico . . . Brother Oscar played in Pittsburgh organization.

Year	Club	Pos.	G	AB	R	H	2B	3B	HR	RBI	SB	Avg.
1979	Montreal	2B	22	40	11	12	2	0	1	8	1	.300
1980	Montreal	2B-SS	82	183	26	41	7	1	5	18	9	.224
1981	Chicago (AL)	2B-SS	106	384	53	106	14	4	6	34	4	.276
1982	Chicago (AL)	2B	137	540	90	138	25	9	11	56	11	.256
1983	Chi (AL)-Seattle	2B	139	533	65	141	34	3	8	56	23	.265
	Totals		486	1680	245	438	82	17	31	172	48	.261

PAT TABLER 26 6-2 195 — Bats R Throws R

After a shaky career that saw him go from Cubs to White Sox to Indians between the end of 1982 and the beginning of 1983, he found a home in Cleveland . . . Called up from Charleston (AAA) after Toby Harrah broke his hand, he had 10 hits in first five games and hit safely in 14 of his first 17 . . . Moved to left when Harrah returned and wound up leading Indian regulars in hitting and finishing third in RBI and doubles . . . Also hit .362 with men in scoring position, the best mark on club . . . Missed a month with pulled left quadricep . . . Hit .296 or better in last five minor-league seasons, including .342 mark for Iowa (AAA) in 1982 . . . Signed with Yankees as their first-round draft choice in June 1976 . . . Born Feb. 2, 1958, in Hamilton, Ohio . . . Grew up in Cincinnati . . . Played high school ball against Richard Dotson, now of White Sox, and Leon Durham, now of Cubs.

Year	Club	Pos.	G	AB	R	H	2B	3B	HR	RBI	SB	Avg.
1981	Chicago (NL)	2B	35	101	11	19	3	1	1	5	0	.188
1982	Chicago (NL)	3B	25	85	9	20	4	2	1	7	0	.235
1983	Cleveland	3B-OF-2B	124	430	56	126	23	5	6	65	2	.293
	Totals		184	616	76	165	30	8	8	77	2	.268

BRETT BUTLER 26 5-10 160 — Bats L Throws L

Worst-kept secret in baseball last year was that he was one of players to be named later in deal that sent pitcher Len Barker to Atlanta in August . . . Confronted Braves' owner Ted Turner to find out if rumors were true and Turner gave him honest answer, causing sticky lame-duck situation that was investigated by commissioner's office . . . Was a bust with Braves in 1982, getting only two extra-base hits, and was sent to minors after opening that season as Atlanta's leadoff hitter . . . Had no such problems in 1983, when he set club record with 39 stolen bases, led NL with 13 triples and played left on regular basis . . . Will play center for Indians . . . Was International League MVP in 1981, when he hit .335 with 44 stolen bases for Richmond (AAA) . . . Born June 15, 1957, in Los Angeles . . . Played freshman baseball at Arizona State, then transferred to Southeastern Oklahoma.

Year	Club	Pos.	G	AB	R	H	2B	3B	HR	RBI	SB	Avg.
1981	Atlanta	OF	40	126	17	32	2	3	0	4	9	.254
1982	Atlanta	OF	89	240	35	52	2	0	0	7	21	.217
1983	Atlanta	OF	151	549	84	154	21	13	5	37	39	.281
	Totals		280	915	136	238	25	16	5	48	69	.260

NEAL HEATON 24 6-1 205 **Bats L Throws L**

Compiled the most wins by a Cleveland left-hander since Herb Score had 16 in 1955 and the most saves by an Indian rookie since Ray Narleski had 13 in 1954 . . . Began season in bullpen, compiling 4-2 record and seven saves in 23 appearances, before moving into rotation May 20 . . . Lost first two starts, but then posted 5-0 record and 1.74 ERA, including three complete games and two shutouts, during June . . . Best effort of year was three-hitter in front of friends and family at Yankee Stadium in September . . . Born March 3, 1960, in Jamaica, N.Y. . . . Made it to big leagues after pitching just 40 games in minors . . . Indians' second-round draft choice in 1981, after compiling 41-6 record and 2.01 ERA during three years at University of Miami . . . Struck out 23 batters in game against Indiana State in 1981 and had 20 strikeouts in seven-inning game during senior year in high school in 1979.

Year	Club	G	IP	W	L	Pct.	SO	BB	H	ERA
1982	Cleveland	8	31	0	2	.000	14	16	32	5.23
1983	Cleveland	39	149	11	7	.611	75	44	157	4.16
	Totals	47	180	11	9	.550	89	60	189	4.35

RICK SUTCLIFFE 27 6-7 200 **Bats R Throws R**

Matched career high in starts . . . Won 10 of first 13 decisions . . . Best game of season was two-hit effort against Kansas City in May . . . Born June 21, 1956, in Independence, Mo., and still lives there . . . Says he wants to play for the Royals . . . Finished fifth in AL with 160 strikeouts . . . Was a member of starting rotation from beginning of season for first time in his career . . . Led AL in ERA in 1982, the first time an Indian had held honor since Luis Tiant in 1968, and he joined Oakland's Steve McCatty as only right-handers to win AL ERA crown in last seven years . . . Was NL Rookie of the Year with Dodgers in 1979, when he set Los Angeles record for wins by rookie, but had personality clash with manager Tommy Lasorda . . . Credits resurrection with Indians to fact they allowed him to throw slider that Dodgers forbade him from using.

Year	Club	G	IP	W	L	Pct.	SO	BB	H	ERA
1976	Los Angeles	1	5	0	0	.000	3	1	2	0.00
1978	Los Angeles	2	2	0	0	.000	0	1	2	0.00
1979	Los Angeles	39	242	17	10	.630	117	97	217	3.46
1980	Los Angeles	42	110	3	9	.250	59	55	122	5.56
1981	Los Angeles	14	47	2	2	.500	16	20	41	4.02
1982	Cleveland	34	216	14	8	.636	142	98	174	2.96
1983	Cleveland	36	243	17	11	.607	160	102	251	4.29
	Totals	168	865	53	40	.570	497	374	809	3.84

DAN SPILLNER 32 6-1 190 Bats R Throws R

Credited with having a rubber arm, but elastic popped in 1983 . . . Got off to strong start with four saves in first five appearances, but had only four more the rest of the season . . . Still managed to lead Indians in saves and appearances, which is as much a gauge of bullpen's ineptitude as anything else . . . Tied Indian records for relief wins (12) and saves (21) in 1982 . . . Ranks sixth on Cleveland all-time save list with 40 and third all-time in wins by a reliever with 24 . . . On verge of being released in 1979, he made squad as 10th pitcher and pumped new life into career . . . Signed five-year contract as free agent after 1980 season . . . Pitched a pair of one-hitters, against Cubs (for San Diego in 1974) and White Sox (for Indians in 1980) . . . Born Nov. 27, 1951, in Casper, Wy.

Year	Club	G	IP	W	L	Pct.	SO	BB	H	ERA
1974	San Diego	30	148	9	11	.450	95	70	153	4.01
1975	San Diego	37	167	5	13	.278	104	63	194	4.26
1976	San Diego	32	107	2	11	.154	57	55	120	5.05
1977	San Diego	76	123	7	6	.538	74	60	130	3.73
1978	San Diego	17	26	1	0	1.000	16	7	32	4.50
1978	Cleveland	36	56	3	1	.750	48	21	54	3.70
1979	Cleveland	49	158	9	5	.643	97	64	153	4.61
1980	Cleveland	34	194	16	11	.593	100	74	225	5.29
1981	Cleveland	32	97	4	4	.500	59	39	86	3.15
1982	Cleveland	65	134	12	10	.545	90	45	117	2.49
1983	Cleveland	60	92	2	9	.182	48	38	117	5.07
	Totals	468	1302	70	81	.464	788	536	1381	4.22

TOP PROSPECTS

BROOK JACOBY 24 5-11 175 **Bats R Throws R**
Got a break when he was traded by Atlanta, where his path to majors was blocked by Bob Horner . . . Acquired in Len Barker deal and will be expected to take over at third base . . . Hit .315 with 25 homers, 100 RBI for Richmond (AAA) . . . Has 86 homers and 347 RBI to show for four years in minors . . . Born Nov. 23, 1959, in Philadelphia . . . Attended Ventura Junior College . . . Was hitless in eight at-bats for Braves last season.

JERRY WILLARD 24 6-2 195 **Bats L Throws R**
Considered a good defensive catcher, he had the highest success ratio throwing out base-stealers in the International League in 1983 . . . Has begun to show signs of life with bat, too . . . Hit .301 with 19 homers and 77 RBI for Charleston (AAA) last year, walking 88 times and striking out 76 times . . . Born March 14, 1960, in Oxnard, Cal. . . . Signed as undrafted player by Philadelphia, out of Oxnard College . . . Came to Indians as part of five-player package for Von Hayes prior to last season.

MANAGER PAT CORRALES: Had a topsy-turvy 1983 season . . . Fired as Philadelphia manager July 15, with club in first place . . . Took over last-place Indians from Mike Ferraro July 29 . . . Indians were 40-60 when he was hired and 30-32 after he came aboard . . . Third tour of duty as big-league manager . . . Was skipper of Texas in 1979 and 1980 and moved into Ranger front office in 1981 . . . After one year as an exec, he returned to dugout to manage Phillies . . . Ran into problems with future Hall of Famers in Phillies' clubhouse, because he was more interested in trying to win than massaging egos . . . Had 17-year playing career, during which he spent parts of 10 seasons in majors . . . Played in only 300 big-league games, spending most of his time watching Johnny Bench catch for Cincinnati . . . Also caught for Philadelphia, St. Louis and San Diego . . . Four-time all-star catcher on minor-league level . . . Has brown belt in karate . . . Born March 20, 1941, in Los Angeles . . . Grew up in Fresno, Cal., along with former big-league pitchers Dick Ellsworth, Jim

Maloney and Dick Selma . . . Overall major-league managerial mark is 310-299.

GREATEST STEALER

Whenever you search for the best players in Indians' history, you'd better plan on a history course. So forget about Miguel Dilone, who set the club record with 61 thefts in 1980. He wasn't around long enough to make a solid imprint upon Indian lore.

Let's head back to shortly after the turn of the century, back to the days of Hall-of-Famer Nap Lajoie and teammates Harry Bay and Elmer Flick. Bay led the AL with 46 stolen bases in 1903 and tied Flick for the lead with 42 the next year. Flick led the league in 1905 with 29. Lajoie came during the middle of the 1902 season and stayed through the end of 1914 and he stole 243 bases.

Lajoie never posted a gaudy single-season total—his high was 29 in 1904—but he was consistent, never falling below double figures in a full season and collecting 380 overall during his 21-year major-league career. However, it is Lajoie's contemporary, Terry (Cotton) Turner, who holds the Indians' career mark with 254, amassed from 1904-18.

ALL-TIME INDIAN SEASON RECORDS

BATTING: Joe Jackson, .408, 1911
HRs: Al Rosen, 43, 1953
RBIs: Hal Trosky, 162, 1936
STEALS: Miguel Dilone, 61, 1980
WINS: Jim Bagby, 31, 1920
STRIKEOUTS: Bob Feller, 348, 1946

DETROIT TIGERS

TEAM DIRECTORY: Chairman of the Board: John Fetzer; Vice-Chairman: Tom Monaghan; Pres.-Chief Exec. Off.: Jim Campbell; Exec. VP-Chief Oper. Off.: William Haase; VP-GM: William Lajoie; VP-Fin.: Alex Callam; Dir. Pub. Rel.: Dan Ewald; Trav. Sec.: Bill Brown; Mgr.: Sparky Anderson. Home: Tiger Stadium (52,806). Field distances: 340, l.f. line; 365, l.c.; 440, c.f.; 370, r.c.; 325, r.f. line. Spring training: Lakeland, Fla.

SCOUTING REPORT

HITTING: The Tigers' attack is balanced. Last season, they had seven players hit 11 or more home runs and seven regulars hit .255 or better en route to a .274 team mark, the third-highest in the AL. The Tigers are strong up the middle, thanks to catcher Lance Parrish (27 homers, 114 RBI), shortstop Alan Trammell (.319), second baseman Lou Whitaker (.320) and center fielder Chet Lemon (24 homers, 69 RBI). Larry Herndon (.302, 20 homers, 92 RBI) had another big year at the plate, too.

But the Tigers don't get the type of production out of the big

Lou Whitaker was third in the AL in hitting at .320.

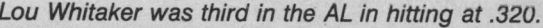

power spots that a team wants. The cast of thousands who played first and third combined for only 18 home runs last season, prompting the signing of free agent Darrell Evans. Evans, who had 30 homers and 82 RBI for the Giants, can play both spots and should be an asset. But the Tigers need stability at the DH spot after using 10 players, including puzzling Kirk Gibson (.227) and reliable John Wockenfuss (.269), in that role in '83.

Though they stole only 93 bases, the Tigers were one of three AL East teams to have four players with at least 10 stolen bases.

PITCHING: With Jack Morris (20-13) and Dan Petry (19-11), manager Sparky Anderson starts with the two pitchers who combined to work more innings (460) than any other duo in the big leagues. Glenn Abbott (7-4) and late-bloomer Juan Berenguer (9-5) give them solid No. 4 and 5 starters, but that third slot remains a puzzle.

The bullpen, led by Aurelio Lopez (18 saves), looked so good during the first four months of last season, but managed only two saves after July 31. The Tigers went into a slump that coincided with the relief drought and that was no coincidence.

Also, there hasn't been a consistent lefty in the Tiger rotation since the days of Mickey Lolich. That is a problem in Tiger Stadium, where right-handed pitchers face difficult days because of the short porch in right field.

DEFENSE: It's good as gold up the middle—good as Gold Glove, that is. Whitaker, Trammell and Parrish all earned those honors in 1983. It doesn't hurt the keystone combo of Whitaker (.983) and Trammell (.979) that they play 81 games on the slow natural grass of Tiger Stadium, because they do seem to have some problems on the faster, artificial surfaces. Few take liberties on Parrish's arm, no matter what the surface.

Given the job in center, and told to do his thing, Lemon blossomed in 1983. Glenn Wilson is a solid right fielder. But there is uncertainty at one of the corners of the infield and in left, where Herndon led AL outfielders with 15 errors.

OVERALL: The Tigers have made a commitment to winning. Prior to the 1982 season, they began giving out long-term contracts and, with the signing of Petry to a five-year deal last winter, the Tigers have the nucleus of their club in the fold through 1985.

They enjoyed their winningest season since 1968 and highest finish (second) since 1972 last year. If they can find a consistent reliever and settle on a No. 3 starter, the Tigers have the basis to do even better in 1984.

DETROIT TIGERS 1984 ROSTER

MANAGER Sparky Anderson
Coaches—Gates Brown, Billy Consolo, Roger Craig, Alex Grammas, Dick Tracewski

PITCHERS

No.	Name	1983 Club	W-L	IP	SO	ERA	B-T	Ht.	Wt.	Born
24	Abbott, Glenn	Sea.-Det.	7-4	129	49	3.63	R-R	6-6	210	2/16/51 Little Rock, AR
60	Bailey, Howard	Detroit	5-5	72	21	4.88	R-L	6-3	195	7/31/58 Grand Haven, MI
40	*Bair, Doug	St. Louis	1-1	30	21	3.03	R-R	6-0	180	6/22/49 Defiance, OH
		Detroit	7-3	56	39	3.88				
44	Berenguer, Juan	Detroit	9-5	158	129	3.14	R-R	5-11	215	11/30/54 Panama
36	Dacko, Mark	Evansville	6-12	143	74	5.29	L-R	6-4	195	8/26/58 Monessen, PA
43	Gumpert, Dave	Evansville	5-1	28	17	2.28	R-R	6-1	190	5/5/58 South Haven, MI
		Detroit	0-2	44	14	2.64				
45	Kelly, Bryan	Birmingham	1-2	25	20	4.68	R-R	6-2	195	2/24/59 Silver Springs, MD
		Evansville	2-4	57	41	6.61				
29	Lopez, Aurelio	Detroit	9-8	115	90	2.81	R-R	6-0	225	10/5/48 Mexico
33	Martin, John	St. Louis	3-1	66	29	3.53	B-L	6-0	190	4/11/56 Wyandotte, MI
		Detroit	0-0	13	11	7.43				
48	Mason, Roger	Birmingham	7-4	127	83	2.06	R-R	6-6	215	9/18/58 Bellaire, MI
		Evansville	5-5	79	43	4.23				
47	Morris, Jack	Detroit	20-13	294	232	3.34	R-R	6-3	200	5/16/55 St. Paul, MN
42	Nail, Charlie	Evansville	8-10	145	79	4.90	R-R	6-4	210	11/22/61 Jackson, MS
49	O'Neal, Randy	Evansville	8-10	140	70	4.23	R-R	6-2	195	8/30/60 Ashland, KY
46	Petry, Dan	Detroit	19-11	266	122	3.92	R-R	6-4	200	11/13/58 Palo Alto, CA
19	Rozema, Dave	Detroit	8-3	105	63	3.43	R-R	6-4	200	8/5/56 Grand Rapids, MI
28	Ujdur, Jerry	Detroit	0-4	34	13	7.15	R-R	6-1	205	3/5/57 Duluth, MN
		Evansville	3-7	107	48	6.24				
39	Wilcox, Milt	Detroit	11-10	186	101	3.97	R-R	6-2	220	4/20/50 Honolulu, HI

CATCHERS

No.	Name	1983 Club	H	HR	RBI	Pct.	B-T	Ht.	Wt.	Born
8	Castillo, Marty	Evansville	50	12	29	.269	R-R	6-1	205	1/16/57 Long Beach, CA
		Detroit	23	2	10	.193				
25	Lowry, Dwight	Birmingham	77	9	44	.267	L-R	6-3	210	10/23/57 Robeson Cty., NC
18	Melvin, Bob	Birmingham	82	10	56	.288	R-R	6-4	205	10/28/61 Palo Alto, CA
		Evansville	27	2	11	.190				
13	Parrish, Lance	Detroit	163	27	114	.269	R-R	6-3	220	6/15/56 Clairton, PA
14	Wockenfuss, John	Detroit	66	9	44	.269	R-R	6-0	190	2/27/49 Welch, WV

INFIELDERS

16	Brookens, Tom	Detroit	71	6	32	.214	R-R	5-10	170	8/10/53 Chambersburg, PA
21	*Cabell, Enos	Detroit	122	5	46	.311	R-R	6-5	185	10/8/49 Fort Riley, KS
59	Chavez, Pedro	Birmingham	11	0	3	.224	R-R	5-11	160	2/23/62 Venezuela
		San Jose	111	6	42	.277				
17	Earl, Scotty	Birmingham	138	10	60	.261	R-R	5-11	165	9/18/60 Seymour, IN
41	Evans, Darrell	San Francisco	145	30	82	.277	L-R	6-2	205	5/26/47 Pasadena, CA
27	Garbey, Barbaro	Evansville	121	14	59	.321	R-R	5-10	170	12/4/56 Cuba
20	Johnson, Howard	Detroit	14	3	5	.212	B-R	6-0	175	11/29/60 Clearwater, FL
		Evansville	2	0	0	.222				
4	Laga, Mike	Evansville	82	16	58	.231	L-L	6-2	210	6/4/60 Ridgewood, NJ
		Detroit	4	0	2	.190				
7	Leach, Rick	Detroit	60	3	26	.248	L-L	6-0	190	5/4/57 Ann Arbor, MI
41	Smith, Jimmy	Denver	93	7	45	.292	R-R	6-3	185	9/8/54 Santa Monica, CA
3	Trammell, Alan	Detroit	161	14	66	.319	R-R	6-0	175	2/21/58 Garden Grove, CA
1	Whitaker, Lou	Detroit	206	12	72	.320	L-R	5-11	160	5/12/57 New York, NY

OUTFIELDERS

23	Gibson, Kirk	Detroit	91	15	51	.227	L-L	6-3	215	5/28/57 Pontiac, MI
30	Grubb, John	Detroit	34	4	22	.254	L-R	6-3	180	8/4/48 Richmond, VA
31	Herndon, Larry	Detroit	182	20	92	.302	R-R	6-3	200	11/3/53 Sunflower, MS
34	Lemon, Chet	Detroit	125	24	69	.255	R-R	6-0	190	2/12/55 Jackson, MS
37	Simmons, Nelson	Birmingham	110	11	64	.272	B-R	6-1	195	6/27/63 Washington, DC
12	Wilson, Glenn	Detroit	135	11	65	.268	R-R	6-1	185	12/22/58 Baytown, TX

*Free agent unsigned at press time

TIGER PROFILES

LANCE PARRISH 27 6-3 220 — Bats R Throws R

Led major-league catchers in home runs for second straight year, despite slight drop from 1982, when he set single-season record for an American League catcher with 32... Has led Tigers in home runs last four years... Finished fourth in AL with 114 RBI and first with 13 sacrifice flies... Dropped into cleanup spot for full season for the first time... Finished strongly with 19 homers and 65 RBI after All-Star break... A devoted weight-lifter, he has won approval of Tiger management after earlier front-office complaints concerning dangers of muscle build-up... Has the strongest arm in AL, but not the quickest release... Born June 15, 1956, in Clairton, Pa.... First-round pick of Detroit in June 1974... Turned down football scholarship to UCLA... Originally a third baseman... Spent one offseason as bodyguard for singer Tina Turner.

Year	Club	Pos.	G	AB	R	H	2B	3B	HR	RBI	SB	Avg.
1977	Detroit	C	12	46	10	9	2	0	3	7	0	.196
1978	Detroit	C	85	288	37	63	11	3	14	41	0	.219
1979	Detroit	C	143	493	65	136	26	3	19	65	6	.276
1980	Detroit	C-1B-OF	144	553	79	158	34	6	24	82	6	.286
1981	Detroit	C	96	348	39	85	18	2	10	46	2	.244
1982	Detroit	C-OF	133	486	75	138	19	2	32	87	3	.284
1983	Detroit	C	155	605	80	163	42	3	27	114	1	.269
	Totals		768	2819	385	752	152	19	129	442	18	.267

LOU WHITAKER 26 5-11 160 — Bats L Throws R

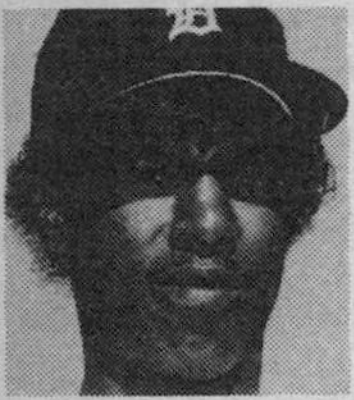

Became first left-handed-hitting Tiger to collect 200 hits in a season since Dick Wakefield in 1943 and third Tiger to reach that plateau since that time, joining Al Kaline (1955) and Ron LeFlore (1977)... Very consistent year at plate... Longest hitless streak of season was three games, average was better than .300 against both left-handers and right-handers, with bases empty and with men in scoring position, against both AL West and AL East teams... Ranked third in AL with .320 mark... Had only 12 home runs in his first four years in big leagues, but has totaled 27 the last two seasons... Since moving to leadoff spot in middle of 1982, he has hit .317... Won AL Rookie-of-the-Year honors in 1978... Born May 12, 1957, in New York City... Second baseman has teamed with shortstop

Alan Trammell since their minor-league days . . . Drafted as third baseman by Tigers in June 1975.

Year	Club	Pos.	G	AB	R	H	2B	3B	HR	RBI	SB	Avg.
1977	Detroit	28	11	32	5	8	1	0	0	2	0	.250
1978	Detroit	2B	139	484	71	138	12	7	3	58	7	.285
1979	Detroit	2B	127	423	75	121	14	8	3	42	20	.286
1980	Detroit	2B	145	477	68	111	19	1	1	45	8	.233
1981	Detroit	2B	109	335	48	88	14	4	5	36	5	.263
1982	Detroit	2B	152	560	76	160	22	8	15	65	11	.286
1983	Detroit	2B	161	643	94	206	40	6	12	72	17	.320
	Totals		844	2954	437	832	122	34	39	320	68	.282

ALAN TRAMMELL 26 6-0 175 — Bats R Throws R

Missed 17 games during middle of season because of problem with right elbow and Tigers were 8-9 without him . . . Closed batting stance to increase power and compiled .471 slugging percentage . . . Combined with Lou Whitaker to become first keystone combination to both hit over .300 since Cass Michaels and Luke Appling did it with 1949 Chicago White Sox . . . Ranked fourth in AL with .319 mark . . . Became first Tiger shortstop to steal as many as 30 bases since Donnie Bush in 1917 . . . After horrible slump to open 1982, he has compiled .316 mark for the last season and a half . . . Selected Southern League's Most Valuable Player with Montgomery (AA) in 1977 . . . Tigers' second-round draft pick in June 1976 . . . Born Feb. 21, 1958, in Garden Grove, Cal. . . . Married high-school sweetheart on his birthday in 1978 . . . Underwent arthroscopic surgery on knee during offseason.

Year	Club	Pos.	G	AB	R	H	2B	3B	HR	RBI	SB	Avg.
1977	Detroit	SS	19	43	6	8	0	0	0	0	0	.186
1978	Detroit	SS	139	448	49	120	14	6	2	34	3	.268
1979	Detroit	SS	142	460	68	127	11	4	6	50	17	.276
1980	Detroit	SS	146	560	107	168	21	5	9	65	12	.300
1981	Detroit	SS	105	392	52	101	15	3	2	31	10	.258
1982	Detroit	SS	157	489	66	126	34	3	9	57	19	.258
1983	Detroit	SS	142	505	83	161	31	2	14	66	30	.319
	Totals		850	2897	431	811	126	30	42	303	91	.280

DARRELL EVANS 36 6-2 205 — Bats L Throws R

After enjoying dream season with Giants, free-agent first baseman-third baseman signed three-year, $2-million-plus contract with Tigers . . . Ranked among NL leaders in several offensive categories and posted his highest homer total since hitting 41 for Atlanta in 1973 . . . Born May 26, 1947, in Pasadena, Cal. . . . Was all-state in baseball and basketball at Pasadena City College, where his coach was Jerry Tarkanian

...Rapped for failure to produce in the clutch, he came through last year with 15 game-winning RBI...Joined Hank Aaron and Dave Johnson as only three teammates in major-league history to hit 40 or more homers in same season, with Atlanta in 1973.

Year	Club	Pos.	G	AB	R	H	2B	3B	HR	RBI	SB	Avg.
1969	Atlanta	3B	12	26	3	6	0	0	0	1	0	.231
1970	Atlanta	3B	12	44	4	14	1	1	0	9	0	.318
1971	Atlanta	3B-OF	89	260	42	63	11	1	12	38	2	.242
1972	Atlanta	3B	125	418	67	106	12	0	19	71	4	.254
1973	Atlanta	3B-1B	161	595	114	167	25	8	41	104	6	.281
1974	Atlanta	3B	160	571	99	137	21	3	25	79	4	.240
1975	Atlanta	3B-1B	156	567	82	138	22	2	22	73	12	.243
1976	Atl.-S.F.	1B-3B	136	396	53	81	9	1	11	46	9	.205
1977	San Francisco	OF-1B-3B	144	461	64	117	18	3	17	72	9	.254
1978	San Francisco	3B	159	547	82	133	24	2	20	78	4	.243
1979	San Francisco	3B	160	562	68	142	23	2	17	70	6	.253
1980	San Francisco	3B-1B	154	556	69	147	23	0	20	78	17	.264
1981	San Francisco	3B-2B	102	357	51	92	13	4	12	48	2	.258
1982	San Francisco	3B-1B	141	465	64	119	20	4	16	61	5	.256
1983	San Francisco	1B-3B	142	523	94	145	29	3	30	82	6	.277
	Totals		1853	6348	956	1607	251	34	262	910	86	.253

LARRY HERNDON 30 6-3 200 **Bats R Throws R**

Has finally lived up to offensive potential since coming to Tigers from Giants in deal for pitchers Dan Schatzeder and Mike Chris prior to 1982 season...Proved 1982 was no fluke last year, when he surpassed .300 mark for first time in pro career and established career high in RBI...In first six major-league seasons, he had 24 home runs and 186 RBI...In two years with Tigers, he has hit 43 homers and driven in 180 runs...Fielding fell off in outfield...After committing only six errors in 1982, he was charged with 15 last year...Despite knee problem, which resulted in offseason surgery, he hit .333 with 13 homers and 54 RBI in second half...Had five hits in one game against California in July...Tied major-league record with home runs in four consecutive plate appearances in 1982...NL Rookie of the Year with San Francisco in 1976...Led Texas League with 50 stolen bases for Arkansas (AA) in 1974...Born Nov. 3, 1953, in Sunflower, Miss....Giants traded him to Houston prior to 1981, but Astro pitcher Ken Forsch vetoed that deal.

Year	Club	Pos.	G	AB	R	H	2B	3B	HR	RBI	SB	Avg.
1974	St. Louis	OF	12	1	3	1	0	0	0	0	0	1.000
1976	San Francisco	OF	115	337	42	97	11	3	2	23	12	.288
1977	San Francisco	OF	49	109	13	26	4	3	1	5	4	.239
1978	San Francisco	OF	151	471	52	122	15	9	1	32	13	.259
1979	San Francisco	OF	132	354	35	91	14	5	7	36	8	.257
1980	San Francisco	OF	139	493	54	127	17	11	8	49	8	.258
1981	San Francisco	OF	96	364	48	105	15	8	5	41	15	.288
1982	Detroit	OF	157	614	92	179	21	13	23	88	12	.292
1983	Detroit	OF	153	603	88	182	28	9	20	92	9	.302
	Totals		1004	3346	427	930	125	61	67	366	81	.278

CHET LEMON 29 6-0 190 **Bats R Throws R**

After difficult season in 1982, he responded to four-year contract by emerging as key player for Tigers . . . "He is stronger mentally than anybody else on our team," said manager Sparky Anderson . . . Led AL in being hit by pitches (20) for third time in four years . . . Was 0-for-7 in stolen bases . . . Was placed on disabled list Aug. 1 with sprained thumb, but talked Tigers out of it . . . Returned to center field at start of season and proved he is better there than in right or left . . . Originally a third baseman, but was moved to center in spring of 1976, after former White Sox owner Bill Veeck saw him taking fly balls in practice . . . Born Feb. 12, 1955, in Jackson, Miss. . . . Attended Fremont High School in Los Angeles, which also produced Willie Crawford, Bob Tolan, Bob Watson, George Hendrick and Dan Ford.

Year	Club	Pos.	G	AB	R	H	2B	3B	HR	RBI	SB	Avg.
1975	Chicago (AL)	3B-OF	9	35	2	9	2	0	0	1	1	.257
1976	Chicago (AL)	OF	132	451	46	111	15	5	4	38	13	.246
1977	Chicago (AL)	OF	150	553	99	151	38	4	19	67	8	.273
1978	Chicago (AL)	OF	105	357	51	107	24	6	13	55	5	.300
1979	Chicago (AL)	OF	148	556	79	177	44	2	17	86	7	.318
1980	Chicago (AL)	OF-2B	147	514	76	150	32	6	11	51	6	.292
1981	Chicago (AL)	OF	94	328	50	99	23	6	9	50	5	.302
1982	Detroit	OF	125	436	75	116	20	1	19	52	1	.266
1983	Detroit	OF	145	491	78	125	21	5	24	69	0	.255
	Totals		1055	3721	556	1045	219	35	116	469	46	.281

GLENN ABBOTT 33 6-6 210 **Bats R Throws R**

Acquired on waivers from Seattle in August . . . Performed well enough that Tigers felt they could let free-agent Milt Wilcox test his market value . . . Was 2-1 with 1.93 ERA and seven walks in 46⅔ innings . . . Always has had control . . . Has averaged 2.25 walks per nine innings since he arrived in majors for keeps in 1976 . . . Missed all of 1982 and first half of 1983 with bone chips in his right elbow, viral meningitis and tendinitis in his right elbow . . . Was last of Mariner expansion acquisitions to play in Seattle . . . Set Seattle record with seven consecutive wins in 1977 . . . Pitched two-hitter against Baltimore in 1981, losing, 1-0, to Steve Stone and Tippy Martinez, who combined on two-hitter of their own . . . Originally signed by Oakland . . . Born Feb. 16, 1951, in Little Rock, Ark. . . . Set major-league record when he combined with Vida Blue, Paul Lindblad and Rollie Fingers to no-hit California, Sept. 28, 1975.

Year	Club	G	IP	W	L	Pct.	SO	BB	H	ERA
1973	Oakland	5	19	1	0	1.000	6	7	16	3.79
1974	Oakland	19	96	5	7	.417	38	34	89	3.00
1975	Oakland	30	114	5	5	.500	51	50	109	4.26
1976	Oakland	19	62	2	4	.333	27	16	87	5.52
1977	Seattle	36	204	12	13	.480	100	56	212	4.46
1978	Seattle	29	155	7	15	.318	67	44	191	5.28
1979	Seattle	23	117	4	10	.286	25	38	138	5.15
1980	Seattle	31	215	12	12	.500	78	49	228	4.10
1981	Seattle	22	130	4	9	.308	35	28	127	3.95
1982	Seattle					(Disabled List)				
1983	Sea.-Det.	21	129	7	4	.636	49	22	146	3.63
	Totals	235	1241	59	79	.428	476	344	1343	4.34

DAN PETRY 25 6-4 200 **Bats R Throws R**

Had career-high 19 wins, thanks to 12-5 mark in second half of season . . . Ranked second in AL to teammate Jack Morris with 12 wild pitches . . . Allowed league-leading 37 home runs, a dramatic increase from 15 he permitted in 1982 . . . Also had dramatic rise in earned-run average, after having posted lowest ERA among Tiger starters the three previous years . . . Combined with Morris to pitch more innings than top two starters on any other AL club . . . Born Nov. 13, 1958, in Palo Alto, Cal. . . . Has won 60 games at a younger age than all but nine other pitchers in major-league history . . . Slider is so good it sets standard for other pitchers . . . Has made only three relief appearances in pro career . . . Never had winning record in three full minor-league seasons and has never had losing record in the majors.

Year	Club	G	IP	W	L	Pct.	SO	BB	H	ERA
1979	Detroit	15	98	6	5	.545	43	33	90	3.95
1980	Detroit	27	165	10	9	.526	88	83	145	3.93
1981	Detroit	23	141	10	9	.526	79	57	115	3.00
1982	Detroit	35	246	15	9	.625	132	100	220	3.22
1983	Detroit	38	266	19	11	.633	122	99	256	3.92
	Totals	138	916	60	43	.583	464	372	837	3.60

JACK MORRIS 28 6-3 200 **Bats R Throws R**

Became first Tiger 20-game winner since Joe Coleman in 1973 and first Tiger to strike out 200 in a season since Mickey Lolich in 1975 . . . Led AL in innings pitched, strikeouts and wild pitches (18) . . . Twelve strikeouts against Yankees in August equalled AL single-game season high . . . Led Tigers in wins for club-record fifth year in a row . . . Has missed only one start in five years . . . Struggled to 3-5 start last year, but then went 15-3 in next 22 starts, averaging more than eight innings per game . . . One-hit Minnesota in 1980 . . . Tied for major-league lead with 14 wins in strike-shortened 1981 . . . Started All-Star Game in 1981 . . . Developed forkball in 1982 and, for awhile, he seemed to lose fastball because of concentrating on new pitch . . . But had 90-plus-mph heater back last year . . . Born June 16, 1955, in St. Paul, Minn. . . . Attended Brigham Young . . . Selected by Tigers in June 1976 draft.

Year	Club	G	IP	W	L	Pct.	SO	BB	H	ERA
1977	Detroit	7	46	1	1	.500	28	23	38	3.72
1978	Detroit	28	106	3	5	.375	48	49	107	4.33
1979	Detroit	27	198	17	7	.708	113	59	179	3.27
1980	Detroit	36	250	16	15	.516	112	87	252	4.18
1981	Detroit	25	198	14	7	.667	97	78	153	3.05
1982	Detroit	37	266	17	16	.515	135	96	247	4.06
1983	Detroit	37	294	20	13	.606	232	83	257	3.34
	Totals	197	1358	88	64	.579	765	475	1233	3.67

AURELIO LOPEZ 35 6-0 225 **Bats R Throws R**

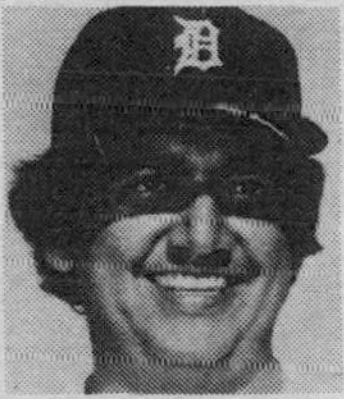

Played big part in Tigers' early success . . . Had saved 16 games by end of July . . . Had only two saves and gave up 20 earned runs in 24 innings the rest of the season . . . Slump began after he signed two-year, $1.2-million contract . . . Victimized by swelling at base of fingers on back of right hand and swelling of right ankle, believed to be caused by gout . . . Has made only nine starts in majors . . . Began 1982 on disabled list, was sent to Evansville (AAA) at midseason and retired in September . . . Decided to return in winter and went to arbitration, where he became first player to have salary cut by arbitrator. He asked for $320,000 for 1983 after making $280,000 in 1982 and was awarded Tiger figure of $250,000 . . . Born Oct. 5, 1948, in Pueblo, Mexico . . . Originally purchased from Mexico by Kansas City in 1974, but Royals released him. St. Louis re-signed him after he had returned to Mexico in 1977 . . . Pitched no-hitter for Mexico City Reds against Carmen in 1969.

Year	Club	G	IP	W	L	Pct.	SO	BB	H	ERA
1974	Kansas City	8	16	0	0	.000	5	10	21	5.63
1978	St. Louis	25	65	4	2	.667	46	32	52	4.29
1979	Detroit	61	127	10	5	.667	106	51	95	2.41
1980	Detroit	67	124	13	6	.684	97	45	125	3.77
1981	Detroit	29	82	5	2	.714	53	31	70	3.62
1982	Detroit	19	41	3	1	.750	26	19	41	5.27
1983	Detroit	57	115	9	8	.529	90	49	87	2.81
	Totals	266	570	44	24	.647	423	237	491	3.47

TOP PROSPECTS

HOWARD JOHNSON 23 6-0 175 Bats S Throws R
Worked out at first base in Florida Instructional League ... After good showing with Tigers in second half of 1982, he was in Detroit lineup to open 1983, but wound up back in Evansville (AAA), where he was sidelined with broken finger ... Has had problems in field at third and in the outfield ... Tigers would like to see him at least platoon at first base ... Born Nov. 29, 1960, in Clearwater, Fla. ... Tigers' No. 1 selection in secondary phase of draft in January 1979, after playing at St. Petersburg Junior College.

BARBARO GARBEY 27 5-10 170 Bats R Throws R
Tigers sent this outfielder to Florida Instructional League to learn to play third base ... Hit .321 with 14 home runs and 59 RBI for Evansville (AAA), despite two suspensions ... One suspension came after he admitted taking part in run-shaving while playing for Cuban national team, the other came after he chased fan while wielding a fungo bat ... Born Dec. 4, 1956, in Santiago, Cuba ... Came to United States on the Freedom Flotilla ... Signed out of tryout camp in 1980 ... Suffered broken jaw when he was hit in face by pitch at Birmingham (AA) in 1981.

MANAGER SPARKY ANDERSON: In fourth full season at

Tiger helm, he guided club to second place in AL East, the best finish by Detroit in the last decade ... Replaced Les Moss in June 1979 and has one year left on contract ... Major-league managerial record of 1,238-912 gives him highest winning percentage (.576) of any active big-league manager with at least 10 years of service ... Managed Cincinnati from 1970-78, guiding Reds to five divisional titles and two world championships ... His Cincinnati clubs finished in first or second place every year except 1971 ... Played one year in the majors, hitting .218 in 152 games as a shortstop for Philadelphia in 1959 ... Spent most of playing career in Dodger organization ... Managed five years in the minors, guiding club to playoffs four times ... Coach with San Diego Padres in 1969 ... Was hired to coach with California in fall of 1969, but 24 hours later, he resigned to take Cincinnati managerial job . . . Born Feb. 22, 1931, in Bridgewater, S.D.

GREATEST STEALER

It doesn't take long to find the name of Hall-of-Famer Ty Cobb in the Tiger record books. He's No. 1 on the all-time list in at-bats, runs, hits, batting average, doubles, triples, RBI, extra-base hits, total bases and, of course, stolen bases.

He's also No. 1 on the all-time AL list with 892 stolen bases, 865 of which came during his tenure with the Tigers, from 1905-26. He set a major-league stolen-base record with 96 thefts in 1915 that stood until Maury Wills stole 104 for the Los Angeles Dodgers in 1962. And Cobb's total remained the best in AL history until Oakland's Rickey Henderson swiped 100 in 1980.

Sixteen times in his career, Cobb surpassed a total of 20 stolen bases in a season, and his 35 thefts of home remain a major-league record that has not been seriously challenged. Lost in the shadow of Cobb was infielder Donie Bush, who had 400 thefts for the Tigers, from 1908-21.

ALL-TIME TIGER SEASON RECORDS

BATTING: Ty Cobb, .420, 1911
HRs: Hank Greenberg, 58, 1938
RBIs: Hank Greenberg, 183, 1937
STEALS: Ty Cobb, 96, 1915
WINS: Denny McLain, 31, 1968
STRIKEOUTS: Mickey Lolich, 308, 1971

MILWAUKEE BREWERS

TEAM DIRECTORY: Pres.: Allan (Bud) Selig; Exec. VP-GM: Harry Dalton; Asst. GM: Walter Shannon; Spec. Assts. to GM: Dee Fondy, Sal Bando; VP-Fin.: Dick Hoffman; Coordinator of Minor League Oper.: Bruce Manno; Dir. Play. Procurement: Ray Poitevint; Dir. Play. Dev.: Bob Humphreys; Dir. Publ.: Tom Skibosh; Trav. Sec.: Jimmy Bank; Mgr.: Rene Lachemann. Home: Milwaukee County Stadium (53,192). Field distances: 315, l.f. line; 362, l.f.; 392, l.c.; 402, c.f.; 392, r.c.; 362, r.f.; 315, r.f. line. Spring training: Sun City, Ariz.

SCOUTING REPORT

HITTING: Harvey's Wallbangers fired blanks in 1983. Oh, the Brewers did manage to compile the second-highest team average in the AL (.277), but were sixth in runs scored. After staging a record-setting home-run assault en route to the AL pennant in 1982, they fell to ninth in the league in long balls last year, with 132.

With the hiring of Rene Lachemann as manager, the Brewers can be expected to exploit their team speed, which has been underrated and overlooked the last few years. Third baseman Paul Molitor is 82-for-97 on thefts the last two seasons.

And Milwaukee still has the makings of a threatening lineup from top to bottom. How many teams can put a 74-RBI man like Jim Gantner (.282) at the bottom of the lineup? The Brewers can, because they have the likes of Cecil Cooper (.307, 30 homers, 126 RBI), Robin Yount (.308, 17 homers, 80 RBI), Molitor (.270), Ted Simmons (.308, 108 RBI) and Ben Oglivie (.280, 66 RBI) to fill the production spots.

PITCHING: There are a lot of questions about an aging rotation led by veterans Don Sutton (8-13), Mike Caldwell (12-11), Moose Haas (13-3) and comebacking Pete Vuckovich (0-2). Jim Slaton (14-6) was sent to California for outfielder Bobby Clark, but there are promising youngsters on hand to help out.

The second-half emergence of Peter Ladd (25 saves), the strong arm of Bob Gibson and optimistic medical reports on former relief ace Rollie Fingers, who hasn't pitched since August 1982, gives the Brewers a strong sense of security about their bullpen. Now, if they could just find a lefty out there. Bob McClure (9-9) could fill the role if he would forget about his personal ambition to be a starter, a role in which he has been average at best.

Robin Yount led AL shortstops with 69 extra-base hits.

FIELDING: It's above average everywhere, except behind the plate and at second base, where Gantner's range is limited and a big problem on fast surfaces. The winter addition of ex-Ranger catcher Jim Sundberg for Ned Yost figures to give the Brewers a big boost. Sundberg, a frequent Gold Glove winner, threw out only 28 percent of potential base-stealers last year, but with a break from the heavy heat of Texas, Sundberg should be stronger this year.

Yount still hears complaints about his defense from people who remember him as an erratic youngster. But at the age of 28 and with 10 years of big-league experience, he has become one of baseball's steadiest shortstops and has a strong arm. First baseman Cooper and center fielder Rick Manning also are very smooth with the glove.

OUTLOOK: The Brewers have had a winning record six years in a row, compiling the third-best record in baseball during that time. The problem is No. 1 and No. 2 during that span were Baltimore and the Yankees, who also call the AL East home. The Brewers may be ready to push ahead of the Yankees this season, but need to develop some pitching stability if they're going to overtake Baltimore.

MILWAUKEE BREWERS 1984 ROSTER

MANAGER Rene Lachemann
Coaches—Pat Dobson, Larry Haney, Tom Trebelhorn, Dave Garcia

PITCHERS

No.	Name	1983 Club	W-L	IP	SO	ERA	B-T	Ht.	Wt.	Born
46	Augustine, Jerry	Milwaukee	3-3	64	40	5.74	L-L	6-0	185	7/24/52 Kewaunee, WI
26	Beene, Andy	Vancouver	13-6	154	95	5.03	R-R	6-3	205	10/12/56 Freeport, TX
		Milwaukee	0-0	2	0	4.50				
48	Caldwell, Mike	Milwaukee	12-11	228	58	4.53	R-L	6-0	185	1/22/49 Tarboro, NC
49	Candiotti, Tom	El Paso	1-0	25	18	2.92	R-R	6-3	205	8/31/57 Walnut Creek, CA
		Vancouver	6-4	99	61	2.81				
		Milwaukee	4-4	56	21	3.23				
47	Cocanower, Jaime	Vancouver	10-10	153	79	4.81	R-R	6-4	190	2/14/57 Canal Zone
		Milwaukee	2-0	30	8	1.80				
34	Fingers, Rollie	Milwaukee	Injured—Did not play				R-R	6-4	200	8/25/46 Steubenville, OH
40	Gibson, Bob	Milwaukee	3-4	81	46	3.90	R-R	6-0	195	6/19/57 Philadelphia, PA
30	Haas, Moose	Milwaukee	13-3	179	75	3.27	R-R	6-0	170	4/22/56 Baltimore, MD
—	Higuera, Teodoro	Juarez	17-8	222	165	2.03	B-L	5-10	178	11/9/58 Mexico
27	Ladd, Pete	Vancouver	0-0	13	16	1.35	R-R	6-3	240	7/17/56 Portland, ME
		Milwaukee	3-4	49	41	2.55				
10	McClure, Bob	Milwaukee	9-9	142	68	4.50	B-L	5-11	170	4/29/53 Oakland, CA
43	Porter, Chuck	Vancouver	0-1	19	10	4.74	R-R	6-3	188	1/12/56 Baltimore, MD
		Milwaukee	7-9	134	76	4.50				
—	Roberts, Scott	Vancouver	6-10	109	69	6.36	R-R	6-4	200	10/7/59 Seattle, WA
20	Sutton, Don	Milwaukee	8-13	220	134	4.08	R-R	6-1	190	4/2/45 Clio, AL
42	Tellmann, Tom	Milwaukee	9-4	100	48	2.80	R-R	6-4	184	3/29/54 Warren, PA
50	Vuckovich, Pete	Milwaukee	0-2	15	10	4.91	R-R	6-4	200	10/27/52 Johnstown, PA
36	Waits, Rick	Cle.-Mil.	0-3	50	33	4.89	L-L	6-3	195	5/15/52 Atlanta, GA
—	Wegman, Bill	Stockton	16-5	187	135	1.30	R-R	6-5	200	12/19/62 Cincinnati, OH
—	Williams, Bruce	Beloit	9-5	75	101	4.58	R-R	6-1	214	12/28/62 West Linn, OR

CATCHERS

No.	Name	1983 Club	H	HR	RBI	Pct.	B-T	Ht.	Wt.	Born
21	Schroeder, Bill	Vancouver	87	20	70	.286	R-R	6-2	200	9/7/58 Baltimore, MD
		Milwaukee	13	3	7	.178				
23	Simmons, Ted	Milwaukee	185	13	108	.308	B-R	6-0	200	8/1/49 Highland Park, MI
—	Sundberg, Jim	Texas	76	2	28	.201	R-R	6-0	195	5/18/51 Galesburg, IL

INFIELDERS

51	Castillo, Juan	El Paso	125	8	62	.271	R-R	5-11	155	1/25/63 Dominican Republic
15	Cooper, Cecil	Milwaukee	203	30	126	.307	L-L	6-2	190	12/20/49 Brenham, TX
17	Gantner, Jim	Milwaukee	170	11	74	.282	L-R	5-11	175	1/5/54 Eden, WI
13	Howell, Roy	Milwaukee	54	4	25	.278	L-R	6-1	194	12/18/53 Lompoc, CA
4	Molitor, Paul	Milwaukee	164	15	47	.270	R-R	6-0	175	8/22/56 St. Paul, MN
7	Money, Don	Milwaukee	17	1	8	.149	R-R	6-1	190	6/7/46 Washington, DC
8	*Picciolo, Rob	Milwaukee	6	0	1	.222	R-R	6-2	185	2/4/53 Santa Monica, CA
2	Ready, Randy	Vancouver	134	13	59	.329	R-R	5-11	180	1/8/60 San Mateo, CA
		Milwaukee	15	1	6	.405				
—	Riles, Earnest	El Paso	166	13	91	.349	L-R	6-1	180	10/2/60 Whigham, GA
11	Romero, Ed	Milwaukee	46	1	18	.317	R-R	5-11	150	12/9/57 Puerto Rico
19	Yount, Robin	Milwaukee	178	17	80	.308	R-R	6-0	170	9/16/55 Danville, IL

OUTFIELDERS

29	Brouhard, Mark	Vancouver	53	5	30	.321	R-R	6-1	210	5/22/56 Burbank, CA
		Milwaukee	51	7	23	.276				
32	Clark, Bobby	California	49	5	21	.231	R-R	6-0	190	6/13/55 Sacramento, CA
—	Felder, Mike	El Paso	156	9	78	.282	B-R	5-8	160	11/18/62 Richmond, CA
14	James, Dion	Vancouver	157	8	68	.336	L-L	6-1	170	11/9/62 Philadelphia, PA
		Milwaukee	2	0	1	.100				
28	Manning, Rick	Cle.-Mil.	140	4	43	.246	L-R	6-1	180	9/2/54 Niagara Falls, NY
22	Moore, Charlie	Milwaukee	150	2	49	.284	R-R	5-11	180	6/21/53 Birmingham, AL
24	Oglivie, Ben	Milwaukee	115	13	66	.280	L-L	6-2	170	2/11/49 Panama
—	Peyton, Eric	El Paso	72	8	40	.343	L-L	5-10	170	11/22/59 San Diego, CA
		Vancouver	56	10	29	.207				

*Free agent unsigned at press time

BREWER PROFILES

CECIL COOPER 34 6-2 190 **Bats L Throws L**

Shared AL lead with 126 RBI, hitting two-run home run in final at-bat of season after being told he needed two to tie . . . Tied Red Sox' Jim Rice, his roommate when both players were in Boston . . . Figure represented Brewer record . . . Finished seventh in AL in home runs and third in runs scored . . . The week before the season ended, he had slumped to .294, but he finished with .586 mark in last six games to post seventh .300-plus season in a row . . . First baseman has driven in 100 or more runs and hit 20 or more home runs the last four full seasons . . . Excellent clutch hitter . . . Wrote column for club newsletter that dealt with mental aspects of game . . . Born Dec. 20, 1949, in Brenham, Tex. . . . Attended Prairie View A&M.

Year	Club	Pos.	G	AB	R	H	2B	3B	HR	RBI	SB	Avg.
1971	Boston	1B	14	42	9	13	4	1	0	3	1	.310
1972	Boston	1B	12	17	0	4	1	0	0	2	0	.235
1973	Boston	1B	30	101	12	24	2	0	3	11	1	.238
1974	Boston	1B	121	414	55	114	24	1	8	43	2	.275
1975	Boston	1B	106	305	49	95	17	6	14	44	1	.311
1976	Boston	1B	123	451	66	127	22	6	15	78	7	.282
1977	Milwaukee	1B	160	643	86	193	31	7	20	78	13	.300
1978	Milwaukee	1B	107	407	60	127	23	2	13	54	3	.312
1979	Milwaukee	1B	150	590	83	182	44	1	24	106	15	.308
1980	Milwaukee	1B	153	622	96	219	33	4	25	122	17	.352
1981	Milwaukee	1B	106	416	70	133	35	1	12	60	5	.320
1982	Milwaukee	1B	155	654	104	205	38	3	32	121	2	.313
1983	Milwaukee	1B	160	661	106	203	37	3	30	126	2	.307
	Totals		1397	5323	796	1639	311	35	196	848	69	.308

ROBIN YOUNT 28 6-0 170 **Bats R Throws R**

Had another strong year, but it paled next to his AL MVP campaign of 1982, which was a once-in-a-lifetime performance . . . Finished tied for ninth in AL batting race with .308 average and was first in triples with 10 in 1983 . . . Also wound up 10th in league with .503 slugging percentage . . . Troubled by back spasms, which required him to wear harness for short period . . . Collected 1,500th hit of career in August . . . In 1982, he became first shortstop to lead AL in home runs and total bases . . . Quit baseball for short time in spring of 1977, claiming he was going to become pro golfer . . . Came to majors at age

18 . . . Born Sept. 16, 1955, in Danville, Ill. . . . Brother Larry pitched in Milwaukee and Pittsburgh organizations.

Year	Club	Pos.	G	AB	R	H	2B	3B	HR	RBI	SB	Avg.
1974	Milwaukee	SS	107	344	48	86	14	5	3	26	7	.250
1975	Milwaukee	SS	147	558	67	149	28	2	8	52	12	.267
1976	Milwaukee	SS-OF	161	638	59	161	19	3	2	54	16	.252
1977	Milwaukee	SS	154	605	66	174	34	4	4	49	16	.288
1978	Milwaukee	SS	127	502	66	147	23	9	9	71	16	.293
1979	Milwaukee	SS	149	577	72	154	26	5	8	51	11	.267
1980	Milwaukee	SS	143	611	121	179	49	10	23	87	20	.293
1981	Milwaukee	SS	96	377	50	103	15	5	10	49	4	.273
1982	Milwaukee	SS	156	635	129	210	46	12	29	114	14	.331
1983	Milwaukee	SS	149	578	102	178	42	10	17	80	12	.308
	Totals		1389	5425	780	1541	296	65	113	633	128	.284

TED SIMMONS 34 6-0 200 — Bats S Throws R

Tied teammate Robin Yount for ninth spot in AL batting parade . . . His .308 average represented return to form after posting marks of .269 and .216 previous two years . . . Said he finally made adjustment to abundance of breaking balls he has seen in AL since coming to Brewers from St. Louis in seven-player swap prior to 1981 season . . . Nine of his 17 game-winning RBI came from the seventh inning on . . . Drove in 46-of-112 runners who were in scoring position when he came to bat . . . Collected 2,000th major-league hit off Yankees' Rudy May June 12 and scored 900th run with home run off Kansas City's Larry Gura Aug. 2 . . . Only Brewer to homer from both left-hand and right-hand sides of the plate in a single game (against Minnesota, May 2, 1982) . . . Holds NL record for career home runs by a switch-hitter (172) . . . Began switch-hitting at age 13 . . . Born Aug. 1, 1949, in Highland Park, Mich. . . . Majored in speech and radio/television at University of Michigan . . . Spends most of his time as DH, because his arm is suspect when he is catching.

Year	Club	Pos.	G	AB	R	H	2B	3B	HR	RBI	SB	Avg.
1968	St. Louis . . .	C	2	3	0	1	0	0	0	0	0	.333
1969	St. Louis . . .	C	5	14	0	3	0	1	0	3	0	.214
1970	St. Louis . . .	C	82	284	29	69	8	2	3	24	2	.243
1971	St. Louis . . .	C	133	510	64	155	32	4	7	77	1	.304
1972	St. Louis . . .	C-1B	152	594	70	180	36	6	16	96	1	.303
1973	St. Louis . . .	C-1B-OF	161	619	62	192	36	2	13	91	2	.310
1974	St. Louis . . .	C-1B	152	599	66	163	33	6	20	103	0	.272
1975	St. Louis . . .	C-1B-OF	157	581	80	193	32	3	18	100	1	.332
1976	St. Louis . . .	C-1B-OF-3B	150	546	60	159	35	3	5	75	0	.291
1977	St. Louis . . .	C-OF	150	516	82	164	25	3	21	95	2	.318
1978	St. Louis . . .	C-OF	152	516	71	148	40	5	22	80	1	.287
1979	St. Louis . . .	C	123	448	68	127	22	0	26	87	0	.283
1980	St. Louis . . .	C-OF	145	495	84	150	33	2	21	98	1	.303
1981	Milwaukee . .	C-1B	100	380	45	82	13	3	14	61	0	.216
1982	Milwaukee . .	C	137	539	73	145	29	0	23	97	0	.269
1983	Milwaukee . .	C	153	600	76	185	39	3	13	108	4	.308
	Totals		1954	7244	930	2116	413	43	222	1195	15	.292

DON SUTTON 38 6-1 190 **Bats R Throws R**

Had eight-game losing streak, matching club record for a starter, set by Clyde Wright in 1974... Had worst record of his career and matched his highest earned-run average... Led Brewers with 135 strikeouts... Hinted at retirement after losing streak, but reconsidered after season... Acquired late in 1982 from Houston for three prospects and posted big wins for Brewers down the stretch that season... Won pennant clincher at Baltimore on the final day of '82 season and Game 3 of AL Championship Series, after California had won first two... Pitched in four All-Star Games for National League, working eight scoreless innings... Has pitched five one-hitters... Born April 2, 1945, in Clio, Ala.... In his first pro year, he went 23-6, including a 15-6 mark at Albuquerque that earned him Texas League Player-of-the-Year honors... Wants to be sportscaster when playing career ends... Won 230 games for Dodgers before signing with Astros as free agent prior to 1981 season.

Year	Club	G	IP	W	L	Pct.	SO	BB	H	ERA
1966	Los Angeles	37	226	12	12	.500	209	52	192	2.99
1967	Los Angeles	37	233	11	15	.423	169	57	223	3.94
1968	Los Angeles	35	208	11	15	.423	162	59	179	2.60
1969	Los Angeles	41	293	17	18	.486	217	91	269	3.47
1970	Los Angeles	38	260	15	13	.536	201	78	251	4.08
1971	Los Angeles	38	265	17	12	.586	194	55	231	2.55
1972	Los Angeles	33	273	19	9	.679	207	63	186	2.08
1973	Los Angeles	33	256	18	10	.643	200	56	196	2.43
1974	Los Angeles	40	276	19	9	.679	179	80	241	3.23
1975	Los Angeles	35	254	16	13	.552	175	62	202	2.87
1976	Los Angeles	35	268	21	10	.677	161	82	231	3.06
1977	Los Angeles	33	240	14	8	.636	150	69	207	3.19
1978	Los Angeles	34	238	15	11	.577	154	54	228	3.55
1979	Los Angeles	33	226	12	15	.444	146	61	201	3.82
1980	Los Angeles	32	212	13	5	.722	128	47	163	2.21
1981	Houston	23	159	11	9	.550	104	29	132	2.60
1982	Houston	27	195	13	8	619	139	46	169	3.00
1982	Milwaukee	7	55	4	1	.800	36	18	55	3.29
1983	Milwaukee	31	220	8	13	.381	134	54	209	4.08
	Totals	622	4357	266	206	.564	3065	1113	3765	3.11

PAUL MOLITOR 27 6-0 175 **Bats R Throws R**

Played third base for second year in a row after spending time at five positions in his first five years in the majors... Showed signs of adapting, cutting errors from 32 to 16... Wrist problem slowed him throughout season and cut down on his offensive production... Finished sixth in league with 41 stolen bases, matching 1982 total... Has been thrown out only 15 times during past two seasons... Twelve of first 13 home runs were bases-empty shots, including 10 leadoff blasts... Set World Series record with five hits in Game 1 against St. Louis in 1982... Scored 136 runs in 1982, the most in AL since Ted Williams scored 150 in 1949... AL Rookie of the Year in 1978... Born Aug. 22, 1956, in St. Paul, Minn.... Spent one year in minors, when he hit .346 for Burlington (A) and was selected MVP of Midwest League in 1977... Was two-time All-American at Minnesota.

Year	Club	Pos.	G	AB	R	H	2B	3B	HR	RBI	SB	Avg.
1978	Milwaukee	2B-SS-3B	125	521	73	142	26	4	6	45	30	.273
1979	Milwaukee	2B-SS	140	584	88	188	27	16	9	62	33	.322
1980	Milwaukee	2B-SS-3B	111	450	81	137	29	2	9	37	34	.304
1981	Milwaukee	OF	64	251	45	67	11	0	2	19	10	.267
1982	Milwaukee	3B-SS	160	666	136	201	26	8	19	71	41	.302
1983	Milwaukee	3B-OF	152	609	95	164	28	6	15	47	41	.269
	Totals		752	3081	518	899	147	36	60	281	189	.292

MOOSE HAAS 27 6-0 170 **Bats R Throws R**

Tied club record with eight-game winning streak from late June to late August... Set Brewer record with .813 winning percentage and also had club-record 28 consecutive scoreless innings... Signed five-year contract late in 1983 season and then missed final month because of a tired arm... Was moved to the bullpen in September 1982 because of the acquisition of Don Sutton... Managed to pick up a win in 1982 World Series against St. Louis... Set Milwaukee strikeout record with 14 against Yankees, April 12, 1978... Born April 22, 1956, in Baltimore... Has a black belt in Tae Kwondo... Amateur magician... Runs locksmith business with father.

Year	Club	G	IP	W	L	Pct.	SO	BB	H	ERA
1976	Milwaukee	5	16	0	1	.000	9	12	12	3.94
1977	Milwaukee	32	198	10	12	.455	113	84	195	4.32
1978	Milwaukee	7	31	2	3	.400	32	8	33	6.10
1979	Milwaukee	29	185	11	11	.500	95	59	198	4.77
1980	Milwaukee	33	252	16	15	.516	146	56	246	3.11
1981	Milwaukee	24	137	11	7	.611	64	40	146	4.47
1982	Milwaukee	32	193	11	8	.579	104	39	232	4.47
1983	Milwaukee	25	179	13	3	.813	75	42	170	3.27
	Totals	187	1191	74	60	.552	638	340	1232	4.06

BEN OGLIVIE 35 6-2 170 **Bats L Throws L**

After hitting better than .500 with eight home runs in spring training, left fielder had one hit in first 16 at-bats... Then he ran off a 16-game hitting streak... Hit three home runs vs. Boston in May, marking third time he has turned trick in his career. Ironically, all have come against teams for which he has played. Other two occasions came against Detroit... Only Lou

Gehrig has more three-homer games in AL, with four . . . Played only 125 games because of nagging injuries, including bruised shoulder, painful heel and strained wrist . . . Average rose, but production dropped . . . Tied Reggie Jackson for AL home-run title with 41 in 1980 . . . Had 26 assists as outfielder for Louisville (AAA) in 1971 . . . Born Feb. 11, 1949, in Colon, Panama . . . Was outstanding soccer player during high school.

Year	Club	Pos.	G	AB	R	H	2B	3B	HR	RBI	SB	Avg.
1971	Boston	OF	14	38	2	10	3	0	0	4	0	.263
1972	Boston	OF	94	253	27	61	10	2	8	30	1	.241
1973	Boston	OF	58	147	16	32	9	1	2	9	1	.218
1974	Detroit	OF-1B	92	252	28	68	11	3	4	29	12	.270
1975	Detroit	OF-1B	100	332	45	95	14	1	9	36	11	.286
1976	Detroit	OF-1B	115	305	36	87	12	3	15	47	9	.285
1977	Detroit	OF	132	450	63	118	24	2	21	61	9	.262
1978	Milwaukee	OF-1B	128	469	71	142	29	4	18	72	11	.303
1979	Milwaukee	OF-1B	139	514	88	145	30	4	29	81	12	.282
1980	Milwaukee	OF	156	592	94	180	26	2	41	118	11	.304
1981	Milwaukee	OF	107	400	53	97	15	2	14	72	2	.243
1982	Milwaukee	OF	159	602	92	147	22	1	34	102	3	.244
1983	Milwaukee	OF	125	411	49	115	19	3	13	66	4	.280
	Totals		1419	4765	663	1297	224	28	208	727	86	.272

PETE VUCKOVICH 31 6-4 200 **Bats R Throws R**

After fighting shoulder problems for two years, he finally saw doctors who discovered torn rotator cuff during spring training . . . Decided to try exercise rehabilitation program instead of surgery and returned to pitch three games in September . . . Brewers didn't push him, hoping he'd be ready for 1984 . . . Did color commentary on pay-TV broadcasts of Brewer games while spending most of summer on disabled list . . . Won AL Cy Young Award in 1982, when he compiled pair of eight-game winning streaks . . . Pitched first shutout in Toronto Blue Jay history when he beat Jim Palmer and Baltimore Orioles in 1977 . . . Spent only two years in minors before debuting with Chicago White Sox . . . Born Oct. 27, 1952, in Johnstown, Pa. . . . Attended Clarion State Teachers College . . . Spent three years with St. Louis before coming over with Rollie Fingers and Ted Simmons prior to 1981.

Year	Club	G	IP	W	L	Pct.	SO	BB	H	ERA
1975	Chicago (AL)	4	10	0	1	.000	5	7	17	13.50
1976	Chicago (AL)	33	110	7	4	.636	62	60	122	4.66
1977	Toronto	53	148	7	7	.500	123	59	143	3.47
1978	St. Louis	45	198	12	12	.500	149	59	187	2.55
1979	St. Louis	34	233	15	10	.600	145	64	229	3.59
1980	St. Louis	32	222	12	9	.571	132	68	203	3.41
1981	Milwaukee	24	150	14	4	.778	84	57	137	3.54
1982	Milwaukee	30	224	18	6	.750	105	102	234	3.34
1983	Milwaukee	3	15	0	2	.000	9	10	15	4.91
	Totals	258	1310	85	55	.607	814	486	1287	3.52

CHARLIE MOORE 30 5-11 180 Bats R Throws R

Continued to adapt to right field after coming to majors as catcher . . . Set career highs in games, hits, doubles and at-bats . . . Good strikeout ratio as he fanned only 42 times in 529 at-bats . . . Led Brewers with 14 of club's 61 sacrifice bunts . . . Hit for cycle vs. California in 1980 . . . Asked Brewers to trade him in spring of 1982, when Ted Simmons was given fulltime catching job . . . Finally was told he could have right-field spot and, after platooning early in the season, he took over job fulltime . . . Born June 21, 1953, in Birmingham, Ala. . . . Turned down football scholarship to Auburn, because he wanted to play baseball . . . Attended Mesa Junior College and Alabama before signing with Brewers.

Year	Club	Pos.	G	AB	R	H	2B	3B	HR	RBI	SB	Avg.
1973	Milwaukee	C	8	27	0	5	0	1	0	3	0	.185
1974	Milwaukee	C	72	204	17	50	10	4	0	19	3	.245
1975	Milwaukee	C-OF	73	241	26	70	20	1	1	29	1	.290
1976	Milwaukee	C-OF-3B	87	241	33	46	7	4	3	16	1	.191
1977	Milwaukee	C	138	375	42	93	15	6	5	45	1	.248
1978	Milwaukee	C	96	268	30	72	7	1	5	31	4	.269
1979	Milwaukee	C	111	337	45	101	16	2	5	38	8	.300
1980	Milwaukee	C	111	320	42	93	13	2	2	30	10	.291
1981	Milwaukee	C-OF	48	156	16	47	8	3	1	9	1	.301
1982	Milwaukee	OF-C-2B	133	456	53	116	22	4	6	45	2	.254
1983	Milwaukee	OF	151	529	65	150	27	6	2	49	11	.284
	Totals		1028	3154	369	843	135	34	30	314	42	.267

PETE LADD 27 6-3 240 Bats R Throws R

Was supposed to be bullpen savior, but, after getting off to an 0-2 start with two saves and an ERA of more than 6.00, he was sent to minors May 20 . . . Got in shape at Vancouver (AAA), pitching 14 innings, during which he struck out 16 and earned five saves and two wins . . . Returned June 21 and, in his final 36 appearances with the Brewers, he was 3-1 with 23 saves and struck out 41 in 49 innings . . . Earned two saves against California in 1982 AL Championship Series . . . Was 43-18 with 69 saves during six years in minors, not counting his brief stay last season . . . Recorded Florida State League-leading 18 saves for Winter Haven (A) in 1978 . . . Born July 17, 1956, in Portland, Maine . . . Attended University of Mississippi . . . Spent winters as jail guard at Cumberland County Jail in home town of Portland . . . His size-17 shoes earned him nickname "Big Foot."

Year	Club	G	IP	W	L	Pct.	SO	BB	H	ERA
1979	Houston	10	12	1	1	.500	6	8	8	3.00
1982	Milwaukee	16	18	1	3	.250	12	6	16	4.00
1983	Milwaukee	44	49	3	4	.429	41	16	30	2.55
	Totals	70	79	5	8	.385	59	30	54	2.96

TOP PROSPECTS

RANDY READY 24 5-11 180 **Bats R Throws R**

Made big impression during September look, finishing season with nine-game hitting streak and .405 average on 15-for-37 for Brewers . . . Hit .329 with 13 home runs, 24 stolen bases and 59 RBI at Vancouver (AAA) . . . Won minor-league batting titles in 1980 (.376 with Butte of Pioneer League) and 1982 (.375 with El Paso of Texas League) . . . Third baseman who could be moved to the outfield . . . Originally signed as a second baseman, he was moved to shortstop and can play third . . . Born Jan. 8, 1960, in San Mateo, Cal. . . . Attended Hayward State and Mesa State.

DION JAMES 21 6-1 170 **Bats L Throws L**

A surprise first-round pick in June 1980 draft, he has surprised the skeptics with his play since signing with the Brewers . . . Born Nov. 9, 1962, in Philadelphia . . . A first baseman and pitcher in high school, he has blossomed into an outstanding center fielder . . . Stole 45 bases for Stockton (A) in 1981 . . . Thefts dropped to 22 in 1983, but he did hit .336 and struck out only 33 times in 467 at-bats for Vancouver (AAA) . . . Could take over center-field spot from weak-hitting Rick Manning.

MANAGER RENE LACHEMANN: The youngest manager in

big leagues . . . Hired the day after the 1983 season ended to replace Harvey Kuenn . . . Began association with pro baseball as batboy for Los Angeles Dodgers in 1959 . . . Attended USC for one year and then signed big bonus contract with Kansas City Athletics . . . Was a top prospect until being hit in face with a pitch at Mobile in 1966 . . . As a 20-year-old, he spent all of 1965 in the majors, combining with 19-year-old Catfish Hunter to comprise the youngest battery in big-league history . . . After the beaning, he played only 26 more games in majors . . . Played in Athletics' farm system until becoming a manager in the A's organization at age 26 . . . Played on same team in Vancouver as Oakland manager Steve Boros and White Sox skipper Tony LaRussa, his longtime minor-league roommate . . . In addition to managing nine years in minors for A's and Seattle, he managed five winters in Latin America . . . Finally got first big-league managerial job when he replaced Maury Wills in Seattle, May 6, 1981 . . . Led Mariners to the best record in their history (76-86) in 1982 and was fired June 25 of last season . . . Brother Marcel is pitching coach for California and brother Bill is minor-league manager for San Francisco . . . Born May 14, 1945, in Los Angeles.

GREATEST STEALER

The home run has been the way home for the Brewers, but hidden by their power displays has been the fleet-footed efforts of Paul Molitor.

He hasn't come close to the franchise's single-season record of 73, set by Tommy Harper when the club was the Seattle Pilots in 1969, but Molitor has led the Brewers in thefts the last six years. He has stolen 41 bases each of the last two seasons, which might not seem like much until it is compared to the totals compiled by the rest of the team. Those 82 thefts have accounted for 44 percent of the team total of 185 and pushed his career total to 189.

And Molitor doesn't get burned often. He was thrown out only 15 times in the last two seasons combined, giving him a success ratio of 84.5 percent.

ALL-TIME BREWER SEASON RECORDS

BATTING: Cecil Cooper, .352, 1980
HRs: Gorman Thomas, 45, 1979
RBIs: Cecil Cooper, 126, 1983
STEALS: Paul Molitor, 41, 1982, 1983
WINS: Mike Caldwell, 22, 1978
STRIKEOUTS: Marty Pattin, 161, 1971

NEW YORK YANKEES

TEAM DIRECTORY: Prin. Owner: George Steinbrenner III; Pres.: Eugene McHale; Adm. VP-Treas.: David Weidler; VP-GM: Murray Cook; VP-Baseball Oper.: Bill Bergesch; Dir. Scouting: Bobby Hofman; Dir. Pub. Rel.: John Fugazy; Dir. Media Rel.: Joseph Safety; Trav. Sec.: Bill Kane; Mgr.: Yogi Berra. Home: Yankee Stadium (57,545). Field distances: 312, l.f. line, 387, l.f.; 430, l.c.; 417, c.f.; 385, r.c.; 353, r.f.; 310, r.f. line. Spring training: Fort Lauderdale, Fla.

SCOUTING REPORT

HITTING: Steve Kemp (.241, 12 homers, 49 RBI) was supposed to give the Yankees the left-handed power threat they have lacked since Reggie Jackson's defection after the 1981 season. Nice idea, but it didn't work. As if Kemp's struggle with the bat wasn't enough, he had his cheekbone fractured by a batting-practice liner and his eyesight makes him a question mark for this season.

There's no question about a middle-of-the-lineup combination of Dave Winfield (.283, 32 homers, 116 RBI) and Don Baylor

There's still lightnin' left in Ron Guidry's arm.

(.303, 21 homers, 85 RBI), but Graig Nettles (20 homers, 75 RBI) is getting along in years and manager Yogi Berra could use another left-handed slugger who can take advantage of that short porch in right field at Yankee Stadium. Ken Griffey (.306), Butch Wynegar (.296) and Don Mattingly (.283) are coming off strong seasons. The Yanks might use versatile Roy Smalley (18 homers, 62 RBI) in the specialty role handled so capably in the past by free-agent defector Oscar Gamble. Fortunately Lou Piniella (.291) has put off retirement for one more season.

PITCHING: The Yankees are well-stocked in left-handed starters with Ron Guidry (21-9), Dave Righetti (14-8), Shane Rawley (14-14) and Ray Fontenot (8-2). And now they have a righty in ex-Brave Phil Niekro (11-10) to go with John Montefusco (14-4 overall), who had a 5-0 September and accounted for the bulk of the nine victories the Yanks got from right-handed starters last season.

Goose Gossage (13-5, 22 saves) blew 12 of his first 25 save opportunities last year, but losing him in the free-agent market last winter was a devastating setback for the Yanks, because he was the only proven stopper they had. With the addition of Mike Armstrong (10-7) from Kansas City to go with George Frazier and Dale Murray, they are loaded with middle-inning relievers.

FIELDING: The numbers don't lie in this case. The Yankees were 11th in the AL in fielding, committing 139 errors. And it's easy to see why. The only positions at which they can feel comfortable about their defense are left field, where Winfield won a Gold Glove, and third base, where Nettles' abilities haven't been significantly diminished by age.

Andre Robertson shows signs of being a classy shortstop—if he can come back from a fractured vertebrae suffered in the August car wreck that ended his season. The center-field situation has become such a jumbled mess that Griffey might be moved back there from first base or Winfield might be moved there from left. Even when he had good vision, Kemp wasn't much to watch in right field.

OUTLOOK: A team in turmoil, the Yankees overcame constant clubhouse bickering to rebound from a 79-win disaster in 1982 to win 91 games in 1983. But a repetition will not be enough to win the tough AL East this year.

The Yankees need some help in the bullpen, from the left side on offense and at a lot of places on defense if they are going to improve in 1984.

NEW YORK YANKEES 1984 ROSTER

MANAGER Yogi Berra

Coaches—Gene Michael, Sammy Ellis, Jeff Torborg, Lee Walls, Roy White

PITCHERS

No.	Name	1983 Club	W-L	IP	SO	ERA	B-T	Ht.	Wt.	Born
—	Armstrong, Mike	Kansas City	10-7	103	52	3.86	R-R	6-3	206	3/7/54 Glen Cove, NY
—	Christiansen, Clay	Columbus	8-9	160	92	5.44	R-R	6-5	205	6/28/58 Wichita, KS
47	Fontenot, Ray	Columbus	3-2	35	36	2.83	L-L	6-0	175	8/8/57 Lake Charles, LA
		New York (AL)	8-2	97	27	3.33				
43	Frazier, George	New York (AL)	4-4	115	78	3.43	R-R	6-5	200	10/13/54 Oklahoma City, OK
49	Guidry, Ron	New York (AL)	21-9	250	156	3.42	L-L	5-11	162	8/28/50 Lafayette, LA
50	Howell, Jay	New York (AL)	1-5	82	61	5.38	R-R	6-3	205	11/26/55 Miami, FL
34	Keough, Matt	Oak.-NY (AL)	5-7	100	54	5.33	R-R	6-3	185	7/3/55 Pomona, CA
45	May, Rudy	Columbus	0-0	7	6	2.45	L-L	6-2	205	7/16/44 Coffeyville, KS
		New York (AL)	1-5	18	16	6.87				
24	Montefusco, John	San Diego	9-4	95	52	3.30	R-R	6-1	192	5/25/50 Keansburg, NJ
		New York (AL)	5-0	38	15	3.32				
48	Murray, Dale	New York (AL)	2-4	94	45	4.48	R-R	6-4	205	2/2/50 Cuero, TX
35	Niekro, Phil	Atlanta	11-10	201	128	3.97	R-R	6-2	180	4/1/39 Blaine, OH
26	Rawley, Shane	New York (AL)	14-14	238	124	3.78	L-L	6-0	180	7/27/55 Racine, WI
19	Righetti, Dave	New York (AL)	14-8	217	169	3.44	L-L	6-3	198	11/28/58 San Jose, CA
—	Rijo, Jose	Ft. Lauderdale	15-5	160	152	1.68	R-R	6-1	160	5/13/65 Dominican Republic
		Nashville	3-2	40	32	2.68				
29	Shirley, Bob	New York (AL)	5-8	108	53	5.08	R-L	5-11	185	6/25/54 Cushing, OK

CATCHERS

No.	Name	1983 Club	H	HR	RBI	Pct.	B-T	Ht.	Wt.	Born
10	Cerone, Rick	New York (AL)	54	2	22	.220	R-R	5-11	185	5/19/54 Newark, NJ
58	Espino, Juan	Columbus	59	10	42	.280	R-R	6-1	190	3/16/56 Dominican Republic
		New York (AL)	6	0	5	.261				
27	Wynegar, Butch	New York (AL)	89	6	42	.296	B-R	6-0	194	3/14/56 York, PA

INFIELDERS

No.	Name	1983 Club	H	HR	RBI	Pct.	B-T	Ht.	Wt.	Born
56	*Campaneris, Bert	New York (AL)	46	0	11	.322	R-R	5-10	160	3/9/42 Cuba
—	Foli, Tim	California	83	2	29	.252	R-R	6-0	175	12/8/50 Culver City, CA
33	Griffey, Ken	New York (AL)	140	11	46	.306	L-L	6-0	200	4/10/50 Donora, PA
—	Hudler, Rex	Ft. Lauderdale	93	2	50	.270	R-R	6-1	180	9/2/60 Tempe, AZ
		Columbus	36	1	11	.305				
20	Meacham, Bobby	Columbus	111	9	60	.262	B-R	6-1	175	8/25/60 Los Angeles, CA
		New York (AL)	12	0	4	.235				
39	Milbourne, Larry	Philadelphia	16	0	4	.242	B-R	6-0	165	2/14/51 Port Norris, NJ
		New York (AL)	14	0	2	.200				
9	Nettles, Graig	New York (AL)	123	20	75	.266	L-R	6-0	185	8/20/44 San Diego, CA
—	Pagliarulo, Mike	Nashville	117	19	80	.260	B-R	6-2	195	3/15/60 Medford, MA
30	Randolph, Willie	New York (AL)	117	2	38	.279	R-R	5-11	166	7/6/54 Holly Hill, SC
18	Robertson, Andre	New York (AL)	80	1	22	.248	R-R	5-10	155	10/2/57 Orange, TX
12	Smalley, Roy	New York (AL)	124	18	62	.275	B-R	6-1	180	10/25/52 Los Angeles, CA
—	Smith, Keith	Nashville	110	8	38	.258	R-R	6-1	175	10/20/61 Los Angeles, CA

OUTFIELDERS

No.	Name	1983 Club	H	HR	RBI	Pct.	B-T	Ht.	Wt.	Born
25	Baylor, Don	New York (AL)	162	21	85	.303	R-R	6-1	210	6/28/48 Austin, TX
62	Dayett, Brian	Columbus	138	35	108	.288	R-R	5-10	180	1/22/57 New London, CT
		New York (AL)	6	0	5	.207				
—	Destrade, Orestes	Ft. Lauderdale	124	18	74	.292	B-R	6-4	210	5/8/62 Cuba
—	Javier, Stan	Greensboro	152	12	77	.311	B-R	6-0	180	9/1/65 Dominican Republic
21	Kemp, Steve	New York (AL)	90	12	49	.241	L-L	6-0	190	8/7/54 San Angelo, TX
46	Mattingly, Don	Columbus	54	8	37	.340	L-L	6-0	175	4/20/61 Evansville, IN
		New York (AL)	79	4	32	.283				
22	Moreno, Omar	Houston	98	0	25	.242	L-L	6-3	188	10/24/52 Panama
		New York (AL)	38	1	17	.250				
52	Nixon, Otis	Columbus	162	0	41	.291	B-R	6-2	180	1/9/59 Evergreen, NC
		New York (AL)	2	0	0	.143				
14	Piniella, Lou	New York (AL)	43	2	16	.291	R-R	6-2	200	8/28/43 Tampa, FL
31	Winfield, Dave	New York (AL)	169	32	116	.283	R-R	6-6	220	10/3/51 St. Paul, MN
—	Winters, Matt	Columbus	126	29	99	.292	L-R	6-3	202	3/18/60 Buffalo, NY

*Free agent unsigned at press time

YANKEE PROFILES

DAVE WINFIELD 32 6-6 220 **Bats R Throws R**

Finished second in AL in game-winning RBI (21), third in total RBI and tied for fifth in home runs . . . Had streaky season . . . From Opening Day through May 31, he had nine home runs and 35 RBI in 45 games . . . Had four homers and 17 RBI in next 35 games . . . Caught fire with .350 average, 12 homers and 44 RBI in following 30 games, then managed only one homer and eight RBI in ensuing 27-game stretch through middle of September . . . His 37 homers in 1982 represented the most by any right-handed-hitter in Yankee history, other than Joe Di-Maggio . . . One of nine players to hit 30 homers in both leagues . . . Born Oct. 3, 1951, in St. Paul, Minn. . . . Went straight from campus of University of Minnesota, where he was 13-1 as pitcher and hit better than .400 in his senior year and was selected 1973 College World Series MVP, to starting lineup of San Diego Padres . . . Also drafted by football's Minnesota Vikings and bas-ketball's Utah Stars and Atlanta Hawks . . . Has played in seven straight All-Star Games . . . Signed huge, long-term contract with Yankees as free agent prior to 1981 season . . . Might wind up moving from left to center on permanent basis.

Year	Club	Pos.	G	AB	R	H	2B	3B	HR	RBI	SB	Avg
1973	San Diego	OF-1B	56	141	9	39	4	1	3	12	0	.27
1974	San Diego	OF	145	498	57	132	18	4	20	75	9	.26
1975	San Diego	OF	143	509	74	136	20	2	15	76	23	.26
1976	San Diego	OF	137	492	81	139	26	4	13	69	26	.28
1977	San Diego	OF	157	615	104	169	29	7	25	92	16	.27
1978	San Diego	OF-1B	158	587	88	181	30	5	24	97	21	.30
1979	San Diego	OF	159	597	97	184	27	10	34	118	15	.30
1980	San Diego	OF	162	558	89	154	25	6	20	87	23	.27
1981	New York (AL)	OF	105	388	52	114	25	1	13	68	11	.29
1982	New York (AL)	OF	140	539	84	151	24	8	37	106	5	.28
1983	New York (AL)	OF	152	598	99	169	26	8	32	116	15	.28
	Totals		1514	5522	834	1568	254	56	236	916	164	.28

DON BAYLOR 35 6-1 210 **Bats R Throws R**

Only problem in first year as a Yankee was his disgust with not playing every day . . . Wound up as most consistent Yankee, posting the high-est average of his career . . . Strongest person-ality on club . . . Was signed as free agent to fill void created by departure of Reggie Jackson . . . Ironically, Baltimore had traded him to Oak-land as part of package for Jackson prior to

1976 season . . . When manager Billy Martin asked each player to submit list of five pitchers who give him problems, this designated hitter turned in blank slip . . . Won AL MVP award in 1979, when he played 162 games for California despite suffering pulled hamstring, separated shoulder, sprained right wrist and dislocated right thumb . . . All-time Angel home-run leader with 141 in six years . . . Born June 28, 1948, in Austin, Tex. . . . Suffered dislocated shoulder playing high-school football and injury has affected his ability to throw and hurt his value as outfielder . . . Turned down football scholarship to University of Texas to sign with Baltimore in 1967 . . . Was selected Minor League Player of the Year with Rochester (.327, 22 homers, 107 RBI) in 1970.

Year	Club	Pos.	G	AB	R	H	2B	3B	HR	RBI	SB	Avg.
1970	Baltimore	OF	8	17	4	4	0	0	0	4	1	.235
1971	Baltimore	OF	1	2	0	0	0	0	0	1	0	.000
1972	Baltimore	OF-1B	102	319	33	81	13	3	11	38	24	.254
1973	Baltimore	OF-1B	118	405	64	116	20	4	11	51	32	.286
1974	Baltimore	OF-1B	137	489	66	133	22	1	10	59	29	.272
1975	Baltimore	OF-1B	145	524	79	148	21	6	25	76	32	.282
1976	Oakland	OF-1B	157	595	85	147	25	1	15	68	52	.247
1977	California	OF-1B	154	561	87	141	27	0	25	75	26	.251
1978	California	OF-1B	158	591	103	151	26	0	34	99	22	.255
1979	California	OF-1B	162	628	120	186	33	3	36	139	22	.296
1980	California	OF	90	340	39	85	12	2	5	51	6	.250
1981	California	1B-OF	103	377	52	90	18	1	17	66	3	.239
1982	California	DH	157	608	80	160	24	1	24	93	10	.263
1983	New York (AL)	OF-1B	144	534	82	162	33	3	21	85	17	.303
	Totals		1656	5991	894	1604	274	25	234	905	276	.268

RON GUIDRY 33 5-11 162 **Bats L Throws L**

Disproved accusations by club owner George Steinbrenner that he was a seven-inning pitcher . . . Finished third in AL in wins and led league with 21 complete games, including nine in a row . . . Didn't overpower hitters as he once did, but still had out pitch when he needed it . . . Has won more games (106) and struck out more batters (1,037) than any other AL pitcher during last six years . . . Has played center field twice in majors, against Toronto in September 1979 and in resumption of pine-tar game against Kansas City last August . . . Won AL Cy Young Award in 1978, when he set Yankee record with 13 consecutive wins . . . Became second unanimous Cy Young selection in history, following in 1968 footsteps of Denny McLain . . . Also had nine shutouts, tying AL record for left-hander that Babe Ruth set in 1916, and set Yankee single-game strikeout record by fanning 18 California Angels in 1978 . . . Led AL in ERA in 1978 and

1979 . . . Born Aug. 28, 1950, in Lafayette, La. . . . Ran track in high school because school had no baseball program.

Year	Club	G	IP	W	L	Pct.	SO	BB	H	ERA
1975	New York (AL)	10	16	0	1	.000	15	9	15	3.38
1976	New York (AL)	20	16	0	0	.000	12	4	20	5.63
1977	New York (AL)	31	211	16	7	.696	176	65	174	2.82
1978	New York (AL)	35	274	25	3	.893	248	72	187	1.74
1979	New York (AL)	33	236	18	8	.692	201	71	203	2.78
1980	New York (AL)	37	220	17	10	.630	166	80	215	3.56
1981	New York (AL)	23	127	11	5	.688	104	26	100	2.76
1982	New York (AL)	34	222	14	8	.636	162	69	216	3.81
1983	New York (AL)	31	250	21	9	.700	156	60	232	3.42
	Totals	254	1572	122	51	.705	1240	456	1362	2.99

GRAIG NETTLES 39 6-0 185 — Bats L Throws R

Despite assorted minor ailments, he put together his best season since 1978 and then spurned re-entry draft to re-sign with Yankees . . . Part of resurrection due to reunion with manager Billy Martin, who was his skipper at Denver in 1968 and brought him to majors for first time with Minnesota in 1969 . . . "He's my all-time gamer," says Martin . . . Became sixth captain in Yankee history in January 1982 . . . Well-known for defense and has earned two Gold Gloves . . . Established major-league records for assists (412) and double plays (54) by a third baseman in 1971 . . . Starred with glove in 1978 World Series vs. Dodgers . . . Led AL in home runs with 32 in 1976 . . . Holds AL career record for home runs by third baseman . . . Born Aug. 20, 1944, in San Diego . . . Played baseball and basketball at San Diego State . . . Brother Jim is a coach for Tacoma in Oakland organization, after playing in majors for Minnesota, Detroit, Cleveland and Kansas City.

Year	Club	Pos.	G	AB	R	H	2B	3B	HR	RBI	SB	Avg.
1967	Minnesota	PH	3	3	0	1	1	0	0	0	0	.333
1968	Minnesota	OF-3B-1B	22	76	13	17	2	1	5	8	0	.224
1969	Minnesota	OF-3B	96	225	27	50	9	2	7	26	1	.222
1970	Cleveland	3B-OF	157	549	81	129	13	1	26	62	3	.235
1971	Cleveland	3B	158	598	78	156	18	1	28	86	7	.261
1972	Cleveland	3B	150	557	65	141	28	0	17	70	2	.253
1973	New York (AL)	3B	160	552	65	129	18	0	22	81	0	.234
1974	New York (AL)	3B-SS	155	566	74	139	21	1	22	75	1	.246
1975	New York (AL)	3B	157	581	71	155	24	4	21	91	1	.267
1976	New York (AL)	3B	158	583	88	148	29	2	32	93	11	.254
1977	New York (AL)	3B	158	589	99	150	23	4	37	107	2	.255
1978	New York (AL)	3B-SS	159	587	81	162	23	2	27	93	1	.276
1979	New York (AL)	3B	145	521	71	132	15	1	20	73	1	.253
1980	New York (AL)	3B-SS	89	324	52	79	14	0	16	45	0	.244
1981	New York (AL)	3B	103	349	46	85	7	1	15	46	0	.244
1982	New York (AL)	3B	122	405	47	94	11	2	18	55	1	.232
1983	New York (AL)	3B	129	462	56	123	17	3	20	75	0	.266
	Totals		2121	7527	1014	1890	273	25	333	1086	31	.251

ANDRE ROBERTSON 26 5-10 155 Bats R Throws R

Fractured neck suffered in early-morning car wreck Aug. 18 ended his season . . . His loss was major factor in club's fade-out, according to team owner George Steinbrenner . . . Injury leaves doubts about future . . . Even if he's healthy, he has to prove that he is strong enough to be consistent for full season . . . Played some at second base when Willie Randolph was hurt, but is considered club's shortstop of the future . . . Struck out 54 times and walked only eight times . . . Was a second baseman at University of Texas, where Met prospect Ron Gardenhire was the shortstop . . . Originally signed by Toronto in 1979 and went to Yankees in 1980, when he made stops at each level of minors . . . Born Oct. 2, 1957, in Orange, Tex. . . . Was fan of San Francisco Giants and Willie Mays.

Year	Club	Pos.	G	AB	R	H	2B	3B	HR	RBI	SB	Avg.
1981	New York (AL)	SS-2B	10	19	1	5	1	0	0	0	1	.263
1982	New York (AL)	SS-2B-3B	44	118	16	26	5	0	2	9	0	.220
1983	New York (AL)	SS-2B	98	322	37	80	16	3	1	22	2	.248
	Totals		152	459	54	111	22	3	3	31	3	.242

WILLIE RANDOLPH 29 5-11 166 Bats R Throws R

When he played, he played well, but he missed 58 games because of hamstring injuries . . . Was disabled twice, from June 17 to June 27 and July 12 to Aug. 16, and appeared in only three of 45 games during troubled stretch . . . In six of his nine years in majors, he has been on divisional title-winner . . . Set AL record for chances by a second baseman (20) and tied major-league record for assists by a second baseman (13) in 19-inning game in 1976 . . . Born July 6, 1954, in Holly Hill, S.C. . . . Grew up in Brooklyn, where he played stickball on streets of Canarsie . . . Brother Terry was drafted by Green Bay Packers in 1977 and also played for New York Jets . . . Originally signed by Pittsburgh Pirates, who traded him to Yankees along with Ken Brett and Dock Ellis for pitcher Doc Medich prior to 1976 season.

Year	Club	Pos.	G	AB	R	H	2B	3B	HR	RBI	SB	Avg.
1975	Pittsburgh	2B-3B	30	61	9	10	1	0	0	3	1	.164
1976	New York (AL)	2B	125	430	59	115	15	4	1	40	37	.267
1977	New York (AL)	2B	147	551	91	151	28	11	4	40	13	.274
1978	New York (AL)	2B	134	499	87	139	18	6	3	42	36	.279
1979	New York (AL)	2B	153	574	98	155	15	13	5	61	33	.270
1980	New York (AL)	2B	138	513	99	151	23	7	7	46	30	.294
1981	New York (AL)	2B	93	357	59	83	14	3	2	24	14	.232
1982	New York (AL)	2B	144	553	85	155	21	4	3	36	16	.280
1983	New York (AL)	2B	104	420	73	117	21	1	2	38	12	.279
	Totals		1068	3958	660	1076	156	49	27	330	192	.272

ROY SMALLEY 31 6-1 180 **Bats S Throws R**

Spent year bouncing around infield, going from shortstop to first to third, and occasionally serving as DH . . . Appendectomy in spring training delayed his start . . . Never has had much range and came under attack from Yankee front office for making errors in critical situations . . . Has played last few years with a back problem . . . Established Yankee record for home runs by a shortstop in 1982, hitting 16 of his homers while playing that position . . . Born Oct. 25, 1952, in Los Angeles . . . Nephew of his former manager at Minnesota, Gene Mauch . . . Father Roy Smalley Jr. played with Cubs, Milwaukee Braves and Philadelphia . . . Was philosophy major while playing on two national championship teams at USC . . . Was drafted five times before finally signing with Texas Rangers, who made him first player selected overall in January 1974 draft and gave him reported $100,000 signing bonus . . . Came to Yankees from Twins in deal that sent reliever Ron Davis to Minnesota.

Year	Club	Pos.	G	AB	R	H	2B	3B	HR	RBI	SB	Avg.
1975	Texas	SS-2B-C	78	250	22	57	8	0	3	33	4	.228
1976	Texas-Minnesota	SS-2B	144	513	61	133	18	3	3	44	2	.259
1977	Minnesota	SS	150	584	93	135	21	5	6	56	5	.231
1978	Minnesota	SS	158	586	80	160	31	3	19	77	2	.273
1979	Minnesota	SS-1B	162	621	94	168	28	3	24	95	2	.271
1980	Minnesota	SS-1B	133	486	64	135	24	1	12	63	3	.278
1981	Minnesota	2B-1B	56	167	24	44	7	1	7	22	0	.263
1982	Minn.-N.Y.(AL)	SS-3B-2B	146	499	57	127	15	2	20	67	0	.255
1983	New York (AL)	SS-3B-1B	130	451	70	124	24	1	18	62	3	.275
	Totals		1157	4157	565	1083	176	19	112	519	21	.261

BUTCH WYNEGAR 28 6-0 194 **Bats S Throws R**

Spent first six weeks of season alternating with Rick Cerone, but finally took command of starting catcher's job . . . Able to beat back challenge of Cerone, but couldn't avoid injuries to hamstring, shoulder and arch of foot that limited him to less than 100 games for the third consecutive season, including strike-shortened 1981 . . . Posted career-high average . . . Third injury-plagued season in a row . . . Was sidelined in second half of 1982 by viral meningitis . . . Opened 1981 on disabled list because of surgery to remove bone chip from right elbow . . . Four-time All-Star selection, including 1976, when he became youngest player ever picked to play in All-Star Game (20 years, 121 days old)... Born March 14, 1956, in York, Pa.... Originally a third baseman, he was converted into catcher in high school... Acquired from Twins in five-player deal in May 1982.

Year	Club	Pos.	G	AB	R	H	2B	3B	HR	RBI	SB	Avg.
1976	Minnesota	C	149	534	58	139	21	2	10	69	0	.260
1977	Minnesota	C-3B	144	532	76	139	22	3	10	79	2	.261
1978	Minnesota	C-3B	135	454	36	104	22	1	4	45	1	.229
1979	Minnesota	C	149	504	74	136	20	0	7	57	2	.270
1980	Minnesota	C	146	486	61	124	18	3	5	57	3	.255
1981	Minnesota	C	47	150	11	37	5	0	0	10	0	.247
1982	Minn.-NY(AL).....	C	87	277	36	74	12	1	4	28	0	.267
1983	New York (AL)	C	94	301	40	89	18	2	6	42	1	.296
	Totals..........		951	3238	392	842	138	12	46	387	9	.260

KEN GRIFFEY 33 6-0 200 **Bats L Throws L**

Bounced back in 1983 after enduring a difficult adjustment to life in the AL in his first season as a Yankee, when he hit 30 points below his career average... Despite a hamstring pull that limited him to 118 games, he was his old self at the plate... Was shifted from the outfield to first base, but could wind up back in the outfield this year... Clashed with former manager Billy Martin concerning his role last season... Knee problems have limited his mobility and cut down on his stolen-base totals in recent seasons... Born April 10, 1950, in Donora, Pa., the birthplace of Stan Musial... Enjoyed his best years with Cincinnati, which made him a 29th-round selection in June 1969... Scored 111 and 117 runs in back-to-back seasons for Reds (1976 and 1977)... Voted MVP of 1980 All-Star Game... Had seven game-winning RBI last season... A quiet man who might prosper under direction of Yogi Berra rather than the volatile Martin... Hopes he'll be a regular at one position rather than a parttime player at two.

Year	Club	Pos.	G	AB	R	H	2B	3B	HR	RBI	SB	Avg.
1973	Cincinnati	OF	25	86	19	33	5	1	3	14	4	.384
1974	Cincinnati	OF	88	227	24	57	9	5	2	19	9	.251
1975	Cincinnati	OF	132	463	95	141	15	9	4	46	16	.305
1976	Cincinnati	OF	148	562	111	189	28	9	6	74	34	.336
1977	Cincinnati	OF	154	585	117	186	35	8	12	57	17	.318
1978	Cincinnati	OF	158	614	90	177	33	8	10	63	23	.288
1979	Cincinnati	OF	95	380	62	120	27	4	8	32	12	.316
1980	Cincinnati	OF	146	544	89	160	28	10	13	85	23	.294
1981	Cincinnati	OF	101	396	65	123	21	6	2	34	12	.311
1982	New York (AL)	OF	127	484	70	134	23	2	12	54	10	.277
1983	New York (AL)	1B-OF	118	458	60	140	21	3	11	46	6	.306
	Totals..........		1292	4799	802	1460	245	65	83	524	166	.304

SHANE RAWLEY 28 6-0 180 **Bats L Throws L**

Found permanent home in Yankee rotation, with streaky results . . . Was 5-1 in August, including four straight wins, but finished with 0-4 mark in September . . . Established career highs in virtually every department . . . Spent first four years in majors with Seattle, where he made only four starts in 205 appearances . . . Finally put into rotation with Yankees, July 5, 1982, and has remained there since . . . Ranks second on Mariner all-time save list with 36 . . . Victim of strange injuries . . . Broke hand in fight after brother was attacked outside a bar during 1980 season . . . Broke left foot while playing basketball in January 1981 . . . Has a pilot's license . . . Born July 27, 1955, in Racine, Wisc. . . . Attended Indian Hill Community College, where he played for Pat Daugherty, who also was his first manager in pro ball . . . Was in minors with Montreal and Cincinnati organizations before finally joining Mariners in 1978 . . . Acquired by Yankees prior to 1982 season for pitchers Gene Nelson and Bill Caudill and outfielder Bobby Brown.

Year	Club	G	IP	W	L	Pct.	SO	BB	H	ERA
1978	Seattle	52	111	4	9	.308	66	51	114	4.14
1979	Seattle	48	84	5	9	.357	48	40	88	3.86
1980	Seattle	59	114	7	7	.500	68	63	103	3.32
1981	Seattle	46	68	4	6	.400	35	38	64	3.97
1982	New York (AL)	47	164	11	10	.524	111	54	165	4.06
1983	New York (AL)	34	238	14	14	.500	124	79	246	3.78
	Totals	286	779	45	55	.450	452	325	780	3.85

DAVE RIGHETTI 25 6-3 198 **Bats L Throws L**

Made his first full season in the majors one to remember . . . No-hit Boston Red Sox July 4, the first no-hitter pitched by a Yankee since Don Larsen's perfect game in the 1956 World Series against Brooklyn . . . Had pitched his first major-league shutout in previous start, against Baltimore June 29 . . . Led Yankee pitchers in strikeouts for second straight year, fanning seven or more batters in 12 games, including a career-high 11 against White Sox Aug. 15 . . . Had hot first half, winning 10-of-13 decisions before All-Star break . . . Born Nov. 28, 1958, in San Jose, Cal. . . . Father Leo was a second baseman in Yankee system . . . Played with Dave Stieb now of Toronto, at San Jose Community College and played against Carney Lansford, now of Oakland, in American Legion ball . . . Was 1981 AL Rookie of the Year, but spent parts of that season and 1982 at Yankees' Columbus (AAA) farm team.

Year	Club	G	IP	W	L	Pct.	SO	BB	H	ERA
1979	New York (AL)	3	17	0	1	.000	13	10	10	3.71
1981	New York (AL)	15	105	8	4	.667	89	38	75	2.06
1982	New York (AL)	33	183	11	10	.524	163	108	155	3.79
1983	New York (AL)	31	217	14	8	.636	169	67	194	3.44
	Totals	82	522	33	23	.589	434	223	434	3.29

PHIL NIEKRO 45 6-2 180 **Bats R Throws R**

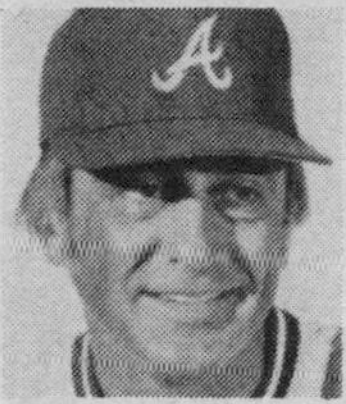

Brings his knuckleball to Yankee Stadium after 19 years with the Braves in Milwaukee and Atlanta . . . Released after the '83 season, he signed a two-year contract at $700,000 a year . . . Oldest player in the majors . . . "His age doesn't bother me at all," says Yogi Berra, who plans to use him as a starter . . . Two years ago he was 17-4 and three times he has won 20 or more . . . Hurled no-hitter against Padres in 1973 . . . Born April 1, 1939, in Lansing, Ohio . . . Brother Joe, six years younger, is the Astro pitcher . . . Was schoolboy teammate of former Celtic John Havlicek.

Year	Club	G	IP	W	L	Pct.	SO	BB	H	ERA
1964	Milwaukee	10	15	0	0	.000	8	7	15	4.80
1965	Milwaukee	41	75	2	3	.400	40	26	73	2.88
1966	Atlanta	28	50	4	3	.571	17	23	48	4.14
1967	Atlanta	46	207	11	9	.550	129	55	164	1.87
1968	Atlanta	37	257	14	12	.538	140	45	228	2.50
1969	Atlanta	40	284	23	13	.639	193	57	235	2.57
1970	Atlanta	34	230	12	18	.400	168	68	222	4.27
1971	Atlanta	42	269	15	14	.517	173	70	248	2.98
1972	Atlanta	38	282	16	12	.571	164	53	254	3.06
1973	Atlanta	42	245	13	10	.565	131	89	214	3.31
1974	Atlanta	41	302	20	13	.606	195	88	249	2.38
1975	Atlanta	39	276	15	15	.500	144	72	285	3.20
1976	Atlanta	38	271	17	11	.607	173	101	249	3.29
1977	Atlanta	44	330	16	20	.444	262	164	315	4.04
1978	Atlanta	44	334	19	18	.514	248	102	295	2.88
1979	Atlanta	44	342	21	20	.512	208	113	311	3.39
1980	Atlanta	40	275	15	18	.455	176	85	256	3.63
1981	Atlanta	22	139	7	7	.500	62	56	120	3.11
1982	Atlanta	35	234	17	4	.810	144	73	225	3.61
1983	Atlanta	34	202	11	10	.524	128	105	212	3.97
	Totals	739	4619	268	230	.538	2912	1452	4218	3.20

DON MATTINGLY 22 6-0 175 **Bats L Throws L**

Played 91 games with Yankees last year ... Showed he could play first base with best of them and could play outfield, too ... Hit .340 in 159 at-bats at Columbus (AAA) last season ... Never hit below .315 in minors ... Not much home-run power, but this line-drive hitter could develop into fine player ... Struck out only 24 times in more than 500 plate appearances at Columbus in 1982 ... Slipped through until 19th round of June 1979 draft because teams thought he was going to go to college ... Born April 20, 1961, in Evansville, Ind. ... Brother Randy played pro football.

Year	Club	Pos.	G	AB	R	H	2B	3B	HR	RBI	SB	Avg.
1982	New York (AL)	OF-1B	7	12	0	2	0	0	0	1	0	.167
1983	New York (AL)	1B-OF	91	279	34	79	15	4	4	32	0	.283
	Totals		98	291	34	81	15	4	4	33	0	.278

TOP PROSPECT

OTIS NIXON 25 6-2 180 **Bats S Throws R**

Converted from second baseman into outfielder ... Didn't slow him down offensively ... Hit .291 with 94 stolen bases at Columbus (AAA) ... Split 1982 between Nashville (AA) and Columbus, combining for 107 stolen bases and 118 walks ... Has stolen 339 bases in five minor-league seasons ... Speed must run in family. Brother Donnell stole 141 bases for Bakersfield in Seattle organization last season, breaking previous pro record, but finishing one behind St. Louis farmhand Vince Coleman, who had 142 thefts for Macon of South Atlantic League ... Born Jan. 9, 1959, in Evergreen, N.C. ... Hit .143 in 14 at-bats with Yankees last season.

MANAGER YOGI BERRA: One of baseball's most storied celebrities, that master of malapropisms, begins

his second stint as Yankee manager, succeeding Billy Martin ... Owner George Steinbrenner hopes Yogi will be more disposed toward following his suggestions than was Martin ... Managed Yankees to 99-win season and American League pennant in 1964, but was fired after club lost World Series to St. Louis ... Managed Mets to NL pennant in 1973, but again lost in

World Series, to Oakland . . . Overall major-league managerial mark is 391–359 . . . Returned to Yankees, with whom he appeared in a record 14 World Series as an active player, as a coach in 1976 . . . Pudgy catcher was AL MVP in 1951, 1954 and 1955 and a 15-time All-Star . . . His 313 career homers as catcher rank him second to Johnny Bench among catchers . . . Has most hits in World Series history (71) . . . His No. 8 was one of eight uniform numbers retired by the Yankees . . . Elected to Hall of Fame in 1972 after posting career mark of .285 with 358 homers and 1,430 RBI from 1946–63 plus a cameo as a Met in 1966 . . . Son Dale is Pirates' shortstop . . . Legendary for his "It's not over 'til it's over" observation, among others . . . Of course, for Yankee managers, sometimes it's over before it's over.

GREATEST STEALER

There wasn't much to distinguish the five years Fritz Maisel spent with the Yankees, from 1913-17. A switch-hitting third baseman, he compiled only a .242 career average, but he could steal bases. He set the Yankee record with 74 in 1914 and his 1915 total of 51 ranks fourth on the club in the single-season category. Despite his limited stay in the Big Apple, he ranks sixth on the all-time Yankee list with 183.

Of course, stealing bases for the Yankees is almost a crime. This is a club that has had only two players exceed 40 thefts in a season since 1931, a club whose all-time stolen-base leader is Hal Chase with 248, a club that, despite its storied past, has led the AL in stolen bases only seven times.

In more recent times, the Yankees' best base-stealer has been Willie Randolph. He has led the team five of the last six years, but has only 42 stolen bases in the past three seasons.

ALL-TIME YANKEE SEASON RECORDS

BATTING: Babe Ruth, .393, 1923
HRs: Roger Maris, 61, 1961
RBIs: Lou Gehrig, 184, 1931
STEALS: Fritz Maisel, 74, 1914
WINS: Jack Chesbro, 41, 1904
STRIKEOUTS: Ron Guidry, 248, 1978

TORONTO BLUE JAYS

TEAM DIRECTORY: Chairman of the Board: R. Howard Webster; Vice-Chairman/Chief Exec. Off.: N. E. (Peter) Hardy; VP-Baseball Oper.: Pat Gillick; VP-Bus. Oper.: Paul Beeston; Dir. Pub. Rel.: Howard Starkman; Trav. Sec.: Ken Carson; Mgr.: Bobby Cox. Home: Exhibition Stadium (43,737). Field distances: 330, l.f. line; 375, l.c.; 400, c.f.; 375, r.c.; 330, r.f. line. Spring training: Dunedin, Fla.

SCOUTING REPORT

HITTING: Youth has been served in Toronto. A patient approach by management has allowed Lloyd Moseby (.315, 18 homers, 81 RBI), Damaso Garcia (.307) and Willie Upshaw (.306, 27 homers, 104 RBI) to blossom into legitimate big-league players. The platoon system of manager Bobby Cox has helped to fill holes at third and behind the plate.

The Blue Jays were so confident about the potential of outfielder Jorge Bell they had no qualms about trading Barry Bonnell to Seattle. If ex-Royal Willie Aikens (.302, 23 homers, 72 RBI) gets a partial reprieve on his one-year drug suspension in May, he'll give Toronto a boost as a DH.

It's far from a one-man show that allowed the Blue Jays to lead the AL in hitting (.277) and finish a close second to Baltimore in home runs (167). Nine Toronto players hit 10 or more home runs—the Blue Jays got a combined 27 from catchers Ernie Whitt and Buck Martinez—and 11 of the 12 Jays who appeared in more than 100 games hit .250 or better.

PITCHING: Dave Stieb (17-12, 3.04 ERA), Jim Clancy (15-11) and Luis Leal (13-12) were the only trio of starters in the AL to work more than 200 innings apiece. The pleasant surprise was midseason-addition Doyle Alexander, who won his final seven decisions, giving the Blue Jays an experienced arm to fill a major void in the rotation.

And during the winter, Toronto acquired Bryan Clark (7-10, 3.94 ERA) from Seattle. He figures to give the Jays a legitimate southpaw pitcher, something they have never really had. He is at his best in the bullpen, which is where the Jays were at their worst. Randy Moffitt led them with 10 saves last year.

If Clark is ready to accept a spot in the bullpen—he pleaded for a regular turn in the rotation during his days in Seattle—the Blue Jays could move up another spot or more in the standings.

This could be year Blue Jays' Dave Stieb gets his 20.

DEFENSE: The Blue Jays have a right to be defensive about slights of their defense. It has made steady strides, just like the rest of the team. They committed only 115 errors last season, two more than AL defensive leaders Texas and Milwaukee. Neither third baseman Garth Iorg nor Rance Mulliniks played enough to qualify for the league lead in fielding percentage, but nobody who played in at least 50 games had a better mark than Iorg's .976 and Mulliniks was No. 2 at .971.

With Bell joining Moseby and Barfield in the outfield, the Jays have three young players whose fielding will require some patience. But the DP combo of shortstop Alfredo Griffin and second baseman Garcia is solid.

OUTLOOK: It didn't seem like things were ever going to get better in Toronto. For six years, the Jays were the doormats of the AL East, but general manager Pat Gillick never panicked. He preached patience and his belief paid off in 1983.

For the first time, the Blue Jays finished ahead of other teams (fourth) and won more games than they lost. They finished .500 or better against every member of the AL West. And, with a starting lineup featuring as many as seven players who are 28 or younger, the expectations of better things to come are realistic.

TORONTO BLUE JAYS 1984 ROSTER

MANAGER Bobby Cox
Coaches—Cito Gaston, John Sullivan, Al Widmar, Jimy Williams

PITCHERS

No.	Name	1983 Club	W-L	IP	SO	ERA	B-T	Ht.	Wt.	Born
31	Acker, Jim	Toronto	5-1	98	44	4.33	R-R	6-2	212	9/24/58 Freer, TX
33	Alexander, Doyle	Kinston	0-0	6	4	0.00	R-R	6-3	200	9/4/50 Cordova, AL
		NY (AL)-Tor.	7-8	145	63	4.41				
55	Cerutti, John	Knoxville	9-13	189	131	3.43	L-L	6-2	195	4/28/60 Albany, NY
18	Clancy, Jim	Toronto	15-11	223	99	3.91	R-R	6-4	207	12/18/55 Chicago, IL
35	Clark, Bryan	Seattle	7-10	162	76	3.94	L-L	6-2	200	7/12/56 Madera, CA
34	Clarke, Stan	Knoxville	2-4	43	51	2.49	R-L	6-1	180	8/9/60 Toledo, OH
		Toronto	1-1	11	7	3.27				
		Syracuse	0-3	53	58	2.89				
28	Eichhorn, Mark	Syracuse	0-5	31	12	1.92	R-R	6-4	200	11/21/60 San Jose, CA
		Knoxville	6-12	121	54	4.33				
38	Gott, Jim	Toronto	9-14	177	121	4.74	R-R	6-4	215	8/3/59 Hollywood, CA
39	Howard, Dennis	Syracuse	9-7	115	64	3.69	B-R	5-11	185	4/24/59 Buffalo, NY
25	Jackson, Roy Lee	Toronto	8-3	92	48	4.50	R-R	6-2	205	5/1/54 Opelika, AL
48	Leal, Luis	Toronto	13-12	217	116	4.31	R-R	6-3	215	3/21/57 Venezuela
49	McKnight, Jack	Knoxville	8-12	172	96	4.13	R-R	6-2	185	6/7/61 Alvin, TX
50	McLaughlin, Joey	Toronto	7-4	65	47	4.45	R-R	6-2	215	7/11/56 Tulsa, OK
17	*Moffitt, Randy	Toronto	6-2	57	38	3.77	R-R	6-3	195	10/13/48 Long Beach, CA
39	Morgan, Mike	Toronto	0-3	45	22	5.16	R-R	6-3	200	10/8/59 Tulare, CA
		Syracuse	0-3	19	17	5.59				
32	Shipanoff, Dave	Knoxville	6-3	70	73	3.36	R-R	6-0	175	12/13/59 Canada
		Syracuse	0-1	11	18	3.27				
37	Stieb, Dave	Toronto	17-12	278	187	3.04	R-R	6-1	190	7/22/57 Santa Ana, CA
45	Williams, Matt	Syracuse	8-8	148	116	3.41	R-R	6-1	200	7/25/59 Houston, TX
		Toronto	1-1	8	5	14.63				

CATCHERS

No.	Name	1983 Club	H	HR	RBI	Pct.	B-T	Ht.	Wt.	Born
13	Martinez, Buck	Toronto	56	10	33	.253	R-R	5-11	200	11/7/48 Redding, CA
14	Petralli, Geno	Syracuse	80	3	40	.245	B-R	6-1	185	9/25/59 Sacramento, CA
		Toronto	0	0	0	.000				
46	Pinkham, Bill	Knoxville	63	10	41	.252	R-R	6-5	215	8/25/59 Worcester, MA
12	Whitt, Ernie	Toronto	88	17	56	.256	L-R	6-2	200	6/13/52 Detroit, MI

INFIELDERS

No.	Name	1983 Club	H	HR	RBI	Pct.	B-T	Ht.	Wt.	Born
24	**Aikens, Willie	Kansas City	124	23	72	.302	L-R	6-2	220	10/14/54 Seneca, SC
1	Fernandez, Tony	Syracuse	131	5	38	.300	B-R	6-2	165	8/6/62 Dominican Republic
		Toronto	9	0	2	.265				
7	Garcia, Damaso	Toronto	161	3	38	.307	R-R	6-0	170	2/7/57 Dominican Republic
4	Griffin, Alfredo	Toronto	132	4	47	.250	B-R	5-11	165	3/6/57 Dominican Republic
16	Iorg, Garth	Toronto	103	2	39	.275	R-R	5-11	170	10/12/54 Arcata, CA
44	Johnson, Cliff	Toronto	108	22	76	.265	R-R	6-4	225	7/22/47 San Antonio, TX
2	Manrique, Fred	Syracuse	130	10	50	.268	R-R	6-1	175	11/5/61 Venezuela
19	McGriff, Fred	Florence	37	7	26	.311	L-L	6-3	200	10/31/63 Tampa, FL
		Kinston	85	21	57	.243				
5	Mulliniks, Rance	Toronto	100	10	49	.275	L-R	6-0	170	1/15/56 Tulare, CA
20	Reynolds, Jeff	Syracuse	95	13	50	.219	R-R	6-1	195	1/27/60 Charleston, WV
26	Upshaw, Willie	Toronto	177	27	104	.306	L-L	6-0	185	4/27/57 Blanco, TX

OUTFIELDERS

No.	Name	1983 Club	H	HR	RBI	Pct.	B-T	Ht.	Wt.	Born
29	Barfield, Jesse	Toronto	98	27	68	.253	R-R	6-1	190	10/29/59 Joliet, IL
11	Bell, George	Syracuse	86	15	59	.271	R-R	6-1	185	10/21/59 Dom. Republic
		Toronto	30	2	17	.268				
10	Collins, Dave	Toronto	109	1	34	.271	B-L	5-10	175	10/20/52 Rapid City, SD
15	Moseby, Lloyd	Toronto	170	18	81	.315	L-R	6-3	205	11/5/59 Portland, AR
21	Shephard, Ron	Syracuse	110	13	62	.272	R-R	6-4	175	10/27/60 Longview, TX
23	Webster, Mitch	Syracuse	120	9	45	.260	B-L	6-1	185	5/16/59 Larned, KS
		Toronto	2	0	0	.182				

*Free agent unsigned at press time
**Suspended for one year pending review

BLUE JAY PROFILES

WILLIE UPSHAW 26 6-0 185 **Bats L Throws L**

Finished 14th in AL batting race with first .300-plus average of career . . . Was eighth in AL in home runs and became first Blue Jay to surpass 100 RBI in a season . . . Also set club record with 16 game-winning RBI . . . Finished strong, hitting .347 with seven homers, 27 RBI in September . . . Committed 10 errors in first 39 games, but only 11 in last 121 . . . Had 50 multi-hit games . . . Originally signed by Yankee scout Pat Gillick, who now runs Blue Jay operation . . . Played some outfield before winning fulltime job as Blue Jays' first baseman in 1982, prompting the trade of John Mayberry . . . Plucked from Yanks' Syracuse farm in December 1977 draft . . . Born April 27, 1957, in Blanco, Tex. . . . Has 14 brothers and sisters . . . Cousin of pro football players Gene and Marvin Upshaw.

Year	Club	Pos.	G	AB	R	H	2B	3B	HR	RBI	SB	Avg.
1978	Toronto	OF	95	224	26	53	8	2	1	17	4	.237
1980	Toronto	1B-OF	34	61	10	13	3	1	1	5	1	.213
1981	Toronto	1B-OF	61	111	15	19	3	1	4	10	2	.171
1982	Toronto	1B	160	580	77	155	25	7	21	75	8	.267
1983	Toronto	1B	160	579	99	177	26	7	27	104	10	.306
	Totals		510	1555	227	417	65	18	54	211	25	.268

DAMASO GARCIA 27 6-0 170 **Bats R Throws R**

Despite nagging foot and knee injuries, second baseman finished 12th in AL in hitting and tied for 11th in stolen bases . . . Accounted for 35 percent of Blue Jays' stolen bases (85-of-246) during last two seasons . . . Had a 21-game hitting streak in 1983 to tie teammate Lloyd Moseby for longest in AL . . . Led off back-to-back games at Detroit with home runs in June . . . Dating back to 1981, he has stolen third base 15 consecutive times . . . Born Feb. 7, 1957, in Moca, Dominican Republic . . . Was a soccer star in high school and college and played soccer for Dominican Republic in Pan Am Games . . . Originally signed by Yankees and became first Yankee to hit into triple play, Sept. 21, 1979 at Toronto . . . Signed by Yankee scout Epy Guerrero, who is now with Toronto . . . Finished fourth in AL Rookie-of-the-Year voting in 1980.

Year	Club	Pos.	G	AB	R	H	2B	3B	HR	RBI	SB	Avg.
1978	New York (AL)	SS-2B	18	41	5	8	0	0	0	1	1	.195
1979	New York (AL)	SS-3B	11	38	3	10	1	0	0	4	2	.263
1980	Toronto	2B	140	543	50	151	30	7	4	46	13	.278
1981	Toronto	2B	64	250	24	63	8	1	1	13	13	.252
1982	Toronto	2B	147	597	89	185	32	3	5	42	54	.310
1983	Toronto	2B	131	525	84	161	23	6	3	38	31	.307
	Totals		511	1994	255	578	94	17	13	144	114	.290

ALFREDO GRIFFIN 27 5-11 165 Bats S Throws R

Only player, other than Baltimore shortstop Cal Ripken Jr., to play in all 162 games last year . . . Only player to have played every game in each of last two seasons . . . Streak of 347 consecutive appearances is longest current stretch in major leagues . . . Shortstop tied for second in AL in triples . . . Led Blue Jays in sacrifice hits (11) for second year in a row . . . Hit for better average right-handed (.287) than left-handed (.227), but had three homers and 32 RBI from left side . . . Tied with Kansas City's Willie Wilson for AL lead in triples in 1980, as both hitters set record for three-base hits by switch-hitter with 15 . . . AL Rookie of the Year in 1979 . . . Began switch-hitting in 1976 . . . Born March 6, 1957, in Santo Domingo, Dominican Republic . . . Attended same high school as former Toronto teammate Rico Carty . . . Signed five-year contract in December.

Year	Club	Pos.	G	AB	R	H	2B	3B	HR	RBI	SB	Avg.
1976	Cleveland	SS	12	4	0	1	0	0	0	0	0	.250
1977	Cleveland	SS	14	41	5	6	1	0	0	3	2	.146
1978	Cleveland	SS	5	4	1	2	1	0	0	0	0	.500
1979	Toronto	SS	153	624	81	179	22	10	2	31	20	.287
1980	Toronto	SS	155	653	63	166	26	15	2	41	18	.254
1981	Toronto	SS-3B-2B	101	388	30	81	19	6	0	21	8	.209
1982	Toronto	SS	162	539	57	130	20	8	1	48	10	.241
1983	Toronto	SS	162	528	62	132	22	9	4	47	8	.250
	Totals		764	2781	299	697	111	48	9	191	66	.251

LLOYD MOSEBY 24 6-3 205 Bats L Throws R

Raw talent finally was translated into production . . . Finished fifth in AL in runs scored and sixth in average . . . Had never hit higher than .236 in majors before 1983 . . . Became first Blue Jay to score more than 100 runs in a season . . . Hit second inside-the-park home run of his career, off Detroit's Dan Petry May 30 . . . His 21-game hitting streak tied him with teammate Damaso Garcia for longest of the year in AL . . . Center fielder had 52 multiple-hit games . . . Equalled career stolen-base total with 26 in 34 attempts in 1983, after getting 26 in 57 attempts previously . . . Born Nov. 5, 1959, in Portland, Ark. . . . Has been youngest player on Blue Jays' 25-man roster last four years . . . Spent only two months at Syracuse (AAA) in making move from Dunedin (A) to majors . . . Cut as a catcher in Little League . . . Blue Jays made him No. 2 pick in the country in June 1978 draft.

Year	Club	Pos.	G	AB	R	H	2B	3B	HR	RBI	SB	Avg.
1980	Toronto	OF	114	389	44	89	24	1	9	46	4	.229
1981	Toronto	OF	100	378	36	88	16	2	9	43	11	.233
1982	Toronto	OF	147	487	51	115	20	9	9	52	11	.236
1983	Toronto	OF	151	539	104	170	31	7	18	81	27	.315
	Totals		512	1793	235	462	91	19	45	222	53	.258

JESSE BARFIELD 24 6-1 190 Bats R Throws R

Still has trouble making contact (110 strikeouts in 388 at-bats), but when he does, watch out . . . Has hit 47 home runs in slightly more than two years in majors, a ratio of one every 18.7 at-bats . . . Finished season strongly . . . After hitting .211 in first half, he hit .288 with 17 homers, 42 RBI after All-Star Game . . . Hit seven home runs between Aug. 29 and Sept. 4, including four in eight at-bats . . . Hit safely in first eight big-league games after being called up in September 1981 . . . Collected first major league home run off White Sox' Britt Burns . . . Born Oct. 29, 1959, in Joliet, Ill. . . . Blue Jays discovered him when they were scouting pitcher Bill Gullickson and made right fielder their ninth-round draft pick in June 1977.

Year	Club	Pos.	G	AB	R	H	2B	3B	HR	RBI	SB	Avg.
1981	Toronto	OF	25	95	7	22	3	2	2	9	4	.232
1982	Toronto	OF	139	394	54	97	13	2	18	58	1	.246
1983	Toronto	OF	128	388	58	98	13	3	27	68	2	.253
	Totals		292	877	119	217	29	7	47	135	7	.247

DAVE STIEB 26 6-1 190 Bats R Throws R

Ranked third in AL in ERA and first in league with 14 hit batsmen . . . Led AL in innings pitched in 1982 and finished second in 1983 . . . Got off to hot start with 8-2 record and 1.04 ERA, including five-game winning streak in which he threw four consecutive complete games . . . Also finished well, winning four of last five . . . Was starting and winning pitcher as AL broke 11-year losing streak in All-Star Game . . . Biggest problems came against former Blue Jay Ken Schrom and the Minnesota Twins, who beat him three straight times . . . Has been All-Star in three of his five major-league seasons . . . Born July 22, 1957, in Santa Ana, Cal. . . . Was outfielder-pitcher at Southern Illinois, after playing on same San Jose City College team as Yankee left-hander Dave Righetti . . . Didn't become fulltime pitcher until 1979, the same year he made it to the majors.

Year	Club	G	IP	W	L	Pct.	SO	BB	H	ERA
1979	Toronto	18	129	8	8	.500	52	48	139	4.33
1980	Toronto	34	243	12	15	.444	108	83	232	3.70
1981	Toronto	25	184	11	10	.524	89	61	148	3.18
1982	Toronto	38	288	17	14	.548	141	75	271	3.25
1983	Toronto	36	278	17	12	.586	187	93	223	304
	Totals.	151	1122	65	59	.524	577	360	1013	3.41

JIM CLANCY 28 6-4 207 — Bats R Throws R

All-time Blue Jay leader in innings pitched and wins . . . Was 4-1 with 2.81 ERA in July, after pitching five consecutive complete games . . . Finished season by losing four of last five decisions . . . Came to Blue Jays in expansion draft . . . Was left unprotected by Texas, be-because owner Brad Corbett didn't want to lose journeyman catcher John Ellis . . . First big-league win was 3-2 complete-game victory over Milwaukee, Aug. 1, 1977 . . . Also got win by forfeit when Baltimore refused to play because of field conditions in 1977 . . . Twice underwent surgery for dislocated tendons in right foot and missed nearly eight weeks of 1979 season . . . Had 20-37 record in minors . . . Born Dec. 18, 1955, in Chicago.

Year	Club	G	IP	W	L	Pct.	SO	BB	H	ERA
1977	Toronto	13	77	4	9	.308	44	47	80	5.03
1978	Toronto	31	194	10	12	.455	106	91	199	4.08
1979	Toronto	12	64	2	7	.222	33	31	65	5.48
1980	Toronto	34	251	13	16	.448	152	128	217	3.30
1981	Toronto	22	125	6	12	.333	56	64	126	4.90
1982	Toronto	40	267	16	14	.533	139	77	251	3.71
1983	Toronto	34	223	15	11	.577	99	61	238	3.91
	Totals.	186	1201	66	81	.449	629	499	1176	4.02

ERNIE WHITT 31 6-2 200 — Bats L Throws R

Platooned at catcher with Buck Martinez . . . His 17 home runs were third-highest by catcher in AL, behind Detroit's Lance Parrish (27) and Chicago's Carlton Fisk (26) . . . Had pair of two-homer games, both against Detroit . . . Committed only four errors, the first of which came Aug. 16 and snapped his streak of 96 errorless games . . . Expansion draft selection from Boston, which signed him as 12th-round draft pick in June 1972 . . . Has been successful on 10-of-17 major-league stolen-base attempts . . . Homered off Milwaukee's Jim Colborn in major-league debut with Boston in September 1976 . . . Spent better part of eight years in minors before finally sticking with Blue Jays in 1980 . . . Born June 13, 1952, in Detroit.

Year	Club	Pos.	G	AB	R	H	2B	3B	HR	RBI	SB	Avg.
1976	Boston	C	8	18	4	4	2	0	1	3	0	.222
1977	Toronto	C	23	41	4	7	3	0	0	6	0	.171
1978	Toronto	C	2	4	0	0	0	0	0	0	0	.000
1980	Toronto	C	106	295	23	70	12	2	6	34	1	.237
1981	Toronto	C	74	195	16	46	9	0	1	16	5	.236
1982	Toronto	C	105	284	28	74	14	2	11	42	3	.261
1983	Toronto	C	123	344	53	88	15	2	17	56	1	.256
	Totals		441	1181	128	289	55	6	36	157	10	.245

LUIS LEAL 27 6-3 215 **Bats R Throws R**

Talk about streaky . . . Lost first three decisions, then won five in a row, lost three straight and won five in a row . . . Threw first career shutout at Chicago July 14 . . . Combines with Dave Stieb and Jim Clancy to give Blue Jays one of best starting trios in baseball, and none of them have turned 30 yet . . . Two of his three wins in 1980 were against Yankees and Tommy John . . . Born March 21, 1957, in Barquisimeto, Venezuela . . . Signed as free agent in November 1978, he made impressive pro debut with 12-2 record and 2.64 ERA for Dunedin (A) and was in big leagues to stay less than a year later . . . Attended Boston rookie camp in 1977, but decided to return home . . . Played for Venezuela in 1978 Pan Am Games . . . Brother Carlos pitches in Blue Jays' system.

Year	Club	G	IP	W	L	Pct.	SO	BB	H	ERA
1980	Toronto	13	60	3	4	.429	26	31	72	4.50
1981	Toronto	29	130	7	13	.350	71	44	127	3.67
1982	Toronto	38	250	12	15	.444	111	79	250	3.93
1983	Toronto	35	217	13	12	.520	116	65	216	4.31
	Totals	115	657	35	44	.443	324	219	665	4.05

RANCE MULLINIKS 28 6-0 170 **Bats L Throws R**

In manager Bobby Cox's platoon set-up, he shared third base with Garth Iorg, but still led the club in doubles . . . Also hit 10 home runs, one more than he had hit in his entire major-league career before 1983 . . . Finished second to Cleveland's Toby Harrah in fielding among AL third basemen and four of his seven errors came vs. Cleveland . . . Originally a shortstop, the position he played for California on Opening Day in 1979 . . . Also has played second during big-league career . . . Posted career minor-league average of .297, including four consecutive seasons above .300, before coming to majors for good in 1980 . . . Has never been given a chance to play every day in big leagues . . . Born Jan. 15, 1956, in Tulare, Cal.

Year	Club	Pos.	G	AB	R	H	2B	3B	HR	RBI	SB	Avg.
1977	California	SS	78	271	36	73	13	2	3	21	1	.269
1978	California	SS	50	119	6	22	3	1	1	6	2	.185
1979	California	SS	22	68	7	10	0	0	1	8	0	.147
1980	Kansas City	SS-2B	36	54	8	14	3	0	0	6	0	.259
1981	Kansas City	2B-SS-3B	24	44	6	10	3	0	0	5	0	.227
1982	Toronto	3B-SS	112	311	32	76	25	0	4	35	3	.244
1983	Toronto	3B-SS	129	364	54	100	34	3	10	49	0	.275
	Totals		451	1231	149	305	81	6	19	130	6	.248

TOP PROSPECTS

TONY FERNANDEZ 21 6-2 165 Bats S Throws R

Only thing that keeps Blue Jays from being satisfied with Alfredo Griffin at shortstop is continuing development of this youngster . . . Was sent to Syracuse (AAA) for second year in a row and was International League All-Star shortstop for second year in a row, hitting .300 with 35 stolen bases . . . Born Aug. 6, 1962, in San Pedro de Macoris, Dominican Republic . . . Great instincts, range and desire . . . Outstanding bat control makes him excellent bunter and allows him to take advantage of his speed . . . Real name is Octavio Antonio Fernandez . . . Hit .265 in 15 games with Toronto last season.

DAVE SHIPANOFF 24 6-0 175 Bats R Throws R

Search for bullpen stopper could be near an end . . . Led Southern League with 18 saves for Knoxville (AA) in 1983, due in large part to 90-plus-mph fastball . . . Set Carolina League record with 30 saves for Kinston (A) in 1982 . . . Native Canadian, which will make him popular with Toronto fans . . . Only Canadian on Blue Jays' 40-man winter roster . . . Born Dec. 13, 1959, in Edmonton, Alberta . . . Attended Wabash Valley Junior College, where he was 16-0 in 1980.

MANAGER BOBBY COX: In his sixth year as a manager, he

compiled best record of his career . . . Led Blue Jays to best record (89-73) in their history and fourth-place finish in 1983 . . . Debuted with Toronto in 1982 by guiding Blue Jays to tie for sixth in AL East, marking first time these expansionists didn't finish last . . . Third manager in Blue Jays' seven-year history . . . Spent 1978-81 as manager of Atlanta, where he developed close friendship with Ted Turner . . . Led Braves to 81-80 mark in 1980, which was Braves' best finish since 1974 . . . Relies extensively on platooning of players, but gets point across without getting anybody upset . . . Managed six years in Yankee system and teams never finished lower than fourth place . . . Developed close relationship with Pat Gillick, now Toronto's VP-baseball operations . . . Coached for Yankees in 1977 . . . Spent only two years of playing career in majors, hitting .224 for Yankees in 1968 and 1969 . . . His 12-year pro playing career ended with him serving as player-manager in Fort Lauderdale in 1971 . . . Had to retire at 30 because of bad knees . . . Originally signed by Los Angeles Dodgers in 1959 . . . Born May 21, 1941, in Tulsa, Okla. . . . Overall major-league managerial record is 433-480.

GREATEST STEALER

The first thing to consider about stolen-base threats in Toronto is that Bob Bailor led the team in 1978 with six. Of course, the Blue Jays have come a long way since then, both in the standings and on the basepaths.

The leader of Toronto's running attack has been second baseman Damaso Garcia. He had never stolen more than 33 bases in a professional season before manager Bobby Cox came aboard in 1982 and turned Garcia loose.

Garcia has stolen 85 bases in the last two years, more than anyone else in the seven-year history of the Blue Jays. He has led the team in stolen bases the last three years and has a career total of 111 for Toronto, 46 more than his closest competitor in club history, Alfredo Griffin.

ALL-TIME BLUE JAY SEASON RECORDS

BATTING: Lloyd Moseby, .315, 1983
HRs: John Mayberry, 30, 1980
RBIs: Willie Upshaw, 104, 1983
STEALS: Damaso Garcia, 54, 1982
WINS: Dave Stieb, 17, 1982, 1983
STRIKEOUTS: Dave Stieb, 187, 1983

CALIFORNIA ANGELS

TEAM DIRECTORY: Chairman of the Board-Pres.: Gene Autry; VP-GM: Buzzie Bavasi; VP-Chief Adm. Off.: Mike Port; Asst. Chairman of the Board: Red Patterson; Dir. Publ. Rel.: Tom Seeberg; Trav. Sec.: Frank Sims; Mgr.: John McNamara. Home: Anaheim Stadium (65,158). Field distances: 333, l.f. line; 386, l.c.; 404, c.f.; 386, r.c.; 333, r.f. line. Spring training: Mesa Grande, Ariz.; Palm Springs, Calif.

SCOUTING REPORT

HITTING: On paper, the Angels can field an awesome lineup. But, like paper, this team, which is as long on years as it is on past accomplishments, can be torn apart with ease. This is a club that saw its 37-year-old cleanup hitter, Reggie Jackson, hit .194 last season and fail to hit a home run after July 31 en route to a total of 14.

If everyone is healthy—and that's a big if in light of the Angels' 15 disabling injuries last year—and plays up to past standards, the Angels can be awesome. They can start a former major-league all-star at every position. The most potent bats belong to Fred Lynn (22 homers, 74 RBI), Doug DeCinces (18 homers, 65 RBI), Rod Carew (.339), Bobby Grich (.292, 16 homers) and Brian Downing (19 homers).

The one thing the Angels haven't featured for nearly a decade is a base-stealing threat. A team that hit only .260 last year, the 12th-best mark in the AL, the Angels stole only 41 bases.

PITCHING: Other than 23-year-old Mike Witt (7-14), the Angels' pitchers look more like a collection for an old-timers' game than the staff of a pennant contender. Geoff Zahn (9-11), Tommy John (11-13), Ken Forsch (11-12) and Bruce Kison (11-5) have an average age of 37.

The bullpen was even worse, as Luis Sanchez led the team with seven of the Angels' league-low total of 23 saves. No wonder this club was a feeble 33-52 in games decided by two or less runs. Ex-Brewer Jim Slaton (14-6), who can start and relieve, former Yankee farmhand Curt Kaufman and ex-Astro Frank LaCorte (4-4, 3 saves), a free-agent signee, were brought in to help.

FIELDING: There's no defense for this defense. With Lynn in center, Rick Burleson at short, Grich at second, DeCinces at third, Downing in left and Bob Boone behind the plate, California would

Rod Carew is dangerous whenever he has a bat in his hands.

seem to have the makings of a solid-fielding squad. But the Angels erred often in 1983.

After finishing second in the AL in defense in 1982, the Angels were ranked 12th last season (.977). They led the AL in double plays (190), but that was as much an indication of the pitching staff's inability to keep people off base as it was a measure of the infield's handiwork. Boone continued to erase the opposition's base-running threats. He has now thrown out 111-of-223 potential base-stealers in his two years with California.

OUTLOOK: Age is creeping up on the Angels. Some of them can't get the job done anymore (Reggie). The others are more susceptible to injuries than they used to be. Boone was the only regular to appear in more than 130 games and Carew was the only other Angel to play more than 120 games.

Injuries were greatly responsible for the Angels' fall from the best in the West in 1982 to a fifth-place tie with Minnesota last year and the threat of more shrouds any expectation of improvement in 1984. The farm system has been raped by trades and the loss of draft choices because of the signing of free agents and doesn't have much to offer to manager John McNamara.

CALIFORNIA ANGELS 1984 ROSTER

MANAGER John McNamara
Coaches—Bob Clear, Preston Gomez, Bobby Knoop, Marcel Lachemann, Jimmie Reese

PITCHING

No.	Name	1983 Club	W-L	IP	SO	ERA	B-T	Ht.	Wt.	Born
46	Aase, Don	California	Injured—Did not play				R-R	6-3	210	9/8/54 Orange, CA
36	Brown, Steve	Edmonton	10-4	124	64	6.15	R-R	6-5	200	2/12/57 San Francisco, CA
		California	2-3	46	23	3.52				
23	Corbett, Doug	California	1-1	17	18	3.63	R-R	6-1	185	11/4/52 Sarasota, FL
		Edmonton	6-6	83	61	4.45				
16	Curtis, John	California	1-2	90	36	3.80	L-L	6-2	185	3/9/48 Newton, MA
43	Forsch, Ken	California	11-12	219	81	4.06	R-R	6-4	215	9/8/46 Sacramento, CA
41	Hassler, Andy	California	0-5	36	20	5.45	L-L	6-5	220	10/18/51 Texas City, TX
25	John, Tommy	California	11-13	235	65	4.33	R-L	6-3	200	5/22/43 Terre Haute, IN
—	Kaufman, Curt	Columbus	6-3	79	93	2.75	R-R	6-2	175	7/19/57 Omaha, NE
		New York (AL)	0-0	9	8	3.12				
—	Kidde, Jay	Edmonton	10-11	174	73	5.32	R-R	6-3	195	4/12/58 Alton, IL
24	Kison, Bruce	California	11-5	127	83	4.05	R-R	6-4	180	2/18/50 Pasco, WA
—	LaCorte, Frank	Houston	4-4	53	48	5.06	R-R	6-1	180	10/13/51 San Jose, CA
27	McLaughlin, Byron	Edmonton	1-2	46	42	5.83	R-R	6-1	175	9/29/55 Van Nuys, CA
		California	2-4	56	45	5.17				
33	Mooneyham, Bill	Nashua	8-6	110	76	4.58	R-R	6-0	175	8/16/60 Livermore, CA
		Edmonton	2-0	36	26	9.84				
21	Moreno, Angel	Edmonton	8-13	163	102	5.73	L-L	5-9	165	6/6/55 Mexico
—	Romanick, Ron	Nashua	9-12	174	112	4.86	R-R	6-4	195	11/6/60 Burley, ID
40	Sanchez, Luis	California	10-8	98	49	3.66	R-R	6-2	210	8/24/53 Venezuela
—	Slaton, Jim	Milwaukee	14-6	112	38	4.33	R-R	6-0	185	6/19/50 Long Beach, CA
—	Smith, Dave W.	Nashua	2-2	36	30	1.98	R-R	6-1	190	8/30/57 Tomball, TX
		Edmonton	6-3	38	26	5.17				
42	Steirer, Rick	Edmonton	7-7	87	58	3.84	R-R	6-4	200	8/27/56 Baltimore, MD
		California	3-2	62	25	4.82				
39	Witt, Mike	California	7-14	154	77	4.91	R-R	6-7	185	7/20/60 Fullerton, CA
38	Zahn, Geoff	California	9-11	203	81	3.33	L-L	6-1	175	2/19/46 Baltimore, MD

CATCHERS

No.	Name	1983 Club	H	HR	RBI	Pct.	B-T	Ht.	Wt.	Born
8	Boone, Bob	California	120	9	52	.256	R-R	6-2	202	11/19/47 San Diego, CA
34	Narron, Jerry	Edmonton	160	27	101	.301	L-R	6-3	205	1/15/56 Goldsboro, NC
		California	3	1	4	.136				

INFIELDERS

No.	Name	1983 Club	H	HR	RBI	Pct.	B-T	Ht.	Wt.	Born
31	Adams, Rick	Edmonton	66	6	38	.316	R-R	6-2	180	1/21/59 Upland, CA
		California	28	2	6	.250				
7	Burleson, Rick	Edmonton	10	0	4	.196	R-R	5-10	160	4/29/51 Lynwood, CA
		California	34	0	11	.286				
29	Carew, Rod	California	160	2	44	.339	L-R	6-0	182	10/1/45 Panama
11	DeCinces, Doug	California	104	18	65	.281	R-R	6-2	195	8/29/50 Burbank, CA
4	Grich, Bobby	California	113	16	62	.292	R-R	6-2	190	1/15/49 Muskegon, MI
15	Jackson, Ron	California	80	8	39	.230	R-R	6-0	217	5/9/53 Birmingham, AL
—	Keedy, Pat	Edmonton	47	14	40	.224	R-R	6-4	204	1/10/59 Birmingham, AL
28	Lubratich, Steve	Edmonton	122	10	78	.321	R-R	6-0	170	5/1/55 Oakland, CA
		California	34	0	7	.218				
30	Schofield, Dick	Edmonton	148	16	94	.284	R-R	5-10	175	11/21/62 Springfield, IL
		California	11	3	4	.204				
6	Sconiers, Daryl	California	86	8	46	.274	L-L	6-2	195	10/3/58 San Bernardino, CA
9	Wilfong, Rob	California	45	2	17	.254	L-R	6-1	185	9/1/53 Pasadena, CA

OUTFIELDERS

No.	Name	1983 Club	H	HR	RBI	Pct.	B-T	Ht.	Wt.	Born
12	Beniquez, Juan	California	96	3	34	.305	R-R	5-11	175	5/13/50 Puerto Rico
37	Brown, Mike	Edmonton	156	22	106	.354	R-R	6-2	195	12/29/59 San Francisco, CA
		California	24	3	9	.231				
5	Downing, Brian	California	99	19	53	.246	R-R	5-10	200	10/9/50 Los Angeles, CA
44	Jackson, Reggie	California	77	14	49	.194	L-L	6-0	208	5/18/46 Wyncote, PA
19	Lynn, Fred	California	119	22	74	.272	L-L	6-1	190	2/3/52 Chicago, IL
20	Pettis, Gary	Edmonton	151	11	52	.285	B-R	6-1	165	4/3/58 Oakland, CA
		California	25	3	6	.294				
17	Valentine, Ellis	California	65	13	43	.240	R-R	6-4	215	7/30/54 Helena, AR

ANGEL PROFILES

FRED LYNN 32 6-1 190 **Bats L Throws L**

Biggest moment came in 1983 All-Star Game, in which he won MVP honors by hitting first grand slam in All-Star history and leading AL to its first win since 1971 . . . Despite assorted injuries which kept him from playing after Sept. 8, center fielder led Angels in home runs, RBI and game-winning RBI (11) . . . Underwent postseason surgery on right knee and had chips removed from right ankle . . . Doesn't like to play if he's not 100 percent and has been plagued with injuries in each of nine big-league seasons . . . Has appeared in nine straight All-Star Games . . . Was voted AL Rookie of the Year and MVP in 1975, when he became first rookie in history to lead either league in slugging percentage (.566) . . . Had 10 RBI in one game against Detroit that year . . . Born Feb. 3, 1952, in Chicago . . . Drafted out of high school by Yankees in 1970 as a pitcher . . . Went to USC and was second-round pick of Boston in 1973.

Year	Club	Pos.	G	AB	R	H	2B	3B	HR	RBI	SB	Avg.
1974	Boston	OF	15	43	5	18	2	2	2	10	0	.419
1975	Boston	OF	145	528	103	175	47	7	21	105	10	.331
1976	Boston	OF	132	507	76	159	32	8	10	65	14	.314
1977	Boston	OF	129	497	81	129	29	5	18	76	2	.260
1978	Boston	OF	150	541	75	161	33	3	22	82	3	.298
1979	Boston	OF	147	531	116	177	42	1	39	122	2	.333
1980	Boston	OF	110	415	67	125	32	3	12	61	12	.301
1981	California.	OF	76	256	28	56	8	1	5	31	1	.219
1982	California.	OF	138	472	89	141	38	1	21	86	7	.299
1983	California.	OF	117	437	56	119	20	3	22	74	2	.272
	Totals		1159	4227	696	1260	283	34	172	712	53	.298

DOUG DeCINCES 33 6-2 195 **Bats R Throws R**

Got off to great start . . . Was hitting .313 with 15 homers and 46 RBI June 24, but then fell victim to back problems and missed 51 of remaining games . . . Did finish season with six-game hitting streak and was given three-year, $3-million contract to pass on free agency . . . Collected 1,000th big-league hit, a home run off Toronto's Doyle Alexander, Sept. 6 . . . Set Angel record with .548 slugging percentage in 1982 and hit three home runs in one game twice in one week that season . . . Had to overcome comparisons to Brooks Robinson, his predecessor at third in Baltimore . . . Born Aug. 29, 1950, in Burbank, Cal.... Attended Pierce Junior College... Acquired from Orioles in swap for Dan Ford after 1981 season.

Year	Club	Pos.	G	AB	R	H	2B	3B	HR	RBI	SB	Avg.
1973	Baltimore.....	3B-2B-SS	10	18	2	2	0	0	0	3	0	.111
1974	Baltimore.....	3B	1	1	0	0	0	0	0	0	0	.000
1975	Baltimore.....	3B-SS-2B-1B	61	167	20	42	6	3	4	23	0	.251
1976	Baltimore.....	3B-2B-SS-1B	129	440	36	103	17	2	11	42	8	.234
1977	Baltimore.....	3B-2B-1B	150	522	63	135	28	3	19	69	8	.259
1978	Baltimore.....	3B-2B	142	511	72	146	37	1	28	80	7	.286
1979	Baltimore.....	3B	120	422	67	97	27	1	16	61	5	.230
1980	Baltimore.....	3B-1B	145	489	64	122	23	2	16	64	11	.249
1981	Baltimore.....	3B-1B-OF	100	346	49	91	23	2	13	55	0	.263
1982	California.....	3B-SS	153	575	94	173	42	5	30	97	7	.301
1983	California.....	3B	95	370	49	104	19	3	18	65	2	.281
	Totals.......		1106	3861	516	1015	222	22	155	559	48	.263

GEOFF ZAHN 37 6-1 175 — Bats L Throws L

Spent a month on disabled list with inflamed left shoulder, keeping him from reaching double figures in wins for first time in seven years... Did lead Angels' staff in ERA and surpassed 200 innings pitched for fourth time ... Career was in jeopardy after he had bone fragments removed from left elbow in 1976 ... Released by Chicago Cubs in 1977, he was signed by Minnesota after a tryout... Credits comeback to strong faith in Christianity... Has a hard slider that is especially tough on left-handed hitters... Born Dec. 19, 1946, in Baltimore... Attended Michigan and was drafted four times before signing with Los Angeles Dodgers in January 1968.

Year	Club	G	IP	W	L	Pct.	SO	BB	H	ERA
1973	Los Angeles............	6	13	1	0	1.000	9	2	5	1.38
1974	Los Angeles............	21	80	3	5	.375	33	16	78	2.03
1975	L.A.-Chi. (NL)..........	18	66	2	8	.200	22	31	69	4.64
1976	Chicago (NL)...........	3	8	0	1	.000	4	2	16	11.25
1977	Minnesota.............	34	198	12	14	.462	88	66	234	4.68
1978	Minnesota.............	35	252	14	14	.500	106	81	260	3.04
1979	Minnesota.............	26	169	13	7	.650	58	41	181	3.57
1980	Minnesota.............	38	233	14	18	.438	96	66	273	4.40
1981	California.............	25	161	10	11	.476	52	43	181	4.42
1982	California.............	34	229	18	8	.692	81	65	225	3.73
1983	California.............	29	203	9	11	.474	81	51	212	3.33
	Totals...............	269	1612	96	97	.497	630	464	1734	3.81

BOB BOONE 36 6-2 202 — Bats R Throws R

Selected club MVP... Was only player on team to appear in at least 130 games... Was only regular who wasn't sidelined by injuries, allaying fears concerning his age... Passed up reentry draft to sign hefty two-year contract with Angels during offseason... In two years as Angels' catcher, he has thrown out impressive 111-of-223 potential base-stealers... Difficult man to strike out . . . Was purchased from Philadelphia Phillies after 1981 season . . . Served as player representative and was actively involved in negotiations during 1981 strike . . . Signed as a third baseman by Philadelphia after being drafted in 20th round in 1969 . . . Moved to catcher as Instructional Leaguer in 1970 . . . Born Nov. 19, 1947, in San Diego . . . Has degree in psychology from Stanford . . . Son of former AL All-Star third baseman Ray Boone.

Year	Club	Pos.	G	AB	R	H	2B	3B	HR	RBI	SB	Avg.
1972	Philadelphia	C	16	51	4	14	1	0	1	4	1	.275
1973	Philadelphia	C	145	521	42	136	20	2	10	61	3	.261
1974	Philadelphia	C	146	488	41	118	24	3	3	52	3	.242
1975	Philadelphia	C-3B	97	289	28	71	14	2	2	20	1	.246
1976	Philadelphia	C	121	361	40	98	18	2	4	54	2	.271
1977	Philadelphia	C-3B	132	440	55	125	26	4	11	66	4	.284
1978	Philadelphia	C-1B-OF	132	435	48	123	18	4	12	62	2	.283
1979	Philadelphia	C-3B	119	398	38	114	21	3	9	58	1	.286
1980	Philadelphia	C	141	480	34	110	23	1	9	55	3	.229
1981	Philadelphia	C	76	227	19	48	7	0	4	24	2	211
1982	California.	C	143	472	42	121	17	0	7	58	0	.256
1983	California.	C	142	468	46	120	18	0	9	52	4	.256
	Totals		1410	4630	437	1198	207	21	81	566	27	.259

BRUCE KISON 34 6-4 180 Bats R Throws R

Has been haunted by injuries since signing free-agent contract with Angels prior to 1980 season . . . Underwent operation for removal of herniated disc after last season . . . Began year in Angels' rotation, but went on disabled list May 30, because of stiffness and spasms in back . . . Returned June 27 and went to bullpen in August . . . Was Angels' only consistent reliever, compiling 3-0 record with two saves and allowing four earned runs in 19⅔ innings (nine appearances) before back forced him out of action in final month . . . Missed most of 1980 and 1981 because of operations on ulnar and medial nerves in right elbow and wrist . . . Did pitch one-hitter for Angels in 1980 and threw one-hitter for Pittsburgh in 1979 . . . Going into last season, he had lifetime record of 27-10 in September and 5-1 mark in postseason play . . . Born Feb. 18, 1950, in Pasco, Wash.

Year	Club	G	IP	W	L	Pct.	SO	BB	H	ERA
1971	Pittsburgh	18	95	6	5	.545	60	36	93	3.41
1972	Pittsburgh	32	152	9	7	.563	102	69	123	3.26
1973	Pittsburgh	7	44	3	0	1.000	26	24	36	3.07
1974	Pittsburgh	40	129	9	8	.529	71	57	123	3.49
1975	Pittsburgh	33	192	12	11	.522	89	92	160	3.23
1976	Pittsburgh	31	193	14	9	.609	98	52	180	3.08
1977	Pittsburgh	33	193	9	10	.474	122	55	209	4.90
1978	Pittsburgh	28	96	6	6	.500	62	39	81	3.19
1979	Pittsburgh	33	172	13	7	.650	105	45	157	3.19
1980	California	13	73	3	6	.333	28	32	73	4.93
1981	California	11	44	1	1	.500	19	14	40	3.48
1982	California	33	142	10	5	.667	86	44	120	3.17
1983	California	26	127	11	5	.688	83	43	128	4.05
	Totals.	338	1652	106	80	.570	951	602	1523	3.57

TOMMY JOHN 40 6-3 200 **Bats R Throws L**

A Jekyll-and-Hyde season . . . Was 8-6 with 2.64 ERA in Anaheim Stadium, 3-7 with 7.13 ERA on the road . . . Ranks 35th on all-time victory list (248) and 15th on all-time start list (569) . . . As member of Chicago White Sox, he picked up victory in first game played at Anaheim Stadium, April 19, 1966 . . . One of nine pitchers to win 20 games in both leagues . . . Ruptured ligament in left elbow and had to have ligament transplant in July 1974 . . . Dr. Frank Jobe said left-hander would never pitch again . . . Named NL Comeback Player of the Year in 1976 and has had 124 victories since the surgery . . . Came to Angels in August 1982 deal with New York Yankees, after Angels had refused to sign him when he left Los Angeles Dodgers as a free agent following 1978 season . . . Born May 22, 1943, in Terre Haute, Ind. . . . Attended Indiana State.

Year	Club	G	IP	W	L	Pct.	SO	BB	H	ERA
1963	Cleveland	6	20	0	2	.000	9	6	23	2.25
1964	Cleveland	25	94	2	9	.182	65	35	97	3.93
1965	Chicago (AL)	39	184	14	7	.667	126	58	162	3.03
1966	Chicago (AL)	34	223	14	11	.560	138	57	195	2.62
1967	Chicago (AL)	31	178	10	13	.435	110	47	143	2.48
1968	Chicago (AL)	25	177	10	5	.667	117	49	135	1.98
1969	Chicago (AL)	33	232	9	11	.450	128	90	230	3.26
1970	Chicago (AL)	37	269	12	17	.414	138	101	253	3.28
1971	Chicago (AL)	38	229	13	16	.448	131	58	244	3.62
1972	Los Angeles	29	187	11	5	.688	117	40	172	2.89
1973	Los Angeles	36	218	16	7	.696	116	50	202	3.10
1974	Los Angeles	22	153	13	3	.813	78	42	133	2.59
1975	Los Angeles					(Disabled List)				
1976	Los Angeles	31	207	10	10	.500	91	61	207	3.09
1977	Los Angeles	31	220	20	7	.741	123	50	225	2.78
1978	Los Angeles	33	213	17	10	.630	124	53	230	3.30
1979	New York (AL)	37	276	21	9	.700	111	64	268	2.97
1980	New York (AL)	36	265	22	9	.710	78	56	270	3.43
1981	New York (AL)	20	140	9	8	.529	50	39	135	2.64
1982	N.Y. (AL)-Cal.	37	222	14	12	.538	68	39	239	3.69
1983	California	34	235	11	13	.458	65	49	287	4.33
	Totals	614	3942	248	184	.574	1983	1045	3850	3.13

BOBBY GRICH 35 6-2 190 **Bats R Throws R**

Missed final five weeks of season with broken hand after being hit by pitch from Yankees' George Frazier, but still was third on Angels with 120 games played . . . Led club with 76 walks . . . In 1981, he became first second baseman to lead AL in home runs since Nap Lajoie in 1901 and first second baseman to lead either league since Rogers Hornsby in 1939 . . . Had back operation midway through 1977 season for injury suffered while moving an air conditioner in his condo . . . Born Jan. 15,

1949, in Muskegon, Mich. . . . Had scholarship to be quarterback at UCLA, but instead signed with Baltimore as Orioles' first-round draft choice in 1967.

Year	Club	Pos.	G	AB	R	H	2B	3B	HR	RBI	SB	Avg.
1970	Baltimore.	SS-2B-3B	30	95	11	20	1	3	0	8	1	.211
1971	Baltimore.	SS-2B	7	30	7	9	0	0	1	6	1	.300
1972	Baltimore.	SS-2B-1B-3B	133	460	66	128	21	3	12	50	13	.278
1973	Baltimore.	2B	162	581	82	146	29	7	12	50	17	.251
1974	Baltimore.	2B	160	582	92	153	29	6	19	82	17	.263
1975	Baltimore.	2B	150	524	81	136	26	4	13	57	14	.262
1976	Baltimore.	2B-3B	144	518	93	138	31	4	13	54	14	.266
1977	California.	SS	52	181	24	44	6	0	7	23	6	.243
1978	California.	2B	144	487	68	122	16	2	6	42	4	.251
1979	California.	2B	153	534	78	157	30	5	30	101	1	.294
1980	California.	2B-1B	150	498	60	135	22	2	14	62	3	.271
1981	California.	2B	100	352	56	107	14	2	22	61	2	.304
1982	California.	2B	145	506	74	132	28	5	19	65	3	.261
1983	California.	2B	120	387	65	113	17	0	16	62	2	.292
	Totals.		1650	5735	857	1540	270	43	184	723	98	.269

ROD CAREW 38 6-0 182 Bats L Throws R

Set Angel record with .339 average, which was second-best mark in AL last season . . . Marked 15th year in a row he has surpassed .300 mark . . . Only Ty Cobb (23), Honus Wagner (17) and Stan Musial (16) had longer streaks of consecutive .300 seasons . . . Ranked third in AL with .411 on-base percentage . . . Nagging injuries forced first baseman to DH more than normal . . . Has averaged 1.26 hits per big-league game . . . Has won seven batting titles, ranking him third all-time behind Cobb (12) and Wagner (8) . . . Ranks 30th on all-time hit list . . . Has been selected to 17 consecutive All-Star teams . . . Was AL MVP with Minnesota in 1977, when he hit .388 and reached 100 level in RBI and runs scored for the only time in his career . . . Signed two-year, $2-million-plus pact in November . . . Born Oct. 1, 1945, in Panama, but was raised in New York City.

Year	Club	Pos.	G	AB	R	H	2B	3B	HR	RBI	SB	Avg.
1967	Minnesota . . .	2B	137	514	66	150	22	7	8	51	5	.292
1968	Minnesota . . .	2B-SS	127	461	46	126	27	2	1	42	12	.273
1969	Minnesota . . .	2B	123	458	79	152	30	4	8	56	19	.332
1970	Minnesota . . .	2B-1B	51	191	27	70	12	3	4	28	4	.366
1971	Minnesota . . .	2B-3B	147	577	88	177	16	10	2	48	6	.307
1972	Minnesota . . .	2B	142	535	61	170	21	6	0	51	12	.318
1973	Minnesota . . .	2B	149	580	98	203	30	11	6	62	41	.350
1974	Minnesota . . .	2B	153	599	86	218	30	5	3	55	38	.364
1975	Minnesota . . .	2B-1B	143	535	89	192	24	4	14	80	35	.359
1976	Minnesota . . .	1B-2B	156	605	97	200	29	12	9	90	49	.331
1977	Minnesota . . .	1B-2B	155	616	128	239	38	16	14	100	23	.388
1978	Minnesota . . .	1B-2B-OF	152	564	85	188	26	10	5	70	27	.333
1979	California . . .	1B	110	409	78	130	15	3	3	44	18	.318
1980	California . . .	1B	144	540	74	179	34	7	3	59	23	.331
1981	California . . .	1B	93	364	57	111	17	1	2	21	16	.305
1982	California . . .	1B	138	523	88	167	25	5	3	44	10	.319
1983	California . . .	1B	129	472	66	160	24	2	2	44	6	.339
	Totals		2299	8543	1313	2832	420	108	87	945	344	.332

REGGIE JACKSON 37 6-0 208 **Bats L Throws L**

Did time catch up to him? Did not hit a home run after July 31 and had only five doubles and nine RBI from that date until end of season . . . Ranked second in AL with 140 strikeouts and first in strikeout ratio (one every 3.1 at-bats) . . . Played on team with losing record for first time since 1967, when he played 35 games as a KC rookie . . . Collected 1,400th career RBI at Boston May 9 and was a strikeout victim for 2,000th time in career, vs. Minnesota's Len Whitehouse, May 13 . . . Set Angel record with 39 homers in 1982, tying him for the AL lead with Gorman Thomas, then of Milwaukee . . . Has tied for AL home-run title three times and won it outright in 1973 . . . Voted AL MVP and World Series MVP with Oakland A's in 1973 . . . Has career .357 average with 10 homers, 24 RBI in five World Series . . . Outfielder-designated hitter leads active players with 478 home runs, 14th on all-time list . . . One of four players in history to amass 400 career homers and 200 stolen bases . . . Born May 18, 1946, in Wyncote, Pa. . . . Played football and baseball at Arizona State . . . Left Yankees to sign with Angels as free agent following 1981 season.

Year	Club	Pos.	G	AB	R	H	2B	3B	HR	RBI	SB	Avg.
1967	Kansas City	OF	35	118	13	21	4	4	1	6	1	.178
1968	Oakland	OF	154	553	82	138	13	6	29	74	14	.250
1969	Oakland	OF	152	549	123	151	36	3	47	118	13	.275
1970	Oakland	OF	149	426	57	101	21	2	23	66	26	.237
1971	Oakland	OF	150	567	87	157	29	3	32	80	16	.277
1972	Oakland	OF	135	499	72	132	25	2	25	75	9	.265
1973	Oakland	OF	151	539	99	158	28	2	32	117	22	.293
1974	Oakland	OF	148	506	90	146	25	1	29	93	25	.289
1975	Oakland	OF	157	593	91	150	39	3	36	104	17	.253
1976	Baltimore	OF	134	498	84	138	27	2	27	91	28	.277
1977	New York (AL) . . .	OF	146	525	93	150	39	2	32	110	17	.286
1978	New York (AL) . . .	OF	139	511	82	140	13	5	27	97	14	.274
1979	New York (AL) . . .	OF	131	465	78	138	24	2	29	89	9	.297
1980	New York (AL) . . .	OF	143	514	94	154	22	4	41	111	1	.300
1981	New York (AL) . . .	OF	94	334	33	79	17	1	15	54	0	.237
1982	California	OF	153	530	92	146	17	1	39	101	4	.275
1983	California	OF	116	397	43	77	14	1	14	49	0	.194
	Totals		2287	8124	1314	2176	393	44	478	1435	216	.268

DARYL SCONIERS 25 6-2 195 **Bats L Throws L**

Has a knack for hitting big home runs . . . Hit two grand slams and two pinch-hit home runs . . . During a seven-game stretch early in the season, he hit three home runs and drove in 11 runs . . . Averaged an RBI per 6.8 at-bats . . . Not too agile around first base . . . Was tried in left field during minor-league career, but complained that it affected his hitting . . . Led

Texas League with .370 average for El Paso (AA) in 1980 and compiled .325 average during final three seasons in minors ... Speed has been diminished by knee surgery early in minor-league career ... Born Oct. 3, 1958, in San Bernardino, Cal. ... Attended Orange Coast College.

Year	Club	Pos.	G	AB	R	H	2B	3B	HR	RBI	SB	Avg.
1981	California........	1B	15	52	6	14	1	1	1	7	0	.269
1982	California........	1B	12	13	0	2	0	0	0	2	0	.154
1983	California........	1B-OF	106	314	49	86	19	3	8	46	4	.274
	Totals..........		133	379	55	102	20	4	9	55	4	.269

TOP PROSPECTS

DICK SCHOFIELD JR. 21 5-10 175 Bats R Throws R

Son of former big-league infielder by same name ... Angels' No. 1 draft choice in 1981 ... Born Nov. 21, 1962, in Springfield, Ill. ... Led Midwest League with .360 average, 10 triples and .483 on-base percentage for Danville (AA) in 1982 ... Continued to make strides at Edmonton (AAA) in 1983, hitting .284 with 16 homers and 94 RBI, but struck out 105 times in 521 at-bats and committed 30 errors ... May have to move from short.

GARY PETTIS 25 6-1 165 Bats S Throws R

Made big impression during September stint with Angels, finishing season with 11-game hitting streak ... That included 4-for-4 effort against Toronto Sept. 27, when he became first Angel to hit an inside-the-park home run since Bobby Bonds in 1977 ... Despite playing only 22 games, he led Angels with eight stolen bases ... Stole 203 bases during last four years in minors ... Began switch-hitting after hitting .318 in rookie ball in 1979 ... Born April 3, 1958, in Oakland ... Shifted from shortstop to center field.

MANAGER JOHN McNAMARA: A nightmarish 1983 season ... Injuries prevented him from putting projected starting lineup on field ... Miserable year was capped by late-season hiring of Gene Mauch to run club from front office ... After Mauch hired Don Zimmer as third-base coach without consulting McNamara, manager resigned ... Was talked out of decision and retained Preston Gomez as third-base coach ... Joined Angels as manager in 1983 after having coached for them in 1978 ... Previously managed at San Diego, Oakland and Cincinnati ... Guided Cincinnati to best record in baseball (66-

42) during 1981, but team finished second in both halves of strike-marred season . . . Reds were 245-186 under his guidance from 1979-81—the best record in NL—but organization's budget-minded player moves led to disaster in 1982 and he was fired . . . Was a minor-league catcher who took up managing at age 26 . . . Managed in minors for nine years and won three pennants before coming to big leagues as coach with Oakland . . . Also coached with San Francisco between managerial jobs . . . Among players he has managed are big-league managers Tony LaRussa, Rene Lachemann, Doug Rader and Pat Corrales . . . Born June 4, 1932, in Sacramento, Cal. . . . Overall major-league managerial record is 670-724.

GREATEST STEALER

The 1975 California Angels, directed by gambling manager Dick Williams, were known around the AL as rabbits. They tried to make up for their mediocre offensive abilities by running the opposition into the ground. They stole 220 bases that year, including four in one inning vs. the Yankees. And the leader of the larceny was Mickey Rivers.

He not only led the Angels with a club-record 70 thefts that year, he led the American League as well, marking the only time an Angel has held that distinction. Rivers wasn't with the club that long—who is?—but in three years he stole 126 bases, ranking him second on the club's all-time list to Sandy Alomar, who had 139.

As further testimony to his raw speed, Rivers grounded into the fewest double plays in the AL in 1976 and 1977, tying the record for most consecutive seasons leading the majors in fewest double-play grounders.

ALL-TIME ANGEL SEASON RECORDS

BATTING: Rod Carew, .339, 1983
HRs: Reggie Jackson, 39, 1982
RBIs: Don Baylor, 139, 1979
STEALS: Mickey Rivers, 70, 1975
WINS: Clyde Wright, 22, 1970
Nolan Ryan, 22, 1974
STRIKEOUTS: Nolan Ryan, 383, 1973

CHICAGO WHITE SOX

TEAM DIRECTORY: Pres.: Eddie Einhorn; Chairman of the Board: Jerry Reinsdorf; VP-GM: Roland Hemond; Dir. Play. Dev.: Bobby Winkles; Dir. Pub. Rel.: Chuck Shriver; Trav. Sec.: Glen Rosenbaum; Mgr.: Tony LaRussa. Home: Comiskey Park (43,695). Field distances: 341, l.f. line; 374, l.c.; 401, c.f.; 374, r.c.; 341, r.f. line. Spring training: Sarasota, Fla.

SCOUTING REPORT

HITTING: The White Sox can get on the scoreboard lots of ways. Carlton Fisk (26 homers, 86 RBI), Greg Luzinski (32 homers, 95 RBI), Ron Kittle (35 homers, 100 RBI) and Harold Baines (20 homers, 99 RBI) made Chicago the only team with four players who drove in 86 or more runs last season.

On the rare occasions the big bats aren't booming, the Sox have the ability to steal a run. Julio Cruz (57 steals) and Rudy Law (77) give them the best base-stealing duo around. They hit

AL Cy Young Award winner LaMarr Hoyt rang up 24 wins.

back-to-back in the order and, when they get on base, they can create havoc.

They've also got a pretty good balance. Luzinski, Kittle, Fisk and Tom Paciorek (.307) are the live bats from the right side and there's not that much of a dropoff from the left side, either, with Baines, Law and Greg Walker, who figures to get better with experience. Then there's left-handed-hitting Jerry Hairston, who led the AL with 17 pinch-hits.

PITCHING: As good as the offense might be, the pitching is even better, especially the starting rotation. From the right side, there's Cy Young winner LaMarr Hoyt (24-10), who has led the AL in wins the last two years, and Richard Dotson (22-7), who is developing into one of the elite. The lefties include power pitchers Floyd Bannister (16-10, 193 strikeouts) and Britt Burns (10-11).

The bullpen doesn't have a key guy on whom manager Tony LaRussa can depend whenever the game is on the line. But LaRussa did orchestrate his relief corps well enough so that the staff earned 48 saves, one less than Kansas City's league-leading total. Dennis Lamp led the Sox with 15 saves and newcomer Ron Reed, who was 9-1 with eight saves for Philadelphia, should be an asset.

FIELDING: The acquisition of Cruz in June solidified an otherwise-shaky infield. He is the most electrifying second baseman in either league, blessed with a great arm, great range and great leaping ability that allows him to complete double-play pivots nobody else would even try to complete.

Fisk, a fine handler of pitchers, has a way of slowing the game down, which leaves the defense a bit flat-footed. That's a problem when the left side of the infield is makeshift at best. Harold Baines (10 assists) is one of the best right fielders ever to make his home at Comiskey Park, but he hasn't been able to inspire the rest of his mates the way Cruz (.983) did in the infield.

OUTLOOK: It doesn't take much to win the AL West (or is that the AL Worst?) and the Sox seemed lulled into a false sense of security by their 99 regular-season wins last year. Reality caught up with this club in the playoffs. Facing a must-win situation for the first time all season, they couldn't respond to the pressure.

It's hard to expect another injury-free year, but even without a bullpen stopper, a third baseman and a shortstop, the White Sox can count on the benefit of limited competition for the division title.

CHICAGO WHITE SOX 1984 ROSTER

MANAGER Tony La Russa
Coaches—Loren Babe, Ed Brinkman, Dave Duncan, Art Kusnyer, Charley Lau, Jim Leyland, Dave Nelson, Joe Nossek

PITCHERS

No.	Name	1983 Club	W-L	IP	SO	ERA	B-T	Ht.	Wt.	Born
50	Agosto, Juan	Denver	4-1	26	19	2.08	L-L	6-0	175	2/23/58 Puerto Rico
		Chicago (AL)	2-2	42	29	4.10				
24	Bannister, Floyd	Chicago (AL)	16-10	217	193	3.35	L-L	6-1	195	6/10/55 Pierre, SD
30	Barojas, Salome	Chicago (AL)	3-3	87	38	2.47	R-R	5-9	160	7/16/57 Mexico
40	Burns, Britt	Chicago (AL)	10-11	174	115	3.58	R-L	6-5	218	6/8/59 Houston, TX
34	Dotson, Richard	Chicago (AL)	22-7	240	137	3.23	R-R	6-0	196	1/10/59 Cincinnati, OH
—	Fallon, Bob	Denver	10-5	138	105	4.29	L-L	6-3	200	2/18/60 New York, NY
45	Hickey, Kevin	Chicago (AL)	1-2	21	8	5.23	L-L	6-1	170	2/25/56 Chicago, IL
47	Hoffman, Guy	Denver	5-3	53	50	3.76	L-L	5-9	175	7/7/56 Ottawa, IL
		Chicago (AL)	1-0	6	2	7.50				
31	Hoyt, LaMarr	Chicago (AL)	24-10	261	148	3.66	R-R	6-1	222	1/1/55 Columbia, SC
49	Jones, Al	Appleton	11-1	102	124	0.97	R-R	6-4	210	2/10/59 Charleston, MS
		Chicago (AL)	0-0	2	2	3.86				
67	Kern, Jim	Chicago (AL)	0-0	1	0	0.00	R-R	6-5	205	3/15/49 Gladwin, MI
36	Koosman, Jerry	Chicago (AL)	11-7	170	90	4.77	R-L	6-2	225	12/23/43 Appleton, MN
53	*Lamp, Dennis	Chicago (AL)	7-7	116	44	3.71	R-R	6-3	210	9/23/52 Los Angeles, CA
33	Martz, Randy	Denver	8-7	128	60	5.12	L-R	6-4	215	5/28/56 Harrisburg, PA
		Chicago (AL)	0-0	5	1	3.60				
43	Mura, Steve	Denver	3-11	121	85	4.82	R-R	6-2	190	2/12/55 New Orleans, LA
		Chicago (AL)	0-0	12	4	4.38				
28	Niemann, Randy	Pittsburgh	0-1	14	8	9.22	R-L	6-4	200	11/15/55 Scotia, CA
		Hawaii	2-3	82	52	4.50				
—	Reed, Ron	Philadelphia	9-1	96	73	3.48	R-R	6-6	225	11/2/42 LaPorte, IN
54	Siwy, Jim	Denver	3-3	51	36	6.14	R-R	6-4	200	9/20/58 Central Falls, RI

CATCHERS

No.	Name	1983 Club	H	HR	RBI	Pct.	B-T	Ht.	Wt.	Born
72	Fisk, Carlton	Chicago (AL)	141	26	86	.289	R-R	6-2	220	12/26/47 Bellows Falls, VT
7	Hill, Marc	Chicago (AL)	30	1	11	.226	R-R	6-3	215	2/18/52 Elsberry, MO
12	Skinner, Joel	Denver	94	12	50	.260	R-R	6-4	198	2/21/61 San Diego, CA
		Chicago (AL)	3	0	0	.273				

INFIELDERS

No.	Name	1983 Club	H	HR	RBI	Pct.	B-T	Ht.	Wt.	Born
16	Cruz, Julio	Sea.-Chi. (AL)	130	3	52	.252	B-R	5-9	150	12/2/54 Brooklyn, NY
20	Dybzinski, Jerry	Chicago (AL)	59	1	32	.230	R-R	6-2	180	7/7/55 Cleveland, OH
1	Fletcher, Scott	Iowa	62	3	31	.237	R-R	5-11	168	7/30/58 Ft. Walton, FL
27	Gray, Lorenzo	Denver	56	4	31	.331	R-R	6-1	180	3/4/58 Mount Bayou, MS
		Chicago (AL)	14	1	4	.179				
32	Hulett, Tim	Denver	130	21	88	.273	R-R	6-0	185	1/12/60 Springfield, IL
		Chicago (AL)	1	0	0	.200				
5	Law, Vance	Chicago (AL)	99	4	42	.243	R-R	6-2	185	10/2/56 Boise, ID
44	Paciorek, Tom	Chicago (AL)	129	9	63	.307	R-R	6-4	210	11/2/46 Detroit, MI
*	Rodriguez, Aurelio	Balt.-Chi. (AL)	12	1	3	.138	R-R	5-11	175	12/28/47 Mexico
—	Sodders, Mike	Orlando	66	9	41	.231	R-R	6-3	190	12/26/58 Compton, CA
		Glens Falls	54	8	36	.251				
25	Squires, Mike	Chicago (AL)	34	1	11	.222	L-L	5-11	198	3/5/52 Kalamazoo, MI
29	Walker, Greg	Chicago (AL)	83	10	55	.270	L-R	6-3	205	10/6/59 Douglas, GA

OUTFIELDERS

No.	Name	1983 Club	H	HR	RBI	Pct.	B-T	Ht.	Wt.	Born
3	Baines, Harold	Chicago (AL)	167	20	99	.280	L-L	6-2	175	3/15/59 Easton, MD
—	Boston, Daryl	Glens Falls	104	18	50	.239	L-L	6-3	185	1/4/63 Cincinnati, OH
		Denver	13	2	7	.255				
17	Hairston, Jerry	Chicago (AL)	37	5	22	.294	B-R	5-10	180	2/16/52 Birmingham, AL
42	Kittle, Ron	Chicago (AL)	132	35	100	.254	R-R	6-4	200	1/5/58 Gary, IN
11	Law, Rudy	Chicago (AL)	142	3	34	.283	L-L	6-1	165	10/7/56 Waco, TX
19	Luzinski, Greg	Chicago (AL)	128	32	95	.255	R-R	6-1	225	11/22/51 Chicago, IL
—	Parsons, Casey	Denver	156	20	95	.300	L-R	6-0	185	4/14/54 Wenatchee, WA
		Chicago (AL)	1	0	0	.200				
8	Stegman, Dave	Denver	132	7	54	.334	R-R	5-11	190	1/30/54 Inglewood, CA
		Chicago (AL)	9	0	4	.170				
—	Yobs, Dave	Denver	65	6	20	.251	L-L	6-0	190	1/17/59 Encino, CA

*Free agent unsigned at press time

WHITE SOX PROFILES

CARLTON FISK 36 6-2 220 Bats R Throws R

Managed only three hits in 17 at-bats as White Sox lost AL playoffs to Baltimore . . . Did a lot better during regular season . . . After miserable first two months, he was moved into No. 2 spot in order June 15 and wound up setting club record for homers by a catcher with 26 . . . Also set Boston record for homers by a catcher, with 26 in 1977 . . . Hit first inside-the-park home run of major-league career, Aug. 21 vs. Texas . . . Combined with Greg Luzinski and Ron Kittle for 93 home runs, most ever by White Sox trio . . . Selected to All-Star Game nine times . . . Signed with White Sox as free agent in spring of 1981 after Red Sox had failed to tender him contract by deadline during winter . . . AL Rookie of the Year in 1972 . . . Wore No. 27 with Boston . . . Changed to No. 72 in Chicago, because it was year son was born and his first year in majors . . . Boston's first-round pick in 1967 draft . . . Born Dec. 26, 1947, in Bellows Falls, Vt. . . . Attended New Hampshire . . . Brother Calvin was catcher in Baltimore organization . . . Brother-in-law is Boston outfielder Rick Miller.

Year	Club	Pos.	G	AB	R	H	2B	3B	HR	RBI	SB	Avg.
1969	Boston	C	2	5	0	0	0	0	0	0	0	.000
1971	Boston	C	14	48	7	15	2	1	2	6	0	.313
1972	Boston	C	131	457	74	134	28	9	22	61	4	.293
1973	Boston	C	135	508	65	125	21	0	26	71	7	.246
1974	Boston	C	52	187	36	56	12	1	11	26	5	.299
1975	Boston	C	79	263	47	87	14	4	10	52	4	.331
1976	Boston	C	134	487	76	124	17	5	17	58	12	.255
1977	Boston	C	152	536	106	169	26	3	26	102	7	.315
1978	Boston	C-OF	157	571	94	162	39	5	20	88	7	.284
1979	Boston	C-OF	91	320	49	87	23	2	10	42	3	.272
1980	Boston	C-OF-1B-3B	131	478	73	138	25	3	18	62	11	.289
1981	Chicago (AL) . .	C-1B-3B-OF	96	338	44	89	12	0	7	46	3	.263
1982	Chicago (AL) . .	C-1B	135	476	66	127	17	3	14	65	17	.267
1983	Chicago (AL) . .	C	138	488	85	141	26	4	26	86	9	.289
	Totals		1447	5162	822	1454	262	40	209	765	90	.282

HAROLD BAINES 25 6-2 175 Bats L Throws L

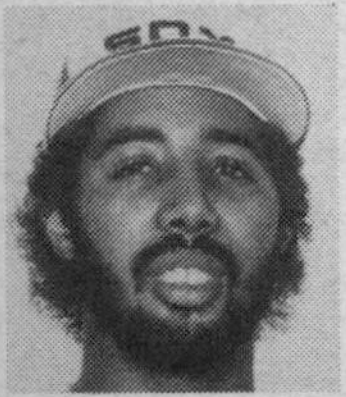

Set AL record with 22 game-winning RBI during regular season, but had none in playoffs, when he went 2-for-16 . . . Had club-leading 19-game hitting streak . . . Was No. 1 draft pick in nation in June 1977 by then-White Sox owner Bill Veeck, who had first seen him as 12-year-old Little Leaguer on Maryland's Eastern Shore . . . Already considered one of most complete players in major leagues . . . Veeck came under attack for passing up such talent as Chicago-area pitcher Bill Gullickson, shortstop Paul Molitor and catcher Terry Kennedy at the time of draft, but Baines has proven Veeck's judgment was based on talent, not sentiment . . . Became youngest White Sox player in history to drive in 100 runs in a season in 1982 . . . That season, he joined with Greg Luzinski to become first double 100-RBI men on White Sox since Zeke Bonura and Luke Appling in 1936 . . . Born March 15, 1959, in Easton, Md. . . . Has displayed strong arm in right field.

Year	Club	Pos.	G	AB	R	H	2B	3B	HR	RBI	SB	Avg.
1980	Chicago (AL)	OF	141	491	55	125	23	6	13	49	2	.255
1981	Chicago (AL)	OF	82	280	42	80	11	7	10	41	6	.286
1982	Chicago (AL)	OF	161	608	89	165	29	8	25	105	10	.271
1983	Chicago (AL)	OF	156	596	76	167	32	2	20	99	7	.280
	Totals		540	1975	262	537	95	23	68	294	25	.272

RON KITTLE 26 6-4 200 **Bats R Throws R**

Broke club record for homers by a rookie, set by Zeke Bonura with 27 in 1934, and finished two short of AL record of 37, set by Cleveland's Al Rosen in 1950 . . . Originally signed by Dodgers . . . Underwent spinal fusion after first season and then was released by Dodgers early in 1978 . . . Went to work in steel mills in Gary, Ind., where he had been born Jan. 5, 1958 . . . Was granted tryout by White Sox on recommendation of former Chicago player Billy Pierce . . . Pacific Coast League MVP in 1982, when he hit .345, with 50 homers, 144 RBI, .729 slugging percentage for Edmonton (AAA) . . . Also won Eastern League MVP honors in 1981, with Glens Falls (AA) . . . Turned down college basketball scholarship offers to play baseball . . . Left fielder was named to All-Star team and won AL Rookie-of-the-Year award.

Year	Club	Pos.	G	AB	R	H	2B	3B	HR	RBI	SB	Avg.
1982	Chicago (AL)	OF	20	29	3	7	2	0	1	7	0	.241
1983	Chicago (AL)	OF	145	520	75	132	19	3	35	100	8	.254
	Totals		165	549	78	139	21	3	36	107	8	.253

TOM PACIOREK 37 6-4 210 **Bats R Throws R**

Had only RBI that White Sox' big five managed in playoffs . . . Complained about manager Tony LaRussa early in season . . . Later on, he walked into manager's office with shoe in his mouth . . . Had earned fulltime job at first base by end of season and finished with third straight .300-plus average . . . One of funniest players in baseball . . . Does several impersonations

...Came to White Sox after demanding trade from Seattle following 1981 season...Originally signed by Dodgers...Career appeared to be over when he was released by Atlanta in April 1978, but he hooked on with Mariners and finally developed into legitimate big-league hitter...Was Minor League Player of the Year for Albuquerque in 1971...Played football and baseball with University of Houston and was drafted by Miami Dolphins as defensive back...Born Nov. 2, 1946, in Detroit...Brother John had career with Astros cut short by congenital back problem...Brother Jim is in Brewer organization.

Year	Club	Pos.	G	AB	R	H	2B	3B	HR	RBI	SB	Avg.
1970	Los Angeles......	OF	8	9	2	2	1	0	0	0	0	.222
1971	Los Angeles......	OF	2	2	0	1	0	0	0	1	0	.500
1972	Los Angeles......	OF-1B	11	47	4	12	4	0	1	6	1	.255
1973	Los Angeles......	OF-1B	96	195	26	51	8	0	5	18	3	.262
1974	Los Angeles......	OF-1B	85	175	23	42	8	6	1	24	1	.240
1975	Los Angeles......	OF	62	145	14	28	8	0	1	5	4	.193
1976	Atlanta.........	OF-1B-3B	111	324	39	94	10	4	4	36	2	.290
1977	Atlanta.........	1B-OF-3B	72	155	20	37	8	0	3	15	1	.239
1978	Atlanta.........	1B	5	9	2	3	0	0	0	0	0	.333
1978	Seattle.........	OF-1B	70	251	32	75	20	3	4	30	2	.299
1979	Seattle.........	OF-1B	103	310	38	89	23	4	6	42	6	.287
1980	Seattle.........	OF-1B	126	418	44	114	19	1	15	59	3	.273
1981	Seattle.........	OF-1B	104	405	50	132	28	2	14	66	13	.326
1982	Chicago (AL).....	1B-OF	104	382	49	119	27	4	11	55	3	.312
1983	Chicago (AL).....	1B-OF	115	420	65	129	32	3	9	63	6	.307
	Totals..........		1074	3247	408	928	196	27	74	420	45	.286

FLOYD BANNISTER 28 6-1 195 **Bats L Throws L**

Bounced back from shaky start to go 13-1 in second half...Lost winning touch in playoffs, giving up three earned runs in six innings and suffering defeat in Game 2...Struck out career-high 12 against former Seattle teammates in September...Led AL in strikeouts in 1982 with 209...Filed for free agency following that season and signed five-year, $4.5-million contract with White Sox...No. 1 player drafted in country in 1976...Pitched only seven games in minors before being called up by Houston in 1977...Born June 10, 1955, in Pierre, S.D....Had 38-6 record, 1.88 ERA during career at Arizona State...Selected College Player of the Year in 1976, when he was 19-2 with 1.45 ERA.

Year	Club	G	IP	W	L	Pct.	SO	BB	H	ERA
1977	Houston..............	24	143	8	9	.471	112	68	138	4.03
1978	Houston..............	28	110	3	9	.250	94	63	120	4.83
1979	Seattle..............	30	182	10	15	.400	115	68	185	4.05
1980	Seattle..............	32	218	9	13	.409	155	66	200	3.47
1981	Seattle..............	21	121	9	9	.500	85	39	128	4.46
1982	Seattle..............	35	247	12	13	.480	209	77	225	3.43
1983	Chicago (AL)...........	34	217	16	10	.615	193	71	191	3.35
	Totals...............	204	1238	67	78	.462	963	452	1187	3.81

GREG LUZINSKI 33 6-1 225 **Bats R Throws R**

Designated hitter became first player in 73-year history of Comiskey Park to hit three balls on or over roof in left field in single season . . . Enjoyed one of his best seasons, but struggled through 2-for-15 playoff performance . . . Endured early-season 3-for-53 slump . . . Homered in five consecutive games in May . . . Combined with Ron Kittle to hit more home runs in a season (67) than any two batters in White Sox history . . . Has not played outfield since playing left for Philadelphia in 1980 World Series . . . Sold to White Sox after that season . . . AL Comeback Player of the Year in 1981 . . . Born Nov. 22, 1950, in Chicago . . . Received 150 college football scholarship offers and was headed for Kansas before finally signing with Philadelphia in 1968.

Year	Club	Pos.	G	AB	R	H	2B	3B	HR	RBI	SB	Avg.
1970	Philadelphia	1B	8	12	0	2	0	0	0	0	0	.167
1971	Philadelphia	1B	28	100	13	30	8	0	3	15	2	.300
1972	Philadelphia	OF-1B	150	563	66	158	33	5	18	68	0	.281
1973	Philadelphia	OF	161	610	76	174	26	4	29	97	3	.285
1974	Philadelphia	OF	85	302	29	82	14	1	7	48	3	.272
1975	Philadelphia	OF	161	596	85	179	35	3	34	120	3	.300
1976	Philadelphia	OF	149	533	74	162	28	1	21	95	1	.304
1977	Philadelphia	OF	149	554	99	171	35	3	39	130	3	.309
1978	Philadelphia	OF	155	540	85	143	32	2	35	101	8	.265
1979	Philadelphia	OF	137	452	47	114	23	1	18	81	3	.252
1980	Philadelphia	OF	106	368	44	84	19	1	19	56	3	.228
1981	Chicago (AL)	DH	104	378	55	100	15	1	21	62	0	.265
1982	Chicago (AL)	DH	159	583	87	170	37	1	18	102	1	.292
1983	Chicago (AL)	DH	144	502	73	128	26	1	32	95	2	.255
	Totals		1696	6093	833	1697	331	24	294	1070	32	.297

BRITT BURNS 24-6-5 218 **Bats L Throws L**

Only White Sox starter with losing record last year, but he tied Richard Dotson for team lead in complete games (eight) and led team in shutouts (four) . . . Lost final game of playoffs to Baltimore, giving up bases-empty home run to Tito Landrum in 10th after having pitched nine shutout innings . . . Began season on disabled list with viral infection in pitching arm . . . Pitched three-hit, 1-0 shutouts against A's and Yankees . . . Also threw one-hitter and two-hitter against Angels . . . During two-month period in 1981, he commuted from bedside of his dying father to where White Sox were playing and did not miss a start . . . Born June 8, 1959, in Houston . . . Was discovered for White Sox by former Chicago Tribune book critic Robert Cromie, who sent then-team owner Bill Veeck a newspaper clipping about Burns striking out 18 batters in high school game in Birmingham, Ala.

Year	Club	G	IP	W	L	Pct.	SO	BB	H	ERA
1978	Chicago (AL)	2	8	0	2	.000	3	3	14	12.38
1979	Chicago (AL)	6	5	0	0	.000	2	1	10	5.40
1980	Chicago (AL)	34	238	15	13	.536	133	63	213	2.84
1981	Chicago (AL)	24	157	10	6	.625	108	49	139	2.64
1982	Chicago (AL)	28	169	13	5	.722	116	67	168	4.04
1983	Chicago (AL)	29	174	10	11	.476	115	55	165	3.58
	Totals	123	751	48	37	.565	477	238	709	3.36

RICHARD DOTSON 25 6-0 196 Bats R Throws R

Was bombed in Game 3 of playoffs, which Sox lost, 11-1 . . . Youngest White Sox pitcher to record a 20-win season since 24-year-old Ewell Russell won 22 in 1913 . . . Ranked second in AL in wins to teammate LaMarr Hoyt . . . Led AL with 106 walks . . . Pitched one-hitter against Baltimore in May, but lost, 1-0, on ninth-inning home run by Dan Ford . . . Won 16-of-18 decisions down stretch, beginning May 23 . . . Came to White Sox after 1977 season as a throw-in from California, which had made him a first-round pick in that June's draft . . . Best pitch is change-up . . . Still needs to learn to maintain composure on the mound . . . Born Jan. 10, 1959, in Cincinnati . . . Has been called a young Tom Seaver ever since high school.

Year	Club	G	IP	W	L	Pct.	SO	BB	H	ERA
1979	Chicago (AL)	5	24	2	0	1.000	13	6	28	3.75
1980	Chicago (AL)	33	198	12	10	.545	109	87	185	4.27
1981	Chicago (AL)	24	141	9	8	.529	73	49	145	3.77
1982	Chicago (AL)	34	197	11	15	.423	109	73	219	3.84
1983	Chicago (AL)	35	240	22	7	.759	137	106	209	3.23
	Totals	131	800	56	40	.583	441	321	786	3.75

LaMARR HOYT 29 6-1 222 Bats R Throws R

Accounted for team's only playoff victory with 2-1 win in opener . . . Cy Young Award winner became first White Sox pitcher to win 20 games in season since Jim Kaat in 1975 and had most wins by a Chicago pitcher since Wilbur Wood won 24 in 1973 . . . Winningest pitcher in major leagues over the last two seasons . . . After a 2-6 start, he won seven of next eight decisions and 22 of final 26 . . . Led AL in wins in 1982, but did not receive a vote in Cy Young balloting that year . . . Set club record for consecutive wins when he combined five straight at end of 1981 with 9-0 start in 1982 . . . Was originally converted into reliever by Tony LaRussa, who was his manager at Knoxville, prior to 1979 season . . . Was returned to fulltime starting status by LaRussa in 1982, with the big-league team . . . Came from Yankees with Oscar Gamble as part of April 1977 deal for Bucky Dent . . . Born Jan. 1, 1955, in Columbia, S.C. . . . Father, a former minor-league pitcher, is also named Dewey LaMarr Hoyt, but he was known as Dewey.

Year	Club	G	IP	W	L	Pct.	SO	BB	H	ERA
1979	Chicago (AL)	2	3	0	0	.000	0	0	2	0.00
1980	Chicago (AL)	24	112	9	3	.750	55	41	123	4.58
1981	Chicago (AL)	43	91	9	3	.750	60	28	80	3.56
1982	Chicago (AL)	39	240	19	15	.559	124	48	248	3.53
1983	Chicago (AL)	36	261	24	10	.706	148	31	236	3.66
	Totals	144	707	61	31	.663	387	148	689	3.73

JULIO CRUZ 29 5-9 160 — Bats S Throws R

A six-year contract in the $4-million range kept this switch-hitting free agent in Chicago . . . Acquired from Seattle June 15 for Tony Bernazard in swap of second basemen . . . Solidifying force in White Sox infield . . . Stole 57 bases and teamed with Rudy Law (77 steals) to give Chicago top stolen-base combo in league . . . Career stolen-base success ratio (82.8 percent) is second on all-time list to Kansas City's Willie Wilson . . . Only player in baseball to surpass 40 stolen bases each of last six years . . . An acrobatic second baseman who leaps to make double-play pivots when most second basemen would have to bail out . . . Has never hit a home run over fence left-handed . . . An expansion selection of Mariners, out of California organization . . . Born Dec. 2, 1954, in Brooklyn, N.Y. . . . Prefers hitting ninth . . . Gets sick when he leads off . . . Shares AL record of 32 consecutive thefts with Wilson.

Year	Club	Pos.	G	AB	R	H	2B	3B	HR	RBI	SB	Avg.
1977	Seattle	2B	60	199	25	51	3	1	1	7	15	.256
1978	Seattle	2B-SS	147	550	77	129	14	1	1	25	59	.235
1979	Seattle	2B	107	414	70	112	16	2	1	29	49	.271
1980	Seattle	2B	119	422	66	88	9	3	2	16	45	.209
1981	Seattle	2B-SS	94	352	57	90	12	3	2	24	43	.256
1982	Seattle	2B-SS-3B	154	549	83	133	22	5	8	49	46	.242
1983	Seat-Chi (AL)	2B	160	515	71	130	19	5	3	52	57	.252
	Totals		841	3001	449	733	95	20	18	202	314	.244

TOP PROSPECT

JOEL SKINNER 22 6-4 198 **Bats R Throws R**
Catcher for Denver (AAA) was voted best prospect in American Association by league's scouts and coaches . . . Youngest son of former big-league outfielder Bob Skinner . . . Became first player ever taken in compensation draft . . . White Sox picked him from Pittsburgh after losing pitcher Ed Farmer prior to 1982 season . . . Born Jan. 21, 1961, in San Diego . . . Has strong and accurate arm . . . Handles pitchers well and keeps game moving . . . Making progress with the bat, but will have to make big leagues with his defense.

MANAGER TONY LaRUSSA: Finally quieted the critics . . . Told in mid-June he had to turn the team around by the All-Star break or he was gone . . . Took White Sox from fifth in standings to their first first-place finish since 1959 . . . Amassed 20-game margin over second-place Kansas City, the biggest bulge in American League history . . . Has law degree and passed Florida bar in 1980 . . . Replaced Don Kessinger as White Sox manager midway through 1979 . . . Originally signed as middle infielder by Kansas City A's and spent majority of 16-year playing career in minors . . . Was roommate of Milwaukee manager Rene Lachemann during minor-league days in A's organization . . . Did see big-league action with A's, Braves and Cubs . . . Had managed White Sox' Knoxville farm into first place in 1978 before joining parent club as coach on July 3 of that year . . . Was sent to Iowa to manage at start of 1979, but that lasted only until Aug. 2, when he took over big-league team . . . Born Oct. 4, 1944, in Tampa . . . Second-youngest manager in big leagues, he is seven months older than Lachemann . . . Second in tenure among AL managers to Sparky Anderson, who took Detroit job 49 days before LaRussa was hired . . . Overall major-league managerial mark is 337-307.

GREATEST STEALER

The first name that comes to mind is Luis Aparicio, who led the AL in stolen bases a record-setting nine consecutive seasons, the first seven times for the White Sox. In all, he played shortstop in Chicago for 10 years and stole 318 bases, but he has already been singled out as Baltimore's greatest base-running thief.

In 1983, Rudy Law sped onto the scene in Chicago. He finished second in the AL with a White Sox-record 77 stolen bases, breaking the mark of 56 that Wally Moses set in 1943 and Aparicio tied in 1959.

But, before any of those three arrived, Eddie Collins was running wild in Chicago, en route to a spot in the Hall of Fame. During his career, Collins stole 743 bases, a total which ranks sixth on the all-time list. He stole 368 of those during his 12 years with the White Sox, a stint that included three of the four seasons he was the major leagues' stolen-base king.

He stole 25 or more bases in 12 seasons in the Windy City, including 1923, when he stole 47 and set the club record for being caught with 29 unsuccessful attempts.

ALL-TIME WHITE SOX SEASON RECORDS

BATTING: Luke Appling, .388, 1936
HRs: Dick Allen, 37, 1972
RBIs: Zeke Bonura, 138, 1936
STEALS: Rudy Law, 77, 1983
WINS: Ed Walsh, 40, 1908
STRIKEOUTS: Ed Walsh, 269, 1908

KANSAS CITY ROYALS

TEAM DIRECTORY: Chairman of the Board: Ewing Kauffman; Vice-Chairman: Avron Fogelman; Pres.: Joe Burke; Exec. VP-GM: John Schuerholz; Exec. VP-Adm.: Spencer Robinson; Dir. Pub. Rel.: Dean Vogelaar; Trav. Sec.: Bill Beck; Mgr.: Dick Howser. Home: Royals Stadium (40,625). Field distances: 330, l.f. line; 385, l.c.; 410, c.f.; 385, r.c.; 330, r.f. line. Spring training: Fort Myers, Fla.

SCOUTING REPORT

HITTING: Even the efforts of George Brett (.310, 25 homers, 93 RBI) and Hal McRae (.311, 82 RBI) and the best season ever by Frank White (.260, 77 RBI) weren't enough for the Royals to make a race of it in the AL West last season. Willie Wilson (.276) became the first defending AL batting champion in a decade to fail to hit .300 before being suspended by the commissioner, along with first baseman Willie Aikens, for their offseason drug convictions. Aikens was traded to Toronto for Jorge Orta, but a favorable ruling by the commissioner in May could shorten Wilson's one-year ban and return him to his usual spot as leadoff man.

If the Royals are going to regain their spot among the top offensive teams in baseball, they are going to have to get some big years from kids like left fielder Butch Davis, catcher Don Slaught and first baseman Steve Balboni. Balboni, the ex-Yankee, has shown power in the minors, but will he be able to make contact often enough in the bigs? Is Davis close to the player he showed in September (.344 in 122 at-bats)? And can Slaught (.312) play a full season without an injury?

PITCHING: Well, there is submarining Dan Quisenberry, who set a major-league record with 45 saves. Counting his five wins, he had a hand in 63 percent of the Royals' 79 victories.

But is he ever going to get any help? And will the Royals have enough starting pitching to get the game far enough along for Quisenberry to get them home with a victory?

Lefty Bud Black (10-7) is the only starter they can count on. Age creates questions about lefties Larry Gura (11-18) and Paul Splittorff (13-8). Joe Beckwith, who made only four starts in more than four years with Los Angeles, and Roger Erickson, a proven big-league starter who spent last year toiling for the Yankees' Columbus farm club, could win spots in the rotation. But how many of the Royals' kid pitchers—Mark Gubicza, Frank Wills and Danny Jackson—are ready to help?

Dan Quisenberry's submarine tosses will keep KC afloat.

FIELDING: As big a culprit as any in the Royals' fall from the elite was their defense. Not only did they rank last in the AL (.974), shortstop U.L. Washington set a club record with 36 errors and his .947 fielding percentage was the lowest of any AL regular.

Balboni's defensive abilities at first are reputed to be fairly good. He can't be any worse than Aikens, anyway. Washington and the rest of the infielders suffered from Aikens' inability to pick up their throws and the pitchers took the blame for the ground balls he couldn't reach.

It was strange that White had one of his most solid years, leading AL second basemen in defense (.990), but had his streak of seven Gold Gloves ended.

OUTLOOK: For a decade, the Royals were the class of the AL West, but in 1983, they hit hard times. They finished below .500 for the first time since 1974. And though they did finish second, they also set a record by finishing 20 games out of first.

The Royals' situation wasn't helped by a drug scandal, which resulted in prison terms for four members of the 1983 team. At least the farm system seems to be getting better. But the Royals need more help than any farm system can provide.

KANSAS CITY ROYALS 1984 ROSTER

MANAGER Dick Howser
Coaches—Howie Bedell, Gary Blaylock, Mike Ferraro, Jose Martinez, Jim Schaffer, Lee May

PITCHERS

No.	Name	1983 Club	W-L	IP	SO	ERA	B-T	Ht.	Wt.	Born
27	Beckwith, Joe	Los Angeles	3-4	71	50	3.55	L-R	6-3	200	1/28/55 Auburn, AL
40	Black, Bud	Omaha	3-1	35	32	3.34	L-L	6-2	180	6/30/57 San Mateo, CA
		Kansas City	10-7	161	58	3.79				
37	Botelho, Derek	Omaha	10-14	153	101	5.42	R-R	6-2	165	8/2/56 Long Beach, CA
—	Cone, David		Injured—Did not play				L-R	6-1	180	1/2/63 Kansas City, MO
—	Cook, Doug	Charleston	2-2	52	55	3.44	R-R	6-2	185	8/2/62 West Palm Beach, FL
		Fort Myers	6-4	71	66	2.92				
21	Creel, Keith	Omaha	4-2	53	41	3.04	R-R	6-2	180	2/4/59 Dallas, TX
		Kansas City	2-5	89	31	6.35				
—	Erickson, Roger	Columbus	9-7	134	59	6.04	R-R	6-3	185	8/30/56 Springfield, IL
		New York (AL)	0-1	17	7	4.32				
—	Ferreira, Tony	Jacksonville	7-11	136	85	4.22	L-L	6-1	160	10/4/62 Riverside, CA
—	Gubicza, Mark	Jacksonville	14-12	196	146	3.08	R-R	6-6	215	8/14/62 Philadelphia, PA
32	Gura, Larry	Kansas City	11-18	200	57	4.90	L-L	6-1	185	11/26/47 Joliet, IL
48	*Hood, Don	Kansas City	2-3	48	17	2.27	L-L	6-3	188	10/16/49 Florence, SC
38	Huismann, Mark	Jacksonville	6-3	61	46	3.23	R-R	6-3	195	5/11/58 Littleton, CO
		Omaha	0-2	24	25	1.85				
		Kansas City	2-1	31	20	5.58				
25	Jackson, Danny	Omaha	7-8	136	93	3.97	R-L	6-0	190	1/5/62 San Antonio, TX
		Kansas City	1-1	19	9	5.21				
22	Leonard, Dennis	Kansas City	6-3	63	31	3.71	R-R	6-1	195	5/8/51 Brooklyn, NY
29	Quisenberry, Dan	Kansas City	5-3	139	48	1.94	R-R	6-2	180	2/7/54 Santa Monica, CA
45	Shaw, Theo	Jacksonville	5-7	106	68	4.43	R-R	6-0	185	5/30/62 Cook County, IL
34	Splittorff, Paul	Kansas City	13-8	156	61	3.63	L-L	6-3	210	10/8/46 Evansville, IN
19	Wills, Frank	Jacksonville	5-2	54	40	2.48	R-R	6-2	200	10/26/58 New Orleans, LA
		Omaha	4-11	95	65	4.64				
		Kansas City	2-1	35	23	4.15				
28	Yuhas, Vinnie	Omaha	7-7	103	65	4.65	R-R	6-1	165	5/23/61 New Brunswick, NJ

CATCHERS

No.	Name	1983 Club	H	HR	RBI	Pct.	B-T	Ht.	Wt.	Born
—	Hansen, Roger	Fort Myers	109	2	62	.282	R-R	6-1	205	8/28/61 Johnstown, PA
7	Slaught, Don	Kansas City	86	0	28	.312	R-R	6-1	190	9/11/58 Long Beach, CA
12	Wathan, John	Kansas City	107	2	33	.245	R-R	6-2	205	10/4/49 Cedar Rapids, IA

INFIELDERS

No.	Name	1983 Club	H	HR	RBI	Pct.	B-T	Ht.	Wt.	Born
66	Balboni, Steve	Columbus	87	27	81	.274	R-R	6-3	225	1/16/57 Brockton, MA
		New York (AL)	20	5	17	.233				
1	Biancalana, Buddy	Omaha	82	5	39	.233	B-R	5-11	160	2/2/60 Larkspur, CA
		Kansas City	3	0	0	.200				
5	Brett, George	Kansas City	144	25	93	.310	L-R	6-0	200	5/15/53 Glendale, WV
2	Concepcion, Onix	Kansas City	53	0	20	.242	R-R	5-6	180	10/5/58 Puerto Rico
35	Johnson, Ron	Omaha	113	10	49	.317	R-R	6-3	220	3/23/56 Long Beach, CA
		Kansas City	7	0	1	.259				
3	Pastornicky, Cliff	Omaha	109	11	52	.270	R-R	5-11	170	11/18/58 Seattle, WA
		Kansas City	4	2	5	.125				
4	Pryor, Greg	Kansas City	25	1	14	.217	R-R	6-0	185	10/2/49 Marietta, OH
—	Scranton, Jim	Jacksonville	98	2	31	.218	R-R	6-0	175	5/5/60 Torrance, CA
30	Washington, U.L.	Kansas City	129	5	41	.236	B-R	5-11	175	10/27/53 Stringtown, OK
20	White, Frank	Kansas City	143	11	77	.260	R-R	5-11	175	9/4/50 Greenville, MS

OUTFIELDERS

No.	Name	1983 Club	H	HR	RBI	Pct.	B-T	Ht.	Wt.	Born
47	Brewer, Mike	Omaha	104	9	42	.252	R-R	6-5	190	10/24/59 Shreveport, LA
33	Davis, Butch	Jacksonville	105	14	63	.317	R-R	6-0	185	6/19/58 Martin County, NC
		Omaha	54	5	21	.316				
		Kansas City	42	2	18	.344				
11	McRae, Hal	Kansas City	183	12	82	.311	R-R	5-11	185	7/10/46 Avon Park, FL
14	Motley, Darryl	Evansville	142	16	60	.281	R-R	5-9	196	1/21/60 Muskogee, OK
		Kansas City	16	3	11	.235				
31	Orta, Jorge	Toronto	58	10	38	.237	L-R	5-10	175	11/26/50 Mexico
16	Roberts, Leon	Kansas City	55	8	24	.258	R-R	6-3	200	1/22/51 Vicksburg, MI
—	Ryal, Mark	Omaha	118	9	56	.260	L-L	6-1	185	4/28/60 Henryetta, OK
15	Sheridan, Pat	Omaha	23	4	14	.307	L-R	6-3	175	12/4/57 Ann Arbor, MI
		Kansas City	90	7	36	.270				
6	**Wilson, Willie	Kansas City	159	2	33	.276	B-R	6-3	195	7/9/55 Montgomery, AL

*Free agent unsigned at press time
**Suspended for one year pending review

ROYAL PROFILES

GEORGE BRETT 30 6-0 200 **Bats L Throws R**

July 24 went down as turning point of his 1983 season . . . In ninth inning of game at Yankee Stadium, he hit home run that gave Royals the lead, but was disallowed by umps because of pine tar on hitting surface of his bat . . . Homer was later reinstated by ruling of then-AL president Lee MacPhail . . . But, for some reason, from that day on, he struggled at plate . . . Had only five home runs and 29 RBI while hitting .254 the rest of the way . . . Still finished eighth in AL in hitting with fifth .300-plus year in a row . . . Has hit .300 or better in eight of nine major-league seasons after never reaching that plateau in minors . . . Also led AL with .553 slugging percentage . . . Would like to move from third base to first or the outfield . . . AL MVP in 1980, when he hit .390 . . . He and Ty Cobb are only players to win three league titles in hits and triples . . . One of five players to hit 20 home runs, 20 doubles and 20 triples in same season (1979) . . . Born May 15, 1953, in Glendale, W. Va. . . . Signed as a shortstop after playing high-school ball with pitcher Scott McGregor in El Segundo, Cal. . . . Brother Ken pitched in majors and brothers John and Bobby played in minors.

Year	Club	Pos.	G	AB	R	H	2B	3B	HR	RBI	SB	Avg.
1973	Kansas City	3B	13	40	2	5	2	0	0	0	0	.125
1974	Kansas City	3B-SS	133	457	49	129	21	5	2	47	8	.282
1975	Kansas City	3B-SS	159	634	84	195	35	13	11	89	13	.308
1976	Kansas City	3B-SS	159	645	94	215	34	14	7	67	21	.333
1977	Kansas City	3B-SS	139	564	105	176	32	13	22	88	14	.312
1978	Kansas City	3B-SS	128	510	79	150	45	8	9	62	23	.294
1979	Kansas City	3B-1B	154	645	119	212	42	20	23	107	17	.329
1980	Kansas City	3B-1B	117	449	87	175	33	9	24	118	15	.390
1981	Kansas City	3B	89	347	42	109	27	7	6	43	14	.314
1982	Kansas City	3B-OF	144	552	101	166	32	9	21	82	6	.301
1983	Kansas City	3B	123	464	90	144	38	2	25	93	0	.310
	Totals		1358	5307	852	1676	341	100	150	796	131	.316

DAN QUISENBERRY 30 6-2 180 **Bats R Throws R**

Shattered major-league single-season save record of 38, set by Detroit's John Hiller in 1973 . . . With 45 saves and five wins, he figured in 63 percent of Royals' 79 victories . . . Not overpowering with submarine delivery, but throws strikes. Two of his 11 walks last season were intentional . . . Has issued only 23 walks in 276 innings over the past two years

...Leads majors with 131 saves over the last four years and is 10th on all-time save list with 136...Has made one start in 568 professional appearances...Born Feb. 7, 1954, in Santa Monica, Cal....Undrafted out of LaVerne College...Signed to fill out Class-A club by Royals in 1975 and worked way up through system...Started throwing sidearm after pitching an amazing 194 innings in college in 1975 and eventually dropped down even lower.

Year	Club	G	IP	W	L	Pct.	SO	BB	H	ERA
1979	Kansas City	32	40	3	2	.600	13	7	42	3.15
1980	Kansas City	75	128	12	7	.632	37	27	129	3.09
1981	Kansas City	40	62	1	4	.200	20	15	59	1.74
1982	Kansas City	72	137	9	7	.563	46	12	126	2.57
1983	Kansas City	69	139	5	3	.625	48	11	118	1.94
	Totals	288	506	30	23	.566	164	72	474	2.47

FRANK WHITE 33 5-11 175 **Bats R Throws R**

Set club record for RBI by a second baseman...Because of injuries to others, he frequently hit third in the lineup, which he credited for increased production and blamed for decrease in average...Equaled personal highs in home runs and triples and posted his second-highest total of doubles...Missed a week with deep bruise in left shoulder after colliding with Baltimore's Rick Dempsey while trying to field ground ball Aug. 29...Became only second baseman in AL history to win six Gold Gloves in 1982...Became first graduate of Royals' baseball academy to be invited to major-league spring training in 1973...Born Sept. 4, 1950, in Greenville, Miss....Raised in Kansas City, but high school did not have baseball team...Signed at tryout camp at Municipal Stadium, the original home of the Royals, in 1970.

Year	Club	Pos.	G	AB	R	H	2B	3B	HR	RBI	SB	Avg.
1973	Kansas City	SS-2B	51	139	20	31	6	1	0	5	3	.223
1974	Kansas City	2B-SS-3B	99	204	19	45	6	3	1	18	3	.221
1975	Kansas City	2B-3B-SS-C	111	304	43	76	10	2	7	36	11	.250
1976	Kansas City	2B-SS	152	446	39	102	17	6	2	46	20	.229
1977	Kansas City	2B-SS	152	474	59	116	21	5	5	50	23	.245
1978	Kansas City	2B	143	461	66	127	24	6	7	50	13	.275
1979	Kansas City	2B	127	467	73	124	26	4	10	48	28	.266
1980	Kansas City	2B	154	560	70	148	22	5	7	60	19	.264
1981	Kansas City	2B	94	364	35	91	17	1	9	38	4	.250
1982	Kansas City	2B	145	524	71	156	45	6	11	56	10	.298
1983	Kansas City	2B	146	549	52	143	34	6	11	77	13	.260
	Totals		1374	4492	547	1159	228	45	70	484	147	.258

LARRY GURA 36 6-1 185 **Bats L Throws L**

Went from 18-game winner to 18-game loser in course of one season . . . Was finally removed from rotation and sent to bullpen for three weeks during September, when he made three scoreless appearances and earned a win . . . In final month, he began experimenting with knuckleball, a pitch he had thrown during his days at Arizona State . . . Smooth fielder . . . Did not commit an error in 1980 or 1981 . . . Fitness fanatic who follows strict dietary and conditioning program, carrying blender with him on road to fix certain foods . . . On Billy Martin's hit list . . . Was dumped by Martin in Texas and New York . . . Born Nov. 26, 1947, in Joliet, Ill. . . . Pitched no-hitters three days apart during 1968 National Baseball Congress tournament.

Year	Club	G	IP	W	L	Pct.	SO	BB	H	ERA
1970	Chicago (NL)	20	38	1	3	.250	21	23	35	3.79
1971	Chicago (NL)	6	3	0	0	.000	2	1	6	6.00
1972	Chicago (NL)	7	12	0	0	.000	13	3	11	3.75
1973	Chicago (NL)	21	65	2	4	.333	43	11	79	4.85
1974	New York (AL)	8	56	5	1	.833	17	12	54	2.41
1975	New York (AL)	26	151	7	8	.467	65	41	173	3.52
1976	Kansas City	20	63	4	0	1.000	22	20	47	2.29
1977	Kansas City	52	106	8	5	.615	46	28	108	3.14
1978	Kansas City	35	222	16	4	.800	81	60	183	2.72
1979	Kansas City	39	234	13	12	.520	85	73	226	4.46
1980	Kansas City	36	283	18	10	.643	113	76	272	2.96
1981	Kansas City	23	172	11	8	.579	61	35	139	2.72
1982	Kansas City	37	248	18	12	.600	98	64	251	4.03
1983	Kansas City	34	200	11	18	.379	57	76	220	4.90
	Totals	364	1853	114	85	.573	724	523	1804	3.56

DENNIS LEONARD 32 6-1 195 **Bats R Throws R**

Has been slowed by injuries the last two seasons . . . Suffered broken fingers when he tried to grab Buddy Bell's line drive in 1982 . . . Tore ligaments in knee fielding grounder against Baltimore in late May last year . . . Had to undergo second knee operation during the winter and will be out at least until July . . . Was 6-3 at time of injury, leaving him short of double figures in victories for the first time in his big-league career . . . Throw in strike of 1981 and he has not pitched a full season since 1980 . . . Has won 136 games since 1975, the most of any AL right-hander . . . Led AL in starts in 1978, 1980 and 1981 . . . Born

May 8, 1951, in Brooklyn, N.Y. . . . Attended Iona College . . . Avid hunter.

Year	Club	G	IP	W	L	Pct.	SO	BB	H	ERA
1974	Kansas City	5	22	0	4	.000	8	12	28	5.32
1975	Kansas City	32	212	15	7	.682	146	90	212	3.78
1976	Kansas City	35	259	17	10	.630	150	70	247	3.51
1977	Kansas City	38	293	20	12	.625	244	79	246	3.04
1978	Kansas City	40	295	21	17	.553	183	78	283	3.33
1979	Kansas City	32	236	14	12	.538	126	56	226	4.08
1980	Kansas City	38	280	20	11	.645	155	80	271	3.79
1981	Kansas City	26	202	13	11	.542	107	41	202	2.99
1982	Kansas City	21	131	10	6	.625	58	46	145	5.10
1983	Kansas City	10	63	6	3	.667	31	19	69	3.71
	Totals	277	1993	136	93	.594	1208	571	1929	3.63

DON SLAUGHT 25 6-1 190 **Bats R Throws R**

Saw spot duty as catcher most of year . . . Took over regular chores Aug. 19 and took off with bat . . . Though he was hitting .250 Aug. 1, he wound up as one of four KC regulars with a .300-plus average . . . Hit .367 (44-for-120) with 12 RBI in 35 games after becoming an everyday player . . . Was able to avoid serious injury for first time in professional career . . . Had been considered mainly a defensive catcher, but struggled some behind the plate in 1983 . . . Made big impression with way he handled pitchers and desire he showed to learn how to set up hitters . . . Singled in his first two big-league at-bats, against Boston's John Tudor in 1982 . . . Born Sept. 11, 1958, in Long Beach, Cal. . . . UCLA teammate of pitcher Matt Young, now of Seattle . . . Two-year starter at quarterback for Rollings Hills High School in California.

Year	Club	Pos.	G	AB	R	H	2B	3B	HR	RBI	SB	Avg.
1982	Kansas City	C	43	115	14	32	6	0	3	8	0	.278
1983	Kansas City	C	83	276	21	86	13	4	0	28	3	.312
	Totals		126	391	35	118	19	4	3	36	3	.302

PAUL SPLITTORFF 37 6-3 210 **Bats L Throws L**

After making team as extra man, he became Royals' most consistent starter, compiling his best earned-run average in five years . . . Led Royals with 13 wins . . . Started 27 games, exactly number he needed to guarantee contract for 1984 . . . Became Kansas City's first 20-game winner in 1973 and lost 19 the following season . . . Has made only 28 relief appearances in majors . . . Pitched one-hitter against Oakland in 1975, retiring final 26 batters . . . No. 1 on Royals in seniority . . . Born Oct. 8, 1946, in Evansville, Ind. . . . Was a 22nd-round selection in 1968 draft, after attending Morningside College.

Year	Club	G	IP	W	L	Pct.	SO	BB	H	ERA
1970	Kansas City	2	9	0	1	.000	10	5	16	7.00
1971	Kansas City	22	144	8	9	.471	80	35	129	2.69
1972	Kansas City	35	216	12	12	.500	140	67	189	3.13
1973	Kansas City	38	262	20	11	.645	110	78	279	3.98
1974	Kansas City	36	226	13	19	.406	90	75	252	4.10
1975	Kansas City	35	159	9	10	.474	76	56	156	3.17
1976	Kansas City	26	159	11	8	.579	59	59	169	3.96
1977	Kansas City	37	229	16	6	.727	99	83	243	3.69
1978	Kansas City	39	262	19	13	.594	76	60	244	3.40
1979	Kansas City	36	240	15	17	.469	77	77	248	4.24
1980	Kansas City	34	204	14	11	.560	53	43	236	4.15
1981	Kansas City	21	99	5	5	.500	48	23	111	4.86
1982	Kansas City	29	162	10	10	.500	74	57	166	4.28
1983	Kansas City	27	156	13	8	.619	61	52	159	3.63
	Totals	417	2527	165	140	.541	1053	770	2597	3.77

JOHN WATHAN 34 6-2 205 **Bats R Throws R**

One of most versatile players in baseball . . . Can catch, play first base, left or right . . . Signed four-year contract with Royals at end of 1983 season instead of filing for free agency . . . Got off to good start but, after losing full-time catching job to Don Slaught, he went into slump . . . Blamed slide on worrying if Royals were going to re-sign him . . . Had only 11 hits and three RBI in final 81 at-bats . . . Utility value was evident in 1980, when he played 126 games without being a regular at any one position . . . Set major-league record for catcher by stealing 36 bases in 1982, despite missing six weeks in middle of season with broken ankle . . . Added 27 thefts last year . . . "They say the legs are the first to go," Wathan said. "I guess I've shown mine are well-rested." . . . Devoted fan of John Wayne . . . Born Oct. 4, 1949, in Cedar Rapids, Iowa. . . . Played baseball and basketball at University of San Diego.

Year	Club	Pos.	G	AB	R	H	2B	3B	HR	RBI	SB	Avg.
1976	Kansas City	C-1B	27	42	5	12	1	0	0	5	0	.286
1977	Kansas City	C-1B	55	119	18	39	5	3	2	21	2	.328
1978	Kansas City	1B-C	67	190	19	57	10	1	2	28	2	.300
1979	Kansas City	1B-C-OF	90	199	26	41	7	3	2	28	2	.206
1980	Kansas City	1B-OF-C	126	453	57	138	14	7	6	58	17	.305
1981	Kansas City	1B-OF-C	89	301	24	76	9	3	1	19	11	.252
1982	Kansas City	C-1B	121	448	79	121	11	3	3	51	36	.270
1983	Kansas City	C-1B	128	437	49	107	18	3	2	32	28	.245
	Totals		703	2189	277	591	75	23	18	242	98	.270

HAL McRAE 37 5-11 185 — Bats R Throws R

Didn't have the banner year that he enjoyed in 1982, but was consistent in 1983 . . . Never went more than two games without a hit and went hitless for that long only five times . . . After the fourth game of the season, his average never fell below .300 . . . Had two eight-game hitting streaks . . . Best month was May, when he hit .374 . . . Despite age, he enjoyed third straight injury-free season . . . Originally an outfielder, he has become a fulltime DH . . . Never played in the field last year and has played a position in only 12 games over the last five seasons . . . Set league DH record for RBI with 133 in 1982 . . . Has lifetime .409 average in three World Series (two with Cincinnati and one with Royals) . . . Career almost ended when he broke his right leg in four places while playing ball in Puerto Rico during the winter of 1968-69 . . . Born July 10, 1946, in Avon Park, Fla. . . . Attended Florida A&M.

Year	Club	Pos.	G	AB	R	H	2B	3B	HR	RBI	SB	Avg.
1968	Cincinnati	2B	17	51	1	10	1	0	0	2	1	.196
1970	Cincinnati	OF-3B-2B	70	165	18	41	6	1	8	23	0	.248
1971	Cincinnati	OF	99	337	39	89	24	2	9	34	3	.264
1972	Cincinnati	OF-3B	62	97	9	27	4	0	5	26	0	.278
1973	Kansas City	OF-3B	106	338	36	79	18	3	9	50	2	.234
1974	Kansas City	OF-3B	148	539	71	167	36	4	15	88	11	.310
1975	Kansas City	OF-3B	126	480	58	147	38	6	5	71	11	.306
1976	Kansas City	OF	149	527	75	175	34	5	8	73	22	.332
1977	Kansas City	OF	162	641	104	191	54	11	21	92	18	.298
1978	Kansas City	OF	156	623	90	170	39	5	16	72	17	.273
1979	Kansas City	DH	101	393	55	113	32	4	10	74	5	.288
1980	Kansas City	OF	124	489	73	145	39	5	14	83	10	.297
1981	Kansas City	OF	101	389	38	106	23	2	7	36	3	.272
1982	Kansas City	OF	159	613	91	189	46	8	27	133	4	.308
1983	Kansas City	DH	157	589	84	183	41	6	12	82	2	.311
	Totals		1736	6271	842	1832	435	62	166	937	109	.292

STEVE BALBONI 27 6-3 225 — Bats R Throws R

After languishing in the Yankees' organization and becoming a minor-league home-run hitting legend, he will finally get his chance . . . The Royals' first-base job has been given to him and the world will find out if he can hit major-league pitching after all . . . Royals, faced with a void at first in the wake of Willie Aikens' difficulties with the law, sent reliever Mike Armstrong to Yanks for pitcher Roger Erickson and this muscular slugger . . . Has shown little in repeated, brief trials with Yankees during last three seasons, but led three minor leagues in home runs with a total of 153 . . . Had 26 homers for Columbus (AAA) and five for the Yankees last season . . . Best minor-league season was 1980, when he hit .301 with 34 homers and 122 RBI for Nashville (AA) . . . Has a reputation as an excellent defensive first baseman . . . Born Jan. 16, 1957, in Brockton, Mass. . . . Led Eckerd College to second-place finish in Division II College World Series in 1977 . . . Selected by Yankees on fourth round of June 1978 draft . . . Nicknamed "Bye Bye" because of his tape-measure blasts and maybe because of all the shuttling he did between New York and Columbus . . . If he produces, his travels might be over.

Year	Club	Pos.	G	AB	R	H	2B	3B	HR	RBI	SB	Avg.
1981	New York (AL)	1B	4	7	2	2	1	1	0	2	0	.286
1982	New York (AL)	1B	33	107	8	20	2	1	2	4	0	.187
1983	New York (AL)	1B	32	86	8	20	2	0	5	17	0	.233
	Totals		69	200	18	42	5	2	7	23	0	.210

George Brett was over .300 for fifth consecutive year.

TOP PROSPECTS

DANNY JACKSON 22 6-0 190 **Bats L Throws L**
Made rapid rise in first year, compiling a combined 17-3 record at Charleston (A) and Jacksonville (AA) in 1982, before suffering stress fracture in thigh . . . Spent 1983 at Omaha (AAA) before being called up in September . . . Was inconsistent while posting 7-8 record and 3.97 ERA at Omaha . . . Did throw back-to-back four-hitters . . . Was 1-1 with 5.21 ERA for Royals . . . Bothered by tendinitis in shoulder late in season . . . Born Jan. 5, 1962, in San Antonio . . . Attended Oklahoma as freshman, then transferred to Trinidad State Junior College to be eligible for draft . . . Chosen as No. 1 overall pick by Royals in January 1982.

BUTCH DAVIS 25 6-0 185 **Bats R Throws R**
Blossomed in 1983 . . . Split year between Jacksonville (AA) and Omaha (AAA), compiling .317 average with 19 HR, 84 RBI and 42 stolen bases before joining Royals in late August . . . Appeared in 33 games for KC, hitting .344 with two doubles, six triples, two HR and 18 RBI . . . Line-drive power in the gaps . . . Weak arm in outfield, but makes up for it with blazing speed and decent instincts . . . Expected to play outfield for couple of years before inheriting DH role from Hal McRae . . . A 13th-round pick out of Eastern Carolina in 1980 . . . Made big hit in debut by winning Gulf Coast MVP honors . . . Born June 19, 1958, in Martin County, N.C.

MANAGER DICK HOWSER: Took command of struggling

Royals from Jim Frey, Aug. 31, 1981, and guided them to second-half title before being swept by Oakland in AL West mini-playoffs . . . Team has been decimated by injuries the past two years . . . Royals finished second both times . . . In major-league managerial debut, he became one of four managers in history to win 100 games in initial year, guiding 1980 Yankees to 103 wins . . . Was forced out after Royals beat Yankees in playoffs . . . Coached third base for Yankees from 1969-78 . . . After leaving Yankees as manager, he coached his alma mater, Florida State, to NCAA regional playoff berth in 1979 . . . Played eight seasons in big leagues, compiling a .248 career average with the Kansas City Athletics, Indians and Yankees . . . Tied AL record by playing 162 games at shortstop for Cleveland in 1964 . . . Voted Florida Amateur Athlete of the Year in 1958 and its Professional Athlete of the Year in 1961 . . . Born May 14, 1937, in Miami . . . Overall major-league managerial mark is 292-227.

GREATEST STEALER

Over the long haul, Amos Otis has been the most consistent base-stealer in Royals' history. He led the AL with 52 in 1971 and set a single-season success mark by stealing in 33-of-35 attempts in 1976. He tied an AL record by swiping seven bases during back-to-back games in 1975 and stole five bases in a game vs. Milwaukee in 1971.

But last season, Willie Wilson (346 career steals) passed Otis (340) on the club's all-time list. Wilson has recorded the top three single-season stolen-base totals in Royals' history, including a club-record 83 in 1979. He set an AL record—since tied by Julio Cruz—by stealing 32 bases in a row during 1980. And his all-time stolen-base success rate of more than 82 percent is the best in major-league history.

As good as Wilson is, however, he could be better. He still relies on pure speed to steal, since he never has learned the techniques of reading pitchers. As a result, only seven of his 59 stolen bases in 1983 came with a left-handed pitcher on the mound.

ALL-TIME ROYAL SEASON RECORDS

BATTING: George Brett, .390, 1980
HRs: John Mayberry, 34, 1975
RBIs: Hal McRae, 133, 1982
STEALS: Willie Wilson, 83, 1979
WINS: Steve Busby, 22, 1974
STRIKEOUTS: Dennis Leonard, 244, 1977

MINNESOTA TWINS

TEAM DIRECTORY: Chairman of the Board-Pres.: Calvin Griffith; VP-Sec.: Thelma Griffith Hayes; Exec. VPs: Clark Griffith, Howard T. Fox, Jr., Bruce Haynes; VPs: William Robertson, James Robertson, George Brophy; Dir. Pub. Rel.: Tom Mee; Mgr.: Billy Gardner. Home: Hubert H. Humphrey Metrodome (55,122). Field distances: 343, l.f. line; 408, c.f.; 327, r.f. line. Spring training: Orlando, Fla.

SCOUTING REPORT

HITTING: A strange composite. The Twins seem to have become so engrossed by the friendly confines of the Metrodome that they don't take advantage of the fact they have the best team speed of any AL club. Ron Washington, who played in only 99 games, led the Twins with 10 of their 44 stolen bases.

And surprisingly the Twins seem to show their power more frequently on the road, where they hit 85 of their 141 home runs. They do, however, score more in the Dome (389 runs to 320). Tom Brunansky still hasn't hit for average (.227), but he is beginning to drive the ball (28 homers, 82 RBI), giving Kent Hrbek (.297, 16 homers, 84 RBI) some protection. He'll have to do even more this year with the loss of home-run threat Gary Ward, who was dealt to Texas. Gary Gaetti (21 homers, 78 RBI), John Castino (.277), Mickey Hatcher (.317) and Dave Engle (.305) must help to pick up the slack.

PITCHING: The Twins have developed an effective bullpen. Ron Davis, armed with his new four-year contract, is the stopper (30 saves in 39 save situations), and the middle-inning quartet of Len Whitehouse (7-1), Pete Filson (4-1), Mike Walters and Rick Lysander do a good job of getting the game to him.

The problem is getting a good enough effort from the starting rotation so that Davis and Co. can do their thing.

Ken Schrom (15-8), the latest in a long line of Twin rehab projects, was the only consistent starter for the club last season. He even seemed to enjoy pitching in the Dome, where he was 7-2 with a 2.77 ERA. But Bobby Castillo (8-12) finished the season with rotator-cuff problems and the Twins can't count on right-hander Al Williams (11-14) or left-handers Frank Viola (7-15), Brad Havens (5-8) and Bryan Oelkers (0-5). That's why they traded Ward to Texas for right-handers Mike Smithson (10-14) and John Butcher (6-6).

Tom Brunansky's 28 homers topped the Twins.

FIELDING: Castino, who may be shifted back to third base or moved to the outfield, is a whiz wherever he plays. He led AL third basemen in fielding in 1981 and set the pace at second base in 1982. Last year, he finished second (.990) at second. Wherever Castino plays, however, is one of the only places the Twins don't need defensive help.

They are going to look at five bodies, including Washington, in an attempt to plug the hole at shortstop. Rookie second baseman Tim Teufel has more limitations than assets with a glove. There is no center fielder, unless Jim Eisenreich can somehow come back from his nervous disorder. And the catching corps is in trouble until Jeff Reed finally shows he can hit enough to hang around.

First baseman Hrbek (.990) is as good with a glove as he is with a bat and Brunansky (16 assists) does a nice job in the outfield.

OUTLOOK: Owner Calvin Griffith's greatest winter activity—besides the Ward-to-Texas trade—was the signing of Davis and Castino to long-term contracts. How long they remain Twins remains to be seen. It was only two years ago that Griffith did the same thing with Butch Wynegar and Roy Smalley and they both were traded before Memorial Day.

The rotation should be better this year, thanks to the acquisition of Smithson and Butcher. And if manager Billy Gardner puts his speed to use, the Twins could show improvement. But there is a lot of room for improvement.

MINNESOTA TWINS 1984 ROSTER

MANAGER Billy Gardner
Coaches—Tom Kelly, Jim Lemon, Johnny Podres, Rick Stelmaszek

PITCHERS

No.	Name	1983 Club	W-L	IP	SO	ERA	B-T	Ht.	Wt.	Born
29	Butcher, John	Texas	6-6	123	58	3.51	R-R	6-4	190	3/8/57 Glendale, CA
37	Castillo, Bobby	Minnesota	8-12	158	90	4.77	R-R	5-10	175	4/18/55 Los Angeles, CA
39	Davis, Ron	Minnesota	5-8	89	84	3.34	R-R	6-4	207	8/6/55 Houston, TX
23	Filson, Pete	Toledo	0-1	7	6	7.71	B-L	6-2	195	9/28/58 Darby, PA
		Minnesota	4-1	90	49	3.40				
27	Havens, Brad	Minnesota	5-8	80	40	8.18	L-L	6-1	192	11/17/59 Highland Park, MI
		Toledo	6-3	70	64	3.88				
36	Hodge, Ed	Toledo	11-6	143	72	3.97	L-L	6-2	192	4/19/58 Bellflower, CA
19	Lysander, Rick	Minnesota	5-12	125	58	3.38	R-R	6-2	188	2/21/53 Huntington Park, CA
33	O'Connor, Jack	Toledo	2-1	43	39	4.98	L-L	6-3	200	6/2/58 Yucca Valley, CA
		Minnesota	2-3	83	56	5.86				
17	Oelkers, Bryan	Minnesota	0-5	34	13	8.65	L-L	6-3	192	3/11/61 Spain
		Toledo	5-7	104	60	5.18				
35	Pettibone, Jay	Orlando	13-7	161	105	3.97	R-R	6-4	182	6/21/57 Mt. Clemens, MI
		Toledo	0-0	22	16	3.32				
		Minnesota	0-4	27	10	5.33				
18	Schrom, Ken	Toledo	3-1	32	20	4.55	R-R	6-2	195	11/23/54 Grangeville, ID
		Minnesota	15-8	196	80	3.71				
—	Smithson, Mike	Texas	10-14	223	135	3.91	R-R	6-8	215	1/21/55 Centerville, TN
16	Viola, Frank	Minnesota	7-15	210	127	5.49	L-L	6-4	209	4/19/60 Hempstead, NY
30	Walters, Mike	Toledo	3-0	46	29	1.96	R-R	6-5	203	10/18/57 St. Louis, MO
		Minnesota	1-1	59	21	4.12				
22	Whitehouse, Len	Minnesota	7-1	74	44	4.15	L-L	5-11	174	9/10/57 Burlington, VT
28	Williams, Al	Minnesota	11-14	193	68	4.14	R-R	6-4	184	5/7/54 Nicaragua
51	Yett, Richard	Orlando	8-10	162	93	3.78	R-R	6-2	187	10/6/62 Pomona, CA

CATCHERS

No.	Name	1983 Club	H	HR	RBI	Pct.	B-T	Ht.	Wt.	Born
20	Engle, Dave	Minnesota	114	8	43	.305	R-R	6-3	210	11/30/56 San Diego, CA
15	Laudner, Tim	Minnesota	31	6	18	.185	R-R	6-3	208	6/7/58 Mason City, IA
21	Reed, Jeff	Orlando	100	6	45	.264	L-R	6-2	185	11/12/62 Joliet, IL
		Toledo	7	0	3	.171				
5	Smith, Ray	Minnesota	34	0	8	.224	R-R	6-1	185	9/18/55 Glendale, CA

INFIELDERS

No.	Name	1983 Club	H	HR	RBI	Pct.	B-T	Ht.	Wt.	Born
2	Castino, John	Minnesota	156	11	57	.277	R-R	5-11	177	10/23/54 Evanston, IL
40	Espinoza, Alvaro	Visalia	155	4	57	.319	R-R	6-0	160	2/19/62 Venezuela
12	Faedo, Lenny	Orlando	11	0	4	.212	R-R	6-0	180	5/13/60 Tampa, FL
		Minnesota	48	1	18	.277				
8	Gaetti, Gary	Minnesota	143	21	78	.245	R-R	6-0	192	8/19/58 Centralia, IL
31	Gagne, Greg	Toledo	100	17	66	.255	R-R	5-11	185	11/12/61 Fall River, MA
		Minnesota	3	0	3	.111				
14	Hrbek, Kent	Minnesota	153	16	84	.297	L-R	6-4	215	5/21/60 Minneapolis, MN
1	Jimenez, Houston	Toledo	16	3	6	.250	R-R	5-8	144	10/30/57 Mexico
		Minnesota	15	0	0	.174				
34	Teufel, Tim	Toledo	152	27	100	.323	R-R	6-0	170	7/7/58 Greenwich, CT
		Minnesota	24	3	6	.308				
38	Washington, Ron	Minnesota	78	4	26	.246	R-R	5-11	163	4/29/52 New Orleans, LA

OUTFIELDERS

No.	Name	1983 Club	H	HR	RBI	Pct.	B-T	Ht.	Wt.	Born
26	Brown, Darrell	Toledo	5	0	5	.217	B-R	6-0	184	10/29/55 Oklahoma City, OK
		Minnesota	84	0	22	.272				
24	Brunansky, Tom	Minnesota	123	28	82	.227	R-R	6-4	210	8/20/60 Covina, CA
25	Bush, Randy	Minnesota	93	11	56	.249	L-L	6-1	186	10/5/58 Dover, DE
4	Eisenreich, Jim	Minnesota	2	0	0	.286	L-L	5-11	194	4/18/59 St. Cloud, MN
48	Hart, Mike	Toledo	141	17	66	.290	L-L	5-11	185	2/17/58 Milwaukee, WI
9	Hatcher, Mickey	Minnesota	119	9	47	.317	R-R	6-2	200	3/15/55 Cleveland, OH
49	Lomastro, Jerry	Orlando	158	21	92	.299	R-R	5-11	185	8/9/58 Miami, FL
50	Meter, Dave	Toledo	143	8	68	.336	R-R	6-0	185	8/8/59 Helena, MT
10	Mitchell, Bobby	Minnesota	35	1	15	.230	L-L	5-10	169	4/7/55 Salt Lake City, UT
45	Weaver, Jim	Orlando	123	15	84	.247	L-L	6-4	200	10/10/59 Kingston, NY
7	Wilson, Tack	Minnesota	1	0	1	.250	R-R	5-10	185	5/16/56 Shreveport, LA
		Toledo	135	3	33	.325				

TWIN PROFILES

KENT HRBEK 23 6-4 215 **Bats L Throws R**

Showed he hasn't forgotten how to hit home runs when he hit eight from Aug. 19 to end of season . . . Finished fifth in AL with 41 doubles, most for a Twin since Zoilo Versalles set club record with 45 in 1965 . . . Tried assorted batting stances, copying parts of ones used by Rod Carew and Oscar Gamble . . . Thirteen errors he committed at first base not a true measure of his considerable defensive abilities . . . Only unanimous selection to 1982 major-league All-Rookie team, but finished second to Baltimore's Cal Ripken Jr. in AL Rookie-of-the-Year balloting . . . Had 23-game hitting streak in rookie season, which was broken when he injured wrist in fight against Detroit . . . In major-league debut, he hit a 12th-inning home run to win game at Yankee Stadium, Aug. 24, 1981 . . . Most popular Twin, stemming in part from fact he is a native of Minnesota . . . Born May 21, 1960, in Minneapolis and grew up down the street from Metropolitan Stadium, original home of Twins.

Year	Club	Pos.	G	AB	R	H	2B	3B	HR	RBI	SB	Avg.
1981	Minnesota	1B	24	67	5	16	5	0	1	7	0	.239
1982	Minnesota	1B	140	532	82	160	21	4	23	92	3	.301
1983	Minnesota	1B	141	515	75	153	41	5	16	84	4	.297
	Totals		305	1114	162	329	67	9	40	183	7	.295

TOM BRUNANSKY 23 6-4 210 **Bats R Throws R**

Average dipped to .227, but he improved his power totals, leading Twins in home runs and finishing third in RBI . . . His 15 game-winning RBI were by far the most of any Twin . . . More than half of his hits went for extra bases . . . Acquired from Angels' Spokane farm in May 1982 deal that sent reliever Doug Corbett and second baseman Rob Wilfong to California . . . Solid defensively in the outfield . . . Hit inside-the-park grand slam against Milwaukee's Jerry Augustine in 1982 . . . Born Aug. 20, 1960, in Covina, Cal. . . . Turned down scholarship offer to play baseball and football at Stanford . . . Angels made him a first-round draft pick in 1978.

Year	Club	Pos.	G	AB	R	H	2B	3B	HR	RBI	SB	Avg.
1981	California	OF	11	33	7	5	0	0	3	6	1	.152
1982	Minnesota	OF	127	463	77	126	30	1	20	46	1	.272
1983	Minnesota	OF	151	542	70	123	24	5	28	82	2	.227
	Totals		289	1038	154	254	54	6	51	134	4	.245

JOHN CASTINO 29 5-11 177 **Bats R Throws R**

Was converted into second baseman early in 1982 after having undergone offseason spinal fusion operation . . . Has maintained defensive excellence that earned him high regard at third base . . . Finished second among AL second basemen in fielding percentage in 1983 . . . Played first 60 games at second in 1982 without committing an error and compiled the best fielding percentage (.995) in majors that year . . . Led AL third basemen in fielding (.975) in 1981 . . . Some talk of moving him to center field to make room for prospect Tim Teufel, which would be a waste of talent . . . Led Twins with 83 runs scored . . . Quiet leader of club with hustling style . . . Born Oct. 23, 1954, in Evanston, Ill. . . . Tied with Toronto's Alfredo Griffin for AL Rookie-of-the-Year honors in 1979.

Year	Club	Pos.	G	AB	R	H	2B	3B	HR	RBI	SB	Avg.
1979	Minnesota	3B-SS	148	393	49	112	13	8	5	52	5	.285
1980	Minnesota	3B-SS	150	546	67	165	17	7	13	64	7	.302
1981	Minnesota	3B-2B	101	381	41	102	13	9	6	36	4	.268
1982	Minnesota	2B-3B-OF	117	410	48	99	12	6	6	37	2	.241
1983	Minnesota	2B-3B	142	563	83	156	30	4	11	57	4	.277
	Totals		658	2293	288	634	85	34	41	246	22	.276

GARY GAETTI 25 6-0 192 **Bats R Throws R**

Don't tell him about the "Homerdome" . . . Hit 14 of his 21 home runs on the road . . . Tied Gary Ward for Twins' lead in games played (157) . . . Erratic defensively at third base, but has power to overshadow shortcomings . . . Cut down on strikeouts from 121 to 107, despite 76 more at-bats in second full big-league season . . . Had 19-game hitting streak, tops on Twins and two short of best in AL last season . . . Tied major-league rookie record with 13 sacrifice flies in 1982 . . . Broke into major leagues in September 1981 by becoming 47th player in history to homer in first at-bat, connecting off Texas knuckleballer Charlie Hough in Arlington Stadium . . . Born Aug. 19, 1958, in Centralia, Ill. . . . Attended Northwest Missouri State before signing with Twins, who selected him in first round of June 1979 secondary draft.

Year	Club	Pos.	G	AB	R	H	2B	3B	HR	RBI	SB	Avg.
1981	Minnesota	3B	9	26	4	5	0	0	2	3	0	.192
1982	Minnesota	3B-SS	145	508	59	117	25	4	25	84	0	.230
1983	Minnesota	3B	157	584	81	143	30	3	21	78	7	.245
	Totals		311	1118	144	265	55	7	48	165	7	.237

DAVE ENGLE 27 6-3 210 **Bats R Throws R**

Made strides in attempt to convert back from outfielder-third baseman into catcher, position he played at USC, but had abandoned after signing with California Angels in 1978 . . . Caught 73 games for the Twins last season . . . Struggled in the early going and wound up throwing out only 16-of-64 runners who attempted steals against him . . . Father, a former minor-league catcher, ran Ted Williams' hitting school . . . Learned art of bat control . . . Succeeded on 6-of-8 attempts to bunt for hit . . . Had average as high as .336, on Aug. 20, before late-season slump . . . Hit first official home run in Metrodome, off Floyd Bannister, April 6, 1982 . . . Born Nov. 30, 1956, in San Diego . . . Has .304 career average in minors, but was hitting .244 overall in big leagues before finishing second in hitting among Twins last year . . . Credits return to minors in 1982 with turning around his career.

Year	Club	Pos.	G	AB	R	H	2B	3B	HR	RBI	SB	Avg.
1981	Minnesota	OF-3B	82	248	29	64	14	4	5	32	0	.258
1982	Minnesota	OF	58	186	20	42	7	2	4	16	0	.226
1983	Minnesota	OF-C	120	374	46	114	22	4	8	43	2	.305
	Totals		260	808	95	220	43	10	17	91	2	.272

MIKE SMITHSON 29 6-8 215 **Bats R Throws R**

Drew Opening Day assignment as a Ranger rookie last year . . . And now he's a Twin as a result of deal that sent outfielder Gary Ward to Texas . . . Tallest player in majors . . . Season high in strikeouts was seven, which he accomplished five times . . . Led American Association with 144 strikeouts for Denver (AAA) in 1982 . . . Pitched 3⅔ scoreless innings for Pawtucket during record-setting 33-inning game against Rochester in 1981 . . . Had made only two starts in two years before joining Ranger organization in 1982 and becoming a starter . . . Has wicked sidearm delivery that makes fastball and slider effective . . . Born Jan. 21, 1955, in Centerville, Tenn. . . . Played basketball and baseball at Tennessee, where he was teammate of former Ranger Rick Honeycutt and Mark Batchko, the Rangers' fulltime bullpen and batting-practice catcher.

Year	Club	G	IP	W	L	Pct.	SO	BB	H	ERA
1982	Texas	8	47	3	4	.429	24	13	51	5.01
1983	Texas	33	223	10	14	.417	135	71	233	3.91
	Totals	41	270	13	18	.419	159	84	284	4.10

RON DAVIS 28 6-4 207 **Bats R Throws R**

After winning controversial salary arbitration that prompted Twins' owner Calvin Griffith to say he felt so sick he could throw up, this reliever made Griffith feel better by becoming fourth Twin to save 30 games . . . Was involved in one-half of Twins' 70 victories and saw ERA drop by more than a run from 1982 mark . . . Had seven saves in seven appearances in August . . . Had third-best strikeout-to-innings-pitched ratio among AL relievers . . . Says he would like to remain in Minnesota, despite trade rumors . . . Has made 273 big-league appearances, all as a reliever . . . Established major-league record for a reliever with nine consecutive strikeouts in games at California and Seattle in 1981 and his eight in a row against Angels tied Nolan Ryan's single-game AL record . . . Set AL record for wins by rookie reliever with 14 as Yankee in 1979 . . . Came to Twins in April 1982 in five-player deal that sent Roy Smalley to New York . . . Born Aug. 6, 1955, in Houston . . . Attended Blinn Junior College before signing with Chicago Cubs in 1976.

Year	Club	G	IP	W	L	Pct.	SO	BB	H	ERA
1978	New York (AL)	4	2	0	0	.000	0	3	3	13.50
1979	New York (AL)	44	85	14	2	.875	43	28	84	2.86
1980	New York (AL)	53	131	9	3	.750	65	32	121	2.95
1981	New York (AL)	43	73	4	5	.444	83	25	47	2.71
1982	Minnesota	63	106	3	9	.250	89	47	106	4.42
1983	Minnesota	66	89	5	8	.385	84	33	89	3.34
	Totals	273	486	35	27	.565	364	168	450	3.33

KEN SCHROM 29 6-2 195 **Bats R Throws R**

Invited to spring training after being released by Toronto, he began season in minors, but finished it leading the Twins in victories . . . Called up May 5 and made three appearances in relief . . . Joined rotation after that and relieved only one more time . . . Won 12 of first 16 decisions, including four in a row during August stretch . . . Pitched first major-league shutout at Texas Sept. 29, his final start of season . . . Was 3-0 against Blue Jays and former teammate Dave Stieb . . . Had not started a game since 1979 before last year . . . Born Nov. 23, 1954, in Grangeville, Idaho . . . Twins originally drafted him out of high school in 1973, but he turned them down to play baseball and football at Idaho . . . Signed with California in 1976 and was traded to Toronto for pitcher Dave Lemanczyk in 1980 . . . Earned only big-league save against Twins in 1980.

Year	Club	G	IP	W	L	Pct.	SO	BB	H	ERA
1980	Toronto	17	31	1	0	1.000	13	19	32	5.23
1982	Toronto	6	15	1	0	1.000	8	15	13	5.87
1983	Minnesota	33	196	15	8	.652	80	80	196	3.71
	Totals	56	242	17	8	.680	101	114	241	4.05

MICKEY HATCHER 29 6-2 200 Bats R Throws R

Made Twins as 25th player in spring training, but wound up reviving career and leading club in hitting . . . Was used mostly as a right-handed DH, but Twins are thinking about giving him a chance to fill an every-day spot in the outfield in 1984 . . . Started a 16-game hitting streak July 20 and wound up hitting in 38-of-43 games . . . Born March 15, 1955, in Cleveland . . . Was drafted by Houston in 1974 and the New York Mets in 1976, but chose to pursue football career at Mesa (Ariz.) Community College and Oklahoma, where he was a punter and wide receiver . . . Signed with Los Angeles Dodgers in 1977 . . . Led Pacific Coast League in hitting with .371 average for Albuquerque in 1979.

Year	Club	Pos.	G	AB	R	H	2B	3B	HR	RBI	SB	Avg.
1979	Los Angeles	3B-OF	33	93	9	25	4	1	1	5	1	.269
1980	Los Angeles	OF-3B	57	84	4	19	2	0	1	5	0	.226
1981	Minnesota	OF-1B-3B	99	377	36	96	23	2	3	37	3	.255
1982	Minnesota	OF-3B	84	277	23	69	13	2	3	26	0	.249
1983	Minnesota	OF-3B	106	375	50	119	15	3	9	47	2	.317
	Totals		379	1206	122	328	57	8	17	120	6	.272

AL WILLIAMS 29 6-4 184 Bats R Throws R

There was no in-between for him in 1983 . . . Won first start and then lost seven of next eight decisions . . . On July 23, he began a 5-3 tear during which he compiled 2.81 ERA . . . Pitched first major-league shutout in five-hit, 11-0 victory at Boston Sept. 1 . . . Complained of elbow problems during final two months of the season . . . Same elbow was bothering him during six-game winning streak in 1982 . . . Born May 7, 1954, in Pearl Lagoon, Nicaragua . . . Originally signed by Pittsburgh in 1975, but couldn't get a visa to pitch in 1977 and 1978, when he was serving as a Nicaraguan freedom fighter . . . Pitched in Inter-American League in 1979 and was signed as a free agent by Twins in January 1980.

Year	Club	G	IP	W	L	Pct.	SO	BB	H	ERA
1980	Minnesota	18	77	6	2	.750	35	30	73	3.51
1981	Minnesota	23	150	6	10	.375	76	52	160	4.08
1982	Minnesota	26	154	9	7	.563	61	55	166	4.22
1983	Minnesota	36	193	11	14	.440	68	68	196	4.14
	Totals	103	574	32	33	.492	240	205	595	4.06

BOBBY CASTILLO 28 5-10 175 **Bats R Throws R**

Nagging injuries slowed him at start of year . . . Had cyst removed from back of right shoulder in spring training, which cost him Opening Night assignment . . . Suffered a strained neck, which knocked him out early in two starts, and a strained lower back, which landed him on the disabled list . . . Ended season with career in doubt, suffering from torn rotator cuff . . . Lost final three decisions . . . Had made only two starts in first 153 big-league appearances before being put in Twins' rotation in May 1982 . . . Wound up that season as team leader in wins, innings pitched and complete games (six) . . . Claims he taught Fernando Valenzuela the screwball when they were aspiring Dodgers in Arizona Instructional League in 1979 . . . Began career as infielder in Kansas City Royals' organization . . . Born April 18, 1955, in Los Angeles and attended Los Angeles State.

Year	Club	G	IP	W	L	Pct.	SO	BB	H	ERA
1977	Los Angeles	6	11	1	0	1.000	7	2	12	4.09
1978	Los Angeles	18	34	0	4	.000	30	33	28	3.97
1979	Los Angeles	19	24	2	0	1.000	25	13	26	1.13
1980	Los Angeles	61	98	8	6	.571	60	45	70	2.76
1981	Los Angeles	34	51	2	4	.333	35	24	50	5.29
1982	Minnesota	40	219	13	11	.542	124	85	194	3.66
1983	Minnesota	27	158	8	12	.400	90	65	170	4.77
	Totals	205	595	34	37	.479	371	267	550	3.87

TOP PROSPECTS

TIM TEUFEL 25 6-0 170 **Bats R Throws R**

Only reason Twins are talking about moving John Castino to outfield spot is to make room for rookie second baseman, who was International League MVP . . . Hit .323 with 27 doubles, six triples, 27 homers and 100 RBI at Toledo (AAA) . . . Hit in 13 of first 14 games after joining Twins in September, but got jammed a lot and was 2-for-24 in final seven games . . . Born July 7, 1958, in Greenwich, Conn. . . . Second-round 1980 draft pick out of Clemson.

JEFF REED 21 6-2 185 **Bats L Throws R**

Has some work to do on his hitting, but has the catching skills needed to play in the big leagues now . . . After hitting .329 at Visalia (A) in 1982, he moved to Orlando (AA) and his average dropped to .261 . . . Will improve, especially in power areas, as his body fills out . . . Twins' first-round pick and 12th overall in 1980 . . . Born Nov. 12, 1962, in Joliet, Ill. . . . Has led league's catchers in assists all four of his years in pro ball.

MANAGER BILLY GARDNER: It's a good thing he has patience with all the kids he has to manage ... Had managed 12 years in minors before replacing John Goryl in Minnesota shortly before strike in 1981 ... Had coached with Boston in 1965 and 1966, with Montreal in 1977 and 1978 and with Twins in opening weeks of 1981 ... In his first full season as Twins' boss, he frequently had eight rookies—and sometimes nine—in the starting lineup ... His 10-year big-league playing career included stop in Minnesota ... Was Twins' first second baseman after club moved from Washington to Twin Cities in 1961 ... Had .237 average to show for big-league stops with New York Giants, Baltimore, Washington/Minnesota, Yankees and Boston ... Played in 1954 World Series with Giants and in 1961 Series with Yankees ... Wife is a former Miss Connecticut ... Born July 19, 1927, in New London, Conn. ... Record with rebuilding Twins is 160-237.

GREATEST STEALER

The Twins seem to ignore their Washington, D.C. roots in developing their all-time records, so Rod Carew is listed as the career leader in stolen bases. He did steal 49 bases in 1976 and has stolen home 17 times, all but once for the Twins. But the best stolen-base artist in Senator/Twin history was George Case.

With the Washington Senators, Case set a major-league record by leading both leagues in stolen bases five consecutive years, from 1939-43. For good measure, he also led the AL in stolen bases for Cleveland in 1946.

In an age when running was almost run out of baseball, Case's natural speed prompted his managers to let him go and he stole 349 bases in his 11-year career. He established a record during his days in Washington by once circling the bases in 13.5 seconds. And some of his theories about base-stealing have become the basis for the wide-open game of the past few decades.

ALL-TIME TWIN SEASON RECORDS

BATTING: Rod Carew, .388, 1977
HRs: Harmon Killebrew, 49, 1964, 1969
RBIs: Harmon Killebrew, 140, 1969
STEALS: Rod Carew, 49, 1976
WINS: Jim Kaat, 25, 1966
STRIKEOUTS: Bert Blyleven, 258, 1973

OAKLAND A's

TEAM DIRECTORY: Pres.: Roy Eisenhardt; Exec. VP: Wally Haas; VP/Baseball Oper.: Sandy Alderson; Dir. Play. Dev.: Karl Kuehl; Dir. Minor League Oper.: Walt Jocketty; Dir. Publ.-Trav. Sec.: Mickey Morabito; Mgr.: Steve Boros. Home: Oakland Coliseum (50,219). Field distances: 330, l.f. line; 372, l.c.; 397, c.f.; 372, r.c.; 330, r.f. line. Spring training: Phoenix, Ariz.

SCOUTING REPORT

HITTING: The signing of free agent Bruce Bochte (idle last year) gave the A's a .300 bat to add to their lineup. But he's left-handed, and so is Joe Morgan (16 homers, 59 RBI), who signed a one-year contract as a free agent. What Oakland needed most was a right-handed power hitter. They thought they had that problem solved by getting Dusty Baker. But Baker vetoed a trade from Los Angeles because Oakland wouldn't hand him Rickey Henderson's job in left field.

With Davey Lopes (.277, 17 homers, 67 RBI) and Jeff Burroughs (.269, 10 homers, 56 RBI) expected to spend more time on the bench than on the field, Carney Lansford (.308) is the only right-handed threat in the lineup. And he wasn't in the lineup nearly enough to make his presence felt last year.

The A's, who set a team record with a .262 team average, do have threats on the bases. Henderson (.292), the only player in big-league history to steal 100 bases in a season three times, led Oakland to an AL-high 234 thefts with 108. Lopes, Mike Davis (.275, 62 RBI) and Bill Almon (.266, 63 RBI) all stole more than 20 last season.

PITCHING: The A's knew they needed help in the arms race and they got it during the winter with the addition of right-handed reliever Bill Caudill. He was not appreciated in Seattle, although he had his second straight 26-save season and blew only three leads.

The A's rotation was the envy of the AL a few years ago, but Billy Burnout left it in shambles. Rick Langford (0-4), Mike Norris (4-5) and Steve McCatty (6-9) remain from those days, but lingering arm problems make them undependable.

Chris Codiroli (12-12) was the only starter who was able to take his regular turn in 1983. But thanks to young arms like those of Mike Warren, Tim Conroy and Bill Kreuger—another question mark due to injury—the A's have reason to expect better things. Former Expo Ray Burris lends an experienced hand.

Record-maker Rickey Henderson stole 100 for third time.

FIELDING: Bochte will help the A's in the field as well as at the plate. He has worked hard to become one of the best at first base, even if he doesn't always look like the most agile. That's more than can be said about the rest of the Oakland infield, although young shortstop Donnie Hill shows signs of big-league potential with his range and his arm. Age had made the gloves and range of second baseman Morgan and utility man Lopes questionable.

Mike Heath has a gun behind the plate—if he stays healthy. And no one can complain about an outfield of Henderson, Dwayne Murphy and Davis (16 assists). They can run the ball down and, once they get to it, they can throw out just about any daring baserunner.

OUTLOOK: Roy Eisenhardt and Co. have pumped money into the farm system, signed players to competitive contracts, hired a steady field boss in Steve Boros and established an excellent reputation for the way they operate.

While the rotation is still a question, the acquisition of Caudill means that if the A's get ahead late in a game, they will usually stay ahead. Bochte and Morgan give the A's stability in the clubhouse, which should carry over to the field. Oakland is the most improved team in the division and could surprise the White Sox.

OAKLAND A's 1984 ROSTER

MANAGER Steve Boros
Coaches—Clete Boyer, Jackie Moore, Bob Didier, Ron Schueler, Billy Williams

PITCHERS

No.	Name	1983 Club	W-L	IP	SO	ERA	B-T	Ht.	Wt.	Born
55	Atherton, Keith	Tacoma	3-8	120	93	3.96	R-R	6-4	200	2/19/59 Matthews, VA
		Oakland	2-5	68	40	2.77				
53	Bradley, Bert	Tacoma	6-5	86	45	2.84	B-R	6-1	190	12/23/57 Athens, GA
		Oakland	0-0	8	3	6.48				
39	Burgmeier, Tom	Oakland	6-7	96	39	2.63	L-L	5-11	180	8/2/43 St. Paul, MN
48	Burris, Ray	Montreal	4-7	154	100	3.68	R-R	6-5	200	8/22/50 Idabel, OK
36	Caudill, Bill	Seattle	2-8	73	73	4.71	R-R	6-1	210	7/13/56 Santa Monica, CA
23	Codiroli, Chris	Oakland	12-12	206	85	4.46	R-R	6-1	160	3/26/58 Oxnard, CA
24	Conroy, Tim	Oakland	7-10	162	112	3.94	L-L	6-1	185	4/3/60 Monroeville, PA
59	Dye, Scott	Tidewater	1-3	37	23	6.08	R-R	6-1	195	1/9/57 Biloxi, MS
		Tacoma	1-0	34	20	3.97				
40	Farmer, Ed	Philadelphia	0-6	27	16	6.08	R-R	6-6	210	10/18/49 Evergreen Park, IL
		Port.-Tacoma	1-1	24	16	4.94				
		Oakland	0-0	10	7	3.48				
13	Heimueller, Gorman	Tacoma	8-4	117	61	3.54	L-L	6-4	195	9/24/55 Los Angeles, CA
		Oakland	3-5	84	31	4.41				
32	Krueger, Bill	Oakland	7-6	110	58	3.61	L-L	6-5	205	4/24/58 McMinnville, OR
22	Langford, Rick	Oakland	0-4	20	2	12.15	R-R	6-0	180	3/20/52 Farmville, VA
54	McCatty, Steve	Oakland	6-9	167	65	3.99	R-R	6-3	210	3/20/54 Detroit, MI
17	Norris, Mike	Oakland	4-5	89	63	3.76	R-R	6-2	170	3/19/55 San Francisco, CA
49	Smith, Mark	Rochester	2-3	49	35	5.33	L-R	6-2	215	11/23/55 Alexandria, VA
		Tacoma	2-2	43	34	3.74				
		Oakland	1-0	15	10	6.75				
—	Stoddard, Tim	Baltimore	4-3	58	50	6.09	R-R	6-7	250	1/24/53 East Chicago, IN
31	*Underwood, Tom	Oakland	9-7	145	62	4.04	R-L	5-11	185	12/22/53 Kokomo, IN
43	Warren, Mike	Albany	6-2	72	87	3.25	R-R	6-1	175	3/26/61 Inglewood, CA
		Tacoma	6-3	79	85	3.53				
		Oakland	5-3	66	30	4.11				
29	Young, Curt	Tacoma	12-9	159	109	5.05	R-L	6-1	175	10/18/59 Saginaw, MI
		Oakland	0-1	9	5	16.00				

CATCHERS

No.	Name	1983 Club	H	HR	RBI	Pct.	B-T	Ht.	Wt.	Born
5	Bathe, Bill	Tacoma	101	16	62	.253	R-R	6-2	200	10/14/60 Downey, CA
—	Essian, Jim	Cleveland	19	2	11	204	R-R	6-1	187	1/2/51 Detroit, MI
2	Heath, Mike	Oakland	97	6	33	.281	R-R	5-11	175	2/5/55 Tampa, FL
57	Tettleton, Mickey	Modesto	92	7	62	.243	B-R	6-2	200	9/16/60 Oklahoma City, OK

INFIELDERS

34	Almon, Bill	Oakland	120	4	63	.266	R-R	6-3	190	11/21/52 Providence, RI
19	Brant, Marshall	Columbus	23	7	19	.193	R-R	6-5	215	9/17/55 Garberville, CA
		Tacoma	38	10	25	.232				
		Oakland	2	0	2	.143				
20	Bochte, Bruce		Did not play				L-L	6-3	200	11/12/50 Pasadena, CA
25	Hill, Donnie	Tacoma	101	14	63	.314	B-R	5-10	160	11/12/60 Pomona, CA
		Oakland	42	2	15	.266				
28	Kiefer, Steve	Albany	102	19	81	.246	R-R	6-1	175	10/18/60 Chicago, IL
4	Lansford, Carney	Oakland	92	10	45	.308	R-R	5-9	195	2/7/57 San Jose, CA
15	Lopes, Davey	Oakland	137	17	67	.277	R-R	5-9	170	5/3/46 E. Providence, RI
7	Meyer, Dan	Oakland	32	1	13	.189	L-R	5-11	180	8/3/52 Hamilton, OH
8	Morgan, Joe	Philadelphia	93	16	59	.230	L-R	5-7	160	9/19/43 Bonham, TX
18	Phillips, Tony	Oakland	102	4	35	.248	B-R	5-10	160	11/9/59 Atlanta, GA
12	Pyznarski, Tim	Albany	116	28	79	.279	R-R	6-2	195	2/4/60 Chicago, IL

OUTFIELDERS

3	Burroughs, Jeff	Oakland	108	10	56	.269	R-R	6-0	200	3/7/51 Long Beach, CA
16	Davis, Mike	Oakland	122	8	62	.275	L-L	6-3	175	6/11/59 San Diego, CA
11	Hancock, Garry	Oakland	70	8	30	.273	L-L	6-0	190	1/23/54 Tampa, FL
56	Harrison, Ron	Albany	116	11	50	.291	L-R	6-2	170	10/15/60 Sacramento, Ca
35	Henderson, Rickey	Oakland	150	9	48	.292	R-L	5-10	180	12/25/58 Chicago, IL
21	Murphy, Dwayne	Oakland	107	17	75	.227	L-R	6-1	180	3/18/55 Merced, CA
6	Page, Mitchell	Oakland	19	0	1	.238	L-L	6-2	205	10/15/51 Los Angeles, CA
31	Romano, Tom	Albany	164	24	89	.320	R-R	5-11	170	10/25/58 Syracuse, NY

*Free agent unsigned at press time

A's PROFILES

CARNEY LANSFORD 27 6-2 195 Bats R Throws R

Only bright part of last season was signing of long-term contract in August . . . His two-year-old son died because of kidney failure during spring training, causing third baseman to miss opening weeks of season . . . After coming back, he was sidelined with sprained wrist . . . Finished season nursing sore ankle and had postseason surgery to remove bone spur . . . Despite playing only half a year, he had 10 home runs and 45 RBI . . . Had 19-game hitting streak in July to raise average from .256 to .303. After going hitless for one game, he ran off a seven-game streak . . . Became first right-handed hitter to win AL batting title since 1970 when he hit .336 in 1981 . . . Played for Santa Clara Little League team that lost to Taiwan in World Series . . . Born Feb. 7, 1957, in San Jose, Cal. . . . Cousin of singer Tex Ritter . . . Brother Phil is in Toronto system and brother Jody is part of San Diego organization.

Year	Club	Pos.	G	AB	R	H	2B	3B	HR	RBI	SB	Avg.
1978	California	3B	121	453	63	133	23	2	8	52	20	.294
1979	California	3B	157	654	114	188	30	5	19	79	20	.287
1980	California	3B	151	602	87	157	27	3	15	80	14	.261
1981	Boston	3B	102	399	61	134	23	3	4	52	15	.336
1982	Boston	3B	128	482	65	145	28	4	11	63	9	.301
1983	Oakland	3B	80	299	43	92	16	2	10	45	3	.308
	Totals		739	2889	433	849	147	19	67	371	81	.294

RICKEY HENDERSON 25 5-10 180 Bats R Throws L

Became only player in history to reach 100-mark in stolen bases three times . . . Led AL with 108 steals after setting major-league records for steals (130) and caught stealings (42) in 1982 . . . Got off to slow start . . . Was hitting .248 and had only 35 thefts July 2 . . . In the two games before All-Star break, he set AL record with seven thefts . . . Added three more in first game after break . . . Has collected eight bases as momentos of base-stealing accomplishments and plans to have them set in floor of trophy room in house he is building . . . Born Dec. 25, 1958, in Chicago . . . Was football player in high school and big fan of O.J. Simpson . . . Mother told him to turn down college football scholarship offers and sign with Oakland, because baseball career offered more longevity . . . One of few players to hit right-handed and throw left-handed.

Year	Club	Pos.	G	AB	R	H	2B	3B	HR	RBI	SB	Avg.
1979	Oakland.	OF	89	351	49	96	13	3	1	26	33	.274
1980	Oakland.	OF	158	591	111	179	22	4	9	53	100	.303
1981	Oakland.	OF	108	423	89	135	18	7	6	35	56	.319
1982	Oakland.	OF	149	536	119	143	24	4	10	51	130	.267
1983	Oakland.	OF	145	513	105	150	25	7	9	48	108	.292
	Totals		649	2414	473	703	102	25	35	213	427	.291

DWAYNE MURPHY 29 6-1 180 — Bats L Throws R

Played all year on sore ankles, then had surgery to remove bone spurs after season ended . . . Considered leader of ballclub . . . Teammates respect his desire to play, even with injuries . . . Thought he was going to benefit from moving down from the No. 2 spot in batting order, where he had to make sacrifices so that leadoff man Rickey Henderson could steal, but didn't find pitches to his liking . . . Reached a season low with .196 mark May 30 . . . Still showed power in spurts . . . Hit four home runs in five games during late July and three homers in four games in August . . . Center fielder owns one of the strongest outfield arms in baseball . . . Born March 18, 1955, in Merced, Cal. . . . Turned down football scholarship to Arizona State to sign with Oakland in 1973.

Year	Club	Pos.	G	AB	R	H	2B	3B	HR	RBI	SB	Avg.
1978	Oakland.	OF	60	52	15	10	2	0	0	5	0	.192
1979	Oakland.	OF	121	388	57	99	10	4	11	40	15	.255
1980	Oakland.	OF	159	573	86	157	18	2	13	68	26	.274
1981	Oakland.	OF	107	390	58	98	10	3	15	60	10	.251
1982	Oakland.	OF-SS	151	543	84	130	16	1	27	94	26	.239
1983	Oakland.	OF	130	471	55	107	17	2	17	75	7	.227
	Totals		728	2417	355	601	73	12	83	342	84	.249

MIKE DAVIS 24 6-3 175 — Bats L Throws L

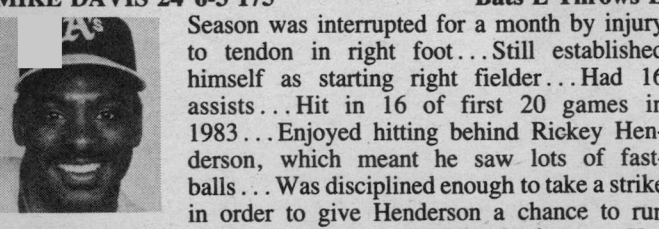

Season was interrupted for a month by injury to tendon in right foot . . . Still established himself as starting right fielder . . . Had 16 assists . . . Hit in 16 of first 20 games in 1983 . . . Enjoyed hitting behind Rickey Henderson, which meant he saw lots of fastballs . . . Was disciplined enough to take a strike in order to give Henderson a chance to run . . . Ranked second on club to Henderson with 32 stolen bases . . . Has averaged 30 stolen bases in seven professional seasons . . . Hit below .300 only once in six minor-league seasons . . . Can also play first base . . . Turned down scholarship to Arizona State to sign with A's in 1977... Born June 11, 1959, in San Diego... Attended same high school as Ted Williams, San Diego's Hoover High ... Brother is standout baseball player at Stanford.

Year	Club	Pos.	G	AB	R	H	2B	3B	HR	RBI	SB	Avg.
1980	Oakland..........	OF-1B	51	95	11	20	2	1	1	8	2	.211
1981	Oakland..........	OF-1B	17	20	0	1	1	0	0	0	0	.050
1982	Oakland..........	OF-1B	23	75	12	30	4	0	1	10	3	.400
1983	Oakland..........	OF-1B	128	443	61	122	24	4	8	62	32	.275
	Totals..........		219	633	84	173	31	5	10	80	37	.273

BILL KRUEGER 25 6-5 205 **Bats L Throws L**

Wasn't on Oakland's Opening Day roster, but joined club the next day... Immediately went into rotation and established himself as solid starter... Strained muscle in left forearm gave him more problems than did AL hitters ... Made last start June 25... Was sent to bullpen to nurse injury and didn't pitch at all after Aug. 2... Best game was four-hit, 1-0 victory over Baltimore May 8... Born April 24, 1958, in McMinnville, Ore.... An unlikely success story... Was first baseman and basketball star at University of Portland and wanted to play pro basketball... When chance didn't come, he went around Northwest League asking for tryout. GM of A's Medford farm team remembered him as a good high-school pitcher and signed him to fill out roster... After so-so first two years, he was 15-9 with 2.83 ERA for West Haven (AA) in 1982.

Year	Club	G	IP	W	L	Pct.	SO	BB	H	ERA
1983	Oakland	17	110	7	6	.538	58	53	104	3.61

MIKE HEATH 29 5-11 175 **Bats R Throws R**

Considered one of the better defensive catchers, but can't defend against injuries which have dotted career... Opened season on disabled list because of back spasms for second year in a row... Spent final month on sideline with same problem... Had played only two games by May 25... Had solid offensive year, finishing with an average that was 38 points above his career mark... Went 13-for-25 during seven-game hit streak in July, raising average to season-high .315... Threw out only 20-of-60 potential base-stealers last season after nabbing 76-of-152 in first three years with Oakland... Played third base and right field as well as catcher... Signed with Yankees as a shortstop in

1973, but was converted into catcher in spring of 1976 . . . Traded to Rangers in multi-player package that brought Dave Righetti to Yankees after 1978 season . . . Acquired by the A's with Dave Chalk for pitcher John Henry Johnson on June 15 trading deadline in 1979 . . . Born Feb. 5, 1955, in Tampa . . . Re-signed with A's during winter.

Year	Club	Pos.	G	AB	R	H	2B	3B	HR	RBI	SB	Avg.
1978	New York (AL)	C	33	92	6	21	3	1	0	8	0	.228
1979	Oakland	OF-C-3B	74	258	19	66	8	0	3	27	1	.256
1980	Oakland	C-OF	92	305	27	74	10	2	1	33	3	.243
1981	Oakland	C-OF	84	301	26	71	7	1	8	30	3	.236
1982	Oakland	C-OF-3B	101	318	43	77	18	4	3	39	8	.242
1983	Oakland	C-OF-3B	96	345	45	97	17	0	6	33	3	.281
	Totals		480	1619	166	406	63	8	21	170	18	.251

DAVEY LOPES 37 5-9 170 — Bats R Throws R

Missed hitting for cycle in strange way . . . Had double, triple and grand-slam home run against Toronto, driving in career-high seven runs June 15, but couldn't get single he needed to complete picture . . . Opened season as A's second baseman, but served as right fielder, third baseman and DH as well . . . Has tutored Rickey Henderson in how to read pitchers . . . Also taught base-stealing for Oakland entry in Arizona Instructional League . . . Has stolen 20 or more bases 11 years in a row . . . Was caught only twice in 24 attempts in 1983 . . . Tied for club lead in home runs with Dwayne Murphy . . . A center fielder when he signed with Dodgers in 1968, he was moved to second base as minor-leaguer in 1971, by Tommy Lasorda . . . Set major-league record with 38 consecutive stolen bases in 1975 . . . Became fifth captain in Dodger history in 1978, then resigned post during 1979 season . . . Born May 3, 1946, in East Providence, R.I. . . . Attended Washburn University and Iowa Wesleyan College . . . Has played in four World Series and four All-Star Games.

Year	Club	Pos.	G	AB	R	H	2B	3B	HR	RBI	SB	Avg.
1972	Los Angeles	2B	11	42	6	9	4	0	0	1	4	.214
1973	Los Angeles	2B-OF-SS-3B	142	535	77	147	13	5	6	37	36	.275
1974	Los Angeles	2B	145	530	95	141	26	3	10	35	59	.266
1975	Los Angeles	2B-OF-SS	155	618	108	162	24	6	8	41	77	.262
1976	Los Angeles	2B-OF	117	427	72	103	17	7	4	20	63	.241
1977	Los Angeles	2B	134	502	85	142	19	5	11	53	47	.283
1978	Los Angeles	2B-OF	151	587	93	163	25	4	17	58	45	.278
1979	Los Angeles	2B	153	582	109	154	20	6	28	73	44	.265
1980	Los Angeles	2B	141	553	79	139	15	3	10	49	23	.251
1981	Los Angeles	2B	58	214	35	44	2	0	5	17	20	.206
1982	Oakland	2B-OF	128	450	58	109	19	3	11	42	28	.242
1983	Oakland	2B-3B-OF	147	494	64	137	13	4	17	67	22	.277
	Totals		1482	5534	881	1450	197	46	127	493	468	.262

CHRIS CODIROLI 26 6-1 160 **Bats R Throws R**

Established himself as No. 1 man in Oakland rotation as a rookie, leading club in wins, starts and innings pitched . . . Only A's starter who remained healthy all year . . . Had streak of 22 scoreless innings during three-game stretch in August that included five-hitter against Minnesota . . . Did make four relief appearances at end of June . . . Was given shot at big leagues after splitting 1982 between Tacoma (AAA) and West Haven (AA), compiling 16-4 record and 2.04 ERA and striking out 130 in 168 innings . . . Was No. 1 pick of Detroit in January 1978 draft . . . Arm problems in 1979 and 1980 led to release . . . Signed by A's in 1981 and quickly rose from Class A to majors . . . Born March 26, 1958, in Oxnard, Cal. . . . Attended San Jose City College and San Jose State.

Year	Club	G	IP	W	L	Pct.	SO	BB	H	ERA
1982	Oakland	3	17	1	2	.333	5	4	16	4.32
1983	Oakland	37	206	12	12	.500	85	72	208	4.46
	Totals.	40	223	13	14	.481	90	76	224	4.44

BILL CAUDILL 27 6-1 210 **Bats R Throws R**

Acquired from Mariners in deal for reliever Dave Beard and catcher Bob Kearney . . . Despite all the questions about what happened to him, he did equal his own Seattle club record with 26 saves and blew a lead only three times . . . Went on disabled list over his own objections in late August, because of sprained ankle . . . Was suggested Mariners did that to keep him from earning incentives of $6,000 per game . . . Still managed to finish sixth in AL with 63 appearances . . . Ranked behind only Yankees' Rich Gossage in strikeouts per nine innings . . . In two years with Mariners, he established club career record of 52 saves . . . Born July 13, 1956, in Santa Monica, Cal. . . . Free spirit who wore out welcome with St. Louis, Cincinnati and Chicago Cub organizations . . . Came to Mariners from Cubs through Yankees . . . Jokes that he deserves "one pinstripe" for having been property of Yanks for 22 minutes.

Year	Club	G	IP	W	L	Pct.	SO	BB	H	ERA
1979	Chicago (NL)	29	90	1	7	.125	104	41	89	4.80
1980	Chicago (NL)	72	128	4	6	.400	112	59	100	2.18
1981	Chicago (NL)	30	71	1	5	.167	45	31	87	5.83
1982	Seattle	70	96	12	9	.571	111	35	65	2.35
1983	Seattle	63	73	2	8	.200	73	38	70	4.71
	Totals.	264	458	20	35	.364	445	204	411	3.69

BRUCE BOCHTE 33 6-3 200 **Bats L Throws R**

Became a free agent after 1982 season with Seattle and spent last year in self-imposed retirement because of "philosophical" differences with the game stemming from what was described as the greed of owners and players . . . Signed with A's in the fall after visiting Boston and Kansas City . . . Hit .297 or better in four of last six big-league seasons . . . Had a .376 average with men in scoring position for Seattle in 1982 . . . Came to big leagues as a solid outfielder, playing all three spots . . . Bursitis in arches, compounded by the artificial surface in Seattle's Kingdome, led to move to first base with the Mariners . . . Born Nov. 12, 1950, in Pasadena, Cal. . . . Was starting forward in basketball as well as a star on the baseball team at Santa Clara University, from where he graduated with degree in commerce . . . One of best breaking-ball hitters in the big leagues.

Year	Club	Pos.	G	AB	R	H	2B	3B	HR	RBI	SB	Avg.
1974	California	OF-1B	57	196	24	53	4	1	5	26	6	.270
1975	California	1B	107	375	41	107	19	3	3	48	3	.285
1976	California	OF-1B	146	466	53	120	17	1	2	49	4	.258
1977	Cal.-Cle	OF-1B	137	492	64	148	23	1	7	51	6	.301
1978	Seattle	OF-1B	140	486	58	128	25	3	11	51	3	.263
1979	Seattle	1B	150	554	81	175	38	6	16	100	2	.316
1980	Seattle	1B	148	520	62	156	34	4	13	78	2	.300
1981	Seattle	1B-OF	99	335	39	87	16	0	6	30	1	.260
1982	Seattle	1B-OF	144	509	58	151	21	0	12	70	8	.297
1983					DID NOT PLAY							
	Totals		1128	3933	480	1125	197	19	75	503	35	.286

TOP PROSPECTS

MIKE WARREN 23 6-1 175 **Bats R Throws R**

No-hit Chicago White Sox Sept. 29, becoming first rookie to throw no-hitter in the majors since Texas' Jim Bibby turned trick against Oakland in 1973 . . . Won his last four starts for A's, the longest winning streak of any A's pitcher last season . . . Earned September look after going 12-5 while splitting summer between Albany (AA) and Tacoma (AAA) . . . Born March 26, 1961, in Inglewood, Cal. . . . So young looking that, before he received his driver's license, he used Oakland media guide with his picture to gain entrance to bar in team's hotel at Kansas City.

DONNIE HILL 23 5-10 160 **Bats S Throws R**

A's No. 1 pick in secondary phase of June 1981 draft quickly progressed and earned shot at majors by middle of 1983 . . . Hit .266 as A's regular shortstop . . . Was hitting .314 with 14 homers and 63 RBI in 322 at-bats at Tacoma (AAA) at the time he was called up . . . Good range and arm . . . Born Nov. 12, 1960, in Pomona, Cal. . . . Signed after junior year at Arizona State, where he helped lead Sun Devils to College World Series title.

MANAGER STEVE BOROS: Had to pick up the pieces . . . Inherited arm-weary pitching staff after replacing Billy Martin as A's manager following 1982 season . . . Led A's to 74-88 record, representing improvement of six games over 1982 mark . . . Has been involved in professional baseball since 1957 . . . Managed six years in the minors in Kansas City (1970-74) and Montreal (1980) organizations . . . His 1974 club at San Jose set modern-day record with 342 stolen bases . . . Coached for Kansas City (1975-79) and Montreal (1981-82) . . . Managed Arecibo in Puerto Rican Winter League in 1973 and 1974 and returned for third tour in winter after 1982 season before getting Oakland job . . . Considered excellent teacher . . . Primarily a third baseman during 13-year pro playing career, which included stops with Detroit, the Chicago Cubs and Cincinnati . . . Compiled .245 average in 422 major-league games . . . Spent short period in A's system at Vancouver in 1968, where he teamed with fellow major-league managers Tony LaRussa and Rene Lachemann . . . Earned a degree in literature at Michigan . . . Born Sept. 3, 1936, in Flint, Mich.

GREATEST STEALER

Think of the A's and you think of base-stealers. You think of Ty Cobb finishing his career with the Philadelphia A's, or Eddie Collins stealing six bases in a game for that club in 1912, or Campy Campaneris surpassing the 50 stolen-base level five times for Kansas City and Oakland.

But don't waste too much time thinking about those gentlemen, because the focus of most of your thoughts should be Rickey Henderson. He has led the A's in stolen bases in each of the five full seasons he has been in the majors and has become the only player in history to steal more than 100 bases in a season three times. His major-league total is 427 and counting.

In 1982, he shattered all major-league stolen-base records by swiping 130 bases. He tied a major-league record in 1983 with seven thefts in back-to-back games. He became only the fourth player in professional baseball history to steal seven bases in a game, for Fresno in 1977. And he's getting better, working with Davey Lopes on how to read pitchers and get a better jump.

ALL-TIME A's SEASON RECORDS

BATTING: Napoleon Lajoie, .422, 1901
HRs: Jimmie Foxx, 58, 1932
RBIs: Jimmie Foxx, 169, 1932
STEALS: Rickey Henderson, 130, 1982
WINS: John Coombs, 31, 1910
Lefty Grove, 31, 1931
STRIKEOUTS: Rube Waddell, 349, 1904

SEATTLE MARINERS

TEAM DIRECTORY: Owner: George Argyros; Pres.-Chief Oper. Off.: Chuck Armstrong; VP-Baseball Oper./GM: Hal Keller; Dir. Play. Dev.: Jeff Scott; Dir. Publ.: Bob Porter; Trav. Sec.: Lee Pelekoudas; Mgr.: Del Crandall. Home: Kingdome (59,438). Field distances: 316, l.f. line; 357, l.c.; 410, c.f.; 357, r.c.; 316, r.f. line. Spring training: Tempe, Ariz.

SCOUTING REPORT

HITTING: The Mariners didn't just finish last in the AL in hitting, they ran away with the distinction, compiling a .240 team average, 15 points less than 13th-place Texas. They also tied Texas for most times shut out (15), and averaged a major-league-low 3.4 runs per game. Pat Putnam, who led the team in home runs (19) and RBI (67), doesn't appear to be in the club's plans for 1984. You figure it out.

Pat Putnam located his misplaced stroke in Seattle.

The Mariners did add a couple of legitimate offensive threats to incumbents Dave Henderson (17 homers, 55 RBI) and Steve Henderson (.292), whom they planned to re-sign as a free agent. But will the winter addition of two-time AL home-run champion Gorman Thomas (22 homers, 69 RBI) from Cleveland and consistent Barry Bonnell (.318) from Toronto compensate for the lack of experience in the Seattle infield? Ken Phelps (.236 in 50 games), Spike Owen (.196 in 80 games), ex-Indian Jack Perconte and rookies Darnell Coles and Harold Reynolds are unproven commodities.

PITCHING: It *was* a strong point. But then reliever Bill Caudill (back-to-back 26-save seasons) was traded to Oakland for a reserve catcher (Bob Kearney) and sore-armed pitcher (Dave Beard). And then lefty Bryan Clark, who can fill any role on the staff, was sent to Toronto for Bonnell, a back-up outfielder.

All that remains from what was a strong nucleus are established veteran Jim Beattie (10-15) and developing youngsters Mike Moore (6-8) and Matt Young (11-15) in the starting rotation, and crafty lefty Ed Vande Berg (5 saves) in the pen. Vande Berg got so worried about a sophomore jinx that he pitched scared in 1983. If he doesn't relax and regain his form, the best the Mariners will have to offer out of the bullpen will be journeymen Mike Stanton (7 saves) and Roy Thomas. Rookie Edwin Nunez has the arm to be a reliever, but his personality makes him a big question.

FIELDING: As a shortstop, Coles was a nightmare for his minor-league managers. But after he came up in September, he was moved to third base and adapted well. He's got a strong arm, good range and a bat that will make up for any fielding problems.

Kearney, the catcher who came from Oakland for Caudill, does have a strong arm, but has lapses in calling a game—a fatal flaw when handling such a young staff. The rest of the group is as average as the Mariners' .978 fielding percentage (10th in the league) would indicate.

OUTLOOK: Every year the Mariners come up with a new plan, but they usually wind up with the same old result—the worst record in the AL (last year it was 60-102). Now they've decided to give up their pitching-first approach and find some offense. They hope they found it in Thomas, whose 1983 season makes him a gamble, and Bonnell, who hasn't been a fulltime starter since 1980.

To get them, they gutted their bullpen. That could lead to another disappointing season.

SEATTLE MARINERS 1984 ROSTER

MANAGER Del Crandall
Coaches—Chuck Cottier, Frank Funk, Ben Hines, Phil Roof

PITCHERS

No.	Name	1983 Club	W-L	IP	SO	ERA	B-T	Ht.	Wt.	Born
36	Beard, Dave	Oakland	5-5	61	40	5.61	L-R	6-5	215	10/2/59 Atlanta, GA
		Modesto	0-0	1	2	0.00				
45	Beattie, Jim	Seattle	10-15	197	132	3.84	R-R	6-6	220	7/4/54 Hampton, VA
39	Best, Karl	Seattle	0-1	5	3	13.50	R-R	6-4	190	3/6/59 Aberdeen, WA
		Salt Lake	7-4	84	108	4.82				
41	Johnson, Mike	Bakersfield	2-7	67	97	2.54	R-R	6-0	190	12/30/60 Minneapolis, MN
43	Langston, Mark	Chattanooga	14-9	198	142	3.59	R-L	6-2	177	8/20/60 San Diego, CA
25	Moore, Mike	Salt Lake	4-4	82	80	3.61	R-R	6-4	205	11/26/59 Eakly, OK
		Seattle	6-8	128	108	4.71				
24	Nelson, Gene	Salt Lake	9-4	99	74	5.18	R-R	6-0	175	12/3/60 Tampa, FL
		Seattle	0-3	32	11	7.88				
30	Nunez, Edwin	Salt Lake	4-4	77	52	7.10	R-R	6-5	235	5/27/63 Puerto Rico
		Seattle	0-4	37	35	4.38				
46	Stanton, Mike	Seattle	2-3	65	47	3.32	R-R	6-2	200	9/25/52 St. Louis, MO
34	Stoddard, Bob	Seattle	9-17	176	87	4.41	R-R	6-1	200	3/8/57 San Jose, CA
49	Thomas, Roy	Seattle	3-1	89	77	3.54	R-R	6-6	200	6/22/53 Quantico, VA
32	Vande Berg, Ed	Seattle	2-4	64	49	3.36	R-L	6-2	175	10/25/58 Redlands, CA
40	Young, Matt	Seattle	11-15	204	130	3.27	L-L	6-3	205	8/9/58 Pasadena, CA

CATCHERS

No.	Name	1983 Club	H	HR	RBI	Pct.	B-T	Ht.	Wt.	Born
11	Kearney, Bob	Oakland	76	8	32	.255	R-R	6-0	180	10/3/56 San Antonio, TX
2	Mercado, Orlando	Seattle	35	1	16	.197	R-R	6-0	180	11/7/61 Puerto Rico
		Salt Lake	20	2	12	.227				
8	Sweet, Rick	Seattle	55	1	22	.221	B-R	6-0	190	9/7/52 Longview, WA

INFIELDERS

No.	Name	1983 Club	H	HR	RBI	Pct.	B-T	Ht.	Wt.	Born
12	Castillo, Manny	Seattle	42	0	24	.207	B-R	5-9	180	4/1/57 Dominican Republic
9	Coles, Darnell	Chattanooga	75	5	24	.283	R-R	6-1	170	6/22/62 San Bernadino, CA
		Salt Lake	74	10	41	.316				
		Seattle	26	1	6	.283				
31	Nixon, Donell	Bakersfield	174	4	51	.321	R-R	6-1	185	12/31/61 Evergreen, NC
7	Owen, Spike	Salt Lake	68	1	32	.266	B-R	5-9	165	4/19/61 Cleburne, TX
		Seattle	60	2	21	.196				
—	Perconte, Jack	Charleston	118	4	45	.346	L-R	5-10	160	8/31/54 Joliet, IL
		Cleveland	7	0	0	.269				
44	Phelps, Ken	Salt Lake	92	24	82	.341	L-L	6-1	205	8/6/54 Seattle, WA
		Seattle	30	7	16	.236				
19	Presley, Jim	Chattanooga	122	14	90	.265	R-R	6-1	180	10/23/61 Pensacola, FL
23	Putnam, Pat	Seattle	126	19	67	.269	L-R	6-1	214	12/3/53 Bethel, VT
3	Ramos, Domingo	Seattle	36	2	10	.283	R-R	5-10	155	3/29/58 Dominican Republic
18	Reynolds, Harold	Salt Lake	165	1	72	.309	B-R	5-11	165	11/26/60 Eugene, OR
		Seattle	12	0	1	.203				
38	Tartabull, Danny	Chattanooga	145	13	66	.301	R-R	6-1	185	10/30/62 Cuba

OUTFIELDERS

No.	Name	1983 Club	H	HR	RBI	Pct.	B-T	Ht.	Wt.	Born
—	Bonnell, Barry	Toronto	120	10	54	.318	R-R	6-3	205	10/27/53 Milford, OH
29	Bradley, Phil	Salt Lake	148	2	41	.323	R-R	6-0	175	3/11/59 Bloomington, IN
		Seattle	18	0	5	.269				
13	Calderon, Ivan	Chattanooga	170	11	80	.311	R-R	5-11	160	3/19/62 Puerto Rico
47	Chambers, Al	Salt Lake	115	12	76	.330	L-L	6-4	217	3/24/61 Harrisburg, PA
		Seattle	14	1	7	.209				
16	Cowens, Al	Seattle	73	7	35	.205	R-R	6-2	200	10/25/51 Los Angeles, CA
42	Henderson, Dave	Seattle	130	17	55	.269	R-R	6-2	210	7/21/58 Dos Palos, CA
28	*Henderson, Steve	Seattle	128	10	54	.294	R-R	6-1	187	11/18/52 Houston, TX
26	Moses, John	Salt Lake	17	0	10	.262	B-L	5-9	165	8/9/57 Los Angeles, CA
		Seattle	27	0	6	.208				
10	Nelson, Rickey	Salt Lake	34	5	27	.333	L-R	6-0	200	5/8/59 Eloy, AZ
		Seattle	74	5	36	.254				
21	Roenicke, Ron	Los Angeles	32	2	12	.221	L-R	6-0	180	8/19/56 Covina, CA
		Seattle	50	4	23	.253				
20	Thomas, Gorman	Mil.-Cle.	112	22	69	.209	R-R	6-3	200	12/12/50 Charleston, SC
22	Zisk, Richie	Seattle	69	12	36	.242	R-R	6-2	220	2/6/49 Brooklyn, NY

*Free agent unsigned at press time

MARINER PROFILES

PAT PUTNAM 30 6-1 214 **Bats L Throws R**

Resurrected from left-handed hitter's graveyard in Texas . . . Collected 49 RBI to earn Mariner MVP honors and fulltime job . . . Regained ability to hit line drives to the gaps . . . Set career highs in homers and RBI and posted second-highest batting average of career last season . . . Has played some games at third and in outfield, but is really a first baseman . . . Has worked hard to improve defensive play . . . Born Dec. 3, 1953, in Bethel, Vt. . . . Rangers' first-round pick in secondary phase of June 1975 draft . . . Minor League Player of the Year in 1976, when he hit .361 and led Western Carolinas League in hits (194), home runs (24) and RBI (142) for Asheville (A).

Year	Club	Pos.	G	AB	R	H	2B	3B	HR	RBI	SB	Avg.
1977	Texas	1B	11	26	3	8	4	0	0	3	0	.308
1978	Texas	1B	20	46	4	7	1	0	1	2	0	.152
1979	Texas	1B	139	426	57	118	19	2	18	64	1	.277
1980	Texas	1B-3B	147	410	42	108	16	2	13	55	0	.263
1981	Texas	1B-OF	95	297	33	79	17	2	8	36	4	.266
1982	Texas	1B-OF	43	122	14	28	8	0	2	9	0	.230
1983	Seattle	1B-OF	144	469	58	126	23	2	19	67	2	.269
	Totals		599	1796	211	474	88	8	61	235	7	.264

MATT YOUNG 25 6-3 205 **Bats L Throws L**

Set club record for wins by a rookie with 11, but could have posted better numbers . . . Ranked seventh in AL in ERA (3.27), setting Mariner record for a starter . . . Got off to a 7-3 start, capped by five-game winning streak . . . Final victory in that stretch was a two-hitter against Yankees . . . Missed one start with a back problem . . . Was knocked out of two games by line drives . . . Boston's Jeff Newman hit him in back of left shoulder with blast May 8 and California's Steve Lubratich hit liner into pitcher's face Aug. 5 . . . Spent following afternoon showing replays of latter liner to teammates in clubhouse . . . Born Aug. 9, 1958, in Pasadena, Cal. . . . Mariners' second-round pick out of UCLA in June 1980 draft, he had been chosen as an outfielder out of high school by Boston Red Sox.

Year	Club	G	IP	W	L	Pct.	SO	BB	H	ERA
1983	Seattle	33	204	11	15	.423	130	79	178	3.27

ED VANDE BERG 25 6-2 175 **Bats R Throws L**

Ranked second in AL in appearances with 68, after setting major-league rookie record with 78 in 1982... Longest stint of career was four-inning scoreless effort against Milwaukee May 22... Used mainly to get left-handed hitters out... Has had fewer innings pitched than appearances... Struggled early in 1983, because he was concerned about sophomore jinx after being selected AL Rookie Pitcher of the Year in 1982... Set Northwest League record with 9-0 mark for Bellingham (A) in 1980 ... Was converted to reliever by Rene Lachemann, his minor-league manager, in 1981, and made it to big leagues the next year... Born Oct. 25, 1958, in Redlands, Cal.... A 13th-round, June 1980 draft choice out of Arizona State, where career was slowed by injuries and personality clash with coach Jim Brock.

Year	Club	G	IP	W	L	Pct.	SO	BB	H	ERA
1982	Seattle	78	76	9	4	.692	60	32	54	2.37
1983	Seattle	68	69	2	4	.333	49	22	59	3.36
	Totals	146	140	11	8	.579	109	54	113	2.83

DAVE BEARD 24 6-5 190 **Bats L Throws R**

Acquired in winter deal that sent Bill Caudill to Oakland... When he was good, he was very good... Wasn't good enough of the time, however... Had three saves and two wins in his first five games... During 11-game stretch from late July to late August, he did not give up a run in 18⅔ innings, winning three games and saving five... Had only two other saves and no wins during other parts of season... Still led A's in saves for second year in a row... Control was big problem... Walked almost as many batters (36) as he struck out (40), after having walked 35 and fanned 73 in 1982... Relieved only once in pro career before joining A's in 1980... Only two of his 118 major-league appearances have been as a starter... ERA was a full run higher than previous worst in pro career, a 4.56 mark at Medicine Hat in rookie ball in 1977... Signed with A's as sixth-round draft pick in June 1977... Born Oct. 2, 1959, in Atlanta.

Year	Club	G	IP	W	L	Pct.	SO	BB	H	ERA
1980	Oakland	13	16	0	1	.000	12	7	12	3.38
1981	Oakland	8	13	1	1	.500	15	4	9	2.77
1982	Oakland	54	92	10	9	.526	73	35	85	3.44
1983	Oakland	43	61	5	5	.500	40	36	55	5.61
	Totals	118	182	16	16	.500	140	82	161	4.10

MIKE MOORE 24 6-4 205 Bats R Throws R

Got off to 0-3 start and was sent back to Salt Lake City before first month ended . . . Returned June 27 and stuck, going 6-5 the rest of the way . . . Snapped personal seven-game losing streak that dated back to 1982 with five-hit, nine-strikeout, 1-0 victory against Detroit . . . Also two-hit Milwaukee in August . . . Has outstanding fastball and maintains 90-plus velocity into ninth inning . . . No. 1 draft choice in nation in June 1981, off campus of Oral Roberts, and was in majors the following spring . . . Drafted out of high school as a catcher by St. Louis . . . Born Nov. 26, 1959, in Eakly, Okla., 13 miles west of Binger, the hometown of Johnny Bench . . . Worked with former big-league pitcher and coach Jim Brewer at Oral Roberts . . . Has great changeup, but won't throw it often enough.

Year	Club	G	IP	W	L	Pct.	SO	BB	H	ERA
1982	Seattle	28	144	7	14	.333	73	79	159	5.36
1983	Seattle	22	128	6	8	.429	108	60	130	4.71
	Totals	50	272	13	22	.371	181	139	289	5.06

STEVE HENDERSON 31 6-1 188 Bast R Throws R

Another reclamation project that paid dividends . . . Coming off worst season of his career with Chicago Cubs in 1982, he led Mariners in hitting with .294 mark after being obtained for pitcher Rich Bordi . . . Opened season as leadoff hitter, but when Del Crandall became manager, he was moved to bench for 10 days and then to lower spot in lineup . . . Excellent artificial-turf hitter . . . Suffered injury to right knee Sept. 17 that ended season, but did not require surgery . . . Originally signed by Cincinnati . . . Has been traded for Tom Seaver (from Reds to Mets in June 1977) and Dave Kingman (from Mets to Cubs before 1981 season) . . . Never has been able to show power that baseball executives demand from an outfielder, but has hit .290 or better in five of his seven big-league seasons . . . Left fielder improved his throwing by working with coach Vada Pinson on getting rid of ball faster . . . Born Nov. 18, 1952, in Houston.

Year	Club	Pos.	G	AB	R	H	2B	3B	HR	RBI	SB	Avg.
1977	New York (NL)	OF	99	350	67	104	16	6	12	65	6	.297
1978	New York (NL)	OF	157	587	83	156	30	9	10	65	13	.266
1979	New York (NL)	OF	98	350	42	107	16	8	5	39	13	.306
1980	New York (NL)	OF	143	513	75	149	17	8	8	58	23	.290
1981	Chicago (NL)	OF	82	287	32	84	9	5	5	35	5	.293
1982	Chicago (NL)	OF	92	257	23	60	12	4	2	29	6	.233
1983	Seattle	OF	121	436	50	128	32	3	10	54	10	.294
	Totals		792	2780	372	788	132	43	52	345	76	.283

JIM BEATTIE 29 6-6 220 **Bats R Throws R**

Scratched from first Opening Day assignment of career because of tendinitis . . . Came back strong to establish personal highs in victories and innings pitched . . . Set Mariner record for low-hit game with one-hitter against Kansas City Sept. 27 in which he did not walk a batter . . . Lost seven in a row and nine of 11, with the only two wins coming against the Royals . . . Combined with Ken Clay to two-hit KC for Yankees in opening game of 1977 AL playoffs . . . Injuries have curtailed each season of his career . . . Born July 4, 1954, in Hampton, Va. . . . Played baseball and basketball at Dartmouth while earning degree in art . . . Hobbies include painting, hiking and squash . . . Wife Martha is one of top crew coaches in the country.

Year	Club	G	IP	W	L	Pct.	SO	BB	H	ERA
1978	New York (AL)	25	128	6	9	.400	65	51	123	3.73
1979	New York (AL)	15	76	3	6	.333	32	41	85	5.21
1980	Seattle	33	187	5	15	.250	67	98	205	4.86
1981	Seattle	13	67	3	2	.600	36	18	59	2.96
1982	Seattle	28	172	8	12	.400	140	65	149	3.34
1983	Seattle	30	197	10	15	.400	132	66	197	3.84
	Totals	144	827	35	59	.372	472	339	818	4.00

DAVE HENDERSON 25 6-2 210 **Bats R Throws R**

Continued to mature at plate . . . Still has to learn to resist reaching for breaking balls down and away . . . For third year in a row, he improved power stats . . . Considered a good center fielder, he found himself in right after late June arrival of manager Del Crandall . . . Original No. 1 draft choice of Mariner organization in June 1977 . . . Was highly recruited out of high school as a football player . . . Mariners got first word of him when he visited University of Washington . . . Underwent arthroscopic surgery to repair damaged cartilage in left knee June 27 . . . Has been Mariners' Opening Night center fielder each of the last three seasons . . . Born July 21, 1958, in Dos Palos, Cal. . . . Uncle Joe Henderson pitched for the Chicago White Sox in 1974.

Year	Club	Pos.	G	AB	R	H	2B	3B	HR	RBI	SB	Avg.
1981	Seattle	OF	59	126	17	21	3	0	6	13	2	.167
1982	Seattle	OF	104	324	47	82	17	1	14	48	2	.253
1983	Seattle	OF	137	484	50	130	24	5	17	55	9	.269
	Totals		300	934	114	233	44	6	37	116	13	.249

GORMAN THOMAS 33 6-3 200 Bats R Throws R

Curiously, he was Brewer franchise's original draft pick as the No. 1 selection of Seattle Pilots in June 1960 . . . And now he's actually in Seattle, traded by Cleveland along with Jack Perconte for Tony Bernazard at the winter meetings . . . Seventeen of his 22 homers last year came after his arrival in Cleveland following June 6 trade from Milwaukee for Rick Manning . . . Despite stiff shoulder, desert fever and difficult recovery from winter knee surgery, center fielder missed only 10 games last year . . . Was more productive than Manning . . . Hit .221 for Indians, while Manning hit .220 for Brewers . . . Has averaged 33 home runs and 96 RBI the last seven years . . . Led AL in home runs in 1979 and tied Angels' Reggie Jackson for homer title in 1982 . . . Holds Brewer record for career home runs (202) . . . Born Dec. 12, 1950, in Charleston, S.C.

Year	Club	Pos.	G	AB	R	H	2B	3B	HR	RBI	SB	Avg.
1973	Milwaukee	OF-3B	59	155	16	29	7	1	2	11	5	.187
1974	Milwaukee	OF	17	46	10	12	4	0	2	11	4	.261
1975	Milwaukee	OF	121	240	34	43	12	2	10	28	4	.179
1976	Milwaukee	OF-3B	99	227	27	45	9	2	8	36	2	.198
1978	Milwaukee	OF	137	452	70	111	24	1	32	86	3	.246
1979	Milwaukee	OF	156	557	97	136	29	0	45	123	1	.244
1980	Milwaukee	OF	162	628	78	150	26	3	38	105	8	.239
1981	Milwaukee	OF	103	363	54	94	22	0	21	65	4	.259
1982	Milwaukee	OF	158	567	96	139	29	1	39	112	3	.245
1983	Mil.-Cle.	OF	152	535	72	112	23	1	22	69	10	.209
	Totals		1164	3770	554	871	185	11	219	646	44	.231

AL COWENS 32 6-2 200 Bats R Throws R

After filing for free agency following the 1982 season, he was given a three-year, $1.2-million contract—the largest in club history—to return to Seattle . . . Had horrible season and there was no apparent reason . . . Reported to spring training three weeks early, at own expense, to get in shape . . . But batting average dropped 65 points . . . Plagued all season by sore right shoulder . . . Outfielder was on disabled list from July 18-Aug. 21 and was used as DH when he came back . . . Expected to be DH in 1984 . . . Born Oct. 25, 1951, in Los Angeles . . . An 84th-round draft choice of Royals in June 1969 . . . As a Royal in 1977, he finished second to Rod Carew in AL MVP race . . . Suffered broken jaw when hit by pitch from Ed Farmer, May 8, 1979 . . . Set Mariner records with 39 doubles, 67 extra-base hits and 14 outfield assists in 1982.

Year	Club	Pos.	G	AB	R	H	2B	3B	HR	RBI	SB	Avg.
1974	Kansas City	OF-3B	110	269	28	65	7	1	1	25	5	.242
1975	Kansas City	OF	120	328	44	91	13	8	4	42	12	.277
1976	Kansas City	OF	152	581	71	154	23	6	3	59	23	.265
1977	Kansas City	OF	162	606	98	189	32	14	23	112	16	.312
1978	Kansas City	OF-3B	132	485	63	133	24	8	5	63	14	.274
1979	Kansas City	OF	136	516	69	152	18	7	9	73	10	.295
1980	Cal.-Detroit	OF	142	522	69	140	20	3	6	59	6	.268
1981	Detroit	OF	85	253	27	66	11	4	1	18	3	.261
1982	Seattle	OF	146	560	72	151	39	8	20	78	11	.270
1983	Seattle	OF	110	356	39	73	19	2	7	35	10	.205
	Totals		1295	4476	580	1214	206	61	79	564	110	.271

TOP PROSPECTS

PHIL BRADLEY 24 6-0 175 **Bats R Throws R**

Has hit above .300 all three years in minors and has stolen 114 bases . . . Outstanding defensive center fielder . . . Selected in third round of June 1981 draft, after playing football and baseball at Missouri . . . Starting quarterback for four years, earning All-Big Eight honors three times and setting Big Eight total offense record . . . Born March 11, 1959, in Bloomington, Ind. . . . Finished work on degree in personnel management last winter.

DARNELL COLES 21 6-1 170 **Bats R Throws R**

An erratic fielder at shortstop, he might have found a home at third base with Mariners during September . . . Never a question about his bat . . . Mariners' first-round pick in June 1980 . . . Turned down football scholarship to UCLA . . . Born June 22, 1962, in San Bernardino, Cal. . . . Split 1983 between Chattanooga (AA), where he hit .283 and Salt Lake City (AAA), where he hit .316 . . . Finished season by hitting in 11 of last 14 games for Mariners (.283 overall) . . . Went to Arizona Instructional League to continue conversion to third base.

MANAGER DEL CRANDALL: Walked into difficult situation

when he replaced popular Rene Lachemann as manager June 25 of last season . . . Fans, players and media were critical of Lachemann's firing. Crandall earned respect by ignoring complaints . . . Said he appreciated respect Lachemann earned and didn't take reaction personally . . . Had managed Milwaukee Brewers from early in 1972 through 1975, compiling records of 65-91, 74-88, 76-86 and 68-94 . . . Played 16 years in majors as catcher, compiling .254 average with 179 homers ... Appeared in five All-Star Games and two World Series with Milwaukee Braves ... Four-time Gold Glove winner ... Began managerial career in Dodger system in 1969 ... Also managed in minors for Milwaukee Brewers and California ... Served as third-base coach for California in 1977 ... Was in fifth year as manager of Dodgers' top farm in Albuquerque (AAA), when Mariners gave him contract through 1986 ... Has been in baseball since 1948, except for two years in military (1951-52) and one year in private business (1978) ... Born May 5, 1930, in Ontario, Cal.

GREATEST STEALER

When Julio Cruz packed his bags last June 15 after being traded to the Chicago White Sox for Tony Bernazard, he took with him virtually every stolen-base record in Mariner history. He led the Mariners in stolen bases in each of his five full seasons with the club, accounting for 242 of the 596 stolen bases those teams amassed.

He is the only player in the majors to have stolen 40 or more bases in each of the last six years. And he doesn't get caught very often. He has been successful on 80.5 percent of his career attempts, ranking him behind only Kansas City's Willie Wilson on the all-time list.

Cruz so dominated the Mariners in setting stolen-base standards that his Seattle total of 289 is more than four times the second-best mark on the club, the 68 amassed by Ruppert Jones during the team's first three years of existence.

ALL-TIME MARINER SEASON RECORDS

BATTING: Tom Paciorek, .326, 1981
HRs: Willie Horton, 29, 1979
RBIs: Willie Horton, 106, 1979
STEALS: Julio Cruz, 59, 1978
WINS: Mike Parrott, 14, 1979
STRIKEOUTS: Floyd Bannister, 209, 1982

TEXAS RANGERS

TEAM DIRECTORY: Chairman of the Board: Eddie Chiles; Pres.: Mike Stone; VP-GM: Joe Klein; Farm Dir.: Tom Grieve; Media Rel. Dir.: Burt Hawkins; Trav. Sec.: Dan Schimek; Mgr.: Doug Rader. Home: Arlington Stadium (41,284). Field distances: 330, l.f. line; 380 l.c.; 400, c.f.; 380, r.c.; 330, r.f. line. Spring training: Pompano Beach, Fla.

SCOUTING REPORT

HITTING: It doesn't seem the Rangers can ever put together a full season, as a team or individually. Just when Larry Parrish (26 homers, 88 RBI), George Wright (18 homers, 80 RBI) and Billy Sample (44 stolen bases) seem ready to make a mess of AL

When it comes to power, Larry Parrish is The Lone Ranger.

pitching, the heart of the Rangers' offense falls apart. Buddy Bell (14 homers, 66 RBI) is coming off a disappointing year and Dave Hostetler (.220, 11 homers, 46 RBI), the big hitter in the early months of 1982, has been unable to locate his lost power stroke.

The Rangers tried to fill the power void by acquiring Gary Ward (19 homers, 88 RBI) from Minnesota. He has been a power threat the past two seasons, but don't overlook the fact that, after he had his cheek shattered by a Dan Petry pitch in August, Ward went homerless in his final 150 at-bats.

PITCHING: Given a chance to start in Texas, knuckleballer Charlie Hough (15-13) has emerged as a consistent contributor. With Dave Stewart (5-2, 2.14 ERA with Texas), Frank Tanana (7-9) and Danny Darwin (8-13) joining him in the rotation, the Rangers have a solid group, especially if rookie Al Lachowicz can come through. The Rangers shouldn't miss the traded Mike Smithson and Rick Honeycutt.

The bullpen is the question. Manager Doug Rader saw glimpses of talent from Odell Jones (10 saves) and Dave Tobik (9 saves), but they lacked consistency.

The Rangers led the AL in earned-run average (3.31), but they should. Arlington Stadium is a graveyard for hitters, thanks to that strong wind that always blows across the outfield from right to left.

FIELDING: Sure, Bucky Dent had the best fielding percentage (.979) of any regular AL shortstop in 1983. But he also probably had the worst percentage of ground balls reached. Curtis Wilkerson may not be as consistent, but he'll make enough other plays to make the Rangers feel better about their shortstop situation.

Traded catcher Jim Sundberg had hit the skids with Ranger management. The front office was upset that he threw out only 28 percent of potential base-stealers. Well, former Brewer Ned Yost, his successor, threw out 8-of-63 last year and this time he'll have to work with a staff that can't hold runners close.

The outfield is strong and will be stronger with the addition of Ward, which will allow Parrish to move to first base or to the DH spot.

OUTLOOK: The Rangers are still without a bullpen, a solid infield—third baseman Bell is the exception—and a catcher, so they will be hard-pressed to approach their performance in the first half of '83, when they were in first place July 4. Rader may have been down on Sundberg, but his exile to Milwaukee may turn out to be a mistake.

TEXAS RANGERS 1984 ROSTER

MANAGER Doug Rader
Coaches—Rich Donnelly, Glenn Ezell, Merv Rettenmund, Dick Such, Wayne Terwilliger

PITCHERS

No.	Name	1983 Club	W-L	IP	SO	ERA	B-T	Ht.	Wt.	Born
33	Cook, Glen	Burlington	4-2	53	59	4.10	R-R	5-11	180	9/8/59 Buffalo, NY
		Tulsa	4-6	72	70	3.13				
		Oklahoma City	0-1	20	16	4.50				
23	Cruz, Victor	Oklahoma City	4-3	33	35	2.16	R-R	5-9	190	12/24/57 Dom. Republic
		Texas	1-3	25	18	1.44				
44	Darwin, Danny	Texas	8-13	183	92	3.49	R-R	6-2	190	10/25/55 Bonham, TX
32	Guzman, Jose	Burlington	12-8	155	146	2.97	R-R	6-2	160	4/9/63 Puerto Rico
35	Henke, Tom	Oklahoma City	9-6	78	90	3.01	R-R	6-5	215	12/21/57 Kansas City, MO
		Texas	1-0	16	17	3.38				
36	Henry, Dwayne	Sarasota	0-0	9	11	4.00	R-R	6-3	205	2/16/62 Elkton, MD
49	Hough, Charlie	Texas	15-13	252	152	3.18	R-R	6-2	190	1/5/48 Honolulu, HI
21	Jones, Odell	Texas	3-6	67	50	3.09	R-R	6-3	174	1/13/53 Tulare, CA
51	Lachowicz, Al	Oklahoma City	5-3	115	96	2.89	R-R	6-3	198	9/6/60 Pittsburgh, PA
		Texas	0-1	8	8	2.25				
16	Mason, Mike	Oklahoma City	5-5	89	50	4.16	L-L	6-2	205	11/21/58 Faribault, MN
		Texas	0-2	11	9	5.91				
34	Musselman, Ron	Oklahoma City	9-11	137	83	5.39	R-R	6-1	195	11/11/54 Wilmington, NC
24	Schmidt, Dave	Texas	3-3	46	29	3.88	R-R	6-1	185	4/22/57 Niles, MI
31	Stewart, Dave	Los Angeles	5-2	76	54	2.96	R-R	6-2	200	2/19/57 Oakland, CA
		Texas	5-2	59	24	2.14				
28	Tanana, Frank	Texas	7-9	159	108	3.16	L-L	6-3	195	7/3/53 Detroit, MI
41	Tobik, Dave	Oklahoma City	3-0	20	14	3.54	R-R	6-1	190	3/2/53 Euclid, OH
		Texas	2-1	44	30	3.68				
38	Wright, Ricky	Los Angeles	0-0	6	5	2.84	L-L	6-3	175	11/22/58 Paris, TX
		Albuquerque	7-6	83	68	4.86				
		Texas	0-0	2	2	0.00				

CATCHERS

No.	Name	1983 Club	H	HR	RBI	Pct.	B-T	Ht.	Wt.	Born
30	Gonzalez, Otto	Burlington	104	12	58	.267	R-R	6-1	188	10/15/63 Puerto Rico
8	Johnson, Bobby	Texas	37	5	16	.211	R-R	6-3	195	7/31/59 Dallas, TX
43	Scott, Donnie	Oklahoma City	94	4	54	.253	B-R	5-11	185	8/16/61 Dunedin, FL
		Texas	0	0	0	.000				
—	Yost, Ned	Milwaukee	44	6	28	.224	R-R	6-1	185	8/19/55 Eureka, CA

INFIELDERS

No.	Name	1983 Club	H	HR	RBI	Pct.	B-T	Ht.	Wt.	Born
14	Anderson, Jim	Texas	22	0	6	.216	R-R	6-0	180	2/23/57 Los Angeles, CA
25	Bell, Buddy	Texas	171	14	66	.277	R-R	6-2	185	8/27/51 Pittsburgh, PA
7	Dent, Bucky	Texas	99	2	34	.237	R-R	5-11	190	11/25/51 Savannah, GA
12	Hostetler, Dave	Texas	67	11	46	.220	R-R	6-4	215	3/27/56 Pasadena, CA
9	O'Brien, Pete	Texas	124	8	53	.237	L-L	6-1	185	2/9/58 Santa Monica, CA
2	Richardt, Mike	Oklahoma City	31	2	13	.267	R-R	6-0	170	5/24/58 Los Angeles, CA
		Texas	13	1	7	.157				
1	Stein, Bill	Texas	72	2	33	.310	R-R	5-10	170	1/21/47 Battle Creek, MI
3	Tolleson, Wayne	Texas	122	3	20	.260	B-R	5-9	160	11/22/55 Spartanburg, SC
—	*Wagner, Mark	Texas	0	0	0	.000	R-R	6-1	175	3/4/54 Conneaut, OH
19	Wilkerson, Curtis	Oklahoma City	107	3	31	.312	B-R	5-9	158	4/26/61 Petersburg, VA
		Texas	6	0	1	.171				

OUTFIELDERS

No.	Name	1983 Club	H	HR	RBI	Pct.	B-T	Ht.	Wt.	Born
20	Buckley, Kevin	Tulsa	150	32	104	.293	R-R	6-1	200	1/16/59 Quincy, MA
27	Canady, Chuckie	Tulsa	144	25	80	.296	R-R	5-11	190	8/12/59 Onslow, NC
4	Capra, Nick	Oklahoma City	113	13	41	256	R-R	5-8	165	3/8/58 Denver, CO
		Texas	0	0	0	.000				
13	Dunbar, Tommy	Oklahoma City	140	4	65	.281	L-L	6-2	192	11/24/59 Graniteville, SC
		Texas	6	0	3	.250				
15	Parrish, Larry	Texas	151	26	88	.272	R-R	6-3	215	11/10/53 Winter Haven, FL
17	Rivers, Mickey	Texas	88	1	20	.285	L-L	5-10	162	10/20/48 Miami, FL
5	Sample, Billy	Texas	152	12	57	.274	R-R	5-9	175	4/2/55 Roanoke, VA
—	Ward, Gary	Minnesota	173	19	88	.278	R-R	6-2	208	12/6/53 Los Angeles, CA
26	Wright, George	Texas	175	18	80	.276	B-R	5-11	180	12/12/58 Oklahoma City, OK

*Free agent unsigned at press time

RANGER PROFILES

BUDDY BELL 32 6-2 185 **Bats R Throws R**

Slumped at plate . . . Had only four home runs and 24 RBI after All-Star break . . . Back problems seemed to ease and he played more games (156) than he had in four years . . . Obtained from Cleveland for Toby Harrah after 1978 season . . . Considered silent leader of Rangers, but manager Doug Rader wanted him to be more vocal . . . Son of former big-league outfielder Gus Bell has expressed desire to wind up career in native Cincinnati . . . Born Aug. 27, 1951, in Pittsburgh . . . Had 21-game hitting streak in 1980 . . . An 11th-round draft choice of Cincinnati in 1969 as an outfielder . . . Has blossomed into premier defensive third baseman.

Year	Club	Pos.	G	AB	R	H	2B	3B	HR	RBI	SB	Avg.
1972	Cleveland	OF-3B	132	466	49	119	21	1	9	36	5	.255
1973	Cleveland	3B-OF	156	631	86	169	23	7	14	59	7	.268
1974	Cleveland	3B	116	423	51	111	15	1	7	46	1	.262
1975	Cleveland	3B	153	553	66	150	20	4	10	59	6	.271
1976	Cleveland	3B-1B	159	604	75	170	26	2	7	60	3	.281
1977	Cleveland	3B-OF	129	479	64	140	23	4	11	64	1	.292
1978	Cleveland	3B	142	556	71	157	27	8	6	62	1	.282
1979	Texas	3B-SS	162	670	89	200	42	3	18	101	5	.299
1980	Texas	3B-SS	129	490	76	161	24	4	17	83	3	.329
1981	Texas	3B-SS	97	360	44	106	16	1	10	64	3	.294
1982	Texas	3B-SS	148	537	62	159	27	2	13	67	5	.296
1983	Texas	3B-SS	156	618	75	171	35	3	14	66	3	.277
	Totals		1679	6387	808	1813	299	40	136	767	43	.284

LARRY PARRISH 30 6-3 215 **Bats R Throws R**

Became first Ranger to hit more than 25 home runs in a season since Bobby Bonds in 1979 . . . Tied Richie Zisk's club record with 17 game-winning RBI and tied for third in AL in that category . . . Had career-high 88 RBI . . . Enjoyed consistent year at plate, in marked contrast from 1982, when he was hitting .186 with six RBI July 1 and broke out of slump by hitting .365 for a week . . . Came from Montreal in spring of 1982 with Dave Hostetler in Al Oliver deal . . . Had been third baseman with Expos . . . Has made smooth adjustment to right field . . . But Rangers are toying with idea of returning him to third, if Buddy Bell is traded, or moving him to first or DH role . . . Doesn't want to be DH . . . Born Nov. 10, 1953, in Winter Haven, Fla. . . . Was MVP of Florida State League for West Palm Beach in 1973.

Year	Club	Pos.	G	AB	R	H	2B	3B	HR	RBI	SB	Avg.
1974	Montreal	3B	25	69	9	14	5	0	0	4	0	.203
1975	Montreal	3B-2B-SS	145	532	50	146	32	5	10	65	4	.274
1976	Montreal	3B	154	543	65	126	28	5	11	61	2	.232
1977	Montreal	3B	123	402	50	99	19	2	11	46	2	.246
1978	Montreal	3B	144	520	68	144	39	4	15	70	2	.277
1979	Montreal	3B	153	544	83	167	39	2	30	82	5	.307
1980	Montreal	3B	126	452	55	115	27	3	15	72	2	.254
1981	Montreal	3B	97	349	42	85	19	3	8	44	0	.244
1982	Texas	OF-3B	128	440	59	116	15	0	17	62	5	.264
1983	Texas	3B-OF	145	555	76	151	26	4	26	88	0	.272
	Totals		1240	4406	557	1163	259	28	143	594	22	.264

GEORGE WRIGHT 25 5-11 180 — Bats S Throws R

Had best offensive year of his pro career . . . Had never hit higher than .275, driven in more than 65 runs or hit more than 11 home runs in a season, including his minor-league days . . . Had extra-base hits in seven straight games in July, falling two games short of the major-league record held by Babe Ruth . . . Invited to camp by Rangers in spring of 1982, he won roster spot with strong showing and wound up in starting lineup due to injury to Mickey Rivers . . . Wound up platooning at midseason, because of problems from left side of plate, which were alleviated after many hours in the batting cage . . . Began switch-hitting in 1980, his fourth year of pro ball . . . Plays shallowest center field in AL, but virtually nothing hit over his head drops in . . . Born Dec. 12, 1958, in Oklahoma City, Okla. . . . Selected fourth by Rangers in 1977 draft.

Year	Club	Pos.	G	AB	R	H	2B	3B	HR	RBI	SB	Avg.
1982	Texas	OF	150	557	69	147	20	5	11	50	3	.264
1983	Texas	OF	162	634	79	175	28	6	18	80	8	.276
	Totals		312	1191	148	322	48	11	29	130	11	.270

CHARLIE HOUGH 36 6-2 190 — Bats R Throws R

Finished fourth in AL with 3.18 ERA . . . Scratched from Opening Day assignment because of spring knee surgery . . . Pitched club-record 36 consecutive scoreless innings, including three shutouts (two of them against Kansas City) . . . Has won 31 games over last two years . . . Won 16 for 1982 team that won only 64 overall . . . Has been strictly starter last two years after making only 23 starts in first 438 major-league appearances . . . Has completed 27-of-74 starts with Texas . . . Born Jan. 5, 1948, in Honolulu, Hawaii . . . Learned knuckleball from Tommy Lasorda and Goldie Holt in 1969, when he was a Dodger minor leaguer who was coming back from an arm injury . . . Tips from Hoyt Wilhelm helped him refine pitch . . . Only knuckleball pitcher in AL . . . Relies on specialty about 80 percent of time.

Year	Club	G	IP	W	L	Pct.	SO	BB	H	ERA
1970	Los Angeles	8	17	0	0	.000	8	11	18	5.29
1971	Los Angeles	4	4	0	0	.000	4	3	3	4.50
1972	Los Angeles	2	3	0	0	.000	4	2	2	3.00
1973	Los Angeles	37	72	4	2	.667	70	45	52	2.75
1974	Los Angeles	49	96	9	4	.692	63	40	65	3.75
1975	Los Angeles	38	61	3	7	.300	34	34	43	2.95
1976	Los Angeles	77	143	12	8	.600	81	77	102	2.20
1977	Los Angeles	70	127	6	12	.333	105	70	98	3.33
1978	Los Angeles	55	93	5	5	.500	66	48	69	3.29
1979	Los Angeles	42	151	7	5	.583	76	66	152	4.77
1980	Los Angeles	19	32	1	3	.250	25	21	37	5.63
1980	Texas	16	61	2	2	.500	47	37	54	3.98
1981	Texas	21	82	4	1	.800	69	31	61	2.96
1982	Texas	34	228	16	13	.552	128	72	217	3.95
1983	Texas	34	252	15	13	.536	152	95	219	3.18
	Totals	506	1422	84	75	.528	932	652	1192	3.51

BILLY SAMPLE 28 5-9 175 — Bats R Throws R

Finally got a chance to play every day and responded with best year of big-league career . . . After stealing only 30 bases in first four-plus seasons with Rangers, he stole 44 in 1983, the third-highest single-season total in club history . . . Was 7-of-8 in attempts to steal third . . . Born April 2, 1955, in Roanoke, Va. . . . Psychology major at James Madison . . . One of the most articulate players in majors . . . Had a radio talk show during strike of 1981 . . . Plagued by injuries during major-league career until last season . . . Had a 19-game hitting streak in 1981 that covered 115 days due to injuries and the strike . . . Compiled .358 average during three minor-league seasons . . . Outfielder led Gulf Coast League with .382 mark for Sarasota in 1976.

Year	Club	Pos.	G	AB	R	H	2B	3B	HR	RBI	SB	Avg.
1978	Texas	OF	8	15	2	7	2	0	0	3	0	.467
1979	Texas	OF	128	325	60	95	21	2	5	35	8	.292
1980	Texas	OF	99	204	29	53	10	0	4	19	8	.260
1981	Texas	OF	66	230	36	65	16	0	3	25	4	.283
1982	Texas	OF	97	360	56	94	14	2	10	29	10	.261
1983	Texas	OF	147	554	80	152	28	3	12	57	44	.274
	Totals		545	1688	263	466	91	7	34	168	74	.276

Billy Sample's finest season included 44 stolen bases.

DAVE STEWART 27 6-2 200 **Bats R Throws R**

Had made only one start with Los Angeles before being traded to Rangers for Rick Honeycutt Aug. 19 . . . Immediately inserted in rotation, he compiled 5-2 record with 2.14 ERA . . . Pitched first complete game . . . Did not face a team with a winning record, except Chicago . . . Was voted a full share of postseason money by Dodger players for bullpen role he filled in LA before trade . . . Was part of package Dodgers offered for Jim Sundberg prior to last season . . . Has overpowering fastball, but curveball gathered dust while he was in bullpen . . . Originally signed as catcher . . . Was 1-6 in first two years of pro ball with Bellingham of Northwest League (A) . . . Began to blossom in 1977, with 17-4 record and 2.15 ERA at Clinton of Midwest League (AA) . . . Born Feb. 19, 1957, in Oakland.

Year	Club	G	IP	W	L	Pct.	SO	BB	H	ERA
1978	Los Angeles	1	2	0	0	.000	1	0	1	0.00
1981	Los Angeles	32	43	4	3	.571	29	14	40	2.51
1982	Los Angeles	45	146	9	8	.529	80	49	137	3.81
1983	Los Angeles	46	76	5	2	.714	54	33	67	2.96
1983	Texas	8	59	5	2	.714	24	17	50	2.14
	Totals	132	326	23	15	.605	188	113	295	3.12

DAVE TOBIK 31 6-1 190 **Bats R Throws R**

Had five of his nine saves early in season ... Was sent to minors after All-Star break ... Returned in September to make 10 appearances, pitching 17 scoreless innings ... Had four saves in four-game span in September... Developed forkball, which Detroit manager Sparky Anderson said would make him next Bruce Sutter ... But Tigers, unwilling to wait, traded him for outfielder Johnny Grubb in spring of 1983 ... Has only two major-league starts ... Born March 2, 1953, in Euclid, Ohio ... Business administration major at Ohio University ... Tigers' No. 1 pick in secondary phase of 1975 draft.

Year	Club	G	IP	W	L	Pct.	SO	BB	H	ERA
1978	Detroit	5	12	0	0	.000	11	3	12	3.75
1979	Detroit	37	69	3	5	.375	48	25	59	4.30
1980	Detroit	17	61	1	0	1.000	34	21	61	3.98
1981	Detroit	27	60	2	2	.500	32	33	47	2.70
1982	Detroit	51	99	4	9	.308	63	38	86	3.56
1983	Texas	27	44	2	1	.667	31	13	36	3.68
	Totals	164	345	12	17	.414	219	133	301	3.65

FRANK TANANA 30 6-3 195 **Bats L Throws L**

Went to spring training with outside shot of making team ... Finally stuck because of impression he made with excellent attitude ... After pitching 17 scoreless innings out of bullpen, he took Jon Matlack's spot in rotation ... Won three of first four decisions ... At age 25, he had 84-61 major-league record, but arm was shot ... Pitched 14 complete games in a row for California early in 1977 and was never the same after that ... Led AL in strikeouts with 269 in 1976 and led league with 2.54 ERA and seven shutouts in 1977 ... Used to claim if he got one run, he should win ... Has become breaking-ball pitcher, but excellent control still allows him to come inside with fastball at times ... Born July 3, 1953, in Detroit ... Turned down college basketball scholarships to sign with Angels, who made him their No. 1 pick in 1971 ... Sat out first year of pro ball with back injury, but was 24-8 in next two years to make it to majors.

Year	Club	G	IP	W	L	Pct.	SO	BB	H	ERA
1973	California	4	26	2	2	.500	22	8	20	3.12
1974	California	39	269	14	19	.424	180	77	262	3.11
1975	California	34	257	16	9	.640	269	73	211	2.63
1976	California	34	288	19	10	.655	261	73	212	2.44
1977	California	31	241	15	9	.625	205	61	201	2.54
1978	California	33	239	18	12	.600	137	60	239	3.65
1979	California	18	90	7	5	.583	46	25	93	3.90
1980	California	32	204	11	12	.478	113	45	223	4.15
1981	Boston	24	141	4	10	.286	78	43	142	4.02
1982	Texas	30	194	7	18	.280	87	55	199	4.21
1983	Texas	29	159	7	9	.438	108	49	144	3.16
	Totals	308	2108	120	115	.511	1506	569	1946	3.26

GARY WARD 30 6-2 202 **Bats R Throws R**

New Ranger—traded by Twins for pitchers Mike Smithson and John Butcher and a minor leaguer—led AL outfielders last year with 24 assists, most in league since Stan Spence had 29 for 1944 Washington Senators . . . But loss of power made him trade bait during the winter . . . Did not hit a home run after Aug. 12 (150 at-bats) . . . Was hit in face by fastball from Detroit's Dan Petry Aug. 30 and missed five games . . . Returned Sept. 5, wearing plastic guard on helmet, and went 4-for-4 against Texas . . . Was about to be released in June 1982, when he became disciple of Karl Kuehl's positive-thinking approach . . . Closed out that season with 22 home runs and 74 RBI after June 16 . . . Has been successful on 21-of-23 stolen-base attempts over last two years . . . Born Dec. 6, 1953, in Los Angeles . . . Was undrafted out of Compton High School, where he played shortstop and pitched, but signed free-agent contract with Twins in August 1972.

Year	Club	Pos.	G	AB	R	H	2B	3B	HR	RBI	SB	Avg.
1979	Minnesota	DH	10	14	2	4	0	0	0	1	0	.286
1980	Minnesota	OF	13	41	11	19	6	2	1	10	0	.463
1981	Minnesota	OF	85	295	42	78	7	6	3	29	5	.264
1982	Minnesota	OF	152	570	85	165	33	7	28	91	13	.289
1983	Minnesota	OF	157	623	76	173	34	5	19	88	8	.278
	Totals		417	1543	216	439	80	20	51	219	26	.285

TOP PROSPECTS

CURTIS WILKERSON 22 5-8 158 **Bats S Throws R**

Began switch-hitting in 1982 and it began to pay dividends last year . . . Hit .312 for Oklahoma City (AAA) . . . Missed a month with broken ankle that cut stolen-base total to 15 . . . Previous career-high average was .261 in 1982 . . . After September promotion, he played second, third and shortstop . . . Has quick hands, so-so arm . . . Born April 26, 1961, in Petersburg, Va. . . . Substitute teacher at alma mater, Dinwiddie High School, during winter.

TOMMY DUNBAR 24 6-2 192 **Bats L Throws L**
Sent to play winter ball and had to show overall improvement if he was going to make big-league team this spring . . . Power dropped off drastically at Oklahoma City (AAA), where he had only four home runs . . . Did hit .281 with 34 doubles and 65 RBI . . . Could take over in right field, despite average arm, if Larry Parrish is moved to another spot . . . Born Nov. 24, 1959, in Graniteville, S.C. . . . Led Middle Georgia College to national junior college title in 1979 and 1980.

MANAGER DOUG RADER: Became club's 12th manager since 1972 season, when he was hired prior to last season . . . Inherited team that lost 98 games in 1982 and had it in first place at All-Star break before severe slump . . . Slide was reversed quickly enough to earn Rangers a 77-85 record and third-place finish, despite no major changes in personnel . . . Played 11 years in majors, the first nine with Houston Astros . . . Won five Gold Gloves at third base . . . With Toronto in 1977, he became only player to ever hit ball in upper deck of left field at Seattle's Kingdome . . . Credited with coining the "Winning Ugly" motto of 1983 AL West-champion Chicago White Sox . . . Managed San Diego's AAA affiliate in Hawaii from 1980-82 after coaching for Padres in 1978 and 1979 . . . Passed over for Padre manager's job in favor of Dick Williams prior to 1982 season . . . Born July 30, 1944, in Chicago.

GREATEST STEALER

In the wind-swept confines of Arlington Stadium, it would be logical to think that stolen bases would be a basic staple of the

Ranger attack. Nothing, however, has ever been logical about this team.

As far as the art of stealing bases is concerned, Davey Nelson, who now teaches White Sox runners how to steal, was the best. But from a numbers standpoint, the edge goes to Bump Wills. Wills set the Ranger single-season record of 52 stolen bases in 1978. And his career total of 161 is No. 1 in club history, ranking him ahead of Toby Harrah (130) and Nelson (125).

But all the Ranger pace-setters could be changing soon. With the arrival of Doug Rader as the Ranger manager in the spring of 1983 came a run-and-have-fun approach. It's going to take awhile before Rader has the type of players he wants, but once he finds them, some theft tradition will be built.

ALL-TIME RANGER SEASON RECORDS

BATTING: Mickey Rivers, .333, 1980
HRs: Jeff Burroughs, 30, 1973
RBIs: Jeff Burroughs, 118, 1974
STEALS: Bump Wills, 52, 1978
WINS: Ferguson Jenkins, 25, 1974
STRIKEOUTS: Gaylord Perry, 233, 1975

INSIDE THE
NATIONAL LEAGUE

By NICK PETERS
Oakland Tribune

	East	*West*
PREDICTED ORDER OF FINISH	Montreal Expos	Los Angeles Dodgers
	Pittsburgh Pirates	Atlanta Braves
	Philadelphia Phillies	Houston Astros
	St. Louis Cardinals	San Diego Padres
	Chicago Cubs	Cincinnati Reds
	New York Mets	San Francisco Giants

Playoff winner: Montreal

EAST DIVISION	Owner		Morning Line Manager
1 EXPOS Running out of time	Charles Bronfman; Scarlet, white & royal blue	1983 W 82 L 80	3-2 Bill Virdon
2 PIRATES A frisky challenger	John Galbreath; Old gold, white & black	1983 W 84 L 78	3-1 Chuck Tanner
3 PHILLIES Miracle finishes exhausted	Bill Giles; Crimson & white	1983 W 90 L 72	5-1 Paul Owens
4 CARDINALS From stud to dud	August A. Busch; Red & white	1983 W 79 L 83	15-1 Whitey Herzog
5 CUBS New jockey might help	Tribune Co./Jim Finks; Royal blue & white	1983 W 71 L 91	50-1 Jim Frey
6 METS Breaking into a trot	N. Doubleday/F. Wilpon; Orange, white & blue	1983 W 68 L 94	100-2 Davey Johnson

EXPOS anxious to erase choke label and have a last chance to do it in two-horse race with frisky **PIRATES**. Lack of savvy and continued confusion take steam out of **PHILLIES**. Speedy **CARDINALS** still wondering why they limped so much last year. **CUBS** closing gap with new jockey, but gimpy **METS** are the only horse they're sure to beat.

Northern Lights Handicap

108th Running. National League Race. Distance: 162 games plus playoff. Payoff (based on '83): $44,000 per losing player, World Series, up to $65,000 per winning player, World Series. A field of 12 entered in two divisions.

Track Record: 116 wins—Chicago, 1906

WEST DIVISION	Owner		Morning Line Manager
1 **DODGERS** Best breeding	Peter O'Malley Royal bluo & white	1983 W 91 L 71	3-2 Tommy Lasorda
2 **BRAVES** Pulls up short	Ted Turner Royal blue & white	1983 W 88 L 74	2-1 Joe Torre
3 **ASTROS** A slow starter	John McMullen Orange & white	1983 W 85 L 77	10-1 Bob Lillis
4 **PADRES** Good and getting better	Ray Kroc Brown, gold & white	1983 W 81 L 81	20-1 Dick Williams
5 **REDS** Difficulty finding the gate	J.R. and W.J. Williams Red & white	1983 W 74 L 88	50-1 Vern Rapp
6 **GIANTS** Ready for pasture	Bob Lurie White, orange & black	1983 W 79 L 83	75-1 Frank Robinson

They're not as formidable as in the past, but **DODGERS** keep coming through because no other horse is as talented, but **BRAVES** will stay on their tail, hoping for a slip. **ASTROS**, the big surprise of 1983 derby, need a break to go all the way, but they're not far behind. **PADRES** do a lot of snorting before fading at finish. **REDS** start feeling their oats and pass **GIANTS**, who have lost their zip.

CHICAGO CUBS

TEAM DIRECTORY: Pres./Chief Exec. Off.: Jim Finks; Exec. VP-GM: Dallas Green; Dir. Minor Leagues/Scouting: Gordon Goldsberry; VP-Adm.: E. R. Saltwell; VP-Fin.: Mark McGuire; VP-Oper.: Terry Barthelmas; Dir. Pub. Rel.: Bob Ibach; Trav. Sec.: John Cox; Mgr.: Jim Frey. Home: Wrigley Field (37,242). Field distances: 355, l.f. line; 400, c.f.; 353, r.f. line. Spring training: Mesa, Ariz.

SCOUTING REPORT

HITTING: The Cubs' attack is good and getting better after the team had ranked last in the league in offense only two years ago. Bill Buckner, prominently mentioned in winter trade talks, slumped last year (.280) along with injured Leon Durham (.258), but the club more than compensated thanks to Keith Moreland, Jody Davis and Ron Cey. In fact, Chicago was No. 1 in the NL in slugging percentage (.401), second in runs scored (701) and third in home runs (140).

Moreland, getting a chance to play regularly, responded with a .302 average; Davis contributed 24 home runs, and Cey, despite adjustment problems at Wrigley Field, finished with 24 homers and 90 RBI. Ryne Sandberg is capable of hitting much higher than .261 and Mel Hall (.283, 17 homers, 56 RBI) showed flashes of brilliance as a rookie. He's on the verge of superstardom, along with Durham. The Cubs are so confident in their attack they swapped promising slugger Carmelo Martinez to San Diego in the deal that brought them Scott Sanderson.

PITCHING: There are more numbers with the addition of injury-prone former Expo Sanderson (6-7, 4.65 ERA) to the rotation, but quality is questionable. Fortunately, new manager Jim Frey can call on Lee Smith, who emerged as the league's best bullpen stopper (1.65 ERA, 29 saves) last year; Bill Campbell, who appeared in the most games (82); and Warren Brusstar, who was a welcome addition to a stout group of relievers.

Sanderson's presence and the availability of Dick Ruthven (13-12) for a full season should strengthen a rotation headed by Chuck Rainey (14-13), but it remains to be seen how much longer Fergie Jenkins (6-9) can contribute effectively. Any improvement would be a big help for a staff that had the worst ERA (4.08) in the league last year.

Catcher Jody Davis slammed 24 homers and drove in 84 runs.

FIELDING: The Cubs were expected to improve afield last season and they did so in convincing fashion, sharing the top spot in the NL rankings with Pittsburgh at .982. Second baseman Sandberg (.986) and shortstop Larry Bowa (.984) were No. 1 at their positions, quite a feat considering it was Sandberg's first full season at second after a switch to accommodate Cey at third.

Buckner still handles himself well at first base and Cey, though lacking range, is adequate at the hot corner. Moreland is no gazelle in the outfield, but he's worked hard to improve. Hall showed signs of being outstanding in center, but Durham likely will wind up either at first base or on another team. Davis can only improve behind the plate. But the way he hits, who cares?

OUTLOOK: It looks encouraging. The farm system shows signs of life and the new regime has turned the club from laughable to capable, despite some obvious shortcomings. The offense has returned to the respectability of the '60s—and it might be even better if Hall and Durham are in the lineup every day and Cey has a big year at the plate following a slow start in '83. With the hitting and fielding fairly solid, it's up to the pitching staff to help the club climb. The Cubs could go as high as fourth if the Cardinals continue to falter. The bench, though, is weak.

CHICAGO CUBS 1984 ROSTER

MANAGER Jim Frey
Coaches—Ruben Amaro, Billy Connors, John Vukovich, Don Zimmer, Johnny Oates

PITCHERS

No.	Name	1983 Club	W-L	IP	SO	ERA	B-T	Ht.	Wt.	Born
45	Banks, Darryl	Midland	12-11	163	97	5.47	R-R	6-2	205	6/12/60 Reno, NV
42	Bordi, Rich	Iowa	7-2	111	80	4.61	R-R	6-7	220	4/18/59 S. San Francisco, CA
		Chicago (NL)	0-2	25	20	4.97				
41	Brusstar, Warren	Chicago (NL)	3-1	80	46	2.35	R-R	6-3	200	2/2/52 Oakland, CA
39	Campbell, Bill	Chicago (NL)	6-8	122	97	4.49	R-R	6-4	200	8/9/48 Highland Park, MI
51	Chris, Michael	Phoenix	3-12	145	94	5.77	L-L	6-2	175	10/8/57 Santa Monica, CA
		San Francisco	0-0	13	5	8.10				
31	Jenkins, Fergie	Chicago (NL)	6-9	167	96	4.30	R-R	6-5	210	12/13/43 Canada
37	Johnson, Bill	Midland	6-6	64	22	4.81	R-R	6-5	205	10/6/60 Wilmington, DE
		Chicago (NL)	1-0	12	4	4.38				
49	Kyles, Stan	Midland	7-11	155	74	3.82	R-R	6-1	165	2/26/61 Chicago, IL
		Iowa	2-1	25	9	3.24				
48	Noles, Dickie	Quad City	0-1	12	12	5.25	R-R	6-2	190	11/19/56 Charlotte, NC
		Chicago (NL)	5-10	116	59	4.72				
52	Patterson, Reggie	Iowa	10-10	172	114	5.23	L-R	6-4	180	11/7/58 Birmingham, AL
		Chicago (NL)	1-2	19	10	4.82				
36	Proly, Mike	Chicago (NL)	1-5	83	31	3.58	R-R	5-10	185	12/15/50 Jamaica, NY
30	Rainey, Chuck	Chicago (NL)	14-13	191	84	4.48	R-R	5-11	195	7/14/54 San Diego, CA
47	Reuschel, Rick	Quad City	3-4	71	56	2.42	R-R	6-3	230	5/16/49 Quincy, IL
		Chicago (NL)	1-1	21	9	3.92				
44	Ruthven, Dick	Phil.-Chi. (NL)	13-12	183	99	4.38	R-R	6-3	190	3/27/51 Sacramento, CA
—	Sanderson, Scott	Montreal	6-7	81	55	4.65	R-R	6-5	195	7/22/56 Dearborn, MI
43	Schulze, Don	Iowa	11-9	169	103	4.27	R-R	6-3	215	9/27/62 Roselle, IL
		Chicago (NL)	0-1	14	8	7.07				
46	Smith, Lee	Chicago (NL)	4-10	103	91	1.65	R-R	6-6	235	12/4/57 Jamestown, LA
34	Trout, Steve	Chicago (NL)	10-14	180	80	4.65	L-L	6-4	189	7/30/57 Detroit, MI

CATCHERS

No.	Name	1983 Club	H	HR	RBI	Pct.	B-T	Ht.	Wt.	Born
7	Davis, Jody	Chicago (NL)	138	24	84	.271	R-R	6-4	200	11/12/56 Gainesville, GA
15	Diaz, Mike	Iowa	77	15	47	.324	R-R	6-2	195	4/15/60 San Francisco, CA
		Chicago (NL)	2	0	1	.286				
16	Lake, Steve	Chicago (NL)	22	1	7	.259	R-R	6-1	180	3/14/57 Inglewood, CA

INFIELDERS

1	Bowa, Larry	Chicago (NL)	133	2	43	.267	B-R	5-10	155	12/6/45 Sacramento, CA
22	Buckner, Bill	Chicago (NL)	175	16	66	.280	L-L	6-1	185	12/14/49 Vallejo, CA
11	Cey, Ron	Chicago (NL)	160	24	90	.275	R-R	5-10	185	2/15/48 Tacoma, WA
19	Owen, Dave	Iowa	110	6	39	.259	B-R	6-2	170	4/25/58 Cleburne, TX
		Chicago (NL)	2	0	2	.091				
17	Rohn, Dan	Iowa	130	8	56	.315	L-R	5-7	165	1/10/56 Alpena, MI
		Chicago (NL)	12	0	6	.387				
23	Sandberg, Ryne	Chicago (NL)	165	8	48	.261	R-R	6-2	190	9/18/59 Spokane, WA
29	Veryzer, Tom	Chicago (NL)	18	1	3	.205	R-R	6-1	180	2/11/53 Port Jefferson, NY

OUTFIELDERS

33	Carter, Joe	Iowa	160	22	83	.307	R-R	6-3	215	3/7/60 Oklahoma City, OK
		Chicago (NL)	9	0	1	.176				
28	Cotto, Henry	Iowa	111	0	35	.261	R-R	6-2	178	1/5/61 Bronx, NY
10	Durham, Leon	Chicago (NL)	87	12	55	.258	L-L	6-2	210	7/31/57 Cincinnati, OH
27	Hall, Mel	Chicago (NL)	116	17	56	.283	L-L	6-1	185	9/16/60 Lyons, NY
24	Hatcher, Bill	Midland	163	10	80	.299	R-R	5-9	175	10/4/60 Williams, AZ
21	Johnstone, Jay	Chicago (NL)	36	6	22	.257	L-R	6-1	190	11/20/45 Manchester, CT
6	Moreland, Keith	Chicago (NL)	161	16	70	.302	R-R	6-0	200	5/2/54 Dallas, TX
25	Woods, Gary	Chicago (NL)	46	4	22	.242	R-R	6-2	190	7/20/53 Santa Barbara, CA

CUB PROFILES

JODY DAVIS 27 6-4 200 Bats R Throws R

Became the first Cub catcher to surpass 20 home runs since Gabby Hartnett in 1934 . . . Georgia native has been especially tough on the Atlanta Braves, against whom he has hit eight homers in 19 games over two years . . . Hit first grand slam June 12 and finished month with six homers and 26 RBI . . . Enjoyed a .323 September and finished season as most underrated catcher in the league . . . Born Nov. 12, 1956, in Gainesville, Ga. . . . Took over catching duties in 1982, shoving Keith Moreland to the outfield . . . Made remarkable recovery following double surgery in 1980 . . . Lost 50 pounds because of a ruptured blood vessel in his intestine that had been originally diagnosed as an ulcer problem . . . One-time Met property was drafted by the Cubs from the Cardinal system after 1980 season.

Year	Club	Pos.	G	AB	R	H	2B	3B	HR	RBI	SB	Avg.
1981	Chicago (NL)	C	56	180	14	46	5	1	4	21	0	.256
1982	Chicago (NL)	C	130	418	41	109	20	2	12	52	0	.261
1983	Chicago (NL)	C	151	510	56	138	31	2	24	84	0	.271
	Totals		337	1108	111	293	56	5	40	157	0	.264

KEITH MORELAND 29 6-0 200 Bats R Throws R

Still a liability defensively, but found a home in right field with productive bat . . . Enjoyed best big-league season with career highs in doubles, homers and game-winning RBI (team-leading 11) . . . Set tone for season with .311 April and batted .336 in June . . . Poor fielding limited him to parttime status in second half of 1982, but he made good on second chance last year . . . Born May 2, 1954, in Dallas . . . Started for Texas as a sophomore linebacker and defensive back . . . Earned All-American honors for Longhorns as a third baseman, but was converted into catcher by Phillies . . . Exhibited major-league potential with 20 homers, 34 doubles and 109 RBI for Oklahoma City (AAA) in 1979 . . . Obtained from Phillies with pitchers Dickie Noles and Dan Larson for pitcher Mike Krukow prior to 1982.

Year	Club	Pos.	G	AB	R	H	2B	3B	HR	RBI	SB	Avg.
1978	Philadelphia . . .	C	1	2	0	0	0	0	0	0	0	.000
1979	Philadelphia . . .	C	14	48	3	18	3	2	0	8	0	.375
1980	Philadelphia . . .	C-3B-OF	62	159	13	50	8	0	4	29	3	.314
1981	Philadelphia . . .	C-3B-1B-OF	61	196	16	50	7	0	6	37	1	.255
1982	Chicago (NL) . .	C-OF-3B	138	476	50	124	17	2	15	68	0	.261
1983	Chicago (NL) . .	OF	154	533	76	161	30	3	16	70	0	.302
	Totals		429	1414	158	403	65	7	41	212	4	.285

BILL BUCKNER 34 6-1 185 Bats L Throws L

Suffered through one of his least productive seasons, but tied Expos' Al Oliver and Pirates' Johnny Ray for NL lead in doubles . . . Best month was July, when he batted .323 with five homers . . . Had no homers and two RBI in a .306 August, apparently wearing out welcome in midst of club's youth movement . . . First baseman was involved in a celebrated scuffle with manager Lee Elia in 1982, but outlasted him despite annual trade rumors . . . Born Dec. 14, 1949, in Vallejo, Cal. . . . Was NL batting champion in 1980, but probably had best overall season in '82, collecting 201 hits and 105 RBI . . . Leg injury reduced effectiveness and made him expendable to Dodgers, who swapped him and shortstop Ivan DeJesus for outfielder Rick Monday prior to 1977 season . . . Attended USC and Arizona State . . . Brother Jim is outfielder in Met organization.

Year	Club	Pos.	G	AB	R	H	2B	3B	HR	RBI	SB	Avg.
1969	Los Angeles......	PH	1	1	0	0	0	0	0	0	0	.000
1970	Los Angeles......	OF-1B	28	68	6	13	3	1	0	4	0	.191
1971	Los Angeles......	OF-1B	108	358	37	99	15	1	5	41	4	.277
1972	Los Angeles......	OF-1B	105	383	47	122	14	3	5	37	10	.319
1973	Los Angeles......	1B-OF	140	575	68	158	20	0	8	46	12	.275
1974	Los Angeles......	OF-1B	145	580	83	182	30	3	7	58	31	.314
1975	Los Angeles......	OF	92	288	30	70	11	2	6	31	8	.243
1976	Los Angeles......	1B-OF	154	642	76	193	28	4	7	60	28	.301
1977	Chicago (NL).....	1B	122	426	40	121	27	0	11	60	7	.284
1978	Chicago (NL).....	1B	117	446	47	144	26	1	5	74	7	.323
1979	Chicago (NL).....	1B	149	591	72	168	34	7	14	66	9	.284
1980	Chicago (NL).....	1B-OF	145	578	69	187	41	3	10	68	1	.324
1981	Chicago (NL).....	1B	106	421	45	131	35	3	10	75	5	.311
1982	Chicago (NL).....	1B	161	657	93	201	34	5	15	105	15	.306
1983	Chicago (NL).....	1B	153	626	79	175	38	6	16	66	12	.280
	Totals..........		1726	6640	792	1964	356	39	119	791	149	.296

RON CEY 36 5-10 185 Bats R Throws R

Batted almost .300 with 15 homers and 52 RBI in second half after a disappointing first half filled with failures in the clutch . . . By season's end, however, he was up to normal production levels and enjoyed his best RBI year since 1977 . . . "The Penguin" batted .255 in the first half, despite a .321 May . . . Took off with eight homers and 21 RBI in July and knocked in 20 runs in September . . . Born Feb. 15, 1948, in Tacoma, Wash. . . . Tied NL record for fewest errors by a third baseman with nine in 1979, but his limited range makes him sub-par defensively now . . . Set major-league single-month record with 29 RBI in April 1977, triggering best season . . . Missed last four weeks with wrist injury in 1981, but returned to bat .350 for Dodgers in World Series... Obtained for two minor-league prospects as part of Dodgers' youth movement prior to last season.

Year	Club	Pos.	G	AB	R	H	2B	3B	HR	RBI	SB	Avg.
1971	Los Angeles......	PH	2	2	0	0	0	0	0	0	0	.000
1972	Los Angeles......	3B	11	37	3	10	1	0	1	3	0	.270
1973	Los Angeles......	3B	152	507	60	124	18	4	15	80	1	.245
1974	Los Angeles......	3B	159	577	88	151	20	2	18	97	1	.262
1975	Los Angeles......	3B	158	566	72	160	29	2	25	101	5	.283
1976	Los Angeles......	3B	145	502	69	139	18	3	23	80	0	.277
1977	Los Angeles......	3B	153	564	77	136	22	3	30	110	3	.241
1978	Los Angeles......	3B	159	555	84	150	32	0	23	84	2	.270
1979	Los Angeles......	3B	150	487	77	137	20	1	28	81	3	.281
1980	Los Angeles......	3B	157	551	81	140	25	0	28	77	2	.254
1981	Los Angeles......	3B	85	312	42	90	15	2	13	50	0	.288
1982	Los Angeles......	3B	150	556	62	141	23	1	24	79	3	.254
1983	Chicago (NL).....	3B	159	581	73	160	33	1	24	90	0	.275
	Totals..........		1640	5797	788	1538	256	19	252	932	20	.265

RYNE SANDBERG 24 6-1 190 **Bats R Throws R**

Probably the most underrated second baseman in the league... Batted a solid .281 in the first half before tailing off... Topped Cubs in stolen bases, but generally didn't play up to caliber of his outstanding rookie season of 1982 ... Nicknamed "Gabby," because he doesn't have much to say... Scored 103 runs in 1982 to tie Billy Williams' record for Cub rookies... Born Sept. 18, 1959, in Spokane, Wash.... Had solid season at third base as a rookie, but was switched to accommodate Ron Cey... Got off to a 1-for-32 start in 1982 before coming on strong... Batted .293 for Oklahoma City (AAA) in 1981 before promotion to Phillies, who swapped him and Larry Bowa for Ivan DeJesus prior to 1982 season.

Year	Club	Pos.	G	AB	R	H	2B	3B	HR	RBI	SB	Avg.
1981	Philadelphia......	SS-2B	13	6	2	1	0	0	0	0	0	.167
1982	Chicago (NL).....	3B-2B	156	635	103	172	33	5	7	54	32	.271
1983	Chicago (NL).....	2B-SS	158	633	94	165	25	4	8	48	37	.261
	Totals..........		327	1274	199	338	58	9	15	102	69	.265

LEON DURHAM 26 6-2 210 **Bats L Throws L**

Limited to 100 games by injuries, "Bull" saw his production drop off drastically from banner 1982 season... Was on his way to a repeat with six homers, 17 RBI and a .343 average in May, but tailed off... Groomed as possible successor to Bill Buckner at first base... Born July 31, 1957, in Cincinnati... Was key man for Cubs in deal that sent Bruce Sutter to Cards prior to 1981 season... Showed why in 1982, when he became first Cub slugger to surpass 20 homers and 20 steals in same season since Frank Schulte in 1911 . . . American Association Rookie of the Year for Springfield (AAA) in 1979, batting .310 with 23 homers . . . Labeled a can't-miss superstar—if he can stay healthy.

Year	Club	Pos.	G	AB	R	H	2B	3B	HR	RBI	SB	Avg.
1980	St. Louis	OF-1B	96	303	42	82	15	4	8	42	8	.271
1981	Chicago (NL)	OF-1B	87	328	42	95	14	6	10	35	25	.290
1982	Chicago (NL)	OF-1B	148	539	84	168	33	7	22	90	28	.312
1983	Chicago (NL)	OF-1B	100	337	58	87	18	8	12	55	12	.258
	Totals		431	1507	226	432	80	25	52	222	73	.287

MEL HALL 23 6-1 185 Bats L Throws L

Powerful and fleet center fielder enjoyed an outstanding rookie season . . . His totals in homers and RBI were especially impressive considering he played only 112 games because of injuries . . . Hit his stride in August, earning NL Player-of-the-Month distinction with a .333 average and nine of his homers . . . Born Sept. 16, 1960, in Lyons, N.Y. . . . Showed signs of brilliance upon promotion in 1982, hitting in nine straight games . . . Tore up the American Association for Iowa (AAA) that year, batting .329 with 32 homers and 125 RBI . . . Father Mel Sr. was a minor leaguer in 1949 . . . Hobbies include painting, drawing and ice skating.

Year	Club	Pos.	G	AB	R	H	2B	3B	HR	RBI	SB	Avg.
1981	Chicago (NL)	OF	10	11	1	1	0	0	1	2	0	.091
1982	Chicago (NL)	OF	24	80	6	21	3	2	0	4	0	.263
1983	Chicago (NL)	OF	112	410	60	116	23	5	17	56	6	.283
	Totals		146	501	67	138	26	7	18	62	6	.275

CHUCK RAINEY 29 5-11 195 Bats R Throws R

Became staff ace after being acquired in trade with Boston for Doug Bird prior to last season . . . Previous major-league high in victories was eight . . . Especially tough after the All-Star break, going a combined 7-3 in July and August . . . Just missed firing first no-hitter by Cub in 11 years . . . Held Cincinnati hitless for 8⅔ innings Aug. 24, but Eddie Milner foiled the bid with single . . . Born July 14, 1954, in San Diego . . . Was erratic for Red Sox in 1982, posting 5.02 ERA despite three shutouts . . . Boston's first selection in January 1974 draft and didn't reach the bigs until 1979 . . . Developed arm problems one year later.

Year	Club	G	IP	W	L	Pct.	SO	BB	H	ERA
1979	Boston	20	104	8	5	.615	41	41	97	3.81
1980	Boston	16	87	8	3	.727	43	41	92	4.86
1981	Boston	11	40	0	1	.000	20	13	39	2.70
1982	Boston	27	129	7	5	.583	57	63	146	5.02
1983	Chicago (NL)	34	191	14	13	.519	84	74	219	4.48
	Totals	108	551	37	27	.578	245	232	593	4.49

DICK RUTHVEN 33 6-3 190 Bats R Throws R

After struggling with a 1-3 record and a 5.61 ERA for Philadelphia, this veteran right-hander went 12-9 with the Cubs and solidified their rotation following midseason trade for Willie Hernandez... An immediate hit, he went 3-1 with a 2.33 ERA in June... Despite relatively high ERAs, he has been a double-digit winner four straight years... Born March 27, 1951, in Sacramento, Cal.... Hardly a tough-luck pitcher, he was 12-7 despite bulging 5.14 ERA in 1981... Attended Fresno State ... Brother-in-law of former major-leaguer Tommy Hutton ... Won Phillies' playoff clincher in 1980... Won 19 of his first 24 decisions after joining Phillies from Braves in 1978, but elbow problems retarded his progress in 1979.

Year	Club	G	IP	W	L	Pct.	SO	BB	H	ERA
1973	Philadelphia	25	128	6	9	.400	98	75	125	4.22
1974	Philadelphia	35	213	9	13	.409	153	116	182	4.01
1975	Philadelphia	11	41	2	2	.500	26	22	37	4.17
1976	Atlanta	36	240	14	17	.452	142	90	255	4.20
1977	Atlanta	25	151	7	13	.350	84	62	158	4.23
1978	Atlanta-Philadelphia	33	232	15	11	.577	120	56	214	3.38
1979	Philadelphia	20	122	7	5	.583	58	37	121	4.28
1980	Philadelphia	33	223	17	10	.630	86	74	241	3.55
1981	Philadelphia	23	147	12	7	.632	80	54	162	5.14
1982	Philadelphia	33	204	11	11	.500	115	59	189	3.79
1983	Phil-Chi (NL)	32	183	13	12	.520	99	38	202	4.38
	Totals	306	1884	113	110	.507	1061	683	1886	4.06

LEE SMITH 26 6-6 235 Bats R Throws R

Probably the most intimidating reliever in the NL because of his imposing size... Topped league with a career-high 29 saves, 12 more than his previous season high, but received little recognition because of club's lowly finish... Registered 20 saves after July 1 last season ... Turned the corner as a relief ace in late 1982, posting 14 of his 17 saves during August and September... More than compensated for loss of Bruce Sutter... Born Dec. 4, 1957, in Jamestown, La.... Also played basketball in high school, but gained attention as a pitcher by going

15-1 in his last two years . . . Struck out 124 in 53 innings as a senior and was drafted No. 2 by the Cubs in June 1975 . . . Became a reliever in 1980, posting 15 saves for Wichita (AAA) . . . Has never enjoyed a winning season as a fulltime big leaguer, going 9-21 the last three years despite dwindling ERA.

Year	Club	G	IP	W	L	Pct.	SO	BB	H	ERA
1980	Chicago (NL)	18	22	2	0	1.000	17	14	21	2.86
1981	Chicago (NL)	40	67	3	6	.333	50	31	57	3.49
1982	Chicago (NL)	72	117	2	5	.286	99	37	105	2.69
1983	Chicago (NL)	66	103	4	10	.286	91	41	70	1.65
	Totals	196	309	11	21	.344	257	123	253	2.53

TOP PROSPECTS

JOE CARTER 24 6-3 215 **Bats R Throws R**

First baseman Carmelo Martinez was regarded as the No. 1 prospect until he was swapped to San Diego along with fellow American Association all-star Fritz Connally . . . That leaves this fellow, a non-roster player last year who batted .307 with 22 homers and 83 RBI for Iowa (AAA) following a strong season (.319, 25 homers, 98 RBI) for Midland (AA) in '82 . . . Born March 7, 1960, in Oklahoma City . . . Carter was a Triple-A all-star, along with second baseman Dan Rohn (.315) . . . Catcher Mike Diaz batted .324 at Iowa and .286 in six games for Chicago.

MANAGER JIM FREY: Gets well-deserved second chance after

guiding Royals to a 127-105 record before his dismissal midway through the 1981 season . . . Managed Kansas City to the World Series in 1980 . . . Received a bad rap for having pitcher Dave Stieb bat in the 1981 All-Star Game. There were no pinch-hitters available because Fred Lynn went to the clubhouse without telling the skipper . . . Born May 26, 1932, in Cleveland . . . Regarded as a solid teacher, may be just what the youthful Cubs need following Lee Elia's embarrassing stint as manager . . . Former minor-league outfielder who batted .302 in 1,206 games before concluding his playing career in 1963 . . . High-school teammate of Don Zimmer . . . Attended Ohio State . . . Named Texas League MVP in 1957, batting .336 for Tulsa . . . Spent 15 years with the Baltimore organization . . . Became 19th manager in major-league history to reach the World Series in first season . . . As coach with Mets last year, he became tutor and confidant of Darryl Strawberry.

GREATEST STEALER

Playing in a ballpark better suited to home-run hitters than speed-burners, the Cubs really haven't done much on the bases since the days of Tinker-to-Evers-to-Chance. Those three were immortalized in a poem regarding their overrated fielding, but there's no denying they could run.

Frank Chance, in fact, holds the Cub record with 67 thefts in 1903 and his 387 career steals also is a Chicago standard. Joe Tinker is No. 2 on the all-time list with 304, followed by Johnny Evers with 281.

Kiki Cuyler won three straight NL stolen-base titles with the Cubs from 1928-30 with 37, 43 and 37 steals respectively. Augie Galan was the league leader in '35 and '37 and Stan Hack became the last Cub to top the NL, doing so in '38 and '39 with 33 thefts each year.

Benefitting from a lack of competition from players of the modern era, Chance easily rates as the premier base thief in club history.

ALL-TIME CUB SEASON RECORDS

BATTING: Rogers Hornsby, .380, 1929
HRs: Hack Wilson, 56, 1930
RBIs: Hack Wilson, 190, 1930
STEALS: Frank Chance, 67, 1903
WINS: Mordecai Brown, 29, 1908
STRIKEOUTS: Ferguson Jenkins, 274, 1970

MONTREAL EXPOS

TEAM DIRECTORY: Chairman of the Board: Charles Bronfman; Pres.-Chief Exec. Off.: John McHale; VP-Play. Dev./Scouting: Jim Fanning; Group VP: Pierre Gauvreau; VP-Dir. Bus. Oper.: Gerry Trudeau; VP-Dir. Fin.: Dennis Bodin; Dirs. Pub. Rel.: Monique Giroux, Richard Griffin. Trav. Sec.: Peter Durso; Mgr.: Bill Virdon. Home: Olympic Stadium (58,838). Field distances: 325, l.f. line; 375, l.c.; 404, c.f.; 375, r.c.; 325, r.f. line. Spring training: West Palm Beach, Fla.

SCOUTING REPORT

HITTING: Anytime you have Andre Dawson, Tim Raines, Gary Carter and Al Oliver in the lineup, good things can happen. The trouble is, the Expos didn't generate enough offense in '83, suggesting a lack of clutch production. The club was third in batting (.264) and first in doubles (297) and had Dawson (.299, 32 homers, 113 RBI), Oliver (.300) and Raines (.298) among the top 12 in batting, yet was only sixth in runs scored (677).

Carter (17 homers, 79 RBI) took some of the blame in what was regarded as a sub-par season for the all-star catcher, and Tim Wallach (19 homers, 70 RBI) also slipped at the plate. If those two snap back, all the pieces might fit for a club that should do better than two games above .500. There is simply too much potential offense in the lineup for the Expos to be regarded as anything less than a contender.

PITCHING: Good and could be even better with the addition of former San Diego left-handed reliever Gary Lucas (17 saves, 2.87 ERA) to complement Jeff Reardon (21 saves, 3.03 ERA). Steve Rogers, Bill Gullickson and Charlie Lea totaled 50 victories, yet that wasn't good enough to rescue the club from mediocrity last year. Something was missing. Maybe Lucas will fill the void for a club that was 18-23 in one-run games and 5-9 in extra innings.

Rogers, regarded as one of the league's premier pitchers, faltered down the stretch to finish 17-12. Lea, finally healthy for an entire season, fulfilled his promise, going 16-11. The club could use a solid No. 4 starter, and it could be Bryn Smith, whose 2.49 ERA suggests a better pitcher than his 6-11 record indicated.

FIELDING: Montreal's .981 fielding percentage was only a shade behind the leaders' last year, so defense can't be used as an excuse, either. Doug Flynn's .986 was as good as Cub Ryne Sandberg's

North of the border, Andre is known as Awesome Dawson.

league-leading figure at second base; Dawson and Raines ranked among the most sure-handed outfielders and Carter stood alone among catchers with a nifty .995 mark. Age has slowed Oliver at first base and Bryan Little and Chris Speier are merely adequate at shortstop, but defense isn't a major problem for the enigmatic Expos.

OUTLOOK: Who knows? This club seems to have enough horses to go all the way, but something always seems to go wrong. Dick Williams did the best job of getting the most out of this talent, but the players complained he was too tough. Jim Fanning and Bill Virdon have been more mild-mannered in their approach, but the club hasn't responded to looser reins, either, so the prima-donna label attached to some of the superstars may be valid.

There is absolutely no reason for the Expos to be dawdling around .500. Chances are a slow start could cost Virdon his job. The other NL East contenders are in a state of transition, so Montreal has a good chance to reach the top. Any club brimming with superstars and solid pitching should be a big winner. Raines, with 133 runs scored and 90 steals, is a one-man offense; Carter is regarded as the majors' best catcher and Dawson is one of the two best players in the league. You tell me why the Expos haven't won a pennant.

MONTREAL EXPOS 1984 ROSTER

MANAGER Bill Virdon

Coaches—Felipe Alou, Galen Cisco, Billy DeMars, Joe Kerrigan, Russ Nixon

PITCHERS

No.	Name	1983 Club	W-L	IP	SO	ERA	B-T	Ht.	Wt.	Born
39	Bargar, Greg	Memphis	4-4	59	50	3.05	R-R	6-2	185	1/27/59 Inglewood, CA
		Wichita	6-2	73	53	4.66				
		Montreal	2-0	20	9	6.75				
59	Dilks, Darren	Wichita	4-6	99	64	6.27	L-L	6-3	210	6/30/60 Canada
50	Grapenthin, Dick	Montreal	0-1	4	3	9.00	R-R	6-2	205	4/16/58 Linn Grove, IA
		Wichita	5-5	70	33	3.84				
34	Gullickson, Bill	Montreal	17-12	242	120	3.75	R-R	6-3	215	2/20/59 Kankakee, IL
37	Harris, Greg	Indianapolis	9-12	152	146	4.14	B-R	6-0	165	11/2/55 Lynwood, CA
38	Hesketh, Joe	Memphis	6-4	74	22	3.04	L-L	6-2	170	2/15/59 Lackawanna, NY
		Wichita	5-5	88	41	5.09				
42	James, Bob	Detroit	0-0	4	4	11.25	R-R	6-4	230	8/15/58 Glendale, CA
		Wichita	4-2	31	40	4.65				
		Montreal	1-0	50	56	2.88				
53	Lea, Charlie	Montreal	16-11	222	137	3.12	R-R	6-4	190	12/25/56 France
25	Lucas, Gary	San Diego	5-8	91	60	2.87	L-L	6-5	200	11/8/54 Riverside, CA
46	Palmer, David		Injured—Did not play				R-R	6-1	205	10/19/57 Glens Falls, NY
41	Reardon, Jeff	Montreal	7-9	92	78	3.03	R-R	6-1	190	10/1/55 Dalton, MA
45	Rogers, Steve	Montreal	17-12	273	146	3.23	R-R	6-1	177	10/26/49 Jefferson City, MO
51	St. Claire, Randy	West Palm Beach	5-7	98	77	2.11	R-R	6-3	180	8/23/60 Glens Falls, NY
43	*Schatzeder, Dan	Montreal	5-2	87	48	3.21	L-L	6-0	195	12/1/54 Elmhurst, IL
28	Smith, Bryn	Montreal	6-11	155	101	2.49	R-R	6-2	210	8/11/55 Marietta, GA

CATCHERS

No.	Name	1983 Club	H	HR	RBI	Pct.	B-T	Ht.	Wt.	Born
8	Carter, Gary	Montreal	146	17	79	.270	R-R	6-2	210	4/8/54 Culver City, CA
44	Ramos, Bobby	Montreal	14	0	5	.230	R-R	5-10	200	11/5/55 Cuba
31	Shines, Ray	Memphis	111	20	63	.286	B-R	6-1	210	7/18/56 Durham, NC
		Wichita	31	1	11	.277				
		Montreal	1	0	0	.500				
11	Wieghaus, Tom	Wichita	63	3	28	.242	R-R	6-0	195	2/1/57 Chicago Heights, IL

INFIELDERS

No.	Name	1983 Club	H	HR	RBI	Pct.	B-T	Ht.	Wt.	Born
23	Flynn, Doug	Montreal	107	0	26	.237	R-R	5-11	172	4/18/51 Lexington, KY
3	Little, Bryan	Montreal	91	1	36	.260	B-R	5-10	160	10/8/59 Houston, TX
24	Mills, Brad	Montreal	5	0	1	.250	L-R	6-0	190	1/19/57 Lemon Cove, CA
		Wichita	86	8	46	.317				
0	Oliver, Al	Montreal	184	8	84	.300	L-L	6-1	195	10/14/46 Portsmouth, OH
6	Salazar, Angel	Wichita	103	1	54	.302	R-R	6-0	170	11/4/61 Venezuela
		Montreal	8	0	1	.216				
4	Speier, Chris	Montreal	67	2	22	.257	R-R	6-1	180	6/28/50 Alameta, CA
29	Wallach, Tim	Montreal	156	19	70	.269	R-R	6-3	200	9/14/58 Huntington Park, CA

OUTFIELDERS

No.	Name	1983 Club	H	HR	RBI	Pct.	B-T	Ht.	Wt.	Born
10	Dawson, Andre	Montreal	189	32	113	.299	R-R	6-3	180	7/10/54 Miami, FL
16	Francona, Terry	Montreal	59	3	22	.257	L-L	6-1	175	4/22/59 Aberdeen, SD
25	Fuentes, Mike	Wichita	134	30	91	.299	R-R	6-3	190	7/11/58 Miami, FL
		Montreal	1	0	0	.250				
27	Johnson, Roy	Wichita	72	5	43	.290	L-L	6-4	205	6/27/59 Parkin, AR
—	McNealy, Rusty	Tacoma	113	0	42	.266	L-L	5-8	160	8/12/58 Sacramento, CA
		Oakland	0	0	0	.000				
30	Raines, Tim	Montreal	183	11	71	.298	B-R	5-8	165	9/16/59 Sanford, FL
47	Roof, Gene	St. L.-Mont.	2	0	1	.133	B-R	6-2	195	1/13/58 Mayfield, KY
		Louisville	139	3	60	.309				
32	Stenhouse, Mike	Wichita	128	25	93	.355	L-R	6-1	195	5/29/60 Pueblo, CO
		Montreal	5	0	2	.125				
33	Vail, Mike	SF-Mont.	19	2	7	.241	R-R	6-0	190	11/10/51 San Francisco, CA
18	*White, Jerry	Montreal	5	0	0	.147	B-R	5-10	175	8/23/52 Shirley, MA
5	Wohlford, Jim	Montreal	39	1	14	.277	R-R	5-11	175	2/28/51 Visalia, CA

*Free agent unsigned at press time.

EXPO PROFILES

AL OLIVER 37 6-1 195 **Bats L Throws L**

First baseman fell off in most areas, but batted more than .300 for eighth straight year . . . Outpolled Padres' Steve Garvey to gain first All-Star Game start . . . Did best hitting in mid-summer with a .325 June and a .360 July that included 21 RBI . . . Became one of oldest batting champs in major-league history when he earned first title at age 35 with a .331 mark for Expos in '82 . . . Born Oct. 14, 1946, in Portsmouth, Ohio . . . Yearned for return to NL, where he started with Pirates, and showed appreciation by leading league in hits, doubles and RBI and winning batting title in '82 . . . Became first man to enjoy 200-hit and 100-RBI season in each league since Nap Lajoie did it shortly after turn of century . . . Obtained from Rangers for Larry Parrish and Dave Hostetler prior to 1982 season . . . Holds AL record for total bases with 21, including four homers, in a 1980 doubleheader for Texas against Detroit.

Year	Club	Pos.	G	AB	R	H	2B	3B	HR	RBI	SB	Avg.
1968	Pittsburgh	OF	4	8	1	1	0	0	0	0	0	.125
1969	Pittsburgh	1B-OF	129	463	55	132	19	2	17	70	8	.285
1970	Pittsburgh	OF-1B	151	551	63	149	33	5	12	83	1	.270
1971	Pittsburgh	OF-1B	143	529	69	149	31	7	14	64	4	.282
1972	Pittsburgh	OF-1B	140	565	88	176	27	4	12	89	2	.312
1973	Pittsburgh	OF-1B	158	654	90	191	38	7	20	99	6	.292
1974	Pittsburgh	OF-1B	147	617	96	198	38	12	11	85	10	.321
1975	Pittsburgh	OF-1B	155	628	90	176	39	8	18	84	4	.280
1976	Pittsburgh	OF-1B	121	443	62	143	22	5	12	61	6	.323
1977	Pittsburgh	OF	154	568	75	175	29	6	19	82	13	.308
1978	Texas	OF	133	525	65	170	35	5	14	89	8	.324
1979	Texas	OF	136	492	69	159	28	4	12	76	4	.323
1980	Texas	OF-1B	163	656	96	209	43	3	19	117	5	.319
1981	Texas	OF-1B	102	421	53	130	29	1	4	55	3	.309
1982	Montreal	1B	160	617	90	204	43	2	22	109	5	.331
1983	Montreal	1B	157	614	70	184	38	3	8	84	1	.300
	Totals		2153	8351	1132	2546	492	74	214	1247	80	.305

ANDRE DAWSON 29 6-3 180 **Bats R Throws R**

Just missed batting .300, but did everything else right last year . . . Entered All-Star Game batting .321, but sagged in September and finished second to Braves' Dale Murphy in MVP balloting . . . Batted above .300 in each of first five months: .343 in April, .312 in May, .304 in June, .319 in July and .317 in August . . . NL Player of the Month in June with nine homers, 27 RBI and nine steals . . . Born July 10, 1954, in Miami . . . NL

Rookie of the Year in '77 and has been a force ever since . . . Equally effective as a fielder, winning Gold Gloves and Silver Bats for his play in center . . . The Sporting News' Player of the Year in '81 . . . Catching up to Gary Carter for Expos' all-time home-run lead, but still trails him, 188-165 . . . Belted two home runs in one inning in Atlanta in '78 . . . Attended Florida A&M . . . Cracked Carter's single-season club homer record by one last season . . . An 11th-round pick in June 1975 draft.

Year	Club	Pos.	G	AB	R	H	2B	3B	HR	RBI	SB	Avg.
1976	Montreal	OF	24	85	9	20	4	1	0	7	1	.235
1977	Montreal	OF	139	525	64	148	26	9	19	65	21	.282
1978	Montreal	OF	157	609	84	154	24	8	25	72	28	.253
1979	Montreal	OF	155	639	90	176	24	12	25	92	35	.275
1980	Montreal	OF	151	577	96	178	41	7	17	87	34	.308
1981	Montreal	OF	103	394	71	119	21	3	24	64	26	.302
1982	Montreal	OF	148	608	107	183	37	7	23	83	39	.301
1983	Montreal	OF	159	633	104	189	36	10	32	113	25	.299
	Totals		1036	4070	625	1167	213	57	165	583	209	.287

GARY CARTER 29 6-2 210 **Bats R Throws R**

Was once again top vote-getting catcher on NL All-Star squad, yet several others had better years behind the plate . . . Reached career batting mark, but tailed off in homers and RBI while belting a career-high total of doubles . . . Brought stats to respectable levels with five homers, 20 RBI and .337 average in August . . . Born April 8, 1954, in Culver City, Cal. . . . Replaced Reds' Johnny Bench as NL's best all-around catcher in late '70s . . . Signed $15-million contract that extends through 1989 before 1982 season . . . A three-sport standout in high school, he turned down scholarships to sign as Expos' third-round choice in June 1972 . . . Required less than three years of minor-league seasoning before reaching Montreal in late '74 . . . Troubled by elbow problem last year . . . Came under verbal fire from club's frustrated owner, Charles Bronfman, at end of year.

Year	Club	Pos.	G	AB	R	H	2B	3B	HR	RBI	SB	Avg.
1974	Montreal	C-OF	9	27	5	11	0	1	1	6	2	.407
1975	Montreal	OF-C-3B	144	503	58	136	20	1	17	68	5	.270
1976	Montreal	C-OF	91	311	31	68	8	1	6	38	0	.219
1977	Montreal	C-OF	154	522	86	148	29	2	31	84	5	.284
1978	Montreal	C-1B	157	533	76	136	27	1	20	72	10	.255
1979	Montreal	C	141	505	74	143	26	5	22	75	3	.283
1980	Montreal	C	154	549	76	145	25	5	29	101	3	.264
1981	Montreal	C-1B	100	374	48	94	20	2	16	68	1	.251
1982	Montreal	C	154	557	91	163	32	1	29	97	2	.293
1983	Montreal	C	145	541	63	146	37	3	17	79	1	.270
	Totals		1249	4422	608	1190	224	22	188	688	32	.269

TIM RAINES 24 5-8 165 Bats S Throws R

Finished fast to enjoy finest major-league season . . . Fleet left fielder topped majors in runs scored and was second only to Rickey Henderson in stolen bases with 90 . . . His 13 game-winning RBI were only one less than total of team leader Andre Dawson . . . Got going with a .333 May, but was at his best down stretch, while other Expos faltered . . . Stole 19 bases in August and crowned season with a .336 September, including 23 thefts . . . Born Sept. 16, 1969, in Sanford, Fla. . . . Sensational 1981 rookie season included 71 steals in only 88 games of strike-torn campaign . . . Voted Minor League Player of the Year in 1980, when he had 77 steals and .354 average for Denver (AAA) . . . Overcame a drug problem in 1982 and put his game together last season.

Year	Club	Pos.	G	AB	R	H	2B	3B	HR	RBI	SB	Avg.
1979	Montreal	PR	6	0	3	0	0	0	0	0	2	.000
1980	Montreal	2B-OF	15	20	5	1	0	0	0	0	5	.050
1981	Montreal	OF-2B	88	313	61	95	13	7	5	37	71	.304
1982	Montreal	OF-2B	156	647	90	179	32	8	4	43	78	.277
1983	Montreal	OF	156	615	133	183	32	8	11	71	90	.298
	Totals		421	1595	292	458	77	23	20	151	246	.287

TIM WALLACH 25 6-3 200 Bats R Throws R

Enjoyed second straight solid year, though RBI total dipped sharply . . . Best month was August, when he had five homers and .340 average . . . Got big break when third baseman Larry Parrish was traded to Texas in Al Oliver deal prior to '82 season . . . Made best of first chance to be a regular with 28 homers and 97 RBI . . . Also hit two grand slams in 1982 . . . Born Sept. 14, 1958, in Huntington Park, Cal. . . . Named College Player of the Year in '79, after leading Cal State-Fullerton to NCAA title with .398 average, 23 homers and 102 RBI . . . Expos' No. 1 pick batted .327 as pro rookie with Memphis (AA) in 1979 and joined Montreal one year later, after blasting 36 homers and driving in 124 runs for Denver (AAA) in 1980 . . . Homered in first official major-league at-bat that September.

Year	Club	Pos.	G	AB	R	H	2B	3B	HR	RBI	SB	Avg.
1980	Montreal	OF-1B	5	11	1	2	0	0	1	2	0	.182
1981	Montreal	OF-1B-3B	71	212	19	50	9	1	4	13	0	.236
1982	Montreal	3B-OF-1B	158	596	89	160	31	3	28	97	6	.268
1983	Montreal	3B-OF	156	581	54	156	33	3	19	70	0	.269
	Totals		390	1410	163	368	73	7	52	182	6	.261

BILL GULLICKSON 25 6-3 215 Bats R Throws R

Emerged with finest major-league season after scratching the surface previous two years . . . His season was just the opposite of Steve Rogers' . . . Was 7-9 in the first half and 10-3 after All-Star break . . . Was 4-1 with a 2.44 ERA in August and 4-0 with 2.84 ERA in September to equal Rogers' overall record . . . Born Feb. 20, 1959, in Kankakee, Ill. . . . No. 2 pick in the nation in June 1977 draft, behind White Sox' Harold Baines . . . Struck out 18 Cubs in September 1981 . . . Posted 23-1 record last two years at Joliet Catholic High . . . Was 10-3 for Memphis (AA) in '79, but didn't reach bigs to stay until he went 6-2 for Denver (AAA) in 1980 before finishing year with Montreal . . . Discovered he was diabetic in '80 and contributes time to fighting the disease.

Year	Club	G	IP	W	L	Pct.	SO	BB	H	ERA
1979	Montreal	1	1	0	0	.000	0	0	2	0.00
1980	Montreal	24	141	10	5	.667	120	50	127	3.00
1981	Montreal	22	157	7	9	.438	115	34	142	2.81
1982	Montreal	34	237	12	14	.462	155	61	231	3.57
1983	Montreal	34	242	17	12	.586	120	59	230	3.75
	Totals	115	778	46	40	.535	510	204	732	3.37

JEFF REARDON 28 6-1 190 Bats R Throws R

Lost nine games, but remained the ace of a spotty bullpen, compiling 21 saves for a two-season total of 47 . . . Was at his peak in July, going 2-0 with a 1.65 ERA and three saves . . . Never had more than eight saves prior to 1982, but got big break when Mets traded him to Montreal as part of package for Ellis Valentine in May 1981, enabling him to escape Neil Allen's shadow . . . Born Oct. 1, 1955, in Dalton, Mass. . . . Selected by Expos in June '73 draft, but opted for college and was a standout at Massachusetts, where he majored in history . . . Signed with Mets and was 30-9 in three minor-league seasons before joining parent club in late '79 . . . Posted solid stats in '80 and Expos got him on their second try in '81 . . . Saved two games in NL division playoffs against Phillies that year . . . Booing of his wife by home fans last year prompted anger and short-lived demand for trade.

Year	Club	G	IP	W	L	Pct.	SO	BB	H	ERA
1979	New York (NL)	18	21	1	2	.333	10	9	12	1.71
1980	New York (NL)	61	110	8	7	.533	101	47	96	2.62
1981	N.Y. (NL)-Mtl.	43	70	3	0	1.000	49	21	48	2.19
1982	Montreal	75	109	7	4	.636	86	36	87	2.06
1983	Montreal	66	92	7	9	.438	78	44	87	3.03
	Totals	263	402	26	22	.542	324	157	330	2.44

CHARLIE LEA 27 6-4 190 — Bats R Throws R

Continued steady improvement last year, topping Expos' starters in ERA . . . Was at his best in August, going 5-0 with a 1.96 ERA . . . Pitched a one-hitter against the Astros in April . . . Fired a no-hitter against Giants, May 10, 1981, at Olympic Stadium . . . Had string of 28⅔ scoreless innings that year, but injuries limited his effectiveness . . . Born Dec. 25, 1956, in Or-eans, France, and grew up in Memphis . . . Spent first three pro ears at Memphis (AA) and earned promotion following 9-0, 0.84 tart in 1980 . . . An avid outdoorsman . . . Has proven he can pitch s well as anyone when he's healthy.

ear	Club	G	IP	W	L	Pct.	SO	BB	H	ERA
980	Montreal	21	104	7	5	.583	56	55	103	3.72
981	Montreal	16	64	5	4	.556	31	26	63	4.64
982	Montreal	27	178	12	10	.545	115	56	145	3.24
983	Montreal	33	222	16	11	.593	137	84	195	3.12
	Totals	97	568	40	30	.571	339	221	506	3.44

STEVE ROGERS 34 6-1 177 — Bats R Throws R

Ranks with finest right-handers in game, but provoked criticism that he is not able to win under pressure by failing the Expos down the stretch . . . Was 12-3 with a 2.77 ERA at the All-Star break and 5-9 with an ERA approaching 4.00 thereafter . . . Started strong with 3-1 April, including two shutouts, and was 4-1 in June . . . Best season was 1982, which included All-Star Game victory at Montreal . . . Former manager Dick Williams questioned his effectiveness in the big games, but he temporarily put that rap to rest in '81 . . . That year, he beat Steve Carlton twice in division playoffs and Dodgers once in NL Championship Series . . . Born Oct. 26, 1949, in Jefferson City, Mo.

...Attended Tulsa, where he was 31-5...Collects coins and is a crossword-puzzle freak.

Year	Club	G	IP	W	L	Pct.	SO	BB	H	ERA
1973	Montreal	17	134	10	5	.667	64	49	93	1.54
1974	Montreal	38	254	15	22	.405	154	80	225	4.46
1975	Montreal	35	252	11	12	.478	137	88	248	3.29
1976	Montreal	33	230	7	17	.292	150	69	212	3.21
1977	Montreal	40	302	17	16	.515	206	81	272	3.10
1978	Montreal	30	219	13	10	.565	126	64	186	2.47
1979	Montreal	37	249	13	12	.520	143	78	232	3.00
1980	Montreal	37	281	16	11	.593	147	85	247	2.98
1981	Montreal	22	161	12	8	.600	87	41	149	3.41
1982	Montreal	35	277	19	8	.704	179	65	245	2.40
1983	Montreal	36	273	17	12	.586	146	78	258	3.23
	Totals	360	2632	150	133	.530	1539	778	2397	3.06

TOP PROSPECTS

MIKE STENHOUSE 23 6-1 195 **Bats L Throws R**

If Expos juggle roster as expected, he could see considerable playing time...Batting champion of American Association with .355 average and 25 home runs for Denver, but had only five hits 21 40 at-bats with Expos...Born May 29, 1960, in Pueblo, Colo. ...Son of former major-league pitcher Dave Stenhouse... Promising outfielder who attended Harvard and is an avid reader ...Club also is high on infielder Angel Salazar, who batted .302 at Wichita (AAA).

MANAGER BILL VIRDON: It was hoped a different, more disciplined approach might extract the best out of Expos last year, but he encountered same problems as his predecessors...From his Texas days, he must have learned you can lead a horse to water, but you can't make it drink...Puzzling Expos proved that again last season...Was the Astros' manager for seven years before his dismissal in August 1982...Manager of the Year in 1980 for leading Houston to its only division title...Reached divisional playoffs in '81...Born June 9, 1931, in Hazel Park, Mich....Was Rookie of the Year with Cardinals in 1955...Was traded to Pirates in '56 and finished that season with career-high .319 average...A fine defensive outfielder who posted .267 career mark...Rookie manager of Pirates in '72 and won division title...Guided Yankees to second-place finish in '74...Overall major-league managerial mark is 931-854.

Despite elbow trouble, Gary Carter caught 145 games.

GREATEST STEALER

Reigning National League base-stealing champion Tim Raines is the most consistently spectacular speedster in the club's short history. Even though he has played only three full major-league seasons and one of those was shortened by a strike, Raines has totaled 246 stolen bases.

The only thing eluding him is the single-season club record, which was set by Ron LeFlore, who had 97 in his only season with the Expos in 1980. But Raines is gradually hiking his total, from 71 in '81 to 78 in '82 to 90 last year, so it seems likely LeFlore's mark will tumble if Raines really wants it.

Raines warmed up for a big splash in the majors by swiping 75 for Denver in 1980. He had 50 steals in 56 games before the strike interrupted the '81 season and went on to lead the majors with 71 in his rookie season. His feats have been overshadowed only by efforts of Oakland's Rickey Henderson the last two years.

ALL-TIME EXPO SEASON RECORDS

BATTING: Al Oliver, .331, 1982
HRs: Andre Dawson, 32, 1983
RBIs: Andre Dawson, 113, 1983
STEALS: Ron LeFlore, 97, 1980
WINS: Ross Grimsley, 20, 1978
STRIKEOUTS: Bill Stoneman, 251, 1971

NEW YORK METS

TEAM DIRECTORY: Chairman of the Board: Nelson Doubleday; Pres.: Fred Wilpon; Exec. VP-GM: Frank Cashen; VP-Baseball Oper.: Lou Gorman; Dir. Scouting: Joe McIlvaine; Dir. Minor Leagues: Steve Schryver; Dir. Pub. Rel.: Jay Horwitz; Asst. GM-Trav. Sec.: Arthur Richman; Mgr.: Davey Johnson. Home: Shea Stadium (55,300). Field distances: 338, l.f. line; 371, l.c.; 410, c.f.; 371, r.c.; 338, r.f. line. Spring training: St. Petersburg, Fla.

SCOUTING REPORT

HITTING: This is definitely the club's strength, especially with Darryl Strawberry emerging as a superstar and Keith Hernandez in the fold for an entire season. Add Mookie Wilson and George Foster, as well as Rusty Staub's pop off the bench, and you have a team capable of scoring more than 3.5 runs per game, as the Mets did last season.

Strawberry could make a big difference. He was like a deer learning how to walk in the early stages of '83, but came on like gangbusters in the second half—too late to elevate the Mets, but not too late to keep hopes kindled for the future. He and Foster,

Jesse Orosco won 13 and saved 17 for last-place Mets.

who bounced back from a miserable '82, combined for 54 homers and 164 RBI, and Hernandez batted .297, giving the club a solid heart of the order. If Wilson (.276, 54 steals) can improve his on-base percentage and the club discovers a solid No. 2 hitter, the Mets will have to be reckoned with offensively. The return of John Stearns from a series of elbow operations would plug the Mets' biggest hole—catcher.

PITCHING: Reliever Jesse Orosco's awesome performance disguised the shabby state of a pitching staff that drove manager George Bamberger, a patient man, to retirement. The pitching starts with Orosco (13-7, 1.47, 17 saves) and ends with him. The Mets annually boast of phenoms who are supposed to make a difference, but they seldom live up to their press clippings. Maybe Ron Darling and Sid Fernandez will be different.

Tom Seaver and Mike Torrez, shadows of their former selves, had to do the bulk of the starting last season and were a combined 19-31, despite some solid work. Ed Lynch (10-10) and rookie Walt Terrell (8-8) were .500 pitchers on their way up, so all isn't lost. But the swap of southpaw reliever Carlos Diaz weakened the bullpen—especially if Orosco doesn't repeat his '83 success.

FIELDING: No longer the worst-fielding team in the league, the Mets climbed to ninth and slashed their errors by 24 last year. The acquisition of first baseman Hernandez (.992) and his Gold Glove definitely helped the infield, where youngsters like second baseman Brian Giles and acrobatic shortstop Jose Oquendo apparently will continue to improve. The same can be said of struggling catcher Junior Ortiz and the strong-armed Strawberry, who is expected to blossom into an all-around standout in right field.

OUTLOOK: There are vivid signs of improvement, but not enough for a climb in the standings. It could be a trying year for rookie manager Davey Johnson, whose patience definitely will be tested. The big question mark is the pitching, which is mediocre, at best. If Orosco falters, the staff could collapse. That is a possibility, because the bullpen ace has very little help.

There is consolation for the club's followers, however. Although the Mets are destined to be losers, they have the makings of an exciting club because of the potentially solid offense. Watching Strawberry develop is worth the price of admission and Hernandez, Foster and Wilson are no slouches at the plate. Unlike the White Sox, who were winning ugly last year, the Mets have the capability of losing pretty. But that pitching is definitely ugly, enough to give Johnson and the fans a season-long migraine.

NEW YORK METS 1984 ROSTER

MANAGER Dave Johnson

Coaches—Vern Hoscheit, Frank Howard, Bill Robinson, Mel Stottlemyre, Bob Valentine

PITCHERS

No.	Name	1983 Club	W-L	IP	SO	ERA	B-T	Ht.	Wt.	Born
46	Bittiger, Jeff	Tidewater	12-10	163	110	4.36	R-R	5-10	175	4/13/62 Jersey City, NJ
44	Darling, Ron	Tidewater	10-9	159	107	4.02	R-R	6-3	195	8/19/60 Honolulu, HI
		New York (NL)	1-3	35	23	2.80				
—	Fernandez, Sid	San Antonio	13-4	153	209	2.82	L-L	6-1	220	10/12/62 Honolulu, HI
		Los Angeles	0-1	6	9	6.00				
45	Gaff, Brent	Tidewater	6-7	112	60	6.04	R-R	6-2	200	10/5/58 Fort Wayne, IN
		New York (NL)	1-0	10	4	6.10				
29	Gorman, Tom	Tidewater	6-1	62	58	2.92	L-L	6-4	200	12/16/57 Portland, OR
		New York (NL)	1-4	49	30	4.93				
28	Holman, Scott	New York (NL)	1-7	101	44	3.74	R-R	6-0	194	9/18/58 Santa Paula, CA
38	Leary, Tim	Tidewater	8-16	160	106	4.38	R-R	6-3	190	12/23/58 Santa Monica, CA
		New York (NL)	1-1	11	9	3.38				
36	Lynch, Ed	New York (NL)	10-10	175	44	4.28	R-R	6-5	207	2/25/56 Brooklyn, NY
47	Orosco, Jesse	New York (NL)	13-7	110	84	1.47	R-L	6-2	185	4/21/57 Santa Barbara, CA
62	Pickett, Rich	Lynchburg	1-0	19	21	1.42	L-L	6-1	190	7/11/59 Crystal Spring, MS
		Tidewater	1-0	32	27	3.98				
41	Seaver, Tom	New York (NL)	9-14	231	135	3.55	R-R	6-1	210	11/17/44 Fresno, CA
39	Sisk, Doug	New York (NL)	5-4	104	33	2.24	R-R	6-2	210	9/26/57 Renton, WA
27	Swan, Craig	New York (NL)	2-8	96	43	5.51	R-R	6-3	210	11/30/50 Van Nuys, CA
49	Terrell, Walt	Tidewater	10-1	87	58	3.12	L-R	6-2	205	5/11/58 Jeffersonville, IN
		New York (NL)	8-8	134	59	3.57				
30	Torrez, Mike	New York (NL)	10-17	222	94	4.37	R-R	6-5	210	8/28/46 Topeka, KS

CATCHERS

No.	Name	1983 Club	H	HR	RBI	Pct.	B-T	Ht.	Wt.	Born
20	Fitzgerald, Mike	Tidewater	105	14	65	.284	R-R	6-0	185	7/13/60 Long Beach, CA
		New York (NL)	2	1	2	.100				
61	Gibbons, John	Jackson	111	18	67	.298	R-R	5-11	187	6/8/62 Great Falls, MT
42	Hodges, Ron	New York (NL)	65	0	21	.260	L-R	6-1	187	6/22/49 Franklin Co., VA
34	Ortiz, Junior	Pitt.-NY (NL)	48	0	12	.249	R-R	5-11	174	10/24/59 Puerto Rico
12	Stearns, John	New York (NL)	0	0	0	.000	R-R	6-0	180	8/21/51 Denver, CO

INFIELDERS

No.	Name	1983 Club	H	HR	RBI	Pct.	B-T	Ht.	Wt.	Born
11	Ashford, Tucker	Tidewater	16	1	8	.327	R-R	6-1	185	12/14/54 Memphis, TN
		New York (NL)	10	0	2	.179				
6	Backman, Wally	Tidewater	114	1	28	.316	B-R	5-9	160	9/22/59 Hillsboro, OR
		New York (NL)	7	0	3	.167				
7	Brooks, Hubie	New York (NL)	147	5	58	.251	R-R	6-0	188	9/24/56 Los Angeles, CA
19	Gardenhire, Ron	Tidewater	111	4	39	.287	R-R	6-0	174	10/24/57 Germany
		New York (NL)	2	0	1	.063				
23	Giles, Brian	New York (NL)	98	2	27	.245	R-R	6-1	162	4/27/60 Manhattan, KS
17	Hernandez, Keith	St. L.-NY (NL)	160	12	63	.297	L-L	6-0	185	10/20/53 San Francisco, CA
26	Kingman, Dave	New York (NL)	49	13	29	.198	R-R	6-6	218	12/21/48 Pendleton, OR
63	Mitchell, Kevin	Jackson	132	15	85	.299	R-R	5-10	186	1/13/62 San Diego, CA
2	Oquendo, Jose	Tidewater	4	0	3	.118	R-R	5-10	155	7/4/63 Puerto Rico
		New York (NL)	70	1	17	.213				
21	Rajsich, Gary	Tidewater	116	28	83	.270	L-L	6-2	200	10/28/54 Youngstown, OH
		New York (NL)	12	1	3	.333				

OUTFIELDERS

No.	Name	1983 Club	H	HR	RBI	Pct.	B-T	Ht.	Wt.	Born
35	Beane, Billy	Jackson	104	11	75	.246	R-R	6-4	195	3/29/62 Orlando, FL
58	Blocker, Terry	Jackson	81	3	54	.308	L-L	6-2	195	8/18/60 Columbia, SC
		Tidewater	73	2	32	.305				
60	Dykstra, Len	Lynchburg	188	8	81	.358	L-L	5-10	160	2/10/63 Santa Ana, CA
15	Foster, George	New York (NL)	145	28	90	.241	R-R	6-1	185	12/1/48 Tuscaloosa, AL
25	Heep, Danny	New York (NL)	64	8	21	.253	L-L	5-11	185	7/3/57 San Antonio, TX
10	Staub, Rusty	New York (NL)	34	3	28	.296	L-R	6-0	225	4/1/44 New Orleans, LA
18	Strawberry, Darryl	Tidewater	19	3	13	.333	L-L	6-6	190	3/12/62 Los Angeles, CA
		New York (NL)	108	26	74	.257				
1	Wilson, Mookie	New York (NL)	176	7	51	.276	B-R	5-10	170	2/9/56 Bamberg, SC
66	Winningham, Herm	Jackson	102	4	41	.354	L-R	6-1	170	12/1/61 Orangeburg, SC
		Tidewater	30	1	11	.265				

MET PROFILES

MOOKIE WILSON 28 5-10 170 **Bats S Throws R**

Continued to play consistently well last year ... His average has been .270 or above all three years as a regular ... Has stolen 112 bases in the last two years ... Holds club single-season record with 58 thefts ... Enjoys baking, especially dishes he learned from grandmother, who gave him his nickname ... Born William Howard Wilson, Feb. 9, 1956, in Bamberg, S.C. ... Speedy center fielder went 655 at-bats without grounding into a double play for Tidewater (AAA) ... Was an All-American at South Carolina, batting .357 in 1977 and sparking Gamecocks to a runnerup finish in the College World Series that season ... Serious enough about baseball to be married at home plate in Jackson, Miss., in 1978 ... Brother John is outfielder in Mets' system ... Walks too rarely and strikes out too frequently to fit mold of a leadoff hitter ... Working on his bunting.

Year	Club	Pos.	G	AB	R	H	2B	3B	HR	RBI	SB	Avg.
1980	New York (NL)	OF	27	105	16	26	5	3	0	4	7	.248
1981	New York (NL)	OF	92	328	49	89	8	8	3	14	24	.271
1982	New York (NL)	OF	159	639	90	178	25	9	5	55	58	.279
1983	New York (NL)	OF	152	638	91	176	25	6	7	51	54	.276
	Totals		430	1710	246	469	63	26	15	124	143	.274

GEORGE FOSTER 35 6-1 185 **Bats R Throws R**

Hit poorly for second straight year, but compensated with long-ball production as he significantly boosted his totals of home runs and RBI from 1982 levels ... Home-run total of 28 was his highest since 1979 ... Belted two grand slams last year, tying Dave Kingman for lead among active major leaguers, with 11 ... Born Dec. 1, 1948, in Tuscaloosa, Ala. ... Left fielder hasn't lived up to expectations of Mets, who gave him a five-year, $10-million-plus contract in 1982 ... Admitted he was pressing during sub-par 1982 season and followed with career-low in batting average last year ... Involved in one of the worst trades in Giants' history, going to Cincinnati for Frank Duffy and Vern Geishert in 1971 ... Became one of majors' most-feared sluggers with Reds, swinging heavy black bat to produce 52 homers and 149 RBI in 1977 ... Enjoys the New York theater.

Year	Club	Pos.	G	AB	R	H	2B	3B	HR	RBI	SB	Avg.
1969	San Francisco.	OF	9	5	1	2	0	0	0	1	0	.400
1970	San Francisco.	OF	9	19	2	6	1	1	1	4	0	.316
1971	S.F.-Cin	OF	140	473	50	114	23	4	13	58	7	.241
1972	Cincinnati	OF	59	145	15	29	4	1	2	12	2	.200
1973	Cincinnati	OF	17	39	6	11	3	0	4	9	0	.282
1974	Cincinnati	OF	106	276	31	73	18	0	7	41	3	.264
1975	Cincinnati	OF-1B	134	463	71	139	24	4	23	78	2	.300
1976	Cincinnati	OF-1B	144	562	86	172	21	9	29	121	17	.306
1977	Cincinnati	OF	158	615	124	197	31	2	52	149	6	.320
1978	Cincinnati	OF	158	604	97	170	26	7	40	120	4	.281
1979	Cincinnati	OF	121	440	68	133	18	3	30	98	0	.302
1980	Cincinnati	OF	144	528	79	144	21	5	25	93	1	.273
1981	Cincinnati	OF	108	414	64	122	23	2	22	90	4	.295
1982	New York (NL)	OF	151	550	64	136	23	2	13	70	1	.247
1983	New York (NL)	OF	157	601	74	145	19	2	28	90	1	.241
	Totals		1615	5734	832	1593	255	42	289	1034	48	.278

DARRYL STRAWBERRY 22 6-6 190 Bats L Throws L

Labeled as the black Ted Williams even before he became a No. 1 overall draft choice as a high-school player in June 1980, he didn't disappoint in his first taste of big-league ball . . . Originally was supposed to stay at Tidewater (AAA) in 1983, but Mets' 6-15 start prompted his promotion on May 4 . . . Right fielder went hitless in his first 11 at-bats and was struggling with a .202 average at the All-Star break before breaking loose . . . Born March 12, 1962, in Los Angeles . . . Batted .294 during the second half and finished with 26 home runs, shattering club rookie record of 19 by Ron Swoboda . . . Voted NL Rookie of the Year, withstanding competition from the Braves' Craig McMurtry and the Cubs' Mel Hall . . . Flashed tremendous potential with 34 homers and 97 RBI in 129 games for Jackson (AA) in 1982.

Year	Club	Pos.	G	AB	R	H	2B	3B	HR	RBI	SB	Avg.
1983	New York (NL)	OF	122	420	63	108	15	7	26	74	19	.257

KEITH HERNANDEZ 30 6-0 185 Bats L Throws L

A June 15 acquisition from Cardinals in deal that sent pitcher Neil Allen to St. Louis, this slick-fielding first baseman batted .306 for Mets and .297 overall . . . Hit nine of his homers with New York . . . Didn't skip a beat after swap, batting .339 in June and improving to .347 in August . . . Hit just below lifetime average . . . Born Oct. 20, 1953, in San Francisco...One of few players to win Gold Glove and Silver Bat for all-around excellence...Became expendable at St. Louis because presence of young outfielders forced switch of George Hendrick to first...Tied Giants' Jack Clark with 21 game-winning RBI in 1982, but slipped to nine last year...Father Tony was outfielder in Cardinals' system...Shared NL MVP honors with Pirates' Willie Stargell in 1979.

Year	Club	Pos.	G	AB	R	H	2B	3B	HR	RBI	SB	Avg.
1974	St. Louis........	1B	14	34	3	10	1	2	0	2	0	.294
1975	St. Louis........	1B	64	188	20	47	8	2	3	20	0	.250
1976	St. Louis........	1B	129	374	54	108	21	5	7	46	4	.289
1977	St. Louis........	1B	161	560	90	163	41	4	15	91	7	.291
1978	St. Louis........	1B	159	542	90	138	32	4	11	64	13	.255
1979	St. Louis........	1B	161	610	116	210	48	11	11	105	11	.344
1980	St. Louis........	1B	159	595	111	191	39	8	16	99	14	.321
1981	St. Louis........	1B-OF	103	376	65	115	27	4	8	48	12	.306
1982	St. Louis........	1B-OF	160	579	79	173	33	6	7	94	19	.299
1983	St. Louis-N.Y. (NL).	1B	150	538	77	160	23	7	12	63	9	.297
	Totals..........		1260	4396	705	1315	273	53	90	632	89	.299

JOSE OQUENDO 20 5-10 155 **Bats R Throws R**

Another good-field, no-hit shortstop who made his share of dazzling plays as a rookie last year...Switch-hitting experiment, which was started in 1981, was abandoned after he reached majors last season...Carolina League All-Star for Lynchburg (A) in 1981...Born July 4, 1963, in Rio Piedras, Puerto Rico...Greatly influenced by countrymen Felix Millan and Ivan DeJesus...Increased his average at Lynchburg from .169 in 1980 to .249 in 1981, but has been woeful at the plate ever since...May have to hit better to keep his job, despite ability to make acrobatic plays at shortstop...An adept base-stealer in minors, but has a problem getting on base.

Year	Club	Pos.	G	AB	R	H	2B	3B	HR	RBI	SB	Avg.
1983	New York (NL)....	SS	120	328	29	70	7	0	1	17	8	.213

TOM SEAVER 39 6-1 210 **Bats R Throws R**

You *can* go home again...Failed to reach double figures in victories for second straight year, but former superstar pitched in hard luck...Was club leader in most pitching categories...Flashed former brilliance with two early-season shutouts, tying Don Sutton for most by any active pitcher with 56...Three-hit Pittsburgh with nine strikeouts April 20 and five-hit Houston May 11 . . . Born Nov. 17, 1944, in Fresno, Cal. . . . Regarded as The Franchise in his previous stint with Mets, earning three Cy Young Awards and winning 20 games five times before being dealt in June 1977 . . . His 14-2 record for Reds in 1981 gave him .875 winning percentage, the best in NL in 22 years . . . No longer Tom Terrific, but still provided big boost to Mets' young pitching staff last year . . . Club exercised its option to renew his contract for another year at a salary of $1 million, including incentives.

Year	Club	G	IP	W	L	Pct.	SO	BB	H	ERA
1967	New York (NL)	35	251	16	13	.552	170	78	224	2.76
1968	New York (NL)	36	278	16	12	.571	205	48	224	2.20
1969	New York (NL)	36	273	25	7	.781	208	82	202	2.21
1970	New York (NL)	37	291	18	12	.600	283	83	230	2.81
1971	New York (NL)	36	286	20	10	.667	289	61	210	1.76
1972	New York (NL)	35	262	21	12	.636	249	77	215	2.92
1973	New York (NL)	36	290	19	10	.655	251	64	219	2.07
1974	New York (NL)	32	236	11	11	.500	201	75	199	3.20
1975	New York (NL)	36	280	22	9	.710	243	88	217	2.38
1976	New York (NL)	35	271	14	11	.560	235	77	211	2.59
1977	New York (NL)-Cincinnati	33	261	21	6	.778	196	66	199	2.59
1978	Cincinnati	36	260	16	14	.533	226	89	218	2.87
1979	Cincinnati	32	215	16	6	.727	131	61	187	3.14
1980	Cincinnati	26	168	10	8	.556	101	59	140	3.64
1981	Cincinnati	23	166	14	2	.875	87	66	120	2.55
1982	Cincinnati	21	111	5	13	.278	62	44	136	5.50
1983	New York (NL)	34	231	9	14	.391	135	86	201	3.55
	Totals	559	4130	273	170	.616	3272	1204	3352	2.73

WALT TERRELL 25 6-2 205 — Bats L Throws R

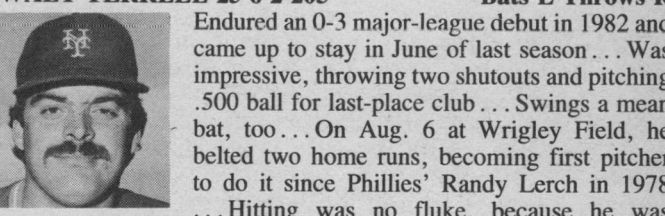

Endured an 0-3 major-league debut in 1982 and came up to stay in June of last season . . . Was impressive, throwing two shutouts and pitching .500 ball for last-place club . . . Swings a mean bat, too . . . On Aug. 6 at Wrigley Field, he belted two home runs, becoming first pitcher to do it since Phillies' Randy Lerch in 1978 . . . Hitting was no fluke, because he was 2-for-5 following his promotion in 1982 . . . Plagued the Cubs again Aug. 12, with his first major-league shutout . . . Born May 11, 1958, in Jeffersonville, Ind. . . . Pitched for former major-leaguer Steve Hamilton at Morehead State . . . Originally drafted by the Rangers in June 1980, he joined Mets as part of package for Lee Mazzilli prior to 1982 season . . . Best full minor-league season was 15-7, 3.10 ERA performance for Tulsa (AA) in 1981.

Year	Club	G	IP	W	L	Pct.	SO	BB	H	ERA
1982	New York (NL)	3	21	0	3	.000	8	14	22	3.43
1983	New York (NL)	21	134	8	8	.500	59	55	123	3.57
	Totals	24	155	8	11	.421	67	69	145	3.54

ED LYNCH 28 6-5 207 **Bats R Throws R**

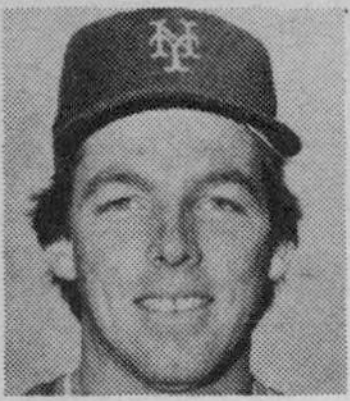

Showed signs of fulfilling promise last year by coming through with finest major-league season... Had never won more than four games in majors previous to 1983, but big breakthrough came in mid-August 1982, when he became a regular starter... Born Feb. 25, 1956, in Brooklyn, N.Y., but grew up in Miami ... Enrolled in South Carolina on a basketball scholarship and was a teammate of Mookie Wilson on the Gamecocks' 1977 College World Series squad... Drafted by Texas and joined Mets along with Mike Jorgensen in Willie Montanez deal in 1979... Once threw only 78 pitches in a victory for Tucson (AAA)... His finest season as Met farmhand was marked by 13-6 record with 3.15 ERA for Tidewater (AAA) in 1980, prompting promotion to majors.

Year	Club	G	IP	W	L	Pct.	SO	BB	H	ERA
1980	New York (NL)	5	19	1	1	.500	9	5	24	5.21
1981	New York (NL)	17	80	4	5	.444	27	21	79	2.93
1982	New York (NL)	43	139	4	8	.333	51	40	145	3.55
1983	New York (NL)	30	175	10	10	.500	44	41	208	4.28
	Totals	95	413	19	24	.442	131	107	456	3.81

JESSE OROSCO 26 6-2 185 **Bats R Throws L**

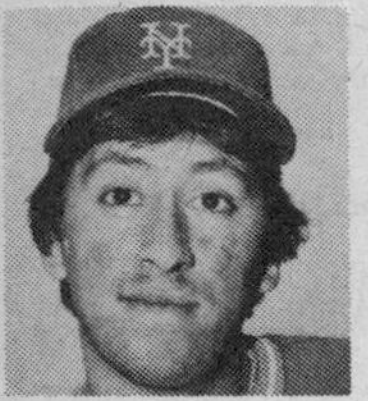

Simply blossomed into one of the NL's two most effective relievers last season, winning 13 games, saving 17 and posting tidy 1.47 ERA ... Set the tone for his parsimonious performance by going 3-0 with a 0.86 ERA in May and was absolutely untouchable in August ... Earned Pitcher-of-the-Month honors that month with a 5-0 record and six saves... From July 22 to Aug. 27, he threw 27⅔ scoreless innings... Born April 21, 1957, in Santa Barbara, Cal.... Began season as club's No. 2 reliever, then became one of best in league after trade of Neil Allen... Credits former manager George Bamberger for his development... Enjoys painting and sculpting as hobbies... Obtained from Twins' organization with Greg Field for Jerry Koosman before 1979 season.

Year	Club	G	IP	W	L	Pct.	SO	BB	H	ERA
1979	New York (NL)	18	35	1	2	.333	22	22	33	4.89
1981	New York (NL)	8	17	0	1	.000	18	6	13	1.59
1982	New York (NL)	54	109	4	10	.286	89	40	92	2.72
1983	New York (NL)	62	110	13	7	.650	84	38	76	1.47
	Totals	142	271	18	20	.474	213	106	214	2.42

RUSTY STAUB 39 6-0 225 **Bats L Throws R**

Nobody did it better than this pinch-hitter deluxe last year . . . Tied major-league record belonging to Joe Cronin (1943) and Jerry Lynch (1961) with his 25th pinch-RBI, which won final game of last season . . . Belted 24 pinch-hits, one shy of Jose Morales' major-league record . . . Erased Ed Kranepool's club marks of 17 pinch-hits and 17 pinch-RBI . . . Had eight consecutive pinch-hits to tie Dave Philley's NL mark (1958) . . . Born April 4, 1944, in New Orleans . . . Three pinch-hit home runs lifted career homer total to 290 and he has amassed 2,685 hits . . . Has played for five major-league clubs, enjoying most of his success with Houston, Montreal and the Mets before becoming a crack DH for Detroit . . . His .375 average topped pinch-hitters in 1982 . . . Owner of restaurant in New York . . . A gourMet.

Year	Club	Pos.	G	AB	R	H	2B	3B	HR	RBI	SB	Avg.
1963	Houston	1B-OF	150	513	43	115	17	4	6	45	0	.224
1964	Houston	1B-OF	89	292	26	63	10	2	8	35	1	.216
1965	Houston	OF-1B	131	410	43	105	20	1	14	63	3	.256
1966	Houston	OF-1B	153	554	60	155	28	3	13	81	2	.280
1967	Houston	OF	149	546	71	182	44	1	10	74	0	.333
1968	Houston	1B-OF	161	591	54	172	37	1	6	72	2	.291
1969	Montreal	OF	158	549	89	166	26	5	29	79	3	.302
1970	Montreal	OF	160	569	98	156	23	7	30	94	12	.274
1971	Montreal	OF	162	599	94	186	34	6	19	97	9	.311
1972	New York (NL)	OF	66	239	32	70	11	0	9	38	0	.293
1973	New York (NL)	OF	152	585	77	163	36	1	15	76	1	.279
1974	New York (NL)	OF	151	561	65	145	22	2	19	78	2	.258
1975	New York (NL)	OF	155	574	93	162	30	4	19	105	2	.282
1976	Detroit	OF	161	589	73	176	28	3	15	96	3	.299
1977	Detroit	DH	158	623	84	173	34	3	22	101	1	.278
1978	Detroit	DH	162	642	75	175	30	1	24	121	3	.273
1979	Detroit	DH	68	246	32	58	12	1	9	40	1	.236
1979	Montreal	1B-OF	38	86	9	23	3	0	3	14	0	.267
1980	Texas	OF-1B	109	340	42	102	23	2	9	55	1	.300
1981	New York (NL)	1B	70	161	9	51	9	0	5	21	1	.317
1982	New York (NL)	OF-1B	112	219	11	53	9	0	3	27	0	.242
1983	New York (NL)	OF-1B	104	115	5	34	6	0	3	28	0	.296
	Totals		2819	9603	1185	2685	492	47	290	1440	46	.280

TOP PROSPECTS

RON DARLING 23 6-3 195 **Bats R Throws R**

Enjoyed success toward end of season, going a misleading 1-3 with 2.80 ERA in his first taste of big-league ball . . . Regarded—along with Sid Fernandez—as the best of the many young Met pitchers . . . Pitched two hitless innings for International League All-Stars against Cleveland Indians and finished 10-9 with a 4.02

ERA for Tidewater (AAA) last year... Born Aug. 19, 1960, in Honolulu, Hawaii... Attended Yale... Mets pulled April Fools joke on Rangers when they acquired him and Walt Terrell for Lee Mazzilli, April 1, 1982... Club also is high on Fernandez, southpaw fastballer who came from Dodgers in December deal for Carlos Diaz and Bob Bailor... Fernandez struck out 209 in 153 innings and was 13-4 at San Antonio (AA) last year... Had 32-11 record in three seasons in minors... Like Darling, he was born in Honolulu—Oct. 12, 1962... Is 6-1, 220, with problem keeping weight down... Right-hander Jeff Bittiger, is another of the pitching hopefuls... He was 12-10 for Tidewater after 12-5 season for Jackson (AA) in 1982... Born April 13, 1962, in Jersey City, N.J.... Next to Darling and Fernandez, Bittiger's a little bit of a guy—5-10, 175.

First baseman Keith Hernandez is glue of Mets' infield.

MANAGER DAVEY JOHNSON: No stranger to some Mets, he managed Darryl Strawberry and Jose Oquendo at Tidewater early last year . . . His appointment to succeed interim skipper Frank Howard was greeted with enthusiasm by Strawberry . . . Guided Tidewater to International League pennant and Little World Series championship last year and also had success with Jackson of Texas League in 1981 . . . Established an NL record for homers by a second baseman with 43 for Atlanta in 1973 . . . His greatest success as a player, however, came with Orioles, for whom he played in four World Series . . . Also played with the Phillies and the Cubs briefly, finishing with a .261 average, 136 home runs and 609 RBI in 1,435 major-league games . . . Also played in Japan . . . Recruited for Mets' organization by GM Frank Cashen, who knew him from their days in Baltimore organization . . . Promised changes in batting order will spur Met offense . . . Insisted upon and received two-year pact . . . Lives in Orlando, Fla., where he was born Jan. 30, 1943.

GREATEST STEALER

There has been no contest ever since Mookie Wilson started to do his thing for the Mets in a serious way in 1982. That was the year Mookie shattered the club single-season record, surpassing Frank Taveras' 42 steals of 1979 by streaking to 58.

By adding 54 last year, Wilson also surpassed the Mets' career record of 139 steals by Lee Mazzilli. Mookie has 143 and, at age 28, he is in a position to push the record out of reach for a few years.

Wilson simply has no competition as the monarch of the Met speedsters. Tommie Agee and Bud Harrelson could scamper effectively in the days of the Miracle Mets, but they lacked the speed of Mookie, who may be reaching his prime as a base thief.

ALL-TIME MET SEASON RECORDS

BATTING: Cleon Jones, .340, 1969
HRs: Dave Kingman, 37, 1976, 1982
RBIs: Rusty Staub, 105, 1975
STEALS: Mookie Wilson, 58, 1982
WINS: Tom Seaver, 25, 1969
STRIKEOUTS: Tom Seaver, 289, 1971

PHILADELPHIA PHILLIES

TEAM DIRECTORY: Pres.: William Y. Giles; Exec. VP: David Montgomery; VP-GM-Mgr.: Paul Owens; VP-Adm.: Tony Siegle; VP-Fin.: Jerry Clothier; VP-Pub. Rel.: Larry Shenk; VP-Dir. Play. Dev./Scouting: Jim Baumer; Trav. Sec.: Eddie Ferenz. Home: Veterans Stadium (65,454). Field distances: 330, l.f. line; 408, c.f.; 330, r.f. line. Spring training: Clearwater, Fla.

SCOUTING REPORT

HITTING: The Phils' attack doesn't figure to be as good without Pete Rose, Joe Morgan and Tony Perez, but the main man remains and Mike Schmidt can do a lot of damage, even in a so-called off year. Schmidt was disappointed with his .255 average and prolonged slumps last year, but he still ranked near the top in most offensive categories, with 40 homers and 109 RBI. His situation mirrored that of the Phillies' offense—the club hit a meager .249, but ranked third in runs scored with 696.

It remains to be seen whether Len Matuszek and Juan Samuel can make the fans forget Rose and Morgan at first and second, respectively, but it's quite likely a healthy Von Hayes (.265) and fellow outfielders Sixto Lezcano (.239) and Joe Lefebvre (.306) will be even more productive than they were last year. Gary Matthews (.258) and Garry Maddox (.275) also can be useful if they accept manager Paul Owens' platooning and realize it is for the good of the club.

PITCHING: With Steve Carlton (15-16) and John Denny (19-6, 2.37 ERA) as solid starters and Al Holland (8-4, 25 saves) and Willie Hernandez (9-4, 8 saves) exemplary in relief, the Phillies are blessed with a pair of formidable one-two punches. Unless age catches up with Carlton, the starting pitching can't be too poor. Rookie Charles Hudson (8-8) came along swiftly last year, so all the club needs is a dependable No. 4 starter.

Denny's Cy Young Award season and Holland's Fireman-of-the-Year credentials were chiefly responsible for the club's collective 3.34 ERA, second only to the Dodgers in the NL. Holland, a terror in the NLCS and World Series, figures to be even better if he's healthy the whole year. Owens will have to fight the urge to overwork Holland and run the risk of the intense reliever burning out by September.

John Denny won most games in NL (19) and Cy Young Award.

FIELDING: An unsettled lineup and the aging process contributed to generally poor fielding by the Phillies, who were 10th in the league with a .976 percentage last year. Schmidt (.959) was the most reliable fielder, finishing a shade behind the Cards' Ken Oberkfell in the fielding percentage rankings among NL third basemen. The outfield is solid defensively, but multiple Gold Glove winner Maddox again is in a fight to keep his job in center.

OUTLOOK: It's never wise to expect a repeat champion in the NL, and the Phillies are likely to miss the intangibles veterans like Rose, Perez and Morgan provided. But the club isn't going to finish too far from the top because it has fairly stable pitching and depth that can be matched only by the Expos among its NL East rivals.

By losing the leadership of the aforementioned veterans, the Phillies may have given the Expos the edge. If the Phillies are to come through, it would be an even greater miracle than last year's fantastic finish. The club has the blessing of The Pope (Owens), but it likely will suffer slightly because of the growing pains that might trouble Matuszek, Samuel and Hudson.

PHILADELPHIA PHILLIES 1984 ROSTER

MANAGER Paul Owens

Coaches—Dave Bristol, John Felski, Deron Johnson, Claude Osteen, Mike Ryan

PITCHERS

No.	Name	1983 Club	W-L	IP	SO	ERA	B-T	Ht.	Wt.	Born
30	Altamirano, Porfi	Portland	5-4	41	39	2.88	R-R	6-0	175	5/17/52 Nicaragua
		Philadelphia	2-3	41	24	3.70				
47	Anderson, Larry	Portland	7-8	70	64	2.05	R-R	6-3	205	5/6/53 Portland, OR
		Philadelphia	1-0	26	14	2.39				
50	Bystrom, Marty	Peninsula	1-0	6	9	0.00	R-R	6-5	210	7/26/58 Coral Gables, FL
		Philadelphia	6-9	119	87	4.60				
32	Carlton, Steve	Philadelphia	15-16	284	275	3.11	L-L	6-5	210	12/22/44 Miami, FL
39	Carmen, Don	Reading	8-5	124	93	2.97	L-L	6-3	190	8/14/59 Oklahoma City, OK
		Philadelphia	0-0	1	0	0.00				
44	Comer, Steve	Sl.C.-Port.	8-4	122	59	3.76	L-R	6-3	205	1/13/54 Minneapolis, MN
		Philadelphia	1-0	9	1	5.19				
40	Denny, John	Philadelphia	19-6	243	139	2.37	R-R	6-3	190	11/8/52 Prescott, AZ
35	Ghelfi, Tony	Portland	1-2	32	28	6.19	R-R	6-3	185	8/23/61 LaCrosse, WI
		Reading	10-3	110	96	3.68				
		Philadelphia	1-1	14	14	3.14				
46	Gross, Kevin	Portland	3-5	80	61	6.75	R-R	6-5	203	6/8/61 Downey, CA
		Philadelphia	4-6	96	66	3.56				
48	Hernandez, Willie	Chi. (NL)-Phil.	9-4	115	93	3.28	L-L	6-2	186	11/14/55 Puerto Rico
19	Holland, Al	Philadelphia	8-4	92	100	2.26	R-L	5-11	205	8/16/52 Roanoke, VA
49	Hudson, Charles	Portland	6-3	64	51	2.67	R-R	6-3	185	3/16/59 Ennis, TX
		Philadelphia	8-8	169	101	3.35				
45	McGraw, Tug	Philadelphia	2-1	56	30	3.56	R-L	6-0	186	8/30/44 Martinez, CA
—	Riley, George	Reading	8-3	82	58	2.42	L-L	6-4	200	10/6/56 Philadelphia, PA
		Portland	5-2	47	27	6.32				

CATCHERS

No.	Name	1983 Club	H	HR	RBI	Pct.	B-T	Ht.	Wt.	Born
—	Cipolloni, Joe	Peninsula	80	5	39	.231	R-R	5-8	180	8/12/60 Philadelphia, PA
10	Daulton, Darren	Reading	95	19	83	.262	L-R	6-0	185	1/3/62 Arkansas City, KN
		Philadelphia	1	0	0	.333				
6	Diaz, Bo	Philadelphia	111	15	64	.236	R-R	5-11	190	3/23/53 Venezuela
17	Virgil, Ozzie	Philadephia	30	6	23	.214	R-R	6-1	205	12/7/56 Puerto Rico

INFIELDERS

No.	Name	1983 Club	H	HR	RBI	Pct.	B-T	Ht.	Wt.	Born
33	Aguayo, Luis	Portland	65	5	33	.284	R-R	5-9	185	3/13/59 Puerto Rico
		Philadelphia	1	0	0	.250				
11	DeJesus, Ivan	Philadelpha	126	4	45	.254	R-R	5-11	175	1/9/53 Puerto Rico
—	Dowell, Ken	Reading	108	2	42	.294	R-R	5-9	160	1/19/61 Sacramento, CA
18	Garcia, Kiko	Portland	39	1	16	.345	R-R	5-11	178	10/14/53 Martinez, CA
		Philadelphia	34	2	9	.288				
15	Jeltz, Steve	Portland	48	0	16	.265	R-R	5-11	170	5/28/59 France
		Philadelphia	1	0	1	.125				
12	Matuszek, Len	Portland	136	24	92	.330	L-R	6-2	190	9/27/54 Toledo, OH
		Philadelphia	22	4	16	.275				
—	Melendez, Francisco	Reading	134	5	75	.298	L-L	6-0	170	1/25/64 Puerto Rico
16	Samuel, Juan	Reading	43	11	39	.243	R-R	5-11	168	12/9/61 Dominican Republic
		Portland	86	15	52	.330				
		Philadelphia	18	2	5	.277				
20	Schmidt, Mike	Philadelphia	136	40	109	.255	R-R	6-2	198	9/27/49 Dayton, OH
—	Schu, Rick	Peninsula	119	14	63	.268	R-R	6-0	170	1/26/62 Philadelphia, PA

OUTFIELDERS

No.	Name	1983 Club	H	HR	RBI	Pct.	B-T	Ht.	Wt.	Born
28	Corcoran, Tim	Portland	141	9	93	.311	L-L	5-11	175	4/19/53 Glendale, CA
		Philadelphia	0	0	0	.000				
29	Dernier, Bob	Reading	13	1	2	.232	R-R	6-0	165	1/5/57 Kansas City, MO
		Philadelphia	51	1	15	.231				
21	Gross, Greg	Philadelphia	74	0	29	.302	L-L	5-11	175	8/1/52 York, PA
9	Hayes, Von	Philadelphia	93	6	32	.265	L-R	6-5	190	8/31/58 Stockton, CA
23	Lefebvre, Joe	SD-Phil.	85	8	39	.306	L-R	5-10	180	2/22/56 Concorde, NH
28	Lezcano, Sixto	SD-Phil.	85	8	56	.239	R-R	5-10	190	11/28/53 Puerto Rico
31	Maddox, Garry	Philadelphia	89	4	32	.275	R-R	6-3	185	9/1/49 Cincinnati, OH
34	Matthews, Gary	Philadelphia	115	10	50	.258	R-R	6-3	205	7/5/50 San Fernando, CA
27	Sanchez, Alejandro	Portland	113	17	74	.247	R-R	6-0	185	2/26/59 Dominican Republic
		Philadelphia	2	0	2	.286				
26	Stone, Jeff	Reading	156	9	67	.317	L-R	6-0	175	12/26/60 Kennett, MO
		Philadelphia	3	0	3	.750				

PHILLIE PROFILES

MIKE SCHMIDT 34 6-2 198 Bats R Throws R

Endured a 1-for-20 World Series after leading the majors in home runs last year . . . Phillies' leading hitter in playoffs with a .467 average, he won Game 1, 1-0, with a home run . . . Belted 25 homers and had 64 RBI after the All-Star break . . . Had nine home runs and 24 RBI in July and repeated those numbers in August . . . Top vote-getter on NL All-Star squad . . . Regarded as finest all-around third baseman in game because of his Gold Glove fielding and slugging prowess . . . Born Sept. 27, 1949, in Dayton, Ohio . . . Topped majors in homers a sixth time and only Babe Ruth has done it more often (nine times) . . . Tied with Johnny Bench for 21st spot on all-time homer list . . . Belted two grand slams to set club record with seven . . . Owns fifth-best homer ratio in history, hitting one every 14.56 at-bats . . . Set Phillies' record with 128 walks . . . Fans voted him the greatest Phillies' player of all time, then booed him in World Series.

Year	Club	Pos.	G	AB	R	H	2B	3B	HR	RBI	SB	Avg.
1972	Philadelphia . . .	3B-2B	13	34	2	7	0	0	1	3	0	.206
1973	Philadelphia . . .	3B-2B-1B-SS	132	367	43	72	11	0	18	52	8	.196
1974	Philadelphia . . .	3B	162	568	108	160	28	7	36	116	23	.282
1975	Philadelphia . . .	3B-SS	158	562	93	140	34	3	38	95	29	.249
1976	Philadelphia . . .	3B	160	584	112	153	31	4	38	107	14	.262
1977	Philadelphia . . .	3B-SS-2B	154	544	114	149	27	11	38	101	15	.274
1978	Philadelphia . . .	3B-SS	145	513	93	129	27	2	21	78	19	.251
1979	Philadelphia . . .	3B-SS	160	541	109	137	25	4	45	114	9	.253
1980	Philadelphia . . .	3B	150	548	104	157	25	8	48	121	12	.286
1981	Philadelphia . . .	3B	102	354	78	112	19	2	31	91	12	.316
1982	Philadelphia . . .	3B	148	514	108	144	26	3	35	87	14	.280
1983	Philadelphia . . .	3B	154	534	104	136	16	4	40	109	7	.255
	Totals		1638	5663	1068	1496	269	48	389	1074	162	.264

GARY MATTHEWS 33 6-3 205 Bats R Throws R

Didn't take to platooning, but prospered in playoffs, when he was MVP . . . Batted .429 with three home runs in NL Championship Series vs. Dodgers, collecting four RBI in Game 3 and adding a three-run homer in Game 4 clincher . . . Limited to 132 games, he had lowest statistical totals of career . . . Left fielder made average respectable with a .369 August . . . Usually overshadowed by teammates, but respected for his aggressiveness and grace under pressure . . . Topped Phillies with 17 game-winning RBI in '82 . . . Born July 5, 1950, in San

Fernando, Cal.... Giants and Braves each made a mistake by letting him get away... A mere $5,000 kept him from staying with Giants as free agent in '76 and Ted Turner let him go in swap for Bob Walk after he had enjoyed four straight solid seasons for Atlanta... Rookie of the Year in 1973 for Giants... Batted .400 in 1981 division playoffs... Called "Sarge" by Phillies because of his take-charge qualities.

Year	Club	Pos.	G	AB	R	H	2B	3B	HR	RBI	SB	Avg.
1972	San Francisco.....	OF	20	62	11	18	1	1	4	14	0	.290
1973	San Francisco.....	OF	148	540	74	162	22	10	12	58	17	.300
1974	San Francisco.....	OF	154	561	87	161	27	6	16	82	11	.287
1975	San Francisco.....	OF	116	425	67	119	22	3	12	58	13	.280
1976	San Francisco.....	OF	156	587	79	164	28	4	20	84	12	.279
1977	Atlanta	OF	148	555	89	157	25	5	17	64	22	.283
1978	Atlanta	OF	129	474	75	135	20	5	18	62	8	.285
1979	Atlanta	OF	156	631	97	192	34	5	27	90	18	.304
1980	Atlanta	OF	155	571	79	159	17	3	19	75	11	.278
1981	Philadelphia......	OF	101	359	62	108	21	3	9	67	15	.301
1982	Philadelphia......	OF	162	616	89	173	31	1	19	83	21	.281
1983	Philadelphia......	OF	132	446	66	115	18	2	10	50	13	.258
	Totals..........		1577	5827	875	1663	266	48	183	787	161	.285

BO DIAZ 31 5-11 190 **Bats R Throws R**

Phillies' leading hitter in World Series, batting .333... Batted close to .300 final month to aid pennant push... Notched career-high five RBI, including ninth-inning, game-winning grand slam, against Mets in April... Enjoyed his first five-hit game, at Chicago in September... Fans were angered by Lonnie Smith swap that brought him to Philly, but he has appeased them somewhat with 33 homers and 149 RBI the last two years... Matched Stan Lopata's club record for homers by a catcher with 18 in 1982... Born March 23, 1953, in Cua, Venezuela... Bo is short for Baudilio... Set Venezuelan Winter League homer record with 20 in 1979-80... Hero in his homeland... Named Venezuelan League MVP in 1977-78 and helped Caracas to Caribbean World Series in '82... Originally signed by Red Sox, but was traded to Indians before 1978 season... Joined Phillies in three-way deal with St. Louis prior to 1982.

Year	Club	Pos.	G	AB	R	H	2B	3B	HR	RBI	SB	Avg.
1977	Boston	C	2	1	0	0	0	0	0	0	0	.000
1978	Cleveland........	C	44	127	12	30	4	0	2	11	0	.236
1979	Cleveland........	C	15	32	0	5	2	0	0	1	0	.156
1980	Cleveland........	C	76	207	15	47	11	2	3	32	1	.227
1981	Cleveland........	C	63	182	25	57	19	0	7	38	2	.313
1982	Philadelphia......	C	144	525	69	151	29	1	18	85	3	.288
1983	Philadelphia......	C	136	471	49	111	17	0	15	64	1	.236
	Totals..........		480	1545	170	401	82	3	45	231	7	.260

GARRY MADDOX 34 6-3 185 — Bats R Throws R

Another malcontent because of platooning, but he thrived under system . . . Batted .317 against left-handers . . . Hit .338 in August . . . Hounded by shoddy fielding in NL playoffs over the years . . . Slipped in Game 2 against Dodgers last year, enabling Pedro Guerrero to belt a two-run triple in the only game Phillies lost . . . Despite status as perennial Gold Glover, this center fielder has done better offensively than defensively in postseason . . . His 10th-inning double decided final game of 1980 playoffs . . . Solo homer off Orioles' Scott McGregor in eighth inning of Game 1 gave Phillies their lone World Series victory over Orioles . . . Born Sept. 1, 1949, in Cincinnati . . . Missed two years of baseball while serving in Vietnam, but compensated with quick climb through Giant system . . . Nicknamed "Secretary of the Defense."

Year	Club	Pos.	G	AB	R	H	2B	3B	HR	RBI	SB	Avg.
1972	San Francisco	OF	125	458	62	122	26	7	12	58	13	.266
1973	San Francisco	OF	144	587	81	187	30	10	11	76	24	.319
1974	San Francisco	OF	135	538	74	153	31	3	8	50	21	.284
1975	S.F.-Phil.	OF	116	426	54	116	26	8	5	50	25	.272
1976	Philadelphia	OF	146	531	75	175	37	6	6	68	29	.330
1977	Philadelphia	OF	139	571	85	167	27	10	14	74	22	.292
1978	Philadelphia	OF	155	598	62	172	34	3	11	68	33	.288
1979	Philadelphia	OF	148	548	70	154	28	6	13	61	26	.281
1980	Philadelphia	OF	143	549	59	142	31	3	11	73	25	.259
1981	Philadelphia	OF	94	323	37	85	7	1	5	40	9	.263
1982	Philadelphia	OF	119	412	39	117	27	2	8	61	7	.284
1983	Philadelphia	OF	97	324	27	89	14	2	4	32	7	.275
	Totals		1561	5865	725	1679	318	61	108	711	241	.284

STEVE CARLTON 39 6-5 210 — Bats L Throws L

Had first losing season in 10 years and his eight complete games were quite a dropoff from 19 he had in 1982 . . . Improved NLCS record to 4-2 with a pair of victories over Dodgers, 1-0 and 7-2 in clincher . . . Was beaten, 3-2, in pivotal Game 3 of World Series . . . "Lefty" became 16th pitcher in history to win 300 games, Sept. 23 at St. Louis . . . Topped majors in strikeouts for fifth time . . . Tied Warren Spahn's record of 17 seasons with 100 or more strikeouts . . . Became all-time strikeout king with 3,709, passing Gaylord Perry (April 16), Walter Johnson (April 27) and Nolan Ryan (June 7) . . . Leads Ryan by 32 entering this season . . . Born Dec. 22, 1944, in Miami . . . Went from 0-4 start to 23-win season in '82 . . . Passed Bob Gibson as all-time

NL strikeout leader in '81 . . . Maintained his vow of silence with press last year after almost wavering when he won No. 300 . . . Allegedly a good guy and a wine connoisseur.

Year	Club	G	IP	W	L	Pct.	SO	BB	H	ERA
1965	St. Louis	15	25	0	0	.000	21	8	27	2.52
1966	St. Louis	9	52	3	3	.500	25	18	56	3.12
1967	St. Louis	30	193	14	9	.609	168	62	173	2.98
1968	St. Louis	34	232	13	11	.542	162	61	214	2.99
1969	St. Louis	31	236	17	11	.607	210	93	185	2.17
1970	St. Louis	34	254	10	19	.345	193	109	239	3.72
1971	St. Louis	37	273	20	9	.690	172	98	275	3.56
1972	Philadelphia	41	346	27	10	.730	310	87	257	1.98
1973	Philadelphia	40	293	13	20	.394	223	113	293	3.90
1974	Philadelphia	39	291	16	13	.552	240	136	249	3.22
1975	Philadelphia	37	225	15	14	.517	192	104	217	3.56
1976	Philadelphia	35	253	20	7	.741	195	72	224	3.13
1977	Philadelphia	36	283	23	10	.697	198	89	229	2.64
1978	Philadelphia	34	247	16	13	.552	161	63	228	2.84
1979	Philadelphia	35	251	18	11	.621	213	89	202	3.62
1980	Philadelphia	38	304	24	9	.727	286	90	243	2.34
1981	Philadelphia	24	190	13	4	.765	179	62	152	2.42
1982	Philadelphia	38	296	23	11	.676	286	86	253	3.10
1983	Philadelphia	37	284	15	16	.483	275	84	277	3.11
	Totals	624	4558	300	200	.600	3709	1524	3993	3.01

IVAN DeJESUS 31 5-11 175 — Bats R Throws R

Definitely the most underrated of the NL champs . . . Led club in games played and was the glue of the defense at shortstop . . . Only two others made fewer errors at the position . . . Batted .300 against left-handers . . . Collected 1,000th hit Aug. 18, against Cardinals . . . Has never missed a game because of injury . . . Joined club in deal that sent Larry Bowa and Ryne Sandberg to Cubs prior to 1982 . . . Born Jan. 9, 1953, in Santurce, Puerto Rico . . . Attended University of Puerto Rico before signing with Dodgers . . . Cubs pulled a coup by landing him and Rick Monday in 1977 swap . . . Did his best hitting at Wrigley Field, but has tailed off in last few years . . . Established NL record for assists by a shortstop in '77, a mark since broken by Ozzie Smith . . . Led NL in runs scored in '78.

Year	Club	Pos.	G	AB	R	H	2B	3B	HR	RBI	SB	Avg.
1974	Los Angeles	SS	3	3	1	1	0	0	0	0	0	.333
1975	Los Angeles	SS	63	87	10	16	2	1	0	2	1	.184
1976	Los Angeles	SS-3B	22	41	4	7	2	1	0	2	0	.171
1977	Chicago (NL)	SS	155	624	91	166	31	7	3	40	24	.266
1978	Chicago (NL)	SS	160	619	104	172	24	7	3	35	41	.278
1979	Chicago (NL)	SS	160	636	92	180	26	10	5	52	24	.283
1980	Chicago (NL)	SS	157	618	78	160	26	3	3	33	44	.259
1981	Chicago (NL)	SS	106	403	49	78	8	4	0	13	21	.194
1982	Philadelphia	SS-3B	161	536	53	128	21	5	3	59	14	.239
1983	Philadelphia	SS	158	497	60	126	15	7	4	45	11	.254
	Totals		1145	4064	542	1034	155	45	21	281	180	.254

JOHN DENNY 31 6-3 190 — Bats R Throws R

Won Cy Young Award and Comeback of the Year Award after slumping to 6-13 due to arm trouble in '82 . . . Posted Phillies' World Series victory, 2-1, in Game 1 . . . Became top winner in NL with a career-high 19 . . . Received only seven runs of support in his six losses and trend continued in playoffs, where he was a 4-1 loser to Dodgers . . . Career-best ERA ranked second in NL . . . Born Nov. 8, 1952, in Prescott, Ariz. . . . Was 3-1 with a 2.25 ERA in April and 6-1 with 2.73 ERA in July . . . Sizzled in September with 6-0 mark and 1.80 ERA . . . A 29th-round draft choice of the Cardinals, who also let Steve Carlton get away . . . Made a big splash in first full major-league season by leading NL in ERA, at age 23, with a 2.52 ERA . . . Cards traded him to Indians along with Jerry Mumphrey for Bobby Bonds in 1980 and he joined Phillies in swap for three minor-leaguers in September '82.

Year	Club	G	IP	W	L	Pct.	SO	BB	H	ERA
1974	St. Louis	2	2	0	0	.000	1	0	3	0.00
1975	St. Louis	25	136	10	7	.588	72	51	149	3.97
1976	St. Louis	30	207	11	9	.550	74	74	189	2.52
1977	St. Louis	26	150	8	8	.500	60	62	165	4.50
1978	St. Louis	33	234	14	11	.560	103	74	200	2.96
1979	St. Louis	31	206	8	11	.421	99	100	206	4.85
1980	Cleveland	16	109	8	6	.571	59	47	116	4.38
1981	Cleveland	19	146	10	6	.625	94	66	139	3.14
1982	Cleveland	21	138	6	11	.353	94	73	126	5.01
1982	Philadelphia	4	22	0	2	.000	19	10	18	4.03
1983	Philadelphia	36	243	19	6	.760	139	53	229	2.37
	Totals	243	1593	94	77	.550	814	610	1540	3.59

AL HOLLAND 31 5-11 205 — Bats R Throws L

This hard-throwing, barrel-chested veteran turned the Phillies around with his stout relief . . . Nicknamed "Mr. T" by teammates for his nasty game face, but is mellow off the field . . . Set club record with 25 saves, despite missing three weeks of the season . . . Injury limited him to six saves and three victories at All-Star break, but he was gangbusters thereafter, saving 19 and winning five in the second half . . . Born Aug. 16, 1952, in Roanoke, Va. . . . Had string of 95 relief appearances without a loss snapped by Pittsburgh in August . . . Was 3-0 with five saves in July and saved nine games under September pennant pressure . . . In final 15 games, he allowed one earned run in 19⅓ innings, saving seven . . . Trend continued in postseason . . . Was unscored upon in 6⅔ innings against Dodgers and Orioles, saving two games . . . Played football at North Carolina

A&T ... Overshadowed in Giants' bullpen by Greg Minton and Gary Lavelle, but broke loose when he became No. 1 man for Phillies after being acquired with Joe Morgan for Mike Krukow, Mark Davis and Charles Penigar prior to last season.

Year	Club	G	IP	W	L	Pct.	SO	BB	H	ERA
1977	Pittsburgh	2	2	0	0	.000	1	0	4	9.00
1979	San Francisco	3	7	0	0	.000	7	5	3	0.00
1980	San Francisco	54	82	5	3	.625	65	34	71	1.76
1981	San Francisco	47	101	7	5	.583	78	44	87	2.41
1982	San Francisco	58	130	7	3	.700	97	40	115	3.33
1983	Philadelphia	68	92	8	4	.667	100	30	63	2.26
	Totals	232	414	27	15	.643	348	153	343	2.52

CHARLES HUDSON 25 6-3 185 **Bats R Throws R**

Went a long way, considering he was a non-roster player in spring training and a minor leaguer at the start of the season ... Lost two World Series games, which had him hanging his head, but he helped Phillies get there ... Posted 7-2 victory over Dodgers' Fernando Valenzuela in Game 3 of the playoffs ... Pitched a no-hitter until Houston's Craig Reynolds ruined it with one out in the ninth July 20 ... Won five straight games at one point ... Born March 16, 1959, in Ennis, Tex. ... Pitched Prairie View A&M to NAIA playoffs in '80 and '81 ... Signed as 12th-round draft choice in June 1981 and reached majors in two-plus years ... Throws hard and is poised for his age ... Posted 15-5 record and league-leading 1.85 ERA for Peninsula (A) in 1982 and was named Carolina League Pitcher of the Year.

Year	Club	G	IP	W	L	Pct.	SO	BB	H	ERA
1983	Philadelphia	26	169	8	8	.500	101	53	158	3.35

VON HAYES 25 6-5 190 **Bats L Throws R**

Came to Phillies with high hopes, but spring injury triggered disappointing season ... Although he raised batting average, he had 50 fewer RBI than in standout 1982 rookie season with Cleveland ... Batted .283 as a regular starter for Phillies and .304 vs. left-handers, but was on bench during stretch drive ... Hitless in five at-bats in postseason play ... Born Aug. 31, 1958, in Stockton, Cal. ... Attended St. Mary's College and was signed by Indians as first baseman ... Took only two years to reach majors after batting .329 with 93 RBI for Charleston in the International League (AAA) in

1981 . . . Belted 11 game-winning RBI for Indianapolis in the American Association (AAA) in 1982 and was swapped to the Phils for five players, including Manny Trillo and Julio Franco . . . Groomed as regular right fielder in '83, but injury contributed to loss of regular status.

Year	Club	Pos.	G	AB	R	H	2B	3B	HR	RBI	SB	Avg.
1981	Cleveland	OF-3B	43	109	21	28	8	2	1	17	4	.257
1982	Cleveland	OF-3B-1B	150	527	65	132	25	3	14	82	32	.250
1983	Philadelphia	OF-1B	124	351	45	93	9	5	6	32	20	.265
	Totals		317	987	131	253	42	10	21	131	56	.256

TOP PROSPECT

LEN MATUSZEK 29 6-2 190 Bats L Throws R
Earns the distinction of being the team's top prospect over second baseman Juan Samuel based on a hot September that helped Phillies win the division . . . Took over at first base for Pete Rose and batted .275 with four homers and 16 RBI . . . Ineligible for postseason, but likely will be first baseman this year . . . Born Sept. 27, 1954, in Toledo, Ohio . . . Flubbed two previous big-league trials, but earned promotion with .330 average, 24 homers and 92 RBI for Portland (AAA) last year.

MANAGER PAUL OWENS: "The Pope" provided some divine

guidance down the stretch to win a pennant . . . It was thought he may return to devoting full attention to general manager's duties, but owner Bill Giles asked him to return in dual capacity in '84 . . . Took over July 18 in a surprise move when Phillies were in first place with 43-42 mark under Pat Corrales . . . Players' complaints led to Corrales' firing . . . New manager also was criticized by veterans who didn't relish platooning . . . Showed them it worked by managing club to a 47-30 mark, including 21 victories in the last 26 regular-season games . . . Born Feb. 7, 1924, in Salamanca, N.Y. . . . Won Pony League batting title with a .407 average for Olean, N.Y., in 1951 . . . Became player-manager of Olean in '55 and won two more batting crowns . . . Ended minor-league managing career with Bakersfield, Cal., in '59 . . . Became a scout and was head of Phillies' farm system when he was named general manager in 1972 . . . That year he replaced Frank Lucchesi as the club's manager for the remainder of the season, going 33-47 and proving "The Pope" isn't infallible.

GREATEST STEALER

Oakland's Rickey Henderson created considerable commotion by stealing 100 or more bases in successive seasons, but that was nothing new to the greatest base-stealer in Phillies' history.

Billy Hamilton isn't regarded among the game's greatest thieves because he did most of his stealing before the turn of the century. But the fact remains Hamilton stole 102 bases in 1890 and followed that with 115 in 1891 to beat Henderson to the punch.

Hamilton finished with 937 career steals, one less than all-time leader Lou Brock. Billy had 508 steals as a member of the Phillies, including 99 in 1894 and 95 in 1895.

Philadelphia's Sherry Magee set a "modern" club record with 55 thefts in 1906 and concluded his Phillies' career with 387 steals. Larry Bowa stole 39 bases in 1974 and is third on the club's all-time list with 288.

ALL-TIME PHILLIE SEASON RECORDS

BATTING: Frank O'Doul, .398, 1929
HRs: Mike Schmidt, 48, 1980
RBIs: Chuck Klein, 170, 1930
STEALS: Sherry Magee, 55, 1906
WINS: Grover Alexander, 33, 1916
STRIKEOUTS: Steve Carlton, 310, 1972

PITTSBURGH PIRATES

TEAM DIRECTORY: Chairman of the Board: John Galbreath; Pres.: Daniel Galbreath; Exec. VP: Harding Peterson; Dir. Scouting: Milt Graff; Dir. Minor Leagues: Branch Rickey III; Publ. Dir: Ed Wade; Trav. Sec.: Charles Muse; Mgr.: Chuck Tanner. Home: Three Rivers Stadium (58,365). Field distances: 335, l.f. line; 375, l.c.; 400, c.f.; 375, r.c.; 335, r.f. line. Spring training: Bradenton, Fla.

SCOUTING REPORT

HITTING: The Lumber Company has turned into The Toothpick Factory, with Dave Parker and Mike Easler gone. The Bucs are attempting to change their image from a hitting team to one with balance. Some big sticks are gone, but the Pirates' overall prospects are good, because of improved pitching.

This isn't to say the club isn't capable at the plate. With the likes of NL batting champion Bill Madlock (.323) and Tony Pena (.301) wielding the mace, the Pirates aren't devoid of punch. Jason

Pirates' Bill Madlock annexed his fourth batting crown.

Thompson (18 homers, 76 RBI) provides the long ball, Johnny Ray (.283) can hit with any second baseman in the league and Lee Lacy (.302) may finally be able to nail down a regular job with Parker and Easler gone. But the departed duo helped the club bat .264 last season, so a mark that high is unlikely without them.

PITCHING: The Bucs have their most impressive collection of starters in years and they've still got relief ace Kent Tekulve (7-5, 1.64, 18 saves), who signed a free-agent, three-year contract for $800,000 a year. Entering the 1983 season, Don Robinson, Rick Rhoden and John Candelaria were regarded as the big three. Robinson, probably a better hitter than a pitcher, no longer is prominent in the club's plans.

This year's cast includes Larry McWilliams (15-8), who blossomed last year; John Tudor (13-12), acquired from Boston in the Easler deal; Jose DeLeon (7-3), a Dominican who did a pretty good imitation of Juan Marichal last season, and young Lee Tunnell (11-6). Add Candelaria (15-8) and Rhoden (13-13) to this group and the Bucs have possibly the best starting depth in the division.

FIELDING: First baseman Thompson, second baseman Ray, third baseman Madlock, center fielder Marvell Wynne and catcher Pena ranked just below the league leaders at their positions, helping the Bucs gain a share of the league lead with a .982 fielding percentage. The Pirates don't strike fans as a great defensive club—compared to the reputation the Cardinals enjoy, for instance—but they keep errors to a minimum and generally are sure-handed, Dale Berra's 30 errors at shortstop notwithstanding. This isn't the most graceful bunch in the league, but somehow the job gets done.

OUTLOOK: If you believe in the premise that good pitching is more important than good hitting, the Bucs' change of emphasis could prove beneficial this summer, especially in a division where stout pitching isn't a strong suit. But there is one glaring weak spot: a bench lacking the club's usual depth.

Otherwise, the club will be in good shape under the guidance of manager Chuck Tanner, who always gets the most out of his material and pulls enough strings to keep his players fresh down the stretch. This club is only one solid outfielder away from a flag.

PITTSBURGH PIRATES 1984 ROSTER

MANAGER Chuck Tanner
Coaches—Harvey Haddix, Grant Jackson, Joe Lonnett, Al Monchak, Bob Skinner

PITCHERS

No.	Name	1983 Club	W-L	IP	SO	ERA	B-T	Ht.	Wt.	Born
26	*Bibby, Jim	Pittsburgh	5-12	78	44	6.69	R-R	6-6	250	10/29/44 Franklinton, NC
55	Bielecki, Mike	Lynn	15-7	164	143	3.19	R-R	6-3	200	7/31/59 Baltimore, MD
45	Candelaria, John	Pittsburgh	15-8	198	157	3.23	B-R	6-7	232	11/6/53 New York, NY
25	DeLeon, Jose	Hawaii	11-6	127	128	3.04	R-R	6-3	210	12/20/60 Dom. Republic
		Pittsburgh	7-3	108	118	2.83				
62	Green, Chris	Hawaii	0-9	77	49	4.31	L-L	6-2	214	9/5/60 Los Angeles, CA
		Lynn	5-6	75	73	3.98				
47	Guante, Cecilio	Hawaii	2-1	26	24	3.51	R-R	6-3	185	2/2/60 Dominican Republic
		Pittsburgh	2-6	100	82	3.32				
61	Krawczyk, Ray	Hawaii	5-7	89	88	3.76	R-R	6-2	185	10/9/59 Sewickley, PA
54	Manzanillo, Ravelo	Alexandria	7-7	105	66	4.44	L-L	5-11	170	10/17/53 Dom. Republic
49	McWilliams, Larry	Pittsburgh	15-8	238	199	3.25	L-L	6-5	175	2/10/54 Wichita, KS
58	Pulido, Alfonso	Mexico City	17-3	187	83	2.02	L-L	5-11	170	1/23/59 Mexico
		Pittsburgh	0-0	2	1	9.00				
29	Rhoden, Rick	Pittsburgh	13-13	244	153	3.09	R-R	6-4	200	5/16/53 Boynton Beach, FL
43	Robinson, Don	Lynn	0-1	7	5	8.10	R-R	6-4	231	6/8/57 Ashland, KY
		Pittsburgh	2-2	36	28	4.46				
38	Sarmiento, Manny	Pittsburgh	3-5	84	49	2.99	R-R	5-11	170	2/2/56 Venezuela
19	Scurry, Rod	Pittsburgh	4-9	68	67	5.56	L-L	6-2	180	3/17/56 Sacramento, CA
35	Sentenney, Steve	Tidewater	0-3	34	39	2.88	R-R	6-2	205	8/7/57 Indianapolis, IN
		Hawaii	4-4	52	55	4.70				
		Pittsburgh	0-0	0	0	0.00				
27	Tekulve, Kent	Pittsburgh	7-5	99	52	1.64	R-R	6-4	175	3/5/47 Cincinnati, OH
—	*Tomlin, Dave	Pittsburgh	0-0	4	5	6.75	L-L	6-2	185	6/22/49 Maysville, KY
—	Tudor, John	Boston	13-12	242	136	4.09	L-L	6-0	185	2/2/54 Schenectady, NY
22	Tunnell, Lee	Pittsburgh	11-6	178	95	3.56	R-R	6-1	180	10/30/60 Tyler, TX
41	Winn, Jim	Pittsburgh	0-0	11	3	7.36	R-R	6-3	190	9/23/59 Stockton, CA
		Hawaii	0-1	39	22	3.96				
44	Zaske, Jeff	Lynn	5-3	70	72	2.18	R-R	6-5	180	10/6/60 Seattle, WA
		Hawaii	1-0	6	4	6.00				
		Pittsburgh	0-0	0	0	0.00				

CATCHERS

No.	Name	1983 Club	H	HR	RBI	Pct.	B-T	Ht.	Wt.	Born
14	May, Milt	SF-Pitts.	49	6	20	.247	L-R	6-0	192	8/1/50 Gary, IN
6	Pena, Tony	Pittsburgh	163	15	70	.301	R-R	6-0	175	11/20/57 Dom. Republic
18	Tenace, Gene	Pittsburgh	11	0	6	.177	R-R	6-0	190	10/10/46 Russelton, PA

INFIELDERS

37	Belliard, Rafael	Lynn	113	2	37	.262	R-R	5-9	139	10/24/61 Dom. Republic
		Pittsburgh	0	0	0	.000				
4	Berra, Dale	Pittsburgh	135	10	52	.251	R-R	6-0	190	12/13/56 Ridgewood, NJ
64	Gonzalez, Denny	Hawaii	121	9	48	.269	R-R	5-11	165	7/22/63 Dominican Republic
10	*Hebner, Richie	Pittsburgh	43	5	26	.265	L-R	6-1	200	11/26/47 Boston, MA
5	Madlock, Bill	Pittsburgh	153	12	68	.323	R-R	5-11	180	1/12/51 Memphis, TN
2	Morrison, Jim	Pittsburgh	48	6	25	.304	R-R	5-11	182	9/23/52 Pensacola, FL
3	Ray, Johnny	Pittsburgh	163	5	53	.283	B-R	5-11	170	3/1/57 Chouteau, OK
30	Thompson, Jason	Pittsburgh	134	18	76	.259	L-L	6-4	220	7/6/54 Hollywood, CA
50	Vargas, Hedi	Lynn	22	2	13	.310	R-R	6-4	205	2/23/59 Puerto Rico
		Hawaii	71	12	46	.348				
15	Wotus, Ron	Hawaii	140	10	62	.301	R-R	6-1	165	3/3/61 Hartford, CT
		Pittsburgh	0	0	0	.000				

OUTFIELDERS

52	Bonilla, Bobby	Alexandria	129	11	59	.256	B-R	6-3	210	2/23/63 New York, NY
28	Davis, Trench	Hawaii	71	0	23	.256	L-L	6-3	185	9/12/60 Baltimore, MD
		Lynn	61	2	16	.279				
—	*Dilone, Miguel	Cleve.-Chi. (AL)	13	0	7	.183	B-R	6-0	160	11/1/54 Dominican Republic
		Pittsburgh	0	0	0	.000				
51	Frobel, Doug	Hawaii	115	24	80	.304	L-R	6-4	196	6/6/59 Canada
		Pittsburgh	17	3	11	.283				
12	Harper, Brian	Pittsburgh	29	7	20	.221	R-R	6-2	195	10/16/59 Los Angeles, CA
17	Lacy, Lee	Pittsburgh	87	4	13	.302	R-R	6-1	175	4/10/48 Longview, TX
11	Mazzilli, Lee	Pittsburgh	59	5	24	.240	B-R	6-1	185	3/25/55 New York, NY
16	Orsulak, Joe	Hawaii	154	10	58	.286	L-L	6-1	185	5/31/62 Parsippany, NJ
		Pittsburgh	2	0	1	.182				
—	Otis, Amos	Kansas City	93	4	41	.261	R-R	5-11	166	4/26/47 Mobile, AL
36	Wynne, Marvell	Tidewater	50	3	29	.286	L-L	5-11	175	12/17/59 Chicago, IL
		Pittsburgh	89	7	26	.243				

*Free agent unsigned at press time

PIRATE PROFILES

BILL MADLOCK 33 5-11 180 Bats R Throws R

"Mad Dog" growled down the stretch to win his fourth batting title, becoming only the 11th player to accomplish that feat . . . Set tempo for .323 season by batting .424 in May and .367 in July, when he connected for five homers . . . Only the sixth player in major-league history to win batting crowns with two clubs, notching two with Pirates and two with Cubs . . . Collected his 1,500th hit last July . . . Born Jan. 12, 1951, in Memphis, Tenn. . . . After winning back-to-back batting titles with Chicago in 1975 and 1976, he was swapped to Giants . . . Candlestick Park didn't agree with his statistics, so third baseman welcomed shift to Pittsburgh in six-player deal in June 1979 and promptly helped push Pirates to world championship that season . . . Batted .375 in '79 World Series vs. Baltimore . . . Became Bucs' clubhouse leader upon Willie Stargell's retirement . . . Injuries limited him to only 130 games last year and Pirates suffered from his absence.

Year	Club	Pos.	G	AB	R	H	2B	3B	HR	RBI	SB	Avg.
1973	Texas	3B	21	77	16	27	5	3	1	5	3	.351
1974	Chicago (NL)	3B	128	453	65	142	21	5	9	54	11	.313
1975	Chicago (NL)	3B	130	514	77	182	29	7	7	64	9	.354
1976	Chicago (NL)	3B	142	514	68	174	36	1	15	84	15	.339
1977	San Francisco.	2B-3B	140	533	70	161	28	1	12	46	13	.302
1978	San Francisco.	2B-1B	122	447	76	138	26	3	15	44	16	.309
1979	SF-Pitts.	3B-2B-1B	154	560	85	167	26	5	14	85	32	.298
1980	Pittsburgh	3B-1B	137	494	62	137	22	4	10	53	16	.277
1981	Pittsburgh	3B	82	279	35	95	23	1	6	45	18	.341
1982	Pittsburgh	3B-1B	154	568	92	181	33	3	19	95	18	.319
1983	Pittsburgh	3B	130	473	68	153	21	0	12	68	3	.323
	Totals		1340	4902	714	1557	270	33	120	643	154	.318

JASON THOMPSON 29 6-4 220 Bats L Throws L

Disappointing down the stretch, he hit only seven homers in second half as production tailed off sharply . . . First baseman had six homers and 23 RBI in July . . . In 1982, he became eighth player to hit 30 homers in one season in each league and 31st to play for each league in All-Star competition . . . That was his option year and he signed a five-year, $5.5-million contract to stay with Bucs . . . Born July 6, 1954, in Hollywood, Cal. . . . Rookie sensation with Tigers in '76, blasting 14 homers in first 16 games . . . Swapped to Angels during 1980 season and batted

.317 with 17 homers and 70 RBI in 102 games for them . . . Traded to Bucs and sent to Yankees for Jim Spencer and money, but deal was voided by commissioner Bowie Kuhn because it violated cash restrictions, much to delight of Pirate players.

Year	Club	Pos.	G	AB	R	H	2B	3B	HR	RBI	SB	Avg.
1976	Detroit	1B	123	412	45	90	12	1	17	54	2	.218
1977	Detroit	1B	158	585	87	158	24	5	31	105	0	.270
1978	Detroit	1B	153	589	79	169	25	3	26	96	0	.287
1979	Detroit	1B	145	492	58	121	16	1	20	79	2	.246
1980	Det.-Calif.	1B	138	438	69	126	19	0	21	90	2	.288
1981	Pittsburgh	1B	86	223	36	54	13	0	15	42	0	.242
1982	Pittsburgh	1B	156	550	87	156	32	0	31	101	1	.284
1983	Pittsburgh	1B	152	517	70	134	20	1	18	76	1	.259
	Totals		1111	3806	531	1008	161	11	179	643	8	.265

TONY PENA 26 6-0 175 — Bats R Throws R

Matched his lifetime average by batting .314 after the All-Star Game . . . Hit .336 in July and .320 in August . . . Best young catcher in NL has stitched together three straight consistent seasons . . . Has excellent speed for a catcher and a strong arm . . . Born Nov. 20, 1957, in Monte Cristi, Dominican Republic . . . Didn't play high-school baseball, but was taught rudiments of the game by his mother, an outstanding softball player . . . A late bloomer, he didn't accomplish much in minors until reaching Buffalo (AA), for which he batted .313 with 34 homers in 1979 . . . After batting .320 for Portland (AAA) in 1980, he showed Pirates he was ready to become their No. 1 catcher.

Year	Club	Pos.	G	AB	R	H	2B	3B	HR	RBI	SB	Avg.
1980	Pittsburgh	C	8	21	1	9	1	1	0	1	0	.429
1981	Pittsburgh	C	66	210	16	63	9	1	2	17	1	.300
1982	Pittsburgh	C	138	497	53	147	28	4	11	63	2	.296
1983	Pittsburgh	C	151	542	51	163	22	3	15	70	6	.301
	Totals		363	1270	121	382	60	9	28	151	9	.301

JOHN TUDOR 30 6-0 185 — Bats L Throws L

Sought by several teams, he was traded by the Red Sox for outfielder Mike Easler of the Pirates . . . Led Red Sox in wins each of last two seasons, becoming first lefty to do that since Mel Parnell in 1953 . . . Has good command of pitches and good knowledge of how to use them . . . Didn't let the Green Monster intimidate him . . . Finished ninth in AL in innings pitched and 10th in strikeouts . . . Was third in AL in home runs allowed (32) . . . Pitched no-hitter for Bristol (AA) against Reading in 1977 . . . Born Feb. 2, 1954, in Schenectady, N.Y. . . . Attended North Shore Community College and Georgia Southern . . . Received degree in criminal justice from Georgia Southern, where he lettered in baseball and basketball . . . Drafted by Mets in 1975, but turned down offer and signed with Red Sox after draft the following January.

Year	Club	G	IP	W	L	Pct.	SO	BB	H	ERA
1979	Boston	6	28	1	2	.333	11	9	39	6.43
1980	Boston	16	92	8	5	.615	45	31	81	3.03
1981	Boston	18	79	4	3	.571	44	28	74	4.56
1982	Boston	32	196	13	10	.565	146	59	215	3.63
1983	Boston	34	242	13	12	.520	136	81	236	4.09
	Totals	106	637	39	32	.549	382	208	645	3.96

JOHN CANDELARIA 30 6-7 232 Bats L Throws L

Elected to remain with Bucs after threatening to leave as free agent prior to last season and responded with best season since 1977 . . . Was 4-0 with a 2.61 ERA in July and 3-0 with 1.36 ERA in September . . . Attained career victory No. 100 last June . . . Except for 1981, when arm injury restricted him to six games, "The Candy Man" has been Bucs' most consistent pitcher since 1976 . . . Born Nov. 6, 1953, in New York City . . . Did not play baseball his final two years in high school, but was an All-American basketball player . . . Declined invitation to try out for Puerto Rican Olympic basketball squad to sign pro baseball contract . . . Pitched no-hitter against Dodgers, Aug. 9, 1976, the first thrown by a Pirate in Pittsburgh since 1907.

Year	Club	G	IP	W	L	Pct.	SO	BB	H	ERA
1975	Pittsburgh	18	121	8	6	.571	95	36	95	2.75
1976	Pittsburgh	32	220	16	7	.696	138	60	173	3.15
1977	Pittsburgh	33	231	20	5	.800	133	50	197	*2.34
1978	Pittsburgh	30	189	12	11	.522	94	49	191	3.24
1979	Pittsburgh	33	207	14	9	.609	101	41	201	3.22
1980	Pittsburgh	35	233	11	14	.440	97	50	246	4.02
1981	Pittsburgh	6	41	2	2	.500	14	11	42	3.51
1982	Pittsburgh	31	175	12	7	.632	133	37	166	2.94
1983	Pittsburgh	33	198	15	8	.652	157	45	191	3.23
	Totals	251	1615	110	69	.615	962	379	1502	3.14

KENT TEKULVE 37 6-4 175 Bats R Throws R

As usual, "Teke" ranked with the finest relievers in the NL, a distinction he first attained by going 10-1 in '77 . . . Best month was July, when he was 2-0 with a 1.29 ERA and had five of his 18 saves . . . Has 139 saves in Pirate career, including club-record 31 twice in '78 and '79 . . . Born March 5, 1947, in Cincinnati . . . Pitched in 101 games, including post-season, in '79 . . . Plans a career in broadcasting . . . Was graduated from Marietta College with degree in education . . . Did not pitch professionally until age 22 and was 28 when he reached majors to stay in '75 . . . Rangy right-hander wears flippers in the shower so he won't slip down the drain, but the jokes are over once he takes the mound and releases his wicked slider.

Year	Club	G	IP	W	L	Pct.	SO	BB	H	ERA
1974	Pittsburgh	8	9	1	1	.500	6	5	12	6.00
1975	Pittsburgh	34	56	1	2	.333	28	23	43	2.25
1976	Pittsburgh	64	103	5	3	.625	68	25	91	2.45
1977	Pittsburgh	72	103	10	1	.909	59	33	89	3.06
1978	Pittsburgh	91	135	8	7	.533	77	55	115	2.33
1979	Pittsburgh	94	134	10	8	.556	75	49	109	2.75
1980	Pittsburgh	78	93	8	12	.400	47	40	96	3.39
1981	Pittsburgh	45	65	5	5	.500	34	17	61	2.49
1982	Pittsburgh	85	129	12	8	.600	66	46	113	2.87
1983	Pittsburgh	76	99	7	5	.583	52	36	78	1.64
	Totals	647	926	67	52	.563	512	329	807	2.63

LEE TUNNELL 23 6-1 180 Bats R Throws R

Tabbed as the club's top prospect last year, he came through following a slow start . . . Was 2-3 with a 4.92 ERA in the first half, but entered the rotation to stay and won nine of his last 12 decisions . . . At his best in September, going 3-1 . . . Born Oct. 30, 1960, in Tyler, Tex. . . . Attended Baylor and was the Pirates' second choice in the June 1981 draft . . . Made quick rise to majors after 12-9 start with Portland (AAA) in '82 . . . In a remarkable debut, he filled in for injured John Candelaria and beat Fernando Valenzuela and Dodgers, 1-0 . . . Has an outstanding sinker.

Year	Club	G	IP	W	L	Pct.	SO	BB	H	ERA
1982	Pittsburgh	5	18	1	1	.500	4	5	17	3.93
1983	Pittsburgh	35	178	11	6	.647	95	58	167	3.65
	Totals	40	196	12	7	.632	99	63	184	3.67

JOSE DeLEON 23 6-3 210 Bats R Throws R

Provided the Pirates with a bonus when he joined the club in an emergency measure in July and exceeded all expectations . . . In four of his first nine starts, this rookie carried a no-hitter into the sixth . . . In his second start, against San Diego in July, he lost a no-hitter on Alan Wiggins' one-out single in the seventh . . . Then the Mets' Hubie Brooks ruined a bid with one out in the ninth of game in which he struck out 11 before leaving with a no-decision after throwing nine scoreless innings . . . Fanned 13 in a two-hitter against the Reds in August, giving up his first hit to

Alan Knicely with two down in the seventh . . . Born Dec. 20, 1960, in LaVega, Dominican Republic . . . Overcame midseason shoulder problems in 1982 to go 10-7 with Portland (AAA) . . . Reputed to have a 90-mph fastball.

Year	Club	G	IP	W	L	Pct.	SO	BB	H	ERA
1983	Pittsburgh	15	108	7	3	.700	118	47	75	2.83

LARRY McWILLIAMS 30 6-5 175 **Bat L Throws L**

In what clearly was a deal that helped both clubs, he was acquired from Braves for Pascual Perez in June 1982 . . . Had never won more than 13 games in any pro season until he tied John Candelaria for staff lead in victories last year . . . May was best month as he went 3-1 . . . Finished April with a one-hit, 3-0 victory over Giants. Bob Brenly's "99-hopper" up the middle with one out in the fifth was the only hit . . . Earlier, he had a two-hit shutout of Houston . . . Born Feb. 10, 1954, in Wichita, Kan. . . . Came up with Braves in 1978 and combined with Gene Garber to halt Pete Rose's 44-game hitting streak . . . After Braves' minor-league pitching coach Johnny Sain hastened his windup in '81, he won 11 of his last 12 games at Richmond (AAA).

Year	Club	G	IP	W	L	Pct.	SO	BB	H	ERA
1978	Atlanta	15	99	9	3	.750	42	35	84	2.82
1979	Atlanta	13	66	3	2	.600	32	22	69	5.59
1980	Atlanta	30	164	9	14	.391	77	39	188	4.94
1981	Atlanta	6	38	2	1	.667	23	8	31	3.08
1982	Atl.-Pitt.	46	159	8	8	.500	118	44	158	3.84
1983	Pittsburgh	35	238	15	8	.652	199	87	205	3.25
	Totals	145	764	46	36	.561	491	235	735	3.88

TOP PROSPECTS

RON WOTUS 23 6-1 165 **Bats R Throws R**

The Pirates figure to need infield help this year and he could be ready following two solid seasons for Portland (AAA) . . . Began 1982 as a utility infielder, but found a home at second base . . . Batted .290 in 1982 and improved to .301 last year . . . Born March 3, 1961, in Hartford, Conn. . . . Infielder Denio Gonzalez and outfielder Joe Orsulak are also highly regarded, as is first baseman Hedi Vargas.

John Candelaria rounds out a decade with his only team.

MANAGER CHUCK TANNER: As usual, this master motivator kept the Pirates in NL East race until a sag in the final two weeks left them six games behind Philadelphia . . . Became the 35th manager to notch 1,000 victories in May . . . Has 1,067-984 record as major-league skipper, guiding eight winning teams since 1970, including the 1979 world champions . . . Born July 4, 1929, in New Castle, Pa. . . . An outfielder who played parts of eight years in majors . . . Homered on his first major-league at-bat, for Milwaukee Braves in 1955 . . . Trademark as a manager is communication and making full use of his roster, keeping club frisky for pennant dash . . . Managed Hawaii (AAA) to best record (98-48) in pro ball in '70 before taking over White Sox . . . Known for rapport with Dick Allen in Chicago . . . Eternal optimist.

GREATEST STEALER

It's difficult to determine the best base-stealer in Pirates' history, because there are three deserving candidates: oldtimers Max Carey and Honus Wagner and modern-day speedster Omar Moreno.

Hall-of-Famer Wagner, regarded as the greatest shortstop ever, was better known for his hitting and fielding skills, but he was good enough on the basepaths to lead the National League in steals five times between 1901 and 1908.

Then Carey came along and doubled Wagner's feat, topping the NL in thefts 10 times between 1913 and 1925. He set a club record with 63 steals in 1916 and went over the 50 mark six times.

Moreno accomplished more in a shorter period of time. He swiped 71 bases in 1978 and placed his single-season record further out of reach with 96 steals two years later. When he left as a free agent prior to last year, Moreno had stolen 412 bases as a member of the Bucs.

Carey ranks No. 1 in club history with 678 steals in a Pirate uniform, closely followed by Wagner, who had 639. Carey also is fourth on the all-time list with 738 stolen bases, so it would be difficult to deny him the honor of being the best of the Bucs' bandits.

ALL-TIME PIRATE SEASON RECORDS

BATTING: Arky Vaughan, .385, 1935
HRs: Ralph Kiner, 54, 1949
RBIs: Paul Waner, 131, 1927
STEALS: Omar Moreno, 96, 1980
WINS: Jack Chesbro, 28, 1902
STRIKEOUTS: Bob Veale, 276, 1965

ST. LOUIS CARDINALS

TEAM DIRECTORY: Chairman of the Board-Pres.: August A. Busch; GM: Joe McDonald; Senior VP: Stan Musial; Dir. Play. Per.: Lee Thomas; Dir. Pub. Rel.: Jim Toomey; Trav. Sec.: C. J. Cherre; Mgr.: Whitey Herzog. Home: Busch Memorial Stadium (50,000). Field distances: 330, l.f. line; 414, c.f.; 330, r.f. line. Spring training: St. Petersburg, Fla.

SCOUTING REPORT

HITTING: Despite the swapping of former NL batting champion Keith Hernandez and a slide in the standings, there was nothing the matter with the Cardinals' hitting last season, so that's not an area of great concern entering this year. Only Atlanta batted higher than St. Louis' .270 team average and the same cast returns, headed by Lonnie Smith (.321) and George Hendrick (.318, 18 homers, 97 RBI).

The pair ranked among the top four batters in the league and Ken Oberkfell (.293) squeezed into the first 15. The Cardinals also made good use of their speed, leading the league in stolen bases (207) and triples (63) while ranking fifth in runs scored (679). The club raced to a world championship with a league-

Cards' George Hendrick lets his bat do his talking.

leading 52 triples and 200 steals in '82, so there actually was an offensive improvement.

A league-low 83 home runs indicates a lack of power, but that didn't deter the Redbirds in '82, when they only hit 67 homers. No, there's nothing the matter with the St. Louis attack, which should continue to improve as the outfield of Smith, Willie McGee and David Green continues to develop.

PITCHING: With Bruce Sutter unable to mask the failings of the starters, the pitching staff took a plunge last year and carried the team with it. The staff earned-run average was 3.79 and the Cards' 27 saves were the league's lowest total, remarkable considering Sutter was on the roster. There simply was no pitcher manager Whitey Herzog could count on, as reflected in the NL pitching statistics. No Cardinal pitcher was among the leaders, with the exception of Sutter (21 saves).

The overall quality of the staff must improve if the club hopes to return to prominence following a disappointing '83. Perhaps it's unfair to place the burden on Sutter, but his 9-10 record and 4.23 ERA of last season suggest he no longer is the league's finest reliever. Given that situation and mediocre starting pitching, it's no wonder the club slipped last year. Former Met Neil Allen (12-13) generally pitched well after joining the club and John Stuper (12-11) is on the rise, but Joaquin Andujar (6-16, 4.16 ERA) and Bob Forsch (10-12, 4.28 ERA)—no-hitter notwithstanding—are capable of pitching much better.

FIELDING: In 1982, the Cardinals led the league in fielding, but last year they slipped to eighth. However, their infield still ranks with the best in the majors and their outfielders can fly, so defense isn't a problem. Shortstop Ozzie Smith's errors climbed from 13 to 21, but he's still regarded as the best. While "The Wizard of Oz" picked up another Gold Glove, third baseman Ken Oberkfell was the NL's best fielder (.960) at his position for the second straight year. Second baseman Tommy Herr tied for the league lead with a .986 percentage, but was limited to 86 games by injury.

OUTLOOK: The Cardinals weren't expected to repeat last year, but they also weren't supposed to have a losing record. Pitching is the big culprit and the club cannot be regarded as a contender until that area is straightened out. A return to form by Sutter would be a big help, making the staff effective even if the starters are merely ordinary. The Redbirds also must improve on the road (35-46 last year) and against their own division (41-49) if they plan to stave off improving Chicago.

ST. LOUIS CARDINALS 1984 ROSTER

MANAGER Whitey Herzog
Coaches—Red Schoendienst, Dave Ricketts, Mike Roarke, Hal Lanier, Nick Levya

PITCHERS

No.	Name	1983 Club	W-L	IP	SO	ERA	B-T	Ht.	Wt.	Born
13	Allen, Neil	NY(NL)-St. Lou.	12-13	176	106	3.94	R-R	6-2	195	1/24/58 Kansas City, KS
49	Andujar, Joaquin	St. Louis	6-16	225	125	4.16	B-R	5-11	180	12/21/52 Dom. Republic
23	Baker, Steve	Oakland	3-3	54	23	4.50	R-R	6-1	200	8/30/56 Eugene, OR
		Tacoma	4-9	85	67	4.55				
		St. Louis	0-1	10	1	1.80				
33	Brito, Jose	Arkansas	2-1	19	19	2.89	R-R	6-2	160	10/28/59 Dom. Republic
		Louisville	3-3	77	56	5.49				
43	Citarella, Ralph	Louisville	7-6	110	64	4.76	R-R	6-0	180	2/7/58 E. Orange, NJ
		St. Louis	0-0	11	4	1.64				
52	Clark, Terry	Arkansas	6-6	81	63	3.21	R-R	6-2	190	10/18/60 Los Angeles, CA
34	Cox, Danny	St. Petersburg	2-2	32	22	2.53	R-R	6-4	230	9/21/59 England
		Arkansas	8-3	86	73	2.29				
		Louisville	0-0	11	8	2.45				
		St. Louis	3-6	83	36	3.25				
31	Forsch, Bob	St. Louis	10-12	187	56	4.28	R-R	6-3	215	1/13/50 Sacramento, CA
35	Hagen, Kevin	Louisville	6-9	131	60	4.32	R-R	6-2	185	3/8/60 Renton, WA
		St. Louis	6-2	22	7	4.84				
49	Horton, Ricky	Louisville	10-6	157	92	4.82	L-L	6-2	195	7/30/59 Poughkeepsie, NY
50	Kepshire, Kurt	Arkansas	3-2	36	23	3.53	L-R	6-1	180	7/3/59 Bridgeport, CT
		Louisville	6-2	83	52	3.67				
32	Lahti, Jeff	Louisville	0-0	2	0	4.50	R-R	6-0	180	10/8/56 Oregon City, OR
		St. Louis	3-3	74	26	3.16				
39	LaPoint, Dave	St. Louis	12-9	191	113	3.95	L-L	6-3	215	7/29/59 Glens Falls, NY
40	Ownbey, Rick	New York (NL)	1-3	35	19	4.67	R-R	6-3	185	10/20/57 Corona, CA
		Louisville	7-5	104	77	3.63				
36	Rucker, Dave	Detroit	1-2	9	6	17.00	L-L	6-1	190	9/1/57 San Bernadino, CA
		Evansville	2-4	30	30	3.34				
		St. Louis	5-3	37	22	2.68				
48	Stuper, John	St. Louis	12-11	198	81	3.68	R-R	6-2	200	5/9/57 Butler, PA
42	Sutter, Bruce	St. Louis	9-10	89	64	4.23	R-R	6-2	190	1/8/53 Lancaster, PA
38	Von Ohlen, Dave	Louisville	1-0	15	13	4.70	L-L	6-2	200	10/25/58 Flushing, NY
		St. Louis	3-2	68	21	3.29				

CATCHERS

No.	Name	1983 Club	H	HR	RBI	Pct.	B-T	Ht.	Wt.	Born
11	Brummer, Glenn	St. Louis	24	0	9	.276	R-R	6-0	200	11/23/54 Olney, IL
29	Geren, Bob	Springfield	115	24	73	.265	R-R	6-3	205	9/22/61 San Diego, CA
23	Nieto, Tom	Louisville	104	5	52	.272	R-R	6-1	193	10/27/60 Downey, CA
15	Porter, Darrell	St. Louis	116	15	66	.262	L-R	6-0	193	1/17/52 Joplin, MO
9	Quirk, Jamie	St. Louis	18	2	11	.209	L-R	6-4	200	10/24/54 Whittier, CA

INFIELDERS

7	Gonzalez, Jose	Louisville	120	3	44	.284	B-R	5-10	155	1/21/60 Dominican Republic
25	Hendrick, George	St. Louis	168	18	97	.318	R-R	6-3	195	10/18/49 Los Angeles, CA
28	Herr, Tommy	St. Louis	101	2	31	.323	B-R	6-0	190	4/4/56 Lancaster, PA
		Arkansas	4	0	1	.444				
30	Lyons, Bill	Louisville	72	5	25	.271	R-R	6-1	175	4/26/58 Alton, IL
		St. Louis	10	0	3	.167				
10	Oberkfell, Ken	St. Louis	143	3	38	.293	L-R	6-1	185	5/4/56 Highland, IL
5	Ramsey, Mike	St. Louis	46	1	16	.263	B-R	6-1	175	3/29/54 Roanoke, VA
12	Rayford, Floyd	Rochester	52	2	38	.361	L-L	6-1	190	9/1/57 San Bernardino, CA
		St. Louis	22	3	14	.212				
1	Smith, Ozzie	St. Louis	134	3	50	.243	B-R	5-10	150	12/26/54 Mobile, AL
18	Van Slyke, Andy	Louisville	81	6	41	.368	L-R	6-1	190	12/21/60 Utica, NY
		St. Louis	81	8	38	.262				

OUTFIELDERS

14	Adduci, Jim	Louisville	131	25	101	.281	L-L	6-4	200	8/9/59 Chicago, IL
		St. Louis	1	0	0	.050				
26	Braun, Steve	St. Louis	25	3	7	.272	L-R	5-10	180	5/8/48 Trenton, NJ
22	Green, David	St. Louis	120	8	69	.284	R-R	6-3	165	12/4/60 Nicaragua
19	Iorg, Dane	St. Louis	31	0	11	.267	L-R	6-0	180	5/11/50 Eureka, CA
51	McGee, Willie	St. Louis	172	5	75	.286	B-R	6-1	175	11/2/58 San Francisco, CA
		Arkansas	8	0	2	.276				
27	Smith, Lonnie	St. Louis	158	8	45	.321	R-R	5-9	170	12/22/55 Chicago, IL

CARDINAL PROFILES

LONNIE SMITH 28 5-9 170 **Bats R Throws R**

Left fielder tailed off in most offensive departments following a sensational 1982, but raised lifetime average with .321 mark . . . Was runnerup to batting champ Bill Madlock of Pirates . . . Made charge for title with a .349 September . . . Regarded as catalyst for 1982 world champions, leading league in runs scored and ranking among NL leaders in seven categories . . . Born Dec. 22, 1955, in Chicago . . . Phillies' No. 1 draft pick in 1974 . . . Averaged .308 and 39 steals in minors . . . Replaced injured Greg Luzinski in 1980 and responded with 33 steals, setting a Phils' rookie record . . . Phillies' fans were furious about three-team swap that sent him to St. Louis and brought Bo Diaz from Cleveland to Philadelphia . . . Batted .321 in 1982 World Series.

Year	Club	Pos.	G	AB	R	H	2B	3B	HR	RBI	SB	Avg.
1978	Philadelphia	OF	17	4	6	0	0	0	0	0	4	.000
1979	Philadelphia	OF	17	30	4	5	2	0	0	3	2	.167
1980	Philadelphia	OF	100	298	69	101	14	4	3	20	33	.339
1981	Philadelphia	OF	62	176	40	57	14	3	2	11	21	.324
1982	St. Louis	OF	156	592	120	182	35	8	8	69	68	.307
1983	St. Louis	OF	130	492	83	158	31	5	8	45	43	.321
	Totals		482	1592	342	503	96	20	21	148	171	.316

WILLIE McGEE 25 6-1 175 **Bats S Throws R**

Proved rookie season was no fluke by enjoying solid sophomore year until late slump dropped him below .300 . . . Batted .311 in first half and lifted average with a .339 July . . . Ranked fourth in All-Star Game voting among outfielders, just missing a start . . . Club's biggest surprise as a rookie in 1982, filling in for injured David Green in center and batting .343 in first 105 at-bats . . . Born Nov. 2, 1958, in San Francisco . . . Thrived in post-season play, belting homer in 1982 NL playoffs and clouting two in Game 3 of World Series to tie a rookie record . . . Batted .322 for Yanks' Nashville farm (AA) in '81, before joining Cards' system in swap for pitcher Bob Sykes . . . His development as a bonafide major leaguer helped to make Keith Hernandez expendable . . . Style of play is tailor-made for synthetic fields.

Year	Club	Pos.	G	AB	R	H	2B	3B	HR	RBI	SB	Avg.
1982	St. Louis	OF	123	422	43	125	12	8	4	56	24	.296
1983	St. Louis	OF	147	601	75	172	22	8	5	75	39	.286
	Totals		270	1023	118	297	34	16	9	131	63	.290

KEN OBERKFELL 27 6-1 185 **Bats L Throws R**

Model of consistency . . . Has never batted below .289 in five major-league seasons . . . Batted .351 in May to get going . . . Began major-league career at second, but was shifted to third to accommodate Tommy Herr . . . Probably the most underrated player on the club . . . Born May 4, 1956, in Highland, Ill. . . . "Obie" swiped second-base job from Mike Tyson in '79 and topped NL with .985 fielding percentage . . . Showed major-league promise early, batting .352 with Johnson City and .351 for St. Petersburg as pro newcomer in 1975 after All-American season at Belleville Area Junior College . . . Batted .292 in '82 World Series.

Year	Club	Pos.	G	AB	R	H	2B	3B	HR	RBI	SB	Avg.
1977	St. Louis	2B	9	9	0	1	0	0	0	1	0	.111
1978	St. Louis	2B-3B	24	50	7	6	1	0	0	0	0	.120
1979	St. Louis	2B-3B-SS	135	369	53	111	19	5	1	35	4	.301
1980	St. Louis	2B-3B	116	422	58	128	27	6	3	46	4	.303
1981	St. Louis	3B-SS	102	376	43	110	12	6	2	45	4	.293
1982	St. Louis	3B-2B	137	470	55	136	22	5	2	34	11	.289
1983	St. Louis	3B-2B	151	488	62	143	26	5	3	38	12	.293
	Totals		674	2184	278	635	107	27	11	199	35	.291

OZZIE SMITH 29 5-10 150 **Bats S Throws R**

"The Wizard of Oz" won fourth straight Gold Glove last year . . . Regarded as best defensive shortstop in majors . . . More than doubled Dave Concepcion's vote total to gain starting nod as NL shortstop in All-Star Game . . . Not regarded as much of a hitter, but .280 second half made average respectable . . . Batted .323 with 18 RBI in July and .316 in August . . . Born Dec. 26, 1954, in Mobile, Ala. . . . Matched previous major-league home-run total with three last year . . . Joined Cardinals in controversial swap with Padres for Garry Templeton prior to 1982 and it turned out to be another St. Louis steal . . . Batted .556 in 1982 playoffs against Braves . . . Did a back flip taking field for Game 7 of World Series, drawing attention to acrobatic agility.

Year	Club	Pos.	G	AB	R	H	2B	3B	HR	RBI	SB	Avg.
1978	San Diego	SS	159	590	69	152	17	6	1	46	40	.258
1979	San Diego	SS	156	587	77	124	18	6	0	27	28	.211
1980	San Diego	SS	158	609	67	140	18	5	0	35	57	.230
1981	San Diego	SS	110	450	53	100	11	2	0	21	22	.222
1982	St. Louis	SS	140	488	58	121	24	1	2	43	25	.248
1983	St. Louis	SS	159	552	69	134	30	6	3	50	34	.243
	Totals		882	3276	393	771	118	26	6	222	206	.235

GEORGE HENDRICK 34 6-3 195 Bats R Throws R

Was trade bait last spring, but quick start made him more valuable to club than Keith Hernandez . . . Moved from outfield to first base last year . . . Batted .339 with six homers and 19 RBI in April, dissuading trade talk . . . Parlayed .349 June into league-leading .347 average at All-Star break . . . Had 58 RBI by midseason . . . Born Oct. 18, 1949, in Los Angeles . . . Won't talk to press, but is very popular with teammates . . . Began career with champion Oakland A's of early '70s, but didn't become a regular until he joined Indians . . . Had three-homer game for Cleveland in 1973 . . . A steal for Cards, he came in 1978 deal with Padres for pitcher Eric Rasmussen . . . Had game-winning hit in final game of '82 World Series and batted .321. .

Year	Club	Pos.	G	AB	R	H	2B	3B	HR	RBI	SB	Avg.
1971	Oakland	OF	42	114	8	27	4	1	0	8	0	.237
1972	Oakland	OF	58	121	10	22	1	1	4	15	3	.182
1973	Cleveland	OF	113	440	64	118	18	0	21	61	7	.268
1974	Cleveland	OF	139	495	65	138	23	1	19	67	6	.279
1975	Cleveland	OF	145	561	82	145	21	2	24	86	6	.258
1976	Cleveland	OF	149	551	72	146	20	3	25	81	4	.265
1977	San Diego	OF	152	541	75	168	25	2	23	81	11	.311
1978	SD-St. Louis	OF	138	493	64	137	31	1	20	75	2	.278
1979	St. Louis	OF	140	493	67	148	27	1	16	75	2	.300
1980	St. Louis	OF	150	572	73	173	33	2	25	109	6	.302
1981	St. Louis	OF	101	394	67	112	19	3	18	61	4	.284
1982	St. Louis	OF	136	515	65	145	20	5	19	104	3	.282
1983	St. Louis	OF	144	529	73	168	33	3	18	97	3	.318
	Totals		1607	5819	785	1647	275	25	232	920	57	.283

DARRELL PORTER 32 6-0 193 Bats L Throws R

Enjoyed best season since 1979, helping to ease residue of ill feeling concerning swap of Ted Simmons to make room for him behind the plate . . . Belted seven home runs in May, collecting 19 RBI . . . Batted .349 in September . . . Solid year was carryover from 1982 post-season, when he batted .556 in playoffs and .286 in World Series to earn MVP honors in both . . . Born Jan. 17, 1952, in Joplin, Mo. . . . Won battle with alcohol and drugs to salvage his career in 1980 . . . Holds .348 average in 15 playoff games . . . Heady catcher who was top priority of Whitey Herzog when Herzog switched from Royals to Cardinals . . . Signed as free agent prior to 1981 . . . Four-time AL All-Star with Kansas City and Milwaukee . . . An All-American quarterback in high school in Oklahoma City.

Year	Club	Pos.	G	AB	R	H	2B	3B	HR	RBI	SB	Avg.
1971	Milwaukee	C	22	70	4	15	2	0	2	9	2	.214
1972	Milwaukee	C	18	56	2	7	1	0	1	2	0	.125
1973	Milwaukee	C	117	350	50	89	19	2	16	67	5	.254
1974	Milwaukee	C	131	432	59	104	15	4	12	56	8	.241
1975	Milwaukee	C	130	409	66	95	12	5	18	60	2	.232
1976	Milwaukee	C	119	389	43	81	14	1	5	32	2	.208
1977	Kansas City	C	130	425	61	117	21	3	16	60	1	.275
1978	Kansas City	C	150	520	77	138	27	6	18	78	0	.265
1979	Kansas City	C	157	533	101	155	23	10	20	112	3	.291
1980	Kansas City	C	118	418	51	104	14	2	7	51	1	.249
1981	St. Louis	C	61	174	22	39	10	2	6	31	1	.224
1982	St. Louis	C	120	373	46	86	18	5	12	48	1	.231
1983	St. Louis	C	145	443	57	116	24	3	15	66	1	.262
	Totals		1418	4592	639	1146	200	43	148	672	27	.250

DAVID GREEN 23 6-3 165 **Bats R Throws R**

Regarded as the key player in huge deal with Milwaukee involving Ted Simmons and Rollie Fingers prior to 1981 . . . Showed Cards were correct about his potential with solid season as fulltime right fielder last year . . . Strong and fast, he was a .300 hitter in first half, batting .383 in June . . . Off to a great start in center field in '82, but his hamstring pull opened door for Willie McGee . . . Went 0-for-15 before belting first major-league hit in 1981 . . . Born Dec. 4, 1960, in Managua, Nicaragua . . . Collected only two hits in '82 World Series—a double and a triple . . . Didn't start playing baseball until he was 14 . . . Ran track in high school . . . Didn't speak English when he signed contract with Brewers in 1978.

Year	Club	Pos.	G	AB	R	H	2B	3B	HR	RBI	SB	Avg.
1981	St. Louis	OF	21	34	6	5	1	0	0	2	0	.147
1982	St. Louis	OF	76	166	21	47	7	1	2	23	11	.283
1983	St. Louis	OF	146	422	52	120	14	10	8	69	34	.284
	Totals		243	622	79	172	22	11	10	94	45	.277

NEIL ALLEN 26 6-2 195 **Bats R Throws R**

Achieved a rarity by shutting out the same team (the Dodgers) with two different clubs last year . . . Longtime bullpen ace of Mets, he reportedly was acquired as relief insurance for Bruce Sutter . . . Joined Cards as part of June swap for Keith Hernandez and was instant success as starter, going 3-1 with two shutouts in July . . . Despite injury-plagued season, he notched 19 saves for Mets in 1982, but his role was diminished by Jesse Orosco's development in 1983 . . . Born Jan. 24, 1958, in Kansas City, Kan. . . . Switched to bullpen after 1-4 start as starter with Mets in '79 and saved 59 games in three years for weak clubs . . . Weighed Big Eight scholarship offers following career as All-American quarterback in high school . . . Had emotional problems early last year, admitting to alcohol problem that didn't exist.

Year	Club	G	IP	W	L	Pct.	SO	BB	H	ERA
1979	New York (NL)	50	99	6	10	.375	65	47	100	3.55
1980	New York (NL)	59	97	7	10	.412	79	40	87	3.71
1981	New York (NL)	43	67	7	6	.538	50	26	64	2.96
1982	New York (NL)	50	65	3	7	.300	59	30	65	3.06
1983	N.Y. (NL)-St. Louis	46	176	12	13	.480	106	84	179	3.94
	Totals	248	504	35	46	.432	359	227	495	3.57

JOHN STUPER 26 6-2 200 **Bats R Throws R**

Tied Dave LaPoint for most wins on team and posted lowest ERA among starters last year . . . Did the bulk of his damage in May, going 5-1 with a 2.64 ERA . . . Was 2-1 with 1.06 ERA in August . . . The surprise of the 1982 staff, he won Game 6 of the World Series, pitching complete game despite 2½ hours of rain delays . . . Including 7-1 stint at Louisville (AAA), he was 16-8 in 1982 . . . Born May 9, 1957, in Butler, Pa. . . . Seemed to be out of Cardinals' picture after posting 6-14 record for Springfield (AAA) in '81 . . . Journalism major at Point Park College . . . Was 34-3 as a collegian . . . Played basketball for Butler Community College . . . Does a nice impersonation of Howard Cosell.

Year	Club	G	IP	W	L	Pct.	SO	BB	H	ERA
1982	St. Louis	23	137	9	7	.563	53	55	137	3.36
1983	St. Louis	40	198	12	11	.522	81	71	202	3.68
	Totals	63	335	21	18	.538	134	126	339	3.55

BRUCE SUTTER 31 6-2 190 **Bats R Throws R**

Injury-torn season cut his save total to 21 and cost him longtime designation as the finest reliever in NL . . . Cards hired Mike Roarke, who helped Sutter's development with Cubs, as a coach for this season to help square away their bullpen ace . . . Was 2-0 in April and 3-1 in June, but 2-7 second half revealed ineffectiveness . . . Awesome in 1982, posting 36 saves and adding two wins and three saves in postseason play . . . Born Jan. 8, 1953, in Lancaster, Pa. . . . Used baffling specialty pitch—a split-finger fastball—to set NL record with 37 saves for Cubs in '79, winning Cy Young Award . . . Winner of two All-Star Games and has saved two others . . . Has 82 saves and 21 victories in three seasons with St. Louis since coming over in deal that sent Leon Durham, Ken Reitz and Ty Waller to Cubs following 1980 season.

Year	Club	G	IP	W	L	Pct.	SO	BB	H	ERA
1976	Chicago (NL)	52	83	6	3	.667	73	26	63	2.71
1977	Chicago (NL)	62	107	7	3	.700	129	23	69	1.35
1978	Chicago (NL)	64	99	8	10	.444	106	34	82	3.18
1979	Chicago (NL)	62	101	6	6	.500	110	32	67	2.23
1980	Chicago (NL)	60	102	5	8	.385	76	34	90	2.65
1981	St. Louis	48	82	3	5	.375	57	24	64	2.63
1982	St. Louis	70	102	9	8	.529	61	34	88	2.90
1983	St. Louis	60	89	9	10	.474	64	30	90	4.23
	Totals	478	765	53	53	.500	676	237	613	2.71

TOP PROSPECTS

RALPH CITARELLA 26 6-0 180 Bats R Throws R

Hard-throwing rookie allowed only two runs in 11 innings after promotion in September . . . Posted 7-6 record with Louisville (AAA) after being biggest winner in American Association when he went 15-6 with same club in '82 . . . Born Feb. 7, 1958, in East Orange, N.J. . . . Outfielder Jim Adduci, who hit 25 homers for Louisville, also is highly regarded.

MANAGER WHITEY HERZOG: Went from penthouse to outhouse in one year, but will be remembered for tremendous job he did to build Cards into 1982 world champions . . . Completely re-designed team after replacing Ken Boyer as manager in 1980, tailoring the club to spacious Busch Stadium by stressing speed . . . While Atlanta was winning a record 13 in a row at start of 1982 season, St. Louis had its best winning streak since 1943, with 12 straight . . . Named The Sporting News' Man of the Year, Manager of the Year and Executive of the Year in 1982 . . . Also won latter award as Cards' general manager in '81 . . . Born Nov. 9, 1931, in New Athens, Ill. . . . Won three straight division titles with Royals from 1976-78 . . . Managed Cardinals to best record in division in 1981 (59-43), but team placed second in each half and didn't reach playoffs . . . Posted .257 career

average for Washington, KC, Baltimore and Detroit from 1956-63 . . . "The White Rat" has 727-628 managerial mark with Texas, California, KC and St. Louis.

GREATEST STEALER

An absolutely unanimous decision, because absolutely nobody did it better than Lou Brock, who tops the all-time list with 938 stolen bases, one more than late-19th-Century star Billy Hamilton.

Brock succeeded Maury Wills as the greatest modern-day base thief and led the National League eight times in nine years from 1966-1974, when he climaxed his pilfering feats with a league-record 118 thefts.

During Brock's reign, he missed leading the NL in thefts only in 1970, when Cincinnati's Bobby Tolan earned top honors. In the four preceding years, larcenous Lou swiped 74, 52, 62 and 53 bases. Following 1970, Brock stole 64, 63, 70 and 118 bases.

Lonnie Smith, who has youth on his side, could well finish his Cardinals' career second to Brock. Smith stole 68 bases in '82 to prove he ranks with the big boys when it comes to base burglaries.

ALL-TIME CARDINAL SEASON RECORDS

BATTING: Rogers Hornsby, .424, 1924
HRs: Johnny Mize, 43, 1940
RBIs: Joe Medwick, 154, 1937
STEALS: Lou Brock, 118, 1974
WINS: Dizzy Dean, 30, 1934
STRIKEOUTS: Bob Gibson, 274, 1970

ATLANTA BRAVES

TEAM DIRECTORY: Chairman of the Board: Bill Bartholomay; Pres.: R. E. (Ted) Turner III; Exec. VP: Al Thornwell, Jr.; VP-GM: John Mullen; VP-Bus. Man.: Charles Sanders; VP-Dir. Play. Dev.: Hank Aaron; Dir. Scouting: Paul Snyder; Dir. Pub. Rel.: Wayne Minshew; Trav. Sec.: Bill Acree; Mgr.: Joe Torre. Home: Atlanta Stadium (52,791). Field distances: 330, l.f. line; 402, c.f.; 330, r.f. line. Spring training: West Palm Beach, Fla.

SCOUTING REPORT

HITTING: The Braves are simply the best offensive team in the league, ranking No. 1 in batting (.272) and runs scored (746) behind the superstar skills of MVP Dale Murphy (.302, 36 homers, 121 RBI). Nobody does it better than Murphy, who gets a lot of plate support from Rafael Ramirez (.297), Chris Chambliss (.280) and Bob Horner (.303, 20 homers, 68 RBI). Teammates Bruce Benedict, Glenn Hubbard and Claudell Washington also are above-average hitters, so the lineup is solid.

Dale Murphy takes aim on third straight NL MVP award.

Letting Brett Butler slip away to Cleveland in the Len Barker deal may have been a mistake. Butler did a good job setting the table for the big boppers last year, so it remains to be seen who steps into the leadoff spot and plays left field. Even more important is keeping Horner healthy. When he went down with a broken thumb last August, the Braves went down with him. With him in the lineup, the club can hit with the best of them.

PITCHING: This was once an Atlanta weakness, but the Braves could have a solid staff if Barker (9-16 overall) proves worthy of all the Braves gave up to get him. The club management feels so confident about its pitching it told Phil Niekro (11-10) to walk away. That could be a mistake if Pascual Perez (15-8) and Craig McMurtry (15-9) don't continue to improve and if Pete Falcone (9-4) shows his '83 success was a fluke.

The bullpen is solid with Steve Bedrosian (19 saves), Terry Forster, Gene Garber and onetime relief ace Rick Camp, who also starts. But it lulled manager Joe Torre into a false sense of security last year and the firemen were exhausted down the stretch. Overall, this has a chance to be an excellent staff, especially if Barker rediscovers his early AL form and stays injury-free.

FIELDING: Not bad, with one notable exception. First baseman Chambliss, second baseman Hubbard, third baseman Horner, catcher Benedict and center fielder Murphy rank with the best at their positions. But Ramirez is a liability at short, making 38 and 39 errors the last two years. His bat is too valuable to keep him out of the lineup, but his glove work leaves a lot to be desired. The Braves also lost excellent fielders when Butler was traded and Niekro was allowed to leave.

OUTLOOK: It looks like another bridesmaid season, but who knows what might have happened one year ago had Horner remained in the lineup? With him healthy and the Braves in front by 6½ games in mid-August, an Atlanta newspaper boldly headlined, "It's Over!" Then Horner was shelved and it was over for the Braves. Torre's victory cigars had turned into bitter stogies.

But this is a good club, one capable of keeping the pressure on the Dodgers. The pitching is no longer laughable, so given the Braves' ample offense, anything can happen. If the Dodgers don't improve after backing into a title last year, Atlanta has the horses to win the NL West in convincing fashion. The bullpen is the key. Despite its growing reputation, something had to go wrong for the Braves to go 19-29 in one-run games and 4-8 in extra innings last year.

ATLANTA BRAVES 1984 ROSTER

MANAGER Joe Torre

Coaches—Tommie Aaron, Bob Gibson, Dal Maxvill, Joe Pignatano, Rube Walker

PITCHERS

No.	Name	1983 Club	W-L	IP	SO	ERA	B-T	Ht.	Wt.	Born
39	Barker, Len	Cleveland	8-13	150	105	5.11	R-R	6-4	215	7/7/55 Fort Knox, KY
		Atlanta	1-3	33	21	3.82				
32	Bedrosian, Steve	Atlanta	9-10	120	114	3.60	R-R	6-3	195	12/6/57 Methuen, MA
48	Brizzolara, Tony	Richmond	9-7	128	90	3.74	R-R	6-5	217	1/14/57 Santa Monica, CA
		Atlanta	1-0	20	17	3.54				
37	Camp, Rick	Atlanta	10-9	140	61	3.79	R-R	6-1	198	6/10/53 Trion, GA
30	Dayley, Ken	Richmond	9-3	91	74	3.28	L-L	6-0	171	2/25/59 Jerome, ID
		Atlanta	5-8	105	70	4.30				
49	Dedmon, Jeff	Savannah	4-1	50	26	2.88	L-R	6-2	200	3/4/60 Torrance, CA
		Richmond	2-2	36	33	1.75				
		Atlanta	0-0	4	3	13.50				
33	Falcone, Pete	Atlanta	9-4	107	59	3.63	L-L	6-2	205	10/1/53 Brooklyn, NY
46	Fisher, Brian	Savannah	8-11	150	103	5.22	R-R	6-3	210	3/18/62 Honolulu, HI
51	Forster, Terry	Atlanta	3-2	79	54	2.16	L-L	6-4	220	1/14/52 Sioux Falls, SD
26	Garber, Gene	Atlanta	4-5	61	45	4.60	R-R	5-10	172	11/13/47 Lancaster, PA
38	Jones, Craig	Savannah	11-7	137	106	4.59	R-R	6-2	195	8/19/58 Natrona Heights, PA
		Richmond	0-1	3	1	3.00				
42	Mahler, Rick	Atlanta	0-0	14	7	5.02	R-R	6-1	202	8/5/53 Austin, TX
		Richmond	12-7	163	103	4.92				
29	McMurtry, Craig	Atlanta	15-9	225	105	3.08	R-R	6-5	195	11/5/59 Temple, TX
31	Moore, Donny	Richmond	0-2	17	9	3.24	L-R	6-0	185	2/13/54 Lubbock, TX
		Atlanta	2-3	69	41	3.67				
47	Payne, Mike	Savannah	10-7	145	97	3.91	R-R	5-11	167	11/15/61 Woonsocket, RI
27	Perez, Pascual	Atlanta	15-8	215	144	3.43	R-R	6-2	162	5/17/57 Dominican Republic
43	Walk, Bob	Richmond	11-12	185	123	5.21	R-R	6-4	203	11/26/56 Van Nuys, CA
		Atlanta	0-0	4	4	7.36				

CATCHERS

No.	Name	1983 Club	H	HR	RBI	Pct.	B-T	Ht.	Wt.	Born
20	Benedict, Bruce	Atlanta	126	2	43	.298	R-R	6-1	190	8/18/55 Birmingham, AL
24	Owen, Larry	Atlanta	2	0	1	.118	R-R	5-11	185	5/31/55 Cleveland, OH
		Richmond	5	1	2	.417				
4	Pocoroba, Biff	Atlanta	32	2	16	.267	L-R	5-10	180	7/25/53 Burbank, CA
14	Sinatro, Matt	Richmond	77	4	41	.211	R-R	5-9	179	3/22/60 Hartford, CT
		Atlanta	2	0	2	.167				

INFIELDERS

No.	Name	1983 Club	H	HR	RBI	Pct.	B-T	Ht.	Wt.	Born
10	Chambliss, Chris	Atlanta	125	20	78	.280	L-R	6-1	215	12/26/48 Dayton, OH
5	Horner, Bob	Atlanta	117	20	68	.303	L-R	6-1	195	8/6/57 Junction City, KS
17	Hubbard, Glenn	Atlanta	136	12	70	.263	R-R	5-8	160	9/25/57 Germany
6	Johnson, Randy	Atlanta	36	1	17	.250	R-R	6-1	190	6/10/56 Escondido, CA
11	Jorgensen, Mike	NY (NL)-Atl.	18	2	11	.250	L-L	6-0	187	8/16/48 Passaic, NJ
28	Perry, Gerald	Richmond	133	13	71	.324	L-R	5-11	180	10/30/60 Savannah, GA
		Atlanta	14	1	6	.359				
16	Ramirez, Rafael	Atlanta	185	7	58	.297	R-R	6-0	170	2/18/59 Dominican Republic
1	Royster, Jerry	Atlanta	63	3	30	.235	R-R	6-0	165	10/18/52 Sacramento, CA
12	Runge, Paul	Richmond	129	15	72	.273	R-R	6-0	175	5/21/58 Kingston, NY
		Atlanta	2	0	1	.250				
22	Sosa, Miguel	Savannah	120	17	93	.245	R-R	5-10	165	5/15/60 Dominican Republic
		Richmond	3	0	2	.333				
8	Watson, Bob	Atlanta	46	6	37	.309	R-R	6-2	200	4/10/46 Los Angeles, CA
18	Zuvella, Paul	Richmond	119	6	64	.287	R-R	6-0	175	10/31/58 San Mateo, CA
		Atlanta	0	0	0	.000				

OUTFIELDERS

No.	Name	1983 Club	H	HR	RBI	Pct.	B-T	Ht.	Wt.	Born
2	Hall, Albert	Richmond	153	1	42	.294	B-R	5-11	155	3/7/59 Birmingham, AL
		Atlanta	0	0	0	.000				
19	Harper, Terry	Atlanta	53	3	26	.264	R-R	6-1	202	8/19/55 Douglasville, GA
7	Komminsk, Brad	Richmond	138	24	103	.334	R-R	6-2	205	4/4/61 Lima, OH
		Atlanta	8	0	4	.222				
3	Murphy, Dale	Atlanta	178	36	121	.302	R-R	6-5	218	3/12/56 Portland, OR
40	Vargas, Leo	Richmond	118	19	75	.289	R-R	6-1	180	9/12/57 Dominican Republic
15	Washington, Claudell	Atlanta	138	9	44	.278	L-L	6-0	190	8/31/54 Los Angeles, CA

BRAVE PROFILES

DALE MURPHY 28 6-5 218 — Bats R Throws R

It all starts with this superstar, the NL MVP the last two years... Started and finished quickly... Batted .348 with seven homers and 21 RBI in April and was Player of the Month for September with .343 average, 10 homers, 29 RBI and 10 steals... Also had seven homers in a .324 June... Has 72 homers last two years, second only to Mike Schmidt's 75... Born March 12, 1956, in Portland, Ore.... NL RBI king after tying for honor in '82... Image as All-American Boy is justified—he is a genuine good guy... Attended Brigham Young... Reached majors as a catcher, but throwing problems prompted switch to center... His offensive potential wasn't realized until fourth year of pro ball, when he amassed .305 average, 22 homers and 90 RBI for Richmond (AAA) in '77... Joined Ernie Banks, Joe Morgan and Schmidt as only players to win NL MVP award two consecutive years.

Year	Club	Pos.	G	AB	R	H	2B	3B	HR	RBI	SB	Avg.
1976	Atlanta	C	19	65	3	17	6	0	0	9	0	.262
1977	Atlanta	C	18	76	5	24	8	1	2	14	0	.316
1978	Atlanta	C-1B	151	530	66	120	14	3	23	79	11	.226
1979	Atlanta	1B-C	104	384	53	106	7	2	21	57	6	.276
1980	Atlanta	OF-1B	156	569	98	160	27	2	33	89	9	.281
1981	Atlanta	OF-1B	104	369	43	91	12	1	13	50	14	.247
1982	Atlanta	OF	162	598	113	168	23	2	36	109	23	.281
1983	Atlanta	OF	162	589	131	178	24	4	36	121	30	.302
	Totals		876	3180	512	864	121	15	164	528	93	.272

BOB HORNER 26 6-1 195 — Bats R Throws R

Could be argued that "Horns" is the *real* MVP of the Braves... After all, club was in first place by 5½ games when he left lineup with a broken wrist and finished three games behind Dodgers without him... Most productive in May, batting .352... Had 13 homers and 44 RBI at All-Star break... Elbow injury sidelined him down stretch in '82... If this third baseman ever puts a whole season together, look out!... Born Aug. 1, 1957, in Junction City, Kan.... Set NCAA record with 58 career home runs for Arizona State... MVP of 1977 College World Series... Before Dale Murphy passed Horner last year, only Hank Aaron had more homers in Atlanta uniform... Refused Atlanta owner Ted Turner's option to Richmond in 1980 and proved point with 35 homers.

Year	Club	Pos.	G	AB	R	H	2B	3B	HR	RBI	SB	Avg.
1978	Atlanta	3B	89	323	50	86	17	1	23	63	0	.266
1979	Atlanta	3B-1B	121	487	66	153	15	1	33	98	0	.314
1980	Atlanta	3B-1B	124	463	81	124	14	1	35	89	3	.268
1981	Atlanta	3B	79	300	42	83	10	0	15	42	2	.277
1982	Atlanta	3B	140	499	85	130	24	0	32	97	3	.261
1983	Atlanta	3B	104	386	75	117	25	1	20	68	4	.303
	Totals		657	2458	399	693	105	4	158	457	12	.282

CLAUDELL WASHINGTON 29 6-0 190 Bats L Throws L

Had nothing to shout about last year, but right fielder reached lifetime average and is club's top returning base-stealer . . . Main man for Braves in '82 title drive, earning Player-of-the-Month honors in September while team's sluggers slumped . . . Joined Babe Ruth and Johnny Mize as the only players to hit three home runs in a game in each league, doing it for White Sox in 1979 and Mets in 1980 . . . Born Aug. 31, 1954, in Los Angeles . . . Couldn't find a permanent home until Ted Turner gave him big contract as a free agent in 1980 . . . Didn't play high-school ball, but was signed by Oakland A's off sandlots . . . Batted .308 in first full major-league season in 1975, after hitting .571 in 1974 World Series.

Year	Club	Pos.	G	AB	R	H	2B	3B	HR	RBI	SB	Avg.
1974	Oakland..........	OF	73	221	16	63	10	5	0	19	6	.285
1975	Oakland..........	OF	148	590	86	182	24	7	10	77	40	.308
1976	Oakland..........	OF	134	490	65	126	20	6	5	53	37	.257
1977	Texas	OF	129	521	63	148	31	2	12	68	21	.284
1978	Texas-Chi (AL)	OF	98	356	34	90	16	5	6	33	5	.253
1979	Chicago (AL)	OF	131	471	79	132	33	5	13	66	19	.280
1980	Chicago (AL)	OF	32	90	15	26	4	2	1	12	4	.289
1980	New York (NL)	OF	79	284	38	78	16	4	10	42	17	.275
1981	Atlanta	OF	85	320	37	93	22	3	5	37	12	.291
1982	Atlanta	OF	150	563	94	150	24	6	16	80	33	.266
1983	Atlanta	OF	134	496	75	138	24	8	9	44	31	.278
	Totals		1193	4402	602	1226	224	53	87	531	225	.279

CHRIS CHAMBLISS 35 6-1 215 Bats L Throws R

Though he is overshadowed by Dale Murphy and Bob Horner, this veteran first baseman is no slouch at the plate . . . Had second straight 20-homer season after never having done it before 1982 . . . Hit for his lifetime average last year . . . At his best in midseason, batting .354 in June and .348 with seven homers and 21 RBI in July . . . Born Dec. 26, 1948, in Dayton, Ohio . . . Tied Hank Aaron's club record with 37 doubles in 1980

...Played at UCLA and set school record with 15 homers ...Cousin of former NBA star Jo Jo White.... AL Rookie of the Year for Indians in 1971...Best remembered for home run in ninth that won 1976 AL Championship Series for Yankees...A consistent and underrated player.

Year	Club	Pos.	G	AB	R	H	2B	3B	HR	RBI	SB	Avg.
1971	Cleveland........	1B	111	415	49	114	20	4	9	48	2	.275
1972	Cleveland........	1B	121	466	51	136	27	2	6	44	3	.292
1973	Cleveland........	1B	155	572	70	156	30	2	11	53	4	.273
1974	Cleve.-NY. (AL) ...	1B	127	467	46	119	20	3	6	50	0	.255
1975	New York (AL)	1B	150	562	66	171	38	4	9	72	0	.304
1976	New York (AL)	1B	156	641	76	188	32	6	17	96	1	.293
1977	New York (AL)	1B	157	600	90	172	32	6	17	90	4	.287
1978	New York (AL)	1B	162	625	81	171	26	3	12	90	2	.274
1979	New York (AL)	1B	149	554	61	155	27	3	18	63	3	.280
1980	Atlanta	1B	158	602	83	170	37	2	18	72	7	.282
1981	Atlanta	1B	107	404	44	110	25	2	8	51	4	.272
1982	Atlanta	1B	157	534	57	144	25	2	20	86	7	.270
1983	Atlanta	1B	131	447	59	125	24	3	20	78	2	.280
	Totals..........		1841	6889	836	1931	373	42	171	893	39	.280

RAFAEL RAMIREZ 25 6-0 170 Bats R Throws R

Proved hot finish in '82 was no fluke last year...His fielding can be both spectacular and shaky, but he earns his pay with his bat... "Rafey" was at his best in August, batting .321...Sparked drive to divisional title in '82, along with Claudell Washington, batting .340 with 18 RBI in September...Born Feb. 18, 1959, in San Pedro de Macoris, Dominican Republic...Converted from outfield to infield in '77...Fielding at short still needs improvement...Belted four hits in third major-league start...Sharpened eye by playing winter ball in homeland after posting mediocre offensive stats in minors.

Year	Club	Pos.	G	AB	R	H	2B	3B	HR	RBI	SB	Avg.
1980	Atlanta	SS	50	165	17	44	6	1	2	11	2	.267
1981	Atlanta	SS	95	307	30	67	16	2	2	20	7	.218
1982	Atlanta	SS	157	609	74	169	24	4	10	52	27	.278
1983	Atlanta	SS	152	622	82	185	13	5	7	58	16	.297
	Totals..........		454	1703	203	465	59	12	21	141	52	.273

GLENN HUBBARD 26 5-9 160 Bats R Throws R

Regarded as the best all-around second baseman in NL...Another unsung hero on a team of hitters, quietly driving in 70 runs and batting a career-high .263...Regarded as a tough clutch hitter...Doesn't make many errors, either... Born Sept. 25, 1957, at Hahn Air Force Base, West Germany...This well-traveled military brat played Little League ball in Taiwan and attended high school in Ogden, Utah, where he was a wrestler... A standout minor-league hitter, including successive .336 seasons for Richmond (AAA) in 1978 and 1979... Set all-time Braves' mark with .991 fielding percentage in '81, making only five errors... An aggressive player with a bright future.

Year	Club	Pos.	G	AB	R	H	2B	3B	HR	RBI	SB	Avg.
1978	Atlanta	2B	44	163	15	42	4	0	2	13	2	.258
1979	Atlanta	2B	97	325	34	75	12	0	3	29	0	.231
1980	Atlanta	2B	117	431	55	107	21	3	9	43	7	.248
1981	Atlanta	2B	99	361	39	85	13	5	6	33	4	.235
1982	Atlanta	2B	145	532	75	132	25	1	9	59	4	.248
1983	Atlanta	2B	148	517	65	136	24	6	12	70	3	.263
	Totals		650	2329	283	577	99	15	41	247	20	.248

BRUCE BENEDICT 28 6-1 190 **Bats R Throws R**

Enjoyed finest season by a Braves' catcher in years with a career-high average.... Set tone for banner season with a .345 April and followed with a .325 May... Offensive work was a bonus because he won job primarily for his defensive skills... Perked up offensively at end of '82, batting .389 from Aug. 23 through the end of season... Born Aug. 18, 1955, in Birmingham, Ala.... Played in 1981 All-Star Game... Earned All-American honors at Omaha... Father played in Yankee and Cardinal systems... Used winter weight program to pump up production.

Year	Club	Pos.	G	AB	R	H	2B	3B	HR	RBI	SB	Avg.
1978	Atlanta	C	22	52	3	13	2	0	0	1	0	.250
1979	Atlanta	C	76	204	14	46	11	0	0	15	1	.225
1980	Atlanta	C	120	359	18	91	14	1	2	34	3	.253
1981	Atlanta	C	90	295	26	78	12	1	5	35	1	.264
1982	Atlanta	C	118	386	34	95	11	1	3	44	4	.246
1983	Atlanta	C	134	423	43	126	13	1	2	43	1	.298
	Totals		560	1719	138	449	63	4	12	172	10	.261

PASCUAL PEREZ 26 6-2 162 **Bats R Throws R**

One helluva pitcher once he finds his way to the mound... After brief stint with Braves in '82, he blossomed along with Craig McMurtry ... NL Pitcher of the Month for April with 4-0 record and 1.74 ERA, which was surprising considering his previous major-league record was 6-12... Also posted a 4-1 record and 1.67 ERA in June to reach All-Star Game at 10-2 with 2.46 ERA... Was only 5-6 the rest of the way and his slump contributed to Atlanta's slide... Born May 17, 1957, in Haina, Dominican Republic... Signed by Pirates, but career took sharp turn for better following June 1982 swap for Larry McWilliams... Gained notoriety in '82 when he got lost on I-95 circling Atlanta and missed a start. Braves had good laugh, won game to snap late-season slump and surged to NL West title.

Year	Club	G	IP	W	L	Pct.	SO	BB	H	ERA
1980	Pittsburgh	2	12	0	1	.000	7	2	15	3.75
1981	Pittsburgh	17	86	2	7	.222	46	34	92	3.98
1982	Atlanta	16	79	4	4	.500	29	17	85	3.06
1983	Atlanta	33	215	15	8	.652	144	51	213	3.43
	Totals	68	392	21	20	.512	226	104	405	3.49

LEN BARKER 28 6-4 215 **Bats R Throws R**

Didn't provide the pennant insurance Braves expected, going 1-3 following swap with Indians... Could be a costly move for Braves, who parted with two top prospects and team stolen-base champ Brett Butler... Was 8-13 with Cleveland at time of deal and was intending to test free-agent waters... Braves signed him to big contract before end of year... Elbow problems make him a gamble, as evidenced by late-season fade four straight years... When he's right, however, he's one of the best... Born July 7, 1955, in Fort Knox, Ky.... Used 96-mph fastball to lead AL in strikeouts in 1980 and 1981... Pitched the first perfect game in the majors in 13 years when he zapped Toronto for Indians, May 15, 1981.

Year	Club	G	IP	W	L	Pct.	SO	BB	H	ERA
1976	Texas	2	15	1	0	1.000	7	6	7	2.40
1977	Texas	15	47	4	1	.800	51	24	36	2.68
1978	Texas	29	52	1	5	.167	33	29	63	4.85
1979	Cleveland	29	137	6	6	.500	93	70	146	4.93
1980	Cleveland	36	246	19	12	.613	187	92	237	4.17
1981	Cleveland	22	154	8	7	.533	127	46	150	3.92
1982	Cleveland	33	245	15	11	.577	187	88	211	3.90
1983	Cleveland	24	150	8	13	.381	105	52	150	5.11
1983	Atlanta	6	33	1	3	.250	21	14	31	3.82
	Totals	196	1079	63	58	.521	811	421	1031	4.23

CRAIG McMURTRY 24 6-5 195 **Bats R Throws R**

Braves' Rookie-of-the-Year candidate became ace of staff with fine debut that included three shutouts... Rated a top prospect before last season, but his production exceeded expectations... Took off with 5-1 record and 2.88 ERA in May, won four games in July and capped season with 3-0 mark and 1.91 ERA in September... String-bean right-hander showed he was ready for majors with 17-9 record at Richmond in '82... Born Nov. 5, 1959, in Temple, Tex.... A JC All-American at McLennan Community College before becoming first-round pick of Braves in January 1980 draft... Three years of minor-league ball, during which he posted 39 victories, prepared him for majors.

Year	Club	G	IP	W	L	Pct.	SO	BB	H	ERA
1983	Atlanta	36	225	15	9	.625	105	88	204	3.08

TOP PROSPECTS

BRAD KOMMINSK 23 6-2 205 Bats R Throws R
First baseman and outfielder tuned up for bigs by blasting International League pitching for .334 average, 24 homers and 103 RBI at Richmond (AAA)... Didn't show much in 36 at-bats with Braves, however, hitting .222... Power hitter who can run... No. 1 draft choice in June 1979... Born April 4, 1961, in Lima, Ohio... Gerald Perry, also a first baseman and outfielder, didn't do as well at Richmond (.324, 13 homers, 71 RBI), but raised some eyebrows with a .359 average in 27 games with Atlanta.

MANAGER JOE TORRE: Maintained composure after Braves

squandered 6½-game lead in August... Also held up well when club dropped 19-of-21 games late in '82, but that time his disposition was ultimately soothed by a final-week rally that won NL West title... Second-guessed when some of his moves went wrong down the stretch, but injuries, more than anything else, caused club's collapse last year... Biggest mistake was burning out reliever Steve Bedrosian, who was 5-2 with 2.67 ERA and 10 saves in the first half and 4-8 with an ERA above 4.00 the rest of the way... Born July 18, 1940, in Brooklyn, N.Y. ... Played 10 years, mostly as a catcher, with Braves, but enjoyed NL MVP-winning season as third baseman for Cardinals in 1971, batting .363... Managed Atlanta to record 13-0 start in 1982... Fired by Mets after posting a 286-420 record in five seasons... Overall major-league mark is 463-557.

GREATEST STEALER

This is not an organization with a rich history of stealing bases. The Braves would rather knock the stuffing out of you with the home run than beat you by flashing speed on the basepaths.

As a result, it may not come as a surprise that the greatest base thief in the history of the franchise, from Boston to Milwaukee to Atlanta, is none other than major-league home-run king Henry Aaron, whose 240 swipes in a Brave uniform are more than anyone else could muster.

Of course, it took Aaron 20 years to accumulate his 240 steals, so that's only an average of 12 per year. On a single-season basis, the Braves' best base bandit was Ralph Myers, who pilfered a club-record 57 in 1913. Another Ralph, named Garr, also could fly, if only for a limited time, but his best stolen-base effort was 35 in 1973.

ALL-TIME BRAVE SEASON RECORDS

BATTING: Rogers Hornsby, .387, 1928
HRs: Eddie Mathews, 47, 1953
Hank Aaron, 47, 1971
RBIs: Eddie Mathews, 135, 1953
STEALS: Ralph Myers, 57, 1913
WINS: Vic Willis, 27, 1902
Charles Pittinger, 27, 1902
Dick Rudolph, 27, 1914
STRIKEOUTS: Phil Niekro, 262, 1977

CINCINNATI REDS

TEAM DIRECTORY: Chairmen of the Board: James R. Williams, William J. Williams; Pres.: Bob Howsam; Scouting Dir.: Larry Doughty; VP-Play. Per.: Sheldon Bender; Dir. Publ.: Jim Ferguson; Trav. Sec.: Steve Cobb; Mgr.: Vern Rapp. Home: Riverfront Stadium (52,392). Field distances: 330, l.f. line; 404, c.f.; 330, r.f. line. Spring training: Tampa Fla.

SCOUTING REPORT

HITTING: The once-proud Reds sank to the depths of the NL batting charts with a .239 average last year and only the Mets scored fewer runs, but help could be on the way. It can be assumed that the many youngsters on the roster will improve with time and, if free-agent signee Dave Parker merely duplicates his performance as a Pirate in 1983 (.279, 12 homers, 69 RBI), the club will have more sock.

Johnny Bench is gone and Dave Concepcion apparently no longer can hit with authority, but Nick Esasky, Dann Bilardello,

Mario Soto's heater made him Red menace to NL hitters.

Paul Householder, Gary Redus and Eddie Milner figure to improve with more seasoning. Redus (17 homers, 51 RBI) has a star quality about him and would have been much more productive as a rookie had he not crashed into a fence or two. Of the hardened veterans, only Dan Driessen (12 homers, 57 RBI) seems capable of making a major contribution at the dish. Cesar Cedeno seems to have worn out his welcome.

PITCHING: There's not much on the Cincy pitching staff to inspire confidence, besides Mario Soto and Joe Price. Soto (17-13, 2.70 ERA) ranks with the finest hurlers in the league and Price (10-6, 2.88) is getting there, but they desperately need help because the Reds' staff is the worst in a pitching-rich division.

The situation is even worse in the bullpen, where once-reliable Tom Hume (9 saves) and Ben Hayes (7 saves) last year used kerosene instead of water in attempts to douse flames. Injuries have taken their toll on Hume, who once ranked with the best in the league and has the paychecks to prove it. Bill Scherrer (10 saves) is the saving grace, having developed into the club's most dependable fireman. But the club had a 3.98 ERA last year and didn't have enough hitting to compensate.

FIELDING: The Reds made the fewest errors (114) in the league last year, so this area is the least of the club's worries. Driessen made only four errors and topped the league's first basemen with a .996 fielding percentage. Householder was No. 1 among NL outfielders with two bobbles and a .991 mark. If nothing else, Concepcion can still pick it at shortstop, Ron Oester is solid at second and Bilardello shows signs of being sturdy behind the plate. The young outfielders are a strength.

OUTLOOK: Not good. Only the stumbling Giants seem capable of replacing the Reds in the cellar. And now the Reds don't have former president Dick Wagner around to take the blame. The new leadership, including new manager Vern Rapp, has improved the lineup with Parker and the bench with returning hero Tony Perez, so that's a start. Who knows? Parker may even return to his late-'70s form in his hometown, away from the Pittsburgh boo-birds.

Pitching remains the key—and the Reds are sorely lacking in that department. Too much of the burden is falling on Soto's shoulders. The club needs at least two other dependable starters and an overhaul in the bullpen to be competitive. There are signs of improvement, but probably not enough to signal substantial improvement.

CINCINNATI REDS 1984 ROSTER

MANAGER Vern Rapp
Coaches—Tommy Helms, Bruce Kimm, George Scherger, Joe Sparks, Stan Williams

PITCHERS

No.	Name	1983 Club	W-L	IP	SO	ERA	B-T	Ht.	Wt.	Born
38	Berenyl, Bruce	Cincinnati	9-14	186	151	3.86	R-R	6-3	215	8/21/54 Sherwood, OH
52	Franco, John	Albuquerque	0-0	15	8	5.40	L-L	5-10	170	9/17/60 Brooklyn, NY
		Indianapolis	6-10	115	54	4.85				
45	Hayes, Ben	Indianapolis	2-0	8	4	4.70	R-R	6-1	180	8/4/57 Niagara Falls, NY
		Cincinnati	4-6	69	44	6.49				
43	Heidenreich, Curt	Waterbury	11-4	119	98	1.73	R-R	6-6	225	7/14/59 Woodstock, IL
		Indianapolis	3-3	41	23	4.57				
47	Hume, Tom	Cincinnati	3-5	66	34	4.77	R-R	6-1	185	3/29/53 Cincinnati, OH
50	Lesley, Brad	Indianapolis	3-1	18	19	2.55	R-R	6-6	230	9/11/58 Turlock, CA
		Cincinnati	0-0	8	5	2.16				
44	Owchinko, Bob	Hawaii	10-6	138	124	4.25	L-L	6-2	195	1/1/55 Detroit, MI
35	Pastore, Frank	Cincinnati	9-12	184	93	4.88	R-R	6-3	205	8/21/57 Alhambra, CA
48	Power, Ted	Cincinnati	5-6	111	57	4.54	R-R	6-4	220	1/31/55 Guthrie, OK
49	Price, Joe	Cincinnati	10-6	144	83	2.88	R-L	6-4	210	11/29/56 Inglewood, CA
25	Puleo, Charlie	Cincinnati	6-12	144	71	4.89	R-R	6-3	200	2/7/55 Bloomfield, NJ
58	Robinson, Ron	Waterbury	7-9	143	82	3.60	R-R	6-4	200	3/24/62 Exeter, CA
		Indianapolis	4-0	31	20	3.23				
46	Russell, Jeff	Indianapolis	5-5	119	98	3.55	R-R	6-4	200	9/2/61 Cincinnati, OH
		Cincinnati	4-5	68	40	3.03				
34	Scherrer, Bill	Cincinnati	2-3	92	57	2.74	L-L	6-4	170	8/4/57 Niagara Falls, NY
53	Smith, Mike	Waterbury	2-5	29	16	2.83	R-R	6-0	175	2/23/61 Jackson, MS
36	Soto, Mario	Cincinnati	17-13	274	242	2.70	R-R	6-0	185	7/12/56 Dominican Republic
59	Toliver, Fred	Indianapolis	8-10	167	112	4.54	R-R	6-1	165	2/3/61 Natchez, MS

CATCHERS

No.	Name	1983 Club	H	HR	RBI	Pct.	B-T	Ht.	Wt.	Born
11	Bilardello, Dann	Cincinnati	71	9	38	.238	R-R	6-0	185	5/26/59 Santa Cruz, CA
23	Gulden, Brad	Columbus	87	9	47	.316	L-R	5-11	175	6/10/56 New Ulm, MN
29	Trevino, Alex	Cincinnati	36	1	13	.216	R-R	5-11	170	8/26/57 Mexico
24	Van Gorder, Dave	Indianapolis	86	5	48	.226	R-R	6-2	205	3/27/57 Los Angeles, CA

INFIELDERS

15	Barnes, Skeeter	Indianapolis	127	7	56	.337	R-R	5-11	175	3/3/57 Cincinnati, OH
		Cincinnati	7	1	4	.206				
13	Concepcion, Dave	Cincinnati	123	1	47	.233	R-R	6-2	175	6/17/48 Venezuela
22	Driessen, Dan	Cincinnati	102	12	57	.277	L-R	5-11	200	7/29/51 Hilton Head, SC
12	Esasky, Nick	Indianapolis	44	14	37	.278	R-R	6-3	200	2/24/60 Hialeah, FL
		Cincinnati	80	12	46	.265				
10	Foley, Tom	Cincinnati	20	0	9	.204	L-R	6-1	175	9/9/59 Columbus, GA
17	Krenchicki, Wayne	Cincinnati	21	0	11	.273	L-R	6-1	175	9/17/54 Trenton, NJ
		Detroit	37	1	16	.278				
61	Lawless, Tom	Indianapolis	118	13	35	.279	R-R	5-11	170	12/19/56 Erie, PA
16	Oester, Ron	Cincinnati	145	11	58	.264	B-R	6-2	190	5/5/56 Cincinnati, OH
—	Perez, Tony	Philadelphia	61	6	43	.241	R-R	6-2	210	5/14/42 Cuba
56	Rowdon, Wade	Waterbury	112	21	76	.233	R-R	6-2	170	9/7/60 Riverhead, NY

OUTFIELDERS

28	Cedeno, Cesar	Cincinnati	77	9	39	.232	R-R	6-2	195	2/25/51 Dominican Republic
55	Davis, Eric	Waterbury	85	15	43	.290	R-R	6-2	165	5/29/62 Los Angeles, CA
		Indianapolis	23	7	19	.299				
21	Householder, Paul	Cincinnati	97	6	43	.255	B-R	6-0	185	9/4/58 Columbus, OH
20	Milner, Eddie	Cincinnati	131	9	33	.261	L-L	5-11	170	5/21/55 Columbus, OH
57	O'Neill, Paul	Tampa	115	8	51	.278	L-L	6-4	200	2/25/63 Columbus, OH
		Waterbury	12	0	6	.279				
39	Parker, Dave	Pittsburgh	154	12	69	.279	L-R	6-2	230	6/9/51 Jackson, MS
2	Redus, Gary	Cincinnati	112	17	51	.247	R-R	6-1	180	11/1/56 Limestone Co., AL
26	Walker, Duane	Cincinnati	53	2	29	.236	L-L	6-0	185	3/13/57 Pasadena, TX
30	Williams, Dallas	Indianapolis	168	11	75	.328	L-L	5-11	170	2/28/58 Brooklyn, NY
		Cincinnati	2	0	1	.056				

RED PROFILES

DAVE CONCEPCION 35 6-2 175 **Bats R Throws R**

Showed signs of his advancing age last season and his playing time may be reduced this year . . . The fluid Venezuelan no longer is regarded as the best all-around shortstop in the league, but what a fabulous career . . . After a solid 1982, highlighted by winning MVP honors at the All-Star Game, he compiled his lowest average since 1972 . . . Missed the All-Star Game after being selected eight straight years . . . Born June 17, 1948, in Aragua, Venezuela . . . An unheralded member of the Big Red Machine, he was the team's glue, earning five Gold Gloves . . . An underrated hitter, he has a .351 average in 15 NL Championship Series games.

Year	Club	Pos.	G	AB	R	H	2B	3B	HR	RBI	SB	Avg.
1970	Cincinnati	SS-2B	101	265	38	69	6	3	1	19	10	.260
1971	Cincinnati	SS-2B-3B-OF	130	327	24	67	4	4	1	20	9	.205
1972	Cincinnati	SS	119	378	40	79	13	2	2	29	13	.209
1973	Cincinnati	SS-OF	89	328	39	94	18	3	8	46	22	.287
1974	Cincinnati	SS-OF	160	594	70	167	25	1	14	82	41	.281
1975	Cincinnati	SS-3B	140	507	62	139	23	1	5	49	33	.274
1976	Cincinnati	SS	152	576	74	162	28	7	9	69	21	.281
1977	Cincinnati	SS	156	572	59	155	26	3	8	64	29	.271
1978	Cincinnati	SS	153	565	75	170	33	4	6	67	23	.301
1979	Cincinnati	SS	149	590	91	166	25	3	16	84	19	.281
1980	Cincinnati	SS-2B	156	622	72	162	31	8	5	77	12	.260
1981	Cincinnati	SS	106	421	57	129	28	0	5	67	4	.306
1982	Cincinnati	SS-1B-3B	147	572	48	164	25	4	5	53	13	.287
1983	Cincinnati	SS	143	528	54	123	22	0	1	47	14	.233
	Totals		1901	6845	803	1846	307	43	86	773	263	.270

RON OESTER 27 6-2 190 **Bats S Throws R**

After getting off to a great start with a .355 April, this smooth second baseman returned to normalcy and finished within .003 of his lifetime average . . . Attained career highs in homers and RBI . . . Realized a boyhood dream by reaching the majors with the Reds . . . Born May 5, 1956, in Cincinnati . . . Became Reds' ninth-round draft choice in June 1974 . . . Batted .311 at Billings in his first year of pro ball and was the best shortstop in the club's minor-league system when he came up in 1979 after batting .281 at Indianapolis (AAA) . . . Switched to second base because of Dave Concepcion's presence . . . Became a regular during 1980 season.

Year	Club	Pos.	G	AB	R	H	2B	3B	HR	RBI	SB	Avg.
1978	Cincinnati	SS	6	8	1	3	0	0	0	1	0	.375
1979	Cincinnati	SS	6	3	0	0	0	0	0	0	0	.000
1980	Cincinnati	2B-SS-3B	100	303	40	84	16	2	2	20	6	.277
1981	Cincinnati	2B-SS	105	354	45	96	16	7	5	42	2	.271
1982	Cincinnati	2B-SS-3B	151	549	63	143	19	4	9	47	5	.260
1983	Cincinnati	2B-3B	157	549	63	145	23	5	11	58	2	.264
	Totals		525	1766	212	471	74	18	27	168	15	.267

DAVE PARKER 32 6-5 230 — Bats L Throws R

Healthy at last, "The Cobra" showed signs of striking back last year, enjoying his most productive season since 1980 . . . It was his option year, however, so fans accused him of salary drive . . . Wore out welcome with Pirates' followers by taking dive after signing lucrative long-term contract . . . And wound up signing a two-year, $800,000 contract with Reds in December . . . Regarded as premier player in NL when he won successive batting titles in 1977 and 1978 . . . Born June 19, 1951, in Cincinnati . . . Weight problems blamed for 1981 slide, but poor 1982 was attributable to thumb injury . . . Won three Gold Gloves in right field during his prime . . . All-Star Game MVP in 1979 . . . A line-drive hitter despite his size and strength.

Year	Club	Pos.	G	AB	R	H	2B	3B	HR	RBI	SB	Avg.
1973	Pittsburgh	OF	54	139	17	40	9	1	4	14	1	.288
1974	Pittsburgh	OF-1B	73	220	27	62	10	3	4	29	3	.282
1975	Pittsburgh	OF	148	558	75	172	35	10	25	101	8	.308
1976	Pittsburgh	OF	138	537	82	168	28	10	13	90	19	.313
1977	Pittsburgh	OF-2B	159	637	107	215	44	8	21	88	17	.338
1978	Pittsburgh	OF	148	581	102	194	32	12	30	117	20	.334
1979	Pittsburgh	OF	158	622	109	193	45	7	25	94	20	.310
1980	Pittsburgh	OF	139	518	71	153	31	1	17	79	10	.295
1981	Pittsburgh	OF	67	240	29	62	14	3	9	48	6	.258
1982	Pittsburgh	OF	73	244	41	66	19	3	6	29	7	.270
1983	Pittsburgh	OF	144	552	68	154	29	4	12	69	12	.279
	Totals		1301	4848	728	1479	296	62	166	758	123	.305

NICK ESASKY 24 6-3 200 — Bats R Throws R

A pleasant surprise following his promotion from Indianapolis, he nailed down the third-base job by hitting .299 with seven homers and 20 RBI in July . . . Also finished strong, batting .323 in September . . . Played in 40 fewer games than Reds' more-heralded rookie Gary Redus, yet had only five fewer RBI . . . Born Feb. 24, 1960, in Hialeah, Fla. . . . Reds' No. 1 draft choice in June 1978 . . . His power asserted itself when he blasted 30 home runs for Waterbury (AA) in 1980 . . . After totaling 44 home runs at Indianapolis in 1981 and 1982, he was deemed ready for the bigs last year and made the best of it.

Year	Club	Pos.	G	AB	R	H	2B	3B	HR	RBI	SB	Avg.
1983	Cincinnati	3B	85	302	41	80	10	5	12	46	6	.265

DAN DRIESSEN 32 5-11 200 **Bats L Throws R**

Despite speculation he'd be traded, this steady first baseman remained with the Reds and posted his highest batting average since 1977 . . . Did most of his damage in the second half, batting .338 in July and .290 in August . . . A solid player who seldom has been appreciated during his major-league career . . . Injuries restricted him to 82 games in 1981 . . . Endured threats of Johnny Bench becoming the regular first baseman in 1982 . . . Born July 29, 1951, in Hilton Head, S.C. . . . Batted .409 in 47 games for Indianapolis in 1973 to win regular job with Reds and eventually prompt club to trade Tony Perez . . . Has a .313 World Series average.

Year	Club	Pos.	G	AB	R	H	2B	3B	HR	RBI	SB	Avg.
1973	Cincinnati	3B-1B	102	366	49	110	15	2	4	47	8	.301
1974	Cincinnati	3B-1B-OF	150	470	63	132	23	6	7	56	10	.281
1975	Cincinnati	1B-OF	88	210	38	59	8	1	7	38	10	.281
1976	Cincinnati	1B-OF	98	219	32	54	11	1	7	44	14	.247
1977	Cincinnati	1B	151	536	75	161	31	4	17	91	31	.300
1978	Cincinnati	1B	153	524	68	131	23	3	16	70	28	.250
1979	Cincinnati	1B	150	515	72	129	24	3	18	75	11	.250
1980	Cincinnati	1B	154	524	81	139	36	1	14	74	19	.265
1981	Cincinnati	1B	82	233	35	55	14	0	7	33	2	.236
1982	Cincinnati	1B	149	516	64	139	25	1	17	57	11	.269
1983	Cincinnati	1B	122	386	57	107	17	1	12	57	6	.277
	Totals		1399	4499	634	1216	227	23	126	642	150	.270

EDDIE MILNER 28 5-11 170 **Bats L Throws L**

Not rated as highly as fellow outfielders Gary Redus and Paul Householder during his minor-league days, center fielder provided a bonus for the Reds by earning a job in his second full major-league season last year . . . Broke up a no-hitter with a two-out, ninth-inning single off Cubs' Chuck Rainey last August . . . Topped Reds in steals, posting a pro career high . . . Born May 21, 1955, in Columbus, Ohio . . . Won three straight batting titles in high school and also was on the wrestling squad . . . Attended Muskingum and Central State . . . Cousin of former major-leaguer John Milner . . . Gradually improved his batting technique in minors and reached majors after hitting career-high .287 with Indianapolis in 1981.

Year	Club	Pos.	G	AB	R	H	2B	3B	HR	RBI	SB	Avg.
1980	Cincinnati	PH	6	3	1	0	0	0	0	0	0	.000
1981	Cincinnati	OF	8	5	0	1	1	0	0	1	0	.200
1982	Cincinnati	OF	113	407	61	109	23	5	4	31	18	.268
1983	Cincinnati	OF	146	502	77	131	23	6	9	33	41	.261
	Totals		273	917	139	241	47	11	13	65	59	.263

BRUCE BERENYI 29 6-3 215 Bats R Throws R

A tough-luck pitcher, he has lost 32 games over the last two years, despite respectable earned-run averages . . . Control problems, however, led to his downfall . . . Started and finished strongly last year, going 2-1 in April and 3-1 in September, but was mere 4-12 in between . . . Luckless trend surfaced in 1982, when 2.44 ERA during one stretch couldn't prevent streak of seven straight defeats . . . Born Aug. 21, 1954, in Sherwood, Ohio . . . Nephew of former major-league pitcher Ned Garver, who also had a tough-luck tag while pitching for the St. Louis Browns . . . Pitched one-hitter against the Expos in 1981 . . . Though he was a so-so 9-9, he topped the American Association with a 2.82 ERA for Indianapolis in 1979.

Year	Club	G	IP	W	L	Pct.	SO	BB	H	ERA
1980	Cincinnati	6	28	2	2	.500	19	23	34	7.71
1981	Cincinnati	21	126	9	6	.600	106	77	97	3.50
1982	Cincinnati	34	222	9	18	.333	157	96	208	3.35
1983	Cincinnati	32	186	9	14	.391	151	102	173	3.86
	Totals	93	562	29	40	.420	433	298	512	3.78

JOE PRICE 27 6-4 210 Bats R Throws L

Finally put it together last year, showing signs of forming a one-two punch with Mario Soto . . . Starting and working in long relief, he enjoyed his finest professional season since going 10-4 for Tampa (A) in 1978 . . . Notched most of his decisions when he was NL Pitcher of the Month for July, going 5-1 with a 1.98 ERA . . . Born Nov. 29, 1956, in Inglewood, Cal. . . . Played baseball at Oklahoma and Oklahoma State . . . Made it to majors in summer of 1980 and went 0-3 against the Giants and 7-0 against rest of the league . . . Basically a starter in the minors, he has shown he can be effective in either role . . . Reds' No. 4 choice in June 1977 draft.

Year	Club	G	IP	W	L	Pct.	SO	BB	H	ERA
1980	Cincinnati	24	111	7	3	.700	44	37	95	3.57
1981	Cincinnati	41	54	6	1	.857	41	18	42	2.50
1982	Cincinnati	59	73	3	4	.429	71	32	73	2.85
1983	Cincinnati	21	144	10	6	.625	83	46	118	2.88
	Totals	145	382	26	14	.650	239	133	328	3.02

MARIO SOTO 27 6-0 185 **Bats R Throws R**

Only Phillies' Steve Carlton had more strikeouts than this dispenser of heat last year . . . Carlton also edged him for workhorse honors, throwing 10 more innings, but Reds' ace led the league with 18 complete games, five more than runnerup Steve Rogers of Expos . . . Was at his mightiest in May, going 4-0 with a 1.40 ERA and fanning 44 in 45 innings . . . Won 17 with a last-place club and is regarded by many to be the best pitcher in the league . . . Born July 12, 1956, in Bani, Dominican Republic . . . His 274 strikeouts in 1982 set Reds' record, topping Jim Maloney's 265 in 1963 . . . Like Bruce Berenyi, he has been a victim of non-support, going 31-26 last two years despite outstanding stuff . . . Named Reds' best pitcher in 1980, his first full season with club . . . Selected as NL All-Star the last two seasons.

Year	Club	G	IP	W	L	Pct.	SO	BB	H	ERA
1977	Cincinnati	12	61	2	6	.250	44	26	60	5.31
1978	Cincinnati	5	18	1	0	1.000	13	13	13	2.50
1979	Cincinnati	25	37	3	2	.600	32	30	33	5.35
1980	Cincinnati	53	190	10	8	.556	182	84	126	3.08
1981	Cincinnati	25	175	12	9	.571	151	61	142	3.29
1982	Cincinnati	35	258	14	13	.519	274	71	202	2.79
1983	Cincinnati	34	274	17	13	.567	242	95	207	2.70
	Totals	189	1013	59	51	.536	938	380	783	3.15

BILL SCHERRER 26 6-4 170 **Bats L Throws L**

Came virtually out of nowhere to become Reds' most effective reliever last year, picking up the slack for Tom Hume and Ben Hayes . . . Resembles a left-handed Kent Tekulve on the mound because of skinny frame . . . Topped club with 10 saves only one year out of Class A . . . Appeared in 73 games, at least 13 more than any other Cincy pitcher . . . Born Aug. 4, 1957, in Niagara Falls, N.Y. . . . Attended Nevada-Las Vegas and was Reds' No. 1 draft choice in January 1977 . . . Had meteoric rise through system in 1982, beginning at Tampa (A), where he had a 17-strikeout performance, and continuing to Waterbury (AA) and Indianapolis (AAA) before ending up in Cincinnati.

Year	Club	G	IP	W	L	Pct.	SO	BB	H	ERA
1982	Cincinnati	5	17	0	1	.000	7	0	17	2.60
1983	Cincinnati	73	92	2	3	.400	57	33	73	2.74
	Totals	78	109	2	4	.333	64	33	90	2.72

GARY REDUS 27 6-1 180 **Bats R Throws R**

Swift and powerful outfielder didn't disappoint in his first full major-league season, despite a mediocre batting average . . . Playing only 125 games, he led team in runs scored and home runs and was second in stolen bases . . . A fearless fly-chaser, he slammed into the wall at Riverfront and fell in a heap, but held onto ball during April game . . . Born Nov. 11, 1956, in Limestone County, Ala. . . . Was NAIA All-American at Athens State . . . Reds' 15th-round draft choice in June 1978 is proving scouts underestimated him . . . Batted .462 and scored 100 runs in 68 games for Billings in Pioneer Rookie League, posting the second-highest average in professional baseball history . . . There was a setback in 1979, but he batted .301 with 48 steals for Tampa (A) in 1980 and was ready for majors after amassing .333 average, 24 homers and 54 steals for Indianapolis in '82.

Year	Club	Pos.	G	AB	R	H	2B	3B	HR	RBI	SB	Avg.
1982	Cincinnati	OF	20	83	12	18	3	2	1	7	0	.217
1983	Cincinnati	OF	125	453	90	112	20	9	17	51	39	.247
	Totals		145	536	102	130	23	11	18	58	39	.243

TOP PROSPECT

JEFF RUSSELL 22 6-4 200 **Bats R Throws R**

Leading the American Association with a 3.55 ERA for Indianapolis when he was promoted to the Reds Aug. 9 and proceeded to turn in a 4-5 record and 3.03 ERA as a major leaguer . . . Born Sept. 2, 1961, in Cincinnati . . . Posted a complete-game victory over San Diego in his debut . . . Hit a two-run homer in victory over the Cubs . . . Held the Giants without a hit for seven innings before losing on a homer Labor Day . . . Reds' No. 5 draft pick in June 1979 . . . Attended Gulf Coast Community College.

MANAGER VERN RAPP: Fits Reds' conservative image

. . . Had problems when he managed the Cardinals and was ousted as manager following 7-11 start in 1978 . . . Begins the season with a 90-90 record as a big-league skipper . . . In 15 years as a minor-league manager, seven of them at Indianapolis, he produced six champions . . . Born May 11, 1928, in St. Louis . . . Began professional baseball career as a catcher in the Cardinals' chain, batting .315 in first pro season in 1946 . . . Never reached the majors . . . Began managing in 1955, working for the Reds' organization most of the time . . . Led the Expos' Denver farm club in 1976 and was named Minor League Manager of the Year . . . One year later, he was tabbed to manage the Cardinals . . . Rejoined the Expos in 1979 and served them as a coach until the Reds hired him as successor to Russ Nixon at end of last season.

GREATEST STEALER

Joe Morgan has exhibited so many skills in his Hall-of-Fame-caliber career, his base burglaries often have been overlooked. But nobody ever did it better in Cincinnati history than little Joe, whose 681 career steals place him sixth on the all-time list.

Morgan stole 406 bases while in a Reds' uniform, 87 more than club career runnerup Bob Bescher. Joe stole 67 bases for the Reds in both '73 and '75 and surpassed 49 thefts in a season seven times in his career, including his Houston days.

Bescher holds the club's single-season record, however, with 80 in 1911. He was the best bandit in the league from 1909-12, leading the NL in steals four straight years with totals of 54, 70, 80 and 67 respectively. Sixty years later, Morgan joined the Reds and rewrote the club record book.

Vada Pinson was the club's premier base-stealer in the '50s and '60s, finishing with 221 swipes for Cincinnati. Of the present-day players, only Dave Concepcion comes close to Morgan. He stole 41 bases in '74 and ranks third on the Reds' career chart.

ALL-TIME RED SEASON RECORDS

BATTING: Cy Seymour, .377, 1905
HRs: George Foster, 52, 1977
RBIs: George Foster, 149, 1977
STEALS: Bob Bescher, 80, 1911
WINS: Adolfo Luque, 27, 1923
Bucky Walters, 27, 1939
STRIKEOUTS: Mario Soto, 274, 1982

HOUSTON ASTROS

TEAM DIRECTORY: Exec. Comm.: John J. McMullen, Jack Trotter, Herb Neyland; Pres.-GM: Al Rosen; Asst. GM: Andy MacPhail; Adm. Asst.-Travel. Sec.: Donald Davidson; Dir. Minor Leagues: Bill Wood; Dir. Scouting: Lynwood Stallings; Dir. Publ.: Mike Ryan; Mgr.: Bob Lillis. Home: Astrodome (45,000). Field distances: 340, l.f. line; 390, l.c.; 406, c.f.; 390, r.c.; 340, r.f. line. Spring training: Cocoa, Fla.

SCOUTING REPORT

HITTING: The Astros improved offensively last season, batting .257 for the sixth spot in the league. Still, only the Mets and the Reds scored fewer runs, so Houston continues to live and die with its pitching. But this is far from a punchless attack. Last year Jose Cruz (.318) and Ray Knight (.304) ranked among the top five batters, Terry Puhl (.292) was not far behind and Dickie Thon

Dickie Thon proves good things come in small packages.

(.286, 20 homers, 79 RBI) emerged as the best offensive shortstop in the NL.

Cruz just missed a batting title and doesn't figure to get any better, but Thon is just reaching his peak and ex-Yankee Jerry Mumphrey showed signs (.336 in 44 games) of finding a permanent home in the Astrodome. Second baseman Bill Doran (.271) also has a bright future as a hitter, and one cannot minimize the punch provided by Phil Garner (14 homers, 79 RBI), who carried the club for half a season. This is a club not known for the long ball, but contact hitters are ideal for the wide-open spaces of their indoor playground.

PITCHING: Following a slump attributed to the demise of their bullpen and the loss of injured Joe Sambito in 1982, the Astros' staff developed some young relievers and ranked third in the league with a 3.45 ERA last season. The pitching comeback, more than anything, returned Houston to the winner's circle, despite an 0-9 start. But now that the bullpen is shored up, there is a need for reliable starters behind the one-two punch of Nolan Ryan (14-9) and Joe Niekro (15-14).

Bob Knepper (6-13) didn't pitch as well as his 3.19 ERA suggests, but there are high hopes for young lefty Mike Madden (9-5). Still, the key remains the bullpen, where it has not been determined whether '83 phenoms Bill Dawley (14 saves) and Frank DiPino (20 saves) are consistent. They must compensate for the absence of Sambito and Frank LaCorte if the Astros are to contend this summer.

FIELDING: With the exception of outfielder Puhl (.991) and a solid full season at first base by Knight (.993), the Astros were average defensively last season, ranking seventh in the league (.977). Thon and Doran, however, have youth on their side and could develop into an excellent double-play combination with more seasoning. Because of their poor run production, the Astros need tight defense to support their pitching and there's definitely room for improvement.

OUTLOOK: Bob Lillis did an outstanding job as a rookie manager last season, posting the fourth-best record in the league, but the club doesn't seem to have improved sufficiently to slip past the Dodgers and the Braves. A better start than last year's surely would help, but it's not likely the pitching will be as stout as it was a year ago. This is a strange club to figure, one that can look very good or very bad and finish anywhere from second to sixth.

HOUSTON ASTROS 1984 ROSTER

MANAGER Bob Lillis
Coaches—Cot Deal, Don Leppert, Denis Menke, Jerry Walker, Les Moss

PITCHERS

No.	Name	1983 Club	W-L	IP	SO	ERA	B-T	Ht.	Wt.	Born
46	Dawley, Bill	Houston	6-6	80	60	2.82	R-R	6-4	240	2/6/58 Norwich, CT
11	DiPino, Frank	Houston	3-4	71	67	2.65	L-L	6-0	175	10/22/56 Syracuse, NY
31	Heathcock, Jeff	Tucson	10-3	110	65	2.77	R-R	6-4	195	11/18/59 Covina, CA
		Houston	2-1	28	12	3.21				
39	Knepper, Bob	Houston	6-13	203	125	3.19	L-L	6-2	210	5/25/54 Akron, OH
51	LaCoss, Mike	Houston	5-7	138	53	4.43	R-R	6-4	190	5/30/56 Glendale, CA
53	Madden, Mike	Tucson	1-1	22	15	3.68	L-L	6-1	190	1/13/58 Denver, CO
		Houston	9-5	95	44	3.14				
—	Mathis, Ron	Tucson	11-13	183	137	4.34	R-R	6-0	180	9/15/58 Kansas City, MO
36	Niekro, Joe	Houston	15-14	264	152	3.48	R-R	6-1	190	11/7/44 Martins Ferry, OH
49	Paris, Zacarias	Daytona Beach	5-3	45	29	4.03	R-R	6-1	155	9/9/57 Dominican Republic
		Columbus	7-6	107	63	5.79				
48	Ruhle, Vern	Houston	8-5	115	43	3.69	R-R	6-1	195	1/25/51 Coleman, MI
34	Ryan, Nolan	Houston	14-9	196	183	2.98	R-R	6-2	195	1/31/47 Refugio, TX
35	Sambito, Joe	Houston	Injured—Did not play				L-L	6-1	190	6/28/52 Brooklyn, NY
33	Scott, Mike	Houston	10-6	145	73	3.72	R-R	6-3	215	4/26/55 Santa Monica, CA
54	Smith, Dave	Houston	3-1	73	41	3.10	R-R	6-1	195	1/21/55 San Francisco, CA
52	Solano, Julio	Tucson	10-7	162	123	4.95	R-R	6-1	160	1/8/60 Dominican Republic
		Houston	0-2	6	3	6.00				

CATCHERS

No.	Name	1983 Club	H	HR	RBI	Pct.	B-T	Ht.	Wt.	Born
14	Ashby, Alan	Houston	58	8	34	.229	B-R	6-2	195	7/8/51 Sugarland, TX
20	Bjorkman, George	Columbus	63	12	36	.252	R-R	6-2	190	8/26/56 Canada
		Tucson	13	0	4	.228				
		Houston	17	2	14	.227				
4	Mizerock, John	Tucson	46	5	31	.261	L-R	5-11	190	12/8/60 Punxsutawney, PA
		Houston	13	1	10	.153				
6	Pujols, Luis	Tucson	28	1	9	.250	R-R	6-1	205	11/18/55 Puerto Rico
		Houston	17	0	12	.195				

INFIELDERS

No.	Name	1983 Club	H	HR	RBI	Pct.	B-T	Ht.	Wt.	Born
7	Clements, Wes	Tucson	123	20	89	.256	R-R	6-4	195	5/26/58 Inglewood, CA
—	Davis, Glenn	Columbus	133	25	85	.299	R-R	6-3	210	3/28/61 Jacksonville, FL
		Tucson	12	1	8	.211				
19	Doran, Bill	Houston	145	8	39	.271	B-R	5-11	175	5/28/58 Cincinnati, OH
3	Garner, Phil	Houston	135	14	79	.238	R-R	5-10	177	4/30/49 Jefferson City, TN
18	*Howe, Art		Injured—Did not play				R-R	6-1	185	12/15/46 Pittsburgh, PA
22	Knight, Ray	Houston	154	9	70	.304	R-R	6-2	185	12/28/52 Albany, GA
1	Pena, Burt	Tucson	94	5	63	.246	R-R	5-11	165	7/11/59 Puerto Rico
		Houston	1	0	0	.125				
12	Reynolds, Craig	Houston	21	1	6	.214	L-R	6-1	175	12/27/52 Houston, TX
16	Spilman, Harry	Houston	13	1	9	.167	L-R	6-1	190	7/18/54 Albany, GA
10	Thon, Dickie	Houston	177	20	79	.286	R-R	5-11	175	6/20/58 South Bend, IN

OUTFIELDERS

No.	Name	1983 Club	H	HR	RBI	Pct.	B-T	Ht.	Wt.	Born
17	Bass, Kevin	Houston	46	2	18	.236	B-R	6-0	180	5/12/59 Redwood City, CA
9	Bullock, Eric	Columbus	131	9	59	.276	L-L	5-11	185	2/16/60 Los Angeles, CA
25	Cruz, Jose	Houston	189	14	92	.318	L-L	6-0	175	8/8/47 Puerto Rico
23	Gainey, Ty	Columbus	107	9	43	.270	R-L	6-1	190	12/25/60 Cheraw, SC
26	Loucks, Scott	Tucson	155	8	58	.287	R-R	6-0	180	11/11/56 Anchorage, AK
		Houston	3	0	0	.214				
28	Mumphrey, Jerry	New York (AL)	70	7	36	.262	B-R	6-2	185	9/9/52 Tyler, TX
		Houston	48	1	17	.336				
21	Puhl, Terry	Houston	136	8	44	.292	L-R	6-1	190	7/8/56 Canada
—	Robles, Rubin	Tucson	48	5	33	.279	R-R	6-2	210	8/13/59 Dominican Republic
20	Scott, Tony	Houston	42	2	17	.226	B-R	6-0	195	9/18/51 Cincinnati, OH
38	Tolman, Tim	Tucson	9	1	6	.375	R-R	6-0	195	4/20/56 Santa Monica, CA
		Houston	11	2	10	.196				
29	Walling, Dennis	Houston	40	3	19	.296	L-R	6-1	185	4/17/54 Neptune, NJ

*Free agent unsigned at press time.

ASTRO PROFILES

RAY KNIGHT 31 6-2 185 Bats R Throws R

Enjoyed second straight solid season with Astros and his finest since '79 campaign with Reds . . . Ranked fifth among NL batters, thanks to a .400 May and a .345 June . . . Married professional golf star Nancy Lopez following 1982 season and credited her for his success . . . Batting style fits in nicely with Astros' style . . . Had 36 doubles last year and has averaged more than 34 per season over last five years . . . Born Dec. 28, 1952, in Albany, Ga. . . . Made successful switch from third base to first base last year . . . Had tough task of replacing Pete Rose at third base for Cincinnati in 1979, but responded in fine style . . . Acquired after 1981 season in deal for Cesar Cedeno.

Year	Club	Pos.	G	AB	R	H	2B	3B	HR	RBI	SB	Avg.
1974	Cincinnati	3B	14	11	1	2	1	0	0	2	0	.182
1977	Cincinnati	3B-2B-OF-SS	80	92	8	24	5	1	1	13	1	.261
1978	Cincinnati	3B-2B-OF-SS	83	65	7	13	3	0	1	4	0	.200
1979	Cincinnati	3B	150	551	64	175	37	4	10	79	4	.318
1980	Cincinnati	3B	162	618	71	163	39	7	14	78	1	.264
1981	Cincinnati	3B	106	386	43	100	23	1	6	34	2	.259
1982	Houston	1B-3B	158	609	72	179	36	6	6	70	2	.294
1983	Houston	1B-3B	145	507	43	154	36	4	9	70	0	.304
	Totals		898	2839	309	810	180	23	47	350	10	.285

PHIL GARNER 34 5-10 177 Bats R Throws R

Unheralded "Scrap Iron" was among NL RBI leaders during first half and has totaled 27 homers and 162 RBI in last two years . . . Became cleanup hitter and shifted from second base to third base last season . . . Belted five homers and knocked in 20 runs in May . . . Only Jose Cruz had more RBI and only Dickie Thon had more game-winning RBI than Garner's 10 among Astros . . . Born April 30, 1949, in Jefferson City, Tenn. . . . An All-American at Tennessee and the Oakland A's No. 1 draft choice in June 1971 . . . Has appeared in All-Star Game for each league, as member of A's in 1976 and as Pirate in 1980 and 1981 . . . Batted .500 with 12 hits in 24 at-bats for the Pirates in 1979 World Series, matching top mark for a seven-game Series . . . A favorite of Chuck Tanner, who managed him at Oakland and Pittsburgh . . . Known as "Yosemite Sam" during days in Oakland, because of his handlebar moustache . . . Acquired from Bucs in August 1981 in deal that sent Johnny Ray to Pittsburgh.

Year	Club	Pos.	G	AB	R	H	2B	3B	HR	RBI	SB	Avg.
1973	Oakland.	3B	9	5	0	0	0	0	0	0	0	.000
1974	Oakland.	3B-SS-2B	30	28	4	5	1	0	0	1	1	.179
1975	Oakland.	2B-SS	160	488	46	120	21	5	6	54	4	.246
1976	Oakland.	2B	159	555	54	145	29	12	8	74	35	.261
1977	Pittsburgh	3B-2B-SS	153	585	99	152	35	10	17	77	32	.260
1978	Pittsburgh	2B-3B-SS	154	528	66	138	25	9	10	66	27	.261
1979	Pittsburgh	2B-3B-SS	150	549	76	161	32	8	11	59	17	.293
1980	Pittsburgh	2B-SS	151	548	62	142	27	6	5	58	32	.259
1981	Pit.-Hou.	2B	87	294	35	73	9	3	1	26	10	.248
1982	Houston	2B-3B	155	588	65	161	33	8	13	83	24	.274
1983	Houston	2B-3B	154	567	76	135	24	2	14	79	18	.238
	Totals		1362	4735	583	1232	236	63	85	577	200	.260

DICKIE THON 25 5-11 175 Bats R Throws R

A steal for the Astros in 1981 swap with the Angels involving Ken Forsch . . . Enjoyed a spectacular season at the plate and afield, earning recognition as the best all-around shortstop in the league . . . Nobody in the NL had more game-winning RBI than his 18 . . . Topped the Astros in stolen bases and home runs and had three two-homer games . . . Never hit more than eight homers in any of his previous professional seasons . . . Born June 20, 1958, in South Bend, Ind., but grew up in Puerto Rico . . . Batted .310 with six homers and 14 RBI last June, after entering last season with total of three major-league homers . . . Batted .394 for Salt Lake City (AAA) in 1980, but still couldn't crack Angel lineup . . . Joined Astros and took shortstop job from Craig Reynolds, stealing a career-high 37 bases in 1982.

Year	Club	Pos.	G	AB	R	H	2B	3B	HR	RBI	SB	Avg.
1979	California.	INF	35	56	6	19	3	0	0	8	0	.339
1980	California.	INF	80	267	32	68	12	2	0	15	7	.255
1981	Houston	2B-SS-3B	49	95	13	26	6	0	0	3	6	.274
1982	Houston	SS-3B-2B	136	496	73	137	31	10	3	36	37	.276
1983	Houston	SS-3B	154	619	81	177	28	9	20	79	34	.286
	Totals		454	1533	205	427	80	21	23	141	84	.279

BILL DORAN 25 5-11 175 Bats S Thrwos R

Touted as the Astros' top prospect last year, he didn't disappoint . . . By looking sharp in a September 1982 trial, he caused shift of Phil Garner from second to third . . . He and Dickie Thon form the best young DP combo in the league . . . Struggled with a .242 average at the All-Star break, but used a .310 August to climb to respectability . . . Born May 28, 1958, in Cincinnati . . . An All-American at Miami of Ohio and drafted in the sixth round by Houston in '79 . . . Gradually hiked his average in the minors, batting .278 for Columbus (AA) in 1981 before posting a .302 mark at Tucson (AAA) in 1982 that prefaced his promotion to the majors . . . An insurance salesman during the offseason.

Year	Club	Pos.	G	AB	R	H	2B	3B	HR	RBI	SB	Avg.
1982	Houston	2B	26	97	11	27	3	0	0	6	5	.278
1983	Houston	2B	154	535	70	145	12	7	8	39	12	.271
	Totals		180	632	81	172	15	7	8	45	17	.272

JOSE CRUZ 36 6-0 175 Bats L Throws L

Just missed becoming oldest batting champion since Ted Williams won one at age 40 in 1958 . . . Was virtually tied with Pirates' Bill Madlock going down the stretch, but slipped to third . . . Posted highest mark of his major-league career . . . A frisky oldtimer, he also stole 30 bases and led the club with career high in RBI . . . Left fielder was especially hot in the second half, batting .375 in July, .322 in August and .356 in September and notching 62 RBI those three months . . . Born Aug. 8, 1947, in Arroyo, Puerto Rico . . . The Astros' most consistent player the last eight years, batting .289 or more six times . . . Tinkers with old cars as a hobby.

Year	Club	Pos.	G	AB	R	H	2B	3B	HR	RBI	SB	Avg.
1970	St. Louis	OF	6	17	2	6	1	0	0	1	0	.353
1971	St. Louis	OF	83	292	46	80	13	2	9	27	6	.274
1972	St. Louis	OF	117	332	33	78	14	4	2	23	9	.235
1973	St. Louis	OF	132	406	51	92	22	5	10	57	10	.227
1974	St. Louis	OF-1B	107	161	24	42	4	3	5	20	4	.261
1975	Houston	OF	120	315	44	81	15	2	9	49	6	.257
1976	Houston	OF	133	439	49	133	21	5	4	61	28	.303
1977	Houston	OF	157	579	87	173	31	10	17	87	44	.299
1978	Houston	OF-1B	153	565	79	178	34	9	10	83	37	.315
1979	Houston	OF	157	558	73	161	33	7	9	72	36	.289
1980	Houston	OF	160	612	79	185	29	7	11	91	36	.302
1981	Houston	OF	107	409	53	109	16	5	13	55	5	.267
1982	Houston	OF	155	570	62	157	27	2	9	68	21	.275
1983	Houston	OF	160	594	85	189	28	8	14	92	30	.318
	Totals		1747	5849	767	1664	288	69	122	786	272	.284

TERRY PUHL 27 6-1 190 Bats L Throws R

Like Jose Cruz, this veteran outfielder reversed a downswing and fashioned his best season since 1977 . . . Matched his career high with 25 doubles and played his usual strong defense in right field . . . Batted .350 in July and .336 in August . . . Born July 8, 1956, in Melville, Sask. . . . Has made amazing progress in baseball considering he didn't play for his high school, which didn't field a team... As a native Canadian, he wanted to play for Montreal, but was rejected by the Expos in a tryout before signing with Houston in 1973... Had seven hits in a doubleheader in 1980... Later that year, he set NL playoff records with 10 hits and a .526 average... Didn't make an error in 1979, when he replaced Cesar Cedeno as the club's center fielder.

Year	Club	Pos.	G	AB	R	H	2B	3B	HR	RBI	SB	Avg.
1977	Houston	OF	60	229	40	69	13	5	0	10	10	.301
1978	Houston	OF	149	585	87	169	25	6	3	35	32	.289
1979	Houston	OF	157	600	87	172	22	4	8	49	30	.287
1980	Houston	OF	141	535	75	151	24	5	13	55	27	.282
1981	Houston	OF	96	350	43	88	19	4	3	28	22	.251
1982	Houston	OF	145	507	64	133	17	9	8	50	17	.262
1983	Houston	OF	137	465	66	136	25	7	8	44	24	.292
	Totals		885	3271	462	918	145	40	43	271	162	.281

JOE NIEKRO 39 6-1 190 **Bats R Throws R**

Allowed one more earned run per game than he did in '82, yet emerged as Astros' biggest winner again... Did his best pitching in July, going 5-1 with a 1.35 ERA... Exceeded previous strikeout high by 22... His 82 victories are more than any other NL right-hander has attained in last five years... Born Nov. 7, 1944, in Martins Ferry, Ohio... Has one of most productive knucklers in majors... Has not yielded a run in 18 playoff innings... NL Pitcher of the Year in 1979, according to The Sporting News... Only Astros pitcher to post back-to-back 20-win seasons, in 1979 and 1980... He and older brother Phil have won 445 games... Former All-American at West Liberty College.

Year	Club	G	IP	W	L	Pct.	SO	BB	H	ERA
1967	Chicago (NL)	35	170	10	7	.588	77	32	171	3.34
1968	Chicago (NL)	34	177	14	10	.583	65	59	204	4.32
1969	Chi. (NL)-S.D.	41	221	8	18	.308	62	51	237	3.71
1970	Detroit	38	213	12	13	.480	101	72	221	4.06
1971	Detroit	31	122	6	7	.462	43	49	136	4.50
1972	Detroit	18	47	3	2	.600	24	8	62	3.83
1973	Atlanta	20	24	2	4	.333	12	11	23	4.13
1974	Atlanta	27	43	3	2	.600	31	18	36	3.56
1975	Houston	40	88	6	4	.600	54	39	79	3.07
1976	Houston	36	118	4	8	.333	77	56	107	3.36
1977	Houston	44	181	13	8	.619	101	64	155	3.03
1978	Houston	35	203	14	14	.500	97	73	190	3.86
1979	Houston	38	264	21	11	.656	119	107	221	3.00
1980	Houston	37	256	20	12	.625	127	79	268	3.55
1981	Houston	24	166	9	9	.500	77	47	150	2.82
1982	Houston	35	270	17	12	.586	130	64	224	2.47
1983	Houston	38	264	15	14	.517	152	101	238	3.48
	Totals	572	2827	177	155	.533	1349	930	2722	3.45

JERRY MUMPHREY 31 6-2 185 Bats S Throws R

Center fielder received a new lease on life when he escaped the Yankees and landed with Houston late in 1983 season . . . Expressed his appreciation by batting .336 in 44 games upon return to NL . . . Was a mediocre .262 hitter with Yankees last year . . . Astros were particularly happy with the swap, too, because they got rid of Omar Moreno, whose performance reflected his sulking . . . Born Sept. 9, 1952, in Tyler, Tex. . . . Yanks soured on him abruptly, after parting with Ruppert Jones, Chris Welch, Tim Lollar and Joe Lefebrve to get him from Padres prior to 1981 season . . . Led Yankees in hitting in first season in New York, but came to regret signing six-year contract to stay with club following that season.

Year	Club	Pos.	G	AB	R	H	2B	3B	HR	RBI	SB	Avg.
1974	St. Louis	OF	5	2	2	0	0	0	0	0	0	.000
1975	St. Louis	OF	11	16	2	6	2	0	0	1	0	.375
1976	St. Louis	OF	112	384	51	99	15	5	1	26	22	.258
1977	St. Louis	OF	145	463	73	133	20	10	2	38	22	.287
1978	St. Louis	OF	125	367	41	96	13	4	2	37	14	.262
1979	St. Louis	OF	124	339	53	100	10	3	3	32	8	.295
1980	San Diego	OF	160	564	61	168	24	3	4	59	52	.298
1981	New York (AL)	OF	80	319	44	98	11	5	6	32	13	.307
1982	New York (AL)	OF	123	477	76	143	24	10	9	68	11	.300
1983	New York (AL)	OF	83	267	41	70	11	4	7	36	2	.262
1983	Houston	OF	44	143	17	48	10	2	1	17	5	.336
	Totals		1012	3341	461	961	140	46	35	346	149	.288

FRANK DiPINO 27 6-0 175 Bats L Throws L

The main reason Astros' bullpen returned to prominence last year . . . Had managed eight saves in entire pro career and none in the majors before registering 20 last season . . . Became relief ace with 3-1 record and 1.42 ERA in May, but didn't win another game . . . Had strong finish with six saves in September . . . Born Oct. 22, 1956, in Syracuse, N.Y. . . . Part of 1982 deal with Milwaukee involving Don Sutton . . . Attended St. Leo College in Florida and signed with Brewers following a tryout . . . Was a combined 10-1 in 1980, firing a no-hitter for Holyoke (AA) against Reading before promotion to Vancouver (AAA) . . . Reached majors to stay at end of 1982 season and struck out 10 Padres in one relief stint.

Year	Club	G	IP	W	L	Pct.	SO	BB	H	ERA
1981	Milwaukee	2	2	0	0	.000	3	3	0	0.00
1982	Houston	6	28	2	2	.500	25	11	32	6.04
1983	Houston	53	71	3	4	.429	67	20	52	2.65
	Totals	61	101	5	6	.455	95	34	84	3.56

NOLAN RYAN 37 6-2 195 **Bats R Throws R**

Enjoyed solid season and ranks behind Phils' Steve Carlton on all-time strikeout list after both passed Walter Johnson . . . Pitched ninth career one-hitter, vs. San Diego Aug. 3, recording his 52nd career shutout. Tim Flannery's one-out single in third prevented a sixth no-hitter for "The Express" . . . Broke Johnson's 55-year-old career strikeout record with his 3,509th, vs. Montreal April 27 . . . Also notched first no-walk complete game of career in five-hit, 2-0 victory over Padres . . . Born Jan. 31, 1947, in Refugio, Tex. . . . NL leader with 1.69 ERA in 1981, one of lowest figures in post-World War II era . . . Struck out 19 batters in a game four times, most recently for California against Toronto in 1977 . . . Despite all of his Hall-of-Fame-caliber statistics, he has registered only two 20-win seasons.

Year	Club	G	IP	W	L	Pct.	SO	BB	H	ERA
1966	New York (NL)	2	3	0	1	.000	6	3	5	15.00
1968	New York (NL)	21	134	6	9	.400	133	75	93	3.09
1969	New York (NL)	25	89	6	3	.667	92	53	60	3.54
1970	New York (NL)	27	132	7	11	.389	125	97	86	3.41
1971	New York (NL)	30	152	10	14	.417	137	116	125	3.97
1972	California	39	284	19	16	.543	329	157	166	2.28
1973	California	41	326	21	16	.568	383	162	238	2.87
1974	California	42	333	22	16	.578	367	202	221	2.89
1975	California	28	198	14	12	.538	186	132	152	3.45
1976	California	39	284	17	18	.486	327	183	193	3.36
1977	California	37	299	19	16	.543	341	204	198	2.77
1978	California	31	235	10	13	.435	260	148	183	3.71
1979	California	34	223	16	14	.533	223	114	169	3.59
1980	Houston	35	234	11	10	.524	200	98	205	3.35
1981	Houston	21	149	11	5	.688	140	68	99	1.69
1982	Houston	35	250	16	12	.571	245	109	196	3.16
1983	Houston	29	196	14	9	.609	183	101	134	2.98
	Totals	516	3521	219	195	.529	3677	2022	2523	3.10

TOP PROSPECT

JEFF HEATHCOCK 24 6-4 195 **Bats R Throws R**

Climbed through system and looked sharp in September trial with Astros, going 2-1 with a 3.21 ERA . . . In second major-league appearance, he yielded only an infield single in 7⅓ innings of relief vs. San Francisco, retiring 22-of-25 batters . . . Born Nov. 18, 1959, in Covina, Cal. . . . Began pro career by going 9-0 for Daytona Beach (A) in '81 . . . Earned promotion to Houston after going 10-3 with a 2.86 ERA for Tacoma (AAA) last year.

MANAGER BOB LILLIS: Guided club to third-place finish and

an 85-77 record despite an 0-9 start, thereby earning some Manager-of-the-Year consideration... Succeeded Bill Virdon in late 1982 and responded with 28-23 record as interim manager... Was a member of the original Houston Colt 45s in expansion year of '62 and was voted the team MVP...Born June 2, 1930, in Altadena, Cal.... Epitome of the company man, he has been involved in all phases of the Astros' organization in the last 22 years...Ended playing career in 1967, with a .236 lifetime average as a good-field, no-hit infielder... Served in Astros' scouting department after retirement and was a coach for the club from 1973 until Aug. 10, 1982, when he became manager... Signed by the Dodgers and began playing career in 1951, reaching majors seven years later... The strong, silent type, just like his predecessor.

GREATEST STEALER

Because the Astros are an expansion franchise, there really is no competition for this distinction. Joe Morgan played only a few years for Houston, so his exploits on the basepaths didn't reach high gear until he became a member of the Reds.

As a result, the greatest base-stealer in Houston history is Cesar Cedeno. Before being traded to Cincinnati, Cesar stole 487 bases for the Astros from 1970-1981, including a club-record 61 in 1977.

Between 1972 and 1977, Cedeno ranked with the finest base thieves in the majors with 55, 56, 57, 50, 58 and 61 thefts respectively. Cesar did not become "another Willie Mays," as some predicted, but he had no peers among the Astros when it came to stealing bases.

ALL-TIME ASTRO SEASON RECORDS

BATTING: Rusty Staub, .333, 1967
HRs: Jimmy Wynn, 37, 1967
RBIs: Bob Watson, 110, 1977
STEALS: Cesar Cedeno, 61, 1977
WINS: Joe Niekro, 21, 1979
STRIKEOUTS: J. R. Richard, 313, 1979

LOS ANGELES DODGERS

TEAM DIRECTORY: Pres.: Peter O'Malley; Exec. VP: Fred Claire; VP-Play. Per.: Al Campanis; VP-Minor Leagues: Bill Schweppe; Dir. Publ.: Steve Brener; Trav. Sec.: Bill DeLury; Mgr.: Tom Lasorda. Home: Dodger Stadium (56,000). Field distances: 330, l.f. line; 370, l.c.; 395, c.f.; 370, r.c.; 330, r.f. line. Spring training: Vero Beach, Fla.

SCOUTING REPORT

HITTING: Last year's batting slide to eighth in the league (.250) was understandable, considering newcomers Mike Marshall, Greg Brock and Jack Fimple cracked the Dodger lineup and Dusty Baker tailed off to a point where he landed on the trading block.

Ken Landreaux (.281, 17 homers, 66 RBI) picked up the slack with a solid season that included 16 game-winning RBI and Marshall (.284, 17 homers, 65 RBI) overcame a slow start to fulfill expectations. Brock, under tremendous pressure as Steve Garvey's successor, batted a mere .224, but made a contribution with 20 homers and 66 RBI, helping the club lead the league with 146 homers.

Pedro Guerrero had 100 or more RBI for second year in row.

The big gun is Pedro Guerrero (.298, 32 homers, 103 RBI), who didn't let the move to third base deter him at the plate. The man can flat out hit and the LA offense will revolve around him for many years to come. Steve Sax (.281) didn't hit as well as he did during his Rookie-of-the-Year season in '82, but he remains a force with his speed on the basepaths (56 steals).

PITCHING: LA boasts the league's finest staff and its best starting rotation. The Dodgers' 3.10 ERA was way below the runnerup Phillies' 3.34. Starters Bob Welch (15-12, 2.65), Alejandro Pena (12-9, 2.75) and Jerry Reuss (12-11, 2.94) ranked among the top six in the ERA race. Add AL ERA champion Rick Honeycutt (14-8, 2.42 for Texas) and Fernando Valenzuela (15-10) to this group and you have a five-deep rotation unmatched in the bigs.

The Dodgers maintained quality control by re-signing Reuss and stealing southpaw reliever Carlos Diaz from the Mets in a winter deal. Diaz (3-1, 2.05) will replace suspended Steve Howe (18 saves, 1.44 ERA). Tom Niedenfuer (8-3, 11 saves, 1.90 ERA) developed into the right-handed bullpen stopper last year, and he has Pat Zachry and Burt Hooton for support. This is unquestionably the finest 10-man staff in the majors.

FIELDING: Well, nobody's perfect. The Dodgers' .974 percentage was 11th in the league and only the Giants made more errors than LA's 168. Defense hasn't been a team strength in recent years, but the Dodgers have the ability to overcome this flaw with superiority in other areas.

Sax is erratic at second, Bill Russell has always been merely average at shortstop and Guerrero is shaky enough at third base (30 errors) to warrant thoughts of shifting him back to the outfield if a third baseman can be found.

OUTLOOK: As usual, the Dodgers are the team to beat because nobody seems better. This organization has the ability to regroup without skipping a beat and the 1983 race was a prime example. The Dodgers had weaknesses, but ultimately came out on top because of superior talent. There's no reason to expect anything different from Tom Lasorda's bunch this year.

When the club is in trouble, resourceful management quickly moves to plug the holes. The acquisition of Honeycutt and Diaz proved that once again. Marshall, Brock, Sax and Guerrero can only improve. The weakness, once again, is defense, especially if Guerrero stays at third. The bench will be just as strong with ex-Met Bob Bailor replacing Derrel Thomas as the supersub.

LOS ANGELES DODGERS 1984 ROSTER

MANAGER Tom Lasorda
Coaches—Joe Amalfitano, Monty Basgall, Mark Cresse, Manny Mota, Ron Perranoski

PITCHERS

No.	Name	1983 Club	W-L	IP	SO	ERA	B-T	Ht.	Wt.	Born
—	Diaz, Carlos	New York (NL)	3-1	83	54	2.05	R-L	6-0	161	1/7/58 Honolulu, HI
55	Hershiser, Orel	Albuquerque	10-8	134	95	4.09	R-R	6-3	190	9/16/58 Buffalo, NY
		Los Angeles	0-0	8	5	3.38				
40	Honeycutt, Rick	Texas	14-8	175	56	2.42	L-L	6-1	190	6/29/54 Chattanooga, TN
		Los Angeles	2-3	39	18	5.77				
46	Hooton, Burt	Los Angeles	9-8	160	87	4.22	R-R	6-1	210	2/7/50 Greenville, TX
57	**Howe, Steve	Los Angeles	4-7	69	52	1.44	L-L	5-11	185	3/10/58 Pontiac, MI
48	Lovelace, Vance	Vero Beach	8-10	115	95	4.77	L-L	6-5	205	8/9/63 Tampa, FL
49	Niedenfuer, Tom	Los Angeles	8-3	95	66	1.90	R-R	6-5	217	8/13/59 St. Louis Park, MN
26	Pena, Alejandro	Los Angeles	12-9	177	120	2.75	R-R	6-3	200	6/25/59 Dominican Republic
41	Reuss, Jerry	Los Angeles	12-11	223	143	2.94	L-L	6-5	217	6/19/49 St. Louis, MO
56	Rodas, Rich	Albuquerque	16-4	186	157	4.16	L-L	6-1	180	11/7/59 Roseville, CA
		Los Angeles	0-0	5	5	1.93				
34	Valenzuela, Fernando	Los Angeles	15-10	257	189	3.75	L-L	5-11	200	11/1/60 Mexico
35	Welch, Bob	Los Angeles	15-12	204	156	2.65	R-R	6-3	190	11/3/56 Detroit, MI
47	White, Larry	Albuquerque	13-8	185	135	3.75	R-R	6-5	190	9/24/58 San Fernando, CA
		Los Angeles	0-0	7	5	1.29				
38	Zachry, Pat	Los Angeles	6-1	61	36	2.49	R-R	6-5	175	4/24/52 Richmond, TX

CATCHERS

No.	Name	1983 Club	H	HR	RBI	Pct.	B-T	Ht.	Wt.	Born
31	Fimple, Jack	Albuquerque	58	10	51	.247	R-R	6-2	185	2/10/59 Darby, PA
		Los Angeles	37	2	22	.250				
43	Morales, Jose	Los Angeles	15	3	8	.283	R-R	6-0	210	12/30/44 Virgin Islands
15	Reyes, Gilberto	San Antonio	35	1	16	.282	R-R	6-2	200	12/10/63 Dom. Republic
		Albuquerque	19	2	15	.306				
		Los Angeles	5	0	0	.161				
22	Sax, Dave	Albuquerque	96	8	59	.343	R-R	6-0	185	9/22/58 W. Sacramento, CA
		Los Angeles	0	0	1	.000				
14	Scioscia, Mike	Los Angeles	11	1	7	.314	L-R	6-2	220	11/27/58 Upper Darby, PA
7	Yeager, Steve	Los Angeles	68	15	41	.203	R-R	6-0	205	11/24/48 Huntington, WV

INFIELDERS

10	Anderson, Dave	Albuquerque	11	0	3	.407	R-R	6-2	185	8/1/60 Louisville, KY
4	Bailor, Bob	New York (NL)	85	1	30	.250	R-R	5-10	160	7/10/51 Connellsville, PA
		Los Angeles	19	1	2	.165				
33	Bream, Sid	Albuquerque	149	32	118	.307	L-L	6-4	215	8/3/60 Carlisle, PA
		Los Angeles	2	0	2	.182				
9	Brock, Greg	Los Angeles	102	20	66	.224	L-R	6-3	200	6/14/57 McMinnville, OR
28	Guerrero, Pedro	Los Angeles	174	32	103	.298	R-R	6-0	195	6/29/56 Dominican Republic
17	Landestoy, Rafael	Cin.-L.A.	11	1	1	.159	B-R	5-11	180	5/28/53 Dominican Republic
25	Rivera, German	Albuquerque	169	24	103	.328	R-R	6-2	195	7/6/59 Puerto Rico
		Los Angeles	6	0	0	.353				
18	Russell, Bill	Los Angeles	111	1	30	.246	R-R	6-0	175	10/21/48 Pittsburg, KS
3	Sax, Steve	Los Angeles	175	5	41	.281	R-R	5-11	185	1/29/60 W. Sacramento, CA
37	Taveras, Alex	Albuquerque	116	8	74	.321	R-R	5-10	170	10/9/55 Dominican Republic
		Los Angeles	0	0	0	.000				

OUTFIELDERS

12	Baker, Dusty	Los Angeles	138	15	73	.260	R-R	6-2	195	6/15/49 Riverside, CA
52	Espy, Cecil	San Antonio	151	4	38	.268	B-R	6-3	195	1/20/63 San Diego, CA
		Los Angeles	3	0	1	.273				
36	Gonzalez, Jose	Lodi	91	6	36	.294	R-R	6-2	190	11/23/64 Dom. Republic
44	Landreaux, Ken	Los Angeles	135	17	66	.281	L-R	5-11	170	12/22/54 Los Angeles, CA
20	Maldonado, Candy	Albuquerque	46	4	20	.319	R-R	5-11	195	9/5/60 Puerto Rico
		Los Angeles	12	1	6	.194				
5	Marshall, Mike	Los Angeles	132	17	65	.284	R-R	6-5	220	1/12/60 Libertyville, IL
51	Miller, Lennie	Albuquerque	179	10	66	.328	R-R	6-1	190	6/2/60 Dallas, TX
16	Monday, Rick	Los Angeles	44	6	20	.247	L-L	6-3	200	11/20/45 Batesville, AR
23	Reynolds, R.J.	San Antonio	170	18	89	.337	R-R	5-11	175	4/19/60 Sacramento, CA
		Los Angeles	13	2	11	.236				
30	*Thomas, Derrell	Los Angeles	48	2	8	.250	B-R	6-0	160	1/14/51 Los Angeles, CA

*Free agent unsigned at press time
**Suspended for one year

DODGER PROFILES

PEDRO GUERRERO 27 5-11 195 Bats R Throws R

Struggled defensively in early going after making move from right field to third base, but improved afield as last season progressed . . . Firmly entrenched as club's big gun . . . Became first Dodger in history to hit at least 30 homers and steal at least 20 bases in 1982 and duplicated that feat last year . . . First LA player to have back-to-back 30-plus-homer seasons . . . Born June 29, 1956, in San Pedro de Macoris, Dominican Republic . . . His two-run triple gave Dodgers the winning run in their sole NL Championship Series victory last season, in Game 2 . . . Shared MVP honors in '81 World Series with Steve Yeager and Ron Cey . . . Started last year with a .329 April and finished with a .307 September that included seven home runs . . . Hit four home runs in '81 postseason . . . A hot hitter since he batted .438 as a sandlot player in homeland . . . Signed by Indians, who virtually gave him to Dodgers prior to 1974 season, trading him for pitcher Bruce Ellingsen and cash.

Year	Club	Pos.	G	AB	R	H	2B	3B	HR	RBI	SB	Avg.
1978	Los Angeles......	1B	5	8	3	5	0	1	0	1	0	.625
1979	Los Angeles......	OF-1B-3B	25	62	7	15	2	0	2	9	2	.242
1980	Los Angeles......	OF-INF	75	183	27	59	9	1	7	31	2	.322
1981	Los Angeles......	OF-3B-1B	98	347	46	104	17	2	12	48	5	.300
1982	Los Angeles......	OF-3B	150	575	87	175	27	5	32	100	22	.304
1983	Los Angeles......	3B-OF	160	584	87	174	28	6	32	103	23	.298
	Totals..........		513	1759	257	532	83	15	85	292	54	.302

DUSTY BAKER 34 6-2 195 Bats R Throws R

Got off to terrible start and was batting .224 June 28 . . . Turned season around, winning Player-of-the-Month honors in July by batting .370 with eight doubles, four homers and 23 RBI, including four game-winners . . . Dodgers' leading hitter in last year's playoffs with .357 mark and he scored twice in their Game 2 victory . . . Enjoyed dream season in '81, making All-Star squad, playing on world championship team and earning a Gold Glove for his play in left field . . . Born June 15, 1949, in Riverside, Cal. . . . A genuine diamond in the rough, he was a 25th-round draft pick by the Braves in June 1967 . . . Joined Dodgers in six-player swap in 1975 and has been a steady, productive performer since . . . Regarded as one of game's best clutch hitters.

Year	Club	Pos.	G	AB	R	H	2B	3B	HR	RBI	SB	Avg.
1968	Atlanta	OF	6	5	0	2	0	0	0	0	0	.400
1969	Atlanta	OF	3	7	0	0	0	0	0	0	0	.000
1970	Atlanta	OF	13	24	3	7	0	0	0	4	0	.292
1971	Atlanta	OF	29	62	2	14	2	0	0	4	0	.226
1972	Atlanta	OF	127	446	62	143	27	2	17	76	4	.321
1973	Atlanta	OF	159	604	101	174	29	4	21	99	24	.288
1974	Atlanta	OF	149	574	80	147	35	0	20	69	18	.256
1975	Atlanta	OF	142	494	63	129	18	2	19	72	12	.261
1976	Los Angeles	OF	112	384	36	93	13	0	4	39	2	.242
1977	Los Angeles	OF	153	533	86	155	26	1	30	86	2	.291
1978	Los Angeles	OF	149	522	62	137	24	1	11	66	12	.262
1979	Los Angeles	OF	151	554	86	152	29	1	23	88	11	.274
1980	Los Angeles	OF	153	579	80	170	26	4	29	97	12	.294
1981	Los Angeles	OF	103	400	48	128	17	3	9	49	10	.320
1982	Los Angeles	OF	147	570	80	171	19	1	23	88	17	.300
1983	Los Angeles	OF	149	531	71	138	25	1	15	73	7	.260
	Totals		1747	6289	860	1760	290	20	221	910	131	.280

STEVE SAX 24 5-11 175 — Bats R Throws R

Had almost an identical season to his Rookie-of-the-Year campaign of 1982 . . . Went through a streak of erratic fielding because of sudden throwing problems, but settled down and finished well . . . Starting second baseman in All-Star Game . . . Set Dodgers' rookie record with 49 steals in 1982 . . . Made LA fans forget Davey Lopes . . . Born Jan. 29, 1960, in Sacramento, Cal. . . . Plays the game with aggressiveness and enthusiasm of Pete Rose, his hero . . . Skipped Triple-A ball by earning Texas League Player-of-the-Year honors and winning batting title with .346 average at San Antonio (AA) in 1981 . . . Only rookie to make NL All-Star squad in 1982, when he became fourth straight Dodger to win Rookie-of-the-Year award.

Year	Club	Pos.	G	AB	R	H	2B	3B	HR	RBI	SB	Avg.
1981	Los Angeles	2B	31	119	15	33	2	0	2	9	5	.277
1982	Los Angeles	2B	150	638	88	180	23	7	4	47	49	.282
1983	Los Angeles	2B	155	623	94	175	18	5	5	41	56	.281
	Totals		336	1380	197	388	43	12	11	97	110	.281

KEN LANDREAUX 29 5-11 170 — Bats L Throws R

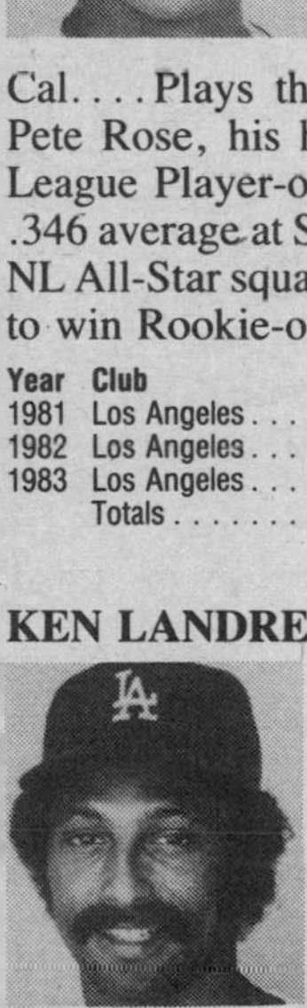

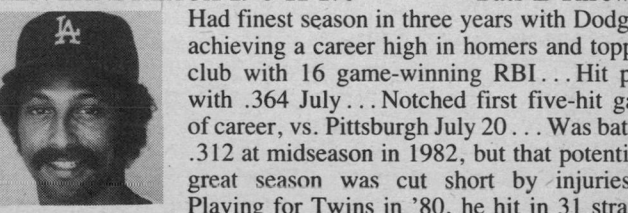

Had finest season in three years with Dodgers, achieving a career high in homers and topping club with 16 game-winning RBI . . . Hit peak with .364 July . . . Notched first five-hit game of career, vs. Pittsburgh July 20 . . . Was batting .312 at midseason in 1982, but that potentially great season was cut short by injuries . . . Playing for Twins in '80, he hit in 31 straight games . . . Born Dec. 22, 1954, in Los Angeles . . . Had three triples for Minnesota against Texas in 1980 . . . Center fielder didn't make an error in '81 . . . Attended Arizona State and batted .413 in his final year there . . . Angels' No. 1 draft pick in June 1976 . . . Was Minor League Player of the Year in '77, hitting a combined .357 for El Paso (AA) and Salt Lake City (AAA) . . . Went from Angels to Twins in Rod Carew deal prior to 1979 . . . Dodgers got him for three players, including Mickey Hatcher, prior to 1981 season.

Year	Club	Pos.	G	AB	R	H	2B	3B	HR	RBI	SB	Avg.
1977	California	OF	23	76	6	19	5	1	0	5	1	.250
1978	California	OF	93	260	37	58	7	5	5	23	7	.223
1979	Minnesota	OF	151	564	81	172	27	5	15	83	10	.305
1980	Minnesota	OF	129	484	56	136	23	11	7	62	8	.281
1981	Los Angeles	OF	99	390	48	98	16	4	7	41	18	.251
1982	Los Angeles	OF	129	461	71	131	23	7	7	50	31	.284
1983	Los Angeles	OF	141	481	63	135	25	3	17	66	30	.281
	Totals		765	2716	362	749	126	36	58	330	105	.276

MIKE MARSHALL 24 6-5 220 Bats R Throws R

Struggled at start of season and was batting only .242 with seven homers and 22 RBI at All-Star break . . . Once outfielder/first baseman adjusted to regular status and learned the pitchers, however, he lived up to preseason billing . . . Batted .311 with 10 homers and 43 RBI during second half to aid pennant push . . . Gained even more attention by romancing rock star Belinda Carlisle . . . Batted .307 at Dodger Stadium . . . Had 14-game hitting streak, matching Steve Sax's team high for last season . . . Born Jan. 12, 1960, in Libertyville, Ill. . . . Reached majors to stay after batting .388 with 14 homers and 58 RBI for Albuquerque (AAA) in '82 . . . Minor League Player of the Year in '81 with .373 average, 34 homers and 137 RBI for Albuquerque . . . Was first PCL Triple Crown winner since Steve Bilko in 1956.

Year	Club	Pos.	G	AB	R	H	2B	3B	HR	RBI	SB	Avg.
1981	Los Angeles	1B-OF	14	25	2	5	3	0	0	1	0	.200
1982	Los Angeles	OF-1B	49	95	10	23	3	0	5	9	2	.242
1983	Los Angeles	OF-1B	140	465	47	132	17	1	17	65	7	.284
	Totals		203	585	59	160	23	1	22	75	9	.274

FERNANDO VALENZUELA 23 5-11 200 Bats L Throws L

Workhorse of staff and Dodgers' only post-season winner, stopping Phillies, 4-1, in Game 2 of playoffs . . . Best month was May, when he went 3-0 with two shutouts . . . Beat Braves three times and had a six-game batting streak . . . Beat Cubs July 26, recording first complete game by an LA pitcher in 33 starts, the longest drought in Dodgers' history . . .

Born Nov. 1, 1960, in Navajoa, Sonora, Mexico . . . Fernandomania has died down, but his glittering start will long be remembered . . . Didn't allow a run in 17⅔ innings at end of '80 . . . Earned Cy Young Award and Rookie-of-the-Year honors in sensational 1981 . . . Won first eight starts of strike-torn season, including five shutouts . . . Held out for three weeks in spring of 1982 before signing for $350,000 with a $100,000 incentive clause.

Year	Club	G	IP	W	L	Pct.	SO	BB	H	ERA
1980	Los Angeles	10	18	2	0	1.000	16	5	8	0.00
1981	Los Angeles	25	192	13	7	.650	180	61	140	2.48
1982	Los Angeles	37	285	19	13	.594	199	83	247	2.87
1983	Los Angeles	35	257	15	10	.600	189	99	245	3.75
	Totals	107	752	49	30	.620	584	248	640	3.00

BOB WELCH 27 6-3 190 — Bats R Throws R

No longer the flame-throwing rookie who fanned Reggie Jackson in the 1978 World Series, but a polished pitcher who is as lethal with his hook as with his heat . . . Tied Fernando Valenzuela for most victories on team last year, but had a much better ERA . . . Pitched his second one-hitter, vs. Phillies June 1 . . . Particularly effective down the stretch . . . Was 4-1 with a 1.95 ERA in August and 3-1 with 2.33 mark in September . . . Born Nov. 3, 1956, in Detroit . . . Hit home run to defeat Reds and Mario Soto, 1-0, June 17 . . . Recurrence of bursitis in left hip hampered playoff performance . . . Won well-publicized bout with alcohol in 1980 and wrote book about it . . . All-American at Eastern Michigan.

Year	Club	G	IP	W	L	Pct.	SO	BB	H	ERA
1978	Los Angeles	23	111	7	4	.636	66	26	92	2.03
1979	Los Angeles	25	81	5	6	.455	64	32	82	4.00
1980	Los Angeles	32	214	14	9	.609	141	79	190	3.28
1981	Los Angeles	23	141	9	5	.643	88	41	141	3.45
1982	Los Angeles	36	236	16	11	.593	176	81	199	3.36
1983	Los Angeles	31	204	15	12	.556	156	72	164	2.65
	Totals	170	987	66	47	.584	691	331	868	3.11

JERRY REUSS 34 6-5 217 — Bats L Throws L

Hard-luck member of Dodger pitching staff—and that includes his salary negotiations with club . . . Was winless for more than two months, losing seven straight games and going 11 starts without a victory . . . Ended tailspin with victory over Giants Aug. 16 and won five in a row . . . Was 3-0 in April and August and 3-1 in September . . . As evidence of tough luck, he went 0-3 with 1.77 ERA in five June starts . . . Born June 19,

1949, in St. Louis... Pitched no-hitter vs. San Francisco, June 27, 1980... One of game's good-humor men, he helped groundskeepers drag the infield during final series against Giants last year... Astros stole him from Cardinals in '72, but didn't realize what they had, giving him to Pirates for Milt May in '73 deal... Became a Dodger in 1979 swap for Rick Rhoden.

Year	Club	G	IP	W	L	Pct.	SO	BB	H	ERA
1969	St. Louis	1	7	1	0	1.000	3	3	2	0.00
1970	St. Louis	20	127	7	8	.467	74	49	132	4.11
1971	St. Louis	36	211	14	14	.500	131	109	228	4.78
1972	Houston	33	192	9	13	.409	174	83	177	4.17
1973	Houston	41	279	16	13	.552	177	117	271	3.74
1974	Pittsburgh	35	260	16	11	.593	105	101	259	3.50
1975	Pittsburgh	32	237	18	11	.621	131	78	224	2.54
1976	Pittsburgh	31	209	14	9	.609	108	51	209	3.53
1977	Pittsburgh	33	208	10	13	.435	116	71	225	4.11
1978	Pittsburgh	23	83	3	2	.600	42	23	97	4.88
1979	Los Angeles	39	160	7	14	.333	83	60	178	3.54
1980	Los Angeles	37	229	18	6	.750	111	40	193	2.52
1981	Los Angeles	22	153	10	4	.714	51	27	138	2.29
1982	Los Angeles	39	255	18	11	.621	138	50	232	3.11
1983	Los Angeles	32	223	12	11	.522	143	50	233	2.94
	Totals	454	2833	173	140	.553	1587	912	2798	3.47

ALEJANDRO PENA 24 6-3 200 — Bats R Throws R

Pleasant surprise for Dodgers... Despite limited minor-league experience, he came through when club needed a starter last spring... Blanked Phillies twice and had three shutouts overall after coming out of bullpen and joining the rotation... Took over ERA lead at 2.18 by blanking Astros Sept. 15, but finished fifth in NL... Started season strong with 3-1 April, including 1.69 ERA, one shutout and one save... Born June 25, 1959, in the Dominican Republic... Was a third baseman as a youngster, but was switched to the mound because of strong arm.

Year	Club	G	IP	W	L	Pct.	SO	BB	H	ERA
1981	Los Angeles	14	25	1	1	.500	14	11	18	2.88
1982	Los Angeles	29	36	0	2	.000	20	21	37	4.79
1983	Los Angeles	34	177	12	9	.571	120	51	152	2.75
	Totals	77	238	13	12	.520	154	83	207	3.06

RICK HONEYCUTT 29 6-1 190 — Bats L Throws L

Finished season in Dodger bullpen after he had posted 14 victories and a league-leading 2.42 ERA for Rangers... Had 5.77 ERA after joining LA, despite 16 scoreless innings against NL-champion Phillies... Came to Dodgers Aug. 19 in swap for pitchers Dave Stewart and Ricky Wright... Sinker more effective in AL, if his NL debut was any indication... Born

June 29, 1954, in Chattanooga, Tenn. . . . All-American first baseman at Tennessee in '76 . . . Posted 2.60 ERA and batted .301 as pitcher and first baseman in first pro season at Niagara Falls in '76 . . . Has had streaky career, going 7-1 in one stretch with Seattle in '80 and getting off to 8-1 start with Rangers in '81 . . . After 0-7 start in '82, he won four in a row before losing 10 of last 11.

Year	Club	G	IP	W	L	Pct.	SO	BB	H	ERA
1977	Seattle	10	29	0	1	.000	17	11	26	4.34
1978	Seattle	26	134	5	11	.313	50	49	150	4.90
1979	Seattle	33	194	11	12	.478	83	67	201	4.04
1980	Seattle	30	203	10	17	.370	79	60	221	3.95
1981	Texas	20	128	11	6	.647	40	17	120	3.30
1982	Texas	30	164	5	17	.227	64	54	201	5.27
1983	Texas	25	175	14	8	.636	56	37	168	2.42
1983	Los Angeles	9	39	2	3	.400	18	13	46	5.77
	Totals	183	1066	58	75	.436	407	308	1133	4.04

TOP PROSPECTS

R. J. REYNOLDS 23 5-11 175 **Bats R Throws R**

The way the Dodgers crank out prospects, your guess is as good as mine who is closest to major-league stardom, but this outfielder came through with some clutch hits for Dodgers down the stretch (11 RBI in 55 at-bats) after batting .337 for San Antonio (AA) . . . Born April 19, 1960, in Sacramento, Cal. . . . First baseman Sid Bream batted .307 with 32 homers and 118 RBI at Albuquerque, but there's no room for him.

MANAGER TOM LASORDA: Earned most of the Manager-of-the-Year votes for winning a division title in what was supposed to be a rebuilding year, according to many observers—but not the 1983 Complete Handbook of Baseball, which predicted a Dodger victory . . . Not every team can win with superior talent—consider the Expos, Angels and Yankees—so he deserves credit for getting so far despite having two rookie starters, a new third baseman and the distractions brought about by the Steve Howe dilemma . . . Born Sept. 22, 1927, in Norristown, Pa. . . . The type of guy you love to hate because of his show-biz demeanor . . . Has a voracious appetite and a bulging belly to prove it . . . Only second NL manager to win pennants in his first two seasons . . . Won five pennants in seven years as minor-league skipper and has four firsts in seven seasons with Dodgers and overall major-league managerial mark of 606-477 . . . Former pitcher once struck out 25 batters in 15-inning game . . . Dodgers departed from tradition, giving him three-year contract to stay with club at end of last season.

GREATEST STEALER

A runaway for Maury Wills, who had 490 of his 586 stolen bases while with the Dodgers and revolutionized the art of base-stealing with his prodigious output in the early '60s.

Wills became the first modern player to surpass the 100 mark with his 104 steals in 1962, erasing Ty Cobb's 96 from the record books. Mercurial Maury led the league six straight years from 1960-65 and exceeded 50 steals in a season four times during that span.

Davey Lopes and Jackie Robinson also rate a mention. Lopes twice led the NL in steals, posting a high of 77 in '75. Robinson broke into the majors with flying spikes in '47, promptly topping the league's base thieves with 29 and repeating as king in '49, with 37.

Lopes finished with 418 steals as a Dodger, second to Wills. Present-day Dodger Steve Sax suggested he may threaten the leaders by swiping 49 as a rookie in 1982.

ALL-TIME DODGER SEASON RECORDS

BATTING: Babe Herman, .393, 1930
HRs: Duke Snider, 43, 1956
RBIs: Tommy Davis, 153, 1962
STEALS: Maury Wills, 104, 1962
WINS: Joe McGinnity, 29, 1900
STRIKEOUTS: Sandy Koufax, 382, 1965

SAN DIEGO PADRES

TEAM DIRECTORY: Owner: Ray Kroc; Pres.: Ballard Smith; VP-Baseball Oper.: Jack McKeon; Senior VP: Elten Schiller; Adm. Minor Leagues/Scouting: Tom Romenesko; Dir. Pub. Rel.: Bob Chandler; Trav. Sec.: John Mattei; Mgr.: Dick Williams. Home: San Diego Jack Murphy Stadium (51,319). Field distances: 330, l.f. line; 405, c.f.; 330, r.f. line. Spring training: Yuma, Ariz.

SCOUTING REPORT

HITTING: A potentially solid lineup fell short of expectations last season, but shows signs of a bright future. Steve Garvey (.294) was limited to 100 games by injury, but he was on a 100-RBI pace with his new club. Terry Kennedy (.284, 17 homers, 98 RBI)

A healthy Steve Garvey could be difference for Padres.

is becoming even more dangerous at the plate than Gary Carter, so the Padres have a solid one-two punch.

But that's where the power stops, unless rookie Kevin McReynolds or newcomer Carmelo Martinez, acquired from the Cubs, cracks the lineup. That's not likely because the outfield seems set with speedsters Alan Wiggins (.276, 66 steals) and Bobby Brown (.267, 27 steals) joining Tony Gwynn, who batted .309 in 86 games. Juan Bonilla, Garry Templeton and Luis Salazar all have hit in the .300 neighborhood in the past, so this has the makings of a solid batting order from one to eight.

PITCHING: The signing of relief ace Rich Gossage (13-5, 2.27 ERA, 22 saves as a Yankee) will be welcomed by the starting corps. Tim Lollar had a great '82 and Dave Dravecky and Eric Show started '83 strongly. But Lollar slumped to 7-12 and Dravecky (14-10) and Show (15-12), a combined 20-10 at the All-Star break, were 9-12 in the second half. The most pleasant surprise was Mark Thurmond (7-3, 2.65 ERA), who finished the season as the most effective starter. Ed Whitson (5-7) and Andy Hawkins (5-7) must do better.

In addition to Gossage, the bullpen has Luis DeLeon (13 saves), former Cub Craig Lefferts (3-4, 3.13 ERA) and Sid Monge (10-3, 3.70 ERA, 7 saves as a Phillie and Padre).

FIELDING: Bonilla (.986) can play second with the best, Kennedy is making strides behind the plate and Gwynn and Wiggins are sure-handed in the outfield, so the Padres can be a solid defensive club if Templeton regains his form at short and Salazar makes an improvement at third base. Garvey doesn't make many errors at first, but his range has been suspect for some time.

OUTLOOK: Despite manager Dick Williams' tendency to produce winners, and the presence of Gossage, this club doesn't have the pitching to finish ahead of the Dodgers, Braves and Astros. There is no starter who can be counted on to win a dozen games for sure.

The Padres will have to score an awful lot of runs. But with Garvey, Kennedy, Gwynn and Wiggins providing a nucleus, offense definitely is a Padre strength. This could be enhanced if Templeton, Bonilla and Salazar regain their previous form and McReynolds does to major-league pitching what he has done to minor-league pitching the last few years.

SAN DIEGO PADRES 1984 ROSTER

MANAGER Dick Williams
Coaches—Harry Dunlop, Jack Krol, Norm Sherry, Ozzie Virgil

PITCHERS

No.	Name	1983 Club	W-L	IP	SO	ERA	B-T	Ht.	Wt.	Born
51	Booker, Greg	Las Vegas	5-6	102	58	5.45	R-R	6-6	230	6/22/60 Lynchburg, VA
		San Diego	0-1	12	5	7.71				
39	Chiffer, Floyd	San Diego	0-2	23	15	3.18	R-R	6-2	180	4/20/56 Long Island City, NY
		Las Vegas	10-4	78	62	3.22				
48	Couchee, Mike	San Diego	0-1	14	5	5.14	R-R	6-0	190	12/4/57 San Jose, CA
		Las Vegas	2-0	27	25	4.05				
44	Decker, Marty	Portland	8-3	96	102	6.66	R-R	5-10	168	6/7/57 Upland, CA
		San Diego	0-0	9	9	2.08	R-R	6-1	153	8/19/58 Puerto Rico
35	DeLeon, Luis	San Diego	6-6	111	90	2.68	R-R	6-1	153	8/19/58 Puerto Rico
43	Dravecky, Dave	San Diego	14-10	184	74	3.58	R-L	6-1	195	2/14/56 Youngstown, OH
54	Gossage, Rich	New York (AL)	13-5	87	90	2.27	R-R	6-3	217	7/5/51 Colorado Springs, CO
40	Hawkins, Andy	Las Vegas	6-4	85	50	6.43	R-R	6-4	200	1/21/60 Waco, TX
		San Diego	5-7	120	59	2.93				
—	Lefferts, Craig	Chicago (NL)	3-4	89	60	3.13	L-L	6-1	180	9/29/51 Germany
48	Lollar, Tim	San Diego	7-12	176	135	4.61	L-L	6-3	195	3/17/56 Poplar Bluff, MO
42	Monge, Sid	Phil.-S.D.	10-3	80	39	3.70	B-L	6-2	200	4/11/51 Mexico
27	Rasmussen, Dennis	Columbus	13-10	181	187	4.57	L-L	6-7	230	4/18/59 Los Angeles, CA
		San Diego	0-0	14	13	1.98				
30	Show, Eric	San Diego	15-12	201	120	4.17	R-R	6-1	185	5/19/56 Riverside, CA
38	Thurmond, Mark	Las Vegas	6-1	63	38	3.29	L-L	6-0	180	9/12/56 Houston, TX
		San Diego	7-3	115	49	2.67				
31	Whitson, Ed	San Diego	5-7	144	81	4.30	R-R	6-3	200	5/19/55 Johnson City, TN
		Las Vegas	1-0	12	11	6.75				
62	Wojna, Ed	Reading	13-7	161	83	3.67	R-R	6-1	185	8/20/60 Bridgeport, CT

CATCHERS

No.	Name	1983 Club	H	HR	RBI	Pct.	B-T	Ht.	Wt.	Born
15	Bochy, Bruce	Las Vegas	44	11	33	.303	R-R	6-4	210	4/16/55 France
		San Diego	9	0	3	.214				
10	Gwosdz, Doug	San Diego	6	1	4	.109	R-R	5-11	180	6/20/60 Houston, TX
16	Kennedy, Terry	San Diego	156	17	98	.284	L-R	6-4	220	6/4/56 Euclid, OH
8	Tingley, Ron	Las Vegas	83	10	48	.202	R-R	6-2	160	5/27/59 Presque Isle, MD

INFIELDERS

No.	Name	1983 Club	H	HR	RBI	Pct.	B-T	Ht.	Wt.	Born
7	Bevacqua, Kurt	San Diego	38	2	24	.244	R-R	6-2	194	1/23/47 Miami, FL
3	Bonilla, Juan	San Diego	132	4	45	.237	R-R	5-9	170	2/12/56 Puerto Rico
—	Connally, Fritz	Iowa	130	22	85	.288	R-R	6-4	210	5/19/58 Bryan, TX
		Chicago (NL)	1	0	0	.100				
11	Flannery, Tim	San Diego	50	3	19	.234	L-R	5-11	170	9/29/57 Tulsa, OK
6	Garvey, Steve	San Diego	114	14	59	.294	R-R	5-10	190	12/22/48 Tampa, FL
57	Guillen, Ozzie	Beaumont	126	2	48	.295	B-R	5-11	150	1/20/64 Venezuela
22	Hinshaw, George	Las Vegas	136	16	67	.283	R-R	6-0	185	10/23/59 Los Angeles, CA
		San Diego	7	0	4	.438				
21	Lansford, Joe	Las Vegas	134	27	116	.254	R-R	6-5	225	1/15/61 San Jose, CA
		San Diego	2	1	2	.250				
—	Martinez, Carmelo	Iowa	115	31	94	.251	R-R	6-1	190	7/28/60 Puerto Rico
		Chicago (NL)	23	6	16	.258				
12	Ramirez, Mario	Las Vegas	12	1	8	.222	R-R	5-9	160	9/12/57 Puerto Rico
		San Diego	21	0	12	.196				
36	Rodriguez, Edwin	Columbus	98	2	52	.249	R-R	5-11	175	8/14/60 Puerto Rico
		San Diego	2	0	0	.167				
4	Salazar, Luis	San Diego	124	14	45	.258	R-R	5-9	180	5/19/56 Venezuela
1	Templeton, Garry	San Diego	121	3	40	.263	B-R	5-11	170	3/24/56 Lockey, TX

OUTFIELDERS

No.	Name	1983 Club	H	HR	RBI	Pct.	B-T	Ht.	Wt.	Born
20	Brown, Bobby	Las Vegas	134	15	70	.331	B-R	6-1	207	5/24/54 Turbeville, VA
		San Diego	60	5	22	.267				
50	Davis, Jerry	Las Vegas	150	23	100	.298	R-R	6-0	185	12/25/58 Trenton, NJ
		San Diego	5	0	1	.333				
19	Gwynn, Tony	Las Vegas	25	0	7	.342	L-L	5-11	185	5/9/60 Los Angeles, CA
		San Diego	94	1	37	.309				
17	*Jones, Ruppert	San Diego	78	12	49	.233	L-L	5-10	171	3/12/55 Dallas, TX
18	McReynolds, Kevin	Las Vegas	168	32	116	.377	R-R	6-1	205	10/16/59 Little Rock, AK
		San Diego	31	4	14	.221				
17	Richards, Gene	San Diego	64	3	22	.275	L-L	6-0	175	9/29/53 Monticello, SC
—	Summers, Champ	San Francisco	3	0	3	.136	L-R	6-2	205	6/15/48 Bremerton, WA
2	Wiggins, Alan	San Diego	139	0	22	.276	B-R	6-2	160	2/17/58 Los Angeles, CA

*Free agent unsigned at press time

PADRE PROFILES

TERRY KENNEDY 27 6-4 220 Bats L Throws R

Established career high in RBI despite tailing off in other offensive categories . . . Had 14 game-winning RBI and, along with Pirates' Tony Pena, he is threatening supremacy of Expos' Gary Carter among NL catchers . . . NL Player of the Month in April, batting .390 with 21 RBI . . . Finished fast with seven homers and 22 RBI in September . . . Born June 4, 1956, in Euclid, Ohio . . . His 40 doubles in 1982 set NL record for a catcher . . . Son of former major-leaguer Bob Kennedy . . . Obtained from Cardinals prior to 1981 season in 11-player deal, the largest in San Diego history . . . No. 1 draft choice as an All-American out of Florida State, where he belted 32 homers and posted .348 average . . . Excellent clutch hitter.

Year	Club	Pos.	G	AB	R	H	2B	3B	HR	RBI	SB	Avg.
1978	St. Louis	C	10	29	0	5	0	0	0	2	0	.172
1979	St. Louis	C	33	109	11	31	7	0	2	17	0	.284
1980	St. Louis	C-OF	84	248	28	63	12	3	4	34	0	.254
1981	San Diego	C	101	382	32	115	24	1	2	41	0	.301
1982	San Diego	C-1B	153	562	75	166	42	1	21	97	1	.295
1983	San Diego	C-1B	149	549	47	156	27	2	17	98	1	.284
	Totals		530	1879	193	536	112	7	46	289	2	.285

LUIS SALAZAR 27 5-9 180 Bats R Throws R

Average wasn't up to standard he set in 1980 and 1981, but he did establish a career high in homers . . . A .297 lifetime hitter in the minors, so Padres are hoping his last two years were a fluke . . . Third baseman's best month was a .307 June . . . Belted nine homers in last two months . . . Came up in Pirates' system, batting .323 with 27 homers for Buffalo (AA) in 1979 . . . Born May 19, 1956, in Barcelona, Venezuela . . . Traded to Padres' organization during 1980 season and divided time with Portland and Hawaii (AAA), batting .316 with 43 steals . . . After being promoted to Padres, he posted a .337 average in 44 games . . . Cracked four hits in seven at-bats in major-league debut against Astros in doubleheader.

Year	Club	Pos.	G	AB	R	H	2B	3B	HR	RBI	SB	Avg.
1980	San Diego	3B-OF	44	169	28	57	4	7	1	25	11	.337
1981	San Diego	3B-OF	109	400	37	121	19	6	3	38	11	.303
1982	San Diego	3B-SS-OF	145	524	55	127	15	5	8	62	32	.242
1983	San Diego	3B-OF	134	481	52	124	16	2	14	45	24	.258
	Totals		432	1574	172	429	54	20	26	170	78	.273

STEVE GARVEY 35 5-10 190 Bats R Throws R

Broke Billy Williams' NL consecutive-game record of 1,117 against Dodgers April 15 and extended it to 1,207 before dislocating left thumb sliding into home plate against Braves July 29, an injury that ended his season... Well-received by new teammates and San Diego fans after leaving Dodgers to sign five-year contract for at least $6.6 million as free agent prior to last year... Got off to a flying start with Padres, batting .333 with five homers in April... Came through with nine game-winning RBI in only 100 games... Born Dec. 22, 1948, in Tampa ... A year of milestones for popular first baseman ... Collected 1,000th RBI April 26 and 2,000th hit May 7, both against Cubs... Manager Dick Williams said that first baseman will be rested periodically now that his consecutive-game streak has been broken... A .346 average in postseason play makes him Mr. October of NL.

Year	Club	Pos.	G	AB	R	H	2B	3B	HR	RBI	SB	Avg.
1969	Los Angeles......	3B	3	3	0	1	0	0	0	0	0	.333
1970	Los Angeles......	3B-2B	34	93	8	25	5	0	1	6	1	.269
1971	Los Angeles......	3B	81	225	27	51	12	1	7	26	1	.227
1972	Los Angeles......	3B-1B	96	294	36	79	14	2	9	30	4	.269
1973	Los Angeles......	1B-OF	114	349	37	106	17	3	8	50	0	.304
1974	Los Angeles......	1B	156	642	95	200	32	3	21	111	5	.312
1975	Los Angeles......	1B	160	659	85	210	38	6	18	95	11	.319
1976	Los Angeles......	1B	162	631	85	200	37	4	13	80	19	.317
1977	Los Angeles......	1B	162	646	91	192	25	3	33	115	9	.297
1978	Los Angeles......	1B	162	639	89	202	36	9	21	113	10	.316
1979	Los Angeles......	1B	162	648	92	204	32	1	28	110	3	.315
1980	Los Angeles......	1B	163	658	77	200	27	1	26	106	6	.304
1981	Los Angeles......	1B	110	431	63	122	23	1	10	64	3	.283
1982	Los Angeles......	1B	162	625	66	176	35	1	16	86	5	.282
1983	San Diego	1B	100	388	76	114	22	0	14	59	4	.294
	Totals..........		1827	6931	927	2082	355	35	225	1051	81	.300

GARRY TEMPLETON 28 5-11 170 Bats S Throws R

Injuries have made him a shadow of his former self... Once regarded as the premier athlete in NL, but now merely good, not great... When he came to San Diego for Ozzie Smith in 1982, he brought a .303 lifetime average with him from St. Louis... Really a phenom when he first broke in with Cardinals... Led NL in triples his first three full seasons, hitting 50 of them from 1977-79... Born March 24, 1956, in Lockey, Tex.... First switch-hitter in history to drill 100 or more hits each way, when he had total of 211 in 1979... Shortstop became unpopular when he snubbed 1979 All-Star Game after not being selected to start . . . Ruffled Redbirds' feathers when he made obscene gesture to St. Louis spectators . . . No. 1 draft choice of Cardinals in June 1974.

Year	Club	Pos.	G	AB	R	H	2B	3B	HR	RBI	SB	Avg.
1976	St. Louis	SS	53	213	32	62	8	2	1	17	11	.291
1977	St. Louis	SS	153	621	94	200	19	18	8	79	28	.322
1978	St. Louis	SS	155	647	82	181	31	13	2	47	34	.280
1979	St. Louis	SS	154	672	105	211	32	19	9	62	26	.314
1980	St. Louis	SS	118	504	83	161	19	9	4	43	31	.319
1981	St. Louis	SS	80	333	47	96	16	8	1	33	8	.288
1982	San Diego	SS	141	563	76	139	25	8	6	64	27	.247
1983	San Diego	SS	126	460	39	121	20	2	3	40	16	.263
	Totals		980	4013	558	1171	170	79	34	385	181	.292

TONY GWYNN 23 5-11 185 — Bats L Throws L

Was considered the club's top prospect last spring, but a fractured wrist suffered in winter ball delayed his start . . . Made up for lost time when he started playing, shortly before All-Star Game . . . In little more than a half-season, he did a lot of hitting, especially down the stretch . . . Batted .325 in August and .355 in September . . . Born May 9, 1960, in Los Angeles . . . A point guard for the San Diego State basketball squad, he was drafted by San Diego Clippers of NBA . . . Signed baseball contract in 1981 and won batting title with a .331 average at Walla Walla (A) before finishing with a .462 mark in 23 games at Amarillo (AA) . . . A .328 start at Hawaii (AAA) in 1982 was final step to majors . . . Outfielder had club-record 25-game hitting streak last year.

Year	Club	Pos.	G	AB	R	H	2B	3B	HR	RBI	SB	Avg.
1982	San Diego	OF	54	190	33	55	12	2	1	17	8	.289
1983	San Diego	OF	86	304	34	94	12	2	1	37	7	.309
	Totals		140	494	67	149	24	4	2	54	15	.302

ALAN WIGGINS 26 6-2 160 — Bats S Throws R

Shattered Gene Richards' club stolen-base record by five and ranked second in NL to Tim Raines with 66 . . . Established since-broken pro stolen-base record of 120 for Lodi (A) in 1980 . . . Major-league progress retarded by a drug problem in 1982 . . . Has averaged 78 steals the last four years . . . Born Feb. 17, 1958, in Los Angeles . . . Signed with Dodgers and struggled first three years in low minors before speed allowed him to break through in 1980 . . . Hit .302 and .312 for Hawaii in 1981 and 1982 before reaching majors for good . . . Pacific Coast League stolen-base champ for Hawaii with 73 in 1981 . . . Saw some action at first and some in outfield.

Year	Club	Pos.	G	AB	R	H	2B	3B	HR	RBI	SB	Avg.
1981	San Diego	OF	15	14	4	5	0	0	0	0	2	.357
1982	San Diego	OF-2B	72	254	40	65	3	3	1	15	33	.256
1983	San Diego	OF	144	503	83	139	20	2	0	22	66	.276
	Totals		231	771	127	209	23	5	1	37	101	.271

LUIS DeLEON 25 6-1 153 — Bats R Throws R

Tailed off slightly from sensational rookie season of '82, but his future remains bright . . . Wasn't main man out of bullpen, but has total of 28 saves in last two years . . . Another great acquisition by Padres' GM Jack McKeon . . . Rangy right-hander came from Cardinals for Alan Olmsted prior to 1982 season as part of Steve Mura-for-Sixto Lezcano deal . . . Emergence as rookie standout in 1982 freed Eric Show and Dave Dravecky for starting duty . . . Born Aug. 19, 1958, in Ponce, Puerto Rico . . . Father and two brothers played pro ball in Puerto Rico . . . Signed by Cardinals and was primarily a reliever in minors, striking out 366 in 385 innings while posting 30-22 record and 2.69 ERA . . . One of Whitey Herzog's mistakes.

Year	Club	G	IP	W	L	Pct.	SO	BB	H	ERA
1981	St. Louis.	10	15	0	1	.000	8	3	11	2.40
1982	San Diego	61	102	9	5	.643	60	16	77	2.03
1983	San Diego	63	111	6	6	.500	90	27	89	2.68
	Totals.	134	228	15	12	.556	158	46	177	2,37

ERIC SHOW 27 6-1 185 — Bats R Throws R

Emerged as staff ace in his first full season as a starter . . . Led staff in victories, innings pitched and shutouts, with two . . . Showed he could start by joining rotation in 1982 and posting best ERA on staff . . . Born May 19, 1956, in Riverside, Cal. . . . One of brightest and most interesting players in majors . . . Pursued a degree in physics at Cal-Riverside . . . An accomplished jazz guitarist . . . Won at every level of minors, compiling 37-20 record in four years and yielding only 399 hits in 480 innings . . . Joined Padres after getting off to 7-3 start with 2.54 ERA for Hawaii in 1981.

Year	Club	G	IP	W	L	Pct.	SO	BB	H	ERA
1981	San Diego	15	23	1	3	.250	22	9	17	3.13
1982	San Diego	47	150	10	6	.625	88	48	117	2.64
1983	San Diego	35	201	15	12	.556	120	74	201	4.17
	Totals.	97	374	26	21	.553	230	131	335	3.49

RICH GOSSAGE 32 6-3 217 Bats R Throws R

Unhappy as a Yankee, "Goose" signed a five-year Padre contract worth more than $5 million in January . . . Led AL relievers with ratio of 9.3 strikeouts per nine innings last year . . . But wasn't as impressive as in years past . . . A seven-time All-Star . . . Was first player Yankees selected in first re-entry draft in 1977 and left Pittsburgh to sign big contract . . . Went into re-entry draft again after last season and said he wouldn't re-sign with Yankees . . . Was named AL Fireman of the Year in 1975, with White Sox, and 1978, with Yanks . . . Set NL record for strikeouts by a reliever (151) in 1977 . . . White Sox tried to convert him to a starter in 1976 without success . . . Born July 5, 1951, in Colorado Springs, Colo. . . . Majored in forestry at Southern Colorado State.

Year	Club	G	IP	W	L	Pct.	SO	BB	H	ERA
1972	Chicago (AL)	36	80	7	1	.875	57	44	72	4.28
1973	Chicago (AL)	20	50	0	4	.000	33	37	57	7.38
1974	Chicago (AL)	39	89	4	6	.400	64	47	92	4.15
1975	Chicago (AL)	62	142	9	8	.529	130	70	99	1.84
1976	Chicago (AL)	31	224	9	17	.346	135	90	214	3.94
1977	Pittsburgh	72	133	11	9	.550	151	49	78	1.62
1978	New York (AL)	63	134	10	11	.476	122	59	87	2.01
1979	New York (AL)	36	58	5	3	.625	41	19	48	2.64
1980	New York (AL)	64	99	6	2	.750	103	37	74	2.27
1981	New York (AL)	32	47	3	2	.600	48	14	22	0.77
1982	New York (AL)	56	93	4	5	.444	102	28	63	2.23
1983	New York (AL)	57	87	13	5	.722	90	25	82	2.27
	Totals	568	1236	81	73	.526	1076	519	988	2.85

MARK THURMOND 27 6-0 180 Bats L Throws L

Replaced Dave Dravecky as club's best lefty down the stretch . . . Recalled from Las Vegas and made big splash with 4-1 July, posting a 1.99 ERA for the month . . . Born Sept. 12, 1956, in Houston . . . An outstanding pitcher at Texas A&M before becoming fifth-round draft choice of Padres in June 1979 . . . Began pro career at Amarillo (AA) and pitched there three straight years, making gradual improvement . . . Was 3-5 with 5.63 ERA as pro rookie in 1979, 10-9 with 3.87 ERA in 1980 and 12-5 with 3.26 ERA in 1981 . . . Got first big-league shot after posting 12-10 record for Hawaii in '82 . . . His emergence made club willing to swap either Dravecky or Tim Lollar.

Year	Club	G	IP	W	L	Pct.	SO	BB	H	ERA
1983	San Diego	21	115	7	3	.700	49	33	104	2.65

Catcher Terry Kennedy led club with 98 RBI.

TOP PROSPECT

KEVIN McREYNOLDS 24 6-1 205 Bats R Throws R
Greatness expected from this powerful outfielder, though paltry .221 mark in 140 at-bats during two major-league trials last year suggests there's still work to be done . . . Born Oct. 16, 1959, in Little Rock, Ark. . . . An All-American at Arkansas and Padres' No. 1 draft pick in June 1981 . . . His two minor-league seasons have been knockouts . . . Batted .376 with 28 homers for Reno (A) and .352 for Amarillo (AA) in '82 . . . At Las Vegas (AAA) last year, he tied for home-run lead with 32, batted .377 and had 116 RBI.

MANAGER DICK WILLIAMS: Guided Padres to 81-81 record

last year, the same record they had under him in 1982 . . . Last year's team got off to a slow start, but went 24-14 before All-Star break to stay in contention . . . Regarded as a tough task-master, he keeps his players alert . . . Tact isn't among his strong points . . . Made it known the Padres were better without Steve Garvey (31-29) than with him (52-50) last year . . . Born

May 7, 1929, in St. Louis . . . Former major-league outfielder who signed with Brooklyn . . . Posted .260 career mark for Brooklyn, Baltimore, Cleveland, KC and Boston . . . Successful at most managerial stops after winning pennant with 1967 Miracle Red Sox as a rookie skipper . . . Won back-to-back World Series with Oakland in 1972 and 1973, after guiding A's to winningest year (101-60) in '71 . . . Also produced Montreal's biggest winner (95-65) in '79 and a club-record, 11-game winning streak for Padres in 1982 . . . Overall major-league managerial mark is 1,207-1,087.

GREATEST STEALER

The Padres are only 15 years old this season, yet they've had their share of players who could run. In 1980, for instance, Gene Richards, Ozzie Smith and Jerry Mumphrey set a major-league record by giving San Diego three players with 50 or more stolen bases in the same season, swiping 61, 57 and 52 respectively.

Richards established the club record with 61 that season, erasing his own mark of 56 in 1977. But Richards has been dethroned by the new king of San Diego swifties: Alan Wiggins. Wiggins set a new single-season standard with 66 thefts last year and, at age 26, has plenty of time to add to his distinction as the Padres' best base burglar.

Wiggins' record pace in '83 is no surprise, of course, because he set a since-broken minor-league mark with 120 stolen bases for Lodi (A) of the California League in 1980. It isn't likely Wiggins will become complacent, either, because fellow Padre outfielders Tony Gwynn and Bobby Brown can run, too, giving Wiggins ample incentive to stay out in front of the race.

ALL-TIME PADRE SEASON RECORDS

BATTING: Clarence Gaston, .318, 1970
HRs: Nate Colbert, 38, 1970
RBIs: Dave Winfield, 118, 1979
STEALS: Alan Wiggins, 66, 1983
WINS: Randy Jones, 22, 1976
STRIKEOUTS: Clay Kirby, 231, 1971

SAN FRANCISCO GIANTS

TEAM DIRECTORY: Pres.: Bob Lurie; Exec. VP-Baseball Oper.: Tom Haller; VP-Bus. Oper.: Pat Gallagher; Exec. VP-Adm.: Corey Busch; Dir. Play. Per.: Bob Fontaine; Dir. Minor Leagues: Ralph E. Nelson, Jr.; Dir. Play. Dev.: Jim Lefebvre; Dir. Publ.: Duffy Jennings; Trav. Sec.: Dirk Smith; Mgr.: Frank Robinson. Home: Candlestick Park (58,000). Field distances: 335, l.f. line; 365, l.c.; 400, c.f.; 365, r.c.; 335, r.f. line. Spring training: Scottsdale, Ariz.

SCOUTING REPORT

HITTING: Unquestionably the toughest club to figure in the league, because of a lack of early winter trading activity. The Giants' .247 average was 10th in the league last year and Darrell Evans, the most productive slugger on the club, left for free agency. Star slugger Jack Clark (20 homers, 66 RBI) all but demanded to

Joel Youngblood topped the Giant hitters with .292.

be traded, so it's hard to figure out what sort of a batting order manager Frank Robinson will be using this summer.

Two certainties are Jeff Leonard and Joel Youngblood, a source of optimism. Leonard (.279, 21 homers, 87 RBI) enjoyed his finest major-league season last year and is on the verge of stardom. Youngblood batted .317 in the second half (.292 overall) while becoming a regular and is certain to start somewhere. The Giants were second in home runs (142) and fourth in runs (687), but that's apt to change without Evans (30 homers, 82 RBI).

PITCHING: Only the league's deepest quality bullpen and some promising young starters give Giant fans hope for respectability. Greg Minton (22 saves) and Gary Lavelle (20 saves) are the best relief tandem in the NL. Forkball specialist Fred Breining (11-12) may return to the bullpen, making it even tougher.

The starting rotation is potentially solid, but it remains to be seen whether Atlee Hammaker (10-9) and Bill Laskey (13-10) bounce back from arm trouble or if Laskey still is with the club. Mike Krukow (11-11) lends stability and promising newcomers Mark Davis and Scott Garrelts are expected to win jobs. It adds up to another busy summer for the bullpen.

FIELDING: Long a thorn in the Giants' paw, defense was a glaring shortcoming last year. The club had the worst fielding percentage in the league (.973) and made the most errors (171). Youngblood had problems at second base, but he'll be moved to the outfield this year to make room for free-agent signee Manny Trillo. Defensive strengths include shortstop Johnnie LeMaster (.964) and outfielders Leonard and Clark (17 assists each).

OUTLOOK: The Giants are much closer to the division cellar than a high finish, despite their contending status in '82. Management made a big mistake in letting Joe Morgan and Al Holland get away last year, giving the Phillies a pennant and the Giants a club devoid of leadership. Evans, despite a great year, felt so unappreciated he wouldn't consider staying with the club.

A flurry of late trading activity was anticipated, so it's impossible to come close to guessing an Opening Day lineup. Chili Davis, mired in a season-long slump following a solid rookie season, Clark, Laskey and Lavelle were all trade bait during the offseason. Pitching, though, remains a strength and that has a tendency to disguise other weaknesses. This is a team in trouble. Management sacrificed present success to build for the future. Robinson likely will pay the price with his job if the club gets off to a slow start.

SAN FRANCISCO GIANTS 1984 ROSTER

MANAGER Frank Robinson

Coaches—Don Buford, Tom McCraw, Danny Ozark, Herm Starrette, John Van Ornum

PITCHERS

No.	Name	1983 Club	W-L	IP	SO	ERA	B-T	Ht.	Wt.	Born
48	Breining, Fred	San Francisco	11-12	203	117	3.82	R-R	6-4	185	11/15/55 San Francisco
32	Calvert, Mark	Phoenix	4-5	86	33	5.88	R-R	6-1	185	9/29/56 Tulsa, OK
		San Francisco	1-4	37	14	6.27				
13	Davis, Mark	Phoenix	6-3	73	64	6.32	L-L	6-4	195	10/19/60 Livermore, CA
		San Francisco	6-4	111	83	3.49				
54	Fowlkes, Alan	Phoenix	9-11	134	78	6.51	R-R	6-2	190	8/08/58 Brawley, CA
50	Garrelts, Scott	Phoenix	5-5	98	89	4.61	R-R	6-4	195	10/30/61 Urbana, IL
		San Francisco	2-2	36	16	2.52				
43	Grant, Mark	Shreveport	10-8	187	159	3.66	R-R	6-2	195	10/24/63 Aurora, IL
14	Hammaker, Atlee	San Francisco	10-9	172	127	2.25	L-L	6-2	195	1/24/58 Carmel, CA
39	Krukow, Mike	San Francisco	11-11	184	136	3.95	R-R	6-4	205	1/21/52 Long Beach, CA
19	Laskey, Bill	San Francisco	13-10	148	81	4.19	R-R	6-5	190	12/20/57 Toledo, OH
46	Lavelle, Gary	San Francisco	7-4	87	68	2.59	R-L	6-1	200	1/3/49 Scranton, PA
29	Lerch, Randy	Phoenix	0-0	8	7	3.24	L-L	6-3	195	10/9/54 Sacramento, CA
		Mont.-SF	2-3	49	30	6.02				
17	Martin, Renie	San Francisco	2-4	94	43	4.20	R-R	6-4	185	8/30/55 Dover, DE
28	McGaffigan, Andy	San Francisco	3-9	134	93	4.29	R-R	6-3	190	10/25/56 W. Palm Beach, FL
38	Minton, Greg	San Francisco	7-11	107	38	3.54	B-R	6-2	190	7/29/51 Lubbock, TX
17	Williams, Frank	Shreveport	7-2	42	54	1.71	R-R	6-1	180	2/13/58 Seattle, WA
		Phoenix	5-3	48	37	3.59				

CATCHERS

No.	Name	1983 Club	H	HR	RBI	Pct.	B-T	Ht.	Wt.	Born
15	Brenly, Bob	San Francisco	63	7	34	.224	R-R	6-2	210	2/25/54 Coshocton, OH
37	Gomez, Randy	Shreveport	116	5	48	.278	R-R	5-10	185	2/4/58 San Mateo, CA
7	Nicosia, Steve	Pitts.-SF	17			.215	R-R	5-10	185	8/6/55 Paterson, NJ
51	Nokes, Matt	Fresno	138	14	82	.322	L-R	6-1	185	10/31/63 San Diego, CA
5	Rabb, John	Phoenix	74	10	49	.343	R-R	6-1	180	6/23/60 Los Angeles, CA
		San Francisco	24	1	14	.231				
34	Ransom, Jeff	Phoenix	65	7	37	.226	R-R	5-11	175	11/11/60 Fresno, CA
		San Francisco	4	1	3	.200				

INFIELDERS

No.	Name	1983 Club	H	HR	RBI	Pct.	B-T	Ht.	Wt.	Born
16	Bergman, Dave	San Francisco	40	6	24	.286	L-L	6-2	180	6/6/53 Evanston, IL
52	Brown, Chris	Shreveport	88	10	58	.273	R-R	6-0	185	8/15/61 Jackson, MS
18	Kuiper, Duane	San Francisco	44	0	14	.250	L-R	6-0	175	6/19/50 Racine, WI
10	LeMaster, Johnie	San Francisco	128	6	30	.240	R-R	6-2	180	6/19/54 Portsmouth, OH
35	O'Malley, Tom	San Francisco	106	5	45	.259	L-R	6-0	180	12/25/60 Orange, NJ
2	Pettini, Joe	San Francisco	16	0	7	.186	R-R	5-9	165	1/26/55 Wheeling, WV
—	Pittman, Joe	Las Vegas	155	3	52	.282	R-R	6-1	180	1/1/54 Houston, TX
21	Sularz, Guy	Phoenix	153	5	58	.316	R-R	5-11	165	11/7/55 Minneapolis, MN
		San Francisco	2	0	0	.100				
—	Trillo, Manny	Cleveland	87	1	29	.272	R-R	6-1	164	12/25/50 Venezuela
		Montreal	32	2	16	.264				
36	Wellman, Brad	Phoenix	52	2	28	.311	R-R	6-0	170	8/17/59 Lodi, CA
		San Francisco	39	1	16	.214				

OUTFIELDERS

No.	Name	1983 Club	H	HR	RBI	Pct.	B-T	Ht.	Wt.	Born
22	Clark, Jack	San Francisco	132	20	66	.268	R-R	6-3	205	11/10/55 New Brighton, PA
30	Davis, Chili	San Francisco	113	11	59	.233	B-R	6-3	195	1/17/60 Jamaica
		Phoenix	13	2	9	.295				
45	Deer, Rob	Shreveport	97	35	99	.217	R-R	6-3	210	9/9/60 Orange, CA
25	Gladden, Dan	Phoenix	153	12	80	.303	R-R	5-11	180	7/7/57 San Jose, CA
		San Francisco	14	1	9	.222				
26	Leonard, Jeff	San Francisco	144	21	87	.279	R-R	6-4	200	9/22/55 Philadelphia, PA
53	Penigar, Charles	Fresno	113	3	37	.257	B-R	6-5	180	7/31/63 Kansas City, KS
49	Venable, Max	San Francisco	50	6	27	.219	L-R	5-10	185	6/6/57 Phoenix, AZ
8	Youngblood, Joel	San Francisco	109	17	53	.292	R-R	5-11	175	8/28/51 Houston, TX

GIANT PROFILES

JACK CLARK 28 6-3 205 **Bats R Throws R**

Endured frustrating season, prompted by desire to be traded, but still finished with 11 game-winning RBI . . . His 61 career game-winning RBI are tops among NL players since that statistic became official in '79 . . . Right fielder belted seven of his homers in May, traditionally his most productive month . . . In 1982, "Jack The Ripper" became first Giant to notch 100 RBI since Bobby Bonds in 1971 . . . Born Nov. 10, 1955, in New Brighton, Pa. . . . An emotional athlete who lets his disenchantment with management affect his play . . . Also has been very critical of Candlestick Park and would have a better mental attitude if he changed uniforms . . . Drafted by Giants in 13th round in June 1973 and converted from a pitcher into an outfielder . . . Pacific Coast League Player of the Year in 1976 with .323 average, 29 doubles, 16 triples and 17 homers for Phoenix (AAA) . . . In second full season as major leaguer in '78, he set club records with 46 doubles and a 26-game hitting streak . . . Has had several run-ins with manager Frank Robinson.

Year	Club	Pos.	G	AB	R	H	2B	3B	HR	RBI	SB	Avg.
1975	San Francisco.	OF-3B	8	17	3	4	0	0	0	2	1	.235
1976	San Francisco.	OF	26	102	14	23	6	2	2	10	6	.225
1977	San Francisco.	OF	136	413	64	104	17	4	13	51	12	.252
1978	San Francisco.	OF	156	592	90	181	46	8	25	98	15	.306
1979	San Francisco.	OF-3B	143	527	84	144	25	2	26	86	11	.273
1980	San Francisco.	OF	127	437	77	124	20	8	22	82	2	.284
1981	San Francisco.	OF	99	385	60	103	19	2	17	53	1	.268
1982	San Francisco.	OF	157	563	90	154	30	3	27	103	6	.274
1983	San Francisco.	OF	135	492	82	132	25	0	20	66	5	.268
	Totals		987	3528	564	969	188	29	152	551	59	.275

JEFF LEONARD 28 6-4 200 **Bats R Throws R**

Blossomed into club's finest all-around outfielder last year . . . Attained career highs in virtually every offensive category and led team in RBI . . . More than doubled his previous season high in home runs . . . Threw out 10 runners at the plate among his 17 assists in left field . . . Had seven homers and 25 RBI in July, six homers and 22 RBI in August . . . Nicknamed "Hack," because he'll swing at anything . . . Born Sept. 22, 1955, in Philadelphia . . . A star shortstop in high school before signing with

Dodgers in 1973 . . . Batted .365 for Albuquerque (AAA) in 1978 and was named Pacific Coast League Player of the Year . . . Traded to Astros and became Sporting News' Rookie of the Year in 1979 . . . Developed reputation as being hard to handle, so was swapped to Giants with Dave Bergman for Mike Ivie during 1981 season and has made gradual improvement as player ever since.

Year	Club	Pos.	G	AB	R	H	2B	3B	HR	RBI	SB	Avg.
1977	Los Angeles	OF	11	10	1	3	0	1	0	2	0	.300
1978	Houston	OF	8	26	2	10	2	0	0	4	0	.385
1979	Houston	OF	134	411	47	119	15	5	0	47	23	.290
1980	Houston	OF-1B	88	216	29	46	7	5	3	20	4	.213
1981	Hou.-SF	OF-1B	44	145	21	42	12	4	4	29	5	.290
1982	San Francisco	OF-1B	80	278	32	72	16	1	9	49	18	.259
1983	San Francisco	OF	139	516	74	144	17	7	21	87	26	.279
	Totals		504	1602	206	436	69	23	37	238	76	.272

MANNY TRILLO 33 6-1 164 Bats R Throws R

As free agent, signed three-year Giant contract in December after being 1983 AL All-Star second baseman as an Indian and finishing season with Expos . . . Batted .272 with one homer and 29 RBI for Indians in 88 games . . . More productive at Montreal with two homers and 16 RBI, including three game-winners in 31 games . . . A perennial All-Star, achieving distinction in brief AL career after starring with bat and glove for Cubs and Phillies . . . With Joe Morgan about to come aboard and Juan Samuel waiting in the wings, Phils swapped him to Indians in five-player package for Von Hayes before last year . . . Hated Cleveland . . . Indians knew he wouldn't sign with them again, so they moved him . . . Born Dec. 25, 1950, in Caritito, Venezuela . . . MVP of 1980 NL Championship Series, batting .381 for Phils . . . Set major-league records by playing in 89 games and handling 472 chances without an error in '82.

Year	Club	Pos.	G	AB	R	H	2B	3B	HR	RBI	SB	Avg.
1973	Oakland	2B	17	12	0	3	2	0	0	3	0	.250
1974	Oakland	2B	21	33	3	5	0	0	0	2	0	.152
1975	Chicago (NL)	2B-SS	154	545	55	135	12	2	7	70	1	.248
1976	Chicago (NL)	2B-SS	158	582	42	139	24	3	4	59	17	.239
1977	Chicago (NL)	2B	152	504	51	141	18	5	7	57	3	.280
1978	Chicago (NL)	2B	152	552	53	144	17	5	4	55	0	.261
1979	Philadelphia	2B	118	431	40	112	22	1	6	42	4	.260
1980	Philadelphia	2B	141	531	68	155	25	9	7	43	8	.292
1981	Philadelphia	2B	94	349	37	100	14	3	6	36	10	.287
1982	Philadelphia	2B	149	549	52	149	24	1	0	39	8	.271
1983	Cleveland	2B	88	320	33	87	13	1	1	29	1	.272
1983	Montreal	2B	31	121	16	32	8	0	2	16	0	.264
	Totals		1275	4529	450	1202	179	30	44	451	52	.265

JOEL YOUNGBLOOD 32 5-11 175 Bats R Throws R

A pleasant surprise after signing with Giants as a free agent before last season . . . Led club in batting after riding bench and carrying a .248 average into the All-Star break . . . Eventually gained regular status at third base and second base and batted .317 in second half . . . Likely to be shifted back to outfield this year . . . Despite playing only 123 games, he established a career high in homers . . . Batted .318 in July and .300 in September . . . Born Aug. 28, 1951, in Houston . . . Well-traveled veteran finally may have found a home . . . Batted .350 and made All-Star team with Mets in '81, yet couldn't find regular work with club in '82 . . . Had the unique distinction of collecting a hit for both the Mets and the Expos on the same day, Aug. 4, 1982, when he was traded to Montreal . . . One of the most versatile performers in the majors.

Year	Club	Pos.	G	AB	R	H	2B	3B	HR	RBI	SB	Avg.
1976	Cincinnati	OF-3B-2B-C	55	57	8	11	1	1	0	1	1	.193
1977	St.L.-N.Y. (NL). . . .	2B-OF-3B	95	209	17	51	13	1	0	12	1	.244
1978	New York (NL)	OF-2B-3B-SS	113	266	40	67	12	8	7	30	4	.252
1979	New York (NL)	OF-2B-3B	158	590	90	162	37	5	16	60	18	.275
1980	New York (NL)	OF-3B-2B	146	514	58	142	26	2	8	69	14	.276
1981	New York (NL)	OF	43	143	16	50	10	2	4	25	2	.350
1982	New York (NL)-Mont.	OF-2B-3B-SS	120	292	37	70	14	0	3	29	2	.240
1983	San Francisco.	OF-2B-3B-SS	124	373	59	109	20	3	17	53	7	.292
	Totals		854	2444	325	662	133	22	55	279	49	.271

JOHNNIE LeMASTER 29 6-2 180 Bats R Throws R

Got off to a great start as club's new leadoff batter, but dropped off sharply . . . Biggest improvement was on the basepaths, where his 39 steals were two more than he had in his previous 701 major-league games . . . "Bones" also beefed up his upper body and doubled his previous home-run output with six, including two in one game . . . Solid glovework at shortstop is his premier attribute . . . Born June 19, 1954, in Portsmouth, Ohio . . . Grew up in Paintsville, Ky., where he was a four-sport star in high school . . . Giants' first-round draft choice in June 1973 . . . Made major-league debut in 1975 and hit inside-the-park homer off Don Sutton in his first at-bat . . . Reached majors to stay after batting .314 for Phoenix in '77, but has been erratic at the plate as a major leaguer.

Year	Club	Pos.	G	AB	R	H	2B	3B	HR	RBI	SB	Avg.
1975	San Francisco.	SS	22	74	4	14	4	0	2	9	2	.189
1976	San Francisco.	SS	33	100	9	21	3	2	0	9	2	.210
1977	San Francisco.	SS-3B	68	134	13	20	5	1	0	8	2	.149
1978	San Francisco.	SS-2B	101	272	23	64	18	3	1	14	6	.235
1979	San Francisco.	SS	108	343	42	87	11	2	3	29	9	.254
1980	San Francisco.	SS	135	405	33	87	16	6	3	31	0	.215
1981	San Francisco.	SS	104	324	27	82	9	1	0	28	3	.253
1982	San Francisco.	SS	130	436	34	94	14	1	2	30	13	.216
1983	San Francisco.	SS	141	534	81	128	16	1	6	30	39	.240
	Totals.		842	2622	266	597	96	17	17	188	76	.228

FRED BREINING 28 6-4 185 — Bats R Throws R

Most underrated pitcher on the staff last year . . . In first full season as a starter, he led club in starts (32) and innings pitched, indicating durability . . . But Giants' need for middle-inning relief may return him to bullpen this season . . . Owns one of finest forkballs in majors, but needs to develop other pitches . . . Has 16-15 record in slightly more than a year as a starter . . . Born Nov. 15, 1955, in San Francisco . . . Became only fourth native son to play for Giants . . . Signed by Pirates in 1974 and joined Giants' system in 1979 swap involving Bill Madlock . . . Combined with Greg Minton, Gary Lavelle and Al Holland to give club the majors' best four-man bullpen in 1981 and 1982 . . . Became a starter for good in '82, after allowing one earned run in a stretch of 21⅔ relief innings in 10 games.

Year	Club	G	IP	W	L	Pct.	SO	BB	H	ERA
1980	San Francisco	5	7	0	0	.000	3	4	8	5.14
1981	San Francisco	45	78	5	2	.714	37	38	66	2.54
1982	San Francisco	54	143	11	6	.647	98	52	146	3.08
1983	San Francisco	32	203	11	12	.478	117	60	202	3.82
	Totals.	136	431	27	20	.574	255	154	422	3.36

ATLEE HAMMAKER 26 6-2 195 — Bats S Throws L

Was National League ERA champion in first full season as a big leaguer last year . . . Became first San Francisco pitcher to win ERA crown since Juan Marichal in 1969 . . . Strangely, he didn't win a game after July 10 and did not pitch after Sept. 10 because of injuries . . . Went out with a blaze of glory, striking out 14 Astros—an NL season high—in final appearance . . . Was 4-1 in June and entered All-Star Game with a 9-4 record and a 1.70 ERA . . . Received a jolt when American Leaguers scored seven runs off him in one inning, but insists that pounding had nothing to do with a 1-5 second half . . . Born

Jan. 24, 1958, in Carmel, Cal. . . . Is of German-Japanese ancestry . . . Attended East Tennessee State on a basketball scholarship . . . Royals' first selection in June 1979 draft . . . Acquired by Giants in Vida Blue deal before start of 1982 season.

Year	Club	G	IP	W	L	Pct.	SO	BB	H	ERA
1981	Kansas City	10	39	1	3	.250	11	12	44	5.54
1982	San Francisco	29	175	12	8	.600	102	28	189	4.11
1983	San Francisco	23	172	10	9	.526	127	32	147	2.25
	Totals	62	386	23	20	.535	240	72	380	3.43

BILL LASKEY 26 6-5 190 Bats R Throws R

Giants' top winner a second straight year, despite missing one month with injuries . . . A streaky pitcher, he started 0-4 before winning seven in a row . . . Was at his best in May, earning NL Pitcher-of-the-Month laurels with 6-0 record and 2.83 ERA . . . Was a solid 3-1 with 2.03 ERA in July before a muscle problem in his side and back retarded his progress . . . Born Dec. 20, 1957, in Toledo, Ohio . . . Attended Kent State . . . Drafted in second round by Royals in June 1978 . . . A nondescript performer in KC system, he blossomed after joining Giants in a trade for Jerry Martin prior to 1982 . . . Started 1982 in Phoenix, but went on to lead Giants with 13 victories . . . Unorthodox delivery places strain on his shoulder and threatens his longevity.

Year	Club	G	IP	W	L	Pct.	SO	BB	H	ERA
1982	San Francisco	32	189	13	12	.520	88	43	186	3.14
1983	San Francisco	25	148	13	10	.565	81	45	151	4.19
	Totals	57	337	26	22	.542	169	88	337	3.61

GARY LAVELLE 35 6-1 200 Bats R Throws L

Absence of Al Holland made him club's top left-handed short reliever once again and he responded with 20 saves, matching his career high set in 1977 . . . Two saves in final two games of season vs. Los Angeles enabled him to join Greg Minton to form only 20-20 bullpen in NL history . . . Their 42 saves set a club record for a tandem . . . At his best during club's 19-7 May, going 2-0 with seven saves and 1.47 ERA that month . . . Club's only reliable reliever until Minton got going in the second half . . . Born Jan. 3, 1949, in Scranton, Pa. . . . Giants' career leader in saves with 115 . . . Drafted in 34th round of June 1967 draft and came up through Giants' farm system as a starter . . . Joined Giants in 1974 and made 434 consecutive relief appearances before making three starts in '81.

Year	Club	G	IP	W	L	Pct.	SO	BB	H	ERA
1974	San Francisco	10	17	0	3	.000	12	10	14	2.12
1975	San Francisco	65	82	6	3	.667	51	48	80	2,96
1976	San Francisco	65	110	10	6	.625	71	52	102	2.70
1977	San Francisco	73	118	7	7	.500	93	37	106	2.06
1978	San Francisco	67	98	13	10	.565	63	44	96	3.31
1979	San Francisco	70	97	7	9	.438	80	42	86	2.51
1980	San Francisco	62	100	6	8	.429	66	36	106	3.42
1981	San Francisco	34	66	2	6	.250	45	23	58	3.82
1982	San Francisco	68	105	10	7	.588	76	29	97	2.67
1983	San Francisco	56	87	7	4	.636	68	19	73	2.59
	Totals................	570	880	68	63	.519	625	340	818	2.82

GREG MINTON 32 6-2 190 **Bats S Throws R**

"Moonie" vowed he would be more serious in his approach to baseball after signing a lucrative contract prior to '83 season... Then his sinker stopped sinking and he had only eight saves at the All-Star break... Added 14 saves in the second half to salvage a so-so season and finished with 22 for a two-year total of 52... Offbeat character who once made a Houston bus driver take him to the ballpark, stranding his teammates at the hotel... Born July 29, 1951, in Lubbock, Tex... Came up in Royals' system, but was acquired by Giants for Fran Healy in 1973... Had spotty minor-league career before reaching majors to stay in 1978... Holds major-league record of 269⅓ innings without yielding a home run, a stretch extending from Sept. 6, 1978 to May 2, 1982... Gave up six in 106⅓ innings last year... Spectacular in 1982, with career-high 10 wins and club-record 30 saves.

Year	Club	G	IP	W	L	Pct.	SO	BB	H	ERA
1975	San Francisco	4	17	1	1	.500	6	11	19	6.88
1976	San Francisco	10	26	0	3	.000	7	12	32	4.85
1977	San Francisco	2	14	1	1	.500	5	4	14	4.50
1978	San Francisco	11	16	0	1	.000	6	8	22	7.88
1979	San Francisco	46	80	4	3	.571	33	27	59	1.80
1980	San Francisco	68	91	4	6	.400	42	34	81	2.47
1981	San Francisco	55	84	4	5	.444	29	36	84	2.89
1982	San Francisco	78	123	10	4	.714	58	42	108	1.83
1983	San Francisco	73	107	7	11	.389	38	47	117	3.54
	Totals................	347	558	31	35	.470	224	221	536	2.95

TOP PROSPECT

SCOTT GARRELTS 22 6-4 195 **Bats R Throws R**

Enjoyed an impressive September with Giants (2-2 with 2.52

ERA), including a shutout of the Astros . . . Defeated the Braves, 2-1, for his other victory . . . Born Oct. 30, 1961, in Urbana, Ill. . . . Excellent strikeouts-to-innings-pitched ratio in minors . . . Was 5-5 at Phoenix (AAA) last year, including a seven-inning no-hitter.

MANAGER FRANK ROBINSON: Guided the club to winning

seasons in 1981 and 1982, but didn't have the horses with which to contend last year and the results were predictable . . . Only source of pride was a 19-7 May and a 13-5 record against arch-rival Dodgers . . . A controversial figure who ranks with the most unpopular managers in the game . . . Has an antagonistic attitude and likes to keep people at a distance . . . A victim of the stereotype that suggests that former great players cannot understand the failings of less-talented athletes . . . Born Aug. 31, 1935, in Beaumont, Tex., but was reared in Oakland . . . Only player to win MVP honors in each major league, doing so with '61 Reds and '66 Orioles . . . Also was MVP of 1971 All-Star Game and 1966 World Series . . . Was Rookie of the Year in '56 and Triple Crown winner in '66 . . . Has hit home runs out of more major-league ballparks (33) than anyone in history . . . Selected to Hall of Fame in his first year of eligibility, in 1982 . . . His 586 career home runs rank him fourth on all-time list . . . His major-league managerial record is 329-319 . . . No longer thought of as major leagues' first black manager, but that is what he became with Cleveland in 1975.

GREATEST STEALER

George Burns holds the club record with 62 stolen bases in 1914, but two modern-day speedsters rank as the best base thieves in Giant history. Willie Mays and Bobby Bonds rate that distinction and each would have been far more prolific on the basepaths had he not been occupied with other duties, such as hitting homers.

Mays led the league in stolen bases four straight years—two in New York and two in San Francisco—from 1956-59 and posted a high of 40 in '56. Bonds never led the league, but his 263 steals in his seven years with the club (1968-74) rank as the top mark in the club's San Francisco history.

Bonds, who had a high of 48 steals in 1970, had his single-season San Francisco record topped by Billy North, who swiped 58 in 1979. Mays finished with 332 steals, 211 of them for San Francisco. Burns stole 334 bases in his career, leading the league twice.

ALL-TIME GIANT SEASON RECORDS

BATTING: Bill Terry, .401, 1930
HRs: Willie Mays, 52, 1965
RBIs: Mel Ott, 151, 1929
STEALS: George Burns, 62, 1914
WINS: Christy Mathewson, 37, 1908
STRIKEOUTS: Christy Mathewson, 267, 1903

ALL-TIME MAJOR LEAGUE RECORDS

National	American
Batting (Season)	
Average	
.438 Hugh Duffy, Boston, 1894	.422 Napoleon Lajoie, Phila., 1901
.424 Rogers Hornsby, St. Louis, 1924	
At Bat	
699 Dave Cash, Phila., 1975	705 Willie Wilson, Kansas City, 198
Runs	
196 William Hamilton, Phila., 1894	177 Babe Ruth, New York, 1921
158 Chuck Klein, Phila., 1930	
Hits	
254 Frank J. O'Doul, Phila., 1929	257 George Sisler, St. Louis, 1920
254 Bill Terry, New York, 1930	
Doubles	
64 Joseph M. Medwick, St. L., 1936	67 Earl W. Webb, Boston, 1931
Triples	
36 J. Owen Wilson, Pitts., 1912	26 Joseph Jackson, Cleve., 1912
	26 Samuel Crawford, Detroit, 1914
Home Runs	
56 Hack Wilson, Chicago, 1930	61 Roger Maris, New York, 1961 (162-game schedule)
	60 Babe Ruth, New York, 1927
Runs Batted In	
190 Hack Wilson, Chicago, 1930	184 Lou Gehrig, New York, 1931
Stolen Bases	
118 Lou Brock, St. Louis, 1974	130 Rickey Henderson, Oakland, 19
Bases on Balls	
148 Eddie Stanky, Brooklyn, 1945	170 Babe Ruth, New York, 1923
148 Jim Wynn, Houston, 1969	
Strikeouts	
189 Bobby Bonds, S.F., 1970	175 Dave Nicholson, Chicago, 1963
Pitching (Season)	
Games	
106 Mike Marshall, L.A., 1974	88 Wilbur Wood, Chicago, 1968
Innings Pitched	
434 Joseph J. McGinnity, N.Y., 1903	464 Edward Walsh, Chicago, 1908
Victories	
37 Christy Mathewson, N.Y., 1908	41 Jack Chesbro, New York, 1904
Losses	
29 Victor Willis, Boston, 1905	26 John Townsend, Wash., 1904
	26 Robert Groom, Wash., 1909
Strikeouts	
(Lefthander)	
382 Sandy Koufax, Los Angeles, 1965	343 Rube Waddell, Phila., 1904
(Righthander)	
303 J.R. Richard, Houston, 1978	383 Nolan Ryan, Cal., 1973
Bases on Balls	
185 Sam Jones, Chicago, 1955	208 Bob Feller, Cleveland, 1938
Earned-Run Average	
(Minimum 200 Innings)	
1.12 Bob Gibson, St. L., 1968	1.01 Hubert Leonard, Boston, 1914
Shutouts	
16 Grover C. Alexander, Phila., 1916	13 John W. Coombs, Phila., 1910

MAJOR LEAGUE YEAR-BY-YEAR LEADERS

AMERICAN LEAGUE MVP

Year	Player, Club
1931	Lefty Grove, Philadelphia Athletics
1932	Jimmy Foxx, Philadelphia Athletics
1933	Jimmy Foxx, Philadelphia Athletics
1934	Mickey Cochrane, Detroit Tigers
1935	Hank Greenberg, Detroit Tigers
1936	Lou Gehrig, New York Yankees
1937	Charley Gehringer, Detroit Tigers
1938	Jimmy Foxx, Boston Red Sox
1939	Joe DiMaggio, New York Yankees
1940	Hank Greenberg, Detroit Tigers
1941	Joe DiMaggio, New York Yankees
1942	Joe Gordon, New York Yankees
1943	Spud Chandler, New York Yankees
1944	Hal Newhouser, Detroit Tigers
1945	Hal Newhouser, Detroit Tigers
1946	Ted Williams, Boston Red Sox
1947	Joe DiMaggio, New York Yankees
1948	Lou Boudreau, Cleveland Indians
1949	Ted Williams, Boston Red Sox
1950	Phil Rizzuto, New York Yankees
1951	Yogi Berra, New York Yankees
1942	Bobby Shantz, Philadelphia Athletics
1953	Al Rosen, Cleveland Indians
1954	Yogi Berra, New York Yankees
1955	Yogi Berra, New York Yankees
1956	Mickey Mantle, New York Yankees
1957	Mickey Mantle, New York Yankees
1958	Jackie Jensen, Boston Red Sox
1959	Nellie Fox, Chicago White Sox
1960	Roger Maris, New York Yankees

Year	Player, Club
1961	Roger Maris, New York Yankees
1962	Mickey Mantle, New York Yankees
1963	Elston Howard, New York Yankees
1964	Brooks Robinson, Baltimore Orioles
1965	Zoilo Versalles, Minnesota Twins
1966	Frank Robinson, Baltimore Orioles
1967	Carl Yastrzemski, Boston Red Sox
1968	Dennis McLain, Detroit Tigers
1969	Harmon Killebrew, Minnesota Twins
1970	Boog Powell, Baltimore Orioles
1971	Vida Blue, Oakland A's
1972	Dick Allen, Chicago White Sox
1973	Reggie Jackson, Oakland A's
1974	Jeff Burroughs, Texas Rangers
1975	Fred Lynn, Boston Red Sox
1976	Thurman Munson, New York Yankees
1977	Rod Carew, Minnesota Twins
1978	Jim Rice, Boston Red Sox
1979	Don Baylor, California Angels
1980	George Brett, Kansas City Royals
1981	Rollie Fingers, Milwaukee Brewers
1982	Robin Yount, Milwaukee Brewers
1983	Cal Ripken Jr., Baltimore Orioles

NATIONAL LEAGUE MVP

Year	Player, Club
1931	Frank Frisch, St. Louis Cardinals
1932	Chuck Klein, Philadelphia Phillies
1933	Carl Hubbell, New York Giants
1934	Dizzy Dean, St. Louis Cardinals
1935	Gabby Hartnett, Chicago Cubs
1936	Carl Hubbell, New York Giants
1937	Joe Medwick, St. Louis Cardinals
1938	Ernie Lombardi, Cincinnati Reds
1939	Bucky Walters, Cincinnati Reds
1940	Frank McCormick, Cincinnati Reds
1941	Dolph Camilli, Brooklyn Dodgers
1942	Mort Cooper, St. Louis Cardinals
1943	Stan Musial, St. Louis Cardinals
1944	Marty Marion, St. Louis Cardinals
1945	Phil Cavarretta, Chicago Cubs
1946	Stan Musial, St. Louis Cardinals
1947	Bob Elliott, Boston Braves

Year	Player, Club
1948	Stan Musial, St. Louis Cardinals
1949	Jackie Robinson, Brooklyn Dodgers
1950	Jim Konstanty, Philadelphia Phillies
1951	Roy Campanella, Brooklyn Dodgers
1952	Hank Sauer, Chicago Cubs
1953	Roy Campanella, Brooklyn Dodgers
1954	Willie Mays, New York Giants
1955	Roy Campanella, Brooklyn Dodgers
1956	Don Newcombe, Brooklyn Dodgers
1957	Hank Aaron, Milwaukee Braves
1958	Ernie Banks, Chicago Cubs
1959	Ernie Banks, Chicago Cubs
1960	Dick Groat, Pittsburgh Pirates
1961	Frank Robinson, Cincinnati Reds
1962	Maury Wills, Los Angeles Dodgers
1963	Sandy Koufax, Los Angeles Dodgers
1964	Ken Boyer, St. Louis Cardinals
1965	Willie Mays, San Francisco Giants
1966	Roberto Clemente, Pittsburgh Pirates
1967	Orlando Cepeda, St. Louis Cardinals
1968	Bob Gibson, St. Louis Cardinals
1969	Willie McCovey, San Francisco Giants
1970	Johnny Bench, Cincinnati Reds
1971	Joe Torre, St. Louis Cardinals
1972	Johnny Bench, Cincinnati Reds
1973	Pete Rose, Cincinnati Reds
1974	Steve Garvey, Los Angeles Dodgers
1975	Joe Morgan, Cincinnati Reds
1976	Joe Morgan, Cincinnati Reds
1977	George Foster, Cincinnati Reds
1978	Dave Parker, Pittsburgh Pirates
1979	Keith Hernandez, St. Louis Cardinals
	Willie Stargell, Pittsburgh Pirates
1980	Mike Schmidt, Philadelphia Phillies
1981	Mike Schmidt, Philadelphia Phillies
1982	Dale Murphy, Atlanta Braves
1983	Dale Murphy, Atlanta Braves

AMERICAN LEAGUE
Batting Champions

Year	Player, Club	Avg.
1901	Napoleon Lajoie, Philadelphia Athletics	.422
1902	Ed Delahanty, Washington Senators	.376
1903	Napoleon Lajoie, Cleveland Indians	.355
1904	Napoleon Lajoie, Cleveland Indians	.381
1905	Elmer Flick, Cleveland Indians	.306
1906	George Stone, St. Louis Browns	.358
1907	Ty Cobb, Detroit Tigers	.350
1908	Ty Cobb, Detroit Tigers	.324
1909	Ty Cobb, Detroit Tigers	.377
1910	Ty Cobb, Detroit Tigers	.385
1911	Ty Cobb, Detroit Tigers	.420
1912	Ty Cobb, Detroit Tigers	.410
1913	Ty Cobb, Detroit Tigers	.390
1914	Ty Cobb, Detroit Tigers	.368
1915	Ty Cobb, Detroit Tigers	.370
1916	Tris Speaker, Cleveland Indians	.386
1917	Ty Cobb, Detroit Tigers	.383
1918	Ty Cobb, Detroit Tigers	.382
1919	Ty Cobb, Detroit Tigers	.384
1920	George Sisler, St. Louis Browns	.407
1921	Harry Heilmann, Detroit Tigers	.393
1922	George Sisler, St. Louis Browns	.420
1923	Harry Heilmann, Detroit Tigers	.398
1924	Babe Ruth, New York Yankees	.378
1925	Harry Heilmann, Detroit Tigers	.393
1926	Heinie Manush, Detroit Tigers	.377
1927	Harry Heilmann, Detroit Tigers	.398
1928	Goose Goslin, Washington Senators	.379
1929	Lew Fonseca, Cleveland Indians	.369
1930	Al Simmons, Philadelphia Athletics	.381
1931	Al Simmons, Philadelphia Athletics	.390
1932	David Alexander, Detroit Tigers-Boston Red Sox	.367
1933	Jimmy Foxx, Philadelphia Athletics	.356
1934	Lou Gehrig, New York Yankees	.365
1935	Buddy Myer, Washington Senators	.349
1936	Luke Appling, Chicago White Sox	.388
1937	Charlie Gehringer, Detroit Tigers	.371
1938	Jimmy Foxx, Boston Red Sox	.349
1939	Joe DiMaggio, New York Yankees	.381
1940	Joe DiMaggio, New York Yankees	.352

Year	Player, Club	Avg.
1941	Ted Williams, Boston Red Sox	.406
1942	Ted Williams, Boston Red Sox	.356
1943	Luke Appling, Chicago White Sox	.328
1944	Lou Boudreau, Cleveland Indians	.327
1945	Snuffy Stirnweiss, New York Yankees	.309
1946	Mickey Vernon, Washington Senators	.353
1947	Ted Williams, Boston Red Sox	.343
1948	Ted Williams, Boston Red Sox	.369
1949	George Kell, Detroit Tigers	.343
1950	Billy Goodman, Boston Red Sox	.354
1951	Ferris Fain, Philadelphia Athletics	.344
1952	Ferris Fain, Philadelphia Athletics	.327
1953	Mickey Vernon, Washington Senators	.337
1954	Bobby Avila, Cleveland Indians	.341
1955	Al Kaline, Detroit Tigers	.340
1956	Mickey Mantle, New York Yankees	.353
1957	Ted Williams, Boston Red Sox	.388
1958	Ted Williams, Boston Red Sox	.328
1959	Harvey Kuenn, Detroit Tigers	.353
1960	Pete Runnels, Boston Red Sox	.320
1961	Norm Cash, Detroit Tigers	.361
1962	Pete Runnels, Boston Red Sox	.326
1963	Carl Yastrzemski, Boston Red Sox	.321
1964	Tony Oliva, Minnesota Twins	.323
1965	Tony Oliva, Minnesota Twins	.321
1966	Frank Robinson, Baltimore Orioles	.316
1967	Carl Yastrzemski, Boston Red Sox	.326
1968	Carl Yastrzemski, Boston Red Sox	.301
1969	Rod Carew, Minnesota Twins	.332
1970	Alex Johnson, California Angels	.329
1971	Tony Oliva, Minnesota Twins	.337
1972	Rod Carew, Minnesota Twins	.318
1973	Rod Carew, Minnesota Twins	.350
1974	Rod Carew, Minnesota Twins	.364
1975	Rod Carew, Minnesota Twins	.359
1976	George Brett, Kansas City Royals	.333
1977	Rod Carew, Minnesota Twins	.388
1978	Rod Carew, Minnesota Twins	.333
1979	Fred Lynn, Boston Red Sox	.333
1980	George Brett, Kansas City Royals	.390
1981	Carney Lansford, Boston Red Sox	.336
1982	Willie Wilson, Kansas City Royals	.332
1983	Wade Boggs, Boston Red Sox	.361

NATIONAL LEAGUE
Batting Champions

Year	Player, Club	Avg.
1876	Roscoe Barnes, Chicago	.403
1877	James White, Boston	.385
1878	Abner Dalrymple, Milwaukee	.356
1879	Cap Anson, Chicago	.407
1880	George Gore, Chicago	.365
1881	Cap Anson, Chicago	.399
1882	Dan Brouthers, Buffalo	.367
1883	Dan Brouthers, Buffalo	.371
1884	Jim O'Rourke, Buffalo	.350
1885	Roger Connor, New York	.371
1886	Mike Kelly, Chicago	.388
1887	Cap Anson, Chicago	.421
1888	Cap Anson, Chicago	.343
1889	Dan Brouthers, Boston	.373
1890	Jack Glassock, New York	.336
1891	Billy Hamilton, Philadelphia	.338
1892	Cupid Childs, Cleveland	.335
	Dan Brouthers, Brooklyn	.335
1893	Hugh Duffy, Boston	.378
1894	Hugh Duffy, Boston	.438
1895	Jesse Burkett, Cleveland	.423
1896	Jesse Burkett, Cleveland	.410
1897	Willie Keeler, Baltimore	.432
1898	Willie Keeler, Baltimore	.379
1899	Ed Delahanty, Philadelphia	.408
1900	Honus Wagner, Pittsburgh	.380
1901	Jesse Burkett, St. Louis Cardinals	.382
1902	C.H. Beaumont, Pittsburgh Pirates	.357
1903	Honus Wagner, Pittsburgh Pirates	.355
1904	Honus Wagner, Pittsburgh Pirates	.349
1905	J. Bentley Seymour, Cincinnati Reds	.377
1906	Honus Wagner, Pittsburgh Pirates	.339
1907	Honus Wagner, Pittsburgh Pirates	.350
1908	Honus Wagner, Pittsburgh Pirates	.354
1909	Honus Wagner, Pittsburgh Pirates	.339
1910	Sherwood Magee, Philadelphia Phillies	.331
1911	Honus Wagner, Pittsburgh Pirates	.334
1912	Heinie Zimmerman, Chicago Cubs	.372
1913	Jake Daubert, Brooklyn Dodgers	.350
1914	Jake Daubert, Brooklyn Dodgers	.329

Year	Player, Club	Avg.
1915	Larry Doyle, New York Giants	.320
1916	Hal Chase, Cincinnati Reds	.339
1917	Edd Roush, Cincinnati Reds	.341
1918	Zack Wheat, Brooklyn Dodgers	.335
1919	Edd Roush, Cincinnati Reds	.321
1920	Rogers Hornsby, St. Louis Cardinals	.370
1921	Rogers Hornsby, St. Louis Cardinals	.397
1922	Rogers Hornsby, St. Louis Cardinals	.401
1923	Rogers Hornsby, St. Louis Cardinals	.384
1924	Rogers Hornsby, St. Louis Cardinals	.424
1925	Rogers Hornsby, St. Louis Cardinals	.403
1926	Bubbles Hargrave, Cincinnati Reds	.353
1927	Paul Waner, Pittsburgh Pirates	.380
1928	Rogers Hornsby, Boston Braves	.387
1929	Lefty O'Doul, Philadelphia Phillies	.398
1930	Bill Terry, New York Giants	.401
1931	Chick Hafey, St. Louis Cardinals	.349
1932	Lefty O'Doul, Brooklyn Dodgers	.368
1933	Chuck Klein, Philadelphia Phillies	.368
1934	Paul Waner, Pittsburgh Pirates	.362
1935	Arky Vaughan, Pittsburgh Pirates	.385
1936	Paul Waner, Pittsburgh Pirates	.373
1937	Joe Medwick, St. Louis Cardinals	.374
1938	Ernie Lombardi, Cincinnati Reds	.342
1939	Johnny Mize, St. Louis Cardinals	.349
1940	Debs Garms, Pittsburgh Pirates	.355
1941	Pete Reiser, Brooklyn Dodgers	.343
1942	Ernie Lombardi, Boston Braves	.330
1943	Stan Musial, St. Louis Cardinals	.330
1944	Dixie Walker, Brooklyn Dodgers	.357
1945	Phil Cavarretta, Chicago Cubs	.355
1946	Stan Musial, St. Louis Cardinals	.365
1947	Harry Walker, St. L. Cardinals-Phila. Phillies	.363
1948	Stan Musial, St. Louis Cardinals	.376
1949	Jackie Robinson, Brooklyn Dodgers	.342
1950	Stan Musial, St. Louis Cardinals	.346
1951	Stan Musial, St. Louis Cardinals	.355
1952	Stan Musial, St. Louis Cardinals	.336
1953	Carl Furillo, Brooklyn Dodgers	.344
1954	Willie Mays, New York Giants	.345
1955	Richie Ashburn, Philadelphia Phillies	.338
1956	Hank Aaron, Milwaukee Braves	.328
1957	Stan Musial, St. Louis Cardinals	.351
1958	Richie Ashburn, Philadelphia Phillies	.350

Year	Player, Club	Avg.
1959	Hank Aaron, Milwaukee Braves	.328
1960	Dick Groat, Pittsburgh Pirates	.325
1961	Roberto Clemente, Pittsburgh Pirates	.351
1962	Tommy Davis, Los Angeles Dodgers	.346
1963	Tommy Davis, Los Angeles Dodgers	.326
1964	Roberto Clemente, Pittsburgh Pirates	.339
1965	Roberto Clemente, Pittsburgh Pirates	.329
1966	Matty Alou, Pittsburgh Pirates	.342
1967	Roberto Clemente, Pittsburgh Pirates	.357
1968	Pete Rose, Cincinnati Reds	.335
1969	Pete Rose, Cincinnati Reds	.348
1970	Rico Carty, Atlanta Braves	.366
1971	Joe Torre, St. Louis Cardinals	.363
1972	Billy Williams, Chicago Cubs	.333
1973	Pete Rose, Cincinnati Reds	.338
1974	Ralph Garr, Atlanta Braves	.353
1975	Bill Madlock, Chicago Cubs	.354
1976	Bill Madlock, Chicago Cubs	.339
1977	Dave Parker, Pittsburgh Pirates	.338
1978	Dave Parker, Pittsburgh Pirates	.334
1979	Keith Hernandez, St. Louis Cardinals	.344
1980	Bill Buckner, Chicago Cubs	.324
1981	Bill Madlock, Pittsburgh Pirates	.341
1982	Al Oliver, Montreal Expos	.331
1983	Bill Madlock, Pittsburgh Pirates	.323

AMERICAN LEAGUE
Home Run Leaders

Year	Player, Club	HRs
1901	Napoleon Lajoie, Philadelphia Athletics	13
1902	Ralph Seybold, Philadelphia Athletics	16
1903	John Freeman, Boston Pilgrims	13
1904	Harry Davis, Philadelphia Athletics	10
1905	Harry Davis, Philadelphia Athletics	8
1906	Harry Davis, Philadelphia Athletics	12
1907	Harry Davis, Philadelphia Athletics	8
1908	Sam Crawford, Detroit Tigers	7
1909	Ty Cobb, Detroit Tigers	9
1910	Garland Stahl, Boston Red Sox	10
1911	Frank (Home Run) Baker, Philadelphia Athletics	9
1912	Frank (Home Run) Baker, Philadelphia Athletics	10
1913	Frank (Home Run) Baker, Philadelphia Athletics	12

Year	Player, Club	HRs
1914	Frank (Home Run) Baker, Philadelphia Athletics	8
	Sam Crawford, Detroit Tigers	8
1915	Bob Roth, Cleveland Indians	7
1916	Wally Pipp, New York Yankees	12
1917	Wally Pipp, New York Yankees	9
1918	Babe Ruth, Boston Red Sox	11
	Clarence Walker, Philadelphia Athletics	11
1919	Babe Ruth, Boston Red Sox	29
1920	Babe Ruth, New York Yankees	54
1921	Babe Ruth, New York Yankees	59
1922	Ken Williams, St. Louis Browns	39
1923	Babe Ruth, New York Yankees	41
1924	Babe Ruth, New York Yankees	46
1925	Bob Meusel, New York Yankees	33
1926	Babe Ruth, New York Yankees	47
1927	Babe Ruth, New York Yankees	60
1928	Babe Ruth, New York Yankees	54
1929	Babe Ruth, New York Yankees	46
1930	Babe Ruth, New York Yankees	49
1931	Babe Ruth, New York Yankees	46
	Lou Gehrig, New York Yankees	46
1932	Jimmy Foxx, Philadelphia Athletics	58
1933	Jimmy Foxx, Philadelphia Athletics	48
1934	Lou Gehrig, New York Yankees	49
1935	Hank Greenberg, Detroit Tigers	36
	Jimmy Fox, Philadelphia Athletics	36
1936	Lou Gehrig, New York Yankees	49
1937	Joe DiMaggio, New York Yankees	49
1938	Hank Greenberg, Detroit Tigers	58
1939	Jimmy Foxx, Boston Red Sox	35
1940	Hank Greenberg, Detroit Tigers	41
1941	Ted Williams, Boston Red Sox	37
1942	Ted Williams, Boston Red Sox	36
1943	Rudy York, Detroit Tigers	34
1944	Nick Etten, New York Yankees	22
1945	Vern Stephens, St. Louis Browns	24
1946	Hank Greenberg, Detroit Tigers	44
1947	Ted Williams, Boston Red Sox	32
1948	Joe DiMaggio, New York Yankees	39
1949	Ted Williams, Boston Red Sox	43
1950	Al Rosen, Cleveland Indians	37
1951	Gus Zernial, Philadelphia Athletics	33
1952	Larry Doby, Cleveland Indians	32
1953	Al Rosen, Cleveland Indians	43

Year	Player, Club	HRs
1954	Larry Doby, Cleveland Indians	32
1955	Mickey Mantle, New York Yankees	37
1956	Mickey Mantle, New York Yankees	52
1957	Roy Sievers, Washington Senators	42
1958	Mickey Mantle, New York Yankees	42
1959	Rocky Colavito, Cleveland Indians	42
	Harmon Killebrew, Washington Senators	42
1960	Mickey Mantle, New York Yankees	40
1961	Roger Maris, New York Yankees	61
1962	Harmon Killebrew, Minnesota Twins	48
1963	Harmon Killebrew, Minnesota Twins	45
1964	Harmon Killebrew, Minnesota Twins	49
1965	Tony Conigliaro, Boston Red Sox	32
1966	Frank Robinson, Baltimore Orioles	49
1967	Carl Yastrzemski, Boston Red Sox	44
	Harmon Killebrew, Minnesota Twins	44
1968	Frank Howard, Washington Senators	44
1969	Harmon Killebrew, Minnesota Twins	49
1970	Frank Howard, Washington Senators	44
1971	Bill Melton, Chicago White Sox	33
1972	Dick Allen, Chicago White Sox	37
1973	Reggie Jackson, Oakland A's	32
1974	Dick Allen, Chicago White Sox	32
1975	George Scott, Milwaukee Brewers	36
	Reggie Jackson, Oakland A's	36
1976	Graig Nettles, New York Yankees	32
1977	Jim Rice, Boston Red Sox	39
1978	Jim Rice, Boston Red Sox	46
1979	Gorman Thomas, Milwaukee Brewers	45
1980	Ben Oglivie, Milwaukee Brewers	41
	Reggie Jackson, New York Yankees	41
1981	Bobby Grich, California Angels	22
	Eddie Murray, Baltimore Orioles	22
	Dwight Evans, Boston Red Sox	22
	Tony Armas, Oakland A's	22
1982	Reggie Jackson, California Angels	39
	Gorman Thomas, Milwaukee Braves	39
1983	Jim Rice, Boston Red Sox	39

NATIONAL LEAGUE
Home Run Leaders

Year	Player, Club	HRs
1900	Herman Long, Boston Nationals	12
1901	Sam Crawford, Cincinnati Reds	16
1902	Tom Leach, Pittsburgh Pirates	6
1903	Jim Sheckard, Brooklyn Dodgers	9
1904	Harry Lumley, Brooklyn Dodgers	9
1905	Fred Odwell, Cincinnati Reds	9
1906	Tim Jordan, Brooklyn Dodgers	12
1907	Dave Brian, Boston Nationals	10
1908	Tim Jordan, Brooklyn Dodgers	12
1909	Jim Murray, New York Giants	7
1910	Fred Beck, Boston Nationals	10
	Frank Schulte, Chicago Cubs	10
1911	Frank Schulte, Chicago Cubs	21
1912	Heinie Zimmerman, Chicago Cubs	14
1913	Gavvy Cravath, Philadelphia Phillies	19
1914	Gavvy Cravath, Philadelphia Phillies	19
1915	Gavvy Cravath, Philadelphia Phillies	24
1916	Dave Robertson, New York Giants	12
	Cy Williams, Chicago Cubs	12
1917	Gavvy Cravath, Philadelphia Phillies	12
	Dave Robertson, New York Giants	12
1918	Gavvy Cravath, Philadelphia Phillies	8
1919	Gavvy Cravath, Philadelphia Phillies	12
1920	Cy Williams, Philadelphia Phillies	15
1921	George Kelly, New York Giants	23
1922	Rogers Hornsby, St. Louis Cardinals	42
1923	Cy Williams, Philadelphia Phillies	41
1924	Jack Fournier, Brooklyn Dodgers	27
1925	Rogers Hornsby, St. Louis Cardinals	39
1926	Hack Wilson, Chicago Cubs	21
1927	Cy Williams, Philadelphia Phillies	30
	Hack Wilson, Chicago Cubs	30
1928	Jim Bottomley, St. Louis Cardinals	31
	Hack Wilson, Chicago Cubs	31
1929	Chuck Klein, Philadelphia Phillies	43
1930	Hack Wilson, Chicago Cubs	56
1931	Chuck Klein, Philadelphia Phillies	31
1932	Chuck Klein, Philadelphia Phillies	38
	Mel Ott, New York Giants	38
1933	Chuck Klein, Philadelphia Phillies	28

Year	Player, Club	HRs
1934	Rip Collins, St. Louis Cardinals	35
	Mel Ott, New York Giants	35
1935	Wally Berger, Boston Braves	34
1936	Mel Ott, New York Giants	33
1937	Joe Medwick, St. Louis Cardinals	31
	Mel Ott, New York Giants	31
1938	Mel Ott, New York Giants	36
1939	Johnny Mize, St. Louis Cardinals	28
1940	Johnny Mize, St. Louis Cardinals	43
1941	Dolph Camilli, Brooklyn Dodgers	34
1942	Mel Ott, New York Giants	30
1943	Bill Nicholson, Chicago Cubs	29
1944	Bill Nicholson, Chicago Cubs	33
1945	Tommy Holmes, Boston Braves	28
1946	Ralph Kiner, Pittsburgh Pirates	23
1947	Ralph Kiner, Pittsburgh Pirates	51
	Johnny Mize, New York Giants	51
1948	Ralph Kiner, Pittsburgh Pirates	40
	Johnny Mize, New York Giants	40
1949	Ralph Kiner, Pittsburgh Pirates	54
1950	Ralph Kiner, Pittsburgh Pirates	47
1951	Ralph Kiner, Pittsburgh Pirates	42
1952	Ralph Kiner, Pittsburgh Pirates	37
	Hank Sauer, Chicago Cubs	37
1953	Eddie Mathews, Milwaukee Braves	47
1954	Ted Kluszewski, Cincinnati Reds	49
1955	Willie Mays, New York Giants	51
1956	Duke Snider, Brooklyn Dodgers	43
1957	Hank Aaron, Milwaukee Braves	44
1958	Ernie Banks, Chicago Cubs	47
1959	Eddie Mathews, Milwaukee Braves	46
1960	Ernie Banks, Chicago Cubs	41
1961	Orlando Cepeda, San Francisco Giants	46
1962	Willie Mays, San Francisco Giants	49
1963	Hank Aaron, Milwaukee Braves	44
	Willie McCovey, San Francisco Giants	44
1964	Willie Mays, San Francisco Giants	47
1965	Willie Mays, San Francisco Giants	52
1966	Hank Aaron, Atlanta Braves	44
1967	Hank Aaron, Atlanta Braves	39
1968	Willie McCovey, San Francisco Giants	36
1969	Willie McCovey, San Francisco Giants	45
1970	Johnny Bench, Cincinnati Reds	45
1971	Willie Stargell, Pittsburgh Pirates	48

Year	Player, Club	HRs
1972	Johnny Bench, Cincinnati Reds	40
1973	Willie Stargell, Pittsburgh Pirates	44
1974	Mike Schmidt, Philadelphia Phillies	36
1975	Mike Schmidt, Philadelphia Phillies	38
1976	Mike Schmidt, Philadelphia Phillies	38
1977	George Foster, Cincinnati Reds	52
1978	George Foster, Cincinnati Reds	40
1979	Dave Kingman, Chicago Cubs	48
1980	Mike Schmidt, Philadelphia Phillies	48
1981	Mike Schmidt, Philadelphia Phillies	31
1982	Dave Kingman, New York Mets	37
1983	Mike Schmidt, Philadelphia Phillies	40

Mike Schmidt: Broken-bat Series, but he won sixth HR title.

CY YOUNG AWARD WINNERS

(Prior to 1967 there was a single overall major league award.)

Year	Player, Club
1956	Don Newcombe, Brooklyn Dodgers
1957	Warren Spahn, Milwaukee Braves
1958	Bob Turley, New York Yankees
1959	Early Wynn, Chicago White Sox
1960	Vernon Law, Pittsburgh Pirates
1961	Whitey Ford, New York Yankees
1962	Don Drysdale, Los Angeles Dodgers
1963	Sandy Koufax, Los Angeles Dodgers
1964	Dean Chance, Los Angeles Angels
1965	Sandy Koufax, Los Angeles Dodgers
1966	Sandy Koufax, Los Angeles Dodgers

AMERICAN LEAGUE

Year	Player, Club
1967	Jim Lonborg, Boston Red Sox
1968	Dennis McLain, Detroit Tigers
1969	Mike Cuellar, Baltimore Orioles
	Dennis McLain, Detroit Tigers
1970	Jim Perry, Minnesota Twins
1971	Vida Blue, Oakland A's
1972	Gaylord Perry, Cleveland Indians
1973	Jim Palmer, Baltimore Orioles
1974	Jim Hunter, Oakland A's
1975	Jim Palmer, Baltimore Orioles
1976	Jim Palmer, Baltimore Orioles
1977	Sparky Lyle, New York Yankees
1978	Ron Guidry, New York Yankees
1979	Mike Flanagan, Baltimore Orioles
1980	Steve Stone, Baltimore Orioles
1981	Rollie Fingers, Milwaukee Brewers
1982	Pete Vuckovich, Milwaukee Brewers
1983	LaMarr Hoyt, Chicago White Sox

Steve Carlton has won the Cy Young Award four times.

NATIONAL LEAGUE

Year	Player, Club
1967	Mike McCormick, San Francisco Giants
1968	Bob Gibson, St. Louis Cardinals
1969	Tom Seaver, New York Mets
1970	Bob Gibson, St. Louis Cardinals
1971	Ferguson Jenkins, Chicago Cubs
1972	Steve Carlton, Philadelphia Phillies
1973	Tom Seaver, New York Mets
1974	Mike Marshall, Los Angeles Dodgers
1975	Tom Seaver, New York Mets
1976	Randy Jones, San Diego Padres
1977	Steve Carlton, Philadelphia Phillies
1978	Gaylord Perry, San Diego Padres
1979	Bruce Sutter, Chicago Cubs
1980	Stevc Carlton, Philadelphia Phillies
1981	Fernando Valenzuela, Los Angeles Dodgers
1982	Steve Carlton, Philadelphia Phillies
1983	John Denny, Philadelphia Phillies

AMERICAN LEAGUE
Rookie of Year

Year	Player, Club
1949	Roy Sievers, St. Louis Browns
1950	Walt Dropo, Boston Red Sox
1951	Gil McDougald, New York Yankees
1952	Harry Byrd, Philadelphia Athletics
1953	Harvey Kuenn, Detroit Tigers
1954	Bob Grim, New York Yankees
1955	Herb Score, Cleveland Indians
1956	Luis Aparicio, Chicago White Sox
1957	Tony Kubek, New York Yankees
1958	Albie Pearson, Washington Senators
1959	Bob Allison, Washington Senators
1960	Ron Hansen, Baltimore Orioles
1961	Don Schwall, Boston Red Sox
1962	Tom Tresh, New York Yankees
1963	Gary Peters, Chicago White Sox
1964	Tony Oliva, Minnesota Twins
1965	Curt Blefary, Baltimore Orioles
1966	Tommie Agee, Chicago White Sox
1967	Rod Carew, Minnesota Twins
1968	Stan Bahnsen, New York Yankees
1969	Lou Piniella, Kansas City Royals
1970	Thurman Munson, New York Yankees
1971	Chris Chambliss, Cleveland Indians
1972	Carlton Fisk, Boston Red Sox
1973	Al Bumbry, Baltimore Orioles
1974	Mike Hargrove, Texas Rangers
1975	Fred Lynn, Boston Red Sox
1976	Mark Fidrych, Detroit Tigers
1977	Eddie Murray, Baltimore Orioles
1978	Lou Whitaker, Detroit Tigers
1979	John Castino, Minnesota Twins
	Alfredo Griffin, Toronto Blue Jays
1980	Joe Charboneau, Cleveland Indians
1981	Dave Righetti, New York Yankees
1982	Cal Ripken, Jr., Baltimore Orioles
1983	Ron Kittle, Chicago White Sox

NATIONAL LEAGUE
Rookie of Year

Year	Player, Club
1947	Jackie Robinson, Brooklyn Dodgers
1948	Al Dark, Boston Braves
1949	Don Newcombe, Brooklyn Dodgers
1950	Sam Jethroe, Boston Braves
1951	Willie Mays, New York Giants
1952	Joe Black, Brooklyn Dodgers
1953	Junior Gilliam, Brooklyn Dodgers
1954	Wally Moon, St. Louis Cardinals
1955	Bill Virdon, St. Louis Cardinals
1956	Frank Robinson, Cincinnati Reds
1957	Jack Sanford, Philadelphia Phillies
1958	Orlando Cepeda, San Francisco Giants
1959	Willie McCovey, San Francisco Giants
1960	Frank Howard, Los Angeles Dodgers
1961	Billy Williams, Chicago Cubs
1962	Kenny Hubbs, Chicago Cubs
1963	Pete Rose, Cincinnati Reds
1964	Richie Allen, Philadelphia Phillies
1965	Jim Lefebvre, Los Angeles Dodgers
1966	Tommy Helms, Cincinnati Reds
1967	Tom Seaver, New York Mets
1968	Johnny Bench, Cincinnati Reds
1969	Ted Sizemore, Los Angeles Dodgers
1970	Carl Morton, Montreal Expos
1971	Earl Williams, Atlanta Braves
1972	Jon Matlack, New York Mets
1973	Gary Matthews, San Francisco Giants
1974	Bake McBride, St. Louis Cardinals
1975	John Montefusco, San Francisco Giants
1976	Pat Zachry, Cincinnati Reds
	Butch Metzger, San Diego Padres
1977	Andre Dawson, Montreal Expos
1978	Bob Horner, Atlanta Braves
1979	Rick Sutcliffe, Los Angeles Dodgers
1980	Steve Howe, Los Angeles Dodgers
1981	Fernando Valenzuela, Los Angeles Dodgers
1982	Steve Sax, Los Angeles Dodgers
1983	Darryl Strawberry, New York Mets

WORLD SERIES WINNERS

Year	A. L. Champion	N. L. Champion	World Series Winner
1903	Boston Red Sox	Pittsburgh Pirates	Boston, 5-3
1905	Philadelphia Athletics	New York Giants	New York, 4-1
1906	Chicago White Sox	Chicago Cubs	Chicago (AL), 4-2
1907	Detroit Tigers	Chicago Cubs	Chicago, 4-0-1
1908	Detroit Tigers	Chicago Cubs	Chicago, 4-1
1909	Detroit Tigers	Pittsburgh Pirates	Pittsburgh, 4-3
1910	Philadelphia Athletics	Chicago Cubs	Philadelphia, 4-1
1911	Philadelphia Athletics	New York Giants	Philadelphia, 4-2
1912	Boston Red Sox	New York Giants	Boston, 4-3-1
1913	Philadelphia Athletics	Boston Braves	Boston, 4-0
1914	Philadelphia Athletics	New York Giants	Philadelphia, 4-1
1915	Boston Red Sox	Philadelphia Phillies	Boston, 4-1
1916	Boston Red Sox	Philadelphia Phillies	Boston, 4-1
1917	Chicago White Sox	New York Giants	Chicago, 4-2
1918	Boston Red Sox	Chicago Cubs	Boston, 4-2
1919	Chicago White Sox	Cincinnati Reds	Cincinnati, 5-2
1920	Cleveland Indians	Brooklyn Dodgers	Cleveland, 5-2
1921	New York Yankees	New York Giants	New York (NL), 5-3
1922	New York Yankees	New York Giants	New York (NL), 4-0-1
1923	New York Yankees	New York Giants	New York (AL), 4-2
1924	Washington Senators	New York Giants	Washington, 4-2
1925	Washington Senators	Pittsburgh Pirates	Pittsburgh, 4-3
1926	New York Yankees	St. Louis Cardinals	St. Louis, 4-3
1927	New York Yankees	Pittsburgh Pirates	New York, 4-0
1928	New York Yankees	St. Louis Cardinals	New York, 4-0
1929	Philadelphia Athletics	Chicago Cubs	Philadelphia, 4-2
1930	Philadelphia Athletics	St. Louis Cardinals	Philadelphia, 4-2
1931	Philadelphia Athletics	St. Louis Cardinals	St. Louis, 4-3
1932	New York Yankees	Chicago Cubs	New York, 4-0
1933	Washington Senators	New York Giants	New York, 4-1
1934	Detroit Tigers	St. Louis Cardinals	St. Louis, 4-3
1935	Detroit Tigers	Chicago Cubs	Detroit, 4-2
1936	New York Yankees	New York Giants	New York (AL), 4-2
1937	New York Yankees	New York Giants	New York (AL), 4-1
1938	New York Yankees	Chicago Cubs	New York, 4-0
1939	New York Yankees	Cincinnati Reds	New York, 4-0
1940	Detroit Tigers	Cincinnati Reds	Cincinnati, 4-3
1941	New York Yankees	Brooklyn Dodgers	New York, 4-1
1942	New York Yankees	St. Louis Cardinals	St. Louis, 4-1
1943	New York Yankees	St. Louis Cardinals	New York, 4-1
1944	St. Louis Browns	St. Louis Cardinals	St. Louis (NL), 4-2
1945	Detroit Tigers	Chicago Cubs	Detroit, 4-3
1946	Boston Red Sox	St. Louis Cardinals	St. Louis, 4-3
1947	New York Yankees	Brooklyn Dodgers	New York, 4-3
1948	Cleveland Indians	Boston Braves	Cleveland, 4-2
1949	New York Yankees	Brooklyn Dodgers	New York, 4-1
1950	New York Yankees	Philadelphia Phillies	New York, 4-0
1951	New York Yankees	New York Giants	New York (AL), 4-2
1952	New York Yankees	Brooklyn Dodgers	New York, 4-3
1953	New York Yankees	Brooklyn Dodgers	New York, 4-2
1954	Cleveland Indians	New York Giants	New York, 4-0
1955	New York Yankees	Brooklyn Dodgers	Brooklyn, 4-3

Orioles' Rick Dempsey homers in fifth game of '83 Series.

Year	A. L. Champion	N. L. Champion	World Series Winner
1956	New York Yankees	Brooklyn Dodgers	New York, 4-3
1957	New York Yankees	Milwaukee Braves	Milwaukee, 4-3
1958	New York Yankees	Milwaukee Braves	New York, 4-3
1959	Chicago White Sox	Los Angeles Dodgers	Los Angeles, 4-2
1960	New York Yankees	Pittsburgh Pirates	Pittsburgh, 4-3
1961	New York Yankees	Cincinnati Reds	New York, 4-1
1962	New York Yankees	San Francisco Giants	New York, 4-3
1963	New York Yankees	Los Angeles Dodgers	Los Angeles, 4-0
1964	New York Yankees	St. Louis Cardinals	St. Louis, 4-3
1965	Minnesota Twins	Los Angeles Dodgers	Los Angeles, 4-3
1966	Baltimore Orioles	Los Angeles Dodgers	Baltimore, 4-0
1967	Boston Red Sox	St. Louis Cardinals	St. Louis, 4-3
1968	Detroit Tigers	St. Louis Cardinals	Detroit, 4-3
1969	Baltimore Orioles	New York Mets	New York, 4-1
1970	Baltimore Orioles	Cincinnati Reds	Baltimore, 4-1
1971	Baltimore Orioles	Pittsburgh Pirates	Pittsburgh, 4-3
1972	Oakland A's	Cincinnati Reds	Oakland, 4-3
1973	Oakland A's	New York Mets	Oakland, 4-3
1974	Oakland A's	Los Angeles Dodgers	Oakland, 4-1
1975	Boston Red Sox	Cincinnati Reds	Cincinnati, 4-3
1976	New York Yankees	Cincinnati Reds	Cincinnati, 4-0
1977	New York Yankees	Los Angeles Dodgers	New York, 4-2
1978	New York Yankees	Los Angeles Dodgers	New York, 4-2
1979	Baltimore Orioles	Pittsburgh Pirates	Pittsburgh, 4-3
1980	Kansas City Royals	Philadelphia Phillies	Philadelphia, 4-2
1981	New York Yankees	Los Angeles Dodgers	Los Angeles, 4-2
1982	Milwaukee Brewers	St. Louis Cardinals	St. Louis, 4-3
1983	Baltimore Orioles	Philadelphia Phillies	Baltimore, 4-1

1983 WORLD SERIES

BALTIMORE ORIOLES

Player	AVG	G	AB	R	H	TB	2B	3B	HR	RBI	GW RBI	SH	SF	HB	BB	SO	SB	CS	E
Ayala	1.000	1	1	1	1	1	0	0	0	1	0	0	0	0	0	0	0	0	0
Bumbry	.091	4	11	0	1	2	1	0	0	1	0	0	1	0	0	1	0	0	0
Cruz	.125	5	16	1	2	2	0	0	0	0	0	0	0	0	1	3	0	0	2
Dauer	.211	5	19	2	4	5	1	0	0	3	0	0	0	0	0	3	0	0	0
Dempsey	.385	5	13	3	5	12	4	0	1	2	1	0	0	0	2	2	0	0	0
Dwyer	.375	2	8	3	3	7	1	0	1	1	0	0	0	0	0	0	0	0	0
Ford	.167	5	12	1	2	5	0	0	1	1	0	0	0	1	1	5	0	0	0
Landrum	—	3	0	0	0	0	0	0	0	0	0	0	0	0	0	0	1	0	0
Lowenstein	.385	4	13	2	5	9	1	0	1	1	0	0	0	0	0	3	0	0	1
Murray . . L	.385	—	13	0	5	11	0	0	2	3	1	0	0	0	1	0	0	0	0
Murray . . R	.000	—	7	0	0	0	0	0	0	0	0	0	0	0	0	4	0	0	0
Murray . . T	.250	5	20	2	5	11	0	0	2	3	1	0	0	0	1	4	0	0	1
Nolan	.000	2	2	0	0	0	0	0	0	0	0	0	0	0	1	0	0	0	0
Ripken	.167	5	18	2	3	3	0	0	0	1	0	0	0	0	3	4	0	0	0
Roenicke	.000	3	7	0	0	0	0	0	0	0	0	0	0	0	0	2	0	0	0
Sakata	.000	1	1	0	0	0	0	0	0	0	0	0	0	0	0	0	0	0	0
Shelby . . L	.667	—	3	0	2	2	0	0	0	0	0	0	0	0	0	1	0	0	0
Shelby . . R	.333	—	6	0	2	2	0	0	0	1	1	0	1	0	0	3	0	0	0
Shelby . . T	.444	5	9	1	4	4	0	0	0	1	1	0	1	0	0	4	0	0	0
Singleton . . L	—	—	0	0	0	0	0	0	0	1	0	0	0	0	1	0	0	0	0
Singleton . . R	.000	—	1	0	0	0	0	0	0	0	0	0	0	0	0	1	0	0	0
Singleton . . T	.000	2	1	0	0	0	0	0	0	1	0	0	0	0	1	1	0	0	0
Boddicker	.000	1	3	0	0	0	0	0	0	1	0	0	1	0	0	1	0	0	0
Davis	.000	1	2	0	0	0	0	0	0	0	0	0	0	0	0	2	0	0	0
Flanagan	.000	1	1	0	0	0	0	0	0	0	0	0	0	0	0	1	0	0	0
T. Martinez	—	3	0	0	0	0	0	0	0	0	0	0	0	0	0	0	0	0	0
McGregor . . L	.000	—	4	0	0	0	0	0	0	0	0	0	0	0	0	0	0	0	0
McGregor . . R	.000	—	1	0	0	0	0	0	0	0	0	0	0	0	0	0	0	0	0
McGregor . . T	.000	2	5	0	0	0	0	0	0	0	0	0	0	0	0	0	0	0	0
Palmer	—	1	0	0	0	0	0	0	0	0	0	0	0	0	0	0	0	0	0
Stewart	.000	3	2	0	0	0	0	0	0	0	0	0	0	0	0	1	0	0	0
Pinch Hitters	.100		10	1	1	1	0	0	0	3	1	0	1	0	2	5	0	0	0
ORIOLES	.213	5	164	18	35	61	8	0	6	17	3	0	3	1	10	37	1	0	4

Pitcher	W	L	ERA	G	GS	CG	GF	SHO	SV	IP	H	R	ER	HR	HB	BB	IBB	SO	WP	BK
Boddicker	1	0	0.00	1	1	1	0	0	0	9.0	3	1	0	0	0	0	0	6	0	0
Davis	1	0	5.40	1	1	0	0	0	0	5.0	6	3	3	0	0	1	0	3	1	0
Flanagan	0	0	4.50	1	1	0	0	0	0	4.0	6	2	2	2	0	1	0	1	0	0
T. Martinez	0	0	3.00	3	0	0	3	0	2	3.0	3	1	1	0	0	0	0	0	0	0
McGregor	1	1	1.06	2	2	1	0	1	0	17.0	9	2	2	2	0	2	0	12	0	0
Palmer	1	0	0.00	1	0	0	0	0	0	2.0	2	0	0	0	0	1	0	1	1	0
Stewart	0	0	0.00	3	0	0	0	0	0	5.0	2	0	0	0	0	2	0	6	0	1
ORIOLES	4	1	1.60	5	5	2	3	1	2	45.0	31	9	8	4	0	7	0	29	2	1

GAME 1
at BALTIMORE
Tuesday, October 11

Philadelphia	0 0 0	0 0 1	0 1 0	2	5	0
Baltimore	1 0 0	0 0 0	0 0 0	1	5	1

DENNY, Holland (8) and Diaz
McGREGOR, Stewart (9), T. Martinez (9) and Dempsey, Nolan (9)
HR: Philadelphia (2)—Morgan and Maddox
Baltimore (1)—Dwyer
T-2:22; A-52,204

GAME 2
at BALTIMORE
Wednesday, October 12

Philadelphia	0 0 0	1 0 0	0 0 0	1	3	0
Baltimore	0 0 0	0 3 0	1 0 x	4	9	1

HUDSON, Hernandez (5), Andersen (6), Reed (8) and Diaz, Virgil (8)
BODDICKER and Dempsey
HR: Baltimore (1)—Lowenstein
T-2:27; A-52,132

GAME 3
at PHILADELPHIA
Friday, October 14

Baltimore	0 0 0	0 0 1	2 0 0	3	6	1
Philadelphia	0 1 1	0 0 0	0 0 0	2	8	2

Flanagan, PALMER (5), Stewart (7), T. Martinez (9) and Dempsey
CARLTON, Holland (7) and Diaz
HR: Philadelphia (2)—Matthews and Morgan
Baltimore (1)—Ford
T-2:45; A-65,792

PHILADELPHIA PHILLIES

Player	AVG	G	AB	R	H	TB	2B	3B	HR	RBI	GW RBI	SH	SF	HB	BB	SO	SB	CS	E
DeJesus	.125	5	16	0	2	2	0	0	0	0	0	0	0	0	1	2	0	0	1
Dernier	—	1	0	1	0	0	0	0	0	0	0	0	0	0	0	0	0	0	0
Diaz	.333	5	15	1	5	6	1	0	0	0	0	0	0	0	1	2	0	0	1
G. Gross	.000	2	6	0	0	0	0	0	0	0	0	0	0	0	0	0	0	0	0
Hayes	.000	4	3	0	0	0	0	0	0	0	0	0	0	0	0	1	0	0	0
LeFebvre	.200	3	5	0	1	2	1	0	0	2	0	0	1	0	0	1	0	0	0
Lezcano	.125	4	8	0	1	1	0	0	0	0	0	0	0	0	0	2	0	0	0
Maddox	.250	4	12	1	3	7	1	0	1	1	1	0	0	0	0	2	0	0	0
Matthews	.250	5	16	1	4	7	0	0	1	1	0	0	0	0	2	2	0	0	0
Morgan	.263	5	19	3	5	13	0	1	2	2	0	0	0	0	2	3	1	2	0
Perez	.200	4	10	0	2	2	0	0	0	0	0	0	0	0	0	2	0	0	0
Rose . . L	.375	—	8	1	3	4	1	0	0	1	0	0	0	0	1	2	0	0	0
Rose . . R	.250	—	8	0	2	2	0	0	0	0	0	0	0	0	0	1	0	0	0
Rose . . T	.313	5	16	1	5	6	1	0	0	1	0	0	0	0	1	3	0	0	0
Samuel	.000	3	1	0	0	0	0	0	0	0	0	0	0	0	0	0	0	0	0
Schmidt	.050	5	20	0	1	1	0	0	0	0	0	0	0	0	0	6	0	0	1
Virgil	.500	3	2	0	1	1	0	0	0	1	0	0	0	0	0	0	0	0	0
Andersen	—	2	0	0	0	0	0	0	0	0	0	0	0	0	0	0	0	0	0
Bystrom	—	1	0	0	0	0	0	0	0	0	0	0	0	0	0	0	0	0	0
Carlton	.000	1	3	0	0	0	0	0	0	0	0	0	0	0	0	1	0	0	0
Denny	.200	2	5	1	1	1	0	0	0	1	0	0	0	0	0	1	0	0	0
Hernandez	—	3	0	0	0	0	0	0	0	0	0	0	0	0	0	0	0	0	0
Holland	—	2	0	0	0	0	0	0	0	0	0	0	0	0	0	0	0	0	0
Hudson	.000	2	2	0	0	0	0	0	0	0	0	0	0	0	0	1	0	0	0
Reed	—	3	0	0	0	0	0	0	0	0	0	0	0	0	0	0	0	0	0
Pinch Hitters	.182		11	0	2	2	0	0	0	1	0	0	0	0	0	1	0	0	0
PHILLIES	.195	5	159	9	31	49	4	1	4	9	1	0	1	0	7	29	1	2	3

Pitcher	W	L	ERA	G	GS	CG	GF	SHO	SV	IP	H	R	ER	HR	HB	BB	IBB	SO	WP	BK
Andersen	0	0	2.25	2	0	0	1	0	0	4.0	4	1	1	0	0	0	0	1	0	0
Bystrom	0	0	0.00	1	0	0	0	0	0	1.0	0	0	0	0	0	0	0	1	1	0
Carlton	0	1	2.70	1	1	0	0	0	0	6.2	5	3	2	1	0	3	0	7	1	0
Denny	1	1	3.46	2	2	0	0	0	0	13.0	12	5	5	1	0	3	2	9	0	0
Hernandez	0	0	0.00	3	0	0	0	0	0	4.0	0	0	0	0	1	1	0	4	0	0
Holland	0	0	0.00	2	0	0	2	0	1	3.2	1	0	0	0	0	0	0	5	0	0
Hudson	0	2	8.64	2	2	0	0	0	0	8.1	9	8	8	4	0	1	0	6	0	0
Reed	0	0	2.70	3	0	0	2	0	0	3.1	4	1	1	0	0	2	1	4	0	0
PHILLIES	1	4	3.48	5	5	0	5	0	1	44.0	35	18	17	6	1	10	3	37	2	0

GAME 4
at PHILADELPHIA
Saturday, October 15

										R	H	E
Baltimore	0	0	0	2	0	2	1	0	0	5	10	1
Philadelphia	0	0	0	1	2	0	0	0	1	4	10	0

DAVIS, Stewart (6), T. Martinez (8) and Dempsey, Nolan (7)
DENNY, Hernandez (6), Reed (6), Andersen (8) and Diaz
HR: NONE
T-2:50; A-66,947

GAME 5
at PHILADELPHIA
Sunday, October 16

										R	H	E
Baltimore	0	1	1	2	1	0	0	0	0	5	5	0
Philadelphia	0	0	0	0	0	0	0	0	0	0	5	1

McGREGOR and Dempsey
HUDSON, Bystrom (5), Hernandez (6), Reed (9) and Diaz
HR: Baltimore (3)—Murray (2) and Dempsey
T-2:21; A-67,064

SCORE BY INNINGS

Baltimore	1	1	1	4	4	3	4	0	0	-	-	18
Philadelphia	0	1	1	2	2	1	0	1	1	-	-	9

E—Cruz (2), Lowenstein, Murray, DeJesus, Diaz, Schmidt
DP—Baltimore (5), Philadelphia (2)
LOB—Baltimore (28), Philadelphia (23)
SB—Landrum, Morgan
S—NONE
SF—Bumbry, Shelby, Boddicker, Lefebvre
WP—Davis, Palmer, Bystrom, Carlton
HBP—Ford (by Hernandez)
ATT—304,139

Official 1983 National League Records

(Compiled by Elias Sports Bureau)

FINAL 1983 STANDINGS

					vs. Eastern Division						vs. Western Division					
EASTERN DIVISION	W	L	PCT	GB	PHIL.	PITT.	MTL.	ST.L.	CHI.	N.Y.	L.A.	ATL.	HOU.	S.D.	S.F.	CIN.
Philadelphia	90	72	.556	--	--	11	10	14	13	12	1	5	8	5	5	6
Pittsburgh	84	78	.519	6	7	--	10	10	9	9	6	6	6	9	6	6
Montreal	82	80	.506	8	8	8	--	9	11	8	5	5	4	8	8	8
St. Louis	79	83	.488	11	4	8	9	--	8	12	3	5	10	6	8	6
Chicago	71	91	.438	19	5	9	7	10	--	9	6	7	5	5	4	4
New York	68	94	.420	22	6	9	10	6	9	--	5	4	3	6	5	5

					vs. Western Division						vs. Eastern Division					
WESTERN DIVISION	W	L	PCT	GB	L.A.	ATL.	HOU.	S.D.	S.F.	CIN.	PHIL.	PITT.	MTL.	ST.L.	CHI.	N.Y.
Los Angeles	91	71	.562	--	--	11	12	6	5	11	11	6	7	9	6	7
Atlanta	88	74	.543	3	7	--	11	9	9	12	7	6	7	7	5	8
Houston	85	77	.525	6	6	7	--	11	12	13	4	6	8	2	7	9
San Diego	81	81	.500	10	12	9	7	--	11	9	7	3	4	6	7	6
San Francisco	79	83	.488	12	13	9	6	7	--	8	7	6	4	4	8	7
Cincinnati	74	88	.457	17	7	6	5	9	10	--	6	6	4	6	8	7

Championship Series: Philadelphia defeated Los Angeles, 3 games to 1

BATTING

INDIVIDUAL BATTING LEADERS

Batting Average	:	.323	Madlock, Pitt.
Slugging Average	:	.540	Murphy, Atl.
Games	:	162	Murphy, Atl.
At Bats	:	638	Wilson, N.Y.
Runs	:	133	Raines, Mtl.
Hits	:	189	Cruz, Hou. & Dawson, Mtl.
Total Bases	:	341	Dawson, Mtl.
Singles	:	160	Ramirez, Atl.
Doubles	:	38	Buckner, Chi., Oliver, Mtl. & Ray, Pitt.
Triples	:	13	Butler, Atl.
Home Runs	:	40	Schmidt, Phil.
Runs Batted In	:	121	Murphy, Atl.
Game-Winning RBI°s	:	18	Thon, Hou.
Sacrifice Hits	:	20	Rogers, Mtl.
Sacrifice Flies	:	18	Dawson, Mtl.
Hit by Pitch	:	9	Dawson, Mtl. & L.Smith, St.L.
Bases on Balls	:	128	Schmidt, Phil.
Intentional Bases on Balls	:	19	Berra, Pitt.
Strikeouts	:	148	Schmidt, Phil.
Stolen Bases	:	90	Raines, Mtl.
Caught Stealing	:	30	S.Sax, L.A.
Grounded into Double Plays	:	21	Concepcion, Cin. & Oliver, Mtl.
Longest Batting Streak	:	25	Gwynn, S.D. August 21(1g) - September 18

Astro Jose Cruz, .318, tied for third in NL batting.

TOP FIFTEEN QUALIFIERS FOR BATTING CHAMPIONSHIP
(*Bats Left-Handed #Switch-Hitter)

Player & Club	PCT	SLUG	G	AB	R	H	TB	2B	3B	HR	RBI	GW	BB	SO	SB
Madlock, Bill, Pitt.	.323	.444	130	473	68	153	210	21	0	12	68	14	49	24	3
Smith, Lonnie, St.L.	.321	.453	130	492	83	158	223	31	5	8	45	3	41	55	43
*Cruz, Jose, Hou.	.318	.463	160	594	85	189	275	28	8	14	92	9	65	86	30
Hendrick, George, St.L.	.318	.493	144	529	73	168	261	33	3	18	97	12	51	76	3
Knight, C. Ray, Hou.	.304	.444	145	507	43	154	225	36	4	9	70	8	42	62	0
Murphy, Dale, Atl.	.302	.540	162	589	131	178	318	24	4	36	121	14	90	110	30
Moreland, B. Keith, Chi.	.302	.460	154	533	76	161	245	30	3	16	70	11	68	73	0
Pena, Antonio, Pitt.	.301	.435	151	542	51	163	236	22	3	15	70	2	31	73	6
*Oliver, Albert, Mtl.	.300	.410	157	614	70	184	252	38	3	8	84	12	44	44	1
Dawson, Andre, Mtl.	.299	.539	159	633	104	189	341	36	10	32	113	14	38	81	25
Guerrero, Pedro, L.A.	.298	.531	160	584	87	174	310	28	6	32	103	13	72	110	23
#Raines, Timothy, Mtl.	.298	.429	156	615	133	183	264	32	8	11	71	13	97	70	90
Ramirez, Rafael, Atl.	.297	.368	152	622	82	185	229	13	5	7	58	10	36	48	16
*Hernandez, Keith, St.L.-N.Y.	.297	.433	150	538	77	160	233	23	7	12	63	9	88	72	9
*Oberkfell, Kenneth, St.L.	.293	.385	151	488	62	143	188	26	5	3	38	6	61	27	12

ALL PLAYERS LISTED ALPHABETICALLY
(*Bats Left-Handed #Switch-Hitter)

Player & Club	PCT	SLUG	G	AB	R	H	TB	2B	3B	HR	RBI	GW	BB	SO	SB
*Adduci, James, St.L.	.050	.050	10	20	0	1	1	0	0	0	0	0	1	6	[illegible]
Aguayo, Luis, Phil.	.250	.250	2	4	1	1	1	0	0	0	0	0	1	2	[illegible]
Allen, Neil, N.Y.-St.L.	.102	.143	46	49	2	5	7	2	0	0	3	0	0	22	0
Altamirano, Porfirio, Phil.	.000	.000	31	2	0	0	0	0	0	0	0	0	0	0	0
Andersen, Larry, Phil.	.000	.000	17	2	0	0	0	0	0	0	0	0	0	0	0
Anderson, David, L.A.	.165	.261	61	115	12	19	30	4	2	1	2	0	12	15	6
#Andujar, Joaquin, St.L.	.082	.096	39	73	2	6	7	1	0	0	2	1	2	38	2
#Ashby, Alan, Hou.	.229	.389	87	275	31	63	107	18	1	8	34	5	31	38	0
Ashford, Thomas, N.Y.	.179	.214	35	56	3	10	12	0	1	0	2	0	7	4	0
#Backman, Walter, N.Y.	.167	.214	26	42	6	7	9	0	1	0	3	0	2	8	0
Bailor, Robert, N.Y.	.250	.282	118	340	33	85	96	8	0	1	30	4	20	23	18
Bair, C. Douglas, St.L.	.000	.000	26	2	0	0	0	0	0	0	0	0	0	2	0
Baker, Johnnie, L.A.	.260	.395	149	531	71	138	210	25	1	15	73	10	72	59	7
Baker, Steven, St.L.	---	---	8	0	0	0	0	0	0	0	0	0	0	0	0
Bargar, Gregory, Mtl.	.167	.167	8	6	0	1	1	0	0	0	1	0	0	4	0
Barker, Leonard, Atl.	.125	.125	6	8	1	1	1	0	0	0	0	0	0	5	0
Barnes, William, Cin.	.206	.294	15	34	5	7	10	0	0	1	4	0	7	3	2
Barr, James, S.F.	.133	.200	53	15	0	2	3	1	0	0	0	0	0	4	0
#Bass, Kevin, Hou.	.236	.333	88	195	25	46	65	7	3	2	18	1	6	27	[illegible]
*Beckwith, T. Joseph, L.A.	.200	.200	42	5	1	1	1	0	0	0	0	0	0	3	0
Bedrosian, Stephen, Atl.	.105	.105	70	19	0	2	2	0	0	0	0	0	0	7	0
Behenna, Richard, Atl.	.333	.583	14	12	1	4	7	0	0	1	2	0	0	5	0
Belliard, Rafael, Pitt.	.000	.000	4	1	1	0	0	0	0	0	0	0	0	1	0
Bench, Johnny, Cin.	.255	.432	110	310	32	79	134	15	2	12	54	7	24	38	0
Benedict, Bruce, Atl.	.298	.348	134	423	43	126	147	13	1	2	43	4	61	24	1
Berenyi, Bruce, Cin.	.218	.273	32	55	5	12	15	3	0	0	5	0	0	19	0
*Bergman, David, S.F.	.286	.457	90	140	16	40	64	4	1	6	24	4	24	21	2
Berra, Dale, Pitt.	.251	.358	161	537	51	135	192	25	1	10	52	4	61	84	8
Bevacqua, Kurt, S.D.	.244	.327	74	156	17	38	51	7	0	2	24	3	18	33	0
Bibby, James, Pitt.	.111	.111	29	18	0	2	2	0	0	0	0	0	0	6	0
Bilardello, Dann, Cin.	.238	.389	109	298	27	71	116	18	0	9	38	6	15	49	2
Bishop, Michael, N.Y.	.125	.250	3	8	2	1	2	1	0	0	0	0	3	4	0
Bjorkman, George, Hou.	.227	.360	29	75	8	17	27	4	0	2	14	0	16	29	0
#Blackwell, Timothy, Mtl.	.200	.267	6	15	0	3	4	1	0	0	2	0	1	3	0
Bochy, Bruce, S.D.	.214	.286	23	42	2	9	12	1	1	0	3	0	0	9	0
Boggs, Thomas, Atl.	---	---	5	0	0	0	0	0	0	0	0	0	1	0	0
Bonilla, Juan, S.D.	.237	.304	152	556	55	132	169	17	4	4	45	6	50	40	[illegible]
Booker, Gregory, S.D.	.000	.000	6	1	0	0	0	0	0	0	0	0	0	0	0
Bordi, Richard, Chi.	.000	.000	11	4	0	0	0	0	0	0	0	0	0	3	0
*Bosley, Thaddis, Chi.	.292	.458	43	72	12	21	33	4	1	2	12	1	10	12	[illegible]
#Bowa, Lawrence, Chi.	.267	.339	147	499	73	133	169	20	5	2	43	8	35	30	7
Bradley, Mark, N.Y.	.202	.327	73	104	10	21	34	4	0	3	5	0	11	35	4
*Braun, Stephen, St.L.	.272	.413	78	92	8	25	38	2	1	3	7	1	21	7	0
*Bream, Sidney, L.A.	.182	.182	15	11	0	2	2	0	0	0	2	0	2	2	0
Breining, Fred, S.F.	.149	.164	32	67	1	10	11	1	0	0	4	0	6	31	0
Brenly, Robert, S.F.	.224	.356	104	281	36	63	100	12	2	7	34	3	37	48	10
Brizzolara, Anthony, Atl.	---	---	14	0	0	0	0	0	0	0	0	0	0	0	0
*Brock, Gregory, L.A.	.224	.396	146	455	64	102	180	14	2	20	66	4	83	81	5
Brooks, Hubert, N.Y.	.251	.321	150	586	53	147	188	18	4	5	58	8	24	96	6
#Brown, Rogers, S.D.	.267	.382	57	225	40	60	86	5	3	5	22	1	23	38	27
Brummer, Glenn, St.L.	.276	.356	45	87	7	24	31	7	0	0	9	1	10	11	1
Brusstar, Warren, Chi.	.000	.000	59	4	0	0	0	0	0	0	0	0	0	3	0
*Buckner, William, Chi.	.280	.436	153	626	79	175	273	38	6	16	66	5	25	30	12
Burris, B. Ray, Mtl.	.231	.282	40	39	2	9	11	2	0	0	2	0	4	15	0
*Butler, Brett, Atl.	.281	.393	151	549	84	154	216	21	13	5	37	2	54	56	39
Bystrom, Martin, Phil.	.237	.263	24	38	2	9	10	1	0	0	4	0	2	14	0

Player & Club	PCT	SLUG	G	AB	R	H	TB	2B	3B	HR	RBI	GW	BB	SO	SB
Calvert, Mark, S.F.	.000	.000	18	8	0	0	0	0	0	0	0	0	1	6	0
Camp, Rick, Atl.	.077	.103	40	39	3	3	4	1	0	0	2	0	0	16	0
Campbell, William, Chi.	.100	.100	82	10	0	1	1	0	0	0	1	0	0	3	0
#Candelaria, John, Pitt.	.138	.154	33	65	4	9	10	1	0	0	2	1	5	17	0
*Carlton, Steven, Phil.	.196	.247	37	97	9	19	24	5	0	0	1	0	2	20	0
*Carman, Donald, Phil.	---	---	1	0	0	0	0	0	0	0	0	0	0	0	0
Carter, Gary, Mtl.	.270	.444	145	541	63	146	240	37	3	17	79	5	51	57	1
Carter, Joseph, Chi.	.176	.235	23	51	6	9	12	1	1	0	1	0	0	21	1
Cato, J. Keefe, Cin.	---	---	4	0	0	0	0	0	0	0	0	0	0	0	0
Cedeno, Cesar, Cin.	.232	.361	98	332	40	77	120	16	0	9	39	4	33	53	13
Cey, Ronald, Chi.	.275	.460	159	581	73	160	267	33	1	24	90	11	62	85	0
*Chambliss, C. Christopher, Atl.	.280	.481	131	447	59	125	215	24	3	20	78	10	63	68	2
Chiffer, Floyd, S.D.	.000	.000	15	1	0	0	0	0	0	0	0	0	0	1	0
*Chris, Michael, S.F.	.000	.000	7	2	0	0	0	0	0	0	0	0	0	0	0
Christenson, Larry, Phil.	.059	.118	9	17	0	1	2	1	0	0	1	0	0	8	0
*Christmas, Stephen, Cin.	.059	.059	9	17	0	1	1	0	0	0	1	0	1	3	0
Citarella, Ralph, St.L.	.000	.000	6	1	0	0	0	0	0	0	0	0	0	0	0
Clark, Jack, S.F.	.268	.441	135	492	82	132	217	25	0	20	66	11	74	79	5
*Comer, Steven, Phil.	.000	.000	3	1	0	0	0	0	0	0	0	0	0	0	0
Concepcion, David, Cin.	.233	.280	143	528	54	123	148	22	0	1	47	8	56	81	14
Connally, Fritzie, Chi.	.100	.100	8	10	0	1	1	0	0	0	0	0	0	5	0
*Corcoran, Timothy, Phil.	---	---	3	0	0	0	0	0	0	0	0	0	0	0	0
Couchee, Michael, S.D.	.500	.500	8	2	0	1	1	0	0	0	0	0	0	0	0
Cox, Danny, St.L.	.074	.074	12	27	1	2	2	0	0	0	0	0	0	12	0
*Cromartie, Warren, Mtl.	.278	.386	120	360	37	100	139	26	2	3	43	8	43	48	8
*Crowley, Terrence, Mtl.	.182	.182	50	44	2	8	8	0	0	0	3	1	9	4	0
*Cruz, Jose, Hou.	.318	.463	160	594	85	189	275	28	8	14	92	9	65	86	30
Darling, Ronald, N.Y.	.100	.100	5	10	0	1	1	0	0	0	0	0	0	3	0
*Daulton, Darren, Phil.	.333	.333	2	3	1	1	1	0	0	0	0	0	1	1	0
#Davis, Charles, S.F.	.233	.352	137	486	54	113	171	21	2	11	59	9	55	108	10
Davis, Gerald, S.D.	.333	.467	5	15	3	5	7	2	0	0	1	0	3	4	1
Davis, Jody, Chi.	.271	.480	151	510	56	138	245	31	2	24	84	8	33	93	0
*Davis, Mark, S.F.	.133	.167	20	30	3	4	5	1	0	0	1	0	3	8	0
Dawley, William, Hou.	.222	.222	48	9	0	2	2	0	0	0	1	0	0	3	0
Dawson, Andre, Mtl.	.299	.539	159	633	104	189	341	36	10	32	113	14	38	81	25
*Dayley, Kenneth, Atl.	.219	.219	25	32	2	7	7	0	0	0	1	0	4	11	0
Decker, D. Martin, S.D.	---	---	4	0	0	0	0	0	0	0	0	0	0	0	0
Dedmon, Jeffrey, Atl.	---	---	5	0	0	0	0	0	0	0	0	0	0	0	0
DeJesus, Ivan, Phil.	.254	.336	158	497	60	126	167	15	7	4	45	7	53	77	11
DeLeon, Jose, Pitt.	.059	.059	15	34	2	2	2	0	0	0	0	0	6	16	0
DeLeon, Luis, S.D.	.143	.143	65	14	3	2	2	0	0	0	0	0	1	8	0
Denny, John, Phil.	.169	.182	36	77	7	13	14	1	0	0	2	0	2	16	2
Dernier, Robert, Phil.	.231	.290	122	221	41	51	64	10	0	1	15	3	18	21	35
Diaz, Baudilio, Phil.	.236	.367	136	471	49	111	173	17	0	15	64	7	38	57	1
Diaz, Carlos, N.Y.	.000	.000	54	5	1	0	0	0	0	0	0	0	1	2	0
Diaz, Michael, Chi.	.286	.429	6	7	2	2	3	1	0	0	1	0	0	0	0
#Dilone, Miguel, Pitt.	---	---	7	0	1	0	0	0	0	0	0	0	0	0	2
*DiPino, Frank, Hou.	.167	.333	53	6	1	1	2	1	0	0	1	0	1	1	0
Dixon, Thomas, Mtl.	---	---	4	0	0	0	0	0	0	0	0	0	0	0	0
#Doran, William, Hou.	.271	.364	154	535	70	145	195	12	7	8	39	2	86	67	12
*Doyle, Jeffrey, St.L.	.297	.432	13	37	4	11	16	1	2	0	2	0	1	3	0
Dravecky, David, S.D.	.098	.131	28	61	4	6	8	2	0	0	1	1	3	19	0
*Driessen, Daniel, Cin.	.277	.420	122	386	57	107	162	17	1	12	57	8	75	51	6
*Durham, Leon, Chi.	.258	.466	100	337	58	87	157	18	8	12	55	5	66	83	12
*Easler, Michael, Pitt.	.307	.441	115	381	44	117	168	17	2	10	54	8	22	64	4
Esasky, Nicholas, Cin.	.265	.450	85	302	41	80	136	10	5	12	46	5	27	99	6
#Espy, Cecil, L.A.	.273	.364	20	11	4	3	4	1	0	0	1	0	1	2	0
*Evans, Darrell, S.F.	.277	.516	142	523	94	145	270	29	3	30	82	15	84	81	6
*Falcone, Peter, Atl.	.115	.115	33	26	0	3	3	0	0	0	2	0	0	5	0
Farmer, Edward, Phil.	.167	.167	12	6	0	1	1	0	0	0	0	0	0	2	0
*Fernandez, C. Sid, L.A.	1.000	1.000	2	1	0	1	1	0	0	0	0	0	0	0	0
Fimple, John, L.A.	.250	.358	54	148	16	37	53	8	1	2	22	1	11	39	1
#Fireovid, Stephen, S.D.	---	---	3	0	0	0	0	0	0	0	0	0	0	0	0
Fitzgerald, Michael, N.Y.	.100	.250	8	20	1	2	5	0	0	1	2	0	3	6	0
*Flannery, Timothy, S.D.	.234	.336	92	214	24	50	72	7	3	3	19	0	20	23	2
Flynn, R. Douglas, Mtl.	.237	.294	143	452	44	107	133	18	4	0	26	3	19	38	2
*Foley, Thomas, Cin.	.204	.265	68	98	7	20	26	4	1	0	9	1	13	17	1
Forsch, Robert, St.L.	.241	.352	37	54	4	13	19	3	0	1	6	1	3	14	0
*Forster, Terry, Atl.	.500	.625	56	8	1	4	5	1	0	0	0	0	0	1	0
Foster, George, N.Y.	.241	.419	157	601	74	145	252	19	2	28	90	12	38	111	1
*Francona, Terry, Mtl.	.257	.352	120	230	21	59	81	11	1	3	22	1	6	20	0
*Frobel, Douglas, Pitt.	.283	.533	32	60	10	17	32	4	1	3	11	1	4	17	1
Fryman, Woodrow, Mtl.	---	---	6	0	0	0	0	0	0	0	0	0	0	0	0
Fuentes, Michael, Mtl.	.250	.250	6	4	1	1	1	0	0	0	0	0	0	2	0
Gaff, Brent, N.Y.	.000	.000	4	3	0	0	0	0	0	0	0	0	0	1	0
Gale, Richard, Cin.	.150	.350	33	20	2	3	7	1	0	1	3	0	2	16	0
Garber, H. Eugene, Atl.	.000	.000	43	3	1	0	0	0	0	0	0	0	2	2	0
Garcia, Alfonso, Phil.	.288	.415	84	118	22	34	49	7	1	2	9	1	9	20	1
Gardenhire, Ronald, N.Y.	.063	.063	17	32	1	2	2	0	0	0	1	0	1	4	0
Garner, Philip, Hou.	.238	.362	154	567	76	135	205	24	2	14	79	10	63	84	18
Garrelts, Scott, S.F.	.222	.222	5	9	1	2	2	0	0	0	0	0	0	4	0
Garvey, Steven, S.D.	.294	.459	100	388	76	114	178	22	0	14	59	9	29	39	4

Player & Club	PCT	SLUG	G	AB	R	H	TB	2B	3B	HR	RBI	GW	BB	SO
Ghelfi, Anthony, Phil.	.250	.250	3	4	0	1	1	0	0	0	0	0	0	0
Giles, Brian, N.Y.	.245	.298	145	400	39	98	119	15	0	2	27	2	36	77
Gladden, C. Daniel, S.F.	.222	.302	18	63	6	14	19	2	0	1	9	2	5	11
*Gorman, Thomas, N.Y.	.250	.250	25	4	0	1	1	0	0	0	0	0	0	2
*Grant, Thomas, Chi.	.150	.200	16	20	2	3	4	1	0	0	2	0	3	4
Grapenthin, Richard, Mtl.	.000	.000	1	1	0	0	0	0	0	0	0	0	0	0
Green, David, St.L.	.284	.422	146	422	52	120	178	14	10	8	69	6	26	76
*Gross, Gregory, Phil.	.302	.376	136	245	25	74	92	12	3	0	29	5	34	16
Gross, Kevin, Phil.	.091	.121	17	33	1	3	4	1	0	0	1	1	1	14
Guante, Cecilio, Pitt.	.091	.091	49	22	1	2	2	0	0	0	0	0	2	14
Guerrero, Pedro, L.A.	.298	.531	160	584	87	174	310	28	6	32	103	13	72	110
Gullickson, William, Mtl.	.134	.232	34	82	10	11	19	5	0	1	3	1	4	27
Gwosdz, Douglas, S.D.	.109	.182	39	55	7	6	10	1	0	1	4	1	7	19
*Gwynn, Anthony, S.D.	.309	.372	86	304	34	94	113	12	2	1	37	6	23	21
Hagen, Kevin, St.L.	.000	.000	9	5	0	0	0	0	0	0	0	0	0	4
#Hall, Albert, Atl.	.000	.000	10	8	2	0	0	0	0	0	0	0	2	2
*Hall, Melvin, Chi.	.283	.488	112	410	60	116	200	23	5	17	56	3	42	101
Hammaker, C. Atlee, S.F.	.102	.102	23	59	1	6	6	0	0	0	2	0	4	19
Hargesheimer, Alan, Chi.	---	---	5	0	0	0	0	0	0	0	0	0	0	0
Harper, Brian, Pitt.	.221	.427	61	131	16	29	56	4	1	7	20	1	2	15
Harper, Terry, Atl.	.264	.383	80	201	19	53	77	13	1	3	26	4	20	43
#Harris, Greg, Cin.	.000	.000	1	1	0	0	0	0	0	0	0	0	0	0
Hawkins, M. Andrew, S.D.	.065	.065	21	31	3	2	2	0	0	0	0	0	4	9
Hayes, Ben, Cin.	.000	.000	60	5	0	0	0	0	0	0	0	0	0	2
*Hayes, Von, Phil.	.265	.370	124	351	45	93	130	9	5	6	32	6	36	55
Heathcock, R. Jeffrey, Hou.	.000	.000	6	6	0	0	0	0	0	0	0	0	0	4
*Hebner, Richard, Pitt.	.265	.395	78	162	23	43	64	4	1	5	26	3	17	28
*Heep, Daniel, N.Y.	.253	.395	115	253	30	64	100	12	0	8	21	3	29	40
Hendrick, George, St.L.	.318	.493	144	529	73	168	261	33	3	18	97	12	51	76
*Hernandez, Guillermo, Chi.-Phil.	.400	.400	74	15	2	6	6	0	0	0	1	0	0	5
*Hernandez, Keith, St.L.-N.Y.	.297	.433	150	538	77	160	233	23	7	12	63	9	88	72
#Herr, Thomas, St.L.	.323	.412	89	313	43	101	129	14	4	2	31	6	43	27
Hershiser, Orel, L.A.	---	---	8	0	0	0	0	0	0	0	0	0	0	0
Hinshaw, George, S.D.	.438	.500	7	16	1	7	8	1	0	0	4	1	0	4
*Hodges, Ronald, N.Y.	.260	.308	110	250	20	65	77	12	0	0	21	2	49	42
Holland, Alfred, Phil.	.000	.000	68	7	0	0	0	0	0	0	0	0	0	5
Holman, R. Scott, N.Y.	.217	.217	35	23	1	5	5	0	0	0	2	0	0	9
*Honeycutt, Frederick, L.A.	.083	.083	9	12	1	1	1	0	0	0	1	0	0	0
Hooton, Burt, L.A.	.160	.200	33	50	5	8	10	2	0	0	7	1	3	15
Horner, J. Robert, Atl.	.303	.528	104	386	75	117	204	25	1	20	68	10	50	63
#Householder, Paul, Cin.	.255	.387	123	380	40	97	147	24	4	6	43	3	44	60
#Howard, Michael, N.Y.	.333	.333	1	3	0	1	1	0	0	0	1	1	0	1
*Howe, Steven, L.A.	.125	.125	46	8	1	1	1	0	0	0	0	0	1	3
Hubbard, Glenn, Atl.	.263	.402	148	517	65	136	208	24	6	12	70	4	55	71
Hudson, Charles, Phil.	.093	.093	27	54	4	5	5	0	0	0	3	0	2	32
Hume, Thomas, Cin.	.000	.000	48	5	0	0	0	0	0	0	0	0	0	2
*Hurdle, Clinton, N.Y.	.182	.242	13	33	3	6	8	2	0	0	2	0	2	10
*Iorg, Dane, St.L.	.267	.362	58	116	6	31	42	9	1	0	11	1	10	11
Jacoby, Brook, Atl.	.000	.000	4	8	0	0	0	0	0	0	0	0	0	1
James, Robert, Mtl.	.286	.286	27	7	0	2	2	0	0	0	1	0	0	4
Jeltz, L. Steven, Phil.	.125	.375	13	8	0	1	3	0	1	0	1	0	1	2
Jenkins, Ferguson, Chi.	.245	.321	33	53	3	13	17	2	1	0	5	0	1	8
Johnson, Randall G., Atl.	.250	.292	86	144	22	36	42	3	0	1	17	5	20	27
#Johnson, Wallace, Mtl.-S.F.	.200	.200	10	10	1	2	2	0	0	0	1	0	1	0
Johnson, William, Chi.	---	---	10	0	0	0	0	0	0	0	0	0	0	0
*Johnstone, John, Chi.	.257	.436	86	140	16	36	61	7	0	6	22	1	20	24
Jones, Jeffrey R., Cin.	.227	.295	16	44	6	10	13	3	0	0	5	1	11	13
*Jones, Ruppert, S.D.	.233	.394	133	335	42	78	132	12	3	12	49	8	35	58
*Jorgensen, Michael, N.Y.-Atl.	.250	.389	95	72	10	18	28	4	0	2	11	0	10	12
*Kaat, James, St.L.	.000	.000	24	4	0	0	0	0	0	0	0	0	0	2
*Keener, Jeffrey, St.L.	---	---	4	0	0	0	0	0	0	0	0	0	0	0
Kennedy, Junior, Chi.	.136	.136	17	22	3	3	3	0	0	0	3	0	1	6
*Kennedy, Terrence, S.D.	.284	.434	149	549	47	156	238	27	2	17	98	14	51	89
Kingman, Brian, S.F.	---	---	3	0	0	0	0	0	0	0	0	0	0	0
Kingman, David, N.Y.	.198	.383	100	248	25	49	95	7	0	13	29	1	22	57
*Knepper, Robert, Hou.	.182	.288	35	66	5	12	19	2	1	1	5	1	2	25
Knicely, Alan, Cin.	.224	.316	59	98	11	22	31	3	0	2	10	1	16	28
Knight, C. Ray, Hou.	.304	.444	145	507	43	154	225	36	4	9	70	8	42	62
Komminsk, Brad, Atl.	.222	.278	19	36	2	8	10	2	0	0	4	1	5	7
*Krenchicki, Wayne, Cin.	.273	.299	51	77	6	21	23	2	0	0	11	2	8	4
Krukow, Michael, S.F.	.254	.333	31	63	3	16	21	2	0	1	8	0	2	15
*Kuiper, Duane, S.F.	.250	.284	72	176	14	44	50	2	2	0	14	1	27	13
LaCorte, Frank, Hou.	.200	.400	37	5	0	1	2	1	0	0	1	0	0	0
LaCoss, Michael, Hou.	.086	.086	38	35	1	3	3	0	0	0	1	0	1	12
Lacy, Leondaus, Pitt.	.302	.406	108	288	40	87	117	12	3	4	13	1	22	36
Lahti, Jeffrey, St.L.	.000	.000	53	10	0	0	0	0	0	0	0	0	0	5
Lake, Steven, Chi.	.259	.365	38	85	9	22	31	4	1	1	7	1	2	6
#Landestoy, Rafael, Cin.-L.A.	.159	.246	71	69	6	11	17	1	1	1	1	0	3	8
*Landreaux, Kenneth, L.A.	.281	.451	141	481	63	135	217	25	3	17	66	16	34	52
Landrum, Terry, St.L.	.200	.600	6	5	0	1	3	0	1	0	0	0	1	2
Lansford, Joseph, S.D.	.250	.625	12	8	1	2	5	0	0	1	2	0	0	3
*LaPoint, David, St.L.	.153	.153	37	59	4	9	9	0	0	0	5	0	7	20

Player & Club	PCT	SLUG	G	AB	R	H	TB	2B	3B	HR	RBI	GW	BB	SO	SB
kin, Patrick, S.F.	.000	.000	5	1	0	0	0	0	0	0	0	0	0	1	0
key, William, S.F.	.106	.106	26	47	5	5	5	0	0	0	1	0	7	21	0
elle, Gary, S.F.	.000	.000	56	14	0	0	0	0	0	0	0	0	0	7	0
, Charles, Mtl.	.114	.129	33	70	6	8	9	1	0	0	3	0	2	29	0
ry, Timothy, N.Y.	.333	.333	2	3	0	1	1	0	0	0	0	0	0	1	0
ebvre, Joseph, S.D.-Phil.	.306	.522	119	278	35	85	145	20	8	8	39	7	33	49	5
ferts, Craig, Chi.	.111	.111	56	18	1	2	2	0	0	0	0	0	1	9	0
aster, Johnnie, S.F.	.240	.307	141	534	81	128	164	16	1	6	30	1	60	96	39
nard, Jeffrey, S.F.	.279	.461	139	516	74	144	238	17	7	21	87	6	35	116	26
ch, Randy, Mtl.-S.F.	.222	.333	26	9	0	2	3	1	0	0	0	0	1	0	0
ley, Bradley, Cin.	---	---	5	0	0	0	0	0	0	0	0	0	0	0	0
cano, Sixto, S.D.-Phil.	.239	.351	115	356	49	85	125	12	2	8	56	8	52	75	1
tle, R. Bryan, Mtl.	.260	.329	106	350	48	91	115	15	3	1	36	4	50	22	4
lar, W. Timothy, S.D.	.241	.345	31	58	7	14	20	1	1	1	11	1	5	12	0
cks, Scott, Hou.	.214	.214	7	14	2	3	3	0	0	0	0	0	1	4	2
iglio, John, Chi.	.000	.000	1	1	0	0	0	0	0	0	0	0	0	1	0
as, Gary, S.D.	.000	.000	62	12	0	0	0	0	0	0	1	0	0	5	0
ch, Edward, N.Y.	.154	.154	30	52	3	8	8	0	0	0	4	0	1	17	0
ns, William, St.L.	.167	.217	42	60	3	10	13	1	1	0	3	0	1	11	3
den, Michael, Hou.	.045	.045	28	22	0	1	1	0	0	0	2	0	1	12	0
dox, Garry, Phil.	.275	.367	97	324	27	89	119	14	2	4	32	0	17	31	7
lock, Bill, Pitt.	.323	.444	130	473	68	153	210	21	0	12	68	14	49	24	3
ler, Richard, Atl.	.000	.000	10	2	0	0	0	0	0	0	0	0	0	1	0
donado, Candido, L.A.	.194	.290	42	62	5	12	18	1	1	1	6	1	5	14	0
shall, Michael, L.A.	.284	.434	140	465	47	132	202	17	1	17	65	11	43	127	7
tin, D. Renie, S.F.	.346	.577	37	26	4	9	15	2	2	0	1	0	0	8	1
tin, John, St.L.	.222	.278	26	18	1	4	5	1	0	0	4	0	0	2	0
tinez, Carmelo, Chi.	.258	.494	29	89	8	23	44	3	0	6	16	1	4	19	0
thews, Gary, Phil.	.258	.374	132	446	66	115	167	18	2	10	50	3	69	81	13
uszek, Leonard, Phil.	.275	.525	28	80	12	22	42	6	1	4	16	0	4	14	0
, Milton, S.F.-Pitt.	.247	.369	73	198	18	49	73	6	0	6	20	4	22	24	2
zilli, Lee, Pitt.	.240	.337	109	246	37	59	83	9	0	5	24	5	49	43	15
affigan, Andrew, S.F.	.067	.133	43	30	0	2	4	2	0	0	3	0	1	20	0
ee, Willie, St.L.	.286	.374	147	601	75	172	225	22	8	5	75	9	26	98	39
raw, Frank, Phil.	.333	.333	34	3	0	1	1	0	0	0	0	0	0	0	0
urtry, J. Craig, Atl.	.086	.086	36	70	2	6	6	0	0	0	3	0	3	40	0
eynolds, W. Kevin, S.D.	.221	.343	39	140	15	31	48	3	1	4	14	2	12	29	2
illiams, Larry, Pitt.	.114	.127	35	79	5	9	10	1	0	0	4	1	1	32	1
bourne, Lawrence, Phil.	.242	.273	41	66	3	16	18	0	1	0	4	2	4	7	2
ls, J. Bradley, Mtl.	.250	.250	14	20	1	5	5	0	0	0	1	0	2	3	0
ner, Eddie, Cin.	.261	.384	146	502	77	131	193	23	6	9	33	1	68	60	41
ton, Gregory, S.F.	.545	.909	73	11	4	6	10	1	0	1	3	0	2	2	0
erock, John, Hou.	.153	.259	33	85	8	13	22	4	1	1	10	1	12	15	0
inaro, Robert, Phil.	.111	.333	19	18	1	2	6	1	0	1	3	1	0	2	0
day, Robert, L.A.	.247	.399	99	178	21	44	71	7	1	6	20	4	29	42	0
ge, Isidro, Phil.-S.D.	.091	.091	61	11	0	1	1	0	0	0	0	0	0	3	0
tefusco, John, S.D.	.053	.053	31	19	1	1	1	0	0	0	1	0	2	11	0
re, Donnie, Atl.	.500	.500	43	8	0	4	4	0	0	0	3	0	0	2	0
ales, Jose, L.A.	.283	.509	47	53	4	15	27	3	0	3	8	1	1	11	0
ales, Julio, Chi.	.195	.299	63	87	11	17	26	9	0	0	11	2	7	19	0
land, B. Keith, Chi.	.302	.460	154	533	76	161	245	30	3	16	70	11	68	73	0
eno, Omar, Hou.	.242	.326	97	405	48	98	132	12	11	0	25	1	22	72	30
gan, Joe, Phil.	.230	.403	123	404	72	93	163	20	1	16	59	7	89	54	18
rison, James, Pitt.	.304	.487	66	158	16	48	77	7	2	6	25	5	9	25	2
kau, Paul, Chi.	.182	.273	8	11	2	2	3	1	0	0	0	0	0	0	0
phrey, Jerry, Hou.	.336	.455	44	143	17	48	65	10	2	1	17	2	22	23	5
phy, Dale, Atl.	.302	.540	162	589	131	178	318	24	4	36	121	14	90	110	30
ray, Richard, S.F.	.200	.200	4	10	0	2	2	0	0	0	1	0	0	3	0
osia, Steven, Pitt.-S.F.	.215	.278	36	79	8	17	22	2	0	1	7	0	4	9	0
denfuer, Thomas, L.A.	.000	.000	66	4	1	0	0	0	0	0	0	0	0	0	0
kro, Joseph, Hou.	.094	.118	38	85	1	8	10	2	0	0	2	0	0	22	0
kro, Philip, Atl.	.185	.215	34	65	3	12	14	2	0	0	5	0	1	12	0
mann, Randy, Pitt.	.000	.000	8	1	0	0	0	0	0	0	0	0	0	0	0
s, Dickie, Chi.	.237	.263	24	38	1	9	10	1	0	0	5	0	1	17	0
hagen, Wayne, Chi.	.143	.257	21	35	1	5	9	1	0	1	4	0	0	5	0
kfell, Kenneth, St.L.	.293	.385	151	488	62	143	188	26	5	3	38	6	61	27	12
ter, Ronald, Cin.	.264	.384	157	549	63	145	211	23	5	11	58	5	49	106	2
ver, Albert, Mtl.	.300	.410	157	614	70	184	252	38	3	8	84	12	44	44	1
lley, Thomas, S.F.	.259	.339	135	410	40	106	139	16	1	5	45	8	52	47	2
ndo, Jose, N.Y.	.213	.244	120	328	29	70	80	7	0	1	17	3	19	60	8
co, Jesse, N.Y.	.333	.333	62	12	0	4	4	0	0	0	2	0	1	3	0
lak, Joseph, Pitt.	.182	.182	7	11	0	2	2	0	0	0	1	0	0	2	0
z, Adalberto, Pitt.-N.Y.	.249	.275	73	193	11	48	53	5	0	0	12	1	4	34	1
inko, Robert, Pitt.	---	---	1	0	0	0	0	0	0	0	0	0	0	0	0
, Dave, Chi.	.091	.182	16	22	1	2	4	0	1	0	2	0	2	7	1
, Lawrence, Atl.	.118	.118	17	17	0	2	2	0	0	0	1	1	0	2	0
ey, Richard, N.Y.	.111	.111	12	9	2	1	1	0	0	0	0	0	0	2	0
s, Kelly, Cin.	.250	.300	56	120	13	30	36	6	0	0	7	0	15	22	8
er, David, Pitt.	.279	.411	144	552	68	154	227	29	4	12	69	10	28	89	12
ore, Frank, Cin.	.186	.271	36	59	6	11	16	2	0	1	5	1	2	19	0
erson, Reginald, Chi.	.000	.000	5	6	1	0	0	0	0	0	0	0	0	2	0
, Adalberto, Hou.	.125	.125	4	8	0	1	1	0	0	0	0	0	2	2	0

Player & Club	PCT	SLUG	G	AB	R	H	TB	2B	3B	HR	RBI	GW	BB	SO
Pena, Alejandro, L.A.	.100	.150	34	60	2	6	9	0	0	1	4	1	0	21
Pena, Antonio, Pitt.	.301	.435	151	542	51	163	236	22	3	15	70	2	31	73
Perez, Atanasio, Phil.	.241	.372	91	253	18	61	94	11	2	6	43	8	28	57
Perez, Pascual, Atl.	.160	.160	33	75	4	12	12	0	0	0	3	0	3	27
*Perry, Gerald, Atl.	.359	.487	27	39	5	14	19	2	0	1	6	1	5	4
Pettini, Joseph, S.F.	.186	.209	61	86	11	16	18	0	1	0	7	0	9	11
*Phillips, Michael, Mtl.	.000	.000	5	2	0	0	0	0	0	0	0	0	0	0
*Pocoroba, Biff, Atl.	.267	.367	55	120	11	32	44	6	0	2	16	1	12	7
*Porter, Darrell, St.L.	.262	.431	145	443	57	116	191	24	3	15	66	5	68	94
Power, Ted, Cin.	.000	.000	49	16	0	0	0	0	0	0	0	0	1	14
Price, Joseph, Cin.	.098	.098	21	41	0	4	4	0	0	0	0	0	3	14
Proly, Michael, Chi.	.091	.091	60	11	1	1	1	0	0	0	0	0	1	3
Pruitt, Ronald, S.F.	.000	.000	1	1	0	0	0	0	0	0	0	0	0	0
*Puhl, Terry, Hou.	.292	.428	137	465	66	136	199	25	7	8	44	5	36	48
Pujols, Luis, Hou.	.195	.218	40	87	4	17	19	2	0	0	12	4	5	14
Puleo, Charles, Cin.	.100	.100	27	50	4	5	5	0	0	0	3	0	4	18
*Pulido, Alfonso, Pitt.	---	---	1	0	0	0	0	0	0	0	0	0	0	0
*Quirk, James, St.L.	.209	.326	48	86	3	18	28	2	1	2	11	1	6	27
Rabb, John, S.F.	.231	.346	40	104	10	24	36	9	0	1	14	0	9	17
#Raines, Timothy, Mtl.	.298	.429	156	615	133	183	264	32	8	11	71	13	97	70
Rainey, Charles, Chi.	.161	.161	34	56	4	9	9	0	0	0	0	0	6	20
*Rajsich, Gary, N.Y.	.333	.500	11	36	5	12	18	3	0	1	3	0	3	1
Ramirez, Mario, S.D.	.196	.308	55	107	11	21	33	6	3	0	12	0	20	23
Ramirez, Rafael, Atl.	.297	.368	152	622	82	185	229	13	5	7	58	10	36	48
Ramos, Roberto, Mtl.	.230	.311	27	61	2	14	19	3	1	0	5	0	8	11
#Ramsey, Michael, St.L.	.263	.337	97	175	25	46	59	4	3	1	16	2	12	23
Ransom, Jeffrey, S.F.	.200	.350	6	20	3	4	7	0	0	1	3	1	4	7
*Rasmussen, Dennis, S.D.	.000	.000	4	3	0	0	0	0	0	0	0	0	0	2
Rasmussen, Eric, St.L.	---	---	6	0	0	0	0	0	0	0	0	0	0	0
#Ray, Johnny, Pitt.	.283	.399	151	576	68	163	230	38	7	5	53	5	35	26
Rayford, Floyd, St.L.	.212	.337	56	104	5	22	35	4	0	3	14	2	10	27
Reardon, Jeffrey, Mtl.	.125	.125	66	8	0	1	1	0	0	0	0	0	0	3
Redus, Gary, Cin.	.247	.444	125	453	90	112	201	20	9	17	51	11	71	111
Reed, Ronald, Phil.	.167	.167	61	6	0	1	1	0	0	0	0	0	0	2
Reuschel, Ricky, Chi.	.143	.143	4	7	0	1	1	0	0	0	0	0	0	2
*Reuss, Jerry, L.A.	.282	.310	32	71	4	20	22	2	0	0	3	0	2	28
Reyes, Gilberto, L.A.	.161	.226	19	31	1	5	7	2	0	0	0	0	0	5
*Reynolds, G. Craig, Hou.	.214	.276	65	98	10	21	27	3	0	1	6	3	6	10
#Reynolds, Robert, L.A.	.236	.345	24	55	5	13	19	0	0	2	11	1	3	11
Reynolds, Ronn, N.Y.	.197	.212	24	66	4	13	14	1	0	0	2	0	8	12
Rhoden, Richard, Pitt.	.151	.163	36	86	2	13	14	1	0	0	5	0	0	19
*Richards, Eugene, S.D.	.275	.386	95	233	37	64	90	11	3	3	22	4	17	17
Rivera, German, L.A.	.353	.412	13	17	1	6	7	1	0	0	0	0	2	2
Robinson, Don, Pitt.	.154	.385	10	13	1	2	5	0	0	1	3	1	0	4
Robinson, William, Phil.	.143	.143	10	7	0	1	1	0	0	0	2	0	1	4
*Rodas, Richard, L.A.	---	---	7	0	0	0	0	0	0	0	0	0	0	0
Rodriguez, Edwin, S.D.	.167	.250	7	12	1	2	3	1	0	0	0	0	1	3
#Roenicke, Ronald, L.A.	.221	.290	81	145	12	32	42	4	0	2	12	3	14	26
Rogers, Stephen, Mtl.	.146	.159	36	82	5	12	13	1	0	0	2	1	1	27
*Rohn, Daniel, Chi.	.387	.613	23	31	3	12	19	3	2	0	6	0	2	2
#Roof, Eugene, St.L.-Mtl.	.133	.267	14	15	3	2	4	2	0	0	1	0	1	3
#Rose, Peter, Phil.	.245	.286	151	493	52	121	141	14	3	0	45	5	52	28
Royster, Jeron, Atl.	.235	.328	91	268	32	63	88	10	3	3	30	3	28	35
*Rucker, David, St.L.	.000	.000	34	4	0	0	0	0	0	0	0	0	0	1
Ruhle, Vernon, Hou.	.105	.105	41	19	1	2	2	0	0	0	2	0	3	11
Runge, Paul, Atl.	.250	.250	5	8	0	2	2	0	0	0	1	0	1	4
Russell, Jeffrey, Cin.	.143	.333	10	21	1	3	7	1	0	1	3	0	1	6
Russell, William, L.A.	.246	.286	131	451	47	111	129	13	1	1	30	7	33	31
Ruthven, Richard, Phil.-Chi.	.210	.242	32	62	6	13	15	2	0	0	3	0	2	16
Ryan, L. Nolan, Hou.	.072	.072	29	69	3	5	5	0	0	0	2	0	2	29
Salazar, Argenis, Mtl.	.216	.297	36	37	5	8	11	1	1	0	1	0	1	8
Salazar, Luis, S.D.	.258	.387	134	481	52	124	186	16	2	14	45	3	17	80
Samuel, Juan, Phil.	.277	.446	18	65	14	18	29	1	2	2	5	0	4	16
Sanchez, Alejandro, Phil.	.286	.286	8	7	2	2	2	0	0	0	2	0	0	2
*Sanchez, Orlando, St.L.	.000	.000	6	6	0	0	0	0	0	0	0	0	0	4
Sandberg, Ryne, Chi.	.261	.351	158	633	94	165	222	25	4	8	48	3	51	79
Sanderson, Scott, Mtl.	.143	.214	18	28	1	4	6	2	0	0	1	0	0	8
Santana, Rafael, St.L.	.214	.214	30	14	1	3	3	0	0	0	2	0	2	2
Sarmiento, Manuel, Pitt.	.000	.000	52	10	0	0	0	0	0	0	0	0	1	4
Sax, David, L.A.	.000	.000	7	8	0	0	0	0	0	0	1	0	0	0
Sax, Stephen, L.A.	.281	.350	155	623	94	175	218	18	5	5	41	2	58	73
*Schatzeder, Daniel, Mtl.	.200	.200	58	10	0	2	2	0	0	0	2	0	0	0
*Scherrer, William, Cin.	.091	.091	73	11	0	1	1	0	0	0	0	0	1	3
Schmidt, Michael, Phil.	.255	.524	154	534	104	136	280	16	4	40	109	12	128	148
Schulze, Donald, Chi.	.000	.000	4	1	0	0	0	0	0	0	0	0	1	1
*Scioscia, Michael, L.A.	.314	.486	12	35	3	11	17	3	0	1	7	1	5	2
#Scott, Anthony, Hou.	.226	.301	80	186	20	42	56	6	1	2	17	3	11	39
Scott, Michael, Hou.	.167	.208	24	48	2	8	10	2	0	0	4	0	1	17
*Scurry, Rodney, Pitt.	.000	.000	61	5	0	0	0	0	0	0	0	0	0	4
Seaver, G. Thomas, N.Y.	.156	.219	34	64	6	10	14	0	2	0	4	0	6	26
Sexton, Jimmy, St.L.	.111	.222	6	9	1	1	2	1	0	0	0	0	1	4
#Shines, A. Raymond, Mtl.	.500	.500	3	2	0	1	1	0	0	0	0	0	0	0

Player & Club	PCT	SLUG	G	AB	R	H	TB	2B	3B	HR	RBI	GW	BB	SO	SB
Show, Eric, S.D.	.172	.188	35	64	3	11	12	1	0	0	2	0	1	23	0
Sinatro, Matthew, Atl.	.167	.167	7	12	0	2	2	0	0	0	2	0	2	1	0
Sisk, Douglas, N.Y.	.500	.500	67	6	0	3	3	0	0	0	0	0	0	2	0
Smith, Bryn, Mtl.	.167	.167	49	30	0	5	5	0	0	0	0	0	2	5	0
Smith, Christopher, S.F.	.328	.493	22	67	13	22	33	6	1	1	11	1	7	12	0
Smith, David, Hou.	.000	.000	42	5	0	0	0	0	0	0	0	0	0	3	0
Smith, Kenneth, Atl.	.167	.417	30	12	2	2	5	0	0	1	2	0	1	5	1
Smith, Lee, Chi.	.111	.111	66	9	0	1	1	0	0	0	0	0	1	5	0
Smith, Lonnie, St.L.	.321	.453	130	492	83	158	223	31	5	8	45	3	41	55	43
Smith, Osborne, St.L.	.243	.335	159	552	69	134	185	30	6	3	50	7	64	36	34
Solano, Julio, Hou.	---	---	4	0	0	0	0	0	0	0	0	0	0	0	0
Sosa, Elias, S.D.	.143	.143	41	7	0	1	1	0	0	0	1	0	0	2	0
Soto, Mario, Cin.	.125	.159	35	88	6	11	14	3	0	0	2	0	1	26	0
Speier, Chris, Mtl.	.257	.341	88	261	31	67	89	12	2	2	22	2	29	37	2
Spilman, W. Harry, Hou.	.167	.244	42	78	7	13	19	3	0	1	9	1	5	12	0
Staub, Daniel, N.Y.	.296	.426	104	115	5	34	49	6	0	3	28	3	14	10	0
Stearns, John, N.Y.	---	---	4	0	2	0	0	0	0	0	0	0	0	0	0
Stenhouse, Michael, Mtl.	.125	.150	24	40	2	5	6	1	0	0	2	1	4	10	0
Stewart, David, L.A.	.143	.143	46	7	0	1	1	0	0	0	1	0	0	3	0
Stone, Jeffery, Phil.	.750	1.750	9	4	2	3	7	0	2	0	3	1	0	1	4
Strawberry, Darryl, N.Y.	.257	.512	122	420	63	108	215	15	7	26	74	11	47	128	19
Stuper, John, St.L.	.136	.136	40	59	2	8	8	0	0	0	6	2	4	32	0
Sularz, Guy, S.F.	.100	.100	10	20	3	2	2	0	0	0	0	0	3	2	0
ummers, John, S.F.	.136	.136	29	22	3	3	3	0	0	0	3	0	7	8	0
utter, H. Bruce, St.L.	.000	.000	60	7	0	0	0	0	0	0	0	0	0	4	0
wan, Craig, N.Y.	.077	.077	27	26	0	2	2	0	0	0	1	0	0	11	0
averas, Alejandro, L.A.	.000	.000	10	4	0	0	0	0	0	0	0	0	0	1	0
ekulve, Kenton, Pitt.	.000	.000	76	8	0	0	0	0	0	0	0	0	0	4	0
empleton, Garry, S.D.	.263	.335	126	460	39	121	154	20	2	3	40	8	21	57	16
enace, F. Gene, Pitt.	.177	.258	53	62	7	11	16	5	0	0	6	0	12	17	0
errell, C. Walter, N.Y.	.182	.409	21	44	3	8	18	1	0	3	8	1	1	17	0
homas, Derrel, L.A.	.250	.375	118	192	38	48	72	6	6	2	8	0	27	36	9
hompson, Jason, Pitt.	.259	.406	152	517	70	134	210	20	1	18	76	11	99	128	1
hompson, V. Scot, Chi.	.193	.250	53	88	4	17	22	3	1	0	10	1	3	14	0
hon, Richard, Hou.	.286	.457	154	619	81	177	283	28	9	20	79	18	54	73	34
hurmond, Mark, S.D.	.054	.081	21	37	1	2	3	1	0	0	0	0	2	6	0
olman, Timothy, Hou.	.196	.375	43	56	4	11	21	4	0	2	10	1	6	9	0
omlin, David, Pitt.	---	---	5	0	0	0	0	0	0	0	0	0	0	0	0
orrez, Michael, N.Y.	.046	.046	39	65	2	3	3	0	0	0	2	1	1	20	0
revino, Alejandro, Cin.	.216	.293	74	167	14	36	49	8	1	1	13	0	17	20	0
rillo, J. Manuel, Mtl.	.264	.380	31	121	16	32	46	8	0	2	16	3	10	18	0
rout, Steven, Chi.	.194	.194	34	62	6	12	12	0	0	0	1	0	2	20	0
unnell, B. Lee, Pitt.	.121	.155	35	58	2	7	9	0	1	0	3	0	1	20	0
urner, John, S.D.	.130	.130	25	23	1	3	3	0	0	0	0	0	1	8	0
ail, Michael, S.F.-Mtl.	.241	.354	52	79	6	19	28	3	0	2	7	2	8	17	0
alenzuela, Fernando, L.A.	.187	.253	36	91	5	17	23	3	0	1	9	1	1	23	0
an Slyke, Andrew, St.L.	.262	.421	101	309	51	81	130	15	5	8	38	2	46	64	21
enable, W. McKinley, S.F.	.219	.364	94	228	28	50	83	7	4	6	27	3	22	34	15
eryzer, Thomas, Chi.	.205	.273	59	88	5	18	24	3	0	1	3	0	3	13	0
irgil, Osvaldo, Phil.	.214	.393	55	140	11	30	55	7	0	6	23	3	8	34	0
on Ohlen, David, St.L.	.143	.143	46	7	0	1	1	0	0	0	0	0	1	3	0
alk, Robert, Atl.	.000	.000	1	1	0	0	0	0	0	0	1	0	0	0	0
alker, Duane, Cin.	.236	.324	109	225	14	53	73	12	1	2	29	3	20	43	6
allach, Timothy, Mtl.	.269	.434	156	581	54	156	252	33	3	19	70	8	55	97	0
alling, Dennis, Hou.	.296	.444	100	135	24	40	60	5	3	3	19	4	15	16	2
ashington, Claudell, Atl.	.278	.413	134	496	75	138	205	24	8	9	44	5	35	103	31
atson, Robert, Atl.	.309	.490	65	149	14	46	73	9	0	6	37	7	18	23	0
elch, Robert, L.A.	.096	.151	31	73	2	7	11	1	0	1	2	1	1	22	0
ellman, Brad, S.F.	.214	.247	82	182	15	39	45	3	0	1	16	1	22	39	5
elsh, Christopher, S.D.-Mtl.	.222	.222	23	18	0	4	4	0	0	0	2	1	1	4	0
hite, Jerome, Mtl.	.147	.176	40	34	4	5	6	1	0	0	0	0	12	8	4
hite, Larry, L.A.	---	---	4	0	0	0	0	0	0	0	0	0	0	0	0
hitson, Eddie, S.D.	.182	.182	31	44	1	8	8	0	0	0	3	0	2	11	0
ieghaus, Thomas, Mtl.	---	---	1	0	0	0	0	0	0	0	0	0	0	0	0
iggins, Alan, S.D.	.276	.324	144	503	83	139	163	20	2	0	22	2	65	43	66
illiams, Dallas, Cin.	.056	.056	18	36	2	2	2	0	0	0	1	0	3	6	0
ilson, William, N.Y.	.276	.367	152	638	91	176	234	25	6	7	51	6	18	103	54
nn, James, Pitt.	---	---	7	0	0	0	0	0	0	0	0	0	0	0	0
ohlford, James, Mtl.	.277	.355	83	141	7	39	50	8	0	1	14	0	5	14	0
oods, Gary, Chi.	.242	.353	93	190	25	46	67	9	0	4	22	3	15	27	5
otus, Ronald, Pitt.	.000	.000	5	3	0	0	0	0	0	0	0	0	0	1	0
ight, J. Richard, L.A.	---	---	6	0	0	0	0	0	0	0	0	0	0	0	0
ynne, Marvell, Pitt.	.243	.355	103	366	66	89	130	16	2	7	26	3	38	52	12
eager, Stephen, L.A.	.203	.379	113	335	31	68	127	8	3	15	41	6	23	57	1
oungblood, Joel, S.F.	.292	.499	124	373	59	109	186	20	3	17	53	6	33	59	7
chry, Patrick, L.A.	.500	.500	40	4	0	2	2	0	0	0	0	0	0	1	0
vella, Paul, Atl.	.000	.000	3	5	0	0	0	0	0	0	0	0	2	1	0

CLUB BATTING

Club	PCT	SLUG	G	AB	R	H	TB	2B	3B	HR	RBI	BB	SO	SB	LOB	SHO
Atlanta	.272	.400	162	5472	746	1489	2187	218	45	130	691	582	847	146	1155	7
St. Louis	.270	.384	162	5550	679	1496	2133	262	63	83	636	543	879	207	1175	1[illegible]
Montreal	.264	.386	163	5611	677	1482	2167	297	41	102	632	509	733	138	1213	1[illegible]
Pittsburgh	.264	.383	162	5531	659	1460	2119	238	29	121	612	497	873	124	1142	7
Chicago	.261	.401	162	5512	701	1436	2212	272	42	140	649	470	868	84	1120	8
Houston	.257	.375	162	5502	643	1412	2062	239	60	97	615	517	869	164	1145	9
San Diego	.250	.351	163	5527	653	1384	1938	207	34	93	592	482	822	179	1103	1[illegible]
Los Angeles	.250	.379	163	5440	654	1358	2061	197	34	146	613	541	925	166	1104	[illegible]
Philadelphia	.249	.373	163	5426	696	1352	2026	209	45	125	649	640	906	143	1154	1[illegible]
San Francisco	.247	.375	162	5369	687	1324	2016	206	30	142	638	619	990	140	1104	6
New York	.241	.344	162	5444	575	1314	1874	172	26	112	542	436	1031	141	1041	1[illegible]
Cincinnati	.239	.356	162	5333	623	1274	1901	236	35	107	577	588	1006	154	1090	1[illegible]
TOTALS	.255	.376	974	65717	7993	16781	24696	2753	484	1398	7446	6424	10749	1786	13546	11[illegible]

PITCHING

INDIVIDUAL PITCHING LEADERS

Earned Run Average	:	2.25	Hammaker, S.F.
Won-Lost Percentage	:	.760	Denny, Phil.
Games Won	:	19	Denny, Phil.
Games Lost	:	17	Torrez, N.Y.
Games	:	82	Campbell, Chi.
Games Started	:	38	Niekro, Hou.
Complete Games	:	18	Soto, Cin.
Games Finished	:	56	Smith, Chi. & Tekulve, Pitt.
Saves	:	29	Smith, Chi.
Shutouts	:	5	Rogers, Mtl.
Batsmen Faced	:	1183	Carlton, Phil.
Innings	:	283	Carlton, Phil.
Hits	:	277	Carlton, Phil.
Runs	:	122	Valenzuela, L.A.
Earned Runs	:	108	Torrez, N.Y.
Home Runs	:	28	Soto, Cin.
Sacrifice Hits	:	27	Valenzuela, L.A.
Sacrifice Flies	:	11	Breining, S.F. & LaPoint, St.L.
Bases on Balls	:	113	Torrez, N.Y.
Intentional Bases on Balls	:	18	Campbell, Chi.
Hit Batsmen	:	7	Bystrom, Phil.
Strikeouts	:	275	Carlton, Phil.
Wild Pitches	:	14	Niekro, Hou.
Balks	:	9	Carlton, Phil.
Games Won, Consecutive	:	9	Orosco, N.Y. (July 22 - September 5)
Games Lost, Consecutive	:	7	McGaffigan, S.F. (May 10 - August 1)
			Pastore, Cin. (April 22 - July 1)
			Reuss, L.A. (June 5 - July 30)

TOP FIFTEEN QUALIFIERS FOR EARNED RUN AVERAGE CHAMPIONSHIP

(*Throws Left-Handed)

Pitcher & Club	W	L	PCT	ERA	G	GS	CG	GF	SV	SHO	IP	H	BFP	R	ER	HR	SH	SF	BB	IB	HB	SO	WP	BK
*Hammaker, C. Atlee, S.F.	10	9	.526	2.25	23	23	8	0	0	3	172.1	147	695	57	43	9	10	4	32	12	3	127	6	2
Denny, John, Phil.	19	6	.760	2.37	36	36	7	0	0	1	242.2	229	983	77	64	9	8	3	53	5	4	139	6	1
Welch, Robert, L.A.	15	12	.556	2.65	31	31	4	0	0	3	204.0	164	828	73	60	13	8	7	72	4	3	156	4	6
Soto, Mario, Cin.	17	13	.567	2.70	34	34	18	0	0	3	273.2	207	1114	96	82	28	8	9	95	6	5	242	2	2
Pena, Alejandro, L.A.	12	9	.571	2.75	34	26	4	4	1	3	177.0	152	730	67	54	7	8	5	51	7	1	120	2	1
*Reuss, Jerry, L.A.	12	11	.522	2.94	32	31	7	0	0	0	223.1	233	935	94	73	12	18	6	50	5	2	143	3	2
Ryan, L. Nolan, Hou.	14	9	.609	2.98	29	29	5	0	0	2	196.1	134	804	74	65	9	7	5	101	3	4	183	5	1
McMurtry, J. Craig, Atl.	15	9	.625	3.08	36	35	6	0	0	3	224.2	204	943	86	77	13	9	5	88	1	1	105	1	2
Rhoden, Richard, Pitt.	13	13	.500	3.09	36	35	7	1	1	2	244.1	256	1012	95	84	13	8	6	68	15	2	153	6	5
*Carlton, Steven, Phil.	15	16	.484	3.11	37	37	8	0	0	3	283.2	277	1183	117	98	20	20	4	84	10	3	275	13	9
Lea, Charles, Mtl.	16	11	.593	3.12	33	33	8	0	0	4	222.0	195	917	87	77	15	4	8	84	4	1	137	8	3
*Knepper, Robert, Hou.	6	13	.316	3.19	35	29	4	2	0	3	203.0	202	867	93	72	12	9	8	71	3	4	125	3	2
Rogers, Stephen, Mtl.	17	12	.586	3.23	36	36	13	0	0	5	273.0	258	1125	108	98	14	12	7	78	12	5	146	6	0
*Candelaria, John, Pitt.	15	8	.652	3.23	33	32	2	0	0	0	197.2	191	797	73	71	15	4	4	45	3	2	157	3	2
*McWilliams, Larry, Pitt.	15	8	.652	3.25	35	35	8	0	0	4	238.0	205	1002	99	86	19	13	6	87	7	3	199	9	4

ALL PITCHERS LISTED ALPHABETICALLY

(*Throws Left-Handed)

Pitcher & Club	W	L	PCT	ERA	G	GS	CG	GF	SV	SHO	IP	H	BFP	R	ER	HR	SH	SF	BB	IB	HB	SO	WP	BK
Allen, Neil, N.Y.-St.L.	12	13	.480	3.94	46	22	5	12	2	3	175.2	179	762	84	77	12	9	2	84	9	1	106	8	1
Altamirano, Porfirio, Phil.	2	3	.400	3.70	31	0	0	11	0	0	41.1	38	173	18	17	9	6	1	15	3	2	24	2	1
Andersen, Larry, Phil.	1	0	1.000	2.39	17	0	0	4	0	0	26.1	19	106	7	7	0	1	1	9	1	0	14	1	1
Andujar, Joaquin, St.L.	6	16	.273	4.16	39	34	5	3	1	2	225.0	215	943	112	104	23	12	3	75	7	3	125	5	6
Bair, C. Douglas, St.L.	1	1	.500	3.03	26	0	0	9	1	0	29.2	24	122	11	10	4	1	1	13	3	0	21	1	0
Baker, Steven, St.L.	0	1	.000	1.80	8	0	0	3	0	0	10.0	10	43	4	2	0	2	1	4	1	1	1	3	0
Bargar, Gregory, Mtl.	2	0	1.000	6.75	8	3	0	1	0	0	20.0	23	94	15	15	6	0	0	8	0	1	9	0	0
Barker, Leonard, Atl.	1	3	.250	3.82	6	6	0	0	0	0	33.0	31	143	17	14	0	3	1	14	2	0	21	2	0
Barr, James, S.F.	5	3	.625	3.98	53	0	0	23	2	0	92.2	106	395	47	41	7	4	9	20	9	1	47	1	0
Beckwith, T. Joseph, L.A.	3	4	.429	3.55	42	3	0	15	1	0	71.0	73	321	40	28	5	7	1	35	11	1	50	1	0
Bedrosian, Stephen, Atl.	9	10	.474	3.60	70	1	0	52	19	0	120.0	100	504	50	48	11	8	4	51	8	4	114	2	0
Behenna, Richard, Atl.	3	3	.500	4.58	14	6	0	1	0	0	37.1	37	160	20	19	7	1	1	12	2	1	17	0	3
Berenyi, Bruce, Cin.	9	14	.391	3.86	32	31	4	1	0	1	186.1	173	816	92	80	9	7	4	102	3	2	151	8	0
Bibby, James, Pitt.	5	12	.294	5.69	29	12	0	6	2	0	78.0	92	367	60	58	10	1	4	51	0	1	44	2	2
Boggs, Thomas, Atl.	0	0	---	5.68	5	0	0	1	0	0	6.1	8	27	4	4	1	1	0	1	0	0	5	1	0

Pitcher & Club	W	L	PCT	ERA	G	GS	CG	GF	SV	SHO	IP	H	BFP	R	ER	HR	SH	SF	BB	IB	HB	SO	WP	BK
Booker, Gregory, S.D.	0	1	.000	7.71	6	1	0	1	0	0	11.2	18	58	10	10	2	1	0	9	0	0	5	0	0
Bordi, Richard, Chi.	0	2	.000	4.97	11	1	0	1	1	0	25.1	34	119	15	14	2	1	0	12	1	0	20	0	0
Breining, Fred, S.F.	11	12	.478	3.82	32	32	6	0	0	0	202.2	202	868	97	86	15	13	11	60	11	5	117	4	1
Brizzolara, Anthony, Atl.	1	0	1.000	3.54	14	0	0	2	1	0	20.1	22	88	8	8	2	3	0	6	0	0	17	0	0
Brusstar, Warren, Chi.	3	1	.750	2.35	59	0	0	21	1	0	80.1	67	335	21	21	1	5	5	37	10	2	46	4	1
Burris, B. Ray, Mtl.	4	7	.364	3.68	40	17	2	6	0	1	154.0	139	641	68	63	13	9	5	56	4	2	100	2	1
Bystrom, Martin, Phil.	6	9	.400	4.60	24	23	1	0	0	1	119.1	136	540	75	61	6	3	8	44	2	7	87	2	1
Calvert, Mark, S.F.	1	4	.200	6.27	18	4	0	5	0	0	37.1	46	190	33	26	2	2	1	34	4	3	14	3	1
Camp, Rick, Atl.	10	9	.526	3.79	40	16	1	4	0	0	140.0	146	590	64	59	16	5	3	38	2	4	61	3	0
Campbell, William, Chi.	6	8	.429	4.49	82	0	0	46	8	0	122.1	128	530	65	61	4	10	5	49	18	1	97	6	1
*Candelaria, John, Pitt.	15	8	.652	3.23	33	32	2	0	0	0	197.2	191	797	73	71	15	4	4	45	3	2	157	3	2
*Carlton, Steven, Phil.	15	16	.484	3.11	37	37	8	0	0	3	283.2	277	1183	117	98	20	20	4	84	10	3	275	13	9
*Carman, Donald, Phil.	0	0	---	0.00	1	0	0	1	1	0	1.0	0	3	0	0	0	0	0	0	0	0	0	0	0
Cato, J. Keefe, Cin.	1	0	1.000	2.45	4	0	0	1	0	0	3.2	2	14	1	1	0	0	0	1	0	0	3	0	0
Chiffer, Floyd, S.D.	0	2	.000	3.18	15	0	0	3	1	0	22.2	17	94	10	8	0	3	0	10	1	0	15	0	1
*Chris, Michael, S.F.	0	0	---	8.10	7	0	0	0	0	0	13.1	16	72	14	12	1	1	1	16	2	2	5	1	0
Christenson, Larry, Phil.	2	4	.333	3.91	9	9	0	0	0	0	48.1	42	203	25	21	2	1	4	17	1	1	44	2	0
Citarella, Ralph, St.L.	0	0	---	1.64	6	0	0	2	0	0	11.0	8	42	2	2	0	0	0	3	1	0	4	1	0
Comer, Steven, Phil.	1	0	1.000	5.19	3	1	0	0	0	0	8.2	11	38	6	5	0	0	0	3	0	0	1	0	0
Couchee, Michael, S.D.	0	1	.000	5.14	8	0	0	2	0	0	14.0	12	63	8	8	1	0	1	6	1	0	5	0	1
Cox, Danny, St.L.	3	6	.333	3.25	12	12	0	0	0	0	83.0	92	352	38	30	6	6	1	23	2	0	36	2	0
Darling, Ronald, N.Y.	1	3	.250	2.80	5	5	1	0	0	0	35.1	31	148	11	11	0	3	0	17	1	3	23	3	2
*Davis, Mark, S.F.	6	4	.600	3.49	20	20	2	0	0	2	111.0	93	469	51	43	14	2	4	50	4	3	83	8	1
Dawley, William, Hou.	6	6	.500	2.82	48	0	0	37	14	0	79.2	51	304	26	25	9	5	0	22	4	1	60	1	0
*Dayley, Kenneth, Atl.	5	8	.385	4.30	24	16	0	3	0	0	104.2	100	436	59	50	12	3	3	39	2	2	70	3	0
Decker, D. Martin, S.D.	0	0	---	2.08	4	0	0	1	0	0	8.2	5	34	2	2	1	0	0	3	0	1	9	1	0
Dedmon, Jeffrey, Atl.	0	0	---	3.50	5	0	0	0	0	0	4.0	10	23	6	6	1	1	0	0	0	0	3	0	0
DeLeon, Jose, Pitt.	7	3	.700	2.83	15	15	3	0	0	2	108.0	75	438	36	34	5	4	3	47	2	1	118	5	2
DeLeon, Luis, S.D.	6	6	.500	2.68	63	0	0	34	13	0	111.0	89	442	34	33	8	7	9	27	7	1	90	1	0
Denny, John, Phil.	19	6	.760	2.37	36	36	7	0	0	1	242.2	229	983	77	64	9	8	3	53	5	4	139	6	1
*Diaz, Carlos, N.Y.	3	1	.750	2.05	54	0	0	20	2	0	83.1	62	339	22	19	1	6	3	35	13	1	64	2	0
*DiPino, Frank, Hou.	3	4	.429	2.65	53	0	0	32	20	0	71.1	52	279	21	21	2	1	3	20	5	1	67	3	0
Dixon, Thomas, Mtl.	0	1	.000	9.82	4	0	0	3	0	0	3.2	6	19	4	4	1	0	1	1	0	1	4	1	0
*Dravecky, David, S.D.	14	10	.583	3.58	28	28	9	0	0	1	183.2	181	756	78	73	18	13	4	44	4	3	74	2	1
*Falcone, Peter, Atl.	9	4	.692	3.63	33	15	2	6	0	0	106.2	102	467	47	43	14	4	4	60	2	1	59	5	0
Farmer, Edward, Phil.	0	6	.000	6.08	12	3	0	3	0	0	26.2	35	137	22	18	2	1	1	20	8	1	16	3	0
*Fernandez, C. Sid, L.A.	0	1	.000	6.00	2	1	0	0	0	0	6.0	7	33	4	4	0	0	0	7	0	1	9	0	0

Fireovid, Stephen, S.D.	0	0	---	1.80	3	0	0	1	0	0	5.0	4	20	2	1	0	1	0	2	0	0	1	1	0
Forsch, Robert, St.L.	10	12	.455	4.28	34	30	6	3	0	2	187.0	190	790	104	89	23	11	8	54	2	3	56	4	1
*Forster, Terry, Atl.	3	2	.600	2.16	56	0	0	29	13	0	79.1	60	316	19	19	3	7	0	31	9	2	54	2	0
*Fryman, Woodrow, Mtl.	0	3	.000	1.00	6	0	0	1	0	0	3.0	8	16	7	7	1	1	0	1	0	0	1	0	0
Gaff, Brent, N.Y.	1	0	1.000	6.10	4	0	0	2	0	0	10.1	18	53	9	7	0	1	1	1	1	0	4	1	0
Gale, Richard, Cin.	4	6	.400	5.82	33	7	0	6	1	0	89.2	103	408	64	58	8	2	2	43	8	1	53	3	1
Garber, H. Eugene, Atl.	4	5	.444	4.60	43	0	0	29	9	0	60.2	72	276	37	31	8	6	6	23	7	2	45	2	1
Garrelts, Scott, S.F.	2	2	.500	2.52	5	5	1	0	0	1	35.2	33	154	11	10	4	3	0	19	4	2	16	4	1
Ghelfi, Anthony, Phil.	1	1	.500	3.14	3	3	0	0	0	0	14.1	15	62	5	5	2	0	0	6	0	0	14	0	1
*Gorman, Thomas, N.Y.	1	4	.200	4.93	25	4	0	9	0	0	49.1	45	204	29	27	3	3	2	15	4	0	30	2	1
Grapenthin, Richard, Mtl.	0	1	.000	9.00	1	0	0	0	0	0	4.0	4	16	4	4	2	0	0	1	0	0	3	0	0
Gross, Kevin, Phil.	4	6	.400	3.56	17	17	1	0	0	1	96.0	100	418	46	38	13	2	1	35	3	3	66	4	1
Guante, Cecilio, Pitt.	2	6	.250	3.32	49	0	0	19	9	0	100.1	90	431	45	37	5	7	2	46	6	2	82	3	0
Gullickson, William, Mtl.	17	12	.586	3.75	34	34	10	0	0	1	242.1	230	990	108	101	19	4	7	59	4	4	120	4	1
Hagen, Kevin, St.L.	2	2	.500	4.84	9	4	0	1	0	0	22.1	34	103	15	12	0	2	0	7	0	0	7	2	0
*Hammaker, C. Atlee, S.F.	10	9	.526	2.25	23	23	8	0	0	3	172.1	147	695	57	43	9	10	4	32	12	3	127	6	2
Hargesheimer, Alan, Chi.	0	0	---	9.00	5	0	0	2	0	0	4.0	6	19	4	4	0	1	0	2	0	0	5	0	0
Harris, Greg, Cin.	0	0	---	7.00	1	0	0	0	0	0	1.0	2	9	3	3	0	1	0	3	2	1	1	0	0
Hawkins, M. Andrew, S.D.	5	7	.417	2.93	21	19	4	1	0	1	119.2	106	501	50	39	8	10	4	48	4	5	59	4	1
Hayes, Ben, Cin.	4	6	.400	6.49	60	0	0	34	7	0	69.1	82	318	53	50	8	3	5	37	6	1	44	1	1
Heathcock, R. Jeffrey, Hou.	2	1	.667	3.21	6	3	0	2	1	0	28.0	19	111	14	10	1	0	1	4	0	1	12	0	1
*Hernandez, Guillermo, Chi.-Phil.	9	4	.692	3.28	74	1	0	31	8	0	115.1	109	478	47	42	9	7	0	32	8	1	93	5	0
Hershiser, Orel, L.A.	0	0	---	3.38	8	0	0	4	1	0	8.0	7	37	6	3	1	1	0	6	0	0	5	1	0
*Holland, Alfred, Phil.	8	4	.667	2.26	68	0	0	53	25	0	91.2	63	371	26	23	8	5	1	30	12	0	100	0	0
Holman, R. Scott, N.Y.	1	7	.125	3.74	35	10	0	10	0	0	101.0	90	439	48	42	7	9	5	52	8	1	44	3	1
*Honeycutt, Frederick, L.A.	2	3	.400	5.77	9	7	1	0	0	0	39.0	46	172	26	25	6	2	0	13	4	2	18	0	1
Hooton, Burt, L.A.	9	8	.529	4.22	33	27	2	0	0	0	160.0	156	684	86	75	21	3	6	59	4	2	87	3	0
*Howe, Steven, L.A.	4	7	.364	1.44	46	0	0	33	18	0	68.2	55	274	15	11	2	5	3	12	7	1	52	3	0
Hudson, Charles, Phil.	8	8	.500	3.35	26	26	3	0	0	0	169.1	158	701	73	63	13	6	4	53	6	0	101	4	3
Hume, Thomas, Cin.	3	5	.375	4.77	48	0	0	33	9	0	66.0	66	301	40	35	8	3	4	41	11	3	34	1	0
James, Robert, Mtl.	1	0	1.000	2.88	27	0	0	16	7	0	50.0	37	208	17	16	3	6	0	23	2	3	56	2	1
Jenkins, Ferguson, Chi.	6	9	.400	4.30	33	29	1	1	0	1	167.1	176	705	89	80	19	7	5	46	5	6	96	2	3
Johnson, William, Chi.	1	0	1.000	4.38	10	0	0	2	0	0	12.1	17	55	6	6	0	2	1	3	1	0	4	0	1
*Kaat, James, St.L.	0	0	---	3.89	24	0	0	9	0	0	34.2	48	162	19	15	5	4	1	10	3	0	19	0	0
Keener, Jeffrey, St.L.	0	0	---	8.31	4	0	0	2	0	0	4.1	6	21	4	4	0	0	1	1	0	1	4	0	1
Kingman, Brian, S.F.	0	0	---	7.71	3	0	0	2	0	0	4.2	10	25	6	4	0	0	0	1	0	0	1	0	0
*Knepper, Robert, Hou.	6	13	.316	3.19	35	29	4	2	0	3	203.0	202	867	93	72	12	9	8	71	3	4	125	3	2
Krukow, Michael, S.F.	11	11	.500	3.95	31	31	2	0	0	1	184.1	189	816	95	81	17	9	3	76	8	3	136	8	1
LaCorte, Frank, Hou.	4	4	.500	5.06	37	0	0	19	3	0	53.1	35	220	32	30	8	5	1	28	3	2	48	5	0

Pitcher & Club	W	L	PCT	ERA	G	GS	CG	GF	SV	SHO	IP	H	BFP	R	ER	HR	SH	SF	BB	IB	HB	SO	WP	BK
LaCoss, Michael, Hou.	5	7	.417	4.43	38	17	2	6	1	0	138.0	142	590	81	68	10	6	6	56	11	2	53	9	1
Lahti, Jeffrey, St.L.	3	3	.500	3.16	53	0	0	13	0	0	74.0	64	305	31	26	2	6	2	29	12	1	26	3	2
*LaPoint, David, St.L.	12	9	.571	3.95	37	29	1	1	0	0	191.1	191	832	92	84	12	17	11	84	7	4	113	11	4
*Larkin, Patrick, S.F.	0	0	---	4.35	5	0	0	4	0	0	10.1	13	48	6	5	1	1	1	3	1	2	6	0	2
Laskey, William, S.F.	13	10	.565	4.19	25	25	1	0	0	0	148.1	151	627	75	69	18	7	4	45	4	3	81	0	1
*Lavelle, Gary, S.F.	7	4	.636	2.59	56	0	0	38	20	0	87.0	73	349	33	25	4	8	3	19	8	0	68	3	1
Lea, Charles, Mtl.	16	11	.593	3.12	33	33	8	0	0	4	222.0	195	917	87	77	15	4	8	84	4	1	137	8	3
Leary, Timothy, N.Y.	1	1	.500	3.38	2	2	1	0	0	0	10.2	15	53	10	4	0	1	1	4	0	0	9	0	1
*Lefferts, Craig, Chi.	3	4	.429	3.13	56	5	0	10	1	0	89.0	80	367	35	31	13	7	0	29	3	2	60	2	0
*Lerch, Randy, Mtl.-S.F.	2	3	.400	6.02	26	5	0	2	0	0	49.1	54	224	33	33	7	2	2	26	3	1	30	1	0
Lesley, Bradley, Cin.	0	0	---	2.16	5	0	0	5	0	0	8.1	9	32	2	2	1	0	1	0	0	0	5	0	0
*Lollar, W. Timothy, S.D.	7	12	.368	4.61	30	30	1	0	0	0	175.2	170	758	98	90	22	9	2	85	1	4	135	5	1
*Lucas, Gary, S.D.	5	8	.385	2.87	62	0	0	41	17	0	91.0	85	391	38	29	9	7	3	34	11	0	60	1	0
Lynch, Edward, N.Y.	10	10	.500	4.28	30	27	1	1	0	0	174.2	208	749	94	83	17	9	7	41	10	3	44	3	2
*Madden, Michael, Hou.	9	5	.643	3.14	28	13	0	7	0	0	94.2	76	387	37	33	4	9	3	45	3	1	44	2	3
Mahler, Richard, Atl.	0	0	---	5.02	10	0	0	1	0	0	14.1	16	66	8	8	0	1	2	9	1	0	7	0	0
Martin, D. Renie, S.F.	2	4	.333	4.20	37	6	0	6	1	0	94.1	95	414	50	44	11	3	3	51	9	3	43	2	2
*Martin, John, St.L.	3	1	.750	3.53	26	5	0	8	0	0	66.1	60	284	31	26	6	5	3	26	4	2	29	3	0
McGaffigan, Andrew, S.F.	3	9	.250	4.29	43	16	0	11	2	0	134.1	131	560	67	64	17	5	2	39	5	1	93	8	7
*McGraw, Frank, Phil.	2	1	.667	3.56	34	1	0	9	0	0	55.2	58	236	24	22	4	0	3	19	4	0	30	0	0
McMurtry, J. Craig, Atl.	15	9	.625	3.08	36	35	6	0	0	3	224.2	204	943	86	77	13	9	5	88	1	1	105	1	2
*McWilliams, Larry, Pitt.	15	8	.652	3.25	35	35	8	0	0	4	238.0	205	1002	99	86	19	13	6	87	7	3	199	9	4
Minton, Gregory, S.F.	7	11	.389	3.54	73	0	0	52	22	0	106.2	117	476	51	42	6	10	5	47	13	0	38	5	0
*Monge, Isidro, Phil.-S.D.	10	3	.769	3.70	61	0	0	32	7	0	80.1	85	354	34	33	8	7	3	37	7	1	39	3	1
Montefusco, John, S.D.	9	4	.692	3.30	31	10	1	9	4	0	95.1	94	398	38	35	6	9	1	32	6	1	52	1	1
Moore, Donnie, Atl.	2	3	.400	3.67	43	0	0	16	6	0	68.2	72	276	30	28	6	3	5	10	3	0	41	0	1
Moskau, Paul, Chi.	3	2	.600	6.75	8	8	0	0	0	0	32.0	44	149	25	24	7	2	0	14	1	0	16	2	0
Niedenfuer, Thomas, L.A.	8	3	.727	1.90	66	0	0	38	11	0	94.2	55	366	22	20	6	7	5	29	11	1	66	1	0
Niekro, Joseph, Hou.	15	14	.517	3.48	38	38	9	0	0	1	263.2	238	1113	115	102	15	13	9	101	5	3	152	14	1
Niekro, Philip, Atl.	11	10	.524	3.97	34	33	2	0	0	0	201.2	212	889	94	89	18	7	5	105	3	2	128	6	3
*Niemann, Randy, Pitt.	0	1	.000	9.22	8	1	0	4	0	0	13.2	20	66	14	14	2	1	1	7	1	1	8	3	0
Noles, Dickie, Chi.	5	10	.333	4.72	24	18	1	2	0	1	116.1	133	506	69	61	9	2	2	37	3	1	59	3	1
*Orosco, Jesse, N.Y.	13	7	.650	1.47	62	0	0	42	17	0	110.0	76	432	27	18	3	4	3	38	7	1	84	1	2
*Owchinko, Robert, Pitt.	0	0	---	----	1	0	0	0	0	0	0.0	2	2	1	1	1	0	0	0	0	0	0	0	0
Ownbey, Richard, N.Y.	1	3	.250	4.67	10	4	0	3	0	0	34.2	31	152	19	18	4	1	0	21	0	1	19	1	2
Pastore, Frank, Cin.	9	12	.429	4.88	36	29	4	2	0	1	184.1	207	791	104	100	20	7	6	64	3	1	93	6	3
Patterson, Reginald, Chi.	1	2	.333	4.82	5	2	0	0	0	0	18.2	17	78	12	10	3	0	1	6	0	2	10	1	0

Pena, Alejandro, L.A.	12	9	.571	2.75	34	26	4	4	1	3	177.0	152	730	67	54	7	8	5	51	7	1	120	2	1
Perez, Pascual, Atl.	15	8	.652	3.43	33	33	7	0	0	1	215.1	213	889	88	82	20	12	4	51	5	4	144	7	0
Power, Ted, Cin.	5	6	.455	4.54	49	6	1	14	2	0	111.0	120	480	62	56	10	4	6	49	3	1	57	1	0
*Price, Joseph, Cin.	10	6	.625	2.88	21	21	5	0	0	0	144.0	118	581	46	46	12	6	4	46	2	0	83	0	0
Proly, Michael, Chi.	1	5	.167	3.58	60	0	0	8	1	0	83.0	79	351	35	33	5	3	4	38	13	1	31	2	1
Puleo, Charles, Cin.	6	12	.333	4.89	27	24	0	0	0	0	143.2	145	649	86	78	18	7	6	91	9	5	71	4	1
*Pulido, Alfonso, Pitt.	0	0	---	9.00	1	1	0	0	0	0	2.0	4	11	3	2	2	0	0	1	0	0	1	0	0
Rainey, Charles, Chi.	14	13	.519	4.48	34	34	1	0	0	1	191.0	219	836	109	95	17	10	7	74	3	3	84	7	1
*Rasmussen, Dennis, S.D.	0	0	---	1.98	4	1	0	1	0	0	13.2	10	58	5	3	1	0	0	8	0	0	13	1	0
Rasmussen, Eric, St.L.	0	0	---	1.74	6	0	0	5	1	0	7.2	16	40	11	10	1	0	0	4	2	0	6	2	0
Reardon, Jeffrey, Mtl.	7	9	.438	3.03	66	0	0	53	21	0	92.0	87	403	34	31	7	8	2	44	9	1	78	2	0
Reed, Ronald, Phil.	9	1	.900	3.48	61	0	0	31	8	0	95.2	89	403	42	37	5	6	3	34	14	1	73	2	0
Reuschel, Ricky, Chi.	1	1	.500	3.92	4	4	0	0	0	0	20.2	18	88	9	9	1	0	1	10	2	0	9	0	0
*Reuss, Jerry, L.A.	12	11	.522	2.94	32	31	7	0	0	0	223.1	233	935	94	73	12	18	6	50	5	2	143	3	2
Rhoden, Richard, Pitt.	13	13	.500	3.09	36	35	7	1	1	2	244.1	256	1012	95	84	13	8	6	68	15	2	153	6	5
Robinson, Don, Pitt.	2	2	.500	4.46	9	6	0	2	0	0	36.1	43	168	21	18	5	2	0	21	3	0	28	2	0
*Rodas, Richard, L.A.	0	0	---	1.93	7	0	0	1	0	0	4.2	4	21	1	1	0	0	0	3	1	0	5	5	1
Rogers, Stephen, Mtl.	17	12	.586	3.23	36	36	13	0	0	5	273.0	258	1125	108	98	14	12	7	78	12	5	146	6	0
*Rucker, David, St.L.	5	3	.625	2.43	34	0	0	9	0	0	37.0	36	158	14	10	1	2	0	18	0	1	22	1	0
Ruhle, Vernon, Hou.	8	5	.615	3.69	41	9	0	11	3	0	114.2	107	480	49	47	13	6	6	36	7	3	43	1	0
Russell, Jeffrey, Cin.	4	5	.444	3.03	10	10	2	0	0	0	68.1	58	282	30	23	7	6	5	22	3	0	40	1	1
Ruthven, Richard, Phil.-Chi.	13	12	.520	4.38	32	32	5	0	0	2	183.0	202	775	101	89	22	8	7	38	3	3	99	1	0
Ryan, L. Nolan, Hou.	14	9	.609	2.98	29	29	5	0	0	2	196.1	134	804	74	65	9	7	5	101	3	4	183	5	1
Sanderson, Scott, Mtl.	6	7	.462	4.65	18	16	0	1	1	0	81.1	98	346	50	42	12	2	1	20	0	0	55	0	0
Sarmiento, Manuel, Pitt.	3	5	.375	2.99	52	0	0	17	4	0	84.1	74	356	35	28	8	10	6	36	8	0	49	0	1
*Schatzeder, Daniel, Mtl.	5	2	.714	3.21	58	2	0	23	2	0	87.0	88	369	34	31	3	5	2	25	6	5	48	5	0
*Scherrer, William, Cin.	2	3	.400	2.74	73	0	0	32	10	0	92.0	73	371	31	28	6	7	6	33	4	0	57	0	0
Schulze, Donald, Chi.	0	1	.000	7.07	4	3	0	0	0	0	14.0	19	67	11	11	1	0	0	7	0	1	8	1	0
Scott, Michael, Hou.	10	6	.625	3.72	24	24	2	0	0	2	145.0	143	612	67	60	8	1	5	46	0	5	73	4	4
*Scurry, Rodney, Pitt.	4	9	.308	5.56	61	0	0	25	7	0	68.0	63	317	45	42	6	3	4	53	7	4	67	6	0
Seaver, G. Thomas, N.Y.	9	14	.391	3.55	34	34	5	0	0	2	231.0	201	962	104	91	18	9	7	86	5	4	135	10	0
Show, Eric, S.D.	15	12	.556	4.17	35	33	4	0	0	2	200.2	201	857	97	93	25	9	4	74	3	6	120	4	2
Sisk, Douglas, N.Y.	5	4	.556	2.24	67	0	0	39	11	0	104.1	88	447	38	26	1	6	4	59	7	4	33	5	1
Smith, Bryn, Mtl.	6	11	.353	2.49	49	12	5	17	3	3	155.1	142	636	51	43	13	14	2	43	6	5	101	5	3
Smith, David, Hou.	3	1	.750	3.10	42	0	0	24	6	0	72.2	72	323	32	25	2	3	5	36	4	0	41	1	1
Smith, Lee, Chi.	4	10	.286	1.65	66	0	0	56	29	0	103.1	70	413	23	19	5	9	2	41	14	1	91	5	2
Solano, Julio, Hou.	0	2	.000	6.00	4	0	0	0	0	0	6.0	5	27	5	4	1	0	0	4	1	0	3	1	0
Sosa, Elias, S.D.	1	4	.200	4.35	41	1	0	9	1	0	72.1	72	314	41	35	7	7	5	30	5	3	45	4	0
Soto, Mario, Cin.	17	13	.567	2.70	34	34	18	0	0	3	273.2	207	1114	96	82	28	8	9	95	6	5	242	2	2

Pitcher & Club	W	L	PCT	ERA	G	GS	CG	GF	SV	SHO	IP	H	BFP	R	ER	HR	SH	SF	BB	IB	HB	SO	WP	BK
Stewart, David, L.A.	5	2	.714	2.96	46	1	0	25	8	0	76.0	67	328	28	25	4	7	3	33	7	2	54	2	0
Stuper, John, St.L.	12	11	.522	3.68	40	30	6	6	1	1	198.0	202	845	95	81	15	5	4	71	3	2	81	8	2
Sutter, H. Bruce, St.L.	9	10	.474	4.23	60	0	0	46	21	0	89.1	90	384	45	42	8	7	3	30	14	1	64	2	2
Swan, Craig, N.Y.	2	8	.200	5.51	27	18	0	4	1	0	96.1	112	424	63	59	14	3	4	42	3	0	43	1	1
Tekulve, Kenton, Pitt.	7	5	.583	1.64	76	0	0	56	18	0	99.0	78	398	27	18	1	9	4	36	12	0	52	1	0
Terrell, C. Walter, N.Y.	8	8	.500	3.57	21	20	4	1	0	2	133.2	123	561	57	53	7	9	5	55	7	2	59	5	0
*Thurmond, Mark, S.D.	7	3	.700	2.65	21	18	2	2	0	0	115.1	104	466	40	34	7	9	3	33	2	2	49	0	1
*Tomlin, David, Pitt.	0	0	---	6.75	5	0	0	0	0	0	4.0	6	20	4	3	0	0	0	1	0	0	5	0	0
Torrez, Michael, N.Y.	10	17	.370	4.37	39	34	5	4	0	0	222.1	227	972	120	108	16	15	4	113	11	1	94	7	1
*Trout, Steven, Chi.	10	14	.417	4.65	34	32	1	0	0	0	180.0	217	789	105	93	13	11	6	59	5	2	80	7	2
Tunnell, B. Lee, Pitt.	11	6	.647	3.65	35	25	5	4	0	3	177.2	167	731	81	72	15	2	6	58	3	2	95	11	5
*Valenzuela, Fernando, L.A.	15	10	.600	3.75	35	35	9	0	0	4	257.0	245	1094	122	107	16	27	5	99	10	3	189	12	1
*Von Ohlen, David, St.L.	3	2	.600	3.29	46	0	0	17	2	0	68.1	71	290	27	25	3	3	5	25	8	3	21	1	0
Walk, Robert, Atl.	0	0	---	7.36	1	1	0	0	0	0	3.2	7	20	3	3	0	1	0	2	0	0	4	0	0
Welch, Robert, L.A.	15	12	.556	2.65	31	31	4	0	0	3	204.0	164	828	73	60	13	8	7	72	4	3	156	4	6
*Welsh, Christopher, S.D.-Mtl.	0	2	.000	4.42	23	6	0	6	0	0	59.0	59	254	35	29	7	2	1	20	1	4	22	5	0
White, Larry, L.A.	0	0	---	1.29	4	0	0	2	0	0	7.0	4	27	1	1	0	0	0	3	0	0	5	0	0
Whitson, Eddie, S.D.	5	7	.417	4.30	31	21	2	4	1	0	144.1	143	617	73	69	23	3	4	50	1	1	81	2	0
Winn, James, Pitt.	0	0	---	7.36	7	0	0	3	0	0	11.0	12	51	9	9	2	0	0	6	0	0	3	1	0
*Wright, J. Richard, L.A.	0	0	---	2.84	6	0	0	3	0	0	6.1	5	26	2	2	0	1	1	2	1	0	5	1	0
Zachry, Patrick, L.A.	6	1	.857	2.49	40	1	0	11	0	0	61.1	63	256	22	17	4	5	3	21	6	1	36	0	0

CLUB PITCHING

Club	ERA	G	CG	SHO	SV	IP	H	BFP	R	ER	HR	SH	SF	BB	IBB	HB	SO	WP	BK
Los Angeles	3.10	163	27	12	40	1464.0	1336	6132	609	505	97	99	45	495	78	20	1000	38	12
Philadelphia	3.34	163	20	10	41	1461.2	1429	6168	635	542	111	65	39	464	77	23	1092	44	18
Houston	3.45	162	22	14	48	1466.1	1276	6117	646	562	94	65	52	570	49	27	904	49	14
Pittsburgh	3.55	162	25	14	41	1462.1	1378	6167	648	577	109	64	46	563	67	18	1061	52	21
Montreal	3.58	163	38	15	34	1471.0	1406	6151	646	585	120	67	37	479	50	33	899	38	9
San Diego	3.62	163	23	5	44	1467.2	1389	6179	653	590	144	96	42	528	52	28	850	33	10
Atlanta	3.67	162	18	4	48	1440.2	1412	6113	640	588	132	75	43	540	47	23	895	34	10
New York	3.68	162	18	7	33	1451.0	1384	6181	680	593	97	83	47	615	82	21	717	46	14
San Francisco	3.70	162	20	9	47	1445.2	1431	6206	697	594	127	78	52	520	95	31	881	53	20
St. Louis	3.79	162	22	10	27	1460.2	1479	6232	710	615	115	88	45	525	73	23	709	55	19
Cincinnati	3.98	162	34	5	29	1441.1	1365	6166	710	638	135	61	58	627	60	20	934	27	9
Chicago	4.08	162	9	10	42	1428.2	1496	6110	719	647	117	80	42	498	83	25	807	43	13

Atlanta's Craig McMurtry was 15-9, 3.09 ERA, in rookie year.

OFFICIAL 1983 AMERICAN LEAGUE RECORDS

compiled by

SPORTS INFORMATION CENTER

FINAL STANDINGS OF CLUBS AT CLOSE OF 1983 SEASON

American League West

	Won	Lost	Pct.	Games Behind
Chicago	99	63	.611	
Kansas City	79	83	.488	20
Texas	77	85	.475	22
Oakland	74	88	.457	25
California	70	92	.432	29
Minnesota	70	92	.432	29
Seattle	60	102	.370	39

American League East

	Won	Lost	Pct.	Games Behind
Baltimore	98	64	.605	
Detroit	92	70	.568	6
New York	91	71	.562	7
Toronto	89	73	.549	9
Milwaukee	87	75	.537	11
Boston	78	84	.481	20
Cleveland	70	92	.432	28

Championship Series: Baltimore defeated Chicago, 3 games to 1

BATTING

TOP FIFTEEN QUALIFIERS FOR BATTING CHAMPIONSHIP
(502 OR MORE PLATE APPEARANCES)

*BATS LEFTHANDED †SWITCH HITTER

BATTER AND CLUB	AVG	G	AB	R	H	TB	2B	3B	HR	RBI	GW RBI	SH	SF	HB	TBB	IBB	SO	SB	CS	GI DP	SLG	OBP
BOGGS, WADE, BOS.*	.361	153	582	100	210	283	44	7	5	74	8	3	7	1	92	2	36	3	3	15	.486	.449
CAREW, ROD, CALIF.*	.339	129	472	66	160	194	24	2	2	44	5	3	3	1	57	9	48	6	7	15	.411	.411
WHITAKER, LOU, DET.*	.320	161	643	94	206	294	40	6	12	72	8	2	8	0	67	8	70	17	10	8	.457	.385
TRAMMELL, ALAN, DET.	.319	142	505	83	161	238	31	2	14	66	8	15	4	0	57	2	64	30	10	7	.471	.383
RIPKEN, CAL, BALT.	.318	162	663	121	211	343	47	2	27	102	17	0	5	0	58	0	97	0	4	24	.517	.373
MOSEBY, LLOYD, TOR.*	.315	151	539	104	170	269	31	7	18	81	11	3	6	5	51	4	85	27	8	10	.499	.380
MCRAE, HAL, K.C.	.311	157	589	84	183	272	41	6	12	82	9	0	5	10	50	7	68	2	3	18	.462	.374
BRETT, GEORGE, K.C.*	.310	123	464	90	144	261	38	2	25	93	12	0	3	1	57	13	38	0	1	9	.563	.387
SIMMONS, TED, MILW.†	.308	153	600	76	185	269	39	3	13	108	17	0	7	2	41	6	51	4	2	22	.448	.355
YOUNT, ROBIN, MILW.	.308	149	578	102	178	291	42	10	17	80	10	1	8	3	72	6	58	12	4	10	.503	.387
COOPER, CECIL, MILW.*	.307	160	661	106	203	336	37	3	30	126	17	3	8	1	37	7	63	2	1	17	.508	.345
GARCIA, DAMASO, TOR.	.307	131	525	84	161	205	23	6	3	38	2	5	5	2	24	3	34	31	17	10	.390	.339
MURRAY, EDDIE, BALT.†	.306	156	582	115	178	313	30	3	33	111	17	0	9	3	86	13	90	5	1	13	.538	.398
UPSHAW, WILLIE, TOR.*	.306	160	579	99	177	298	26	7	27	104	16	3	7	5	61	8	98	10	7	8	.515	.377
RICE, JIM, BOS.	.305	155	626	90	191	344	34	1	39	126	14	0	5	6	52	10	102	0	2	31	.550	.364

INDIVIDUAL BATTING
(ALL PLAYERS LISTED ALPHABETICALLY)

* BATS LEFTHANDED † SWITCH HITTER

BATTER AND CLUB	AVG	G	AB	R	H	TB	2B	3B	HR	RBI	GW RBI	SH	SF	HB	TBB	IBB	SO	SB	CS	GI DP	SLG	OBP
ADAMS, RICK, CALIF.	.250	58	112	22	28	36	2	0	2	6	0	3	0	3	5	0	12	1	1	2	.321	.300
AIKENS, WILLIE, K.C.*	.302	125	410	49	124	221	26	1	23	72	4	0	1	2	45	9	75	0	0	16	.539	.374
ALLEN, JAMIE, SEA.	.223	86	273	23	61	83	10	0	4	21	2	6	0	1	33	0	52	6	5	8	.304	.309
ALLEN, ROD, SEA.	.167	11	12	1	2	2	0	0	0	0	0	0	0	0	0	0	1	0	0	0	.167	.167
ALLENSON, GARY, BOS.	.230	84	230	19	53	73	11	0	3	30	1	5	5	2	27	0	43	0	1	8	.317	.317
ALMON, BILL, OAK.	.266	143	451	45	120	163	29	1	4	63	5	5	11	2	26	3	67	26	8	8	.361	.309
ANDERSON, JIM, TEX.	.216	50	102	8	22	25	1	1	0	6	0	4	0	0	5	0	8	1	2	3	.245	.252
ARMAS, TONY, BOS.	.218	145	574	77	125	260	23	2	36	107	10	0	8	2	29	0	131	0	1	31	.453	.258
ARMSTRONG, MIKE, K.C.	—	59	0	0	0	0	0	0	0	0	0	0	0	0	0	0	0	0	0	0	—	—
ATHERTON, KEITH, OAK.	.000	29	1	0	0	0	0	0	0	0	0	0	0	0	0	0	1	0	0	0	.000	.000
AYALA, BENNY, BALT.	.221	47	104	12	23	42	7	0	4	13	2	0	2	0	9	0	18	0	0	2	.404	.283
BAINES, HAROLD, CHGO.*	.280	156	596	76	167	264	33	2	20	99	22	3	6	1	49	13	85	7	5	15	.443	.336
BALBONI, STEVE, N.Y.	.233	32	86	8	20	37	2	0	5	17	2	0	1	0	8	0	23	0	0	2	.430	.298
BANDO, CHRIS, CLEV.†	.256	48	121	15	31	46	3	0	4	15	1	1	1	0	15	0	19	0	1	5	.380	.338
BANNISTER, ALAN, CLEV.	.265	117	377	51	100	148	25	4	5	45	2	7	4	3	31	0	43	6	6	7	.393	.326
BARFIELD, JESSE, TOR.	.253	128	388	58	98	198	13	3	27	68	9	1	5	4	22	0	110	2	5	8	.510	.300
BARRETT, MARTY, BOS.	.227	33	44	7	10	13	1	1	0	2	0	0	1	0	3	0	1	0	0	1	.295	.277
BAYLOR, DON, N.Y.	.303	144	534	82	162	264	33	3	21	85	8	2	8	13	40	11	53	17	7	10	.494	.366
BELL, BUDDY, TEX.	.277	156	618	75	171	254	35	3	14	66	7	0	6	4	50	5	48	3	5	24	.411	.335
BELL, GEORGE, TOR.	.268	39	112	5	30	49	5	4	2	17	1	0	0	2	4	1	17	1	1	4	.438	.305
BENIQUEZ, JUAN, CALIF.	.305	92	315	44	96	120	15	0	3	34	5	6	1	4	15	0	29	4	2	9	.381	.344
BERNAZARD, TONY, CHGO.-SEA.†	.265	139	533	65	141	205	34	3	8	56	4	9	7	2	55	3	97	23	9	9	.385	.336
BIANCALANA, BUDDY, K.C.†	.200	6	15	2	3	3	0	0	0	0	0	0	0	0	0	0	7	1	0	0	.200	.200
BIITTNER, LARRY, TEX.*	.276	66	116	5	32	39	5	1	0	18	0	0	2	0	9	5	16	0	0	0	.336	.328
BOGGS, WADE, BOS.*	.361	153	582	100	210	283	44	7	5	74	8	3	7	1	92	2	36	3	3	15	.486	.449
BONNELL, BARRY, TOR.	.318	121	377	49	120	177	21	3	10	54	4	2	5	0	33	5	52	10	7	8	.469	.373
BONNER, BOB, BALT.	—	6	0	0	0	0	0	0	0	0	0	0	0	0	0	0	0	0	0	0	—	—

BOONE, BOB, CALIF.	.256	142	468	46	120	165	18	0	9	52	5	10	7	0	24	1	42	4	3	19	.353	.293
BRADLEY, PHIL, SEA.	.269	23	67	8	18	20	2	0	0	5	0	1	1	0	8	0	5	3	1	0	.299	.347
BRANT, MARSHALL, OAK.	.143	5	14	2	2	2	0	0	0	2	0	0	0	0	0	0	3	0	0	0	.143	.143
BRETT, GEORGE, K.C.*	.310	123	464	90	144	261	38	2	25	93	12	0	3	1	57	13	38	0	1	9	.563	.387
BROOKENS, TOM, DET.	.214	138	332	50	71	108	13	3	6	32	2	5	6	2	29	2	46	10	4	3	.325	.281
BROUHARD, MARK, MILW.	.276	56	185	25	51	84	10	1	7	23	3	1	1	2	9	0	39	0	4	7	.454	.316
BROWN, DARRELL, MINN.†	.272	91	309	40	84	94	6	2	0	22	2	3	0	1	10	0	28	3	3	9	.304	.297
BROWN, MIKE, CALIF.	.231	31	104	12	24	40	5	1	3	9	1	0	0	0	7	0	20	1	0	2	.385	.279
BRUNANSKY, TOM, MINN.	.227	151	542	70	123	241	24	5	28	82	15	1	3	4	61	4	95	2	5	13	.445	.310
BULLING, BUD, SEA.	.000	5	5	0	0	0	0	0	0	0	0	0	0	0	0	0	0	0	0	0	.000	.000
BUMBRY, AL, BALT.*	.275	124	378	63	104	135	14	4	3	31	2	4	3	0	31	2	33	12	5	1	.357	.330
BURGMEIER, TOM, OAK.*	—	51	0	1	0	0	0	0	0	0	0	0	0	0	0	0	0	0	0	0	—	—
BURLESON, RICK, CALIF.	.286	33	119	22	34	41	7	0	0	11	2	2	1	0	12	0	12	0	2	5	.345	.351
BURROUGHS, JEFF, OAK.	.269	121	401	43	108	155	15	1	10	56	6	0	7	0	47	4	79	0	2	16	.387	.346
BUSH, RANDY, MINN.*	.249	124	373	43	93	156	24	3	11	56	4	0	1	7	34	8	51	0	1	7	.418	.324
BUTERA, SAL, DET.	.200	4	5	1	1	1	0	0	0	0	0	0	0	0	0	0	0	0	0	0	.200	.200
CABELL, ENOS, DET.	.311	121	392	62	122	170	23	5	5	46	6	5	6	1	16	2	41	4	8	14	.434	.340
CAMPANERIS, BERT, N.Y.	.322	60	143	19	46	51	5	0	0	11	1	3	1	0	8	0	9	6	7	4	.357	.358
CAPRA, NICK, TEX.	.000	8	2	2	0	0	0	0	0	0	0	0	0	0	0	0	0	0	0	0	.000	.000
CAREW, ROD, CALIF.*	.339	129	472	66	160	194	24	2	2	44	5	3	3	1	57	9	48	6	7	15	.411	.411
CASTILLO, CARMELO, CLEV.	.278	23	36	9	10	17	2	1	1	3	0	0	0	1	4	0	6	1	1	0	.472	.366
CASTILLO, MANNY, SEA.†	.207	91	203	13	42	54	6	3	0	24	4	1	4	1	7	2	20	1	1	4	.266	.237
CASTILLO, MARTY, DET.	.193	67	119	10	23	33	4	0	2	10	1	6	0	0	7	0	22	2	0	4	.277	.238
CASTINO, JOHN, MINN.	.277	142	563	83	156	227	30	4	11	57	8	10	4	1	62	1	54	4	2	11	.403	.350
CERONE, RICK, N.Y.	.220	80	246	18	54	67	7	0	2	22	4	4	0	1	15	1	29	0	0	5	.272	.267
CHAMBERS, AL, SEA.*	.209	31	67	11	14	20	3	0	1	7	1	0	0	0	18	1	20	0	1	1	.299	.376
CIAS, DARRYL, OAK.	.333	20	18	1	6	7	1	0	0	1	0	0	0	0	2	0	4	1	0	0	.389	.400
CLARK, BOBBY, CALIF.	.231	76	212	17	49	75	9	1	5	21	3	3	1	0	9	0	45	0	0	7	.354	.262
COLES, DARNELL, SEA.	.283	27	92	9	26	36	7	0	1	6	1	1	0	0	7	0	12	0	3	8	.391	.333
COLLINS, DAVE, TOR.†	.271	118	402	55	109	132	12	4	1	34	5	2	2	2	43	1	67	31	7	6	.328	.345
CONCEPCION, ONIX, K.C.	.242	80	219	22	53	70	11	3	0	20	0	6	2	1	12	0	12	10	3	4	.320	.284
COOPER, CECIL, MILW.*	.307	160	661	106	203	336	37	3	30	126	17	3	8	1	37	7	63	2	1	17	.508	.345
COWENS, AL, SEA.	.205	110	356	39	73	117	19	2	7	35	3	0	3	2	23	0	38	10	2	13	.329	.257

*BATS LEFTHANDED †SWITCH HITTER

BATTER AND CLUB	AVG	G	AB	R	H	TB	2B	3B	HR	RBI	GW RBI	SH	SF	HB	TBB	IBB	SO	SB	CS	GI DP	SLG	OBP
CRUZ, JULIO, SEA.-CHGO.†	.252	160	515	71	130	168	19	5	3	52	8	5	7	4	49	1	66	57	12	12	.326	.322
CRUZ, TODD, SEA.-BALT.	.199	146	437	37	87	136	13	3	10	48	7	10	3	3	22	2	108	4	7	14	.311	.242
CULMER, WIL, CLEV.	.105	7	19	0	2	2	0	0	0	1	0	0	1	0	0	0	4	0	1	1	.105	.105
DAUER, RICH, BALT.	.235	140	459	49	108	142	19	0	5	41	5	7	5	2	47	2	29	1	1	20	.309	.309
DAVIS, BUTCH, K.C.	.344	33	122	13	42	62	2	6	2	18	2	2	2	0	4	0	19	4	3	3	.508	.365
DAVIS, MIKE, OAK.*	.275	128	443	61	122	178	24	4	8	62	3	5	4	5	27	1	74	33	14	9	.402	.324
DAYETT, BRIAN, N.Y.	.207	11	29	3	6	8	0	1	0	5	1	1	0	0	2	0	4	0	0	0	.276	.258
DE CINCES, DOUG, CALIF.	.281	95	370	49	104	183	19	3	18	65	6	1	8	0	32	2	56	2	0	13	.495	.338
DEMPSEY, RICK, BALT.	.231	127	347	33	80	112	16	2	4	32	1	5	5	3	40	1	55	1	1	9	.323	.315
DENT, BUCKY, TEX.	.237	131	417	36	99	124	15	2	2	34	1	7	2	1	23	0	31	3	7	3	.297	.279
DILONE, MIGUEL, CLEV.-CHGO.†	.183	36	71	16	13	18	3	1	0	7	0	0	0	0	10	0	5	6	1	1	.254	.284
DOWNING, BRIAN, CALIF.	.246	113	403	68	99	173	15	1	19	53	5	1	2	5	62	4	59	1	2	7	.429	.353
DUNBAR, TOMMY, TEX.*	.250	12	24	3	6	6	0	0	0	3	0	0	0	0	5	0	7	3	1	1	.250	.379
DWYER, JIM, BALT.*	.286	100	196	37	56	99	17	1	8	38	6	1	1	0	31	3	29	1	1	3	.505	.383
DYBZINSKI, GERRY, CHGO.	.230	127	256	30	59	74	10	1	1	32	3	11	3	2	18	0	29	11	4	8	.289	.286
EASTERLY, JAMIE, MILW.-CLEV.*	.000	54	1	0	0	0	0	0	0	0	0	1	0	0	0	0	0	0	0	0	.000	.000
EDLER, DAVE, SEA.	.190	29	63	2	12	18	1	1	1	4	1	2	1	1	5	0	11	3	3	2	.286	.261
EDWARDS, MARSHALL, MILW.*	.297	51	74	14	22	25	1	1	0	5	0	3	1	0	1	0	9	5	5	1	.338	.307
EISENREICH, JIM, MINN.*	.286	2	7	1	2	3	1	0	0	0	0	0	0	0	1	0	1	0	0	0	.429	.375
ENGLE, DAVE, MINN.	.305	120	374	46	114	168	22	4	8	43	4	0	5	1	28	1	39	2	1	13	.449	.355
ESPINO, JUAN, N.Y.	.261	10	23	1	6	9	0	0	1	3	0	0	1	0	1	0	5	0	0	0	.391	.292
ESSIAN, JIM, CLEV.	.204	48	93	11	19	29	4	0	2	11	0	1	2	0	16	0	8	0	1	1	.312	.321
EVANS, DWIGHT, BOS.	.238	126	470	74	112	205	19	4	22	58	8	0	2	2	70	5	97	3	0	12	.436	.339
FAEDO, LENNY, MINN.	.277	51	173	16	48	58	7	0	1	18	2	3	2	0	4	1	19	0	0	4	.335	.294
FAHEY, BILL, DET.*	.273	19	22	4	6	7	1	0	0	2	0	0	0	0	5	1	3	0	0	0	.318	.407
FERGUSON, JOE, CALIF.	.074	12	27	3	2	2	0	0	0	2	0	1	0	0	5	0	8	0	0	3	.074	.219
FERNANDEZ, TONY, TOR.†	.265	15	34	5	9	12	1	1	0	2	0	1	0	1	2	0	2	0	1	1	.353	.324
FISCHLIN, MIKE, CLEV.	.209	95	225	31	47	62	5	2	2	23	2	11	2	2	26	0	32	9	2	2	.276	.296
FISK, CARLTON, CHGO.	.289	138	488	85	141	253	26	4	26	86	9	2	3	6	46	3	88	9	6	8	.518	.357
FLETCHER, SCOTT, CHGO.	.237	114	262	42	62	97	16	5	3	31	5	7	2	2	29	0	22	5	1	8	.370	.317

FOLI, TIM, CALIF.	.252	88	330	29	83	99	10	0	2	29	3	11	2	1	5	1	18	2	3	5	.300	.265
FORD, DAN, BALT.	.280	103	407	63	114	179	30	4	9	55	10	3	6	3	29	1	55	9	2	9	.440	.333
FRANCO, JULIO, CLEV.	.273	149	560	68	153	217	24	8	8	80	9	3	6	2	27	1	50	32	12	22	.388	.309
GAETTI, GARY, MINN.	.245	157	584	81	143	242	30	3	21	78	2	0	8	4	54	2	121	7	1	18	.414	.313
GAGNE, GREG, MINN.	.111	10	27	2	3	4	1	0	0	3	0	0	2	0	0	0	6	0	0	0	.148	.111
GAMBLE, OSCAR, N.Y.*	.261	74	180	26	47	82	10	2	7	26	5	0	0	3	25	1	23	0	0	3	.456	.361
GANTNER, JIM, MILW.*	.282	161	603	85	170	242	23	8	11	74	8	11	4	6	38	5	46	5	6	11	.401	.331
GARCIA, DAMASO, TOR.	.307	131	525	84	161	205	23	6	3	38	2	5	5	2	24	3	34	31	17	10	.390	.339
GEDMAN, RICH, BOS.*	.294	81	204	21	60	84	16	1	2	18	2	3	0	1	15	6	37	0	1	4	.412	.345
GERONIMO, CESAR, K.C.*	.207	38	87	2	18	22	4	0	0	4	2	0	0	2	2	0	13	0	1	1	.253	.242
GIBSON, KIRK, DET.*	.227	128	401	60	91	166	12	9	15	51	6	5	4	4	53	3	96	14	3	2	.414	.323
GONZALEZ, JULIO, DET.	.143	12	21	0	3	4	1	0	0	2	0	1	0	0	1	0	7	0	0	1	.190	.182
GRAHAM, LEE, BOS.*	.000	5	6	2	0	0	0	0	0	1	0	0	1	0	0	0	0	0	1	0	.000	.000
GRAY, LORENZO, CHGO.	.179	41	78	18	14	20	3	0	1	4	0	1	0	0	8	0	16	1	0	3	.256	.256
GRICH, BOBBY, CALIF.	.292	120	387	65	113	178	17	0	16	62	3	4	3	7	76	2	62	2	3	11	.460	.417
GRIFFEY, KEN, N.Y.*	.306	118	458	60	140	200	21	3	11	46	7	3	2	2	34	3	45	6	1	3	.437	.356
GRIFFIN, ALFREDO, TOR.†	.250	162	528	62	132	184	22	9	4	47	2	11	3	3	27	0	44	8	10	5	.348	.290
GROSS, WAYNE, OAK.*	.233	137	339	34	79	133	18	0	12	44	6	4	2	3	36	4	52	3	5	5	.392	.312
GRUBB, JOHN, DET.*	.254	57	134	20	34	55	5	2	4	22	5	0	1	2	28	1	17	0	0	5	.410	.390
GUIDRY, RON, N.Y.*	—	32	0	0	0	0	0	0	0	0	0	0	0	0	0	0	0	0	0	0	—	—
GULLIVER, GLENN, BALT.*	.213	23	47	5	10	13	3	0	0	2	1	0	1	0	9	0	5	0	1	1	.277	.339
GURA, LARRY, K.C.*	—	35	0	0	0	0	0	0	0	0	0	0	0	0	0	0	0	0	0	0	—	—
GUTIERREZ, JACKIE, BOS.	.300	5	10	2	3	3	0	0	0	0	0	0	0	0	1	0	1	0	1	1	.300	.364
HAAS, MOOSE, MILW.	—	26	0	0	0	0	0	0	0	0	0	0	0	0	0	0	0	0	0	0	—	—
HAIRSTON, JERRY, CHGO.†	.294	101	126	17	37	63	9	1	5	22	0	0	2	0	23	4	16	0	1	1	.500	.403
HANCOCK, GARRY, OAK.*	.273	101	256	29	70	107	7	3	8	30	3	3	1	1	5	4	13	2	0	3	.418	.290
HARGROVE, MIKE, CLEV.*	.286	134	469	57	134	172	21	4	3	57	8	7	7	5	78	5	40	0	6	10	.367	.393
HARRAH, TOBY, CLEV.	.266	138	526	81	140	192	23	1	9	53	5	4	3	7	75	1	49	16	10	11	.365	.365
HASSEY, RON, CLEV.*	.270	117	341	48	92	131	21	0	6	42	3	2	5	2	38	2	35	2	2	10	.384	.346
HATCHER, MICKEY, MINN.	.317	106	375	50	119	167	15	3	9	47	3	3	2	1	14	0	19	2	0	12	.445	.344
HEATH, MIKE, OAK.	.281	96	345	45	97	132	17	0	6	33	4	1	1	1	18	4	59	3	4	9	.383	.319
HENDERSON, DAVE, SEA.	.269	137	484	50	130	215	24	5	17	55	4	2	6	1	28	3	93	9	3	5	.444	.310
HENDERSON, RICKEY, OAK.	.292	145	513	105	150	216	25	7	9	48	6	1	1	4	103	8	80	108	19	11	.421	.415

* BATS LEFTHANDED † SWITCH HITTER

BATTER AND CLUB	AVG	G	AB	R	H	TB	2B	3B	HR	RBI	GW RBI	SH	SF	HB	TBB	IBB	SO	SB	CS	GI DP	SLG	OBP
HENDERSON, STEVE, SEA.	.294	121	436	50	128	196	32	3	10	54	6	1	3	0	44	2	82	10	14	9	.450	.358
HERNANDEZ, LEO, BALT.	.246	64	203	21	50	76	6	1	6	26	3	0	1	0	12	1	19	1	0	4	.374	.288
HERNDON, LARRY, DET.	.302	153	603	88	182	288	28	9	20	92	9	0	6	3	46	6	95	9	3	20	.478	.354
HILL, DONNY, OAK.†	.266	53	158	20	42	55	7	0	2	15	0	5	2	0	4	0	21	1	1	2	.348	.284
HILL, MARC, CHGO.	.226	58	133	11	30	39	6	0	1	11	1	4	0	0	9	2	24	0	1	4	.293	.275
HOFFMAN, GLENN, BOS.	.260	143	473	56	123	161	24	1	4	41	8	11	2	2	30	1	76	1	1	5	.340	.307
HOSTETLER, DAVE, TEX.	.220	94	304	31	67	113	9	2	11	46	5	0	2	5	42	1	103	0	2	10	.372	.325
HOWELL, ROY, MILW.*	.278	69	194	23	54	87	9	6	4	25	0	2	0	0	15	0	29	1	2	4	.448	.330
HRBEK, KENT, MINN.*	.297	141	515	75	153	252	41	5	16	84	8	0	7	3	57	5	71	4	6	12	.489	.370
HUDGENS, DAVE, OAK.*	.143	6	7	0	1	1	0	0	0	0	0	0	0	0	0	0	3	0	0	0	.143	.143
HULETT, TIM, CHGO.	.200	6	5	0	1	1	0	0	0	0	0	0	0	0	0	0	0	1	0	0	.200	.200
HUPPERT, DAVE, BALT.	—	2	0	0	0	0	0	0	0	0	0	0	0	0	0	0	0	0	0	0	—	—
IORG, GARTH, TOR.	.275	122	375	40	103	141	22	5	2	39	5	2	3	1	13	3	45	7	0	10	.376	.301
IVIE, MIKE, DET.	.214	12	42	4	9	13	4	0	0	7	2	0	1	0	2	1	4	0	0	2	.310	.250
JACKSON, REGGIE, CALIF.*	.194	116	397	43	77	135	14	1	14	49	3	0	5	4	52	5	140	0	2	5	.340	.294
JACKSON, RON, CALIF.	.230	102	348	41	80	122	16	1	8	39	5	1	0	3	27	2	33	2	3	10	.351	.291
JAMES, DION, MILW.*	.100	11	20	1	2	2	0	0	0	1	0	0	0	0	2	0	2	1	0	0	.100	.182
JIMENEZ, ALFONSO, MINN.	.174	36	86	5	15	22	5	1	0	9	1	0	2	0	4	0	11	0	1	0	.256	.211
JOHNSON, BOBBY, TEX.	.211	72	175	18	37	60	6	1	5	16	2	0	1	1	16	0	55	3	0	7	.343	.281
JOHNSON, CLIFF, TOR.	.265	142	407	59	108	199	23	1	22	76	9	1	4	5	67	8	69	0	1	10	.489	.376
JOHNSON, HOWARD, DET.†	.212	27	66	11	14	23	0	0	3	5	0	0	0	1	7	0	10	0	0	1	.348	.297
JOHNSON, RON, K.C.	.259	9	27	2	7	7	0	0	0	1	0	0	0	0	3	0	1	0	0	0	.259	.333
JONES, BOBBY, TEX.*	.222	41	72	5	16	23	4	0	1	11	2	0	2	2	5	1	17	0	2	2	.319	.291
JONES, LYNN, DET.	.266	49	64	9	17	22	1	2	0	6	0	3	0	0	3	0	6	1	0	1	.344	.299
JURAK, ED, BOS.	.277	75	159	19	44	60	8	4	0	18	0	3	2	1	18	1	25	1	2	4	.377	.354
KEARNEY, BOB, OAK.	.255	108	298	33	76	111	11	0	8	32	6	4	1	4	21	1	50	1	4	12	.372	.313
KEMP, STEVE, N.Y.*	.241	109	373	53	90	149	17	3	12	49	9	1	2	2	41	3	37	1	0	17	.399	.320
KITTLE, RON, CHGO.	.254	145	520	75	132	262	19	3	35	100	9	0	3	8	39	8	150	8	3	10	.504	.316
KLUTTS, MICKEY, TOR.	.256	22	43	3	11	20	0	0	3	5	0	0	0	1	1	1	11	0	1	0	.465	.289
KRENCHICKI, WAYNE, DET.*	.278	59	133	18	37	47	7	0	1	16	1	2	2	1	11	0	27	0	0	1	.353	.338

KUNTZ, RUSTY, CHGO.-MINN.	.211	59	142	19	30	43	4	0	3	6	1	0	1	0	18	0	41	1	0	5	.303	.300
LAGA, MIKE, DET.*	.190	12	21	2	4	4	0	0	0	2	0	0	0	0	1	0	9	0	0	1	.190	.227
LANDRUM, TITO, BALT.	.310	26	42	8	13	18	2	0	1	4	0	0	1	0	1	0	11	0	2	1	.429	.326
LANSFORD, CARNEY, OAK.	.308	80	299	43	92	142	16	2	10	45	6	0	4	3	22	4	33	3	8	8	.475	.361
LAUDNER, TIM, MINN.	.185	62	168	20	31	58	9	0	6	18	2	0	1	0	15	0	49	0	0	2	.345	.251
LAW, RUDY, CHGO.*	.283	141	501	95	142	185	20	7	3	34	3	4	2	2	42	2	36	77	12	4	.369	.341
LAW, VANCE, CHGO.	.243	145	408	55	99	142	21	5	4	42	4	6	5	1	51	1	56	3	1	7	.348	.328
LEACH, RICK, DET.*	.248	99	242	22	60	86	17	0	3	26	3	0	0	1	19	1	21	2	2	6	.355	.305
LEMON, CHET, DET.	.255	145	491	78	125	228	21	5	24	69	11	4	4	20	54	1	70	0	7	12	.464	.352
LOPES, DAVEY, OAK.	.277	147	494	64	137	209	13	4	17	67	7	4	10	2	51	7	61	22	4	9	.423	.347
LOWENSTEIN, JOHN, BALT.*	.281	122	310	52	87	149	13	2	15	60	9	0	6	1	49	1	55	2	1	2	.481	.381
LUBRATICH, STEVE, CALIF.	.218	57	156	12	34	43	9	0	0	7	0	13	1	0	4	0	17	0	1	2	.276	.238
LUZINSKI, GREG, CHGO.	.255	144	502	73	128	252	26	1	32	95	10	0	10	11	70	6	117	2	1	10	.502	.358
LYNN, FRED, CALIF.*	.272	117	437	56	119	211	20	3	22	74	11	0	6	2	55	10	83	2	2	7	.483	.356
MALER, JIM, SEA.	.182	26	66	5	12	16	1	0	1	3	0	0	0	2	5	0	11	0	3	3	.242	.260
MANNING, RICK, CLEV.-MILW.*	.246	158	569	60	140	188	20	4	4	43	4	3	4	1	38	5	62	18	5	13	.316	.294
MARTIN, JERRY, K.C.	.318	13	44	4	14	22	2	0	2	13	2	0	3	0	1	0	7	1	0	0	.500	.333
MARTINEZ, BUCK, TOR.	.253	88	221	27	56	100	14	0	10	33	4	1	2	0	29	0	39	0	1	7	.452	.340
MATTINGLY, DON, N.Y.*	.283	91	279	34	79	114	15	4	4	32	3	2	2	1	21	5	31	0	0	8	.409	.336
MCBRIDE, BAKE, CLEV.*	.291	70	230	21	67	80	8	1	1	18	3	1	2	1	9	2	26	8	2	8	.348	.321
MCCATTY, STEVE, OAK.	—	39	0	0	0	0	0	0	0	0	0	0	0	0	0	0	0	0	0	0	—	—
MCNEALY, RUSTY, OAK.*	.000	15	4	5	0	0	0	0	0	0	0	0	0	0	0	0	0	0	1	0	.000	.000
MCRAE, HAL, K.C.	.311	157	589	84	183	272	41	6	12	82	9	0	5	10	50	7	68	2	3	18	.462	.374
MEACHAM, BOB, N.Y.†	.235	22	51	5	12	14	2	0	0	4	0	0	0	1	4	0	10	8	0	0	.275	.304
MERCADO, ORLANDO, SEA.	.197	66	178	10	35	53	11	2	1	16	3	2	2	1	14	0	27	2	2	3	.298	.259
MEYER, DAN, OAK.*	.189	69	169	15	32	44	9	0	1	13	0	1	2	0	19	2	11	0	0	8	.260	.271
MILBOURNE, LARRY, N.Y.†	.200	31	70	5	14	18	4	0	0	2	0	0	0	1	5	0	10	1	1	0	.257	.263
MILLER, RICK, BOS.*	.286	104	262	41	75	95	10	2	2	21	2	1	1	1	28	1	30	3	3	6	.363	.357
MITCHELL, BOBBY, MINN.*	.230	59	152	26	35	46	4	2	1	15	2	0	0	1	28	2	21	1	1	3	.303	.354
MOLINARO, BOB, DET.*	.000	8	2	3	0	0	0	0	0	0	0	0	0	0	1	0	1	1	1	0	.000	.333
MOLITOR, PAUL, MILW.	.270	152	608	95	164	249	28	6	15	47	7	7	6	2	59	4	74	41	7	12	.410	.336
MONEY, DON, MILW.	.149	43	114	5	17	25	5	0	1	8	1	1	2	0	11	1	17	0	0	3	.219	.224
MOORE, CHARLIE, MILW.	.284	151	529	65	150	195	27	6	2	49	4	14	3	4	55	5	42	11	4	14	.369	.355

* BATS LEFTHANDED † SWITCH HITTER

BATTER AND CLUB	AVG	G	AB	R	H	TB	2B	3B	HR	RBI	GW RBI	SH	SF	HB	TBB	IBB	SO	SB	CS	GI DP	SLG	OBP
MOORE, KELVIN, OAK.	.210	42	124	12	26	45	4	0	5	16	0	0	1	1	10	0	39	2	4	3	.363	.274
MORENO, OMAR, N.Y.*	.250	48	152	17	38	52	9	1	1	17	1	3	0	0	8	0	31	7	3	4	.342	.288
MORRIS, JACK, DET.	—	44	0	3	0	0	0	0	0	0	0	0	0	0	0	0	0	0	0	0	—	—
MOSEBY, LLOYD, TOR.*	.315	151	539	104	170	269	31	7	18	81	11	3	6	5	51	4	85	27	8	10	.499	.380
MOSES, JOHN, SEA.†	.208	93	130	19	27	33	4	1	0	6	0	0	0	1	12	0	20	11	5	4	.254	.280
MOTLEY, DARRYL, K.C.	.235	19	68	9	16	30	1	2	3	11	1	0	1	1	2	0	8	2	1	3	.441	.268
MULLINIKS, RANCE, TOR.*	.275	129	364	54	100	170	34	3	10	49	4	3	2	1	57	5	43	0	2	14	.467	.374
MUMPHREY, JERRY, N.Y.†	.262	83	267	41	70	110	11	4	7	36	5	2	5	0	28	3	33	2	3	11	.412	.332
MURCER, BOBBY, N.Y.*	.182	9	22	2	4	9	2	0	1	1	1	0	0	0	1	0	1	0	0	3	.409	.217
MURPHY, DWAYNE, OAK.*	.227	130	471	55	107	179	17	2	17	75	8	7	6	0	62	4	105	7	5	16	.380	.317
MURRAY, EDDIE, BALT.†	.306	156	582	115	178	313	30	3	33	111	17	0	9	3	86	13	90	5	1	13	.538	.398
NAHORODNY, BILL, DET.	.000	2	1	0	0	0	0	0	0	0	0	0	0	0	1	0	0	0	0	0	.000	.500
NARRON, JERRY, CALIF.*	.136	10	22	1	3	6	0	0	1	4	1	0	0	0	1	0	3	0	0	0	.273	.174
NELSON, JAMIE, SEA.	.219	40	96	9	21	27	3	0	1	5	0	1	1	0	13	1	12	4	2	2	.281	.312
NELSON, RICKEY, SEA.*	.254	98	291	32	74	108	13	3	5	36	6	2	1	0	17	3	50	7	4	4	.371	.295
NETTLES, GRAIG, N.Y.*	.266	129	462	56	123	206	17	3	20	75	5	0	3	3	51	2	65	0	1	9	.446	.343
NEWMAN, JEFF, BOS.	.189	59	132	11	25	38	4	0	3	7	0	2	1	2	10	1	31	0	1	4	.288	.257
NICHOLS, REID, BOS.	.285	100	274	35	78	120	22	1	6	22	3	3	1	3	26	2	36	7	5	5	.438	.353
NIXON, OTIS, N.Y.†	.143	13	14	2	2	2	0	0	0	0	0	0	0	0	1	0	5	2	0	0	.143	.200
NOLAN, JOE, BALT.*	.277	73	184	25	51	79	11	1	5	24	2	0	0	2	16	1	30	0	0	5	.429	.342
NYMAN, CHRIS, CHGO.	.286	21	28	12	8	14	0	0	2	4	0	0	0	1	4	0	7	2	2	0	.500	.394
O BERRY, MIKE, CALIF.	.167	26	60	7	10	14	1	0	1	5	0	2	0	0	3	0	11	0	0	1	.233	.206
O BRIEN, PETER, TEX.*	.237	154	524	53	124	182	24	5	8	53	7	3	2	1	58	2	62	5	4	11	.347	.314
OFFICE, ROWLAND, N.Y.*	.000	2	2	0	0	0	0	0	0	1	0	0	1	0	0	0	0	0	0	0	.000	.000
OGLIVIE, BEN, MILW.*	.280	125	411	49	115	179	19	3	13	66	10	0	8	4	60	12	64	4	6	9	.436	.377
ORTA, JORGE, TOR.*	.237	103	245	30	58	100	6	3	10	38	1	0	4	0	19	0	29	1	2	6	.408	.292
OTIS, AMOS, K.C.	.261	98	356	35	93	127	16	3	4	41	7	0	1	0	27	3	63	5	2	7	.357	.313
OWEN, SPIKE, SEA.	.196	80	306	36	60	83	11	3	2	21	3	5	3	2	24	0	44	10	6	2	.271	.259
PACIOREK, TOM, CHGO.	.307	115	420	65	129	194	32	3	9	63	8	4	4	3	25	4	58	6	1	11	.462	.350
PAGE, MITCHELL, OAK.*	.241	57	79	16	19	22	3	0	0	1	0	1	0	2	10	0	22	3	3	2	.278	.341

PAGEL, KARL, CLEV.*	.300	8	20	1	6	6	0	0	0	1	1	0	0	0	0	0	5	0	0	0	.300	.300
PARRISH, LANCE, DET.	.269	155	605	80	163	292	42	3	27	114	14	0	13	1	44	7	106	1	3	21	.483	.320
PARRISH, LARRY, TEX.	.272	145	555	76	151	263	26	4	26	88	17	0	9	3	46	8	91	0	0	20	.474	.331
PARSONS, CASEY, CHGO.*	.200	8	5	1	1	1	0	0	0	0	0	0	0	0	2	1	1	0	0	0	.200	.429
PASTORNICKY, CLIFF, K.C.	.125	9	32	4	4	10	0	0	2	5	2	0	0	0	0	0	3	0	0	4	.313	.125
PERCONTE, JACK, CLEV.	.269	14	26	1	7	8	1	0	0	0	0	0	0	0	5	0	2	3	1	0	.308	.387
PERKINS, BRODERICK, CLEV.*	.272	79	184	23	50	60	10	0	0	24	2	0	4	0	9	3	19	1	5	3	.326	.306
PETERS, RICKEY, OAK.†	.287	55	178	20	51	58	7	0	0	20	3	2	5	1	12	0	21	4	9	2	.326	.335
PETRALLI, GENO, TOR.†	.000	6	4	0	0	0	0	0	0	0	0	0	0	0	1	0	1	0	0	0	.000	.200
PETTIS, GARY, CALIF.†	.294	22	85	19	25	42	2	3	3	6	0	1	0	0	7	0	15	8	3	1	.494	.348
PHELPS, KEN, SEA.*	.236	50	127	10	30	57	4	1	7	16	1	1	3	0	13	0	25	0	0	0	.449	.307
PHILLIPS, TONY, OAK.†	.248	148	412	54	102	132	12	3	4	35	3	11	3	2	48	1	70	16	5	5	.320	.329
PICCIOLO, ROB, MILW.	.222	14	27	2	6	9	3	0	0	1	0	1	1	0	0	0	4	0	0	0	.333	.222
PINIELLA, LOU, N.Y.	.291	53	148	19	43	60	9	1	2	16	2	0	0	1	11	3	12	1	1	4	.405	.344
POWELL, HOSKEN, TOR.*	.169	40	83	6	14	17	0	0	1	7	1	0	1	0	5	0	8	2	0	1	.205	.216
PRYOR, GREG, K.C.	.217	68	115	9	25	32	4	0	1	14	1	2	1	0	7	0	8	0	0	3	.278	.262
PUTNAM, PAT, SEA.*	.269	144	469	58	126	210	23	2	19	67	8	1	5	3	39	8	57	2	1	12	.448	.329
QUINONES, LUIS, OAK.†	.190	19	42	5	8	12	2	1	0	4	1	1	1	0	1	0	4	1	1	0	.286	.209
RAMOS, DOMINGO, SEA.	.283	53	127	14	36	46	4	0	2	10	0	1	0	1	7	0	12	3	1	4	.362	.326
RANDOLPH, WILLIE, N.Y.	.279	104	420	73	117	146	21	1	2	38	1	3	0	1	53	0	32	12	4	11	.348	.361
READY, RANDY, MILW.	.405	12	37	8	15	25	3	2	1	6	0	0	0	0	6	1	3	0	1	0	.676	.488
REMY, JERRY, BOS.*	.275	146	592	73	163	189	16	5	0	43	7	12	3	0	40	2	35	11	3	12	.319	.321
REYNOLDS, HAROLD, SEA.†	.203	20	59	8	12	18	4	1	0	1	0	1	1	0	2	0	9	0	2	1	.305	.230
RHOMBERG, KEVIN, CLEV.	.476	12	21	2	10	10	0	0	0	2	0	0	1	0	2	0	4	1	1	0	.476	.522
RICE, JIM, BOS.	.305	155	626	90	191	344	34	1	39	126	14	0	5	6	52	10	102	0	2	31	.550	.364
RICHARDT, MIKE, TEX.	.157	22	83	9	13	20	2	1	1	7	0	0	1	0	2	0	11	2	1	2	.241	.176
RIPKEN, CAL, BALT.	.318	162	663	121	211	343	47	2	27	102	17	0	5	0	58	0	97	0	4	24	.517	.373
RIVERS, MICKEY, TEX.*	.285	96	309	37	88	108	17	0	1	20	3	5	3	1	11	0	21	9	4	1	.350	.312
ROBERTS, LEON, K.C.	.258	84	213	24	55	86	7	0	8	24	1	1	2	1	17	1	27	1	1	6	.404	.316
ROBERTSON, ANDRE, N.Y.	.248	98	322	37	80	105	16	3	1	22	1	7	3	3	8	0	54	2	4	8	.326	.273
RODRIGUEZ, AURELIO, BALT.-CHGO.	.138	67	87	1	12	16	1	0	1	3	0	2	1	1	0	0	16	0	0	1	.184	.148
ROENICKE, GARY, BALT.	.260	115	323	45	84	154	13	0	19	64	6	4	5	4	30	2	35	2	2	9	.477	.331
ROENICKE, RONALD, SEA.†	.253	59	198	23	50	74	12	0	4	23	0	2	2	2	33	1	22	6	2	2	.374	.365
ROMERO, ED, MILW.	.317	59	145	17	46	56	7	0	1	18	1	3	2	0	8	0	8	1	0	2	.386	.353

* BATS LEFTHANDED † SWITCH HITTER

BATTER AND CLUB	AVG	G	AB	R	H	TB	2B	3B	HR	RBI	GW RBI	SH	SF	HB	TBB	IBB	SO	SB	CS	GI DP	SLG	OBP
SAKATA, LENN, BALT.	.254	66	134	23	34	50	7	0	3	12	3	1	0	1	16	0	17	8	4	4	.373	.338
SAMPLE, BILLY, TEX.	.274	147	554	80	152	222	28	3	12	57	4	4	4	5	44	2	46	44	6	7	.401	.333
SCHOFIELD, DICK, CALIF.	.204	21	54	4	11	22	2	0	3	4	0	1	0	1	6	0	8	0	0	2	.407	.295
SCHROEDER, BILL, MILW.	.178	23	73	7	13	26	2	1	3	7	0	2	0	1	3	0	23	0	1	0	.356	.221
SCHROM, KEN, MINN.	—	34	0	0	0	0	0	0	0	0	0	0	0	0	0	0	0	0	0	0	—	—
SCONIERS, DARYL, CALIF.*	.274	106	314	49	86	135	19	3	8	46	4	2	1	0	17	2	41	4	2	8	.430	.311
SCOTT, DONNIE, TEX.†	.000	2	4	0	0	0	0	0	0	0	0	0	0	0	0	0	0	0	0	0	.000	.000
SHELBY, JOHN, BALT.†	.258	126	325	52	84	118	15	2	5	27	2	6	0	0	18	2	64	15	2	2	.363	.297
SHERIDAN, PAT, K.C.*	.270	109	333	43	90	127	12	2	7	36	7	4	0	0	20	0	64	12	3	3	.381	.312
SIMMONS, TED, MILW.†	.308	153	600	76	185	269	39	3	13	108	17	0	7	2	41	6	51	4	2	22	.448	.355
SIMPSON, JOE, K.C.*	.168	91	119	16	20	26	2	2	0	8	0	2	1	2	11	2	21	1	1	1	.218	.250
SINGLETON, KEN, BALT.†	.276	151	507	52	140	221	21	3	18	84	2	2	3	1	99	19	83	0	2	22	.436	.395
SKINNER, JOEL, CHGO.	.273	6	11	2	3	3	0	0	0	1	0	0	0	0	0	0	1	0	0	2	.273	.273
SKUBE, BOB, MILW.*	.200	12	25	2	5	8	1	1	0	9	0	0	0	0	4	0	7	0	0	2	.320	.310
SLAUGHT, DON, K.C.	.312	83	276	21	86	107	13	4	0	28	6	1	2	0	11	0	27	3	1	8	.388	.338
SMALLEY, ROY, N.Y.†	.275	130	451	70	124	204	24	1	18	62	5	5	4	2	58	2	68	3	3	9	.452	.360
SMITH, RAY, MINN.	.224	59	152	11	34	39	5	0	0	8	1	3	1	1	10	0	12	1	0	4	.257	.276
SQUIRES, MIKE, CHGO.*	.222	143	153	21	34	43	4	1	1	11	1	2	1	2	22	3	11	3	3	2	.281	.328
STAPLETON, DAVE, BOS.	.247	151	542	54	134	197	31	1	10	66	7	6	8	2	40	2	44	1	1	19	.363	.301
STEFERO, JOHN, BALT.*	.455	9	11	2	5	6	1	0	0	4	2	0	0	0	3	0	2	0	0	0	.545	.571
STEGMAN, DAVE, CHGO.	.170	29	53	5	9	11	2	0	0	4	0	0	2	0	10	0	9	0	1	1	.208	.302
STEIN, BILL, TEX.	.310	78	232	21	72	95	15	1	2	33	4	0	2	0	8	0	31	2	3	6	.409	.333
STEWART, SAMMY, BALT.	—	59	0	0	0	0	0	0	0	0	0	0	0	0	0	0	0	0	0	0	—	—
SUNDBERG, JIM, TEX.	.201	131	378	30	76	96	14	0	2	28	4	7	1	2	35	0	64	0	4	8	.254	.272
SWEET, RICK, SEA.†	.221	93	249	18	55	67	9	0	1	22	4	2	1	0	13	1	26	2	2	11	.269	.260
TABLER, PAT, CLEV.	.291	124	430	56	125	176	23	5	6	65	5	0	5	1	56	1	63	2	4	18	.409	.374
TEUFEL, TIM, MINN.	.308	21	78	11	24	42	7	1	3	6	3	2	0	0	2	0	8	0	0	1	.538	.325
THOMAS, GORMAN, MILW.-CLEV.	.209	152	535	72	112	203	23	1	22	69	4	4	8	2	80	3	148	10	4	13	.379	.314
THORNTON, ANDRE, CLEV.	.281	141	508	78	143	223	27	1	17	77	12	0	8	2	87	14	72	4	2	10	.439	.389
TOLLESON, WAYNE, TEX.†	.260	134	470	64	122	148	13	2	3	20	2	7	2	2	40	0	68	33	10	8	.315	.320

TRAMMELL, ALAN, DET.	.319	142	505	83	161	238	31	2	14	66	8	15	4	0	57	2	64	30	10	7	.471	.388
TRILLO, MANNY, CLEV.	.272	89	320	33	87	105	13	1	1	29	2	4	2	0	21	2	46	1	3	13	.328	.317
ULLGER, SCOTT, MINN.	.190	35	79	8	15	19	4	0	0	5	1	0	0	1	5	0	21	0	2	6	.241	.247
UPSHAW, WILLIE, TOR.*	.306	160	579	99	177	298	26	7	27	104	16	3	7	5	61	8	98	10	7	8	.515	.377
VALDEZ, JULIO, BOS.†	.120	12	25	3	3	3	0	0	0	0	0	0	0	1	1	0	4	0	0	0	.120	.185
VALENTINE, ELLIS, CALIF.	.240	86	271	30	65	118	10	2	13	43	2	1	4	0	18	0	48	2	1	6	.435	.287
VELEZ, OTTO, CLEV.	.080	10	25	1	2	2	0	0	0	1	0	0	0	0	3	0	6	0	0	0	.080	.179
VUKOVICH, GEORGE, CLEV.*	.247	124	312	31	77	103	13	2	3	44	1	3	4	2	24	4	37	3	4	8	.330	.305
WAGNER, MARK, TEX.	.000	2	2	0	0	0	0	0	0	0	0	0	0	0	0	0	1	0	0	0	.000	.000
WALKER, CHICO, BOS.†	.400	4	5	2	2	6	0	2	0	1	0	0	0	0	0	0	0	0	0	0	1.200	.400
WALKER, GREG, CHGO.*	.270	118	307	32	83	135	16	3	10	55	9	0	3	2	28	3	57	2	1	3	.440	.335
WARD, GARY, MINN.	.278	157	623	76	173	274	34	5	19	88	4	1	5	3	44	2	98	8	1	24	.440	.328
WASHINGTON, RON, MINN.	.246	99	317	28	78	103	7	3	4	26	5	3	1	1	22	1	50	10	5	7	.325	.297
WASHINGTON, U.L., K.C.†	.236	144	547	76	129	175	19	6	5	41	7	7	1	1	48	0	78	40	7	3	.320	.299
WATHAN, JOHN, K.C.	.245	128	437	49	107	137	18	3	2	32	4	2	2	1	27	0	57	28	7	13	.314	.290
WEBSTER, MITCH, TOR.†	.182	11	11	2	2	2	0	0	0	0	0	0	0	0	1	0	1	0	0	0	.182	.250
WHITAKER, LOU, DET.*	.320	161	643	94	206	294	40	6	12	72	8	2	8	0	67	8	70	17	16	8	.457	.385
WHITE, FRANK, K.C.	.260	146	549	52	143	223	35	6	11	77	10	4	6	0	20	4	51	13	5	18	.406	.286
WHITT, ERNIE, TOR.*	.256	123	344	53	88	158	15	2	17	56	11	1	5	0	50	5	55	1	1	9	.459	.350
WILFONG, ROB, CALIF.*	.254	65	177	17	45	60	7	1	2	17	3	2	1	0	10	1	25	0	2	2	.339	.294
WILKERSON, CURTIS, TEX.†	.171	16	35	7	6	8	0	1	0	1	0	0	0	0	2	0	5	3	0	0	.229	.216
WILSON, GLENN, DET.	.268	144	503	55	135	205	25	6	11	65	6	0	2	3	25	1	79	1	1	8	.408	.307
WILSON, TACK, MINN.	.250	5	4	4	1	2	1	0	0	1	0	0	0	0	0	0	0	0	0	0	.500	.250
WILSON, WILLIE, K.C.†	.276	137	576	90	159	203	22	8	2	33	1	1	0	1	33	2	75	59	8	4	.352	.316
WINFIELD, DAVE, N.Y.	.283	152	598	99	169	307	26	8	32	116	21	0	6	2	58	2	77	15	6	30	.513	.348
WOCKENFUSS, JOHN, DET.	.269	92	245	32	66	103	8	1	9	44	7	0	2	0	31	1	37	1	1	5	.420	.351
WRIGHT, GEORGE, TEX.†	.276	162	634	79	175	269	28	6	18	80	12	1	3	2	41	9	82	8	7	9	.424	.322
WYNEGAR, BUTCH, N.Y.†	.296	94	301	40	89	129	18	2	6	42	3	1	2	1	52	1	29	1	1	7	.429	.401
YASTRZEMSKI, CARL, BOS.*	.266	119	380	38	101	155	24	0	10	56	5	0	1	2	54	11	29	0	0	13	.408	.360
YOST, NED, MILW.	.224	61	196	21	44	69	5	1	6	28	1	8	1	0	5	0	36	1	0	6	.352	.244
YOUNG, MIKE, BALT.†	.167	24	36	5	6	10	2	1	0	2	1	4	0	1	2	0	8	1	0	1	.278	.231
YOUNT, ROBIN, MILW.	.308	149	578	102	178	291	42	10	17	80	10	1	8	3	72	6	58	12	4	10	.503	.387
ZISK, RICHIE, SEA.	.242	90	285	30	69	117	12	0	12	36	4	0	3	0	30	3	61	0	0	6	.411	.314

TOP FIFTEEN DESIGNATED HITTERS
(BASED ON TIMES AT BAT)

BATTER	BATS	CLUB	AVG	G	AB	R	H	TB	2B	3B	HR	RBI	GW RBI	SH	SF	HB	TBB	IBB	SO	SB	CS	GI DP	SLG	OBP
MCRAE	R	K.C.	.311	156	588	84	183	272	41	6	12	82	9	0	5	10	50	7	68	2	3	18	.463	.375
BAYLOR	R	N.Y.	.303	136	508	82	154	254	31	3	21	83	8	2	8	12	40	11	52	16	7	10	.500	.368
SINGLETON	S	BALT	.275	150	506	52	139	220	21	3	18	83	2	2	3	1	99	19	83	0	2	22	.435	.394
LUZINSKI	R	CHI	.253	139	495	73	125	248	25	1	32	92	10	0	9	11	68	6	115	2	1	10	.501	.355
THORNTON	R	CLEV	.288	114	413	66	119	188	24	0	15	65	10	0	6	1	75	13	54	3	1	8	.455	.399
BURROUGHS	R	OAK	.271	114	395	43	107	154	15	1	10	56	6	0	7	0	46	3	78	0	2	16	.390	.347
JOHNSON	R	TOR	.271	130	380	56	103	192	21	1	22	74	8	1	4	5	64	8	68	0	1	10	.505	.383
YASTRZEMSKI	L	BOS	.271	107	362	38	98	150	22	0	10	54	4	0	1	2	50	10	27	0	0	13	.414	.362
BUSH	L	MINN	.248	103	347	39	86	143	23	2	10	49	4	0	1	7	32	8	48	0	1	6	.412	.324
HOSTETLER	R	TEX	.218	88	293	28	64	110	9	2	11	46	5	0	2	5	41	1	98	0	2	9	.375	.324
ZISK	R	SEA	.238	84	281	30	67	115	12	0	12	36	4	0	3	0	28	2	60	0	0	6	.409	.307
SIMMONS	S	MILW	.329	66	258	37	85	134	21	2	8	56	6	0	3	2	16	0	24	2	1	9	.519	.373
JACKSON REG	L	CAL	.176	62	227	23	40	64	9	0	5	23	1	0	3	2	34	3	85	0	1	1	.282	.289
RIVERS	L	TEX	.290	53	210	27	61	78	14	0	1	16	3	5	1	1	9	0	13	4	4	0	.371	.323
GIBSON	L	DET	.252	66	210	33	53	91	7	5	7	28	3	3	2	1	34	3	47	7	3	2	.433	.359

PITCHING

TOP FIFTEEN QUALIFIERS FOR EARNED-RUN LEADERSHIP
(162 OR MORE INNINGS)

*THROWS LEFTHANDED

PITCHER AND CLUB	W	L	PCT	ERA	G	GS	CG	GF	SHO	SV	IP	H	TBF	R	ER	HR	SH	SF	HB	TBB	IBB	SO	WP	BK
HONEYCUTT, RICK, TEX.*	14	8	.636	2.42	25	25	5	0	2	0	174.2	168	693	59	47	9	3	6	6	37	2	56	1	2
BODDICKER, MIKE, BALT.	16	8	.667	2.77	27	26	10	1	5	0	179.0	141	711	65	55	13	4	3	0	52	1	120	5	0

STIEB, DAVE, TOR	17	12	.586	3.04	36	36	14	0	4	0	278.0	223	1141	105	94	21	6	9	14	93	6	187	5	1
HOUGH, CHARLIE, TEX	15	13	.536	3.18	34	33	11	1	3	0	252.0	219	1030	96	89	22	5	5	3	95	0	152	6	1
MCGREGOR, SCOTT, BALT.*	18	7	.720	3.18	36	36	12	0	2	0	260.0	271	1072	101	92	24	8	10	1	45	2	86	0	0
DOTSON, RICHARD, CHGO	22	7	.759	3.23	35	35	8	0	1	0	240.0	209	997	92	86	19	4	7	8	106	1	137	7	0
HAAS, MOOSE, MILW	13	3	.813	3.27	25	25	7	0	3	0	179.0	170	729	66	65	12	4	6	1	42	5	75	2	0
YOUNG, MATT, SEA.*	11	15	.423	3.27	33	32	5	0	2	0	203.2	178	851	86	74	17	4	8	7	79	2	130	4	2
ZAHN, GEOFF, CALIF.*	9	11	.450	3.33	29	28	11	1	3	0	203.0	212	852	90	75	22	6	8	0	51	3	81	4	0
MORRIS, JACK, DET	20	13	.606	3.34	37	37	20	0	1	0	293.2	257	1204	117	109	30	8	9	3	83	5	232	18	0
BANNISTER, FLOYD, CHGO.*	16	10	.615	3.35	34	34	5	0	2	0	217.1	191	902	88	81	19	4	4	2	71	3	193	8	1
GUIDRY, RON, N.Y.*	21	9	.700	3.42	31	31	21	0	3	0	250.1	232	1024	99	95	26	4	9	2	60	3	156	4	2
RIGHETTI, DAVE, N.Y.*	14	8	.636	3.44	31	31	7	0	2	0	217.0	194	900	96	83	12	10	4	2	67	2	169	10	1
DARWIN, DANNY, TEX	8	13	.381	3.49	28	26	9	0	2	0	183.0	175	780	86	71	9	7	7	3	62	3	92	2	0
BURNS, BRITT, CHGO.*	10	11	.476	3.58	29	26	8	0	4	0	173.2	165	732	79	69	14	6	3	5	55	2	115	6	0

INDIVIDUAL PITCHING

*THROWS LEFTHANDED

PITCHER AND CLUB	W	L	PCT	ERA	G	GS	CG	GF	SHO	SV	IP	H	TBF	R	ER	HR	SH	SF	HB	TBB	IBB	SO	WP	BK
ABBOTT, GLENN, SEA.-DET.	7	4	.636	3.63	21	21	3	0	1	0	129.0	146	541	58	52	14	5	3	4	22	3	49	2	2
ACKER, JIM, TOR.	5	1	.833	4.33	38	5	0	8	0	1	97.2	103	426	52	47	7	1	2	8	38	1	44	1	0
AGOSTO, JUAN, CHGO.*	2	2	.500	4.10	39	0	0	13	0	7	41.2	41	166	20	19	2	5	4	1	11	1	29	2	0
ALEXANDER, DOYLE, N.Y.-TOR.	7	8	.467	4.41	25	20	5	3	0	0	145.0	157	603	76	71	20	1	4	1	33	1	63	4	0
ANDERSON, BUD, CLEV.	1	6	.143	4.08	39	1	0	27	0	7	68.1	64	290	34	31	8	5	2	0	32	6	32	4	0
APONTE, LUIS, BOS.	5	4	.556	3.63	34	0	0	18	0	3	62.0	74	276	28	25	7	4	1	2	23	3	32	1	0
ARMSTRONG, MIKE, K.C.	10	7	.588	3.86	58	0	0	33	0	3	102.2	86	432	53	44	11	3	4	3	45	3	52	5	0
ATHERTON, KEITH, OAK.	2	5	.286	2.77	29	0	0	21	0	4	68.1	53	277	22	21	7	2	5	1	23	4	40	1	1
AUGUSTINE, JERRY, MILW.*	3	3	.500	5.74	34	7	1	9	0	2	64.1	89	304	45	41	11	4	3	1	25	4	40	1	0
BAILEY, HOWARD, DET.*	5	5	.500	4.88	33	3	0	15	0	0	72.0	69	302	45	39	11	3	1	2	25	3	21	1	0
BAIR, DOUG, DET.	7	3	.700	3.88	27	1	0	10	0	4	55.2	51	233	27	24	8	2	0	1	19	4	39	0	0
BAKER, STEVE, OAK.	3	3	.500	4.33	35	1	0	18	0	5	54.0	59	244	32	26	4	4	3	2	26	4	23	3	0
BANNISTER, FLOYD, CHGO.*	16	10	.615	3.35	34	34	5	0	2	0	217.1	191	902	88	81	19	4	4	2	71	3	193	8	1
BARKER, LEN, CLEV.	8	13	.381	5.11	24	24	4	0	1	0	149.2	150	633	92	85	16	10	5	2	52	3	105	6	0
BARNES, RICHARD, CLEV.*	1	1	.500	6.94	4	2	0	1	0	0	11.2	18	59	10	9	0	0	1	0	10	2	2	1	0
BAROJAS, SALOME, CHGO.	3	3	.500	2.47	52	0	0	29	0	12	87.1	70	355	24	24	2	3	2	5	32	2	38	1	0

*THROWS LEFTHANDED

PITCHER AND CLUB	W	L	PCT	ERA	G	GS	CG	GF	SHO	SV	IP	H	TBF	R	ER	HR	SH	SF	HB	TBB	IBB	SO	WP	BK
BEARD, DAVE, OAK.	5	5	.500	5.61	43	0	0	26	0	10	61.0	55	268	39	38	8	3	3	2	36	5	40	3	0
BEATTIE, JIM, SEA.	10	15	.400	3.84	30	29	8	0	2	0	196.2	197	834	89	84	12	3	2	3	66	6	132	6	1
BEENE, ANDY, MILW.	0	0	—	4.50	1	0	0	1	0	0	2.0	3	10	3	1	0	0	0	0	1	1	0	1	0
BEHENNA, RICK, CLEV.	0	2	.000	4.15	5	4	0	0	0	0	26.0	22	111	13	12	0	1	0	1	14	1	9	1	0
BERENGUER, JUAN, DET.	9	5	.643	3.14	37	19	2	7	1	1	157.2	110	650	58	55	19	1	2	6	71	3	129	3	1
BEST, KARL, SEA.	0	1	.000	13.50	4	0	0	0	0	0	5.1	14	36	9	8	2	0	0	2	5	0	3	1	0
BIRD, DOUG, BOS.	1	4	.200	6.65	22	6	0	7	0	1	67.2	91	303	52	50	14	0	4	2	16	4	33	1	0
BLACK, BUD, K.C.*	10	7	.588	3.79	24	24	3	0	0	0	161.1	159	672	75	68	19	4	5	2	43	1	58	4	0
BLUE, VIDA, K.C.*	0	5	.000	6.01	19	14	1	4	0	0	85.1	96	382	62	57	12	4	5	2	35	0	53	6	2
BLYLEVEN, BERT, CLEV.	7	10	.412	3.91	24	24	5	0	0	0	156.1	160	660	74	68	8	2	5	10	44	4	123	5	1
BODDICKER, MIKE, BALT.	16	8	.667	2.77	27	26	10	1	5	0	179.0	141	711	65	55	13	4	3	0	52	1	120	5	0
BOYD, OIL CAN, BOS.	4	8	.333	3.28	15	13	5	2	0	0	98.2	103	413	46	36	9	1	5	1	23	0	43	3	1
BRADLEY, BERT, OAK.	0	0	—	6.48	6	0	0	2	0	0	8.1	14	40	7	6	1	0	1	0	4	1	3	1	0
BRENNAN, TOM, CLEV.	2	2	.500	3.86	11	5	1	2	1	0	39.2	45	167	22	17	3	0	2	1	8	1	21	0	0
BROWN, CURT, CALIF.	1	1	.500	7.31	10	0	0	7	0	0	16.0	25	73	13	13	1	0	1	0	4	1	7	1	0
BROWN, MIKE, BOS.	6	6	.500	4.67	19	18	3	0	1	0	104.0	110	454	62	54	12	5	6	2	43	1	35	4	4
BROWN, STEVE, CALIF.	2	3	.400	3.52	12	4	2	4	1	0	46.0	45	195	19	18	4	1	2	0	16	1	23	0	0
BURGMEIER, TOM, OAK.*	6	7	.462	2.81	49	0	0	22	0	4	96.0	89	409	33	30	2	10	2	0	32	8	39	2	2
BURNS, BRITT, CHGO.*	10	11	.476	3.58	29	26	8	0	4	0	173.2	165	732	79	69	14	6	3	5	55	2	115	6	0
BUTCHER, JOHN, TEX.	6	6	.500	3.51	38	6	1	14	1	5	123.0	128	522	50	48	8	4	2	1	41	4	58	4	0
CALDWELL, MIKE, MILW.*	12	11	.522	4.53	32	32	10	0	2	0	228.1	269	970	125	115	35	4	4	1	51	1	58	3	1
CALLAHAN, BEN, OAK.	1	2	.333	12.54	4	2	0	1	0	0	9.1	18	52	16	13	0	1	1	0	5	1	2	0	0
CAMACHO, ERNIE, CLEV.	0	1	.000	5.06	4	0	0	1	0	0	5.1	5	23	3	3	1	0	0	1	2	0	2	0	0
CANDIOTTI, TOM, MILW.	4	4	.500	3.23	10	8	2	1	1	0	55.2	62	233	21	20	4	0	2	2	16	0	21	0	0
CASTILLO, BOBBY, MINN.	8	12	.400	4.77	27	25	3	0	0	0	158.1	170	686	91	84	17	6	2	1	65	4	90	3	1
CASTILLO, MANNY, SEA.	0	0	—	23.63	1	0	0	0	0	0	2.2	8	19	7	7	3	0	0	1	3	0	2	1	0
CASTRO, BILL, K.C.	2	0	1.000	6.64	18	0	0	6	0	0	40.2	51	190	34	30	4	0	3	5	12	1	17	1	0
CAUDILL, BILL, SEA.	2	8	.200	4.71	63	0	0	54	0	26	72.2	70	317	39	38	10	1	4	2	38	6	73	4	1
CLANCY, JIM, TOR.	15	11	.577	3.91	34	34	11	0	1	0	223.0	238	955	115	97	23	4	12	1	61	0	99	3	0
CLARK, BRYAN, SEA.*	7	10	.412	3.94	41	17	2	7	0	0	162.1	160	697	82	71	14	6	3	3	72	6	76	10	0
CLARKE, STAN, TOR.*	1	1	.500	3.27	10	0	0	5	0	0	11.0	10	46	4	4	2	1	1	0	5	0	7	0	1
CLEAR, MARK, BOS.	4	5	.444	6.28	48	0	0	33	0	4	96.0	101	448	71	67	10	1	6	3	68	5	81	2	0

COCANOWER, JAMIE, MILW.	2	0	1.000	1.80	5	3	1	0	0	0	30.0	21	118	8	6	1	0	0	1	12	0	8	1	0
CODIROLI, CHRIS, OAK.	12	12	.500	4.46	37	31	7	3	2	1	205.2	208	884	115	102	17	10	6	7	72	4	85	2	2
CONROY, TIM, OAK.*	7	10	.412	3.94	39	18	3	6	1	0	162.1	141	715	89	71	17	3	4	2	98	2	112	8	1
COOPER, DON, TOR.	0	0	—	6.75	4	0	0	1	0	0	5.1	8	23	4	4	3	0	0	0	0	0	5	0	0
CORBETT, DOUG, CALIF.	1	1	.500	3.63	11	0	0	7	0	0	17.1	26	80	10	7	1	1	0	1	4	2	18	0	0
CREEL, KEITH, K.C.	2	5	.286	6.35	25	10	1	9	0	0	89.1	116	404	66	63	17	1	3	2	35	0	31	1	0
CRUZ, VICTOR, TEX.	1	3	.250	1.44	17	0	0	13	0	5	25.0	16	103	7	4	2	3	2	1	10	3	18	0	0
CURTIS, JOHN, CALIF.*	1	2	.333	3.80	37	3	0	14	0	5	90.0	89	394	44	38	5	2	5	2	40	11	36	8	0
DARWIN, DANNY, TEX.	8	13	.381	3.49	28	26	9	0	2	0	183.0	175	780	86	71	9	7	7	3	62	3	92	2	0
DAVIS, RON, MINN.	5	8	.385	3.34	66	0	0	61	0	30	89.0	89	382	34	33	6	6	6	3	33	3	84	4	1
DAVIS, STORM, BALT.	13	7	.650	3.59	34	29	6	0	1	0	200.1	180	831	90	80	14	5	4	2	64	4	125	7	2
DOTSON, RICHARD, CHGO.	22	7	.759	3.23	35	35	8	0	1	0	240.0	209	997	92	86	19	4	7	8	106	1	137	7	0
EASTERLY, JAMIE, MILW.-CLEV.*	4	3	.571	3.67	53	0	0	25	0	4	68.2	83	306	32	28	4	5	2	4	32	5	45	1	0
ECKERSLEY, DENNIS, BOS.	9	13	.409	5.61	28	28	2	0	0	0	176.1	223	787	119	110	27	1	5	6	39	4	77	1	0
EICHELBERGER, JUAN, CLEV.	4	11	.267	4.90	28	15	2	5	0	0	134.0	132	577	80	73	10	2	4	2	59	3	56	9	0
ERICKSON, ROGER, N.Y.	0	1	.000	4.32	5	0	0	2	0	0	16.2	13	69	8	8	1	0	0	0	8	1	7	2	0
FARMER, ED, OAK.	0	0	—	3.48	5	1	0	1	0	0	10.1	15	42	4	4	1	0	1	0	0	0	7	0	0
FILSON, PETE, MINN.*	4	1	.800	3.40	26	8	0	10	0	1	90.0	87	379	34	34	9	1	2	1	29	0	49	1	2
FLANAGAN, MIKE, BALT.*	12	4	.750	3.30	20	20	3	0	1	0	125.1	135	528	53	46	10	4	6	2	31	2	50	1	0
FONTENOT, RAY, N.Y.*	8	2	.800	3.33	15	15	3	0	1	0	97.1	101	408	41	36	3	2	1	1	25	0	27	0	0
FORSCH, KEN, CALIF.	11	12	.478	4.06	31	31	11	0	1	0	219.1	226	920	107	99	21	4	3	4	61	6	81	6	0
FRAZIER, GEORGE, N.Y.	4	4	.500	3.43	61	0	0	30	0	8	115.1	94	479	44	44	5	6	10	3	45	4	78	5	0
GEISEL, DAVE, TOR.*	0	3	.000	4.64	47	0	0	16	0	5	52.1	47	230	28	27	4	1	0	2	31	5	50	2	1
GIBSON, BOB, MILW.	3	4	.429	3.90	27	7	0	16	0	2	80.2	71	357	40	35	6	4	6	1	46	2	46	5	1
GLYNN, ED, CLEV.*	0	2	.000	5.84	11	0	0	5	0	0	12.1	22	66	11	8	2	0	1	0	6	0	13	4	0
GOLTZ, DAVE, CALIF.	0	6	.000	6.22	15	6	0	2	0	0	63.2	81	301	48	44	10	3	3	1	37	2	27	1	1
GOSSAGE, RICH, N.Y.	13	5	.722	2.27	57	0	0	47	0	22	87.1	82	367	27	22	5	5	6	1	25	5	90	0	0
GOTT, JIM, TOR.	9	14	.391	4.74	34	30	6	2	1	0	176.2	195	776	103	93	15	4	3	5	68	5	121	2	0
GROSS, WAYNE, OAK.	0	0	—	.00	1	0	0	1	0	0	2.1	2	11	0	0	0	0	0	1	1	0	0	0	0
GUIDRY, RON, N.Y.*	21	9	.700	3.42	31	31	21	0	3	0	250.1	232	1024	99	95	26	4	9	2	60	3	156	4	2
GUMPERT, DAVE, DET.	0	2	.000	2.64	26	0	0	17	0	2	44.1	43	179	16	13	1	1	4	0	7	3	14	2	0
GURA, LARRY, K.C.*	11	18	.379	4.90	34	31	5	1	0	0	200.1	220	881	119	109	23	5	17	8	76	6	57	0	0
HAAS, MOOSE, MILW.	13	3	.813	3.27	25	25	7	0	3	0	179.0	170	729	66	65	12	4	6	1	42	5	75	2	0
HASSLER, ANDY, CALIF.*	0	5	.000	5.45	42	0	0	20	0	4	36.1	42	160	22	22	2	4	0	0	17	8	20	5	0

*THROWS LEFTHANDED

PITCHER AND CLUB	W	L	PCT	ERA	G	GS	CG	GF	SHO	SV	IP	H	TBF	R	ER	HR	SH	SF	HB	TBB	IBB	SO	WP	BK
HAVENS, BRAD, MINN.*	5	8	.385	8.18	16	14	1	0	0	0	80.1	110	378	75	73	11	1	9	0	38	3	40	6	0
HEATON, NEAL, CLEV.*	11	7	.611	4.16	39	16	4	19	3	7	149.1	157	637	79	69	11	3	5	1	44	10	75	1	0
HEIMUELLER, GORMAN, OAK.*	3	5	.375	4.41	16	14	2	2	1	0	83.2	93	362	43	41	8	6	1	1	29	2	31	3	0
HENKE, TOM, TEX.	1	0	1.000	3.38	8	0	0	5	0	1	16.0	16	65	6	6	1	0	0	0	4	0	17	0	0
HICKEY, KEVIN, CHGO.*	1	2	.333	5.23	23	0	0	13	0	5	20.2	23	98	14	12	5	0	0	0	11	2	8	1	0
HOFFMAN, GUY, CHGO.*	1	0	1.000	7.50	11	0	0	4	0	0	6.0	14	32	5	5	1	0	1	0	2	0	2	0	0
HONEYCUTT, RICK, TEX.*	14	8	.636	2.42	25	25	5	0	2	0	174.2	168	693	59	47	9	3	6	6	37	2	56	1	2
HOOD, DON, K.C.*	2	3	.400	2.27	27	0	0	15	0	0	47.2	48	199	20	12	5	4	3	2	14	2	17	3	0
HOUGH, CHARLIE, TEX.	15	13	.536	3.18	34	33	11	1	3	0	252.0	219	1030	96	89	22	5	5	3	95	0	152	6	1
HOWELL, JAY, N.Y.	1	5	.167	5.38	19	12	2	3	0	0	82.0	89	368	53	49	7	1	5	3	35	0	61	2	1
HOYT, LA MARR, CHGO.	24	10	.706	3.66	36	36	11	0	1	0	260.2	236	1034	115	106	27	4	8	1	31	4	148	1	1
HUISMANN, MARK, K.C.	2	1	.667	5.58	13	0	0	5	0	0	30.2	29	135	20	19	1	1	1	0	17	3	20	4	1
HURST, BRUCE, BOS.*	12	12	.500	4.09	33	32	6	0	2	0	211.1	241	903	102	96	22	3	4	3	62	5	115	1	2
JACKSON, DANNY, K.C.*	1	1	.500	5.21	4	3	0	0	0	0	19.0	26	87	12	11	1	1	0	0	6	0	9	0	0
JACKSON, ROY LEE, TOR.	8	3	.727	4.50	49	0	0	19	0	7	92.0	92	402	48	46	6	7	7	3	41	2	48	0	0
JAMES, BOB, DET.	0	0	—	11.25	4	0	0	3	0	0	4.0	5	19	5	5	2	0	0	0	3	0	4	0	0
JEFFCOAT, MIKE, CLEV.*	1	3	.250	3.31	11	2	0	1	0	0	32.2	32	140	13	12	1	1	0	1	13	1	9	1	1
JOHN, TOMMY, CALIF.*	11	13	.458	4.33	34	34	9	0	0	0	234.2	287	1010	126	113	20	8	7	2	49	5	65	11	0
JOHNSON, JOHN HENRY, BOS.*	3	2	.600	3.71	34	1	0	19	0	1	53.1	58	234	28	22	3	3	5	1	20	4	51	1	0
JONES, AL, CHGO.	0	0	—	3.86	2	0	0	1	0	0	2.1	3	10	1	1	0	0	0	0	2	0	2	0	0
JONES, JEFF, OAK.	1	1	.500	5.76	13	1	0	5	0	0	29.2	43	138	19	19	7	1	0	2	8	1	14	0	0
JONES, ODELL, TEX.	3	6	.333	3.09	42	0	0	33	0	10	67.0	56	281	28	23	4	4	2	2	22	1	50	1	0
KAUFMAN, CURT, N.Y.	0	0	—	3.12	4	0	0	1	0	0	8.2	10	39	3	3	0	0	2	0	4	0	8	0	0
KEOUGH, MATT, OAK.-N.Y.	5	7	.417	5.33	26	16	0	3	0	0	99.2	109	456	71	59	19	2	3	2	51	1	54	3	1
KERN, JIM, CHGO.	0	0	—	.00	1	0	0	0	0	0	0.2	1	3	1	0	0	0	0	0	0	0	0	1	0
KISON, BRUCE, CALIF.	11	5	.688	4.05	26	17	4	5	1	2	126.2	128	540	59	57	13	7	2	4	43	4	83	0	0
KOOSMAN, JERRY, CHGO.*	11	7	.611	4.77	37	24	2	6	1	2	169.2	176	730	96	90	19	5	5	6	53	2	90	6	0
KRUEGER, BILL, OAK.*	7	6	.538	3.61	17	16	2	0	0	0	109.2	104	473	54	44	7	0	5	2	53	1	58	1	1
LACEY, BOB, CALIF.*	1	2	.333	5.19	8	0	0	4	0	0	8.2	12	35	5	5	1	0	0	0	0	0	7	0	0
LACHOWICZ, AL, TEX.	0	1	.000	2.25	2	1	0	0	0	0	8.0	9	34	2	2	0	0	0	0	2	0	8	1	0
LADD, PETE, MILW.	3	4	.429	2.55	44	0	0	40	0	25	49.1	30	194	17	14	3	0	3	1	16	2	41	3	0
LAMP, DENNIS, CHGO.	7	7	.500	3.71	49	5	1	31	0	15	116.1	123	483	52	48	6	2	1	4	29	7	44	0	0

LANGFORD, RICK, OAK.	0	4	.000	12.15	7	7	0	0	0	0	20.0	43	112	28	27	4	1	3	2	10	1	2	0	0
LAROCHE, DAVE, N.Y.*	0	0	—	18.00	1	0	0	1	0	0	1.0	2	5	2	2	1	0	0	0	0	0	0	0	0
LEAL, LUIS, TOR.	13	12	.520	4.31	35	35	7	0	1	0	217.1	216	918	113	104	23	3	5	6	65	5	116	2	2
LEONARD, DENNIS, K.C.	6	3	.667	3.71	10	10	1	0	0	0	63.0	69	270	29	26	3	0	2	0	19	1	31	1	0
LEWIS, JIM, MINN.	0	0	—	6.50	6	0	0	0	0	0	18.0	24	82	13	13	5	0	0	1	7	0	8	0	0
LOPEZ, AURELIO, DET.	9	8	.529	2.81	57	0	0	46	0	18	115.1	87	473	36	36	12	4	5	1	49	7	90	7	1
LYSANDER, RICK, MINN.	5	12	.294	3.38	61	4	1	19	1	3	125.0	132	543	63	47	8	10	8	2	43	12	58	5	1
MARTIN, JOHN, DET.*	0	0	—	7.43	15	0	0	5	0	1	13.1	15	56	11	11	2	0	1	0	4	1	11	0	0
MARTINEZ, DENNIS, BALT.	7	16	.304	5.53	32	25	4	3	0	0	153.0	209	688	108	94	21	3	5	2	45	0	71	2	0
MARTINEZ, TIPPY, BALT.*	9	3	.750	2.35	65	0	0	51	0	21	103.1	76	406	30	27	10	3	5	0	37	3	81	6	0
MARTZ, RANDY, CHGO.	0	0	—	3.60	1	1	0	0	0	0	5.0	4	23	2	2	0	0	0	0	4	0	1	0	0
MASON, MIKE, TEX.*	0	2	.000	5.91	5	0	0	2	0	0	10.2	10	50	7	7	0	2	0	1	6	0	9	0	0
MATLACK, JON, TEX.*	2	4	.333	4.66	25	9	2	7	0	0	73.1	90	330	43	38	7	2	5	3	27	1	38	4	0
MAY, RUDY, N.Y.*	1	5	.167	6.87	15	0	0	4	0	0	18.1	22	90	15	14	1	2	0	1	12	1	16	2	0
MCCATTY, STEVE, OAK.	6	9	.400	3.99	38	24	3	11	2	5	167.0	156	725	79	74	16	4	6	1	82	4	65	5	0
MCCLURE, BOB, MILW.*	9	9	.500	4.50	24	23	4	0	0	0	142.0	152	625	75	71	11	0	4	5	68	1	68	4	6
MCGREGOR, SCOTT, BALT.*	18	7	.720	3.18	36	36	12	0	2	0	260.0	271	1072	101	92	24	8	10	1	45	2	86	0	0
MCLAUGHLIN, BYRON, CALIF.	2	4	.333	5.17	16	7	0	2	0	0	55.2	63	250	32	32	3	2	4	2	22	3	45	0	0
MCLAUGHLIN, JOEY, TOR.	7	4	.636	4.45	50	0	0	31	0	9	64.2	63	285	33	32	11	2	3	0	37	7	47	3	0
MIRABELLA, PAUL, BALT.*	0	0	—	5.59	3	2	0	1	0	0	9.2	9	45	6	6	1	1	0	0	7	0	4	0	0
MOFFITT, RANDY, TOR.	6	2	.750	3.77	45	0	0	33	0	10	57.1	52	247	27	24	5	5	3	1	24	6	38	0	0
MONTEFUSCO, JOHN, N.Y.	5	0	1.000	3.32	6	6	0	0	0	0	38.0	39	157	14	14	3	0	2	1	10	0	15	0	0
MOORE, MIKE, SEA.	6	8	.429	4.71	22	21	3	1	2	0	128.0	130	556	75	67	10	1	6	3	60	4	108	7	0
MORGAN, MIKE, TOR.	0	3	.000	5.16	16	4	0	2	0	0	45.1	48	198	26	26	6	0	1	0	21	0	22	3	0
MOROGIELLO, DAN, BALT.*	0	1	.000	2.39	22	0	0	8	0	1	37.2	39	160	10	10	1	1	1	1	10	3	15	1	0
MORRIS, JACK, DET.	20	13	.606	3.34	37	37	20	0	1	0	293.2	257	1204	117	109	30	8	9	3	83	5	232	18	0
MURA, STEVE, CHGO.	0	0	—	4.38	6	0	0	3	0	0	12.1	13	57	11	6	1	0	1	0	6	0	4	5	0
MURRAY, DALE, N.Y.	2	4	.333	4.48	40	0	0	21	0	1	94.1	113	415	56	47	5	6	6	1	22	4	45	4	1
NELSON, GENE, SEA.	0	3	.000	7.88	10	5	1	2	0	0	32.0	38	153	29	28	6	2	0	1	21	2	11	1	0
NIPPER, AL, BOS.	1	1	.500	2.25	3	2	1	1	0	0	16.0	17	67	4	4	0	0	1	1	7	0	5	0	0
NORRIS, MIKE, OAK.	4	5	.444	3.76	16	16	2	0	0	0	88.2	68	365	42	37	11	5	2	3	36	0	63	1	1
NUNEZ, EDWIN, SEA.	0	4	.000	4.38	14	5	0	4	0	0	37.0	40	170	21	18	3	1	0	3	22	1	35	0	2
O CONNOR, JACK, MINN.*	2	3	.400	5.86	27	8	0	9	0	0	83.0	107	383	59	54	13	3	4	0	36	1	56	3	0
OELKERS, BRYAN, MINN.*	0	5	.000	8.65	10	8	0	1	0	0	34.1	56	167	34	33	7	0	1	0	17	0	13	0	0

*THROWS LEFTHANDED

PITCHER AND CLUB	W	L	PCT	ERA	G	GS	CG	GF	SHO	SV	IP	H	TBF	R	ER	HR	SH	SF	HB	TBB	IBB	SO	WP	BK
OJEDA, BOB, BOS.*	12	7	.632	4.04	29	28	5	0	0	0	173.2	173	746	85	78	15	6	11	3	73	2	94	2	0
PALMER, JIM, BALT.	5	4	.556	4.23	14	11	0	1	0	0	76.2	86	330	42	36	11	4	3	0	19	0	34	1	1
PASHNICK, LARRY, DET.	1	3	.250	5.26	12	6	0	4	0	0	37.2	48	181	27	22	5	1	3	3	18	1	17	0	0
PERRY, GAYLORD, SEA.-K.C.	7	14	.333	4.64	30	30	3	0	1	0	186.1	214	811	108	96	24	11	6	4	49	4	82	6	0
PETRY, DAN, DET.	19	11	.633	3.92	38	38	9	0	2	0	266.1	256	1115	126	116	37	5	5	6	99	7	122	12	0
PETTIBONE, JAY, MINN.	0	4	.000	5.33	4	4	1	0	0	0	27.0	28	111	16	16	8	1	0	2	8	0	10	0	1
PORTER, CHUCK, MILW.	7	9	.438	4.50	25	21	6	1	1	0	134.0	162	595	72	67	9	4	7	2	38	2	76	0	0
QUISENBERRY, DAN, K.C.	5	3	.625	1.94	69	0	0	62	0	45	139.0	118	536	35	30	6	6	4	0	11	2	48	0	0
RAMIREZ, ALLAN, BALT.	4	4	.500	3.47	11	10	1	0	0	0	57.0	46	233	22	22	6	1	1	0	30	1	20	1	0
RASMUSSEN, ERIC, K.C.	3	6	.333	4.78	11	9	2	1	1	0	52.2	61	236	28	28	4	2	1	0	22	0	18	0	0
RAWLEY, SHANE, N.Y.*	14	14	.500	3.78	34	33	13	1	2	1	238.1	246	1010	111	100	19	7	6	3	79	1	124	5	1
REED, JERRY, CLEV.	0	0	—	7.17	7	0	0	1	0	0	21.1	26	95	19	17	4	1	1	0	9	1	11	0	0
RENKO, STEVE, K.C.	6	11	.353	4.30	25	17	1	2	0	1	121.1	144	536	63	58	9	4	4	0	36	1	54	4	0
RIGHETTI, DAVE, N.Y.*	14	8	.636	3.44	31	31	7	0	2	0	217.0	194	900	96	83	12	10	4	2	67	2	169	10	1
ROZEMA, DAVE, DET.	8	3	.727	3.43	29	16	1	7	0	2	105.0	100	441	50	40	10	3	5	1	29	6	63	1	3
RUCKER, DAVE, DET.*	1	2	.333	17.00	4	3	0	0	0	0	9.0	18	52	17	17	2	0	0	1	8	0	6	0	0
SANCHEZ, LUIS, CALIF.	10	8	.556	3.66	56	1	0	33	0	7	98.1	92	417	42	40	6	9	2	3	40	14	49	2	0
SCHMIDT, DAVE, TEX.	3	3	.500	3.88	31	0	0	20	0	2	46.1	42	191	20	20	3	1	1	1	14	1	29	2	0
SCHROM, KEN, MINN.	15	8	.652	3.71	33	28	6	2	1	0	196.1	196	843	92	81	14	7	9	9	80	3	80	2	1
SHIRLEY, BOB, N.Y.*	5	8	.385	5.08	25	17	1	3	1	0	108.0	122	467	71	61	10	9	6	0	36	3	53	1	1
SIMPSON, JOE, K.C.*	0	0	—	3.00	2	0	0	2	0	0	3.0	4	15	1	1	0	0	0	0	2	0	1	0	0
SLATON, JIM, MILW.	14	6	.700	4.33	46	0	0	26	0	5	112.1	112	490	57	54	12	9	10	3	56	5	38	3	0
SMITH, MARK, OAK.	1	0	1.000	6.75	8	1	0	2	0	0	14.2	24	70	11	11	0	1	0	1	6	1	10	1	0
SMITHSON, MIKE, TEX.	10	14	.417	3.91	33	33	10	0	0	0	223.1	233	960	102	97	14	6	8	8	71	2	135	8	2
SORENSEN, LARY, CLEV.	12	11	.522	4.24	36	34	8	2	1	0	222.2	238	941	112	105	21	5	7	2	65	9	76	9	1
SPILLNER, DAN, CLEV.	2	9	.182	5.07	60	0	0	41	0	8	92.1	117	418	54	52	7	0	7	2	38	9	48	4	0
SPLITTORFF, PAUL, K.C.*	13	8	.619	3.63	27	27	4	0	0	0	156.0	159	667	77	63	9	3	5	1	52	2	61	3	0
STANLEY, BOB, BOS.	8	10	.444	2.85	64	0	0	53	0	33	145.1	145	602	56	46	7	11	4	3	38	12	65	4	0
STANTON, MIKE, SEA.	2	3	.400	3.32	50	0	0	23	0	7	65.0	65	274	26	24	3	5	2	1	28	5	47	1	3
STEIRER, RICK, CALIF.	3	2	.600	4.82	19	5	0	7	0	0	61.2	77	282	40	33	3	3	3	3	18	4	25	1	0
STEWART, DAVE, TEX.	5	2	.714	2.14	8	8	2	0	0	0	59.0	50	237	15	14	2	2	1	2	17	0	24	1	0
STEWART, SAMMY, BALT.	9	4	.692	3.62	58	1	0	21	0	7	144.1	138	624	60	58	7	6	3	1	67	4	95	9	0

STIEB, DAVE, TOR.	17	12	.586	3.04	36	36	14	0	4	0	278.0	223	1141	105	94	21	6	9	14	93	6	187	5	1
STODDARD, BOB, SEA.	9	17	.346	4.41	35	23	2	4	1	0	175.2	182	739	95	86	29	9	3	4	58	0	87	5	4
STODDARD, TIM, BALT.	4	3	.571	6.09	47	0	0	34	0	9	57.2	65	261	39	39	10	4	4	1	29	4	50	2	1
SUTCLIFFE, RICK, CLEV.	17	11	.607	4.29	36	35	10	0	2	0	243.1	251	1061	131	116	23	8	9	6	102	5	160	7	3
SUTTON, DON, MILW.	8	13	.381	4.08	31	31	4	0	0	0	220.1	209	925	109	100	21	8	7	5	54	2	134	2	0
SWAGGERTY, BILL, BALT.	1	1	.500	2.91	7	2	0	3	0	0	21.2	23	92	8	7	1	0	0	0	6	0	7	0	0
TANANA, FRANK, TEX.*	7	9	.438	3.16	29	22	3	1	0	0	159.1	144	667	70	56	14	7	3	7	49	5	108	6	1
TELLMANN, TOM, MILW.	9	4	.692	2.80	44	0	0	26	0	8	99.2	95	415	34	31	7	8	3	2	35	4	48	2	1
THOMAS, ROY, SEA.	3	1	.750	3.45	43	0	0	12	0	1	88.2	95	386	44	34	3	3	4	2	32	3	77	3	0
TIDROW, DICK, CHGO.	2	4	.333	4.22	50	1	0	27	0	7	91.2	86	396	50	43	13	4	3	1	34	8	66	1	0
TOBIK, DAVE, TEX.	2	1	.667	3.68	27	0	0	24	0	9	44.0	36	176	18	18	2	0	1	0	13	3	30	0	0
TRAVERS, BILL, CALIF.*	0	3	.000	5.91	10	7	0	2	0	0	42.2	58	201	32	28	4	2	3	2	19	1	24	4	0
TUDOR, JOHN, BOS.*	13	12	.520	4.09	34	34	7	0	2	0	242.0	236	1022	122	110	32	5	5	4	81	3	136	8	2
TUFTS, BOB, K.C.*	0	0	—	8.10	6	0	0	3	0	0	6.2	16	42	8	6	1	0	0	1	5	0	3	1	0
UJDUR, JERRY, DET.	0	4	.000	7.15	11	6	0	4	0	0	34.0	41	161	33	27	6	0	0	1	20	1	13	2	0
UNDERWOOD, PAT, DET.*	0	0	—	8.71	4	0	0	2	0	0	10.1	11	44	10	10	1	0	0	0	6	0	2	1	0
UNDERWOOD, TOM, OAK.*	9	7	.563	4.04	51	15	0	15	0	4	144.2	156	627	69	65	13	1	10	2	50	4	62	7	0
VANDE BERG, ED, SEA.*	2	4	.333	3.36	68	0	0	30	0	5	64.1	59	270	32	24	6	4	3	1	22	6	49	4	1
VIOLA, FRANK, MINN.*	7	15	.318	5.49	35	34	4	0	0	0	210.0	242	949	141	128	34	5	2	8	92	7	127	6	2
VUCKOVICH, PETE, MILW.	0	2	.000	4.91	3	3	0	0	0	0	14.2	15	69	9	8	0	0	0	1	10	1	10	0	0
WAITS, RICK, CLEV.-MILW.*	0	3	.000	4.89	18	2	0	5	0	0	49.2	62	225	33	27	2	3	5	0	20	3	33	3	0
WALTERS, MIKE, MINN.	1	1	.500	4.12	23	0	0	10	0	2	59.0	52	242	31	27	4	5	2	2	20	4	21	0	1
WARREN, MIKE, OAK.	5	3	.625	4.11	12	9	3	1	1	0	65.2	51	262	33	30	4	2	4	1	18	1	30	2	0
WELCHEL, DON, BALT.	0	2	.000	5.40	11	0	0	3	0	0	26.2	33	124	18	16	1	2	1	0	10	1	16	1	0
WHITEHOUSE, LEN, MINN.*	7	1	.875	4.15	60	0	0	27	0	2	73.2	70	323	34	34	6	6	4	2	44	11	44	6	0
WILCOX, MILT, DET.	11	10	.524	3.97	26	26	9	0	2	0	186.0	164	775	89	82	19	2	3	4	74	6	101	10	2
WILLIAMS, AL, MINN.	11	14	.440	4.14	36	29	4	3	1	1	193.1	196	829	105	89	21	4	4	4	68	6	68	4	3
WILLIAMS, MATT, TOR.	1	1	.500	14.63	4	3	0	1	0	0	8.0	13	45	13	13	5	0	1	1	7	0	5	0	0
WILLS, FRANK, K.C.	2	1	.667	4.15	6	4	0	1	0	0	34.2	35	152	17	16	2	0	2	0	15	0	23	3	0
WITT, MIKE, CALIF.	7	14	.333	4.91	43	19	2	15	0	5	154.0	173	683	90	84	14	5	7	6	75	7	77	8	0
WORTHAM, RICH, OAK.*	0	0	—	INF	1	0	0	0	0	0	0.0	3	4	1	1	0	0	0	0	1	0	0	0	0
WRIGHT, RICKY, TEX.*	0	0	—	.00	1	0	0	0	0	0	2.0	0	8	0	0	0	2	0	0	1	0	2	0	0
YOUNG, CURT, OAK.*	0	1	.000	16.00	8	2	0	0	0	0	9.0	17	50	17	16	1	0	0	1	5	0	5	1	0
YOUNG, MATT, SEA.*	11	15	.423	3.27	33	32	5	0	2	0	203.2	178	851	86	74	17	4	8	7	79	2	130	4	2
ZAHN, GEOFF, CALIF.*	9	11	.450	3.33	29	28	11	1	3	0	203.0	212	852	90	75	22	6	8	0	51	3	81	4	0

TV/RADIO ROUNDUP

NETWORK COVERAGE

ABC-TV: Coverage on ABC will include Monday Night Baseball, late-season Sunday afternoon games, the 1984 All-Star Game and the American and National League Championship Series.

NBC-TV: The Saturday Game of the Week and the World Series will highlight NBC's baseball calendar.

USA CABLE NETWORK: The USA Cable Network will present regular-season games on Thursday nights.

NATIONAL LEAGUE

ATLANTA BRAVES: WCNN radio (680) and WTBS-TV (Channel 17) are the anchor stations for the Braves' network. Ernie Johnson, Pete Van Wieran, John Sterling and Skip Carey provide the coverage.

CHICAGO CUBS: Harry Caray, Milo Hamilton and Steve Stone describe the action for WGN-TV (Channel 9), while Lou Boudreau, Vince Lloyd and Hamilton do the honors for WGN radio (720).

CINCINNATI REDS: Ray Lane and Ken Wilson are on WLWT-TV (Channel 5), while Joe Nuxhall and Marty Brennaman call 'em as they see 'em over WLW radio (700).

HOUSTON ASTROS: KRBE (1070) and KRBE-FM (104) are the radio flagship stations, while KTXH (Channel 20) is the club's TV home. Gene Elston, Dewayne Staats and Larry Dierker handle TV and Elston and Staats double up on radio.

LOS ANGELES DODGERS: Vin Scully, Ross Porter and Jerry Doggett broadcast over KABC radio (790) and KTTV-TV (Channel 11). Spanish coverage is provided by Jaime Jarrin and Rene Cardenas on KTNQ radio (950).

MONTREAL EXPOS: Dave Van Horne and Duke Snider work the games for the English-speaking audience on CFCF radio (600)

The camera captures peppy play of Dodger Steve Sax.

and the CBC-TV network. Jacques Doucet and Claude Raymond say it in French for radio CKAC (730), but the French play-by-play announcers for CBC-TV were not determined at press time.

NEW YORK METS: Ralph Kiner, Tim McCarver and Steve Zabriskie handle television on WOR (Channel 9) and will be joined by Bud Harrelson on SportsChannel. Bob Murphy and Steve LaMar have radio duties for WHN (1050).

PHILADELPHIA PHILLIES: Harry Kalas, Andy Musser, Chris Wheeler and Richie Ashburn describe the action on WCAU radio (1210) and WTAF-TV (Channel 29).

PITTSBURGH PIRATES: Lanny Frattare, Jim Rooker and John Sanders line up for KDKA radio (1020) and also do the honors for KDKA-TV (Channel 2).

ST. LOUIS CARDINALS: Jack Buck, Mike Shannon and Dan Kelly are on KMOX radio (1120) and are joined by Jay Randolph on KSDK-TV (Channel 5).

SAN DIEGO PADRES: Jerry Coleman and Dave Campbell handle the play-by-play for KFMB radio (760) and KCST-TV (Channel 39).

SAN FRANCISCO GIANTS: David Glass and Hank Greenwald team up on radio station KNBR (680), while Gary Park and Greenwald work the television side for KTVU (Channel 2).

AMERICAN LEAGUE

BALTIMORE ORIOLES: Jon Miller and Tom Marr describe the action for radio station WFBR (1300), while Chuck Thompson and Brooks Robinson perform the chores for WMAR-TV (Channel 2).

BOSTON RED SOX: Ken Coleman and Joe Castiglione broadcast over the Campbell Sports Network, including Boston flagship station WHDH (850), while Ned Martin and Bob Montgomery handle television on WSBK (Channel 38).

CALIFORNIA ANGELS: Bob Starr and Ron Fairly describe the action on KMPC radio (710). Television arrangements were not determined at press time.

CHICAGO WHITE SOX: Ken Harrelson and Don Drysdale are the television crew for Sportsvision cable (Channel 60) and WGN-TV (Channel 9). Joel McConnell and Early Wynn call the action on radio station WMAQ (670).

CLEVELAND INDIANS: Herb Score and Nev Chandler are behind the mike for WWWE (1100), the flagship station for a four-state radio network. Joe Tait and a partner who was not yet chosen at press time work the telecasts for WUAB-TV (Channel 43).

DETROIT TIGERS: Ernie Harwell and Paul Carey broadcast on a radio network originating with WJR (760). George Kell and Al Kaline handle the chores for WDIV-TV (Channel 4).

KANSAS CITY ROYALS: Denny Trease, Denny Matthews and Fred White call the shots for WDAF-TV (Channel 4), while White and Matthews share radio time on a network headed by KCMO (810) and WIBW (580).

MILWAUKEE BREWERS: Steve Shannon and Mike Hegan describe the action for WVTV-TV (Channel 18), while the announcers for the Wisconsin Sports Network (WSN cable TV) were undetermined at press time. Bob Uecker and a partner who was unnamed at press time work the radio for WTMJ (620).

MINNESOTA TWINS: Bob Kurtz and Larry Osterman preside over the telecasts on KMSP (Channel 9), while Ron Weber and Herb Carneal call the plays for a radio network headed by WCCO (830).

NEW YORK YANKEES: Frank Messer, Phil Rizzuto, Bill White and Bobby Murcer share duties on a TV network headed by WPIX (Channel 11), while Mel Allen and Fran Healy join them in describing the action for SportsChannel cable. John Gordon works with Messer, Rizzuto and White on a radio network originating with WABC (770).

OAKLAND A's: Bill King, Lon Simmons and Wayne Hagin do the play-by-play on KFSO radio (560) and are joined by Bill Rigney on KBHK-TV (Channel 44).

SEATTLE MARINERS: Dave Niehaus and Rick Rizzs do the honors for radio station KVI (570) and Wes Stock joins them on telecasts for KSTW (Channel 11).

TEXAS RANGERS: Eric Nadel, Steve Busby and Mark Holtz form the team that works the games for WBAP radio (820) and KXAS-TV (Channel 5).

TORONTO BLUE JAYS: Tom Cheek and Jerry Howarth do the radio play-by-play on a network that originates with CJCL (1430). Don Chevrier, Tony Kubek and Fergie Olver are behind the mike for the CTV Network's television coverage.

OFFICIAL 1984 AMERICAN LEAGUE SCHEDULE

BOLD = SUNDAY   ( ) = HOLIDAY   = NIGHT DAY   TN = TWI-NIGHT   DH **[2]** = DH   TBA = TO BE ANNOUNCED

	AT SEATTLE	AT OAKLAND	AT CALIFORNIA	AT TEXAS	AT KANSAS CITY	AT MINNESOTA	AT CHICAGO
SEATTLE	81 HOME DATES 62 NIGHTS	May 7*,8,9 Aug. 3 TN,4,**5**	April 27*,28,**29**,30* July 23*,24*,25*	June 1*,2*,**3*** Sept. (3*),4*,5*	June 4*,5*,6*,7* Sept. 7*,8*,**9**	April 13*,14,**15** July 30*,31* Aug 1	June 25*,26*,27* Sept. 21*,22,**23**
OAKLAND	April 16*,17*,18 July 27*,28*,**29**	79 HOME DATES 38 NIGHTS	May 1*,2* Aug. 9*,10*,11*,**12**	June 8*,9*,**10***,11* Sept. 24*,25*,26*	June 25*,26 TN,27* Sept. 21*,22*,**23**	May 4*,5,**6** July 23*,24*,25*	May 31*, June 1*,2*,**3** Sept. (3),4*,5*
CALIFORNIA	May 4*,5*,**6** Aug. 6*,7*,8	April 12,13*,14,**15** July 30*,31* Aug. 1	81 HOME DATES 61 NIGHTS	June 25*,26*,27* Sept. 27*,28*,29*,**30**	June 8*,9*,**10** Sept. 24*,25*,26*	April 16*,17*,18* July 27*,28*,**29**	June 4*,5*,6* Sept. 6*,7*,8,**9**
TEXAS	June 15*,16*,**17** Sept. 10*,11*,12*,13*	June 22*,23,**24** Sept. 17*,18*,19	June 18*,19*,20* Sept. 21*,22,**23**	81 HOME DATES 72 NIGHTS	May 18*,19*,**20** Aug. 28*,29*,30*	June 4*,5*,6*,7 Sept. 7*,8,**9**	May 10*,11*,12 **13** Aug. 13*,14*,15*
KANSAS CITY	June 12*,13*,14 Sept. 14*,15*,**16**	June 18*,19*,20 Sept. 28*,29,**30**	June 22*,23*,**24** Sept. 17*,18*,19*,20*	May (28*),29*,30* Aug. 16*,17*,18*,**19***	80 HOME DATES 64 NIGHTS	May 31* June 1*,2*,**3** Sept. 10*,11*,12*	May 14*,15*,16* Aug. 31* Sept. 1*,**2**
MINNESOTA	May 1*,2*,3* Aug. 9*,10*,11*,**12**	April 27*,28,**29[2]** Aug. 6*,7*,8	May 7*,8*,9* Aug. 2*,3*,4*,**5**	June 12*,13*,14* Sept. 14*,15*,**16**	June 15*,16*,**17** Sept. (3*),4*,5*	81 HOME DATES 52 NIGHTS	June 8*,9,**10** Sept. 24*,25*,26*
CHICAGO	June 18*,19*,20 Sept. 27*,28*,29*,**30**	June 15*,16,**17** Sept. 10*,11*,12	June 12*,13*,14* Sept. 14*,15*,**16**	May 25*,26*,**27** Aug. 20*,21*,22*	May 21*,22*,23* Aug. 24*,25*,**26**,27*	June 22*,23*,**24** Sept. 17*,18*,19*,20	81 HOME DATES 54 NIGHTS

MILWAUKEE	April 6*,7*,**8** July 16*,17*,18	April 3*,4* July 19*,20*,21,**22**	April 10*,11* July 12*,13*,14*,**15**	May 22*,23*,24* Aug. 31* Sept. 1*,**2**	April 13*,14*,**15** Aug. 7*,8*,9*	May 25*,26,**27** Aug. 13*,14*,15*	May 7*,8*,9* Aug 10*,11*,**12**
DETROIT	May 25*,26*,**27** Aug. 28*,29*,30*	May (28*),29*,30 Aug. 31* Sept. 1,**2**	May 22*,23*,24* Aug. 24*,25*,**26**	April 25*,26* July 5*,6*,7*,**8***	May 7*,8*,9* Aug. 10*,11*,**12**	April 3,5 July 12,13*,14*,**15**	April 6,7,**8** July 2*,3*,(4*)
CLEVELAND	June 22*,23*,**24** Sept. 17*,18*,19*	June 12*,13,14 Sept. 14*,15,**16**	June 15*,16*,**17** Sept. 11*,12*,13*	April 3*,5* July 12*,13*,14*,**15***	April 6*,7*,**8** July 16*,17*,18*	June 19*,20*,21 Sept. 21*,22,**23**	April 10*,11 July 5,6*,7,**8**
TORONTO	April 4*,5* July 19*,20*,21*,**22**	April 9*,10* July 12,13*,14,**15**	April 6*,7,**8** July 16*,17*,18*	April 13*,14,**15** Aug. 6*,7*,8*	April 27*,28*,**29** July 23*,24*,25*	May 15*,16 Aug. 24*,25,**26**,27*	May (28*),29*,30* Aug. 17*,18*,**19**
BALTIMORE	May (28*),29*,30 Aug. 31* Sept. 1*,**2**	May 22*,23,24 Aug. 24*,25,**26**	May 25*,26,**27** Aug. 27*,28*,29	May 4*,5*,**6** July 23*,24*,25*	April 25*,26* July 19*,20*,21,**22**	April 6*,7,**8** July 2*,3*,(4*)	April 23*,24* June 28*,29*,30* July **1**
NEW YORK	May 22*,23*,24* Aug. 24*,25*,**26**	May 25*,26,**27** Aug. 27*,28*,29*	May (28),29*,30* Aug. 31* Sept. 1*,**2**	April *6,7,**8** July 2*,3*,(4*)	April 2,4*,5* June 29*,30 July **1**	April 25*,26 July 5*,6*,7*,**8**	April 30* May 1*,2* July 27*,28,**29**
BOSTON	April 10*,11* July 12*,13*,14*,**15**	April 6*,7,**8** July 16*,17*,18	April 2*,4*,5* July 20*,21,**22**	May 8*,9* Aug. 9*,10*,11*,**12***	May 11*,12*,**13** Aug. 13*,14*,15*	May 18*,19*,**20** Aug. 28*,29*,30*	April 27*,28 **29** July 30*,31* Aug. 1*

ALL-STAR GAME AT CANDLESTICK PARK, SAN FRANCISCO, JULY 10

OFFICIAL 1984 AMERICAN LEAGUE SCHEDULE

BOLD = SUNDAY ( ) = HOLIDAY = NIGHT DAY TN = TWI-NIGHT DH **[2]** = DH TBA = TO BE ANNOUNCED

	AT MILWAUKEE	AT DETROIT	AT CLEVELAND	AT TORONTO	AT BALTIMORE	AT NEW YORK	AT BOSTON
SEATTLE	April 20*,21,**22** July 2*,3*,(4)	May 14*,15*,16* Aug. 17*,18*,**19**	June 8*,9,**10[2]** Sept. 25*,26*	April 23,24* July 5*,6*,7,**8**	May 18*,19*,**20** Aug. 20*,21*,22*	May 11*,12*,**13** Aug. 14*,15,16*	April 25*,26* June 28*,29*,30 July **1**
OAKLAND	April 23*,24* July 5*,6*,7*,**8**	May 18*,19*,**20** Aug. 20*,21*,22*	June 4*,5*,6* Sept. 7*,8,**9**	April 25*,26 June 28*,29*,30 July **1**	May 11*,12*,**13** Aug. 14*,15*,16*	May 14*,15*,16* Aug. 17*,18*,**19**	April 20*,21,**22** July 2*,3*,(4)
CALIFORNIA	April 25*,26 June 28*,29*,30* July **1**	May 11*,12,**13** Aug. 14*,15*,16	June 1*,2*,**3** Sept. (3*),4*,5*	April 20,21,**22** July (2),3*,4*	May 14*,15*,16* Aug. 17*,18,**19**	May 18*,19,**20** Aug. 20*,21*,22*	April 23*,24* July 5*,6*,7,**8**
TEXAS	May 15*,16*,17 Aug. 24*,25,**26**	April 10,12 July 19*,20*,21*,**22**	April 23,24 June 28*,29*,30* July **1**	April 30* May 1*,2* July 27*,28*,**29**	April 27*,28*,**29** July 30*,31* Aug. 1*	April 20*,21,**22** July 16*,17*,18	April 17*,18*,19 Aug. 3*,4,**5**
KANSAS CITY	May 1*,2*,3 July 27,28*,**29**	April 17*,18* Aug. 3*,4,**5[2]**	April 20,21,**22** July 2*,3*,(4)	May 4*,5,**6** July 30*,31* Aug. 1*	April 10*,11* July 5*,6*,7*,**8**	April 23*,24 July 12*,13*,14,**15**	May 25*,26,**27** Aug. 20*,21*,22*,
MINNESOTA	May 11*,12,**13** Aug. 21*,22*,23	April 23*,24* June 29 TN,30* July **1**	June 26*,27* Sept. 27*,28*,29,**30**	May 21,22*,23* Aug. 31* Sept. 1,**2**	April 20*,21*,**22** July 16*,17*,18*	April 10,12* July 19*,20*,21,**22**	May (28),29*,30* Aug. 17*,18,**19**
CHICAGO	April 17,19 Aug. 3*,4,**5**,6*	April 20*,21,**22** July 16*,17*,18*	April 25,26 July 19*,20*,21,**22**	May 17*,18*,19,**20** Aug. 28*,29*	April 2,4 July 12*,13*,14*,**15**	April 13*,14,**15** Aug. 7*,8,9*	May 4*,5,**6** July 24*,25*,26*

MILWAUKEE	80 HOME DATES 49 NIGHTS	June 21*,22*,23,**24** Sept. 17*,18*,19*	May (28*),29*,30* Aug. 17*,18*,**19**	June 19*,20 Sept. 20*,21*,22,**23**	June 4*,5*,6* Sept. 7*,8*,**9**	April 27*,28*,**29** July 30*,31* Aug. 1*,2*	June 7*,8*,9,**10** Sept. 10*,11*,12*
DETROIT	June 15*,16*,**17** Sept. 24*,25*,26*	78 HOME DATES 51 NIGHTS	May 4*,5,**6** July 23*,24*,25*,26*	June 11*,12*,13* Sept. 7*,8,**9**	June 8*,9(2),**10** Sept. 10*,11*,12*	June 25*,26*,27* Sept. 27*,28*,29,**30**	April 13,**15**,16 Aug. 6*,7*,8*
CLEVELAND	May 18*,19*,**20** Aug. 27*,28*,29*,30	April 27*,28,**29** July 31* Aug. 1*,2	80 HOME DATES 49 NIGHTS	May 25*,26,**27[2]** Aug. 21*,22*,23	April 30* May 1*,2 July 27*,28*,**29**	May 7*,8*,9*,10* Aug. 3*,4*,**5**	May 21*,22*,23* Aug. 24*,25,**26**
TORONTO	June 25 TN,26*,27 Sept. 28*,29,**30**	June 4*,5*,6*,7 Sept. 14*,15,**16**	May 11*,12,**13** Aug. 14*,15*,16*	80 HOME DATES 45 NIGHTS	May 7*,8*,9* Aug. 3*,4*,**5**	June 8*,9*,**10** Sept. (3),4*,5*	June 21*,22*,23,**24** Sept. 24*,25*,26*
BALTIMORE	June 11*,12*,13*,14 Sept. 14*,15,**16**	June 1*,2,**3** Sept. (3*),4*,5*	April 14,**15**,16 Aug. 6*,7*,8*,9*	April 17,18,19 Aug. 10*,11,**12**,13*	80 HOME DATES 61 NIGHTS	June 15*,16,**17** Sept. 17*,18*,19*	June 19*,20* Sept. 27*,28*,29,**30**
NEW YORK	May 4*,5*,**6** July 23*,24*,25*	June 18*,19*,20* Sept. 21*,22,**23**	April 17*,18* Aug. 10*,11*,**12**,13*	June 1*,2,**3** Sept. 10*,11*,12*,13*	June 21*,22*,23*,**24** Sept. 24*,25*,26*	81 HOME DATES 55 NIGHTS	June 11*,12*,13*,14* Sept. 7*,8,**9**
BOSTON	June 1*,2,**3** Sept. (3),4*,5*	May 1*,2*,3 July 27 TN,28*,**29**	May 14*,15*,16*,17* Aug. 31* Sept. 1,**2**	June 15*,16,**17** Sept. 17*,18*,19*	June 25*,26*,27* Sept. 20*,21*, 22(TBA),**23**	June 4*,5*,6* Sept. 14*,15*,**16**	81 HOME DATES 53 NIGHTS

ALL-STAR GAME AT CANDLESTICK PARK, SAN FRANCISCO, JULY 10

OFFICIAL 1984

EAST

	AT CHICAGO	AT MONTREAL	AT NEW YORK
Chicago		June 5*, 6*, 7* Aug. 9*, 10*, 11, **12** Sept. 5*, 6*	May 1*, 2* July 27,* 28, **29, 29** Sept. 7*, 8*, **9**
Montreal...............	June 11, 12, 13 Aug. 2, 3, 4, **5** Sept. 12, 13		April 17, 18, 19 June 22*, 23, **24** Sept. 21*, 22, **23**
New York	April, 13, 14, **15** Aug. 6, 7, 8 Sept. 14, 15, **16**	April 23, 24, 25 June 8*, 9*, **10** Sept. 28*, 29*, **30**	
Philadelphia	June 14, 15, 16, **17** July 30, 31, Aug. 1 Sept. 10, 11	April 13, 14, **15** Aug. 6*, 7*, 8,* Sept. 7*, 8*, **9**	April 27*, 28, **29** June 19*, 20*, 21 Sept. 24*, 25*, 26
Pittsburgh	April 20, 21, **22** June 25, 26, 27 Sept. 18, 19, 20	June 14*, 15*, 16, **17** July 24*, 25*, 26* Sept. 3, 4*	June 11*, 12*, 13* Aug. 9*, 10*, 11*, **12** Sept. 12*, 13
St. Louis...............	April 17, 18, 19 June 22, 23, **24** Sept. 28, 29, **30**	April 27, 28, **29** June 18*, 19*, 20* Sept. 24*, 25*, 26*	May 31*, June 1*, 2*, **3** July 23*, 24*, 25 Sept. 10*, 11*
Atlanta	May 22, 23, 24 Aug, 24, 25, **26**	May 4*, 5, **6** July 16*, 17*, 18*	May 9*, 10 June 28*, 29*, 30*, July **1**
Cincinnati.............	May 25, 26, **27**, 28 Aug. 28, 29	May 9*, 10 July 12*, 13*, 14*, **15**	May 7*, 8* July 5*, 6*, 7*, **8**
Houston	May 18, 19, **20** Aug. 20, 21, 22	May 7*, 8 July 5*, 6*, 7*, **8**	May 4*, 5*, **6** July 2*, 3*, 4*
Los Angeles	May 9, 10 July 12, 13, 14, **15**	May 28*, 29*, 30* Aug 31*, Sept. 1, **2**	May 25*, 26, **27** Aug. 27*, 28*, 29*
San Diego.............	May 4, 5, **6** July 16, 17, 18	May 22*, 23* Aug. 24*, 24*, 25*, **26**	May 28, 29*, 30* Aug. 31*, Sept. 1*, **2**
San Francisco.......	May 7, 8 July 19, 20, 21, **22**	May 25*, 26*, **27** Aug. 27*, 28*, 29*	May 22*, 23*, 24* Aug. 24*, 25*, **26**

*NIGHT GAME
HEAVY BLACK FIGURES DENOTE SUNDAY
NIGHT GAMES: ANY GAME STARTING AFTER 5:00 p.m.

NATIONAL LEAGUE SCHEDULE

EAST

	AT PHILADELPHIA	AT PITTSBURGH	AT ST. LOUIS
Chicago	May 31*, June 1*, 2, **3** July 23*, 24*, 25 Sept. 3*, 4*	April 27*, 28,* **29** June 19*, 20*, 21* Sept. 24*, 25*, 26*	April 23*, 24*, 25 June 8*, 9*, **10** Sept. 21*, 22, **23**
Montreal	April 30*, May 1*, 2* July 27*, 28*, **29** Sept. 14*, 15*, **16**	May 31*, June 1*, 2*, **3** July 30*, 31*, Aug. 1* Sept. 10*, 11*	April 20*, 21*, **22** June 25*, 26*, 27* Sept. 18*, 19*, 20*
New York	April 20*, 21, **22** June 25*, 26*, 27* Sept. 17*, 18*, 19*	June 4*, 5*, 6* Aug. 2*, 3*, 4*, **5** Sept. 5*, 6*	June 14*, 15*, 16*, **17** July 30*, 31*, Aug. 1 Sept. 3*, 4*
Philadelphia		April 17, 18, 19 June 22*, 23*, **24** Sept. 21*, 22*, **23**	June 4*, 5*, 6* Aug. 2*, 3*, 4*, **5** Sept. 5*, 6*
Pittsburgh	April 24*, 25* June 8*, 8*, 9*, **10** Sept. 28*, 29*, **30**		April 13*, 14*, **15** Aug. 6*, 7*, 8* Sept. 14*, 15, **16**
St. Louis	June 11*, 12*, 13* Aug. 9*, 10*, 11*, **12** Sept. 12*, 13*	April 30*, May 1*, 2* July 27*, 28, **29** Sept. 7*, 8*, **9**	
Atlanta	May 7*, 8* July 5*, 6*, 7, **8**	May 18*, 19*, **20** Aug. 20*, 21*, 22*	May 15*, 16*, 17 Aug. 17*, 18, **19**
Cincinnati	May 4*, 5*, **6** July 2*, 3*, 4*	May 22*, 23*, 24* Aug. 24*, 25*, **26**	May 18*, 19*, **20** Aug. 13*, 14*, 15*
Houston	April 10, 11* June 28*, 29*, 30*, July **1**	May 14*, 15*, 16* Aug. 17*, 18*, **19**	May 21*, 22*, 23 Aug. 31*, Sept. 1*, **2**
Los Angeles	May 22*, 23*, 24* Aug. 24*, 25, **26**	May 4*, 5, **6** July 16*, 17*, 18*	May 7*, 8* July 19*, 20*, 21, **22**
San Diego	May 25*, 26*, **27** Aug. 27*, 28*, 29*	May 7*, 8* July 19*, 20*, 21*, **22**	May 9*, 10 July 12*, 13*, 14*, **15**
San Francisco	May 28*, 29*, 30* Aug. 31*, Sept. 1*, **2**	May 9*, 10 July 12*, 13*, 14, **15**	May 4*, 5*, **6** July 16*, 17*, 18*

JULY 10 — ALL-STAR GAME AT SAN FRANCISCO
AUGUST 13 — HALL OF FAME GAME at COOPERSTOWN, NY
(Detroit Tigers vs. Atlanta Braves)

OFFICIAL 1984

WEST

	AT ATLANTA	AT CINCINNATI	AT HOUSTON
Chicago	May 29*, 30* Aug. 30*, 31*, Sept. 1, **2**	May 15*, 16*, 17 Aug. 17*, 18*, **19**	May 11*, 12, **13*** Aug. 13*, 14*, 15*
Montreal	April 6*, 7*, **8** July 2, 3*, 4*	April 9*, 10*, 11 June 29*, 30*, July **1**	April 3*, 4* July 19*, 20*, 21*, **22***
New York	April 10*, 11* July 12*, 13*, 14*, **15**	April 2, 4* July 19*, 20*, 21*, **22**	April 6*, 7*, **8*** July 16*, 17*, 18*
Philadelphia	April 3*, 4* July 19*, 20*, 21, **22**	April 6*, 7, **8** July 16*, 17*, 18*	May 9*, 10* July 12*, 13*, 14*, **15***
Pittsburgh	May 11*, 12*, **13** Aug. 14*, 15*, 16*	May 29*, 30* Aug. 30*, 31*, Sept. 1*, **2**	May 25*, 26*, **27***, 28* Aug. 28*, 29*
St. Louis	May 25*, 26, **27**, 28* Aug. 28*, 29*	May 11*, 12, **13** Aug. 20*, 21*, 22*	May 29*, 30* Aug. 23*, 24*, 25*, **26***
Atlanta		April 17*, 18 June 1*, 1*, 2*, **3** Sept. 25*, 26*, 27*	April 27*, 28, **29*** July 30*, 31*, Aug. 1* Sept. 10*, 11*, 12*
Cincinnati	April 24*, 25*, 26* June 14*, 15*, 16*, **17** Sept. 19*, 20*		April 13*, 14*, **15*** June 11*, 12*, 13* Sept. 21*, 22*, **23***
Houston	April 20*, 21*, **22** June 25*, 25*, 26*, 27* Sept. 3*, 4*	May 1*, 2*, 3 Aug. 10*, 11*, **12** Sept. 28*, 29, **30**	
Los Angeles	June 22*, 23, **24** Aug. 6*, 7*, 8*, 9* Sept. 17*, 18*	June 19*, 20*, 21* Aug. 3*, 4, **5** Sept. 14*, 15*, **16**	April 16*, 17*, 18* June 14*, 15*, 16*, **17*** Sept. 19*, 20*
San Diego	May 1*, 2*, 3* Aug. 10*, 11*, **12** Sept. 28*, 29*, **30**	June 22*, 23*, **24** Aug. 6*, 7*, 8*, 9* Sept. 17*, 18	June 19*, 20*, 21* Aug. 3*, 4*, **5*** Sept. 14*, 15, **16***
San Francisco	June 19*, 20*, 21* Aug. 3*, 4*, **5** Sept. 14*, 15*, **16**	April 27*, 28, **29, 29** July 31*, Aug. 1*, 2* Sept. 11*, 12*	June 22*, 23*, **24*** Aug. 6*, 7*, 8*, 9* Sept. 17*, 18*

*NIGHT GAME
HEAVY BLACK FIGURES DENOTE SUNDAY
NIGHT GAMES: ANY GAME STARTING AFTER 5:00 p.m.

NATIONAL LEAGUE SCHEDULE

WEST

	AT LOS ANGELES	AT SAN DIEGO	AT SAN FRANCISCO
Chicago	April 9*, 11* June 28*, 29*, 30*, July **1**	April 6*, 7*, **8** July 2*, 3*, 4*	April 3, 5* July 5*, 6*, 7, **8**
Montreal	May 18*, 19*, **20** Aug. 20*, 21*, 22	May 14*, 15*, 16*, 17 Aug. 17*, **19**	May 11*, 12, **13** Aug. 14*, 15, 16*
New York	May 11*, 12, **13** Aug. 13*, 14*, 15*	May 18*, 19*, **20** Aug. 20*, 21*, 22*	May 15*, 16 Aug. 17*, 18, **19, 19**
Philadelphia	May 14*, 15*, 16* Aug. 17*, 18*, **19**	May 11*, 12*, **13** Aug. 14*, 15*, 16	May 18*, 19, **20** Aug. 20*, 21*, 22
Pittsburgh	April 6*, 7, **8** July 2*, 3*, 4*	April 3*, 5 July 5, 6*, 7*, **8**	April 10*, 11 June 28*, 29*, 30, July **1**
St. Louis	April 3, 5* July 5*, 6*, 7*, **8**	April 10*, 11* June 28*, 29*, 30*, July **1**	April 6*, 7, **8** July 3, 4, 4
Atlanta	June 7*, 8*, 9, **10** July 24*, 25*, 26* Sept. 5*, 6*	April 12*, 13*, 14*, **15** June 11*, 12* Sept. 21*, 22*, **23**	June 4*, 5*, 6 July 27*, 28, **29** Sept. 7*, 8, **9**
Cincinnati	June 4*, 5*, 6* July 27*, 28, **29** Sept. 7*, 8*, **9**	June 7, 8*, 9*, **10** July 24*, 25*, 26 Sept. 5*, 6	April 19*, 20*, 21, **22** June 25*, 26*, 27 Sept. 3, 4*
Houston	April 23*, 24*, 25* June 1*, 2*, **3** Sept. 24*, 25*, 26*	June 4*, 5*, 6* July 27*, 28*, 28*, **29** Sept. 7*, **9**	June 7*, 8*, 9, **10** July 24*, 25, 26* Sept. 5*, 6
Los Angeles		April 26, 27*, 28*, **29** July 30*, 31*, Aug. 1* Sept. 11*, 12*	April 30*, May 1*, 2 Aug. 10*, 11, **12** Sept. 21*, 22, **23**
San Diego	April 19*, 20*, 21, **22** June 25*, 26*, 27* Sept. 3*, 4*		April 17*, 18 June 1*, 2, **3, 3** Sept. 24*, 25*, 26
San Francisco	April 13*, 14, **15** June 11*, 12*, 13 Sept. 28*, 29, **30**	April 23*, 24*, 25* June 14, 15*, 16*, **17** Sept. 19*, 20	

JULY 10 — ALL-STAR GAME AT SAN FRANCISCO
AUGUST 13 — HALL OF FAME GAME at COOPERSTOWN, NY
(Detroit Tigers vs. Atlanta Braves)